Praise for *Treat Me Like Dirt*

"The book tells the story of Ontario's punk movement in the words of the players, often in shockingly lurid and graphic detail. It's the straight goods, no holds barred."
— Graham Rockingham, *Hamilton Spectator*

"Being a huge champion of Toronto punk rock and the untold story of its origins, I thought it was great to read a lot of stuff that I knew but also tons that I didn't: the inception of bands from Simply Saucer to the Viletones to the Diodes. It's a really fun read."
— Damian Abraham (Fucked Up), Pitchfork Guest List

"If you want to know where Canadian alt-rock came from, you need to read this."
— Alan Cross

"An incredible document of a self-contained world."
— Lindsay Hutton, The Next Big Thing

"This book, seriously, you will not be able to put down."
— Paul Robinson, The Diodes

"Like most oral histories worth their salt, Worth's book is informative and a great historical document on bands like the Diodes, Teenage Head, Simply Saucer and the Viletones, and clubs like the Crash 'n' Burn. But it's her ability to step aside and let the characters tell their own stories that gives the book a true sense of time and place."
— Johnson Cummins, *Montreal Mirror*

"*Treat Me Like Dirt* is Canada's answer to *Please Kill Me* . . . but what the book lacks in names you've heard of, it makes up for with a good share of dropping acid and going to get a VD test on Halloween, bands storming the stage and stealing each other's instruments, heroin, forced electro-shock treatments, biker attacks, venues being burned to the ground, riots, full-body casts due to car crashes, women peeing in jukeboxes, gangs . . ."
— *Vice*

"This is the finest oral history of one punk scene I've ever seen. A regional document, it lacks the span (and name recognition) of the three U.S.-wide giants of that era, what led up to it, and what followed, from the Velvets to the Voidoids, Please Kill Me, and Our Band Could Be Your Life. But with vivid storytelling from nearly every participant in the Toronto (and Hamilton) punk explosion, it's equal in quality and interest to those essential tomes."
— *Big Takeover*

Treat Me Like Dirt

An Oral History of Punk in Toronto and Beyond
1977-1981

By Liz Worth

Edited by Gary Pig Gold

Published by ECW Press
665 Gerrard Street East, Toronto, ON M4M 1Y2
416-694-3348 / info@ecwpress.com

Originally published by Bongo Beat Books, 2049 Melrose, Montreal, Quebec, Canada, H4A 2R6
www.bongobeat.com

NOTE: The publisher does not condone or endorse and is not liable for the opinions, comments, conjectures, accusations, theories, complaints, or possible misinformation as expressed by the individuals interviewed for this book and which are presented here within the context of an oral history of a particular time and place. Wherever possible we have tried to verify for accuracy, and we are more than happy to correct any mistakes in future editions of this book and related websites.

Library and Archives Canada Cataloguing in Publication

Worth, Liz, 1982-
Treat me like dirt : an oral history of punk in Toronto and beyond,
1977-1981 / Liz Worth.

ISBN 978-1-77041-067-1
Also Issued As: 978-1-77090-056-1 (PDF); 978-1-77090-055-4 (ePUB)

1. Punk rock music—Ontario—Toronto—History and criticism. 2.
Punk rock musicians—Ontario—Toronto—Interviews. I. Title.

ML3534.6.C2W9322 2011   782.4216609713541   C2011-902834-4

Editor: Gary Pig Gold
Cover and text design: Ralph Alfonso

PRINTED AND BOUND IN CANADA

The publication of *Treat Me Like Dirt* has been generously supported by the Canada Council for the Arts, which last year invested $20.1 million in writing and publishing throughout Canada, by the Ontario Arts Council, by the OMDC Book Fund, an initiative of the Ontario Media Development Corporation, and by the Government of Canada through the Canada Book Fund.

preface

Two questions persistently followed me during the course of working on this book. People wanted to know, first, how I got into these bands, and second, why I chose to document Toronto punk.

The answer to the first question is perhaps telling of how obscure Toronto punk history had become over the years. Having been born in 1982, I obviously wasn't around for punk's first wave, but it wasn't hard to be exposed to it. The Ramones, Sex Pistols, Clash, X-Ray Spex, Velvet Underground, X, and all the rest of the American and English brands were picked up as mandatory history lessons for a lot of us in who were seriously into music in the 1990s.

It actually wasn't until I came across a novel called *1978* by Daniel Jones of Toronto that I learned there had been a first wave punk scene right here. While the story of a group of downtown kids living in chaos is fictional, the bands and venues referenced are all true. After reading names like the Diodes, the Viletones, and the Poles, I took a trip to a favourite music store. My timing couldn't have been better — a lot of Toronto punk recordings had just recently been released on CD back then.

I had been thinking of undertaking a project like *Treat Me Like Dirt* for a couple years before I actually decided to do it. For a long time I had been happy in my role as a fan of these bands, but eventually I found myself getting bored. I knew that artists like Bad Brains and Henry Rollins were Viletones fans. I knew that like in New York, London, and Los Angeles, the women in Toronto's punk scene had strong, visible presences. I could sense the danger and rock 'n' roll ethos around a band like the Ugly. And I knew that the Forgotten Rebels and Teenage Head had been relentlessly playing ever since they started. The Diodes had made some phenomenal albums that still stand up today. I've seen more bands cover the Demics than I can count.

Obviously these bands had made an impact, and I wanted to know the stories of these musicians and the people around them. Unfortunately, the more questions I had, the more I realized the answers were scarce.

It was in the spring of 2006 that I started working on *Treat Me Like Dirt* with the intention of finally getting to know the backstory I had long been looking for. I hadn't originally intended for it to become an oral history, but it only took about five or six interviews before I could hear how each person's story was falling in place against the others, and I realized that the best way to tell this story — especially since it was one that had been silent for so long — was through the voices of those who were there.

Treat Me Like Dirt had a momentum of its own when it came to gathering support from Toronto's punk scene, as well as from friends, family, and colleagues. Resistance really came from Canadian editors and literary agents. For the most part, no one wanted to touch a book about punk in Toronto that so obviously excluded the rest of Canada. That's just the Canadian way. It's an attitude I hope won't last much longer.

I had to explain that I hadn't set out to create an encyclopedia about punk in Canada. I wanted to tell a story about a time and a place and a specific group of people. And most of all, I wanted to create the book about Toronto punk that I, as a fan, have always wanted to read. This is something that goes beyond a music genre and its geographic boundaries. It's about dreams and disappointments, successes and setbacks, and all of the chaotic nights and incredible insights that happen in between.

— *Liz Worth, Toronto 2008*

cast of characters

Elizabeth Aikenhead: Director of punk film *Bollocks*. Fan. Girlfriend.

Ralph Alfonso: Manager of the Diodes and Crash 'n' Burn club. Rock writer, photographer.

Cleave Anderson: Drummer for the Battered Wives, Tyranna, Toby Swann Band, the Sidewinders, Handsome Ned and the Hayseed Hellions, Blue Rodeo, and Screamin' Sam.

Mike Anderson (*aka* Motor X): Drummer for the Viletones, the Secrets, and Arson.

Iain Atkinson: Bassist for the Demics.

Caroline Azar: Vocalist, co-lyricist, and keyboardist for Fifth Column. Director, actor, and playwright.

John Balogh: Hamilton promoter, comedian.

Christopher Barnes: Son of Margaret Barnes-DelColle and Freddy Pompeii.

Margaret Barnes-DelColle (*aka* Margarita Passion): Proprietor of Toronto's first punk store, New Rose. Power Street resident.

Slash Booze (Brian Baird): Source of Teenage Head's inspiration.

Anna Bourque: Bassist for the Curse and True Confessions. Filmmaker.

Julia (Jula) Bourque (*aka* Trixie Danger): Guitarist for the Curse and True Confessions.

Rodney Bowes: Photographer. Former Bomb Records employee.

Gambi Bowker: Proprietor of the 404 speakeasy. Fan.

Edgar Breau: Vocalist and guitarist for Simply Saucer.

James Bredin: Fan.

Tony Brighton: Bassist for the Ugly and Zro4.

AA Bronson: Artist and member of Toronto artists' group General Idea from 1964 to 1994.

John Brower: Promoter.

Wayne Brown: Vocalist for the Fits and Thee Immaculate Hearts.

Colin Brunton: Former employee of the Original 99 Cent Roxy, New Yorker Theatre. Filmmaker, director, producer. Credits include *The Last Pogo*, *Bollocks*, *Duality of Self*, *A Trip Around Lake Ontario*, *The Mysterious Moon Men of Canada*, *Roadkill*, *Highway 61*, *Blood & Donuts*, and *Hedwig and the Angry Inch*.

Bob Bryden (*aka* Simon De Beaupré): Producer for the Forgotten Rebels; manager of Star Records. Solo recording artist.

Stephen Burman: Forgotten Rebels manager.

Carmen Bycok (*aka* Cram Savage): Fan.

David Byers: Guitarist and altered/electrified woodwind player for Simply Saucer.

Deane Cameron: President of EMI Canada. Former member of the A&R team of Capitol Records of Canada.

Peter Case: Bassist for the Nerves.

Sally Cato: Lead vocalist for the Androids and Smashed Gladys.

John Catto: Guitarist for the Diodes.

Fred Chagpar: Larry's Hideaway accountant and booking agent.

Kevin Christoff: Bassist for Simply Saucer.

Cheetah Chrome: Guitarist for the Dead Boys. Solo recording artist.

Richard Citroen: Drummer for the Loved Ones.

David Clarkson: Bassist and founding member of the Eels, the Diodes, and Martha and the Muffins. Founding member of Toronto's YYZ gallery and the director of Gallery 76 at OCA from 1982–87. Artist.

William Cork: Founder of the Shock Theatre. Member of the Wild Things with Mike Nightmare.

Gary Cormier: One half of promoting team The Garys. Formerly of the New Yorker Theatre. Promoted at the Horseshoe and the Edge.

Len Cramer: Brother of Simply Saucer drummer Don Cramer. Simply Saucer roadie.

Karla Cranley: Fan. Girlfriend.

Captain Crash: The Viletones roadie.

Andy Crosbie: Co-founding partner of Ready Records.

Joe Csontos: Drummer for the Forgotten Rebels.

Alex Currie (*aka* Runt): Artist. Former employee of the New Yorker Theatre and the Hotel Isabella.

Nora Currie: Fan.

Steven Davey: Drummer for the Dishes. Founder of the Everglades. Writer and critic.

Michael Dent: Drummer for the Dents.

Mickey DeSadist (Mike Grelecki): Singer; Forgotten Rebels.

Greg Dick: Vocalist for the Dream Dates.

Mark Dixon: Bassist for The Mods.

Paul Eknes: Front man for the Wads and Dick Duck and the Dorks.

Dave Elley: Guitarist and vocalist for the Orphans, the Loudmouths, the Mad Daddys, the Moon Crickets, the Chosen Few. Punker House proprietor.

Bruce Eves: Artist and member of the Centre for Experimental Art and Communication.

Ken Farr: Bassist for the Dishes and Drastic Measures.

Barrie "Bear" Farrell: Guitarist for the Toyz, the Existers, Australia, and Babyoil. Roadie for the Romantics and the Ugly.

Sam Ferrara (*aka* Sam Sinatra, Screamin' Sam): Bassist for the Ugly and the Viletones.

Danny Fields: Former manager of the Stooges, Jonathan Richman (Modern Lovers), and Ramones. Former employee of Elektra Records and former executive of Atlantic Records. Author.

Ricki Landers Friedlander: Entertainment executive producer/promoter. Co-founder of RLF Entertainment Productions and R&B Music Productions with Bob Gallo.

Bob Gallo: Producer for the Diodes.

Mark Gane: Guitarist for Martha and the Muffins.

Johnny Garbagecan (Zoltan Lugosi): The Ugly roadie, zine maker.

Jeremy Gluck: Writer for *The Pig Paper*, *Sounds*, and *Mojo*. Founder and vocalist of the Barracudas. Solo recording artist. Novelist.

Gary Pig Gold: Founder of *The Pig Paper* and Pig Records. Member of the Loved Ones.

Chris Haight (*aka* Chris Hate, real name Chris Paputts): Bassist for the Viletones. Guitarist for the Secrets.

John Hamilton: Member of the Daily Planet and Zoom. Drummer for the Diodes. Bassist for the Secrets.

George Higton: Founder and editor of *Shades* magazine. Guitarist and vocalist for the Existers. Solo recording artist. Screenwriter.

Chris Houston: Bassist for the Forgotten Rebels and the One Eyed Jacks. Solo recording artist.

Dan Husband: Fan.

Martha Johnson: Organist for Oh Those Pants! Member of the Doncasters. Lead vocalist for Martha and the Muffins.

Michaele Jordana: Artist. Lead vocalist for the Poles.

John Kancer: Fan.

Joe Keithley (*aka* Joey Shithead): Front man for D.O.A.

Nip Kicks (Lawrence Makoto Kabayama): Roadie / security guard for Ugly and the Viletones.

Paul Kobak: Founder of Hamilton's Star Records. Former manager of Teenage Head. Founder of Teen Agency.

Alex Koch: Drummer for Buick McKane, Crash Kills Five, the One Eyed Jacks, and Tony Balony and the Rubes.

Steve Koch: Guitarist for Crash Kills Nine, the Viletones, the Demics, the One Eyed Jacks, and Handsome Ned.

Imants Krumins: Fan. Record collector. Former radio host at CFMU-FM.

Bob Lanois: Co-founder of Master Sound and Grant Avenue Studio. Solo recording artist.

Larry LeBlanc: Music critic. Writer for *Record World*. Former host on Q107 FM.

Steven Leckie (*aka* Nazi Dog, Natzee Dog): Lead vocalist for the Viletones.

Linda Lee (*aka* Patsy Poison): Drummer for the Curse and True Confessions.

Mike Lengyell: Drummer for the Diodes.

Gordie Lewis: Guitarist for Teenage Head.

David Liss: Fan.

Pete Lotimer (*aka* Pete Treason):
Drummer for the Forgotten Rebels.

Lydia Lunch: Vocalist for Teenage Jesus & the Jerks, solo recording artist, actor, poet, and writer.

Ian Mackay: Bassist for the Diodes.

Johnny MacLeod: Front man for Johnny and the G-Rays.

Stephen Mahon: Bassist for Teenage Head.
Bassist for the Forgotten Rebels in a later incarnation.

Fred Mamo: Promoter. Band financer.

Gail Manning: The Curse manager.
Former employee of Teen Agency and Jack Morrow.

Scott Marks: Guitarist for the Mods.

Blair Martin: Drummer for the Androids (1978–1980); front man for the Raving Mojos (1981–1985); drummer for Teenage Head (1985).

Henry Martinuk: Fan. Bassist and vocalist for the Anemics. Filmmaker and event producer.

Andrew McGregor: Fan.

Andy Ramesh Meyers: Guitarist, bassist, vocalist, songwriter, and saxophone player for the Scenics.

Carmela Morra: Fan.

Bruce Farley Mowat: Music journalist, broadcaster, archivist, radio host, liner note writer.

Raymi Mulroney: Guitarist for The Ugly.

Nash the Slash (Jeff Plewman): Co-founder of the band FM. Solo recording artist.

Suzanne Naughton: Filmmaker. Credits include punk films *Afternoon At New Rose* and *Mondo Punk*. Screenplay writer and photographer.

Mike Niederman: Fan, friend, and supporter of the Demics.

Mike Nightmare (deceased): Lead vocalist for the Ugly and the Wild Things.

Jeff Ostofsky: Fan. Roadie for various groups.

Harri Palm: Guitarist for the Eels and Johnny and the G-Rays.

Stephen "Sparky" Park: Guitarist for Teenage Head, the Loved Ones, and Simply Saucer.

Chick Parker (*aka* Chick Kunte): Guitarist for the Ugly, Zro4, Dick Duck and the Dorks, and Arson.

Gerard Pas: Artist and fan.

Andy Paterson: Guitarist and vocalist for The Government.

Enzo Petrungaro: Fan. Toronto music promoter.

Bryan Pietersma: Fan.

Stewart Pollock: Teenage Head road manager.

Freddy Pompeii: Guitarist for the Viletones. Front man for the Secrets. Bassist and vocalist for Thee Immaculate Hearts.

Larry Potvin (*aka* Larry Electrician):
Drummer for the Forgotten Rebels.

Doug Pringle:
Keyboardist and synthesizer player for the Poles.

Don Pyle: Fan. Photographer. Vocalist for Crash Kills Five. Drummer for Shadowy Men on a Shadowy Planet. Record producer.

David Quinton: Drummer, pianist, and songwriter for the Androids, the Mods and Stiv Bators. Solo recording artist. Drummer for the Jitters, Strange Advance, and Lost & Profound. Entertainment lawyer.

Dave Rave: Guitarist for the Shakers.
Vocalist for Teenage Head during the 1980s.

Paul Robinson: Vocalist for the Diodes.

Cynthia Ross: Bassist for the B-Girls, the Survivors, the Mystery Girls, the Chris Bond Band, the Renegades, the Handsome Neds, Shotgun Shack. Backup vocalist on Blondie's *AutoAmerican* and Stiv Bators's solo album.

Lucasta Ross: Lead vocalist for the B-Girls.
Lead vocalist for Minutes From Downtown.

Rosy Ruin: Elusive and mysterious *Shades* contributor.

Glenn Schellenberg: Keyboardist for the Dishes.
Member of the Everglades.

Bob Segarini: Soundman for the Crash 'n' Burn. Producer for the B-Girls. Recording artist, singer songwriter, composer, radio host. Member of the Family Tree (1966–1968), Roxy (1968–1970), The Wackers (1970–1973), All the Young Dudes (1973–1976).

Michael Severin (*aka* Sev Micron): Drummer and vocalist for the Roll Ons, Hoi Polloi, and Tulpa.

Greg Shaw (deceased): Fanzine publisher. Founder of Bomp Records.

Mr. Shit: Fan.

Rob Sikora: Fan.

Mickey Skin: Lead vocalist for the Curse and Bangkok.

Xenia Splawinski (aka Xenia Holiday): Lead vocalist and guitarist for the B-Girls. Backup vocalist for Certain General and Swaha.

Sandy Stagg: Local entrepreneur. Founder of the Peter Pan Restaurant and the Fiesta.

Edie Steiner: Photographer.

Joe Sutherland: Director, camera operator/cinematographer.

Tibor Takacs: The Viletones manager, Cardboard Brains manager. Filmmaker.

Tank (Dave Roberts): The Viletones roadie. The Garys bouncer.

Ross Taylor: Photographer.

Marty Thau: Founder of Red Star Records.

Gary Topp: One half of Toronto promoters The Garys. Founder of the Original 99 Cent Roxy and New Yorker Theatre. Promoter at the Horseshoe and the Edge.

Rick Trembles: Guitarist for the Electric Vomit. Bassist and guitarist for the American Devices.

Greg Trinier: Vocalist for The Mods.

Anya Varda: Model; fan; vocalist for Land of Giants.

Frankie Venom (Frank Kerr, deceased): Front man for Teenage Head.

Tony Vincent (*aka* Tony Torcher): Drummer for the Ugly and the Viletones.

Kerry Wade: Fan.

Jimmy "J.D." Weatherstone: Drummer for the Demics.

Keith Whittaker (deceased): Front man for the Demics and Hoi Polloi.

Tom Williams: Co-founder of Attic Records.

Zero: Proprietor of 404 speakeasy; lead vocalist for Zro4.

Part One:
1969-1977

1. nowheresville

John Hamilton, Chris Haight / photo by Gail Bryck

Chris Haight: One of the saddest days of my life was when my parents moved to Scarborough.

I grew up just on the other side of the Don River. I was a city kid all the way. I grew up here and all my friends were still here, and I still remember them taking us to this Nowheresville. I didn't even know what a plaza was, that's how bad it was. It was so desolate. The first thing that hit you was you need a car to live here, that kind of bullshit.

That's where I ran into Johnny.

John Hamilton: Chris Haight and I had always been playing together. We came out of the old Toronto school, and the old Toronto school was you always went and jammed around; that's how you learned stuff. You'd meet a guy and his band would rehearse and you'd go and sit in and you'd play a song and then they'd say, "Oh, what was that chord change you did?" or whatever. So we were always doing that, jamming.

Chris Haight: At the time the big deal was rhythm and blues. Don't get me wrong, there were still bands like the Ugly Ducklings and all that shit, which were more on the rock end of things, and there was that greasers-and-hippies shit that you could cut with a knife in high school. I never conformed to the hair and the paisley shit and stuff like that. I just kind of followed my heart, so I was weaned on rhythm and blues, basically, and I still love the shit; I still love Motown and all that stuff.

It wasn't till later that I actually relented and started experimenting with rock. In the East End, at the intersection of Jones and Dundas, there's a whole two blocks of garages — actual car garages. And my very first musical experience was in one of those garages. I don't think they even made PAs back then. There was a microphone and an amplifier, and I remember it was just a drummer, bass, and guitar, but the guitar and bass were plugged in the same amplifier. I guess they couldn't afford another one.

They had their eyes closed and they knocked me dead. And that's when it all first happened, and I guess that was my very first taste of garage music.

John Hamilton: I was playing gigs every weekend from the time when I was sixteen in high school. I was gonna be a drummer and that was gonna be my trade, like a plumber. And then I got sick of that and started playing guitar, and I wanted to write songs and I started reading too many books and I started wanting to be intellectual. So I didn't fit into that old Toronto scene, that Ronnie Hawkins-type scene anymore.

Chris Haight: I met John through a rhythm and blues outfit. At the time we were still going to high school.

We would be playing non-union gigs. The union gigs were for established bands that belonged to Local 149, and they would have to pay dues, but they were guaranteed of making so much money an hour and that certain things were right in the venue that they were performing. But when you hit the non-union thing, well, anything goes. It could have been a gig from a rec room to a church recreation hall. It could've been anything. But there was *so* much shit going down. Every time you turned around there was a dance or something. The whole city was just buzzing with bands.

There were agencies in town at the time and one of the agencies was called Top Ten. These were basically agents that had their end of the market on certain clubs and sometimes their connections would stretch out to the East Coast and stuff. So I remember this one guy from Top Ten, he asked us some personal questions first and then he fitted us up with these really dorky suits, matching suits and shit, and he sent us to the Promised Land out east.

John Hamilton: We had a band called the Three Little Pigs and it was like a heavy metal trio. We went out east and we rented a house trailer and played around Fredericton and Moncton and all that.

I came down with hepatitis while we were out there because I'd been shooting up. Toronto was the speed capital of the world in 1969; you can't *believe* how much methedrine there was in this city.

It was unbelievable, unbelievable. We were shipping it into the United States; like I knew dealers and stuff like that. Everybody was doing speed and shooting it up. We were all crazy.

Chris Haight: We closed up shop for Top Ten because we just weren't in synch with the word "professionalism." We just weren't.

Johnny had hepatitis. He looked like a walking banana. He was delirious and this and that.

John Hamilton: We had reached our limit on the East Coast and were running out of money and we couldn't pay our rent on the trailer park. We were like the original *Trailer Park Boys*, literally. It came down to the landlord banging on the front door of our house trailer as we were jumping out the back door and climbing into our truck. I had hepatitis and was barely getting around. I think I'd been eating all these oranges to try to fight the jaundice and I'd broken out in hives, too. But we had to do one more gig to get enough money to get back to Toronto.

We had one more gig booked at a community centre or something for a hundred and fifty bucks. So we booked ourselves into a hotel there downtown. I think it was called the Colonial Inn. I managed to play the gig with a fever of probably a hundred and ten or something like that. The next day we skipped out on our hotel bill by climbing out the window. We were bad people; we were bad.

We took off to head back to Toronto, and by this time we were fighting amongst ourselves like crazy. That kind of pressure and starvation and all that and getting on each other's nerves like bands always do — of course Chris Haight and I were at each other's throats.

So anyway, we were leaving Fredericton in the dead of winter.

Chris Haight: We were on our way home after we successfully closed shop for Top Ten, ha ha ha, with two tins of Hi-C and some baloney sandwiches. Things just didn't pan out, and we were taking these amphetamines so we could just drive straight through all the way home. We didn't have any money for lodgings.

Just out of Fredericton there was a snowstorm coming down. And I remember the last thing was Johnny screaming, "You're going too fast! You're going too fast!"

John Hamilton: Chris Haight is the worst driver in the world. He's been in so many accidents. He was going too fast and I kept saying, "Slow down, slow down, slow down," and he didn't, and he hit a patch of black ice or some snow.

Chris Haight: So next thing I know we're off the highway and we're doing these rolls in the truck. We were out there and there was gear all over the ravine and stuff like that.

John Hamilton: The back doors came off the truck and all the gear went flying into the snow.

Chris Haight: Everybody's just wired on amphetamines for starters, and Johnny's walking around with this condition and he's going, "Aw jeez. I'm just gonna phone my mom." He was saying all the wrong things. We were like in shock and there's shit all over the gear, and we were wondering how the hell we were even gonna make it home. The van wouldn't even start.

Myself and Bruce, the bass player, we kind of threw everything down. And it was really funny because we had rope with us, and we just tied two or three laps of rope around the whole van so it would keep the side and the back doors intact. I'm looking at Bruce going, "If we hang around with John, we might just have to kill him." Ha ha ha.

John Hamilton: At that point I just said, "I'm going back to Fredericton." I had a girlfriend there who would take care of me. So I took a cab back to her house and she nursed me back to health. A woman named Donna Greer — I probably would have died if it wasn't for her. And those guys, they bungee-corded the back doors of the truck and put the gear back in; in the winter with no heater. It was a total disaster. That was our first tour.

Chris Haight: We jumped back in the van and just headed for Montreal, where I was pleasantly surprised later because Bruce pulled out a credit card that wasn't his. It was one of the big, big hotels in downtown Montreal where you pull in front, and some guy comes running out with the white gloves and … gets this van that's rolled about five or six times off the highway. He takes the van away and we're room serviced and this and that.

Eventually, we all made it back home.

John Hamilton: The Toronto music scene had really deteriorated from the days of Yorkville when there were original bands. In the Yorkville days the drinking age in Toronto was twenty-one, so all the younger people went to coffeehouses where you got a lot of original music being made. Then they dropped the drinking age to eighteen and all the people started getting into bars, so then it became bar band music and the whole scene that gave birth to Neil Young and the Paupers and Kensington Market — that all died out.

When I was first starting out, the clubs in Toronto were the Gasworks, the Generator, the Coal Bin, and then later on the El Mocambo. But basically what they were was the whole room was full of tables and chairs and there would be a dance floor the size of a postage stamp because they didn't want to give any floor space away to a table where they could sell beer. They would have cover bands playing there all the time, and they would just herd the people in, pour as much draft beer into them as possible — which they would be watering by about fifty per cent after a couple hours — and then pour them out again at night. And all the bands were cover bands, and they all had to belong to an agency, to a musicians' union, so it was really controlled.

*　　*　　*　　　*　　　　*

Blair Martin: Aleister Crowley once said Toronto makes a Scottish fishing village on a Sunday morning look like an opium dream. That's sort of an indication of what a dreary, miserable place this really was. My mother remembers, for example, that there was really not much of a cosmopolitan feeling about Toronto until probably 1956 or '57, when a couple of Hungarian restaurants opened on Bloor Street. That was really the beginning of our multicultural, cosmopolitan experience.

If the sky was overcast and you walked out onto Yonge Street on a Sunday morning and everything was closed and you'd look down from Bloor right down to Wellesley, you'd see nobody else on the street but you. You would really feel like you were in downtown Peterborough. There's not a lot of difference. And I don't think that feeling is there anymore because you'll never be on Yonge Street alone anymore. So Toronto was small-town-y, but becoming this big city.

*　　*　　*　　　*　　　　*

Freddy Pompeii: As soon as I graduated from art school I took a trip up to Toronto because I was real curious about what Toronto was like, having another country next door. So I came up to the Mariposa Folk Festival on Toronto Island because I also wanted to see this black blues band that everybody was talking about, the Screaming Nighthawks. I came up to see them specifically. That was Buddy Guy's band from Chicago.

So I came up from Philadelphia and I met my future wife, Margarita. We got along very well when I was there and we kept in touch by letters and by telephone and whatnot. We were sort of courting over the phone, and then I started making frequent trips up to Toronto for weekends or a week at a time. I started to get to know the people and made a lot of friends really fast.

Eventually I was so disillusioned with the United States and the Vietnam War and that kind of stuff. I had already beaten the draft; I didn't have to go into service. I managed to get out of it on my own. But I still liked Canada because the whole attitude and atmosphere was different than the United States. United States was just so violent and it seemed to be like a hopeless situation. All of that went into making my decision on coming up there to live.

I had made so many friends and had so many places that I could crash I decided to come up and see what there was for me in the music biz, so that's what I did. I wasn't engaged or anything with Margaret; at that point we were really good friends and I was getting to know her better and better.

Margaret Barnes-DelColle: I lived north of Toronto in a place called Nobleton. I met Freddy at the Mariposa Folk Festival. Because he was American and seven years older than me, he was just really something different. I was pretty naïve and kind of country girlish. He was an artist, he was a musician, he was cute, and he had long hair. He was easygoing, he was very hip, he was very knowledgeable about music; not just one kind of music but everything, so I think all of those things attracted me to him.

Freddy Pompeii: The whole United States was a bad trip so I figured living somewhere else like Toronto would be a nice thing for me and for my head, so that's what I did. I moved there in '71.

Captain Crash: We lived in a house. It was at Islington and Bloor where those high-rises are now. They were these big Tudor homes and they were gonna be torn down to put those high-rises in. So the deal was, "You can have this house, but it's only gonna last for six months. We're not doing repairs or nothing." It was really cheap.

So we rented it, but it was like three years before they ended up kicking us out. But they wouldn't do any repairs on the house. The basement had that much fuckin' water in it and stuff. Fred and I used to go down there with hockey sticks and golf balls, and there was nothing in the basement. It was cement walls, right? We used to slap-shot these golf balls in the basement and the balls would ricochet off the walls twice as fast as you hit them, ha ha ha. You'd have to duck from these golf balls ricocheting off the walls. All the windows were broken down there because of these golf balls bouncing around. What beer will do, eh?

This was all when Fred first came to Canada. Fred met Margaret at Mariposa and went back to Philadelphia and he was in love, so he came up here.

This would have been in the mid-'70s, I guess.

I met Margaret in the hospital. I was a teenage father and she was a teenage mother and we had mutual friends. But Margaret and I didn't know each other yet. I was in for a car accident and my wife was in having kids, and Margaret was down the hall having kids, too.

Freddy Pompeii: I fell in love and we ended up getting a house together, and she already had a son who was a year old so I became a father. We set up house on Queen and Parliament.

We had a house right on the corner there which became a gathering place for friends and other people; it was kind of like a party house. We all sort of dressed the same way and talked the same language and listened to the same music.

It was a nice house: Three-story, very spartan, easy to keep clean. Every winter I had to put plastic on the windows to keep the cold out. We had one winter where we had to stand on the chairs in the kitchen because the heat rose. Even though we had it all insulated and everything it was still freezing cold, so we ended up having to stand on the chairs in the kitchen to keep our noses warm.

The house was owned by the Catholic Church. It was a tax write-off kind of thing. In fact, it was facing the church; our front window was facing directly across the street to the cathedral and the sun used to shine off of it and flash into our living room and light the whole room.

We were living like poor people. We *were* poor people. Some days you'd wake up and the whole house was frozen. The water wouldn't run and the heater was off, things like that. Any artist that lives the life of art has to put up with that kind of shit. You can't get away with it. If you decide you're gonna live that kind of life, you're gonna be broke most of the time. It was either I'd have to work weekend jobs or part-time jobs. I was a commercial artist by trade. I worked steady in Philadelphia but in Toronto I couldn't get a leg up. They didn't like Americans very much.

Dan Aykroyd, the actor, had a bar on Queen Street called the Club 505. He wasn't famous yet. He was working for Second City and they did an improv thing. And he was doing some modelling and doing some stage stuff. Around '71, I had met him because he had this speakeasy at 505 Queen.

Everybody from John Candy to the Mackenzie Brothers to Catherine O'Hara would hang out there. All the bars would close at twelve o'clock so people would open up speakeasies because the entertainers had nowhere to go at night. You'd walk in at any given night and there'd be Belushi hanging out or Chevy Chase or Cue Ball, who were the blues band in Toronto.

I had a band with Dan's brother, Peter Aykroyd, called Wheelchair that we were gigging around with. It started out as a duo and then ended up as a six-piece band. If that had lasted it would have been considered like a new wave or a punk band, but it didn't last. He was too much into his acting and comedy and stuff. Music wasn't that important to him.

Our place wasn't a speakeasy, but it was just as popular as 505 because we were a little younger and we used to play real loud music all the time and sit around and party. It was always Stooges and MC5 and garage rock, stuff that we liked. It sort of became known to a small crowd of people. Everybody talked about Power Street — "Let's go over to Power Street." If there was nothing else happening around, "Let's go over to Power Street, something's bound to be happening," which was pretty much true. We didn't mind. We were young and we had set up house and we couldn't really go out because we had a kid, so it was better that people came over to our house for companionship and entertainment and socializing. We couldn't go out to bars because we'd have to pay for a babysitter or something and couldn't really afford that.

There was an underground happening to Toronto at that time. There was like a group of people who had the same likes and dislikes and a distinct attitude about what was cool and what was rock 'n' roll and what wasn't. We all shared this attitude; this show business attitude that the established stuff was passé and that there had to be something else in the wind. It's funny that all these people, we all partied together; we all shared the same attitudes. Our house was sort of like a gathering place for a lot of the freaks; people used to come over to our house and party. It was pretty much an open door policy because it was a small crowd of people.

Freddy Pompeii / photo by Gail Bryck

Gary Topp: I was probably the world's first headbanger. I would bet on it. When I was five years old I used to sit in a little room next to my bedroom and there was a record player on the floor. I would sit on the floor and listen to my records and bang my head against the wall to the music. I would be willing to bet there was nobody else in the world who was doing that in 1950.

I went to Centennial College for a few years. Because of the Rolling Stones my high school years were terrible. So I started this film society in college and I'd get busted for showing Andy Warhol films.

The second of my two jobs where I was not working for myself was at a little cinema and film distribution company at Yonge and Charles. They owned a theatre called CineCity. It was at the northeast corner that was an old post office. It was a two-hundred-and-fifty-seat cinema and they used to distribute *Gimme Shelter* and Jean-Luc Godard movies and the '60s underground films and all that stuff. The owner of the company was the guy who was initially producing the Festival Express [The Festival Express was a tour across Canada featuring The Band, The Grateful Dead, and Janis Joplin. Because the tour itself was a financial failure, a documentary film capturing the event was shelved shortly after the festival ended]. The whole tour was such a fiasco that it took the whole film company down with it.

When the company went down, I quit and started my own company distributing movies. At one point a guy knocked on the door and said, "I got a movie about Jimi Hendrix, do you want to distribute it?" So I go, "Yeah, I'm gonna make my millions." But it was a fifty-minute concert and the theatre chains didn't want to run it. So I thought, I'm gonna do it myself, fuck them.

There was this theatre out at Greenwood and Danforth that hadn't been used for a few years. It hadn't even been swept. It stunk. So I rented the theatre and showed the movie. We ran the movie for about five weeks. I had always wanted my own theatre so I thought, this is great, we'll continue. We played two different movies every night at ninety-nine cents and called it the Original 99 Cent Roxy Theatre.

Colin Brunton: It was an infamous theatre from the start because you could smoke pot there. They showed really good, amazing, smart, clever double-bills, everything from Kenneth Anger to crazy B movies to the hottest thing from New York or whatever. Me and my buddy started hanging out there and we just got friendly with them. When they started showing *Reefer Madness*, that's when the place got really popular. They said, "Hey, do you guys want to watch the door? Because we have people sneaking in. We'll pay you twenty bucks a night." And we're like, "Yeah, sure," and it went on from there.

I started at the Roxy Theatre as an usher when I was probably fourteen or fifteen years old. I found Gary to be probably the smartest person I ever met, and also the coolest person I ever met. I lived in East York and I was kind of into rock music. I really dug Hendrix the first time I heard him and all that kind of stuff. So whatever cool factor I had within me, it was just multiplied tenfold just by being with Gary. He would just come out and say the odd little thing and it was like, "Yes, wise one."

Gary Topp: I think the whole idea behind the theatre was to be different and do it yourself. Nobody was doing what we were doing with these very specialized movies and all that stuff. It drew a specific crowd, and this was sort of in the era when rock music or pop music was pretty dead. There were some interesting bands, like Roxy Music and I guess Bowie were all getting started. And I used to play all that stuff in the theatre.

The people that came were really into what we were doing there. A lot of weed was being smoked and wine being drunk and nobody ever got busted. The people that came, this was something new for them.

Colin Brunton: If Gary knew that on the weekend he was gonna have a double-bill of Jean-Luc Godard films or something, he would spend a couple of hours at home at night with his reel-to-reel tape recorder and make the perfect music to play at intermission. And so few people got it; so few people got the detail.

At the Roxy we only had a very few number of projectionists that could handle us, because we actually wanted them to not only work but to *think* and maybe be creative. There would be rules like, "Okay, as soon as you hear the final chord of the song, that's when you simultaneously dim the lights, slowly open the curtain, put on this trailer ..." These detailed things. So you'd get these projectionists who fuckin' hated us because we really kept them on their toes.

A couple of guys, this guy Bob Carswell in particular, just loved it. He said, "Oh my god, I'm actually treated like I have a brain here." And on top of that was all this other goofy stuff.

Alex Currie: I lived in the East End and went all the time. I remember the Roxy stunk of dope, every night. I would come home and all my clothes would just stink of pot. I was a huge movie nut. I mean, it was so weird because at the time I was like twelve years old and I was there for two, three times a week. If I wasn't home my mom would just phone the Roxy and ask if I was there. It was pretty cool. They really dug my mom a lot because she was like fifty and she'd come to all these freaky shows and she'd leave me there. I think they liked her more than they liked me.

Gary Pig Gold: Years before I'd ever even *seen* a marijuana cigarette — I was from the nice, genteel suburbs, remember — someone dragged me straight out of school and into the Roxy to see a midnight screening of *Night Of The Living Dead*. Afterwards, everyone was hanging around outside with buckets of Kentucky Fried Chicken, pretending to be flesh-eating zombies and acting out entire scenes from the movie. And this was years before *Rocky Horror* ever became this kind of phenomenon, I'll have you know.

Later, those Roxy double bills were absolutely essential to my audio-visual education. I mean, where else could you see *Magical Mystery Tour* AND the Monkees' incredible *Head*, plus get a lung full of reefer . . . and all for less than one Canadian dollar?!

*   *   *   *   *

Steven Leckie ["The Viletones: Now and Then, and When?" by Lola Michael, *Impulse*, 1978]: I am one of those kids that can distinctly remember being born. My mother had me when she was seventeen and my parents were really into rock 'n' roll; my father drove a convertible; they were kind of loose.

Anyway, I was in Grade 1 and I was listening to the radio and I asked my mother what made that sound and she said electric guitar. Electric guitar, eh? Boy that sounds good, I thought.

Margaret Barnes-DelColle: I worked at these stores on Yonge Street. One was called Long John's, the other was Juicy Lucy's. They were the two really hip stores to go shopping in and at the time it was the whole glam rock thing happening with David Bowie. Everybody was wearing satin pants and bright colours and lots of makeup; the guys were wearing lots of makeup and shag haircuts.

There was that hair salon on Yonge Street called House of Lords. On a Saturday — nowadays you can't even imagine it — but imagine a hair salon having a lineup outside of people wanting to get a shag haircut. I lived thirty minutes outside the city and yet I took a bus into town to go stand in line at House of Lords to get a shag haircut. So there was that whole glam rock thing that everybody was really into.

Steven Leckie: I was completely, religiously entangled in glitter rock. I was quite young; I'd be fourteen, fifteen, decked out as English as I possibly could, which was kind of hard in Toronto. There were only a couple of spots where you could buy the gear at.

Barrie Farrell: I remember Steve Leckie when he was called Ariel, back in the glam rock days.

Him and myself, and Dennis from the Existers, we used to all hang out. We were the platform-wearing kids into the Sweet and David Bowie.

Steven Leckie: I lived for that. At the time there were a couple of faux English rock bars like the Gasworks, but what really made it was all the gay clubs that were in Toronto in the '70s.

Barrie Farrell: Yeah, he would have this English accent and he would be trying to bum drugs. He was like Ziggy Stardust. He was doing the pills; he was getting guys fucked up on pills. He looked like a rooster. He had this red hair. Then the next time I saw him he was Nazi Dog. No shock. It was a perfect transformation. He was a hurricane from early on.

Some of the guys just live it, others espouse the philosophy. They just self-destruct and off they go.

Steven Leckie: I was a very outgoing kid, had loads of friends; my dad lived in Montreal so I had my own apartment that he would have to pay for because I was young. I was the one who had all the parties so I knew everyone, and particularly in this context was very close with Lucasta and Xenia and Anya. They were top-notch global groupies. Guys in New York and London knew to look up Lucasta and Xenia. They were my street sisters, these platonic, gorgeous girls.

Lucasta Ross: Steve Leckie and I had been friends since we were eleven or twelve, and then Xenia and I started hanging out when we were about fifteen. We were down-town kids and we all hung around the downtown scene, which was partly the gay scene. They really accepted us because we weren't just like your average kids.

Paul Eknes: I was born in 1956 so I grew up with the whole ethos of, "I hope I die before I get old." When I was growing up the Beatles sucked. The Rolling Stones were cool but inaccessible. Animals and the Who, that's who it was — "I hope I die before I get old." Yeah, me too!

Steven and I, we both grew up in Scarborough. He was a glam rocker. Platforms, makeup, fake nose ring. We used to take the all-night bus on Bloor. We took it downtown. There was a girl called Anya Varda. We both had the hots for her. He had the hots for her but perhaps he more had the hots for me.

This is back in the glam days, pre-punk, and we all shared an affinity for Iggy Pop and the Stooges, who we didn't consider punk at that point because "punk" was not coined as a term yet. I think that's a Legs McNeil thing, '75.

Back then Iggy and the Stooges was like killer rock, motherfucker. And at the same time we still had a little bit of Ozzy affection, not so much Led Zeppelin; I'm thinking about us growing up 1967, '68, '69, yeah, there was like hard rock influences that I think we grew up with. And then when '73 ended, glam started.

It took a while to take hold in Canada, especially Toronto, so we were spending time having to listen to Peter Frampton. It just seemed that music was making us pissed off and any opportunity that we had to change that would be a good thing as far as we were concerned.

Lucasta Ross: We didn't fit in at high school. We didn't fit in anywhere. We were really into more underground things like Iggy Pop and the New York Dolls and MC5 and things like that, so we dressed strange and people sort of looked at us like we were strange, so we just gravitated toward each other.

We'd hang out in gay bars because for some reason they'd let us buy liquor even though we were teenagers. There was weird stuff in the street scene, like guys deciding they wanted boobs so they'd start taking hormones.

Paul Eknes: Around that time there were only a few people from Scarborough who were coming downtown to check out the scene because Scarborough's so far away. And we all tended to meet each other because you had to *save* each other. Because you were taking the all-night bus back at three o'clock in the morning to Scarborough and you were wearing lime-green hair and pierced noses and lipstick and platform heels, you'd tend to get together just to save each other's butts and such. Steve Leckie was one of them.

Steven Leckie: At Massey Hall, there'd be a concert, and Lucasta and Xenia would tell me not only where to go to get the limo, but what hotel and what hotel room, and I would just live for that. Bowie I saw at O'Keefe Centre in the tour that became *David Live*, where he had the big huge hand that opened up on the stage and he walked down out of his hand. That was the last time that was done because after the Toronto segment the next gig was Philly and they just simply couldn't afford the staging any longer, so I was quite fortunate to see all this.

All my poetry and thinking and judgments were based on Velvet Underground records, for real. No parenting at all. I mean *at all*. It was just the street and I really knew it, I really understood it.

I would get into trouble a great deal. I was always on probation, like *always*. For stupid little things, nothing heavy, stuff like thievery.

Then I also had the other streak in me that was somehow very, very *Clockwork Orange*. Cinema gave me a lot of identification too.

That was all my oxygen, all my REM, all my everything. To do that was a full-time job. Friday at four in the afternoon, I had to start getting ready for midnight. The ceremony was that huge. Girls would come over; we had to get ready. That was enough. It was a lot of crazy teenage sex and underage drinking behind Rosedale subway.

Blair Martin: When I met Steve Leckie it was the last day of school at the end of the 1972–73 school year and I stole six beers from my dad.

Me and these two little sleazy friends of mine, we went to what we called Itchycoo Park, which is behind Rosedale subway station. Steve Leckie is two years older; he was fifteen, and he looked like Aladdin Sane. He had this bright red hair and a pink silk shirt and green satin pants, and I've always remembered the big platform boots as being white. He was the first David Bowie fan I ever met.

He was pretty cool and we drank our beers and we gave him some money to buy more. Because these kids were wearing the platform shoes they'd be taller, so they'd be able to go into the liquor store and buy booze. So we all got up five bucks and he went to buy some fuckin' cheap shit, like sparkling wine, which with the beer probably made us kind of sick, but we probably thought we were drunk.

He was this older kid and he was really watching out for us; he was all mature and concerned. He's only a little kid himself, but he's still asking other kids this question, saying, "Well, we're outside the law here, how much drinking can you handle? Because none of us want to get in trouble." Even knowing that he had to ask that instead of just running off to the store and buying us booze; he was always a really poised guy. That was the cool thing about him. Poised and kind of mature. There's a commonality of people who come from the same neighbourhood and who have walked over the same rocks and through the same footpaths and smoked joints in the same bushes as kids.

*   *   *   *   *

Freddy Pompeii: When I was eighteen years old I was in a band [The band was called Bubble. They released one 45 and while there were plans for releases beyond that, nothing else materialized.] and I had a recording contract with Dot Records in Philadelphia. It was a major label. It didn't go anywhere. I was a singer and then I taught myself how to play guitar and I basically accompanied myself.

I needed something for my voice so I learned how to do that and in doing that I learned how to play the right songs. The way I played acoustic guitar, it sounded like a whole band, so all I had to do was add bass and drums and bring the volume up on the guitar and it would be the same thing.

I did a stint in jail for about six months. I got caught selling pot; a large quantity of marijuana, very large. It took until about the end of '74 before the trial came up and I only did four of the six months. While I was in there I applied for the House of Concord, and it was a really experimental jail. There was no bars and no fences or anything like that. It was like a farm run by the Salvation Army. We had rooms with our own keys and there were beautiful television sets and pool tables. Basically you were on your own. You couldn't leave because if you left you would get caught and you would go back to jail to finish your time.

They were anxious for you to do anything that would increase your self-esteem and pry you away from the criminal way of life. That was their idea; that's why they founded this jail. Like I said, it was an experiment. So while I was in there, they gave me a room that they had. It was like a little empty room that nothing was being done in, and I was allowed to bring an electric guitar and an amp, and there was a few other people in there that played guitars and they brought their amps in, and we would spend our days jamming. Basically that's where I learned to play electric guitar.

I had seen the Stooges and I saw the New York Dolls and was really influenced by them, blown away by them, and I wanted to play guitar like that, with that kind of openness. And they were really short on leads. It was mostly a rhythm guitar with bass and drums and they played really hard and driving, and that's what I wanted to do.

So that's what I was doing while I was in the joint and that's the kind of band I tried to put together after I got out. I stopped playing acoustic guitar altogether and just started looking for people that would be into doing that stuff. And people would just look at me crazy because of the way I looked. I had my hair cut really short. Everybody had their hair down to their shoulders and bell-bottom pants and I just had this self-tailored rock 'n' roll look that I came up with. It was sort of like a '50s thing but not. And there were other people in Toronto doing that, but you had to find them.

Margaret Barnes-DelColle: Freddy was playing music and came up with the name Peter Panic for himself. He was trying to create a feeling and I think he was trying to create what eventually happened, but he wasn't finding the right people that were understanding what he was trying to do and where he wanted to take it.

So when he did perform it was like a transitional stage for him in terms of his music and in terms of the people that he was making music with.

Nora Currie: I was hanging out with some people, some guys, and these two friends of mine, Captain Crash and Michael Windsor, took me to hear Peter Panic. He was doing kind of a folk "Fuck you": It was one guy with a guitar, he was doing all his own material, and he was in the bar scene.

That was my first time I ever saw Fred. I was on acid. I immediately fell in love with him and went home to his place after and met Margaret who I fell in even more love with, and they had a place for rent. I would use their place as a benchmark; not that a scene originated in one place or one house, but Power Street became a doorway very quickly.

Freddy Pompeii: I used to play at a place called the Gasworks on Yonge Street. It was a rock 'n' roll bar and I opened up for guys like Rush.

I would play in the afternoon. I played like a punk rock acoustic guitar show and that was my way of getting my music out there. I never called it "punk" or anything like that; it just was what it was. The music I wrote was on acoustic guitar but it was upbeat and very fast and the nerves were all jammed in there.

I had run into Steven Leckie. At that point he had his New York Dolls look. He looked like David Johansen with his hair all teased up and had really tight pants on and platform boots. He looked just like one of the New York Dolls and that was right around when they came out. He had jumped up onstage when I was playing and he had wanted to sing along with me.

I ended up having to kick him off the stage because he was getting me into trouble. In fact, I even got fired because of it.

Steven Leckie: I'd see this character from time to time in the day doing a matinee at the Gasworks, and he called himself Peter Panic. I would say to him, "Hey, man, can I introduce you?" And this would be at the Gasworks in front of ten people. He'd go, "Yeah, yeah, sure." He'd get a kick out of it.

I was wearing lamé halter tops. I looked like a girl with no breasts, but in those days you'd wear cock rings because the New York Dolls did. It was all part of a fucked up '70s sexuality weird thing.

Nora Currie: It was a time when there was a lot of experimentation going on around music, around drugs, around gender, around sex, around language. It was a very exciting time where change was natural and experimentation was very positive and very open.

You could afford at that time to make a lot of mistakes and learn from them and actually fall forward. It actually was positive to do that. It was the '70s and it was a time when those things all colluded to creating a scene.

Of course, there was also great resistance. We were just coming of age.

2. STEEL TOWN

Simply Saucer, John LaPlante (aka Ping Romany), Edgar Breau, Don Cramer, Kevin Christoff / press photo

Edgar Breau: We lived in Guelph for about three years because my father was a guard at the penitentiary there. We came back home to Hamilton because my mom couldn't handle being away from the old Steel Town.

About 1971, even '69, when I was in high school, I was a pretty avid record collector and I met somebody who was also a big record collector. We were both into a lot of the British bands like the Soft Machine and the early Pink Floyd and the Yardbirds and American bands like the Velvet Underground and Moby Grape.

This guy I met, Paul, was a keyboard player. I had a Fender Telecaster and I was kind of a budding songwriter. So we started playing together and we met some other people that were also your record-collecting types.

David Byers: I met Paul Collili and Edgar Breau on January 8, 1972 at a party that was given by a guy that worked at a record store in downtown Hamilton. The store was kind of a local hangout for offbeat musicians and offbeat characters.

I remember the date because it was strange. It was the weekend *after* New Year's and I thought, It was just New Year's Eve the week before. Why have a party? And I remember that Edgar, Paul and I each brought about three or four albums with us and we kind of dominated the record player.

Edgar Breau: David Byers was also a songwriter. He was into stuff like Terry Riley and the Velvet Underground and Dutch bands like Savage Rose. The three of us started playing together and we added some electronics.

David Byers: We found a rehearsal space and that was up on the Hamilton Mountain. It was like a small, dance hall–type of thing called Wright's Music Centre.

It was a combination music store and where you'd put receptions on and things like that. So we were able to rent that but our biggest problem was that we had to leave a lot of our equipment there, like the big amplifiers and things like that. Paul was the keyboard player so he couldn't tote his organ back and forth. We found that was a big problem because we were worried about it being stolen.

So we did that for two months in the fall of 1972, and then after that I found an apartment above a store, so we moved all the equipment there and used that as a rehearsal space until the spring of 1973. Then by that time John, Ed's foster brother, joined.

Edgar Breau: We had somebody called Ping [John LaPlante] who had been influenced a lot by Eno and Stockhausen and Sun Ra. He happened to be my foster brother as well. My family had taken him in, and his sister, actually. So he was kind of the electronic side of the band.

I had a theremin at the time so we had a six-piece band. It was really highly improvisational and experimental and loud.

I read Kerouac and all that, and I thumbed out west and had my own Canadian *On the Road* experiences in '72. I had a sidekick and we were on the TransCanada Highway going across the country to Vancouver and back and had all kinds of experiences on the road. When I came back I was pretty immersed in all the counter-cultural things that were going on.

There was a writer that wrote for *Fusion* magazine by the name of Wayne McGuire who really influenced me. He was interesting because the kind of music he listened to was John Fahey and Robbie Basho, John Coltrane, Yoko Ono, Sun Ra, the Velvet Underground, the Stooges. He read medieval authors like Wolfram von Eschenbach. It was just a huge kind of mix with him. Also he liked the Inklings, which was that whole C.S. Lewis, Tolkien, Charles Williams, Dorothy L. Sayers, English writers he admired, along with some really cool musicians. He was somebody I really admired because he wasn't the predictable anti-Western cultural thing that was going on at the time. He was more nuanced and he had a broader appreciation of things.

I started reading a lot of the writers that he recommended and listened to the music. I always kept that in my musical tastes. I liked that kind of blend of the avant-garde that's traditional. Even in those early Saucer days I was listening to folk music. And it was exciting to be doing something musically that was experimental.

Kevin Christoff: I met Edgar I guess through his brother Paul. The way that came about was we were all at school together. I guess a couple of my friends found themselves in a class with Paul. One thing led to another, they started talking about music — Syd Barrett and the likes.

Edgar Breau: I was a chartered member of the Syd Barrett Appreciation Society in the early '70s. I was the first Canadian member. I think one of the first American members was a guy called Craig Bell who eventually ended up playing with Rocket From The Tombs. We used to correspond way back then, so it was an exciting time. I'd have to say it was that excitement, that's what turned me on.

Kevin Christoff: That prompted Paul to mention that his brother had a band and that they were needing a bass player, and my buddies suggested me. Basically that's how that happened. I met Edgar about a week or so after that at my first audition.

When I met those guys they were into listening to Hawkwind, Savage Rose, that kind of thing. I think just by and by I started learning a lot about the music that they were playing and it opened up a whole vista for me. I stuck I guess, you know?

There were not demands, but I do remember my first visit with them and Edgar turning to me — I'll never forget this, actually — he told me that he wanted the bass to sound like I was walking through a wet field of tall grass. And I thought, *whoa*, ha ha ha, I can't imagine this. But I did my level best and it was that kind of thing that spurned me on.

David Byers: At that time this apartment rehearsal space was too small. We had so much equipment and it wasn't a very big apartment to begin with, so I found a loft down in the centre, right smack in the middle of downtown Hamilton, a third floor loft. I decided to give up the apartment and live in the loft and we would be able to keep our equipment there.

Kevin Christoff: When I first joined, I don't believe that they had a name. I was pretty new with the band and I sort of found out about the name, I wouldn't say accidentally, but we were all hanging out and the two of them, it might have been Ed and Dave, were talking about, "Well, is this the name we're gonna stick with? Is Simply Saucer the name?" And I remember thinking, *What?* Simply *what?* I'm sure a lot of people had a similar reaction to the name. Of course now I think it's a great name.

It's a hybrid. It's a combination of ideas that came from Ed and Paul. Paul at the time was a big Pink Floyd fan, particularly of their early years. The Saucer half of it came from the *Saucerful of Secrets* LP, and I think Ed at the time was a fan of Elton Dean and a band from England called Just Us and I think he added the Simply as a nod in that direction.

Edgar Breau: We had just gotten the idea of automatic music — "Let's just make music that just happens and we don't have to be there." We had two audio generators and a theremin. We had all the amps up full and the guitars through echo chambers and fuzz distortion units. There were two electric guitars, we had a bass and we had a sax feeding back and the mini Moog and we just jacked it up.

Kevin Christoff: I just laid my bass up against the amplifier I was using and that was my contribution.

David Byers: We were really into ambient sound and whatever strange, long, drone-y feedback things we could make. So we decided to turn all our amps up and the guitars up and the electronics, and Paul put some bricks on his organ. We tried to get the loudest, strangest sound we could, so we did.

Edgar Breau: It got so loud we just ran out of the room.

David Byers: So we left and went down — we were on the third floor — we went down and locked the door.

Kevin Christoff: That's part of the eye-opening experiences of Saucer. That's just not the kind of thing that I did in my basement groups.

David Byers: We just wanted to walk around a few blocks. This was right down the middle of a commercial part of Hamilton and it sounded pretty strange, but we loved it.

Kevin Christoff: All the windows were opened and we just strolled around downtown. It was great fun checking out the reactions and all that. Yeah, it made one heck of a racket I'll tell ya. Everybody's looking like they're expecting UFOs to land any second now and we were just kind of digging the whole thing, ha ha ha.

David Byers: But after a while we thought, Oh we better stop. Too many people were starting to notice.

Edgar Breau: We got about a block and a half away and it was still really, *really* loud and when we got back there were cops there; there were two cop cars in the alley.

David Byers: Lo and behold, in putting the key in the lock I broke it. I think we had another key but the tip of the key was still in the lock. At that time we were panicking and the police and the fire department eventually came and they were able to fish that little part of the key out. I had to run upstairs and pull all the plugs so they wouldn't realize what was going on. We just told them we had left one amp on.

Edgar Breau: David ran upstairs to turn it all off because he thought maybe we were going to get fined or something like that, and the key broke in the door just prolonged it. One cop looked at us and shook his head and said, "I haven't heard noise like that since the Second World War."

*   *   *   *   *

David Byers: We used to go see the New York Dolls on probably their first tour outside of New York. It was a thrilling experience. They were quite something for their time. The audience was very small. I think we'd also seen Iggy and the Stooges there and it was great. Those were great concerts. We didn't know what to expect.

Captain Crash: Things were pretty staid, but when the New York Dolls played on the corner here at Spadina and Dundas at the old Victory Theatre in Toronto, that was an awakening.

William Cork: I saw Iggy and the Stooges at the Victory Burlesque in 1973. I was walking down Spadina and they have this particular breed of mutant in Michigan, the Psychedelic Ranchers. They're like these seven-foot-tall hippies with straight black hair going down to their asses. So I met one of these guys on Spadina Avenue and got to talking to him and he asked me if I wanted to buy some acid. So I bought three hits of Window Pane from him and slammed them all into my face and he went, "Holy shit, man, did you do *all* of those?" I said, "Yeah." He said, "What are you gonna do now?" I said, "I don't know." He said, "Why don't you come and see this band? Actually, their singer Iggy set me up out here to sell acid to people coming into the gig." And I said "Yeah, okay," and I went in there.

I realized on these three hits of Window Pane that I had never seen a rock 'n' roll band before Iggy and the Stooges. They were what the Rolling Stones *should* have evolved into.

Kevin Christoff: I never really got too much into the Dolls for some reason, but I saw the Stooges at the Victory Theatre. That was the *Raw Power* lineup and Iggy did his thing, jumped into the crowd.

I think we were already there in terms of being influenced by it. We listened to a lot of spacey stuff, a lot of weird things: Arthur Brown, *Galactic Zoo,* all that kind of stuff. But I remember on the turntable almost constantly was either *Raw Power* or the first Stooges album or the Pink Fairies or something like that. So when we went to see the Stooges it was like preaching to the converted. We already knew and we were there just to see the man in action.

The concert notwithstanding, Iggy had a big impact I think on a portion of our sound, as did Lou Reed and Syd and all those kind of things. You kind of go through influences and we were heavily influenced by a lot of that at the time.

*   *   *   *   *

Edgar Breau: I remember one night the six of us all got bottles and were just banging on bottles for an hour. There was this Terry Riley composition, "In C," that sounded like bottles. We were trying to duplicate that. We were listening to a lot of Krautrock in those days. There was a lot of experimentation. It was important. When we rehearsed we improvised a lot.

In the early days we'd do really long songs, twenty-minute songs. But the six-piece band never played anywhere. We didn't seem to get hired.

David Byers: For a university town, Hamilton *still* is a dire cultural place. There was no scene happening. There were no bands playing, as far as to our knowledge, the type of music we were trying to achieve, and there were no places to play. We occasionally had people over because the loft was a pretty big space, so I think there were times we had small groups there but we never played outside the loft at all.

In the fall the lease came up so we had to move. At the time I decided to leave the band. I had my reasons. Paul also quit that same day; I don't know why, I didn't discuss it with him. So that was the end of my tenure with the band, although we parted on good terms.

It was only natural for the band to evolve into one person, which was Edgar. He had the vision. In the beginning it was a collective and then it focused into Edgar's vision, which I'm totally in agreement with. That's the way it was supposed to be.

Kevin Christoff: Everything coincided. We were practicing down on King Street, downtown Hamilton, and Dave and Paul leaving sort of coincided with us getting new digs on Kenilworth Avenue and I guess that's where the story really starts.

This new space was affectionately called The Office. It was an old pet shop that was just up for rental. It was around the end of '73 that we got that place and found ourselves as a four-piece and we started. Eddy at that point was, and probably remained, the primary source of material. The songs, although they had an electronic slant to them — obviously Ping played a really big part in the sound in the early days — but there was a lot more emphasis in songs themselves, and it kind of just sort of developed from that point on.

Edgar Breau: I lived right in the practice place where we rehearsed at first. I slept on a quarter-inch piece of foam. I didn't have a bed or a couch or a shower or a bath there or anything. It was a pretty primitive place to live. The walls were painted black. I would just write all day long. People would bring me meals. I was really focused on music and wrote most of *Cyborgs Revisited* in that little storefront. That's where most of it came from.

Kevin Christoff: "Illegal Bodies" was one of the very first songs that Ed presented to us when we settled into Kenilworth Avenue. "Bullet Proof Nothing" was another one. They all came in pretty fast succession. There was a real burst of creativity once we got settled in.

I don't want this to be taken the wrong way, but it was sort of the liberation of having the band paired down to a smaller lineup. It made the material come forward quicker, I think. A lot of songs ended up being dropped in favour of new material because the newer material was more representative of us at the moment.

Edgar Breau: I remember we rehearsed on Christmas Day one year. It was pretty well every day of the week that we would rehearse. It must have been hard, I guess, for the rest of the band, but most of the time they'd show up.

Kevin Christoff: It was, "Go and have Christmas dinner and enjoy yourself, but be here for seven thirty," ha ha ha, and we did. The music in the band meant quite a bit to us. I would say right from that point on, we rehearsed every day without fail.

We were staking our turf musically, I guess. There wasn't anybody in Hamilton really playing or listening to anything remotely like we were, or so it would seem in the mainstream, let's put it that way.

Edgar Breau: It was one of those in-the-wilderness experiences, similar to Rocket From The Tombs in Cleveland. I think they had the same kind of feeling that it was kind of isolated. The early band especially, when we were doing the electronic stuff, the audiences were at times puzzled by what we were doing. We emptied a few places out when we started.

Kevin Christoff: It's pretty accurate to say we were determined that people were going to like us for what we were, rather than what we should be.

Our first gig, we featured a song, and it may have something to do with the fact that we didn't really have a whole lot of material, ha ha ha, but we did one song for, oh, about thirty-five minutes.

Edgar Breau: We did this one song called "Noise" that was twenty minutes long and it was just noise, electronic noise and feedback.

Our first gig ever was in an Anglican church hall and we were doing really experimental stuff. It was in the east end of Hamilton and all these fights broke out. It was kind of like a riot going. The police came and they were hauling people out of there.

Kevin Christoff: Obviously this song had various parts and at one point our drummer got out from behind the kit, wearing a top hat if I recall, and was manically playing a violin. I don't know if it can be akin to performance art, but we were definitely still in that phase of doing exploratory kind of things.

This was 1974. It's pretty hard to imagine what venues would support the kind of music that was being put out by us at the time.

Edgar Breau: We got thrown off the stage at this place in Oakville called the 707 Club. They just kind of bodily threw the drummer off the stage and kicked us out. They pulled our plug and then the bouncers picked the drummer up and threw him outside. The electronics player had come onstage in a scuba diving outfit and I don't think they could understand what we were doing.

Kevin Christoff: We played some very, very ... well, the places themselves weren't strange, but they were strange in light of what we were. We played high schools. Not so much in Hamilton. Hamilton always was a tough place for us to get work.

We acquired a manager. It was a guy who kind of knew the other guys, Ed and Paul and Dave. He ran a record store in Hamilton. That seemed to be a natural place to meet people. This fellow offered to manage us, and he did. He mounted a couple of — it wouldn't be accurate to call them tours; we ended up doing a lot of one-nighters and one-night stands in places like Hawkesbury, Carleton Place, St. Catharines, Smiths Falls, Kitchener. A lot of out-of-the-way places.

Edgar Breau: We played Carleton Place in the early days and we pretty well emptied an arena, but there were a few people left that said they loved us.

Kevin Christoff: I think this might have been in Pembroke. We were hired to play this teen dance. It just didn't wash. Everybody basically walked out on us but we kept on playing.

We played the whole night, and at the end we noticed at the far end of the gymnasium were about three or four people just leaning up against the wall listening, and then they started walking towards us. It was like that scene out of *Clockwork Orange*. They came up to us and said, "You know, people in this town don't know anything, man. You guys were just great. You were awesome." So it made your night, and I mean that, because when you're doing something like that, it's rewarding that you reach *somebody*. Everybody else in the room hated us, but these three or four people dug it.

Edgar Breau: Our manager, Rick Bissell, was an old style manager. He would do everything for you. He would sell ice to an Eskimo. He called this high school and they said, "We're looking for a band that's appropriate for a high school prom." And he said, "Yeah, Simply Saucer." He told them we were just a perfect compliment to that evening.

Kevin Christoff: We promptly cleared the place. It was a little demoralizing.

Edgar Breau: I remember I was on my belly, screaming into the microphone, and after our first set the principal of the school came into the dressing room. He was almost to the point of tears saying, "Can you guys play something that we know?" Rick would always promise the world and we went out there and did the same thing all over again.

They did that snake dance where they all line up, so they seemed to be having a good time by the end of it. That's the kind of gig we did in the early days. They were kind of bizarre.

Kevin Christoff: The Office was quite a scene. We met a lot of people. We were right off the street, so we were easy to find. There would be a knock on the door and there would be some people saying, "Oh jeez, we've been passing by here for six months listening to you guys and we're just curious what's going on in here," that kind of thing. We attracted a lot of attention, as you probably could guess.

Actually, one night we were playing, going full throttle for a good hour and a half or so, and we decided to take a break and walk outside. Our practice space was right across the road from two pretty popular bars at the time, and we were faced with a mini riot. There were paddy wagons and cops everywhere and people getting arrested and taken down on the street. It was a huge brawl that had erupted in one of these bars, and here we were supplying the soundtrack to it. It must have been kind of weird if you'd happened to be on the street, watching this take place, to have Simply Saucer supplying the vibes to it all.

*   *   *   *   *

Edgar Breau: Our manager took us over to the Lanois studio in 1974, where Danny Lanois and Bob Lanois were working out of their mom's basement. We were one of the early bands that they produced there.

Kevin Christoff: That was really special. None of us had ever done that before and, of course, working with Daniel and Bob Lanois, although then they were just a couple guys, in retrospect it's another level of significance.

Bob Lanois: Simply Saucer came in just before I started building Grant Avenue Studio.

We had been working with Raffi before that. As a matter of fact, when I did Saucer it was actually at the tail end of the basement studio time. We had already been going at it for a few years and when I did Saucer, I already had in mind plans to make a move to the big city of Hamilton.

At that time we were in Ancaster. We were in just a plain little house in Ancaster in the basement, right below my mother's bedroom. Drums are not her favourite instrument.

When Saucer knocked on my door I guess I was just ready for them and we went nuts. I took it seriously. At the age I was at, I forget how old I was; I think it was somewhere around twenty-four years old. I was kind of primed to just really *live it.*

But they just kind of showed up. I didn't know a whole lot about their music or about them, but as I might have done in other cases I just gave them a good set-up so they could do their stuff. That's all, really, so that they could really bloom and be themselves and yell at each other in front of me if they had to and all that stuff. So I think they just felt at home, they just did what they do, and I just got it on tape.

I was a real freak myself at the time. I guess I still am, sort of, but I was a full-blown freak then and so I think I fit right in to their band.

I think without realizing it I like anything that's different, and I suppose I was a little bit musically sheltered to tell you the truth. I'm not sure how open-minded I was musically, and frankly this may have been somewhat of an education even for *me.* So I was really learning as we went, and it was very exciting because I find the learning process for anything a very alive feeling, and even today I'm that way. So I think something new was being revealed to me and I think I was loving it.

What I remember is that they were typical young guys kind of being a bit rough with one another. Serious, and kind of a little bit somber. It was not a giggly, silly atmosphere. There wasn't a lot of humour going on. They had to be in a slightly darker mood to pull it off and so they kept that demeanor, and they were probably those kinds of people, anyway.

I think they were borrowing from, and they were adding their huge, original slant on music, but they were *not* doing a parody of anything and that suits me just fine.

Gary Pig Gold: At the risk of sounding at all overblown or even pretentious, I'd really equate that half-hour recorded at the Lanois' Master Sound studio to Elvis Presley's *Sun Sessions.*

It really is that preposterous, and incongruous a project for its time and place. Not to mention, especially in retrospect, bravely historic. I guess it's only too bad that there were no Sam or Dewey Phillips, not to mention Colonel Tom Parkers, in Hamilton in 1974.

Edgar Breau: Rick took the tapes from those sessions and got turned down. He went to all the major record companies in Canada with the tapes we made with the Lanois brothers and he could not get anybody to put that thing out, so it kind of really hurt because we had such high expectations … Rick did everything he could.

Kevin Christoff: Rick organized these little jaunts here, there, and everywhere. He would put together, on occasion, package deals where we actually played a handful of gigs at high school gyms and this is really kind of funny when I reminisce about it now.

John Balogh came along through Rick I think. At the time, I guess John was a bit of a promoter and what have you, but he was also a stand-up comedian along the lines of Cheech and Chong. It was druggie-type humour. He would go onstage and he would open up for us by delivering a performance of his various stories and situations and he would be followed by a folk singer.

This girl named Melinda would get up onstage, God bless her, armed with nothing but an acoustic guitar and sing. She wrote a few songs and then she'd do some Judy Collins and stuff, and then on would come us. So it was an interesting package. That's how I remember John Balogh coming into the picture and I'm sure it was through an association with Rick, because Rick knew a lot of people in those days.

John Balogh: We didn't have agents and managers back then so we were friends in this little community. There was a chap out of Burlington by the name of Rick Bissell who had promoted a few shows in and around town, so obviously every band and would-be comedian and roadie and everybody would have been stuck to this guy like the human tick just because he was somewhat in it; he was on the inside, we were on the outside.

So somehow we convinced this poor guy to put together a tour. I would have been the emcee, and then we would have had Simply Saucer on the bill and there were a few other unknown artists. There was Melinda Madden and there was another band I think. I never heard of the other ones after that. Maybe everybody married and lived happily every after.

Back then, there were no clubs like we have today where bands can go and play all the time. This was pre–all that, and Rick went out and sold this show, or this revue if you will – it was like a two-, three-hour show – to high schools.

So we were touring with bands and with people like myself who people had literally never heard of — ever, ever, *ever* heard of. And then when the bands get onstage: Simply Saucer's music was like Pink Floyd, LSD; it was a creative endeavour. So if somebody like my mom and dad were in the audience, they would have looked at each other and said, "This guy's on dope," and walked out.

Simply Saucer would be playing and they'd finish a set — one song might have been a half-hour long — and then the song would finish and this is what you'd hear: *nothing*. Because people didn't know whether they were supposed to clap or whether they were supposed to yell. They heard the band; they didn't know if they liked it or not. It was new and they just didn't know what to do — to clap, to cry, to throw something.

We toured like that probably for about a year, year and a half with Saucer. There was like this three-hour tour that we did. It should have been called the Gilligan's Island Tour. But this guy Rick — and I don't know if he was an armed thug or how he talked these high schools into booking this entourage — but I must say the guy had it down; he was pretty polished.

He was probably a short-hair and had a nice suit with some cologne so he'd go in and tell you how great the bands were, and nobody had any idea that there'd be some Moog half-hour solo by Simply Saucer, because back then stuff like that was unheard of. Like I said, end of the song nobody would know whether to laugh, clap, leave, or wait to see if there was another song coming. And he slugged it through. He would have been a pioneer. He was a promoter before I was a promoter.

People used to tell me, "You'll never make a living in the music business. This is Hamilton. What are you, *nuts?*" Well, thankfully enough, we *were* nuts. Because if we had have been conformists like everyone else, instead of sitting here speaking to you today, I would be across the counter from you saying, "Would you like double cream in that?" Or, "Was it Export A or du Maurier?"

And that's sort of what would have happened to us, because none of the guys from Simply Saucer or from Teenage Head or myself, none of us were Rhodes scholars. We had some artistic exploration that had to be done, and thankfully enough we lived in a country where you weren't shot if you displayed some artistic inquisition, you know what I mean?

There was no real place here to play bands. It was a Steel City. So I went to the people that just built the Lloyd D. Jackson Square Mall in Hamilton and said, "You've got a four-acre rooftop garden up there, which is beautiful, with grass and trees and you can hear the wind and you've got a waterfall, but there's really nothing happening and it's not like an old stoner movie where they say, 'Build it and they will come.' They will not come unless you do something there. It needs some activity."

Edgar Breau: It was fairly new, the Jackson Square Mall, right in the centre of Hamilton, downtown. John Balogh was a comic who opened for us on a tour and he booked us into that Jackson Square.

John Balogh: Everybody just wanted to work. They just wanted to play, and I just wanted to tell dirty jokes, and everybody just wanted to do what they thought they were gonna do the rest of their life, but there was nowhere to do it.

At the same time Teenage Head was just being put together, too, and everybody was sort of cutting their wings then. We would all have been sixteen, seventeen years old. As far as a music scene in Hamilton, there was none. We were the creators of the music scene, because if you went to anybody and said, "Oh, we're in the music business in Hamilton," they'd go, "Yeah, and on the weekends you're at *what* institution?"

When you look back that far ago when I started doing the shows on top of Jackson Square, what was the reason or ideology? Well, my only reasoning then was definitely not money. My idea was I had all these friends that were in bands, but they had nowhere to play. They were always dying to fuckin' go to Toronto. So my idea of that whole thing came about to give these guys somewhere to play so they *don't* have to go to Toronto, and make it open to all ages. Because back then when I started doing that stuff, the booze thing wasn't as big a deal as it is now.

Edgar Breau: We played I think the same day Pink Floyd played Ivor Wynne Stadium. It was in the middle of the afternoon and we had a fairly big crowd out there. Shoppers were stopping by to listen to the music. We were pretty hot that day. It was a really good gig. Some days you feel like the muse is visiting you, and that day my fingers were just flying on that fret board. We really let it rip.

I don't know what the shoppers thought of it all.

Kevin Christoff: Somebody wrote in comparing how somebody would have to pay exorbitant amounts of money to go and see Pink Floyd, who were legendary at that time, but Simply Saucer are doing it for free and doing it better and all this stuff. That prompted a few responses from other people and what have you. We didn't get a great deal of publicity about it, but we did get *some* reaction.

John Balogh: I still think to this day a good tour would have been Simply Saucer and Pink Floyd. They were happening at the same time, but Pink Floyd were commercially prostituted far beyond that of mortal men. Simply Saucer were in a league by themselves, in that the stuff that they played wasn't as socially acceptable. I mean, London had a much larger underground, which would have afforded a band like Pink Floyd that momentum, if you will. Where, really, here we were in the city of Hamilton – the Steel City. Our strength was steel; our product was people.

Kevin Christoff: I would say one of the hardest times for the band was after the guitars got stolen. We were lined up to play at McMaster University and we had two nights. And the first night, despite the fact that we still had the electronics and so we were still pretty out there, we had a really large crowd, and apparently people were lined up to come in and see us so it was a really, really good night and the band was in good form.

And that next afternoon the guitars were stolen, but we still had a show to do. So we scrounged around and we got some substitutes, but they were very cheap instruments and we weren't familiar with them and that night was an absolute disaster.

It was very demoralizing, not to mention the fact that after it was all said and done we had to face the fact that we had no instruments. We, being Ed and I, had insurance coverage for any kind of loss or theft with the Musicians' Union, so it took a long time for the claim to come through. So there was a really long period of time where we didn't have instruments, therefore we had no way of doing what we do.

We'd still all get together as if it were some ritual, but there was no music being played, no songs being written. That was a pretty bleak period. There was definitely momentum lost, absolutely.

3. freaks of nature

Teenage Head / photo by Ralph Alfonso

Frankie Venom: When we came over from Glasgow I was only, what, three years old, and my sister, she's three years younger than me. So we lived in this alley, Melbourne, off of Locke Street in Hamilton. There was an abundance of rats so we had jars of rat poison. So I told my sister, Christine's her name, I told her, "They're wee mints." They looked like little rabbit stools. So my parents were out with my aunts, my aunt Agnes, my aunt Chrissy, my uncle John, blah, blah, blah, blah, blah. I'm babysitting Christine so I feed her this rat poison. She turns *blue.* Like I said, I was four years old, she was two. So our parents come back — this is true — fortunately my parents came back and had to take her to the hospital, get her stomach pumped.

"Frankie, what'd you do? What'd you do to Christine?"

So I run into the alley, up the tree — I'm up the tree, thirty feet up. My dad's there, he was real stocky, saying, "Come here!" I'm frozen. They had to call the fire department. The crane comes up to get me. I'm just like a frozen cat. I didn't know what I was in for. So they get me down.

Well, I attempted to kill my sister. You know what my dad did? *Hugged* me! He said, "Don't you poison your sister again, son." Ha ha ha.

True. That's true. I'm not bullshitting you. I don't bullshit. He just gave me a hug.

Well, she survived because they pumped her stomach. To this day, my sister and I are tight. She says, "Frankie, don't poison me again," ha ha ha, and we wink.

Stephen Mahon: I was too young to know, "I want to do that," but I saw the Beatles on television and I was sort of drawn to it like a moth to a light. I wasn't even at the age where I could say, "Oh, that's a great riff," or, "That's a great song." That's my first memory of what music was and how it could impress me.

We moved from Ancaster to Hamilton. That was when I started Grade 3. Ancaster and Hamilton were only about a ten-mile difference. I think we were busing to school, me and my sister, and I think they wanted us to get closer so we could walk or ride our bikes to school. It was closer for my dad to go to work, too.

Nick [Stipanitz] was the first guy I met. He was in my homeroom class. Nick had an older brother. His parents were really tolerant of their sons playing instruments and having bands and things, because his brother had his own band in the basement of his house and that was a big deal for me and Nick to hear this band practise.

When I'd come over on the weekend we weren't allowed downstairs because we were pests, but we'd stand by the basement window and listen and that was my first memory of, like, wow, this is too cool, these guys are really doing it. They've got their amps plugged in and there's drums and there's mics and a PA, so that's kind of what got me excited.

I'm sure Nick wasn't as excited because he kind of grew up with it. Then at one point, I think it was the summer of Grade 8, his mom and dad let him get drums. I remember thinking, Oh shit, *I* wanted to play drums. But he was my best bud so I was like, "Okay, cool, you got drums," right? I still had nothing.

Gordie Lewis: Believe it or not, I knew I was going to do this from the time I was six years old. I wanted to do this. I wasn't old enough to see the Beatles on *Ed Sullivan,* but my first interest in music was probably Beatles cartoons as a kid.

By the time I was in adolescence *The Monkees* were on, around 1967, and that's when I knew I wanted to do it. It was more I wanted to be part of a group dynamic more than just be a musician. There was something about that group dynamic, and playing music, that I really liked. And I started buying magazines like *Hit Parader,* which actually printed lyrics to songs. That was the most amazing thing I ever saw in my life at the time, actually seeing the lyrics printed out. You have to remember there wasn't a whole lot of media. Things were very primitive as far as what you could obtain outside of the radio. You really had to do some digging. It was very limited, and to find things took a lot of searching.

I would have been ten, eleven years old and I still hadn't played a musical instrument yet, but I was still fascinated with music. And it wasn't really encouraged in the schools at the time. There weren't any music classes. If you wanted to do music you really had to do it on your own, you really did. It just wasn't there.

Dave Rave: Gordie and Steve and me, we were all in chemistry class in Westdale. Steve was a great artist. Stephen and me, we were chemistry partners, which meant no chemistry was being done. We both failed miserably. Gord was always smart and sat in the back and stayed away from us and got his marks. Ha ha ha. We were too distracted, drawing amps and talking about the Stones' new record coming out, *Exile on Main Street.*

I think Westdale mixed a lot of different people. We had posh people, we had Jewish, we had low class, and we had middle and we had working class. All of us were all going to this same big school and because of that mix — this is looking back in retrospect — we had a wide variety of people who were influencing us all. Entertainment and all that stuff was in the air. Jack Blum, who went off to be Spaz in *Meatballs,* he was from our school. Back then Jack was a Renaissance guy.

He could act, he could play guitar, he could debate the teachers. He was ahead of the curve in human behaviour, and watching that brought me out into something else.

My guitar playing was encouraged, and I'd meet other guys who played guitar and we'd have these assemblies. And at the time tradition didn't mean much, but Martin Short came from our school, Eugene Levy; so we had a bit of a tradition of people who had come from the school and achieved something. We were pretty irreverent about it, but it was still in the back of our minds. So I think that's what it was: A wide range of people, where other schools would have had a more suburban point of view at the time.

Gordie Lewis: We all met more or less at Westdale High School in Hamilton. We probably ran into each other at different places but that's where we more got our musical ideas together before we even had a band. Just kind of talking at the locker. We met as kids playing baseball and stuff like that. Actually, the first time I met Frank was in Grade 9 phys. ed.

Frankie Venom [*Shades* no. 4, Spring, 1979]: In Grade 9 and 10 I took a couple of smacks on the back in the hallways and got my head crammed in the lockers.

Gordie Lewis: We were put together as wrestling partners because we were the two smallest kids in the class. I didn't know who he was at the time.

Frankie Venom: I was wild, cantankerous, obnoxious, abusive, insensitive — bullshit. What do you think?

We just grew up with the influences of New York Dolls, Stooges, MC5, Eddie Cochran, Gene Vincent. We were the only guys that went to high school with tight jeans. Everybody was wearing bell bottoms and all that kind of shit. We weren't punks. We're *still* not punks.

We used to open our lockers and we had little pictures of New York Dolls, MC5, and I saw their lockers, they saw mine. We were all connected. "Let's get a band together," and that was it. That was the inspiration; that was the start.

We weren't outcasts, but liked to be different. Back then we took a lot of heckling, a lot of bullshit. "Fuck you," pardon my language. "Fuck off." Let's say we got expelled a few times. So what?

Stephen Mahon: By Grade 9 Nick and I had met Gordie and obviously hit it off. Gord was right at the same place except that he'd gotten a bass guitar. I'm sure I was right in the middle of that, saying, "Cool, Nick has drums and you've got a bass, you guys should jam some-how." Gord would end up coming over when Nick would have his little turn in the basement. I guess I was just glad to be part of it, even though I was just watching.

Gordie Lewis: It was just guys getting together and goofing off, that's really what we were doing, because none of us knew how to play.

The very first thing I remember was with Nick: he actually played the drums and *had* drums. And Frank played drums, too, so they had musical backgrounds as drummers. I had a bass guitar by that time and I just went down one day with my bass and an amp — I don't know *where* I got an amp from — and Nick drummed for about fifteen minutes. And that was about it. That was our first rehearsal. A drummer and a bass player for fifteen minutes, that was about all we could get through. But it was a start, you know?

Stephen Mahon: Not too long after that happened, for some reason Gord came to the next practise with a guitar, and I don't know why. It was obviously a good move for Gord because he's turned into an amazing guitar player. But because of that decision, that left the bass just sitting there, so you fill in the gap and I picked it up.

I could never figure out how the bass worked. It's like you're *feeling* it, and you're *hearing* it, but it's weird. I'm going back to when I was eight or nine and my mom took me to the Canadian National Exhibition. Actually, that was the first time I saw a band. We walked in the Princess Gates and 1050 CHUM had a little stage set up where they had a DJ going live and there was a stage with some band on it. This was probably ten o'clock in the morning when we got there. I was holding my mom's hand because I was that small — well, not that small, but it was, like, Toronto and you're with your mom — and I must have looked at her, and looked at the band, and she looked at me and she just let my hand go. I know it sounds corny but it's true. And off I went and stood right up front; you'd go right to the edge because there was nobody watching this band, who knows who the hell they were, and that was just such a buzz for me to watch that band play.

But I had no idea how to play. I'm left-handed, Gord isn't, so the bass was right-handed. Do you think I knew? When I picked it up I just flipped it over in the left-handed way that felt comfortable and started playing it. It took two years for someone to go, "Hey, you know you're playing that backwards, right?"

I'm like, "What?" And they had to explain it to me — "It's supposed to be like *this,* with the big E string on top." I said, "Really? So what, who cares?" And I just left it that way.

Frank was one year older than us, but he had drums. Frank wasn't a singer yet; he was just this other kid from across the tracks who already had kids coming into his basement. Again, it was kindred spirits.

We'd lost Nick to his brother's band and at some point we were asked to come to Frank's place and jam. We were getting a little bit better, slowly. We were cranking the amps on Saturdays when his parents let us jam. Nick's parents lived about a block from Frank's parents, so every Saturday he knew we were having our little jam session.

Well, he missed it. I mean Nick was our buddy. The songs his brother's band was doing were all Top 40. He'd come over every Saturday with excuses to borrow pieces of equipment his brother needed or to give back something maybe he'd borrowed, but it wasn't really important. He just wanted to be a part of it.

Slash Booze: There are a lot of incarnations of the early Teenage Head. The rehearsals centred around Frank's basement and Nick's house. Saturdays were when they'd congregate. Frank's parents were pretty tolerant, to a point. Ha ha ha. The police weren't always quite so tolerant.

Chris Houston: They came every Saturday.

Stephen Mahon [CIUT-FM interview with Greg Dick, 2007]: The cops *would* come, but they were really nice. They'd say, "Well, look, guys, just try to turn it down a little bit, because it's in the middle of the day, so ..." And they'd actually tell us we were getting better every time they'd come. They were nice. We didn't care that they came.

Gordie Lewis [CIUT-FM interview with Greg Dick, 2007]: They got to know us.

Slash Booze: Frank's dad used to yell down, "Get that bass down, the cat can't walk." The floor would be shaking. Steve managed to acquire what we called the Fridge. It was a Fender Reflex Bassman. He wasn't shy about turning it up and that thing shook the floor.

Stephen Mahon: There wasn't really a problem with the way we wanted it to sound because we wanted it garage-y, trashy, just like Iggy, just like Alice Cooper, just like the Dolls. That's what we wanted and that's really the only style we could play. It wasn't like one guy was a great virtuoso. We all started on the same level playing field and that was never a problem, we always just seemed to gel. We always had an agreement of what sounded cool and what didn't.

Gordie Lewis: The name came from a band called the Flamin' Groovies.

How we picked up our information was through magazines. I had this *CREEM* magazine and on the

back was (an offer): If you got a subscription, (you got) this free album called *Teenage Head* by the Flamin' Groovies. I just thought, Wow, what a cool name for a band, Teenage Head. This is 1971; I hadn't even picked up a guitar yet I don't think. I thought, This is the name of my band. This band that I was thinking of back when I was six years old, back when I was ten and watching the Monkees, and it was, "Okay, now I've got the *name* of my band."

Stephen Mahon: To make a long story short, at some point Frank maybe went upstairs for a phone call; Frank seems to remember that he hurt his wrist drumming — whatever reason, obviously Nick ended up getting behind Frank's drums and that left Frank to attempt to sing somehow. Because, see, for the longest time we didn't miss singing. When you're just a band starting out, you just want to get through the song musically. That is just such a buzz when you do that, even if it's just a two-chord song, you feel like you've climbed a mountain. But then you'd sit back and you'd think, "Oh yeah, but there's *singing*," so at that point we probably thought, We need that. If we're going to get anywhere we need someone to sing. So that was just cool, because that led to Frank becoming a singer and the rest is history.

Dave Rave: Frank was a great musician, great drummer. I've always called him the most talented guy I've ever known because anything he picked up he was a natural at. So natural that it was almost to his detriment in a way because he never thought about it.

I grabbed my guitar and started singing these Beatles songs. Frank started singing "I Should Have Known Better." So I knew he could sing a tune, even though *he* didn't know he could sing a tune. He had that natural, beautiful Scottish voice when he sang. So I knew he had a nice voice, but he was playing the kit.

But I always thought that Frank, because he was a drummer first, was insecure about his singing. Because I don't think he came in going, "I'm going to be a singer." But he was so natural — and this is how I'm illustrating the point of how natural a musician he was — he could do it and suddenly he's the most amazing front man ever, from being a *drummer*. He's fantastic. He's got all the attitude, everything it takes to do it.

But because he didn't plan to be a front man, or he didn't want it and he wasn't playing out all these stage moves in his room like the rest of us who would look in the mirror and pretend we were Alice Cooper. He wasn't doing that . . . Looking back, maybe at first he was a bit nervous.

Frankie Venom: I wanted to be in a band to get girls and get laid and get drunk and have some drugs.

Gordie Lewis: When we were in high school as a band, we were freaks of nature. Nobody was in a band; that was unheard of, guys being in a band. The only thing that was going on was folk music in schools. Being in a band was a really strange thing to do.

But because it was that way, no one discouraged us because no one understood exactly what we were doing every weekend.

David Liss: Those guys were in some ways *destined* to be in a band. They never did anything else from the age of twelve.

Stephen Mahon [*Shades* no. 4, Spring, 1979]: One thing that made up our minds was when we went to see the New York Dolls. We were about sixteen and managed to sneak up to their hotel room. We saw these five guys with literally no talent at all, with all this booze and chicks running in and out all the time. We were just standing against the wall, holding it up and Gordie said to me, "Look, this is a real tough life." And here we are.

*   *   *   *   *

Gordie Lewis [*Blitz* Magazine, March/April 1982]: The first unofficial Teenage Head gig was at the Hillview Street Dance. That was the street that Frank lived on. They are all Scottish on that street. Every year they have a great big street dance with different bands. And we played there. It was Steve Park on bass, Frank on drums, and me on guitar. We hired Dave Rave for the day as a singer.

We did "Teengenerate" by the Dictators, "Down on the Street" by the Stooges, "Lookin' For a Kiss" by the New York Dolls, an MC5 song and stuff like that. No originals. Those might as well have been original tunes when you consider the number of people that knew those songs back then.

Dave Rave: I remember in the beginning Teenage Head were doing covers, and they were getting a hard time because nobody knew around here what these guys were doing. Nobody liked glam rock, not in the clubs. Everybody still wanted rock 'n' roll like the Doobie Brothers, that's what the clubs were playing.

I've always had an open mind and I love inventors and I love inventions, so I kept looking over there going, "These guys are having a hell of a time."

We'd all be reading these New York magazines and we'd see all these groovy pictures, but we couldn't get the records. But the pictures were intriguing enough that they interested me in the music. I always had this thing where I want to see the inventors.

The Stooges had disbanded and we were waiting for Iggy to come back. The Dolls were sort of over, too.

And the Dictators were happening, and it's funny, the Dictators were rampaged in the press. Lauren Agnelli, God bless her, wrote this amazing review called "Heavy Metal Will Stand" of the Dictators and I remember going, "That's got to be right." Gordie of course got the record because *Rolling Stone* killed it — they said it's a bunch of shit, worse than you've ever heard — but Lauren went, "It's great," and I went, "I'll trust a girl any day." Guys never get rock right. The girls liked Elvis, the guys didn't like him, so I trusted her opinion more than the stodgy rock critics.

So there was a vacuum happening between '74, '75, and we're getting these articles and looking in the papers.

Gordie Lewis: Hamilton at the time was folk and blues; that's basically what it was then. So therefore anyone following what was going down in New York was pretty unique. There was nothing like that here, so we were kind of isolated from the musical community.

Frankie Venom [*Shades* no. 4, Spring, 1979]: One thing about our band, though, is that we spent a solid summer in the basement, none of us ever seeing the sun. We were in there every fucking day for about six hours for an entire summer, and we didn't come out until we thought we were good enough.

Gordie Lewis: The Westdale High School coffeehouse at the end of the year, in October '75, let us play. We had probably about ten, twelve songs that we had learned. I can't remember a whole lot about it except we got through the songs and everyone seemed to like it. Nobody said anything bad about us.

It just felt like we'd accomplished something. Like, "Okay, we're a band now." We had our first gig under our belt so it was, "What can we do next? Is there *anything* we can do next?"

At that point we were just doing cover songs like New York Dolls songs, Mott the Hoople, Sweet, whatever we could come up with at the time. Aerosmith, because they were just starting. Then it was, "Okay, let's *write* songs." That's what I always wanted to do; I didn't want to be a cover band. I wanted to play original material. So that was the next step — How do we write? And that's what we started doing.

Stephen Mahon: We all knew all the bands that we loved, like Iggy and the Dolls and stuff, they all wrote their own songs. We knew that; we knew you had to. Any kid that got into that game knew that right from the get-go. I mean, the Stones went through the same thing — the first song they did was the Buddy Holly song "Not Fade Away," but not too long afterwards they started writing. So that was sort of a given; we knew that, and thank God Gord had the talent to do it.

He's basically the creator of most of the songs. Everybody else threw their two cents in. Frank would write lyrics and Nick would help him and I threw in the bass line and stuff. It didn't take long. We knew we weren't gonna be one of those clone bands. We knew that we needed to do our own thing.

Slash Booze: Everybody in Teenage Head got along well and that, but they were really treading water because at this time there was no what they'd call the "punk scene" now.

They were really doing good at starting to write their own songs and work on how a song is structured and that sort of thing. They did a lot of covers, too, but no bars around this time were going to hire a band like that. Like, "What's this music you're playing?" At that time the covers would consist of KISS songs, New York Dolls, and the Dictators. There was no Ramones yet. People were looking at this like, "What's this crap?" They didn't really get it.

Gordie Lewis: We were definitely on our own.

*   *   *   *   *

Paul Kobak: My cousin and I started out in the '70s listening to rock and going to concerts almost every week in Toronto. We thought the prices of vinyl LPs were too high and figured there's money to be made by cutting down on the profit margin and relying upon volume sales. We opened a store in Oshawa in 1973 but his family persuaded him that I should open my own store somewhere. I wasn't ambitious enough to be the best vinyl store in Toronto, so I decided upon Hamilton and opened Star Records there in March of 1975.

When I arrived in Hamilton, the bar scene was more profound then. Downtown was more vibrant and the steel companies employed a larger chunk of the population, providing younger adults with much spending money. The radio stations were playing awful stuff that all the bar bands would interpret as a signal of what people en masse would enjoy. The only existing real bands were Crowbar and Rush, but they became big quick and didn't play locally much. Max Webster and Goddo had only started playing the bar circuit and were about to release their first LPs.

Dave Rave: I remember one day on our break from school we took the bus and went downtown. There was this store at the corner of King and James [upstairs] called Star Records. I went, "*Cool.*" So we walked upstairs and it was really cheap, like three ninety-nine and four ninety-nine for all these records, and I went, "What a cool little store." Slowly, Star Records would

get these records that nowhere else had. That was a big part, like seeing the Flamin' Groovies *Shake Some Action*. They were getting records that they weren't getting anywhere else.

Paul Kobak: The only typical thing for me about Star Records was that there were long hours working at a fast pace. On opening day, I had four boxes of sealed records to sell. Within nine months I had about five thousand, within three years there were twenty-five thousand. I took usually two trips a week to the warehouses in Toronto because the stock was just flying out the doors then. The big boom in records had arrived. My time spent behind the counter increasingly decreased because I'd be too busy doing advertising, dealing with other business affairs, trying to have affairs of my own, constantly liaising with other store owners, getting complimentary concert tickets weekly from the record companies and basically trying to keep tabs on what the trends were in music and who was hot.

Whoever was behind the counter, myself included, would open the doors in the morning, turn on the stereo and then people would walk in and out all day, keeping oneself fairly engaged in conversation and activities. My trips to the warehouse were exciting for all. I'd be excited like a kid in a candy store, picking out any records I wanted. My workers got excited at being able to open up brand new records and hear them for the first time. Then between us and the customers, we'd endlessly talk about the latest releases, who's touring, and every kind of music existing. There was no way anyone could get bored.

Star Records seemed to be the music information hub of Hamilton. First of all it had a superior location. You couldn't be more downtown than James Street. You just had to find the doorway to walk upstairs and "save a buck." The other stores were corporate chain stores and charged twenty to forty per cent more and had staffing who seemed indifferent about music and their jobs.

My store was used as a meeting place for lots of people. "Meet you between three and four?" "Okay, I'll see you over at Star." Very common. So yeah, Star was a catalyst to the Hamilton music scene, whether for buying albums or catching up on what's happening anywhere. It turned out to be the place to go to first.

Stephen Mahon: Me and Gordie and Nick were already buying and collecting albums and would certainly go there. It was the first store in Hamilton that would actually sell used records, so that was really cool. We didn't have a penny so to think that you could go buy an album that was used but a lot cheaper, that attracted us, so we would go there. You know that *Empire Records* thing where record stores seem to become more than just a place to buy records? It was like that, for me anyways.

Paul Kobak: Most of my acquaintances came through my record store. One day a couple of my regular customers came into my store thrilled that they'd just played their first gig at the coffeehouse in their high school, and proclaimed that the name of their band was Teenage Head.

Gordie Lewis: I guess we were probably all meeting or congregating up there at Star Records and just out of conversation we had probably started talking to Paul and eventually said, "We've got a band."

Whatever it was that connected us with Paul, there was some common fondness for whatever certain type of music that was happening at the time. Which would have been the Ramones, Flamin' Groovies, Runaways, Slade, Bay City Rollers, you know, all that stuff. Paul had the store and it was a place for us to go and buy records and just hang around. One thing led to another and we became friends.

Paul Kobak: I enjoyed the same music they were into and went to see them rehearse at the ex-rhythm guitarist Stephen Park's basement. They didn't have any original tunes at that time, but I was impressed enough at the way they handled themselves and had such laughs with them that I offered to do what I could to find them some gigs.

Stephen Mahon: Paul just took an interest in wanting to be involved with a band as a manager. And we were certainly in need of anybody helping us in any way, especially someone like that who was able to help financially. You couldn't think of a better way of helping a band with nothing. The guy had a car and a record store. It was perfect. He was like a father figure.

Paul Kobak: Let's get something straight: During the '70s, I chauffeured Teenage Head to every gig they did.

Slash Booze: When we went to see the New York Dolls at the Queensbury Arms, well, of course Kobak was driving, he was the only one who had a car —

Chris Houston: With a beer fridge in it, too.

Stephen Mahon: The New York Dolls played at the Queensbury Arms in the west end for a whole week. That was the first time I saw Steven Leckie. Me and Gordie went, actually made it somehow, every night. I can remember seeing the two girls from the B-Girls, Lucasta and Xenia; they were there all dressed up. They were kind of like the Toronto groupies. Steven, I don't think he even had the Viletones yet, in '76.

Rob Sikora: I was there every night. I lived around the corner. Not many people there, but I remember Lucasta and Xenia were pretty visible.

Steve [Leckie] and his bunch were there. He was pretty aloof. He had sunglasses and black hair, sort of Ramones'd out. Steve's hair changed a lot.

Stephen Mahon: The Dolls were already on their second version. It wasn't with Johnny Thunders, it wasn't with Jerry Nolan.

Rob Sikora: It was this weird bridge period where they weren't a glam rock band anymore and they were embracing different kinds of music. Like there would be a disco song playing before they came on, and Syl would start playing and singing along to it and people weren't digging that.

But these guys were from New York. They listened to that music *for real.*

Stephen Mahon: So it was just the end with the glam era and it was just starting to touch base with what was going to become the new punk thing, in Toronto anyway. That's why we all went. Anybody that was sort of anybody at that time was at the Queensbury Arms that week.

Imants Krumins: At that point I sort of noticed that Teenage Head were becoming more serious about [being] a band because I don't think I came back some nights, and they went *every* night, rather than me just going two nights. They were so into it. That was what they wanted to do; you could really tell at that point.

Paul Kobak: When I first saw them practise in a basement, I knew that here were some guys that had potential. They were very cohesive the moment they felt they were quote unquote onstage. As raw as they were in the beginning, they always maintained a sense of professionalism and wanted to buck the current trends at the time by going back to the roots. The more they started writing their own tunes, the more impressed I became. We were all comparing notes constantly on what was going on in New York, London, and elsewhere and could sense an underlying explosion or "new wave" about to hit.

Gordie Lewis: We did have a few people that kind of were interested, like Paul, who picked up on what we were doing and helped us out. But it was very, very low-key and it was very minimal as far as the people who would really pick up on what we were trying to do.

Paul Kobak: They envied New York City. There seemed an underlying current about them; that they wanted to be famous and play the States. They got tighter rapidly and started writing their own tunes and I became increasingly impressed in the belief that they could've been a major talent.

Gordie Lewis: Paul let us party in his apartment, he bought us beer and wine and stuff, food. Ha ha ha. He helped us out. He believed in us in a time when there weren't a whole lot of people that did.

Dave Rave: Paul took an interest in Teenage Head and the band rehearsed there at Star Records. And he became the first manager of the band, which is a very common thing in rock 'n' roll. The record store guys usually get screwed because they know how to run a record store, not be a manager. You're in the record store half the time anyhow and the manager knows it, and you're not buying anything but you're still somehow coming into the store. Are they stealing? Can't prove it. They must be in a band. Ha ha ha. And so that was very important. Paul nurtured the band and gave them a place to rehearse.

Paul Kobak: What sort of experience did one require in the mid-'70s to manage a bar band? That's all they were until they started to write their own tunes. Any fool could manage a bar band.

To go through all the bullshit I went through, I would not wish upon anyone. The first few months of managing Teenage "Fred" were like the first few years. Lotsa going-out-of-one's-way to pitch the band, just to have lotsa doors shut in your face.

Dave Rave: There was resistance all around. I remember I had an agent and I was bringing Gord down after school and I'd say, "Book Teenage Head!" And they'd say, "We want show bands." And the show bands would have been the bands that were playing the rock music that was already big and already around.

Paul Kobak: I put on a free Christmas party at a local hall and had some band open for Teenage Head and they were hooked. They were headlining and had their name in the paper. A few months later we opened for Max Webster at the Delta Theatre and more doors started to open at that point.

They called me their manager and it was a big ego boost to me. Imagine, being twenty years old and having the hippest record store west of Toronto and managing a cutting-edge band.

After the first couple of gigs, I would envision them playing in front of concert settings and going on tours and stuff. Onstage and in practice, they became an increasingly tight unit.

1975, l-r: Gordie Lewis, Stephen Mahon, Nick Stipanitz, Frankie Venom, Stephen Park / photo by Peter Bauce, courtesy Teenage Head

Teenage Head, Crash 'n' Burn Club, 1977

l-r: Stephen Mahon, Slash Booze, Jan Sikora, Gordie Lewis, Frank Venom, Nick Stipanitz, Paul Kobak, Xenia, Rob Sikora, Lucasta, Eden Mohler

/ photo by Ralph Alfonso

4. death by design

John Hamilton: There seemed to be a lot of people in Toronto around the same age at the same time who wanted to do something different. It might have been a blip in the birth rate or something that we all came to the same age at the same time and we didn't like what we'd inherited.

You've got the Ontario College of Art at Dundas and McCaul, and that begot the Beverley Tavern because all the art students had to go somewhere and have beer. So when I first went to the Beverley Tavern it was because a guy I went to high school with was going to OCA.

Queen Street at that time was really just a quiet area with lots of cheap housing, cheap spaces to rent. The artists naturally gravitated to it because there were a lot of buildings that I guess once upon a time probably had offices above them or something like that. But they'd all gone to the 'burbs or somewhere else, so you had stores with second and third floors that were virtually abandoned.

Johnny MacLeod: Queen Street was this derelict area of the city. There was nothing; there was no celebrity scene around it then. So it felt like you were at the outpost of civilization, you could go this way or that way.

Mark Gane: The 1970s culture, the mainstream culture, was just so incredibly bland. The '60s were a very revolutionary time, though it never fulfilled its promises, I don't think. Then in the '70s, it was like the '60s got blanded out. It was the same sort of hippie idea but was all blanded out, and you were getting songs on the radio like "Tie a Yellow Ribbon Around an Old Oak Tree" and all that crap.

It was bound to happen. Punk was just inevitable. Somebody was going to go, "I just can't stand this anymore." It was so pukey.

John Hamilton: Everybody was sort of kicking against what a dismal scene it was in Toronto, and that you couldn't play any original music. I'd been in England for a while and I'd seen people playing original music over there and I wanted to do the same thing.

The only club around at that time where you could play original music was the Beverley Tavern. It had been the old art scene bar for years. In the '60s it had blues bands playing in it, then it had fallen off and anybody could basically play there as long as you showed up for Thursday, Friday, and Saturday. I think they paid you a hundred and eighty dollars for three days.

Murray Ball, The Dishes / photo by Ralph Alfonso

I started playing there with a band called the Daily Planet, doing original material.

Queen Street at that time, nobody went there. The street was really bad to drive on because of the streetcars; it was all broken up, so most people who drove downtown would avoid it. There was no reason to go there.

There was only one or two restaurants. It was like being in a small town on Queen Street. It was quiet. When you walked down the street you would virtually know just about everybody. It was an ethnic area, too, with Polish and Ukrainian people, so it wasn't a scary area like Queen Street East where you had some serious white trash who were dangerous and violent.

Queen Street West might have been sort of crappy, but it wasn't scary. There was nobody at the Beverley Tavern who would beat you up. It was next to a chicken slaughterhouse, which would definitely keep away people who wanted to like disco. And that kept the posers away really bad. When you went to the Beverley Tavern the chicken blood would be running down the gutters in the summer at ninety-eight degrees. It was pretty raw; you had to be a pioneer to go there.

Johnny MacLeod: My reality of it is when I was growing up, the Velvet Underground was a rock band, or the Stooges were a rock band, or the MC5. A lot of us north of the city up around Thornhill and so on were playing music that was influenced by all those things, plus Captain Beefheart and all *those* things. They were creeping in there.

But there really was nowhere to play. The drinking age at that time was kind of going from twenty-one down to eighteen, but there hadn't really developed a bar scene for music and the high school scene had kind of died off, which was the real bread and butter of the Toronto music scene at that time because the audience couldn't go to bars. But in the early '70s, there was absolutely nothing for original music.

Ken Farr: We were a bunch of kids from the suburbs, a story that's often been told. Ha ha ha. At the time there really wasn't an independent band scene in Toronto at all. Everybody was over on Yonge Street.

At the time people played guitars in stairwells in high schools. The acoustics were really good in those concrete buildings from the '70s. So I guess there was a music scene in Thornhill in the high school, kind of more folky, and it developed from there.

The Dishes started out as a band playing in Andy Zeeley's basement in a house in Thornhill, and I think that had a lot to do with the shape of the music. Then after his parents couldn't stand it anymore we played in *my* parents' basement.

My mom used to go around and take the pictures off the wall that were going to fall down. I look back on it now and I just can't believe anyone would tolerate a six-piece band playing in the basement of a small house.

It was your standard kids in high school — start a band and away you go.

Steven Davey: The Dishes were my brother's band and they were, like, five years younger and they brought me in to be their manager. The first thing I said was, "You need a drummer, so I'll be the drummer until you can find one because I can keep basic time." So that's how I ended up as the drummer, but I was also the manager and sort of conceptualist. I did the image thing and aligned us up with the art people.

I always knew that all you had to do was appeal to people who worked in boutiques. We used to follow Rough Trade around; I was the first person to ever write about Rough Trade and was very instrumental in their very early days. They started out at Grossman's [Tavern] and I saw how they attracted this trendy, elite core, and I realized if you could get those people to like your band it would snowball from there. And of course we did — the photographers, the fashion people, people who owned stores. Those are people who are usually up on new things and hip things. Not to say the Dishes weren't serious musicians.

Glenn Schellenberg: I started to go to music school at U of T [University of Toronto], and I quit after two weeks and joined the Dishes because I wanted to be a pop star.

With the Dishes, it was very arty and also it had this kind of gay thing going on. There was some sexual ambiguity with Rough Trade, but with women it's not as threatening. I mean, it's just not. Little girls can be tomboys or whatever, but if a little boy dresses up in a dress people go berserk, right? The Dishes were very cool. Tony and Murray were queer, and Michael too at the time and I was a queer guy, so it was appealing. Oh, and Steven, too. Ha ha ha.

Ken Farr: It was the standard suburban thing — you go downtown. That's where it was happening. Steven, who was the promotional artistic brilliance behind everything, already had lots of connections in the city.

Glenn Schellenberg: Steven was more like the producer. He was the oldest kid and he had the most connections. Steven was also more in charge of the look and the aesthetic. He would always make the posters. The rest of it, other than the music writing, was really Steven.

Martha Johnson: It was the Ontario College of Art that got things going.

Mark Gane: There was no "D" on the end of it then. Everybody who went to OCA at that time loathes the "D." As if art has to be legitimized by design.

Martha Johnson: Death by design.

Steven Davey: People I grew up with north of Toronto, we all went to York University or U of T and then moved downtown. And a lot of the people who took film courses or video art courses got jobs on staff at OCA, so that was our "in" there. They had a building just south of the main campus which was the experimental arts wing and they had a recording studio and video equipment and they would have parties in there all the time and have really horrible blues bands play. Me and my friends would go, "Wait a minute, we have our own band." And so that was the nucleus.

There was a jokey sort of band called Oh Those Pants!, and they played songs like "Kung Fu Fighting" really badly on purpose. But they would play in front of three hundred drunken students and in front of films being projected on the wall and the whole thing, so it was a real multimedia experience. But it was a joke; it wasn't anything serious, it was all covers. There were two drummers. Neither of them could play. Martha was the keyboard player and had never played before in her life. I played the saxophone and didn't know how. But we'd just play these old rock 'n' roll songs that everybody sort of knew, so you didn't even have to rehearse them and the audience would all get up and dance.

Martha Johnson: I was a very minor part in Oh Those Pants! I was the token girl. I think there were eleven people in the band at that time. It was pretty much a cover band. But they always had a theme, like this wrestling theme where the two lead singers would dress up as wrestlers.

Oh Those Pants! / photo by Ralph Alfonso

Anna Bourque: They were the first band I'd ever seen I think. Apparently they were sitting around trying to figure out a name and one of them said, "Okay, the next thing that comes out of someone's mouth is our band name." And someone went, "Oh those pants are … oops!" So they were called Oh Those Pants!, which I still think is one of the best band names ever.

Seeing them was kind of when you started to see the world turn in a way.

Mark Gane: I remember Oh Those Pants! played at OCA and the lead singer came out in a tennis costume walking with a tennis ball and then went into "The In Crowd." I thought that was totally great.

Martha Johnson: We played for nothing. Oh Those Pants! used to play for a case of beer.

Steven Davey: The people who were in Oh Those Pants! were also on staff at OCA. And so after work they would all go down to the Beverley because it was the closest bar, obviously. It was even closer than the Rex. So the staff would all hit this bar at two o'clock in the afternoon, as well as the technicians, and would sit there all afternoon drinking away. They used to have quarts of Black Label for ninety cents, so it didn't pay to be sober.

Rodney Bowes: That's where we'd go every day. It was kind of like the school cafeteria except there was beer. It's funny because people say, "So what'd you guys all do, go and get drunk?" It was like no, that wasn't really what the thing was at the Beverley. It was really like a cafeteria. After school that's where you would go and all your friends would be there and you'd hang out there. There really weren't any places to go. You could buy a tray of draft for like a buck or something.

It was disgusting in there. It was all smoky and really raunchy and it was all full of rubbies and semi-homeless people, and then bikers were downstairs. It was kind of a weird thing but there was no bar. There was no sanctuary, no place to go, so we just kind of took that place over. And it was right at the bottom of the street. It was totally convenient. That's what you'd tell all your friends — "Okay, I'll meet you at the Beverley after class."

Mark Gane: The Beverley Tavern was like OCA's living room.

Steven Davey: At nine o'clock a horrible country and western band would come on. I just realized, Wait a minute, *we* could start putting shows on here. So I approached the manager and the Dishes started playing there in early 1976.

Ken Farr: I think the first show was really the oddest, or in a way the most memorable, because people just stood in the audience and couldn't believe what we were doing; couldn't believe what they were hearing. It was the only time I've ever played a set where people just sort of looked blank. Completely puzzled would be the way to describe it.

What we really wanted, I think, was music that sounded like the background music to really old animated cartoons from the 1930s. That chunky, bouncy music where toothpaste tubes are dancing and they've got arms and legs and they sing, that kind of thing. So it started out as two-beat, chunky music. It was really kind of odd 1930s cartoon jazz music.

At the time Queen Street West, where the Beverley Tavern was, there was a chicken processing factory next door which added to the ambience of the place. People would be chopping the heads off chickens with the door open. MuchMusic was just an empty warehouse. We often thought, "Oh, that would make a great recording studio or something." It was really a fun time to be in Toronto. There was just a sense of unbridled possibility, and for music it certainly was. It was a scene that grew very quickly.

Gary Pig Gold: You know, my father used to go to the Beverley, so it was always there. When I used to come home he'd go, "Where do you stay out to till two in the morning?" Because Toronto closes at eight o'clock at night, right? And I said, "There's this place on Queen Street called the Beverley Tavern." He goes, "Upstairs?" And I thought, Well, he doesn't hang out with the Dishes or anything. But he used to go there after work years earlier.

Steven Davey: We had to start the Beverley. To play in this city anyway you had to be in the Musicians' Union to play, or so they told you, and you had to be represented by an agent if you wanted to play one of the eight clubs in town that put bands on. It was closed to us; there was nowhere to play. So when we saw Rough Trade at Grossman's, and then they started playing Tuesday nights in a discotheque when things were normally closed, and then coupled with everything that was happening in New York, it made us say, "Well, we've got this place with cheap beer, and art students are a block away."

John Hamilton's first band played at the Beverley before the Dishes did, but they were terrible. They played in front of an empty audience. They were sort of a half-bar band, like they played all covers and then they did a couple of their own songs. But they were long-haired and there was nothing new about them. But they did play there before the Dishes did.

Johnny MacLeod: The Dishes played the Beverley more than other people because they were getting the whole thing started. They were really the only band that could ever fill the Beverley at the early stages. They were the only band to play all original material all night and they were really a focal point. Anybody who started a band would show up at their gigs at the Beverley.

Ken Farr: The Beverley kind of became our place. We played there a lot. They'd book you in for several nights at a time, so that saved us from having to move the freakin' piano up and down the stairs every time, which takes away from the excitement of being in a band if you have to move a piano around at two in the morning.

Being installed there, it was a fun place. The downstairs was the old bar and there were some grizzled old guys who would sit down there and drink beer and the upstairs was kind of like a big club house. It was always a really positive scene with lots of friendly people.

As time went by we gathered a modest but loyal following, and it turned out to be something like being at someone's cottage. It was kind of rec roomy — wood panels and low ceilings. Everybody smoked at the time of course which made for good lighting. I guess a couple of things that added some style was that Steven Davey was very good at graphic work and posters. That doesn't sound like a big deal now, but making a nice poster then was a little bit more involved.

Steven Davey: We were the first band to do posters. They used to have telephone poles back then made out of wood. Ha ha ha. At first, half of the scene were OCA students and half of them were from Thornhill from the same sort of crowd that we'd grown up with through high school and university. And then of course it attracted more and more people.

Steven Davey / photo by Ralph Alfonso

5. no place to go

Gary Topp: I left the Roxy in '75 and moved to the New Yorker Theatre. I continued my movie policy. I knew what was going on down in New York and I was showing a movie called *Blank Generation* and I brought up the filmmaker, Amos Poe. We were playing it on Saturday, midnights.

I was sitting at the back of the theatre and I knew about these bands and thought, We should build a stage in front of the screen and bring these bands up.

Colin Brunton: When Gary Topp got the New Yorker Theatre I went right there and was first the assistant manager, then the manager.

Alex Currie: When they opened the New Yorker they had a job opening at the snack counter and I started working there. When I got the job my mom was really concerned about it and she went down and talked to Jeff [Silverman] and made him say that I wouldn't be exposed to any marijuana or anything like that.

I was a heavy metaller; I listened to Genesis and AC/DC, and all the people I worked with there had really, really eclectic tastes in music. Topp and Brunton knew a really good history of music. I was amazed at the size of their collections and the stuff they listened to. It was just sort of daunting because I was listening to Aerosmith. Ha ha ha.

There was me and this other kid, Philip, who worked there. Then there was Mr. Peepers who was this really tall, middle-aged guy who wore these really thick glasses and was a total pain in the ass. There was also this woman getting a sex change, Joan. She was great; she worked there for a long time at the snack bar too. She was actually the first man/woman — I always thought of her as a woman — to lick my ear.

The New Yorker was my first exposure to freaks, and finding out I *like* freaks.

Colin Brunton: We'd crank our intermission music, because it was completely relevant to whatever was playing that night. I would say probably a couple of times a week I'd get people going, "Excuse me, could you turn the music down?" I'd say, "No, I'm sorry, we can't do that. You can go to another theatre if you want. Everyone else plays it really quiet but we don't do that." Other theatres were so afraid of offending somebody.

Toronto was way more uptight back then. It was really boring. Gary did this great stuff and it was so standout.

The Ramones / photo by Ralph Alfonso

He would have done a great job in New York City and he'd be known there, but because Toronto is just so bloody dull — I think it's a *great* city — but back then it just wasn't that exciting. If I had to nail Toronto down in a couple of words, I'd say it was pretty boring back in those days. We had a well-deserved rep for being this uptight, boring place.

Suzanne Naughton: When I moved to Toronto nothing was open on Sundays. Abso-fucking-lutely nothing. No stores, no restaurants, no bars, no movie theatres. This was Toronto the Good when I moved here, and it was horrible.

Long weekends, nothing was open. My mother used to come here and there was nothing we could do but sit in the apartment. If you didn't buy food, you were screwed. Toronto was a bad place to be; it was boring. That's why things like speakeasies started springing up. They existed long before the punk scene.

We used to try to find one on weekends because the bars closed at one and what were you gonna do, go home? There was no booze at home. So we'd look for booze cans. Everybody we knew was trying to make their rent and they'd throw a booze can every three months.

I think culture itself was trying to find its own feet. Toronto certainly was.

Gary Topp: My wife's brother and some of his friends who lived up in Huntsville came down and built this huge, concrete stage. So then I needed to book an artist, so I thought, I want to book the Ramones.

I had the stage but I didn't have anything else, so I went to this guy named David Bluestein. He's a middle-of-the-road agent; he's done everything under the sun. So I said, "First of all, what do I need on the stage if I want to have a band?" He said, "Oh you need power and blah blah blah." Then he said, "Who do you want?" I said, "The Ramones." He said, "*Who* do you want?" I said, "I want a band called the Ramones." He said, "I've never heard of them but I'll try to find them."

A few days later he said, "I found the Ramones, they want five thousand bucks." I wanted to do three shows. So I got them.

Just after I booked the Ramones I wanted to have a candy bar built in the theatre that could service people on the street as well. We were bringing up Nathan's hot dogs from New York and stuff. So a friend who worked at A&M Records said, "You should talk to Gary Cormier, he's a really good carpenter."

Gary Cormier: I had been an agent. I managed a couple of acts. I managed Rough Trade when they were a little baby band working at Grossman's for two hundred and seventy-five dollars on the weekend including a matinee on Saturday, and within six months had them working at the Colonial upstairs for two thousand dollars for two days.

But I went into carpentry because of the artistes. Rock 'n' roll's a vicious game. It's hard to work with other people unless everybody sees things the same way, and artistes feel that a manager should be there to pump money into the band. I was trying to create a situation where the band generated enough to take care of their needs. I didn't have money.

One day a friend suggested that I go over to the theatre and ask for Gary and talk to him. Somebody had built a candy counter for the New Yorker Theatre, some industrial art student, and the clerk serving the candy bars couldn't *see* the candy bars. It was built all rather incongruously.

I'm one of those fortunate souls that can make a living at whatever it is I decide to do at that given moment in time. My life bounced back and forth between rock 'n' roll and carpentry for years. So I went to the theatre to meet Gary Topp and his partner at the time Jeffrey Silverman, and discussed the candy counter. Then Gary brought me into the theatre and showed me where they were building the stage and what his plans were. Then I was riding my bicycle home and I thought, God, I probably *forgot* more about what you need to do to do a show than these guys know. I should hook up with them. You know when you meet somebody in your life and you know you look at things the same way? That's what I sensed immediately with Gary.

So as I was riding home I decided I was going to call them. As I arrived home the phone was ringing as I'm running up the stairs to make the call. I was excited like a little schoolboy. Sure enough, it was them phoning to say, "Hey, it just dawned on us. You probably forgot more than we know. Why don't you come down here and hook up with us?" At which point I did.

Gary Topp: So we met and through the construction became really good friends and realized that we had an interest in the same sort of music. Eventually I just said, "Do you want to be part of the company?" He had been an agent years before and quit because he got fed up with the music business. So we became partners.

Colin Brunton: The first time I met Steven Leckie was within an hour of me putting up the first Ramones poster on the front door of the New Yorker. He walked by and he looked at it and he came in and goes, "Yeah, I knew you guys would bring the Ramones here. I knew it, I knew it."

Alex Currie: I can't think of anywhere else where they could have played. I don't think any other bars really knew the potential of them. And when they first came they didn't draw many people. I don't remember the Ramones ever selling out.

Ross Taylor: We didn't really have anything going on here. Then the Ramones showed up.

Danny Fields: We adored Toronto. We said, "*Oooh,* this city is ripe, but there is no place to go."

The city was so civilized and big. I thought it was fabulous. I thought it was a gorgeous city and beautifully located and modern and chic and much nicer than America. I loved it. I thought that they should have everything, and they did.

Gary Topp: I knew something was happening when the Ramones walked onstage the first time. When they walked onstage it was all white light and it was loud.

Steven Leckie: They were devastating. That first Ramones show was *beyond*. Everything you think about how great they were in the beginning was ten times more than that. It was unbelievable.

When they strutted out there and Johnny and Dee Dee took their legs-askew stance and Joey just stood there, and Dee Dee would yell out "One-two-three-four!" and went into "Beat on the Brat," you never heard anything like it. It was really, really strange.

Beautiful. And one note more would have been unnecessary. The thirty minutes was enough, because in thirty minutes they did probably twenty songs.

Margaret Barnes-DelColle: When the Ramones played at the New Yorker, that just threw *everybody*. They were just like, "What is this?"

Up until then, I think for most people you'd heard about punk rock — or I don't even know if they called it that — but you heard about different things happening in England and in New York, but that was truly the first real live experience that everybody here had was when the Ramones came. And I actually remember at Power Street, like we always did, we'd get home from our jobs, barely ate, and everybody would spend hours getting ready; just primping and hanging out and smoking pot and drinking. Then you would go out late; usually you didn't go out till eleven or something. We went to the New Yorker and we just went crazy. We just couldn't believe it was the Ramones.

Cynthia Ross: A lot of the people at that concert, we all sort of looked a certain way. We just found each other. You'd go, "Well, that person looks cool, who are they?" And you'd start talking to them. If there was a band in town you'd find that you'd see the same people going to the same types of music. The same people would always be there.

Freddy Pompeii: When Gary Topp and Gary Cormier started bringing these crazy shows to the New Yorker and kept bringing movies in like *Charlie Is My Darling*, a Rolling Stones documentary, there were these young kids that started coming out. You could see the audience that was forming, this grassroots audience, and these were the kids that started coming to the punk rock shows.

The first one that I saw was when the Ramones came to town. The place was packed. Not to capacity, but it was packed with these kids a little younger than me. And it wasn't a Big Rock Star rock show. It was this band coming out of New York that nobody knew about. Except for these kids, and they packed the place.

You sort of saw the scene coming together. You saw these people that you didn't see anywhere else. You wouldn't see them hanging around; it was only at shows that you would see them. They were the ones that went to those shows: Young kids disillusioned with pop music.

Colin Brunton: I sure didn't have a sense of anger. I wasn't angry about much. I had great, working class parents. I think the more common thing for everyone who was starting to gather around this music was boredom. We were tired of what we had been given before then, and I think really the Ramones were the ones that said, "Look, you can play three chords and hit a drum. Why don't you do your *own* thing?"

Suddenly, Gary Topp was bringing this great culture to the city, and I was really in the eye of the hurricane the whole time. I was just right there, soaking it all in.

Gary Cormier: The Ramones show did get a lot of attention from the press. There were a lot of people at the show, many of whom walked out before the show was halfway through. And considering the band only played for twenty minutes, that's saying something.

Gary Topp: All the press was bad. "These guys can't play, these guys are too loud." Peter Gabriel was recording when they came to Toronto. He came to the New Yorker and left in fifteen minutes and said it was shit. It was well documented that he was there.

Nobody liked it; everybody just panned it. The media's always like that. The media's fickle. Nobody really cared.

Gary Cormier: I had been through this enough with people who I would try to get to come out to see bands like Rough Trade. They would come in and be amused for a few minutes and leave, not taking any of it seriously. I would sense that they were sort of laughing at me as opposed to laughing with me. These were the kind of people who, months later, would come up to me at a function, put their arm around me and say, "I knew what you were doing was right all along," and you know darn well they didn't.

For something to be successful, I think it's got to polarize people. When I was growing up you were either a long-hair and liked the Beatles, or you had short hair and you liked Otis Redding. This was polarizing audiences. There were people on one side who supported the whole punk and new wave thing, and then there were all of the other people who supported corporate rock and disco and everything that goes along with it.

I had a conversation once, one of those days when I was an agent. I had booked a band out into London, Ontario, and it happened to be a bunch of guys that had inspired me to actually want to be in the rock 'n' roll industry.

I had moved here from Montreal as a kid. When I was about seventeen, eighteen, my parents moved to Whitby, Ontario; then as soon as I was nineteen or twenty I moved to Toronto on my own. When I was going to dances in Whitby when I was still in high school, there was a really hot R&B scene in Toronto. So I ended up booking one of these bands who had later gone on to form something else later, a big American band, called Rhinoceros.

The singer was a guy called John Finley. I had to go to the gig and collect the money because they hadn't paid the agency the money that was due to them. Basically I was going there to take all of the money that was being generated from the show in order to pay all of the back commissions. When I got there I sat down with John and explained who I was and what I was going to do. And he said to me, "You'll never make a mistake in your life as long as you believe in your heart of hearts that what you're doing is right. It doesn't matter who says what, as long as you believe that what you're doing is right, you won't make a mistake."

I knew that when we started doing this. We believed that these guys had every bit as much to offer to the world as anybody who was out there doing it, and we were basically going to provide a platform for them. These were our unsung heroes. We undertook it upon ourselves to do it because we wanted to see these bands and we were prepared to put our money where our mouths were.

Gary Topp: I always wanted to do what I do. I remember when I asked Bluestein to find me the Ramones, because I wasn't really that knowledgeable on the whole thing, I had no idea how many people were going to come. It was something that I wanted to do that I thought was good for the theatre and would sort of bring the interest back into my life. You know, booking that many movies over a period of time, there are only so many you can get or that you want to show.

Quite honestly, when I booked the Ramones, I was certainly not thinking *punk rock*, even though that's how they were sort of labelled by New York media and that's all who was really covering them at that time. I just booked them because they sounded interesting and my musical tastes are quite unusual.

I'd been reading about them and reading about all these other bands, and I just thought they sounded great. I wasn't looking to do it as a slap in the face to anybody or because this was a new underground thing. But when I did the show I realized that there was something happening and that there are people who want to hear these bands. It was something different that I really wanted to do.

I liked different things. You've got to keep it interesting. The Ramones was what I really wanted, and nobody really cared at the time.

Margaret Barnes-DelColle: When it was over, we all went back to Power Street. Everybody came back and it was like a big party because everybody was just so psyched, the adrenaline was just going. It just kind of inspired everybody. It must have been this electricity that passed through the city, and just about everybody planned to start a band that same night.

Freddy Pompeii: Once the Ramones played in Toronto it was like Toronto caught the fever. Everybody wanted to have a band that played three chords.

Ralph Alfonso [*Cheap Thrills* magazine, Sept, 1976]: It sounds amusing because the term punk rock is as much a musical ideal as it is form. It involves equal parts attitude, ragged musicianship and the all-encompassing obsession on the musician's part that makes any imperfection trivial, even irrelevant, to the whole. Whatever ingredients, the resulting charisma is always magnetic and the reason why some groups are revered long after the fact while others allowed to vanish from existence.

Steven Leckie ["The Viletones: Now and Then, and When?" by Lola Michael, *Impulse,* 1978]: I saw the Ramones the first time they played Toronto and I thought wow, *anybody* can do better than *that —*

I am going to do it better and have a greater relationship with the kids. I mean, the kids can't relate to people in the CIA.

*   *   *   *   *

Harri Palm: David Clarkson and I went to the Ramones show on Yonge Street and we were blown away. This was cool, new, kind of exciting. We had sort of been talking about doing something and right then and there we said, "Okay, let's start a band."

David Clarkson: Harri was playing guitar and I told him I could play bass so we had half a band right there. He said, "What should we be called?" and I said, "We should be Evil." I was thinking probably that it was Evel Knievel but he fortunately I guess misheard me and that's how we started this group called the Eels. It was I think technically supposed to be the Electric Eels, which I still like better because it had this primordial and technological aspect to it, but it got shortened just to the Eels.

We got this drummer Bent Rasmussen and then the other guy we recruited was this fellow Rob Rogers, who was easy to find because he was another OCA student.

Ian Mackay: When the Eels first played, Steven Davey was in the audience, who was in the Dishes at the time, and they were just starting up *their* band. Our idea for the Eels was to do a wall of sound; we wanted to be as loud as we possibly could be. We were nineteen, twenty years old at the time.

I was the soundman of the Eels; I wasn't onstage. Dave Clarkson was up there, I think we had a drummer — it might have been Bent Rasmussen, Harri was up there, and they were singing and misbehaving generally. I remember being their soundman and looking up there saying, "That's what I want to do. I want to be up there and I want to play the bass," or actually, I wanted to play the guitar. I managed to get my way onto stage fairly quickly.

David Clarkson: A lot of the songs were improvised and spontaneous. We kind of re-thought the pop song so that it only was choruses and then this jammed instrumental part and then a bunch of the same choruses. We did away with verses and things because we were in such a rush and they seemed kind of extraneous. The lyrics were something like, "Television, television, watch you every day, television, television, nothin' more to say."

Harri Palm: We didn't think it would take off. It wasn't a joke, but we just did it for fun. Everyone was blown away by it and we said, "We're onto something."

We did one other show after that. We did two or three shows or whatever we did and sort of made history at OCA.

Ian Mackay: Our first idea with the Eels was that we were going to project a wall of sound as a sound sculpture and the idea would be we might submit that as an art project.

The idea of the wall of sound, we were literally trying to create the physical presence of a wall. That was related somehow to a conceptual art idea but at the same time had a pop sensibility. If you look at some of Warhol's work, he was a conceptual artist in many ways and yet he had this pop sensibility and spin to what he was doing. A lot of artists who had this ironic pop sensibility but are actually doing tight and sophisticated intellectual art worked with this curve ball that it's all thrown at you with this ironic pop twist to it. If you look at the minimalists combined with the pop art, there was a convergence there in the late '60s and '70s where people were mixing and matching all these themes. So it was easier for us to take that on and say, "Yeah, we can do something that has intellectual rigour, a sound sculpture, but use the instruments of a rock band to manifest it."

Harri Palm: The Eels' history is short, but it was right at the beginning. Nothing had really gotten going yet. The first time, I think we opened for Oh Those Pants!

David Clarkson: We only played a little bit and I can't remember exactly what happened. I think Harri started playing with Johnny and the G-Rays and Ian Mackay basically said that he would like to have a band, too. So Ian found Paul Robinson, who was an art student from York, and Ian found John Catto who was also at OCA, and we started to play and became the Diodes.

John Catto: I was an art student at the time I was sort of going to shows around Toronto and so on. I think I used to start seeing Paul at that time but I didn't really know him.

What actually happened was there were a couple of people playing around OCA. There was this band called the Eels which I think did one gig back then, and I turned up at a rehearsal for them and I was just hanging around and playing guitar and stuff. And after the rehearsal, Paul, who was also just hanging around, came chasing after me. He'd just come in, he'd been in Montreal or something like that, and he was just kind of lurking around Toronto. He comes after me and says, "They're breaking up, why don't we get their bass player and drummer and put something together?" That's kind of how I met him.

Supposedly he'd come to my painting show and all this stuff at the time. Anything's possible there. He just kind of approached me. I think he liked my shoes, to be honest. Ha ha ha.

Rodney Bowes: Paul Robinson was not from OCA. He was more serious into actually doing it.

He was the guy that first brought in a Ramones tape and played it for us. I remember the first time I heard that I was like, "Wow, 'now the kids wanna sniff some glue,' that's so cool. 'Beat on the brat?' It's so cool what these guys are singing about, who *are* these guys?" And that's really how it all evolved. It was kind of a synchronous thing. I always find it funny when people say, "Well, the scene started here or started there." It's like the scene kind of just started.

Paul Robinson [CIUT-FM, Greg Dick interview, 2007]: I was nineteen when they were drafting people into the Vietnam War and my parents thought that it was a good idea that I move up to Canada, which is why I moved and went to Concordia University. I finished university at Concordia and I came to graduate school at York University in Toronto.

Ian Mackay: In the fall of '76 we ran into John and Paul. Paul was a graduate student at York doing his masters in fine arts. We were all getting together for a lecture by a sculptor ... was it Donald Judd? It was one of the great modern sculptors of the time. We met there and one of us was playing the Ramones out of our little tape player and Paul heard and yelled, "I know these guys. This is great!"

David Clarkson: I remember when I met Paul it was just on the front steps of OCA. Ian had organized this by having Paul come and me meet him.

We didn't have anything to talk about except I had to check him out, to see that he'd be a good singer, and he wasn't even singing, ha ha. He was good looking and that was probably half of it. And I liked him. He was trying to talk to me about art, about sculpture, so we had something to talk about. I could tell he really wanted to be in the band and that's about all it took, you know? So we gave him a shot.

Rodney Bowes: Paul Robinson was a very bright guy. He was an art history major. He was kind of an outsider and he just appeared and was very vocal and very kind of an aggressive guy, and then became the singer of the band. But he kind of propelled them to take it more seriously. Everybody else there wanted to be an artist, wanted to become a filmmaker, do video and stuff, and he sort of kept that whole thing going.

Ian Mackay: I can't remember all the details of how we really started up, but we started to rehearse almost immediately. Paul was kind of a driving force. He grappled with the concept, loved the idea, and thought this could be really fun — "Let's go, let's do it, let's make something happen," and so we all followed along. John Catto was pretty instrumental as well.

I was of two minds. I was quite serious about fine art at the time, about moving into electronic video and conceptual art, which was cresting in '76, so I had to make a choice somewhere along the line, which I did.

Paul Robinson: We were trying to think of a name that sounded modern, which I think any band does in their time.

Originally, Dave Clarkson was in another band with someone called Harri Palm who was in Johnny and the G-Rays, and they were called the Eels. I kind of liked the name the Eels but they thought it was too slimy. We wanted "the" before the name because again that was very modern; it was going back to the Beatles, it was the return of "the." So we wanted "the," that was definite. I remember distinctly wanting "the."

One of the bands of the time that I really liked the name of was the Tubes, and they were a band from San Francisco, I think. I really liked the name the Tubes so I said, "That sounds like a really modern name." This photographer called Rodney Bowes who did our first photographs said, "Well, what about the Diodes?" And it kind of just stuck.

Ian Mackay: It was a very interesting point in history on the Queen Street scene because you had OCA feeding onto Queen Street, and you also had the emergence of all of these electronics and hobby computing stores popping up along Queen Street. So the name the Diodes was loosely related to the fact that there was this microcomputer revolution happening at the same time the punk revolution was happening.

I was seriously into computing at the time and I was studying what's now called New Media Studies at OCA, which back then was called Cybernetics, Software Design for Computing, Computer Graphics, Computer Music; I was taking all these courses in my fourth year. So I was very interested in the blend of the new wave punk scene with what was happening with microcomputers.

John Catto started building his own pedals. We were into electronics in some way, but not so much into the electronic music. We were more into the raw energy of the punk scene. But a lot of our friends and a lot of the people in the emerging microcomputer business were real punk fans, so it was a very interesting thing that happened in that period.

John Catto: We had this straight-up idea that we were gonna do this more hard rock thing because none of the other bands that were floating around were like that.

If you think back to it, there were all these bands around Toronto. Rough Trade was getting going and there were all of Steven Davey's things. John Hamilton's band was around, Zoom, and they were almost a heavy power poppy thing. That's the way I remember them, anyway. I think I saw one gig. Mostly all the bands that were floating around were all these kinds of bands like the Dishes and so on. Very light. And at the same time there was that Yonge Street bar scene going on around then, Goddo and all those bands.

The main thing that we wanted was to *not* do something like the Dishes. We were rock people and that's how it came out, really.

Paul Robinson: There wasn't a lot out there when we formed the band. There were very few alternative bands and most of them were in the States. We were going to see these bands; it started with Iggy Pop and the New York Dolls. But there were very few bands in Canada to compare us to, and we kind of just took the initiative to start our own band.

I think it came about in seeing these bands that we said, "Hey, we can do this ourselves, there's nothing like this." We did it under our own initiative and really for ourselves because we never really thought it was going to be anything commercial, and in some ways it wasn't. Alternative bands were not selling a lot of records.

Ian Mackay: I think I came up with the more middle of the road set of interests. I hate to say it, but in '71 I was into James Taylor, Joni Mitchell in '72. I liked the Stones, I liked the Beatles, I loved the Who, Supertramp, Pink Floyd. I was into all the big bands. By '75, '76, I was listening to Lou Reed, I was listening to Roxy Music; it was starting to converge in that direction and the influences were starting to mount. I liked the New York Dolls but I wasn't a big New York Dolls fan like John Catto was, but they were there so early. I loved Iggy Pop, just the rawness. I liked the Detroit heavy metal scene. I was even into Black Sabbath in their day. I would say my interests were very diverse.

Television, I saw them live at CBGB's in '76 just as the Diodes were starting up and that was the epiphany for me. When I saw Tom Verlaine and his band playing up there onstage, I thought they were the best band I'd heard in years. They were so fantastic. "Marquee Moon" as a rock anthem of that era was tremendous.

Mark Gane: There was a trip to New York every year at OCA in March. They'd rent a bus and everybody who wanted to go down would go down.

People would be reading fanzines and music magazines from London and New York like *NME* and *Melody Maker* and *Interview*. There was this yearly trip where everybody would go down and go to clubs and see exhibits. So you'd go down and see this stuff and you'd see New York bands down there and it was hugely influential because everybody would come back and say, "I just saw Talking Heads."

John Catto [CIUT-FM, Greg Dick interview, 2007]: This would be the second of the OCA New York trips that I went on. Paul by this point had appeared at OCA and was smuggled onto the bus. He tucked himself up on the luggage rack or something, ha ha ha.

Paul Robinson [CIUT-FM, Greg Dick interview, 2007]: We met the people from *Rock Scene* magazine and Ian, John and I ended up having dinner with them at a place called the Ocean Club. There was a band on, I can't remember what it was — all right, the Feelies — and we were sitting at a table with John Cale. For some reason John Cale just had a go at me like I couldn't believe. The guy just devastated me. I told him, "Oh, I really love all the things you've done," or whatever, and he was just on my case. It was just unbelievable.

I think we eventually ended up being in *Rock Scene*.

Anyways, Ian got completely pissed. I mean he was *so* drunk, just leglessly drunk. We ended up walking around Soho looking at all the art galleries; there were just a handful at the time, but there was the Leo Castelli Gallery, which was one of the major, major galleries of pop art. I mean, he was Warhol's dealer and Lichtenstein's dealer and Robert Rauschenberg's dealer. Ian looked at it and he went, "*Fuck* art*!* Fuck *art!*"

Then he picked up this brick and he threw it through the window of the Leo Castelli Gallery. Then he picked up another one and he threw it through the window of the Sonnabend Gallery, which was next door. And we're just going, "Oh my god, oh my god, Ian what are you doing?" And he's just going, "*Fuck art! Fuck art!*"

It was like a revelation.

Ian Mackay [CIUT-FM, Greg Dick interview, 2007]: Actually, Paul was cheering me on the whole time. And before we did that, we actually went into a number of clubs chanting, "Fuck art!" People were looking at us strangely like, "*What* are you saying?" I guess at that point we decided we weren't going to be artists; we were going to be musicians instead.

Paul Robinson [CIUT-FM, Greg Dick interview, 2007]: The next day we went back down to see the damage that was done, and they had bordered up the window on the Castelli Gallery.

They had used a Robert Rauschenberg crate, signed with his signature on it, and I thought that that was just so appropriate that they bordered up the hole with this Rauschenberg that was signed.

But "fuck art" was the end of us being artists, really.

John Catto: It's funny looking back on it now, sort of like who was around and who wasn't around.

At the time we came together there were virtually no English bands that we knew about, but there were New York bands that we knew about. Television were already around, Ramones were around. One band that was definitely around was the Talking Heads.

Paul Robinson: We were playing for friends at OCA. There were no venues that would book us. There just wasn't any infrastructure like there is today for anything that was independent or alternative to what the mainstream music in Canada was.

And the mainstream music in Canada was pretty god awful. There were a whole slew of bar bands that were pretty well supported by an industry that wanted bands to do covers of bigger bands. Really, that's what we came out of; we came out of this whole culture. People weren't trying to do anything original, they were just trying to do covers of bands that were big at the time. So you had all these bands doing Led Zeppelin covers and things like that. They took one look at us and they certainly wouldn't book us.

There was also a big blues tradition, like Long John Baldry who had come over from England. That was really big in Canada. So when we started out there was no place for us to play. There was no hope of getting a record contract because we weren't a heavy rock band. Rush was the best known band in Canada. There was nowhere for us to go except to start our own culture. There were a handful of us that started a whole new scene, which was an alternative to the mainstream.

John Catto: My best friend in art college was the person who booked all the entertainment at OCA and we were saying that we really had to do a gig. We found out the Talking Heads were doing a show at A Space.

Freddy Pompeii: The Talking Heads were playing around Toronto when they were still a trio at A Space. You saw these people that you didn't see anywhere else. You wouldn't see them hanging around, it was only at shows that you would see them. They were the people that were the entertainers from '77 on.

John Catto: They were a three-piece then. They were doing the A Space show and we were going, "Well, we can co-opt their management and say, 'Hey, would you

like to play another gig when you're in Toronto and we'll give you money?'" So that's what we did. We called them up and sorted it out and of course they went, "Wow, great, we can come to Toronto and do *two* things." We booked ourselves in as the opening act. It was a funny gig because everyone from the same period was at that gig.

It was January 28 in '77. We got together in October or something like that. We went into a little recording studio in the annex of OCA and did a little demo before we did anything. Paul went off to Boston and started hanging around people like Oedipus, who was a DJ at the time and played our demo on Boston radio. When he came back, we did the gig.

Rodney Bowes: I remember the curtains opening and there were the Diodes. Everybody knows that it's the guys from the school and here they are all kind of decked out like that, pretending that they're rock stars doing this thing and making really horrendous noise.

Steven Davey: With the Diodes, it was pretty heavily gestured. There was always a sense of irony with the Toronto bands.

Ian Mackay: I would say that after our first live gig with the Talking Heads we knew [this] was a very different thing: It was the rock business.

Paul Robinson: I kind of knew at a very early age that I wanted to do something. I had a drive to do something in my late teens or early twenties. I wanted to be a painter and that was what I was putting all my energies into. John and Ian were also painters and they were putting all of their energies into that. Then it just grew from art into music and the punk scene exploded. It wasn't all contrived; we didn't try to do anything, but what we were doing was of our time. What we were doing was absolutely right.

Diodes, 1976, OCA. Robinson, Clarkson, Mackay / photo by Ralph Alfonso

6. one day these poets will exist

Steven Leckie: I grew up in the Annex, went to school at Yonge and St. Clair, Deer Park. We had Glenn Gould coming by the little plaza there where there'd be a fountain where the kids would go for lunch. And here was this older man that wore a long coat no matter how warm it was. It was a pretty artistic school and everyone knew that was Glenn Gould, and that was pretty cool.

Then I went to Northern [Secondary School] and got expelled a couple months before the end of the year for mugging a kid. All through the first few months of being at Northern I refused to compromise my identity as a glitter rock kid in an era where everyone basically kind of looked like Lynyrd Skynyrd or Nirvana. I'd be wearing velvet and satin. Then I went to a couple of free schools, then eventually just stopped going.

Freddy Pompeii: I had stopped listening to pop music. The only people I was listening to was the Stooges, the Velvet Underground, the Modern Lovers, and MC5. I had a steady diet of that everyday. I woke up in the morning and that's what I would listen to the minute I got up and that's the only kind of music that excited me. It wasn't like any of the other music that was out there at the time. You couldn't tell one band from the other the way it got so watered down.

Steven Leckie: Rock 'n' roll was my absolute religion. Like, *religion*. It was absolutely everything to me and it saved my life many times just by taking life advice from David Bowie saying, "Oh no, love, you're not alone." That was really important to me.

I went to every concert that was cool at Massey Hall that you can imagine. I saw the Dolls the first time they were here at the Victory Burlesque when Rush opened. I would have been fifteen at that point. I saw the Dolls when KISS opened for them, I saw Mott the Hoople, Sweet, Raspberries, Sparks, Roxy Music. Really theatrical and devastating bands. Alice Cooper was always a big thread that weaved through my life. You could always count on Alice Cooper to just turn it on.

Then I had a guy, a couple years older than me, that sat me down for a whole summer. I was a real face on the street scene before then; everyone knew me. And he sat me down and gave me the ABCs on the Velvet Underground. I had an encyclopedic knowledge on the Velvets after that and got hip to what all of that meant,

Steven Leckie, first gig / photo by Ralph Alfonso

l-r: Jackie Death, Freddy Pompeii, Steven Leckie, Motor X first gig, Colonial Underground / photo by Ralph Alfonso then led into things like the Flamin' Groovies, MC5, and the Stooges. And then after those bands I saw that the musical horizon was impossible, in my opinion, to top. That was the epicentre.

Before that I thought, Jim Morrison's awfully fuckin' cool, he's really writin' some cool shit. But it wasn't like "TV Eye." It wasn't like "Kick out the jams, motherfucker!" It had a different resonation in my heart and soul, so that's what I knew I could do and be, and not fake it at all in any way.

Freddy Pompeii: I was really anxious to put a band together that was completely different than anything that was going on. And all that was going on at the time, in Canada especially, was these heavy metal bands with really long hair like Triumph and Rush. They all sort of fit into that same category and all the bar bands were like that. They were either folky country rock or this heavy metal distillation that was either boring or repetitive.

So of course this idea that I had was a hare-brained idea as far as anybody in the music business was concerned. Anybody I tried to explain it to was like, "Oh you're crazy," and they just wouldn't call me back. I'd go to a rehearsal space and meet some people and play some of my original material and never hear from them again. This went on for quite a while.

Ian Mackay: The Beverley Tavern, for the OCA people, was the place to hang out.

Harri Palm: I lived at the Beverley. I would go to the Beverley every single day. I would walk through the door and Johnny would be waiting. He'd have my quart opened. In those days I would often drink from noon till one in the morning.

One day I'm sitting there, I can't remember who I'm with, and this guy walks in, sits down about ten tables away, and there's only about four of us upstairs, and he's staring at me. He's this weird looking guy. He's got the black hair and he's got the black leather jacket. Punks in those days were still pretty new. And he's looking at me and he drinks a beer. Finally he stands up and says, "You! You're Harri Palm and I want you in my band." I just looked at him and he's almost drooling and I just said, "Fuck off you fuckin' asshole, go back to Scarborough where you're from," because in those days we used to get a lot of posers coming down from Scarborough.

Well, that was Steven Leckie.

Ian Mackay: He calls himself Nazi Dog. We don't know who the heck he is, but he's coming in and he makes himself known.

He starts talking to us and before we know it we're talking to him about his band and he's talking about how he's gonna cut himself. He's only sixteen or seventeen years old; we were older than he was, but he became very attached to what we were trying to do.

Steven Leckie: My old man lived in Montreal so I had my own spot. I put an ad in the *Toronto Star* and I referenced the MC5, Stooges, and I hired the very first three guys that answered. The first one was Mike Anderson, who I renamed Motor X.

Mike Anderson: Steven was a young guy living on his own with his dog in a basement apartment. He was very knowledgeable in a lot of obscure bands that I liked, too, like the MC5. He had that persona of being a lead man, a lead singer. He had the look.

I think he was a little bit of a chameleon; he was able to change his looks. I'd seen pictures of him before where he was in his Bowie stage or whatever. He was able to do that. But it was a feeling; we all had the same kind of feeling. We just did our own thing. To me it was all rock 'n' roll; that "punk" handle came after.

Steven Leckie: And then we got Freddy Pompeii, who as luck would have it was from Philly so he was a real dead-end kid. He had a whole groove going; that soulful thing you can only get in a place like Philly.

Freddy Pompeii: He had no idea who I was when I answered this ad that he had put in the paper. The ad was worded, "Ramones/Iggy Pop stylist seeking the same," and a phone number. And I'm telling you, nobody ever put an ad like *that* in the paper. It was all real serious, like "Serious people only apply and blah blah blah," real uptight requests. So when I saw this ad I thought, Maybe I can do something with this guy because he seems like he's a little ahead of his time.

So I called him up and he seemed real nice on the phone and he says, "Do you want to come over and we'll talk about it and bring some of your material and your guitar?" So I went over and he was living in this little basement apartment. It had swastikas all over the walls and he had real short, spiky hair, kind of like Johnny Rotten but this was before Johnny Rotten. And I was in the same boat. I had been wearing my hair really short for at least five or six years and my wife would taper my pants like skin-tight all the way down to my ankles and I'd wear Beatle boots which completed the look.

Of course I was sort of singled out in the downtown scene in Toronto because I was one of the few people that came out in daylight looking that way. Sometimes we wore makeup; sometimes we dyed our hair.

We were anti-hippie. Anything that was '60s and early '70s that was real popular like long hair and beards and German shepherds and that kind of thing; anything that was like that, me and my friends were *anti-*that because it was so played out and so uncool.

Steven turned out to be one of these people like me and my friends and I thought, Whoa, this is interesting: You're somebody who's on the same page as me, and we hit it off right away. And he said he had a drummer lined up, which was Motor, and he had a bass player which was this kid named Jackie, Jackie Death. We decided to try to put something together.

He heard the way I played guitar and I listened to him sing a few tunes and he wasn't bashful by any means. And when he opened the door and I seen him I thought, This is that fuckin' asshole that got me fired from the Gasworks!

Toward the end of our quote unquote interview I said to him, "You remember me don'tcha?" And he says, "No, no, what do you mean?" And I says, "You're the motherfucker who got me fired from the Gasworks." He says, "Oh no, I didn't do that! No!" I said, "Steve, you did," and I refreshed his memory and he remembered. And he says, "I got you fired?" And I says, "Yeah, man, you got me fired, thanks a lot!" I was laughing about it; it was not the kind of thing you get uptight about and carry a grudge the rest of your life. It was kind of a funny thing. That was really the way we met.

Steven Leckie: History, history, history. Ego. History. I'd read enough — I mean a *lot*, a real lot. I knew that history was for those who want to make it happen. I had an encyclopedic knowledge of the Situationist movement. I knew that history was for those who just take it.

I had my work cut out for me here where it's not a hero-oriented culture. It's become so, though; it's become a lot more so, but then it was not. So I think that's what motivated me.

And I think what's behind that is like Dennis Hopper — this is just me, I have to talk in analogies — but when he was doing *Rebel Without a Cause*, everybody knew the word on Dean preceded him. They're doing the chicken run scene where the first guy who chickens out going off a cliff loses. So anyway, the director calls, "Cut!" and everybody goes to the food, but Dean stayed in character behind the wheel, smoking in his red jacket. Hopper was going crazy and grabbed him and said, "How do you do this, how do you do what you do?" And Dean apparently slowly looked at him, blew out the smoke, and said, "Well, don't you hate your parents?" And there was something to that; maybe not hate, but the idea of usurping what the societal expectation of you is.

Alice Cooper's father was a minister, but that sure didn't mean Alice thought he needed to be one. Good rock 'n' roll always comes out of a lower economic bracket and when I was an adolescent that was the case for me and my dad, because he had custody of me. It meant more to me to buy velvet pants that cost a week's wages, because to me that showed I'm not poor when you're looking at me.

Freddy Pompeii: The thing that clicked with us all was we were really passionate about it, and the chemistry was astounding. We played together so well.

As far as quality, we really stunk in the beginning but after three or four shows we were on our way to being professionals. I'd never played electric guitar with a band, I'd only played acoustic. So it was a first for me, picking up an electric guitar and making a sound with it. I was in bands before, but as a vocalist in the '60s. And Steven boasted of being in a few different bands but they never got up onstage or anything. They never got out of the rehearsal space. So what I brought to the party was I got this band to start playing gigs, which was sort of my forte. I was able to be a coach. I was able to whip 'em into shape.

Steven Leckie: We knew Viletones was a dead cool name. It just fit for the time. Essentially it comes from the idea of when you put "tones" at the end of the name it gave a feeling of the '60s, and I read that "vile" was one of the worst words you could say. At this time, I'm only nineteen, so I'm still learning these things. So "Vile-tones," wow, that means you're doing the sickest songs ever.

Arthur Rimbaud, who wrote *A Season in Hell* and *The Drunken Boat* and stopped writing when he was nineteen and fled to Abyssinia, he said in one of his poems that one day these poets will exist, one day my voice will be understood. Like speaking into the future, which I find so heartbreaking, so heartbreakingly beautiful.

*　　*　　*　　　*　　　*

John Catto: From about the time we got together we were aware of the fact that the Viletones were floating around, but they'd never played anywhere at all. They'd just turn up with jackets with writing on the back and hang around. When we did the Talking Heads gig everyone came out because from what I picked up later, certainly Steven and all them turned up for that gig. But then they'd turned up to every OCA gig leading up to it. They were just kind of lurking around and trying to do this *look*, you know? More biker at first.

We did that one gig and what I picked up from John Hamilton via his guitar player Chris Haight, who eventually joined them, was that they were about to break up. And they went to our gig and said, "Well, they can't fucking do it." So they stayed together and next thing you know there's two or three bands all of a sudden.

Steven Davey: When Steven Leckie first came to see the Dishes he was a glitter rocker. He wore platform shoes and had a long, long shag and satin pants. He was just this trendy guy who hung around discotheques. I remember one week he showed up and had shaved all his hair off.

The Viletones had the black leather jackets before they even had their instruments. They said "Viletones" on the back and they would just go to parties and menace people. But they were all sucks underneath.

John Hamilton: Chris Haight and I went down to the New Yorker and we saw the Ramones and I think it was about one-third full or half full, and I think we mooched our way in because we were broke. And we saw the Ramones and we thought, This is sort of like what we're trying to do but they've got it figured out a little bit more so we're gonna go along in this direction. So we started doing similar stuff in a band called the Zoom, and we'd got the old Colonial Underground going and we were playing there.

I knew there was something going on when Steven Leckie and the Viletones showed up at a Zoom gig when we were playing the Underground. People started showing up and you could really see that there was something happening; that there was a real movement. It wasn't just a couple of freaks, it was more people coming every day. They were looking for something and if you had a little bit of it they'd come to you.

The Zoom would never have made it as a punk band because we were sort of leftover glam and stuff like that, but we had a little bit of punk so we attracted some of the original people. Then you really saw that things were happening.

Johnny MacLeod: The Viletones would go to gigs and throw bottles at people and get chased out of the gig, so the last thing you'd see would be the logos on their jackets.

Freddy Pompeii: Steve was pushing the envelope. We had just started rehearsing but we didn't have all the personnel yet so the band didn't really exist. But Steven and Motor used to go out and they had their leather jackets. They got these big white stick-on letters that you could buy in the art store and they spelled out VILETONES on the back.

They used to go to all the bars and hang out and be seen. That was it: It was a promotional thing, which Steven Leckie is a genius at. He knows how to get his name around, or whoever he's involved with, he knows how to get it out there.

Steven Leckie [*The Pig Paper* no. 8, April 1978]: I had all the PR ideas. We used to put Viletones posters up even though we weren't playing anywhere. All of us except Fred used to walk around in black leather jackets that said Viletones and Viletonettes on the back. We used to go to OCA and get in as many fights as possible.

Freddy Pompeii: He'd go out and start fights and kick over tables and get so drunk that he couldn't even talk. Him and Motor would be side by side kicking over tables together and chattin' up girls. Then people would say to him, "What's Viletones, is it a gang?"

"The Viletones is my band and it ain't no faggot art school band." That's the kind of stuff he would say. Before we even played a gig we were already famous.

Steven Leckie: That was wild. I was never guessing it was going to happen, so it was "Yeah, let's put Viletones on the back of our jackets." I think that was inspired by the movie *The Warriors*.

And I hate to say it — it was a different era, so keep this in mind — but I loved my Saturday night fights and I was good, I was a good scrappy guy. But in those days there weren't guns and this, that, and the other. In those days you could beat a guy up and then buy him a beer after, you know what I'm saying? It was part of what rock 'n' roll still meant. It wasn't lethargic. It was almost like when you went to a concert you could hardly sleep the night before because it all seemed like an event.

We went to a couple of other shows. Before we played I saw the Diodes at OCA, I saw the Talking Heads at A Space. I saw the Dishes, which were a little light in the wrist for me but I knew if they had've gone to London, let's say, they would have killed. They were good for that genre. They were smart, they were all good looking, great package. We'd see them at the Beverley.

We were really into promoting this apocalypse to come, and it came. It came. We did it.

Mike Anderson: We were just sort of hanging out and going to parties and that. We kind of stood out a lot. I went to parties, OCA kind of parties, mostly to do with the art crowd, the art students. That's where the scene kind of started. Maybe mentally we were art students and just didn't have a place to do our studies. We took our art to the street.

Steven Leckie: Freddy had a three-story house, still there, on Power Street. His girlfriend was Margarita Passion. I remember their kid when he was little. Power Street at Parliament and Queen and it was a three-story, big Victorian home and all bets were off; we could do anything we wanted.

He had an obsession with Catholicism and symbolism around the church and it was very important and private to him. He would have these inordinately gorgeous crosses of Christ and what it really was, was that when you're from Philly that shit's for real; that's in your DNA.

Freddy Pompeii: I had a hobby of collecting paintings and statues and crucifixes and all kinds of Catholic and Protestant and Jewish religious articles. I had my whole living room and hallway and other things sprinkled around in the house, you know, in the bathroom and in the guest room. We had lots of crucifixes, big ones and little ones and there was a big statue of the Blessed Mother. I had this portable church, like a last rites kit. It was a really cool-looking living room.

Being a Catholic I was just fascinated by the paganism, the false idols. I was really amazed at the paradox of the Catholic Church being the one true religion but also being a pagan religion because it worshipped idols; a contradiction. I was a big Catholic kid. I wanted to be a priest and everything and I broke away from it in my teenage years. But I always had this amazing thing about all the statues and the rosary beads and all the artifacts that went along with the religion. I knew what paganism was and I knew what Catholicism was, but it didn't make sense to me. You had all these things that were like, "Pray to St. Anthony for this," and, "Pray to the Blessed Mother for that," and, "Pray to St. Jude for hopeless cases." I mean, that was straight out of Roman paganism. They had a god for everything. They had a god for walking through a doorway and a god for the doorway and a god for the wood that built the doorway. They had a god for everything. I mean, it's the same thing, isn't it? I was just fascinated by that, so it sort of led me to collect it and put it up.

Mike Anderson: We had a little bit of a scuffle in Freddy's house and we fell on his record player and broke it. Ha ha ha. It was like, "Guys, get out of here and don't come back." Then we came and knocked at the door once and he wouldn't open the door.

"Freddy, come and rehearse."

"I'm not going anywhere with you guys."

It was just a lovers' quarrel I guess.

Freddy Pompeii: I had quit the band right before we did our first gig because I didn't see any gigs coming. Finally to Steven I was like, "Man, you're a fuckin' asshole and this is not gonna happen because you're not doing the work." Him and Motor fell on my stereo turntable and they broke it; flattened it like a pancake. So I threw them out of my house.

John Hamilton: We started booking bands at the Colonial Underground. We met the Viletones and booked them in there. There was a lot of enthusiasm because there was only a couple of clubs where people who were into a certain kind of music could go to. And people were really sick of Fleetwood Mac-middle-aged-boring music.

Freddy Pompeii: About five days later they both came to knocking on my door. There was a plate glass window in the front door and then there was a vestibule and then there was a window with frosted glass that you couldn't see through. But from the front door you could see through and here's Steven and Motor standing like a couple of sad puppies that were just scolded. They're going, "Please let us in, Freddy. Please let us in. Please will you come back in the band again, we got a gig, we got a gig." And I was like, "Aw, get outta here, you guys are full of shit. You're just trying to torture me some more." And it was, "No, no, please let us in, let us in."

This went on for a while and finally I let them in. They had a case of beer with them and we started drinking and I said, "All right, tell me about this gig." They told me about this underground discotheque and I said, "Well, when is this gig?" And they said, "This weekend." I said, "*This* weekend? We don't even have any songs yet." And Steve says, "We can do it, we can do it."

I said, "Well, you know, if you think we can do it, I'll do it. But this is the only gig I'm gonna do. If this doesn't work and I get embarrassed by you assholes, I'm gonna quit and I'm not comin' back." They said, "All right, just one, just one gig. I promise you'll stay in the band after just one gig."

We had to rehearse before our first show. It was the dead of winter and the place that we had to rehearse was the basement of this rehearsal building, the only room they had. The whole floor was covered with glass and broken concrete, broken bottles; there was a big hole in the wall where the snow and the rain was coming in and it was ice cold in there. We're trying to practise and in the meantime Steven's doing his rolling around on the stage act, except he's rolling around in glass. So he cut himself up real bad rolling around in the glass in this rehearsal space. These are the kind of conditions we had to try to get ready for a show coming up, so you can imagine how tough we were getting because of the circumstances. Anyway, he cut himself up real bad and as soon as we were done practicing he went out and made the rounds at all the bars with his open wounds and blood dripping off of him and told everybody that we were practicing for a show and he was practicing for his stage act.

We spent a week writing all the material. We wrote enough for three sets of material, which was a pretty astounding achievement. It was all guitar-based and it was like we started getting a sound when all of a sudden I just figured, this isn't going anywhere. All these guys want to do is get drunk and go out and party. I felt like I was the only one doing any work, so that's why I took such a stance and that's all they really needed. That's all Steven really needed was to be pushed into it with some force. When we started practicing, we were serious.

All the jokes aside, we were very serious about being the first and the best punk rock band in Toronto. The best and fastest and best looking and that whole thing.

I don't know how we did it, but in a week's time we had three sets of material.

*   *   *   *   *

Chris Haight: I guess my first experience with them would be when they were hanging around the Beverley pulling the wool over with their jackets. I remember Dog was so smart and he just talked a great game when he didn't even have a band. They were just kind of hanging around. I think they had Viletones on their jackets, but they didn't have a band.

And then I actually saw them play for the first time at a bar called the Underground in the basement of the Colonial Tavern. And I remember it took them about two or three nights for them to clear the regulars out, which at the time consisted mainly of older, drunken men who couldn't care less about loud music. So after two or three gigs to clear 'em all out of there, that's when the action started happening.

Imants Krumins: They played Thursday, Friday, and Saturday. It was ninety-nine cents to get in and I do remember it was free to go to bars before punk rock started, so you can blame punk rock for charging admission to bars. The original bassist was Jackie Death that weekend. They were great. The first weekend I think there was a buzz, but it wasn't full.

Freddy Pompeii: Jackie Death did the very, very first show we did at the Underground. It was a half-assed crowd. We played two sets and we didn't play that good. I thought it was a pretty sloppy set.

Gordie Lewis: In my opinion, love him or hate him, Steve Leckie single-handedly started the punk scene in Toronto by that show. He was the first one.

The very first show I went to was at OCA and that seemed to be where the germ actually started, from my opinion or my first time seeing what was going on there. We went to this show called The 3D Show and there was the Doncasters, Diodes, and the Dishes. And the things I remember the most about that musically is, again, it was *original* music. They stand for playing original songs; this is incredible! And I remember the Doncasters doing a Kinks song, "I'm Not Like Everybody Else," and for me at that age, what a perfect song: I'm not like everybody else; I'm a misfit. And so that kind of told me that there's something happening in this city that I really want to be part of, and Steve Leckie was there. We met him. We both talked and we said, "I've got a band, I've got a band." We probably didn't say much more than that.

Doncasters, OCA, 3D show. Martha Johnson on vocals / photo by Ralph Alfonso

Paul Kobak: Since I was in the music business and pretty much driving to Toronto twice a week, I'd always be keeping my ear to the ground on what was happening and would often snag flyers off telephone poles to put up in my store.

We decided to check out The 3D Show at the Ontario College of Art. Many people acknowledge that show as the first official new wave gig in Toronto. Initially, all the bands were called "new wave," with "punk" being a sub-category. All three bands were attending the art college. You could certainly tell the Dishes were, anyways. Their music was for select tastes. The Doncasters you could loosely say were like the Talking Heads, and the Diodes were pretty raw but were at least more exciting than the others.

Stephen Mahon: I remember them coming back and saying, "We're gonna blow 'em away because they all stink," ha ha ha.

I think that 3D gig was ground zero for the whole movement.

Gordie Lewis: We stayed in touch with the Underground and what was going on there. Steven Leckie was the leader of the Viletones and he was a real punk, but a real go-getter.

It was kind of a competition thing; no one had heard each other's bands yet, but we knew of *this* guy. Then he put posters up, which was really unheard of at the time: you didn't put posters on poles. It was the whole DIY thing that was just starting to take place and also, again, *original music*. Plus I remember he handed out what was called the "Viletones Manifesto" or something like that. I don't know what it was; how to be a Viletone or something.

He really promoted, and we got wind of that and we went and it was great. So we said, "Let's play here, too!" The Viletones couldn't play every week so we worked our way into that.

Ralph Alfonso [*Cheap Thrills*, April 1977]: Pamphlets given out at the door say… "We're tired of the old ways. We think it's about time rock and roll was given back to the young in this city. The war must start."

Steven Leckie: I wrote a manifesto and typed it up and put it on all the tables before we played. And it said basically the new order — The War Has Begun, like language like that, and how antiquated the current rock stars in the city are and their days, I swear to you, are numbered, and how two of the Viletones are only eighteen. I think I wanted Motor to be my age. He wasn't too much older, but he was the closest anyway.

I put them on the tables. It worked. It was something people hadn't seen. You never saw that before … The written word really hits you if it's done right.

I was looking to accomplish a couple of things with that. One was to sort of raise the cultural stakes a bit, and to serve notice to Rough Trade and Goddo, because they ruled, those two especially. And I thought, Fuck you, you know? That was what the head-spinning thing in punk was. There'd be this group of people that would go, "Why wouldn't you try to make friends with them, and then you could open for them?" But I was so sure the way to play it was to bury rock 'n' roll, not praise it, as Brutus said in *Julius Caesar*. I think that was one of the things, and the other was to take advantage of the cultural climate.

The '70s were frenetic. It was extremely liberal. A thing like punk would be so popular in that kind of era. I'd heard everything and read everything where people said the '20s were the best, the wildest, until the stock market crashed and by the 1970s the people were, in a sense, kind of ready for something like this. It was bringing *Clockwork Orange* to life. At least that's how I would have thought about it.

Gordie Lewis: Steve was Nazi Dog, the bass player Jackie Death, Motor Mike, and Freddy Pompeii, and that was the band. All I remember thinking was, This is great, and *finally* I've got a place where I can do my thing, too. The door was opened and people came.

"The Viletones: Destructive Punk Rock Masochism," **by Steven Davey** [*Metropolitan*, April 25, 1977]: "No more Beatles, no more Stones, we want to hear the Viletones!" the capacity crowd chanted at the Colonial Underground on a prematurely warm March evening. Previous attendance records set by Rush and Rough Trade were smashed as two hundred of Toronto's dilettantes packed this hang-out to witness the debut performance of the Viletones. Whether they were there to cheer, jeer or leer, everyone knew it was going to be a spectacular evening. And it was.

Ralph Alfonso [*Cheap Thrills*, April 1977]: "I've got a mission for this city," says lead singer Nazi Dog, 18, whose short-cropped, carrot-top red hair, missing teeth, and safety pins holding his clothes together make him a frightening bastard son of the English and American new rock scenes, "And I'd kill myself for it."

"The Viletones: Destructive Punk Rock Masochism," **by Steven Davey** [*Metropolitan*, April 25, 1977]: Without having played one note, the Viletones were already notorious. They'd thrown ashtrays at Carole Pope, hurled bottles at the Talking Heads, and been in more fights per capita — often with each other — than any gang of toughs this side of the Don River. It was only natural they formed the Viletones.

Steven Leckie: It was '77 when the Viletones had their first show at the Colonial Underground. It was sold out. It had a lot to do with our pre-promotion from wearing the Viletones things, but when I looked out over the audience there were the cats from Teenage Head.

It felt like I was going into a firefight. It was sold out, which didn't surprise me, because I've got to be honest, man, some of this is about fuckin' ego. Some of the other people in the Toronto scene are not imbued with the true show business ego. They don't have the bravado you need.

Chris Haight: They had 'em lined up. I don't know if it was because it was a novelty, but they had them lined up outside and down the block. And I guess it was like a curiosity thing more than anything to find out what was going on. You'd look around and you'd see the prototypes of what would become fashionable gadgets like safety pins and the right amount of rips and a certain amount of duct tape.

VILETONES

DON'T THINK ABOUT GROUPS FROM ENGLAND OR THE STATES,
JUST THINK ABOUT TORONTO GROUPS.

BRUTUS, ROUGH TRADE, GODDO, HOTT ROXX, MORNINGTON DRIVE.
IN FACT, ALL THE TORONTO UNION GROUPS HAVE BEEN AROUND
FOR MUCH TOO LONG. I CAN'T THINK OF ONE THAT HAS
MEMBERS UNDER 20 YEARS OLD.

TWO OF THE VILETONES ARE ONLY 18.

TO QUOTE "MOTOR", DRUMMER OF THE VILETONES, "WE THINK
ITS ABOUT TIME ROCK AND ROLL WAS GIVEN BACK TO THE
YOUNG IN THIS CITY. WE'RE TIRED OF THE OLD WAYS".

THE WAR MUST START.

THE NEW ORDER IS THE VILETONES

NAZI DOG   - SINGER AND FOUNDER
FREDDIE   - GUITAR
JACKKIE DEATH - BASS
MOTOR MIKE   - DRUMS

Margaret Barnes-DelColle: They kept pumping everybody up so that when they finally *did* play the Underground — I think it was three nights they did — the first night I can't even tell you … It was as if you'd went to see the band of the moment, like if there was some band now that was really hot and you were like, "Oh yeah, yeah, they're in town, I gotta go see them," and you get there and the street's full of people and you can't get in and there's that real energy in the air and excitement because you're going to see a band that you love.

But this was a band that nobody had ever heard a single note of; had never seen them perform, knew nothing about them except for when they went out. And when they went out, the four of them always walked into a bar just like, "Here we are," with a real attitude and stuff, so people always noticed them. So that first night, the place was packed. I mean, just *packed.*

Ross Taylor: Some friends had said, "The Viletones are playing, do you want to check them out?" I brought my camera of course.

There was about five of us that were gonna go. Two of them got to the front doors and said, "No way." They wouldn't go into the place and they turned around and left. The rest of us went in and I remember we were plastered back against the back wall. We were as far away from the stage as you could possibly get. The crowd was all leather, safety pins, torn shirts, and I'd never seen that before. They were breaking glass left, right, and centre. Glasses were smashing and bottles were smashing and there were chunks of broken glass everywhere and flying through the air. I thought, This is crazy, the band hadn't even started at this point, this was just the *audience.* I thought, This is why the other people left; maybe I should have gone with them.

"The Viletones: Destructive Punk Rock Masochism," **by Steven Davey** [*Metropolitan*, April 25, 1977]: Unceremoniously, they took to the stage. Freddy plugged in his guitar and emitted an ear-bursting feedback howl that set the musical standard of the evening. Flanking him were Jackie Death on bass, and the somnambulant Motor Mike behind the drums. Lead singer, Nazi Dog, walked onstage to join the group and casually put a cigarette out on his arm.

The Viletones launched into their premiere number. Already the Underground was electrified. Sporadic pogo-dancing broke out immediately.

Ross Taylor: The band comes on, start playing, and the lights were fairly low. Steve comes out of the wings, sauntering up to the stage, smoking a cigarette. He butts the cigarette out on his arm, flicks the butt away, grabs a beer bottle off the table in front of the stage, smashes it, and proceeds to start cutting his arm. He hasn't even sung a note yet! I'm thinking, Oh my god, what's going on here? He was seventeen or eighteen, really had a baby face, and I thought, This is a kid with problems.

Ralph Alfonso [*Cheap Thrills*, April 1977]: It's times like this you wonder whether you're supposed to applaud, find a doctor, or get the hell out of there.

Colin Brunton: Man, the word of the day at that show was amyl nitrate. And all I remember was the Colonial Underground was jam-packed and all these people were passing around these teeny little bottles of amyl nitrate and taking sniffs and pretty much almost collapsing on the ground, then kind of getting up and stumbling around. Meanwhile Steven Leckie's up there and I think he might have cut himself open. They just breathed danger and it was just, "Fuck, this is *great,* man!"

I used to really like Max Webster, so we brought Max Webster to the New Yorker and they played two nights. Unbelievable excessive amount of equipment and lights, but whatever, I kind of liked them. Our thing at the New Yorker was let people in and then go sit and watch the show. So I sit and watch the show and Kim Mitchell has this shtick. He does his songs, he's got a couple of funny things he does, and he talks to the audience. So the second show, it's fuckin' word for word. So this guy has even his so-called ad libs rehearsed. And they're written. He knows exactly what he's going to say and there's no spontaneity. There's tons of musical craft and maybe artistry, but there's nothing spontaneous here.

But when you saw Steven Leckie, you really felt like wherever this anger or energy's coming from, it feels legit.

"The Viletones: Destructive Punk Rock Masochism," **by Steven Davey** [*Metropolitan*, April 25, 1977]: Nazi Dog is eighteen years old. He has spikey, taped and sprayed red hair. He wears the standard ripped T-shirt, straight jeans, sneakers, dog collar and leash when onstage. And around his neck, a six-inch safety pin hangs open against his skin. His pale complexion, visible through his torn clothes, is a map of scars and stitches. He's missing his front teeth, too.

Ralph Alfonso [*Cheap Thrills*, April 1977]: "I'm going to keep on doing this till I'm 25," said Nazi Dog between sets while Eva, his girlfriend, bandaged up his face and arms. "And then I plan on dying."

"The Viletones: Destructive Punk Rock Masochism," by **Steven Davey** [*Metropolitan*, April 25, 1977]: As the band careened recklessly through their set, Nazi Dog fell around the stage like a whirling dervish off his rocker. Mike stands fell about pal mal. Nazi Dog stumbled into the drums and occasionally kicked Jackie and Freddy. The audience was invited to throw their glasses at the stage. Some twenty or thirty glasses were hurled through the air. Freddy and Jackie left the stage, their amps on full and their guitars endlessly screaming feedback. Motor Mike kept a spasmodic beat.

Nora Currie: Oh god, it was insane. All hell broke loose. There was a huge fucking fight, Leckie was cutting himself, bottles were being thrown. It was kind of a revolution in a band, in a club, on a certain night that epitomized everything that came after. It kind of reopened the doors; it was a statement and there was no looking back after that. The course was set, although no one really knew what it was.

It's interesting because the whole thing of cutting and blood, it can be looked at in different ways, and it *should* be looked at in different ways. There was a joy about it, and a political statement of resistance and a revolution about it that was not ideological and hard to balance with the fact that there was blood, people were cutting themselves, and there was a violent element to it.

My experience was not about it being violent. The violence was there but it was more of a using that tool of the violence to make a statement.

Steven Leckie's super smart and very political, and I believe that for him also there was a revolutionary politicism involved in what he was doing. So the violence was there, but for me it was not negative; it was not about doing harm to anybody. It was about joy. It sounds so incongruous and contradictory to say that, but it was violence as a tool to resist or shift or change. It was almost like a performance piece; it was part of the performance versus a violent act designed to do harm.

Harri Palm: That was a magic moment, that first night that the Viletones played at the Colonial. I had to go check out this band that I was supposed to be in, and me and Ian went down.

I was blown away. I was just *floored*. It was an incredible show, it really was. I have seen a bajillion bands and I know when I see history in the making, and *that* was history in the making. When he did that first show and broke that first beer bottle and cut himself, it was just electric. And the guys at the Colonial, they didn't know what to think. Ha ha ha, this world famous jazz club with him in the basement, it was priceless. It was perfect; it was just perfect. That was a magical night.

"The Viletones: Destructive Punk Rock Masochism," by **Steven Davey** [*Metropolitan*, April 25, 1977]: "Where do you want me to cut myself?" Nazi Dog inquired. "Your face! Your arms!" screamed the audience.

He grabbed a draft from the front table where his girlfriend sat, downed it in one gulp, smashed it on the mike stand, and chuckled, "suicide." He collapsed onstage and began running the glass across his forehead and arms. By now the audience of thrill-seekers realized this was the real thing. His arms and face trickled blood. He placed slivers of broken glass in his mouth. He took another glass and crushed it in his hand. The band returned and Nazi Dog started singing the Viletones theme song, "I Never Feel Sad."

He then accepted a rose from a fan in the front row, stuck out his tongue and ran the thorns across it, biting off the blood-red bloom on the end and swallowing the whole thing.

Margaret Barnes-DelColle: There was this kind of weird energy in the air. At one point they were performing and Steven was talking about killing himself, and he cut himself and he was spitting at everybody in the audience and they were all grossed out but they were all lovin' it.

I went in the ladies' room and there were girls in there younger than me, and they were *crying* and they were wrecking the bathroom, shoving beer bottles down the toilets. It was kind of like when people get charged up and they don't even know how to act with it; you're just so full of adrenaline that you don't know where to funnel it. And that's what it was like that night. It was unbelievable. After that I think things just kind of broke open.

Ross Taylor: The audience was going nuts and the glasses were flying all night. I eventually started sort of relaxing because I was far enough away that I wasn't in the line of fire, but still, my heart was racing through the whole thing. It was a profound experience.

"The Viletones: Destructive Punk Rock Masochism," by **Steven Davey** [*Metropolitan*, April 25, 1977]: Backstage after the show, his girlfriend applied band-aids as he laughed. He took fourteen stitches after that show.

The Viletones are simultaneously the best and the worst band of all time, dead-centre in the danger zone, putting the vile back in violence.

Whether the Viletones are a metaphor for a sick society anesthetized into numbness and dumbness, a death trip, or merely a jolt of shock therapy, is something you'll have to decide before they're stopped by the morality squad or some anti-defamation league.

Steven Leckie: That was it. Once we did that gig we were Number One in Toronto.

Chris Haight: To me, I thought they had a lot of nerve when I first caught them. I thought, They've got more nerve than a toothache, these guys. But when I seen what they were kind of representing as far as going back to you know, "We don't really care, we're not gonna conform to what the labels want us to record, blah blah blah, we're just gonna do our own thing and be the rogues that we are," that's when it overwhelmed me. I just liked their approach. It was fresh, it was vigorous, and they pulled all the stops. I just couldn't believe how fast they progressed in such a short space of time with just a handful of tunes.

There was something about them; I can't really put my finger on it, but they had some kind of magnetism, they had some kind of attraction. You see that once in a while and I figured what the heck, these guys feel the way I do and who knows?

* * *   * *

Freddy Pompeii: Jackie was so young and inexperienced and he got his girlfriend pregnant and he couldn't come to Toronto from Hamilton. It was a mess. It was truly a punk rock band in every respect with making all the mistakes that young people make.

Jackie had this long Brian Jones hair. That kind of haircut except longer, in a bob with the bangs. So he had this really great look. He was tiny, which was kind of cool, too, because if everybody is the same size in a band it looks a little better. We were pretty little guys, except for Motor; he was kind of tall.

Jackie got kicked out because he was very irresponsible. We were irresponsible, too ... about everything but music. We all had the same problem in that we were immature and all we wanted to do was play music. We were pretty much like Jackie in that sense, but he was over the line with it. He would miss practices altogether and we'd say to him, "Hey, next time you miss a practice you're out." "Oh no, no, no, don't kick me out, don't kick me out," that kind of thing. So he ends up with a girlfriend and he gets her pregnant and all of a sudden he's not showing up for practices.

So we kicked him out. Jackie was like, "Oh no, man, Freddy, you can't do this to me. It's just for now, it's not gonna be forever." Yeah, only a year and a half, or maybe two years, or maybe twelve years. Ha ha ha. He was crying and stuff.

Mike Anderson: Jackie's mother was mad at him; she thought we were bad characters.

But it turned out *he* was the bad character.

After that he got caught doing B&Es. So we didn't have a bass player.

Chris Haight: I was playing in a band called Zoom. It was a trio. John Hamilton played drums and this other guy played bass. It was Johnny's gig. He kind of found the Beverley and he'd come down with this original thing and there definitely would be some of the Dishes and the Diodes — before we got to know each other, they'd come down to check it out. Steve and them were checking us out. As fate would have it, there were some internal rebuildings going on.

Freddy Pompeii: Because Jackie was being sporadic, the stage was set. And Chris, we already knew what a good guitar player he was, and a songwriter.

It was mentioned that Chris had been talking about playing bass, and I thought, Wow, this fuckin' guy is good. So I went for it right away. Everybody else did, too, because they knew he was a real musician; somebody who was gonna do what he had committed to do.

Chris Haight: At the time, the Diodes were experimenting with their own little thing. And through the grapevine — that's all we had was the grapevine — I heard the Viletones were looking for a bass player. And I knew that Zoom wasn't gonna last because we weren't all on the same page.

Freddy Pompeii: It was immediate that Chris got in the band. A week after we played the Underground we made the phone calls and told everybody who was concerned that they were no longer concerned. It was a very quick transition, and smooth.

I was actually ecstatic because Chris was a good guitar player first. He liked the band so much he picked up the bass and started playing *that*. The guy had way more experience in showmanship and all that. He was definitely a better guy than Jackie. Jackie was in it for a lark. Chris was like, "Let's play. Let's travel. Let's see the world." Which is a good attitude for being in a band.

Chris Haight: When I first hooked up with that group we were rehearsing at some joint and it was like a little cubbyhole, like a doghouse in the basement of a studio. And the Dog would really go to extra measures just to see where our breaking point was, like to the point where he wouldn't even use the washroom. He'd just turn around in the corner and do what a dog does and expect us to just be right there. It was disgusting at times, but I think it would have taken a lot more than that to put a frown on our heads.

But he had his own little way of testing you.

I'm not sure what was going through his mind, but I remember the stench. I guess he was thinking if they can put up with that, it must be solid. You'd just want to kick him right up the ass.

Freddy Pompeii: Chris played on the second show, which is what we really considered the first show, because that's the band that made the noise.

Steven Leckie: There was no nervousness. I didn't know what to really wear when I got there so I had my girlfriend at the time wrap me up in gaffer's tape, which at the time was an odd thing to see.

Johnny Garbagecan: I think Steven Leckie was much more gory and gruesome and ballsy than Iggy Pop and Johnny Rotten. He made them look terrible. Seriously. I saw all three of them and I saw Steve Leckie live many times, and he did crazier shit than anybody. Okay, Iggy Pop jumped through mirrors, big deal. So he cut himself up. But Steven didn't do a bad job of that himself.

He had gaffer's tape wrapped around his whole torso. It pulls off a layer of skin when you're pulling it off. It is so strong that you can use it in construction; that's where they use it. They use it to tape ductwork together, and he had his torso wrapped in that. When he pulled it off — I was in the dressing room — when they pulled it off he was bleeding all over. Who did stuff like that?

Chris Haight: I still remember Jimmy the Worm [Chris Haight's brother. Booker at the Colonial Underground. Deceased] chasing the Dog with the cash box at the end of the night. I think it was two bucks or something to get in, and the Dog was always doing one of these when it came to the pay out. And I still remember Jimmy chasing him all around the club and the Dog had the cash box under his arm and he's going, "What do you think you're doing?" And this and that. He was overstepping his bounds, which he developed into an art later. Ha ha ha.

From that very first day I always kept one eye on the Dog and his little antics.

Steven Leckie: The next morning I woke up to the cover of the *Globe and Mail* in the Entertainment section, *Fanfare*, the next day.

Blair Martin: I remember my dad showing me the article. It was on the cover of the *Fanfare* section, this guy wearing gaffer's tape as a shirt which he ripped off his body and he cut himself with glass and he's calling himself Nazi Dog. And I'm really suspicious of someone calling himself Nazi Dog. I don't think it's really too cool; it wouldn't strike me initially as too cool, so I was

really not turned on to the thing.

Then I went to school and my friend Tony Fares was talking about it — "Oh, you should have seen this! He ripped off the gaffer's tape and he cut himself and blah, blah, blah, blah." Then Peter Doig came to the north doors of Jarvis Collegiate and he said, "Hey, man, see that fuckin' thing in the newspaper this morning? That was Steve Leckie."

I remember once in the New Yorker Theatre a friend of mine said, "Oh hey look, it's Steve Leckie," and he's dressed like Lou Reed. I think he'd dyed his hair black and he was wearing the big shades, sitting in the New Yorker Theatre sort of giving off a New Yorker buzz. So when Peter Doig told us this guy on the front, this Nazi Dog on the front of the *Fanfare* section was Steve Leckie, it really made absolute, complete sense to me. And that was the one thing that struck me as cool about it was that it was Steve Leckie. Because I went, "Oh, of course. What *else* would a guy like that do?"

Freddy Pompeii: We were in all the papers and magazines. The headline was "Not Them! Not Here!" It was real big, across half of the page. Like in other words, "Oh no, the barbarian hordes are attacking, lock up your daughters." It was a very comic book kind of thing.

When I saw that title for the story I was on the floor; I couldn't catch my breath from laughing so much.

Steven Leckie: I thought, Holy fuck, we're riding on the exact right time. It was that soon.

It was unlike other movements, from rockabilly to doo-wop to the Beach Boys sound. Punk happened so rapidly; so incredibly quick. Mick Jones said it happened in one hundred days; there was an *ultra* time.

I wish I knew you a million lifetimes to tell you how I felt about having that knowledge that we were in the right place at the right time, because it was *quick*. And it never stopped for the Viletones.

Paul Kobak: There was lots of rehearsing and trying new songs. Frank got a job at a transmission shop that lasted one day. We played a correctional institute for young offenders, things like that.

Gordie Lewis: We just played wherever we possibly could. We even played a few youth detention centres, one in Hagersville and one in Oakville. It was great. They loved us. That's the type of thing we were doing.

Gambi Bowker: The first time I saw Teenage Head was at a school in Hamilton, so that must have been 1975 or '76, maybe. I'm not that great on dates.

I was just blown away, right? It was the coolest thing I'd ever seen. Frankie Venom at that point, and for the next two years, was probably the most mesmerizing performer around.

Gordie Lewis: Hamilton was home for us and it still is, but we realized it was very limited as far as where we could play and who would let us play. We knew Toronto was the place we could probably get away with this, more than in Hamilton.

7. one of THe Pioneers

Frankie Venom / photo by Ross Taylor

Paul Kobak: Chris Paputts' brother Jimmy [the Worm] was booking the [Colonial] Underground. Within a week of the Underground opening I'd approached Jimmy saying I was managing a band from Hamilton called Teenage Head and we'd like to play there. We were at the doorway surrounded by people and it was pretty noisy and Jimmy thought I'd said *Talking* Heads and hustled me into his office.

While he was initially disappointed and had never heard of Hamilton, I got a gig out of it. We started out playing some middle-of-the-week dates that were sparsely attended but it didn't take long before it became weekend dates playing to packed houses.

Stephen Mahon: This would have been the spring of '77. That was the Year of the Punks. There wasn't really anything happening in Toronto until the spring of '77. That was the first time we played in Toronto, at the Colonial. That was our coming out, so to speak.

Gordie Lewis: The Underground was very similar to what happened with CBGB's. It was a desolate club and then a few bands come in and pick up the pieces. It was very urban. It was very downtown. There was a lot of art influence.

I wouldn't miss a show. I'd always go. I went to everything that happened. I wanted to be a part of it. I saw a place where I could do my thing.

Frankie Venom: Oh fuck — debauchery at its finest. Brilliant, absolutely. Downstairs it was us, the Viletones, and who else was on the bill?

It was fuckin' madness, but *fun* madness, you know? No one got hurt. Well, *we've* seen some ugly things in our career. Bottles in the head and ...

One time I got smashed in the face with the mic and it hit my front tooth. Some idiot shoved it and *pop!* Oh, thanks a lot, blood's just drippin', kept singin'. Everyone's like, "Oh cool, man!" And after the show I was like, "This doesn't feel so good," but it looked cool. It's part of your pay for being in the business for our type of music. You know, I mean, we're not fuckin' the Carpenters, you know what I mean?

Paul Eknes: There was a club on Yonge and Dundas called the Colonial. Upstairs they used to have the Commodores and A-name acts, and downstairs for a while they made it a punk club because obviously it was, "Oh, what's happening? We can make money off of this."

I remember seeing Viletones and Teenage Head, double header, and Frankie Venom was jumping up and down so much that he actually broke through the dance floor, fell down, cut himself on the chin, and went,

"Look at me! I'm a Teenage Head." To this day I've seen fifteen million bands live, and to me I just loved him for that.

Back then he was the sexiest guy in Toronto, even though he wasn't *from* Toronto.

Slash Booze: The stage was so rotted out that there were boot holes in it. Frank actually went down into this hole on the riser and he surfaced in another hole ten feet away. With the microphone, too, ha ha ha.

Steven Leckie: I loved things like Teenage Head. I got along very well with them. They were really boys' boys.

They were a hell of a lot of fun, they had great senses of humour; they were really just top fuckin' musicians. They didn't care. When you hear Frankie singing he only opens his mouth *this* much, like Roy Orbison. That's because Frank doesn't really care. And the songs were fuckin' good. "Disgusteen," that's a good song, you know? "I took a shot of whisky, started looking for the bar." That's cool. "Picture My Face" — "One day I needed a buck, today I need a bank." That's rock 'n' roll.

Frankie Venom: We had a great deal involved with putting an end to disco. It was a shitty era.

We started in '74 and along came the fuckin' Bay City Rollers and fuckin,' pardon my language, but we were just a three-chord band. Now we know four chords. But it's all attitude, intensity; you know, sweat, cuts and glass, and it's rock 'n' roll.

Imants Krumins: At the Colonial, Slash Booze played harmonica on one song for them. He always gets credit on their records. So we're at the Colonial and it comes time for Slash to do his song and he's on the balcony when Frank calls him down. So he dives off the balcony onto the stage, lands on his foot. But unfortunately it broke. So he plays his harmonica bit for the song, obviously in total pain, and he walks off and we see him the next six weeks with a cast on his leg. Ha ha ha.

Dave Rave: The lads kept working and working, and I think the breakthrough really came when they started playing Toronto at the Underground. I think they really started finding their groove and Gord was starting to feel positive about shows.

At that point I could see it was still tough; there was resistance and they were trying to find their home. I still don't think it was punk rock yet, but it was happening. They had found a niche. Because I knew they had to bypass all that other music. Their music was not in that department.

It didn't fit the other groups at the time, so that was I think when they started finding other like-minded people and I remember going to their shows and it was exciting.

Slash Booze: I knew that Teenage Head had the potential to go further when they got to Toronto and there was an acceptance of that sort of thing. When any band played, the whole same group of people would go there. They'd all show up and I realized there was a scene going on.

Little did we know, it was happening all over the world.

Paul Kobak: I'd agree that the Colonial Tavern in Toronto was when Teenage Head really started happening. The Colonial was the first real outlet for the new wave scene and bands were starting to form overnight, playing their own original music.

The Head had written some tunes by this time and were experimenting via crowd response. Seemed like whenever we'd come back to play T.O. there'd be at least a couple of new tunes to be tried. We'd play to ten people some nights but that didn't last too long, because it didn't take long to maintain a dedicated following. A fortunate bonus for Teenage Head is that a number of friends/fans from Hamilton would follow the band to wherever they'd play.

Gary Pig Gold: In my opinion, in '77 in Southern Ontario, Teenage Head were the best band of any band. They were *so* good live. The Viletones were always entertaining, and Edgar Breau would have the X factor — you never knew what was going to happen. But Teenage Head were the perfect band: Hardcore, hard rock, a hard-*something* type of band. They were incredible.

Larry LeBlanc: I saw them open for Eddie and the Hot Rods at the Masonic Temple. I mean, they were *so* good, that band.

Gary Pig Gold: Gord's an excellent guitar player. For me he had all the right elements. Steve Jones from the Pistols was a poor imitation of Gord. Gord *had it.* Deservedly, they're in the history books now.

When I would drag my friends out of the suburbs to see these bands, *anyone* would be able to relate to Teenage Head. Even if you were into Alice Cooper you could relate. When I brought my Deadhead friend Larry of all people down to see them, he said the same thing — "These guys are *good.*" And this was a very jaded man. It was everything you could do just to get him to come down.

John Catto: When Teenage Head first came to Toronto, Frankie had really long hair and stuff. I think they saw themselves like a different sort of thing; they just got sucked into it all. In fact, come to think of it, they *all* had long hair.

I remember that Lucasta was hanging around with Frankie. She kind of took him and got his hair cut. I went at the end of that week or something, so I didn't even see the shows at the beginning of the week when he had long hair. The only moment in history he's ever had long hair and I missed it, ha ha ha.

Don Pyle: I remember that my perception of it at the time was quite different than what reality was.

I think the reality was that things were very conservative; that you had to dress this way or you were not accepted, that you had to only listen to these records or you were not accepted, that the gender roles were still very much kept in place. I think there was certainly some breaking out of that in certain places, but for all of its so-called rebellious spirit I think punk rock was extremely conservative. Lyrically, obviously there's the whole spectrum of things, but it surprises me now when I listen to some lyrics by the Sex Pistols and the conservative attitudes that are in those songs.

Teenage Head were the only band pretty much at that time that were allowed to have long hair. They were accepted by the punks. I think people somehow forgave them because they were from Hamilton, and also because they were so good. But long hair was definitely not allowed.

Gordie Lewis: We were from Hamilton. Again, it was an urban art type of crowd, so they always tried to give us a hard time about being from Hamilton.

But we had one up over on them. See, they were all just starting out in their bands. They didn't know that we'd been rehearsing for the last two or three years and we actually did have gigs under our belt. So when we went to play it was, "Hey, they can *play.*" We were good. So as much as they gave us a hard time, we could get up there and as far as they were concerned we were the best band out of the bunch because we knew how to play and we were rehearsing. It wasn't new to us. And we'd been together since 1975 in one form or another. So we were able to stand up for ourselves.

It was good-natured, but definitely there was a resistance. There was definitely something going on between Hamilton and Toronto. They definitely thought of us as foreign.

Xenia Splawinski: Teenage Head I think was probably the best. They had a sound that really, really worked and it was different than the others. It was their own thing.

I wish I could describe it better, but their music to me, whenever I hear it, I *still* think it's fantastic. It really has lived through it. It just had the right energy. And yet even as a Toronto band ... *Hamilton?* We had a hard time accepting them. If they were from Hamilton you did accept them, their music was great, but it really did feel pickier. Toronto had that attitude towards London [Ont], too.

Toronto had an attitude.

*   *   *   *   *

Ian Mackay: The Diodes played the Colonial, the Viletones played there, and Teenage Head played there all within a few weeks of each other. That was it: Boom! Instant scene.

Dave Rave: Boom, there it was. It was exciting.

I remember reading this Beatles book and I was like, "Oh god, why can't that happen in *our* lives? Our lives are so dull." It was fine for learning and playing chords and that, musically it was ripe, but when you played the bar it was nothing special. You'd do your show and you'd get paid, but it was not this Hamburg experience that I was reading about in this book.

When it happened here it was like, "It's here, we've *got* it!" It was like a miracle. I remember taking the train back to Hamilton from Toronto after Teenage Head played the Colonial and saying to my girlfriend, "I think it's back. I think we've got it. It's here."

Going to see these shows, to be honest with you, the intensity could be frightening. And I *liked* that, being frightened. The music was being played with so much passion that it was almost violent; it was a violent passion. I could recognize that it was true. And anything could happen, and did, at certain times. It was very, very exciting.

Gordie Lewis: The scene was in its infancy, because it was able to let us be one of the leaders and one of the dominating forces in the scene. That's important.

What I miss about the '70s is the competition. That was what I really liked. I liked the "My band's better than your band." I really enjoyed that. That was great. It made you want to be better all the time and I thought that was really healthy.

Stephen Mahon: You know what? It sounds cocky, but we never felt competition from anybody. We started *pre-*punk, so when the whole thing hit in '77 when we went to Toronto and played, we just knew. It was like we'd already played a couple of seasons.

I *wished* the bands were better. I'd come offstage and it would have been nice to watch other bands that I was into, but there really wasn't anybody else around that was that good, really. That does sound conceited but it was true; I think it was true, anyway.

Gordie Lewis: By being on the ground floor we were able to establish our ground and stake our ground in the scene that was going on, so therefore we could say we helped start this thing, we were one of the pioneers. We might not have been able to do that if we got in later. I'm glad we got in when we got in.

Frankie Venom, Colonial Underground, 1977 / photo by Ralph Alfonso

l-r: Nick Stipanitz, Stephen Mahon, Frankie Venom, Gordie Lewis, / photo by Arthur Usherson, courtesy Teenage Head

8. disaster land

Anya Varda: I remember the first time I was aware of anything Toronto punk oriented was seeing the Diodes play at the Colonial. They were the first L.A. kind of punk band that I saw.

The Dishes, oh god, I just remember I was the president of their, not *fan* club, but *fun* club, ha ha ha. I remember when the Viletones formed. I remember sitting there talking with Steven who I'd known since I was fifteen. Steven Leckie, who we used to call Steven Lucky. When his dad would leave town he would turn their home into what we referred to as the Lucky Hotel and we would all go crash there.

I loved the Diodes. They were like us. They were hip and cool. None of us knew each other at the time. We all started gravitating towards this English sound that was coming out, and the style.

The Diodes, CEAC basement, 1977
l-r: John Catto, Paul Robinson, John Hamilton,
Ian Mackay, John Korvette
/ photo by Ralph Alfonso

We were all kind of far-flung. We were from Scarborough, Etobicoke, North York; we were children of the suburbs, a lot of us. There were a lot of kids from OCA and then there was the beginning of the Queen Street scene that Sandy Stagg really kind of started in a great way, because she took over that greasy spoon Peter Pan in the mid-'70s and made that the hip joint. She started it, getting that scene right in that neighbourhood, for sure.

Sandy Stagg: Up until about '76 I was just doing my shop, Amelia Earhart Originals, antique clothing, and working a bit with General Idea, the artist group. I was sort of being a model for some of their stuff and generally a patron and all that. And then we opened the Peter Pan in '76, which is kind of when things got going because members of a lot of the bands worked in the Peter Pan.

I met a woman named Grenada and she took me up to General Idea's studio. I started to be invited to things, you know, you sort of make contact that way. They seemed to find something in me they liked so I got invited to do stuff and I became one of the group, really. It was all very casual in those days. I wasn't really that connected with OCA, really; more artists in general and A Space.

The Dishes, the Diodes, a lot of people from those bands worked as waiters and cooks and whatever. I don't know how that happened, but it did. I tried to do good for a lot of people during those years. I gave jobs to a lot of people and encouraged a lot of people and tried to promote Toronto. It really was small but perfectly formed and much enjoyed by lots of visitors from other towns, like London and New York.

AA Bronson: We were the first people to set up our studio on Queen Street West and then Sandy and her partners opened up the Peter Pan a few months later, and then it became this extremely lively spot where all the art slash music slash theatre etcetera scene would go out and hang out and eat. It was a good late-night spot. It's hard to imagine now; the scene was so small then that there really wasn't any place to go. Now there's countless little artsy restaurants in Toronto, but then there was really only the one.

Mark Gane: The atmosphere on a wide level was that there were always people who were outsiders. It was primed to happen. And what was happening mainly in New York and London was a huge influence.

The Toronto scene was very, very small and totally undocumented. It all revolved around OCA, Queen Street — which you would never recognize. It would look totally dull to you in 1976. But behind all those funky old buildings were artists' studios and the Peter Pan.

It was this big mix of artists and a lot of people couldn't play, but that was the whole punk ethos, it didn't matter. In a lot of periods of history where there's been a really heavy music and art interaction, that's not a new idea. In Italy just before World War One, the Futurists were doing noise concerts and people would just build machines that made noise. In a way, punk is just an extension of these weird ideas of what music was and how you made music.

Anya Varda: At that time in Toronto, and maybe even so now — and I'm not sure if you could even say that happened anywhere else on the planet — but in Toronto the music, the art scene, anything that was cool, hip, and fabulous, was all part and parcel of exactly the same crowd. If you were into the Diodes you were also into General Idea. And General Idea were three very attractive men, very young at the time but several years older than we were ... I remember I was nineteen and they were turning thirty, and I thought they were just *so* sophisticated. But they were just gorgeous and fun and hip and went to all the concerts, too, and they were doing this really cool, cutting edge, original type of performance art. Anybody who was going to the concerts by the Diodes were also going to all the openings of General Idea, so it was one big, happy, dysfunctional family, but all very, very attractive and very well-dressed. A little incestuous, too.

Ken Farr: General Idea, they were so cool. Again, just a great audience of people who were creative and interesting. And the whole General Idea scene, they set out to be famous. That was step one. "What do we want to be? We want to be famous." So the idea was to be famous from the beginning. And they were good graphic artists. They had picked up on that style of Bauhaus from the 1930s and that grainy, black and white style of art, and they were really good at it and stylish in their own way. So being associated with them just added to what we were doing.

Anything connected with General Idea was always great. It was kind of like the Algonquin Roundtable or something like that. You just never knew who you were going to meet, the cross-section of talented and creative people.

David Clarkson: It was very glamourous, but kind of fake. It was a lot of gay camp and irony and it was very sophisticated.

Although I was really quite intrigued and interested in a lot of things those guys did, it was easier for me to interact with this other camp, which was in fact closer to the art school and they were called CEAC, which was the Centre for Experimental Art and Communication. They were interested in many of the same things, but it was a little grittier and it was more overtly political. They were less interested in a cultural spectacle and more interested in spontaneous performances in using the actual context of where you actually were and incorporating that within the art performance rather than planning everything out.

That was the great deal of difference between General Idea and the CEAC guys.

Bruce Eves: There was the whole A Space, General Idea crowd and then there was the whole CEAC, leftist politics, gay liberation stuff at the other end, butting heads.

General Idea were johnny-come-latelies. They rewrite their own history. Everything they say I would take with a giant grain of salt.

AA Bronson, he was very hostile to the whole thing. He was like a total careerist. He wanted to work in a national gallery. He wanted big name galleries. We just held that in such contempt. This is what I'm meaning about the competing agendas. I have no axes to grind.

David Clarkson: The CEAC guys had their own clubhouse, store, and library, which was this big warehouse building. It was this mammoth building and they had their own library there; performance spaces, showed movies, had some exhibition rooms and meeting places. It was a great resource.

General Idea had been around from the `60s so they were sort of older and more established, and I guess this probably was the only real thing that drew me a little bit more to CEAC: They were new.

We met these guys, Bruce Eves and Amerigo Marras, that were running it, and they had made some contacts with some OCA students that were a little ahead of me. If they brought somebody in from Europe to do a performance, they would do the performance at CEAC and then what the heck, they'd bring them up to OCA and they could make fifty dollars or something doing a class.

So little by little, because me and Ian were good students and kind of well-known, we would go to these things and introduce ourselves and ask questions and in a very genuine way we just kind of met them.

These guys really liked us because we were young art students who were interested in them. That's exactly what they wanted. They wanted to have a youthful and exciting audience and so it was a good symbiosis between those two places. Harri Palm and I did a performance night at CEAC and I also remember Ian and I shooting a videotape down in the basement of CEAC, so we had some kind of interchange with them through the three of us being down at their events.

Paul Robinson: We kind of got asked to leave Ontario College of Art. They didn't want us to rehearse there anymore. I think we were making too much noise. We got involved with this group called Centre for Experimental Art and Communication.

Ian Mackay: General Idea represented post-modernist pastiche bordering on sexual politics, later to be tumbled into it with AIDS.

CEAC represented Marxist political art in Canada, and was snuffed out. We had aligned with a shaky but potent ally.

Paul Robinson: They had a building on Duncan Street. They owned this building and they went away for the summer and said we could rehearse in the basement. It was an art gallery but on the first floor it housed the Liberal Party of Ontario, their head office, who basically left at about six o'clock in the evening. We could rehearse after that because they wouldn't allow us to rehearse during the day.

Ian Mackay: We got the space first without question. Full stop period.

I know I made a lot happen. I sat in their office and went over the loose terms. It is a vague memory; it was a very sunny day. I remember sitting in a low seating arrangement, sitting on the floor before a large square table, and I think sharing something illegal, and then CEAC offering it up to us as their idea. Little did they realize the discontinuity we all started. Then we acted.

Paul Robinson: The Diodes were never purely out to shock. We actually had something quite intelligent to purvey. We wanted desperately to express, and did it through music and art. This was a very small window in our lives. Unrepeatable.

It was the Mackay/Clarkson connection that brought CEAC into the picture and yes, they, CEAC, wanted an alternative to the General Idea/A Space domination of the Toronto art scene. GI were really a phenomenon, musically rooted in Roxy Music and 1930s camp glamour. GI wanted to create a post-Warhol Factory alternative in Toronto. They were tied into Duggie Fields and Andrew Logan as well as Gilbert & George in the UK; extremely international for the time.

CEAC saw a window of opportunity with punk. They connected to the political lyrics of the UK scene something that didn't exist in North America. The Ramones, Talking Heads, Television, Heartbreakers, etcetera, were not very political in the CEAC way.

Bruce Eves: I think it was more the DIY aesthetic we liked about punk rather than any specific interest. It was sort of taking history by the throat and doing it yourself. I mean, most of the bands were all art students, so there was already this kind of affinity between upstairs and downstairs. They needed the space, we had the space, we thought it was a good idea.

Paul Robinson: Right at the end of the college year Dave decided that he wanted to concentrate more on his photography and so he left the band. Also, Bent Rasmussen, who was the drummer, decided he was going to leave too.

David Clarkson: The reason I stopped being in the Diodes is it was very obvious that we had succeeded in this initial idea to use it as this kind of exploration of popular culture. I could just see it. We had been very successful in a very short amount of time. We were self-conscious throughout about creating an image and working socially and building good songs and making sure people knew about them.

So you know, all of that had happened and the only next step was that it was going to get all legal, and just bigger, and I wasn't that committed to it, you know? I was interested in doing my art projects of which Diodes was just one, and I just couldn't see quitting school and going on tour for a couple of years. And I couldn't really see just working with bigger and bigger record companies and doing bigger and bigger shows. It just seemed repetitive to me. It all seemed like larger versions of the trajectory we had done in eight months. That's why I stopped.

I guess Bent must have dropped out at that time, too, and went to play with his friend Harri in the G-Rays. I never spoke to Bent about why he quit, or if I did I don't remember. We played pretty good together and he might not have had the confidence if I wasn't there, because they hadn't mastered their instruments. I really don't know why he stopped, but by that time the G-Rays were a really excellent band.

John Hamilton: By that point in '77, everything was in a state of flux. The Diodes' drummer had quit because he'd bought a red sports car and wanted to drive across Canada. Zoom had broken up because Chris had been courted by the Viletones, and our bass player was sort of a fugitive from the Holiday Inn.

So I got a call from the Diodes and they said, "Do you want to come and audition to be our drummer?" So I said, "Yeah, okay."

So I went down to the basement of a place called CEAC. There was a stage there because they'd just had a play called something like *Disaster Land*; it was supposed to be some sort of apocalypse at the end of the world. So you went in there and there were like mounds of dirt and construction rubble that were at least six feet high in this fifteen hundred square foot warehouse space. And the Diodes were rehearsing onstage. So I came in and I met them and they still had a different bass player then.

I'd been playing in bands since about 1966, when I was in high school. All kinds of bands — R&B bands, country western bands, stuff like that. But I don't think the Diodes had ever been in a band before in their lives. My first impression of them was that they had a lot of talent, but they were pretty unformed. They didn't even know how to wrap up their guitar cords at that point.

The first time I rehearsed with them I think John Catto spent most of the time kicking his amplifier because it wouldn't work. So I played some songs with them and I was kind of undecided whether I wanted to throw my lot in with them. I thought Paul had a pretty good voice. They were really green, but I thought they had something. They were artists and I was sort of an old tradesman, I guess, with a bit of an artistic streak. But anyway, that night Steven Davey phoned me up and told me I *had* to join the Diodes, and gave me a great big sales pitch about how they were really going to go places. He probably talked me into it actually. So I threw my lot in with the Diodes.

John Catto: John Hamilton was floating around because his band had broken up. We liked him. He had this cool Chinese guy outfit that he used to walk around in with a bowl haircut and everything. We went, "Oh he looks really cool, and he plays great drums," so that was really the thing.

Getting John in was pretty important with the band, because he'd done a lot more than everyone else had at that point. So he sort of came in and went, "Oh you don't do this, you do *this*." We'd been flying blind totally.

*　　*　　*　　　*　　　*

Ralph Alfonso: The Diodes were like nothing I had seen before.

I had seen them at The 3D Show and they had a slideshow projection happening behind them. One of them had a shirt that had the letter "T" on it and another guy had a shirt that said "V" on it and they had these crazy matching haircuts. Ian, he was the guitar player then, he had this haircut you would never see again until Phil Oakey from the Human League, where this big thing of hair covered up half your face. The guy from the Cramps had it, too. This was way before any of that, and Ian had it. And the singer just stood there and he had his lyrics taped on to the mic stand and he was just spewing them out and it was just great. I mean, the whole night was great because in the audience, of course, were the Teenage Head guys. Everybody that would later rise to prominence was in the audience.

The Dishes had been around for quite a while; they were sort of like Sparks. They were like the vestige of glam, Roxy Music–type stuff. They were part of the Rough Trade crowd; Steven Davey was part of that gang. So the Dishes were kind of the bridge, but the Diodes were definitely the future. And the Doncasters were another kind of bridge because that was Martha Johnson's first band. The Doncasters were more of a '60s cover band; they would do pop-type stuff and they dressed the part. So you had this really interesting cross section of old — Doncasters had the '60s aesthetic, the last of the '70s glam ethic, which was the Dishes — and then spearheading the new was the Diodes.

Caroline Azar: The '70s Toronto punk scene was so pure because it was a mix of really wild glam street trash mixed with egghead art school intellectualism.

I really loved being the audience for the Curse and the Biffs and the Demics. The Diodes — they were writing songs as good as the Who. The Mods were good — musically more like Bruce Springsteen, but they were dressed like mods.

Ralph Alfonso: And it all worked, because you could see that just on a superficial level they all connected.

The Diodes, the way they presented themselves and the way they dressed was very similar to the Dishes, very similar to the Doncasters, so right away you could see that they had all inadvertently discovered that the energy that held all those genres together was now poised to emerge as something else; like almost a distillation. Because everybody was into Roxy Music and Slade and the '70s glam, but yet the energy of old garage rock. Now you could see it morphing into something new.

A friend of mine was Dean Motter, who was a teacher at OCA and was actually a very famous comic book creator. He created Mister X and he's worked at DC Comics. And another friend of mine was going to OCA called Ken Stacey, and he was part of the comics world, which was part of where I come from, and so they introduced me to Paul and Ian.

I was going to write this whole piece on the scene. I think the U of T beat me to it and somebody did a whole rundown of what was happening. I had my own column in *Cheap Thrills* magazine called Bomp de Bomp, and I had just started writing about — there was no name for it yet — this new music that was about to explode. So I got a hold of Paul's number and we started talking and six hours later … We just hit it off so well because he's a really intelligent guy.

He's also a very persuasive guy, so next thing I know I've not only agreed to become their manager but I'm going to help open their club and all this stuff.

Meanwhile I'm living in Mississauga so I have no car. I was going to Sheridan College at the time. I was studying journalism. So I hitchhiked in with my camera gear. I go to their rehearsal space, which would later become the Crash 'n' Burn. It was the basement of this building, and I just went in there and started taking all these great shots of them and posing them and I guess nobody had ever done that with them before. The drummer, John Hamilton, was really impressed by that and we hit it off.

Paul Robinson [CIUT-FM, Greg Dick interview, 2007]: Steven Leckie came up to me at the Colonial Underground and said, "Have you heard of this band called Crash And Burn? They are going to be huge. They are way better than any of the Toronto bands," referencing the Diodes, "and they're about to get a huge deal." He wanted to see how I would react, or maybe he was thinking of using the name and putting out feelers to see if I'd heard of a band called that.

John Hamilton [CIUT-FM, Greg Dick interview, 2007]: It turned out to be a bunch of old hippies from the Toronto Island called Moonfood that I knew from a previous incarnation that I got Jimmy the Worm to book because they had a big following who drank. Anyway, I heard about this incident and thought that Crash And Burn was a good name for the club and suggested it.

Bruce Eves: We owned the building at 15 Duncan Street. The top floor was the artists' space and the two middle floors were rented. The main floor was actually rented to the Liberal Party, ha ha ha, and the basement level was vacant.

I'm not sure who it was, whether it was the Diodes or whether it was Ralph Alfonso that actually approached us with the idea of doing a one-day-a-week series of punk rock performances and we basically said, "Fine, go with it, run with it, just don't break the law. Make sure there are party permits that you can sell beer, all the money goes to the bands, we don't want any money, we'll pay the hydro bill," and that was that. I was the liaison between upstairs and downstairs.

Ralph Alfonso: The Diodes did a performance in London, Ontario, for Applegarth Follies in March or April '77 as part of the CEAC deal to get the basement. I tagged along. There were twenty to thirty people there — all kind of, "What the . . .?" But it went down very well and may have trickled down to the local scene about to bloom there.

John Catto: We moved into their basement, and the very first thing that happened was we did this performance art thing which was eventually what came out as the "Raw/War" single with Mickey Skin of the Curse.

Paul Robinson: They [CEAC] wanted the Diodes and the Curse to be political, and manipulated "Raw/War" to this end. It all seems a bit contrived now on hearing it again, but it was interesting and very them.

It is interesting to note that both GI and CEAC were heavily into gay politics, although they had nothing in common with each other. Jorge [Zontal] and [Felix Partz] of [GI] died of AIDS-related illnesses.

Bruce Eves: The quote unquote art world thought we were just bonkers. It was like, "What are you doing? What is this all about?" when CEAC got involved with this. We were doing performance, and we were trying to push the boundaries of what we were doing. It just seemed natural. We did some performance art and punk rock. It was like breaking the mold of what art is, what music is.

Ian Mackay: CEAC wanted a response to General Idea's runaway success of *FILE* magazine, but in a more pure performance space, because in post-Marxist art the performance is the pure art form. Crash 'n' Burn represented proletariat performance to them, and a pop art infiltration.

Steven Davey: The people who owned the building, CEAC, had tons of government funding. It was this rich Italian guy, and the family bought this building and it was all very cutting edge and weird.

John Catto: The first thing that happened was the guys that owned the place, or the guys that ran CEAC, took off to Europe for the summer, leaving, like, an accountant in charge.

Bruce Eves: We were on a European tour. It was, like, two weeks. I mean, I would have loved to have been in Europe all summer. No, we were there for two weeks. And the accountant, ha ha ha, was one of the central people in CEAC, Amerigo's boyfriend, and he worked at a bank. He had a straight job. It makes it sound like we were sitting up there with calculators.

No. I was there every night, just to make sure — I was there to protect the real estate. I mean let's face it, I was there to make sure the place didn't get burned down. And knock on wood that the cops don't show up, which they never did because again, no one was around to complain.

John Hamilton: It wasn't like we'd walked into an empty warehouse and said, "Hey! Let's start a club." We had to throw out all the garbage that the hippies had left from their play, which took probably about a week's worth of backbreaking effort on our part. I don't know how many green garbage bags we filled with construction rubble, but it was probably equivalent to doing a house reno three times over. And then there were a couple of broken down bathrooms we got a friend of my dad's who was a plumber to fix. Then John and Paul started doing this artistic stuff, putting up things on the walls to make it look kind of cool. Ian and I were a bit more the handymen.

Ralph Alfonso: I got all the weird pieces of wood and I built benches out of it, and we found a bathtub and that became the bar. You'd just fill it with ice and put beer in it, and then the bar itself was I think two doors that we found and we put them over something.

John Hamilton: We actually did get legitimate liquor permits to run the Crash 'n' Burn through CEAC. We got these Special Occasion permits through the city to run special presentations and shows.

We'd gone out of our way and put in all of the things you're supposed to have, like fire extinguishers, which   I think we stole from the Royal York Hotel.

Paul Robinson: We planned to open it up on weekends, and we would bring bands in and we went out and got all the beer ourselves and put it in a bathtub with ice. We did everything ourselves. We wired the place up and got a sound system in there and did pretty well everything.

*   *   *   *   *

Johnny MacLeod building the stage, Crash'n'Burn / photo by Ralph Alfonso

Ralph Alfonso: I think the one time the Diodes ventured out of the Crash 'n' Burn I was out of town, of course, and I come back and I find out there had been this horrible brawl at the Colonial Underground. That solidified the scene even more.

Stephen Mahon: Even though we weren't playing that night we had to hang out, so we went. The Diodes were just doing their thing. These bouncers from upstairs just decided this had to stop.

The upstairs was a legitimate club; it was kind of like an El Mocambo and they'd get international acts in and there was a cover charge and it was just a nice place. I guess the noise must have annoyed somebody somehow, so these bouncers just came down and let loose.

John Catto: Long John Baldry was playing upstairs and he had this idea to play this acoustic set, but said, "That band downstairs is making too much noise." So they sent the bouncers down, they went, "Turn it down," and we were kind of like, "Well, fuck you." So up they go again, and then down come more bouncers.

Chris Haight: The biggest guys I've ever seen came through that door with pool cues. And it's kind of funny because the first thing that I thought of was, What are they gonna do with those? There aren't any pool tables down here.

John Catto: All these guys from bands and stuff are all lining up in front of the stage. The bouncers, for some reason — I have no idea why they did this, but they started wading into the audience and attacking people with pool cues.

Stephen Mahon: It was really kind of bizarre. It wasn't like anybody threw a firebomb up into the club or anything like that. There was a whole look to the crowd. Who knows?

Steven Davey: A lot of the violence in punk was gestural violence, and then somebody would come along and take it seriously. I think that happened in punk a lot, where people would come along who were drawn to that violence, that meathead thing. People took it literally, which I guess you could understand why.

David Clarkson: That was the last show I remember playing with the Diodes. We were playing a good show and it just turned into this brawl. It was kind of out of the blue, you know? I remember being on stage and turning around and some guy throwing a chair past my head.

I don't know if Leckie started it, but he was there and he was continually courting trouble wherever he went.

Paul Robinson: They pulled the plugs on us and came at us with some very, very heavy Detroit bouncers and started attacking the crowd. The entire place just erupted and we grabbed our stuff and got the hell out of there.

A lot of people were injured and it was a huge problem. The police were called; we were already out of there by then, we just got out of there. Steven Leckie got hit over the head with a pool cue and he was bleeding. It was pretty awful ... I think the Viletones prevented them from coming towards the stage and it was amazing — that's when the whole scene really had solidarity.

Steven Leckie: It was not my fight. It was the Diodes'. And I knew they were toast. The Diodes, holy fuck, you could have taken all four of them. But John Hamilton was pretty tough so he knew the ropes.

But the bouncers kept beating up more than the band. I think they hightailed it pretty quick, the Diodes.

Frankie Venom: It was extremely ugly. Myself and Steve, the bass player, we ran away because these guys, they were huge and they were swinging. Our road manager at that time, Paul Kobak, got smashed in the head with a pool cue.

Steven Leckie: Kobak was trying to be the voice of reason — "Hey, let's talk about this" kind of thing — and *whack!*

They didn't want to talk about it. It was pretty scary. It was for real.

Paul Kobak: I was in the corner taping the show — my machine kept running — and I noticed Slash Booze was onstage and a bouncer had just poked him in the gut with the bottom of a pool cue. I went running up and got between them, raised my hands in the air and shouted at the bouncer, "Cool it!" Next thing I knew, the bouncer whacked me over the head with his stick and I went unconscious.

Stephen Mahon: No one was expecting to be beaten on, that was the last thing people were thinking. They were just having a good time.

Gordie Lewis: I was one of the only guys that didn't get hit. I can't figure out why I didn't. I just remember seeing it. Me and whoever I was with ran into this elevator shaft and just took the elevator upstairs and got out of the place, but I didn't get hit.

Stephen Mahon: It was fairly quick; it wasn't like it lasted hours and hours. They did their beating, some people got hurt, some didn't, and then it was over.

John Catto: Unbelievable mess. Effectively, right after it happened I think John ran up and down Yonge Street pulling down flyers and stuff so nobody knew we were playing. Obviously the management of the place knew this was a really bad thing. You don't really have your bouncers attack your clients with pool cues en masse, randomly. So basically all the guys got shipped out of Toronto the next day. They were all from Detroit or whatever, all the bouncers.

One guy from Hamilton got really, really badly beaten up and maybe a couple of other people. I think they eventually extradited those bouncers out to Detroit. I don't know much more than that, other than it was a pretty nasty thing. That was the first really, really sort of bad, violent gig that occurred during the period. Prior to that everything was kind of playtime — no real weapons and no real stuff happening. I'm pretty sure that finished the Colonial club off. That would be a given, I think.

Freddy Pompeii: They must have been playing pretty fuckin' loud because we never got any complaints about volume, so I don't know. There was such a distance between the upstairs and the downstairs. I never heard any kind of interruption when there was a show there, so I think it might have been a set-up. They got sick of having the punk rockers down there and just wanted to get rid of them, and these bouncers had the opportunity to beat up some punk rockers and jumped at the opportunity.

The Colonial got written up — not in a very favourable light, but it was a big article. Steve was pissed off because they got the outrageous headlines, and that's the kind of stuff *he* wanted to get.

Lucasta Ross: It was in the newspaper. That was one of the nights we were hauling the wounded into the bathroom to bandage them up. That's one night I'll never forget.

Paul Kobak: Next thing I knew, I was in the hospital with stitches in my head. The following day, there was a photo on page 10 of the *Toronto Sun* of me laying prostrate with a towel over my head and Sally Cato kneeling beside me holding my hand and crying, looking up into the camera. The newspapers mistakenly said that Teenage Head was the band because our amplifiers were onstage.

Oh well, free publicity is free publicity.

Stephen Mahon: It was kind of a like a little version of Kent State except no one was shot. Thank God it was just pool cues.

It had nothing to do with the Diodes. It could have been any band. It was just wrong place, wrong time.

The Diodes, Crash'n'Burn / photo by Ross Taylor

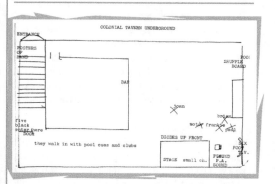

Colonial Tavern brawl diagram courtesy Crash'n'Burn News

Simply Saucer, Saucer House, 1977, Kevin Christoff, Don Cramer, Stephen Park (aka Sparky), Edgar Breau / press photo

9. rock shock

Kevin Christoff: I wouldn't say we'd split up; it's not like we decided to break up the band, but we were on a hiatus.

We had been evicted from Kenilworth Avenue on failure to pay rent, ha ha ha. It's kind of a rock 'n' roll thing. We tried, but we failed. We weren't gigging a lot. That's the story about Saucer.

We ended up gigging a lot more in the second phase because there were more places to play and I think our sound changed a little bit. The electronics were gone. John had left the group by then. But even at that point we weren't making a great deal of money. It was beer money, mostly, so we had to leave Kenilworth Avenue, sadly.

Everybody kind of went their separate ways. I was playing in a wedding band at the time just to make some extra money and waiting to see what everybody else was doing. Don and Ed I think were living together at the time and I think it was Don Cramer that actually found this house to practise in. So it seemed like it was a really long hiatus but really, it was only about maybe four to six weeks.

So we were sort of floating in limbo and then we found the house and we turned that into another event, another story.

Chris Houston: Hamilton has a history of these famous party houses. Saucer House is one of them. These are the type of places you'd go to where the front windows were smashed out. They'd move to places that were closest to the liquor store and it was like twenty-four hour insanity.

Saucer House was on Ferguson and Main. It was owned by some gas station guy. It was a very small cottage-like house. The front porch faced the railway tracks, so maybe there was a foot between the train and the front porch. Saucer rehearsed so loud in the basement that you couldn't hear the trains going by. They would rehearse every day of the week. They would write a new record a week.

I think Saturdays it was Open House, and they would premiere the new record they wrote that week. I heard *so* much music that disappeared into those walls. Supposedly they found a Satanic altar upstairs. I was shown the location of it. Edgar had to de-spook the place.

Len Cramer: Ed's closet? Oh, Ed discovered a passage in there and he found an old Ouija board, some bandages covered in blood, and newspaper articles on something from the '40s.

And I remember he ended up getting some holy water from St. Patrick's church and sprinkling it all over the room.

Imants Krumins: I'm pretty sure it was haunted. I remember seeing weird things going on there. But there was a lot of drug and alcohol abuse going on there as well, so ...

I remember seeing blood coming out of the walls one night. I never took dope — I'm not a good doper, I've never done LSD or any of that stuff. I would hear noises, but the people that lived there would hear them more than I would. Curtains moving when they aren't supposed to, that kind of thing. Maybe it was our imaginations, who knows?

Edgar Breau: It *was* kind of haunted there. It seemed like it, with lights going on and off in the middle of the night and noises.

All I found in my room was this little secret door in my wall. It had all been covered over with wallpaper and I crawled — it was just really a crawl space — and I found a Ouija board and that was about the extent of all of that. But there was no Satanic altar; boy, stories really get out of hand.

Chris Houston: Edgar would hold court upstairs. It was very small, but that's where I heard all the records for the first time. They had a big stereo and they'd have Metal Machine Music Day. They'd get four different stereos and play all four different sides of *Metal Machine Music* in different rooms simultaneously while everyone was kind of baked. I remember hearing the Television album for the first time, and that's where Imants Krumins said, "I've found this new band, Chris. They're angry like you, Chris, they're called the Sex Pistols."

Len Cramer: My brother, Ed, a couple of the roadies all lived in the house together, so when everybody from high school was going to dances or doing whatever I was hanging out at the band's house and going to see their shows and stuff. So I basically grew up in the Saucer House, getting all the influence. Everybody else in school was listening to Max Webster or disco music, and I was hanging out learning about T.Rex and Can, so it was like a bonus for me.

Chris Houston: Len's brother had this stereo system that was the best stereo system drug money could buy. It was so fuckin' loud. So you would get the latest records and they'd all listen to them and analyze them. And if it was *really* good they'd get pissed off because they thought it was a challenge to them.

Len Cramer: Usually they'd start practicing around six or seven. The drinking and the drugs would start about eight. They'd practise serious until about eleven and then after that it was just a party till the next morning and it was chaos.

And the railroad tracks: The good thing about those was they used to jump on the train and ride home because they were too drunk to walk.

Chris Houston: The trains ran right by the front porch. So you'd be wasted out of your mind on the porch and there's that gap between the front porch and the railway tracks. Saucer were so loud that if you had a fuckin' freight train going by you could hear them in the basement.

Len Cramer: They had the one manager who ended up parking his car on the tracks when they were getting ready for a show and they had to stop the train.

Chris Houston: The manager used to tie his dog to that fire hydrant, so they'd have to stop the train to get the dog out of there. Then after a while the train guys knew that they were partying all the time so they'd stop the trains right here, go and have a beer with them, and come out again.

Len Cramer: It wasn't always intended to be public, but it was turned into that because the house was sort of open. They'd say people could come in the house but you weren't supposed to come in the basement during rehearsal. But after everybody got hammered they'd just meander down anyway.

It was basically open all the time. There'd be three of them living there and some nights there would be forty or fifty people in there.

Kevin Christoff: There's two stories to Simply Saucer: There's the first phase with all the improvisation, and gradually that led to losing the instruments and going on hiatus for a while and recharging and going in a new direction. It was a long, strange trip, but it was good.

*   *   *   *   *

Edgar Breau: I went to The 3D Show, and *that* was when I realized there was something going on in Toronto. It was the Diodes, Dishes, and the Doncasters, and I remember in the lobby the Viletones kind of prowling around, making insulting remarks about the Diodes, I think. It looked like they wanted to rumble, ha ha ha. I just remember Nazi Dog prowling around with the leather; there was almost a '50s thing about them, rumble in the jungle or something.

Ralph Alfonso [*Bomp!* Newsletter, March 22, 1977]: In the audience were a bunch of punk-toughs called the Viletones. They're supposed to be a group, but no one's seen them play. They just hang around, cause trouble, pick fights and inevitably get beat up.

David Clarkson: I think it was at the 3D show that Steve Leckie pulled the fire alarm.

Edgar Breau: But it was definitely a cool concert. It was one of my favourite concerts of all the ones that I went to. It was amazing. I really loved the Doncasters, actually. They were the band I liked the best that night. I met a fellow named John Pinto, who was a friend of Gary Pig. I think the Doncasters did a Kinks song, "I'm Not Like Everybody Else," and I don't know, I made some remark and John Pinto turned around and he said, "You like the Kinks? Well, a friend of mine is doing a fanzine on the Kinks."

Gary Pig Gold: *The Pig Paper* actually began as hand-written correspondence in the early '70s between my oldest friend Doug Pelton, who worked summers at a camp in Northern Ontario, and me, who was stuck home in Mississauga with nothing to do, nowhere to go, and nothing on the radio.

Before the Internet it was really hard to connect with people that were not into the usual stuff, which in those days was two camps: Sabbath and Deep Purple, or singer/songwriters like Elton and Carly Simon. So if you didn't fit in with either of those, you sort of got back into '50s and '60s music by default.

You would meet up at record conventions. There were no bands playing this kind of music, so we had to put together our own bands and that's how we eventually, by college age, were all connecting. Teenage Head were playing Alice Cooper songs when I first ran across them. They were part Cooper, part Dolls, but they also had the '50s, '60s element. That's why we liked them. Simply Saucer, same thing. They were into the Troggs and the Kinks. And no one was into this stuff at the time. *No one*. It's easier nowadays because there are blogs and whatever, but that didn't exist back then. That's why we needed fanzines.

In 1975, the Who played Toronto for the first time in ages, and my friends and I all camped out overnight in the slush on Carlton Street, foolishly thinking we'd score really good advance tickets. Of course, all the choice seats weren't even for sale; they'd been claimed already by industry and friends and whatever. So John Pinto and I, who'd lined up with me, decided we'd publish and distribute an angry little literary broadside to "expose" this grave music business injustice. One thing led to another, we got ambitious — plus John snuck

me in to where he worked after hours so we could use all their typewriters and office equipment — so now we had twenty-eight pages filled with vintage Who articles clipped from old magazines, plus new, um, "interviews" we made up with the band. We packaged it all together as a mock Official Who Concert Programme and sold them for a buck apiece outside Maple Leaf Gardens the night of the show … until we got frightened off by some guy who said he was a rep from MCA Records and was gonna call the cops on us. But that was the first real *Pig Paper*, and with our seventy dollars profit from outside the Gardens we thought we'd start publishing regularly.

The next cool band coming through town was the Kinks in early '77, so we were looking to do a *Pig Paper* on them. John discovered Edgar Breau at the OCA 3D concert, noticed they had the "K" as in "Kinks" word in "kommon," so we arranged to head out to the only house on Ferguson Avenue South in Hamilton to do an interview.

Kevin Christoff: I don't know what my first inkling was of a scene in Toronto, but I guess it would be when Ed came back from the 3D concert and was talking about people that he had seen and talked to and what have you. And it wasn't long after that that we started getting work in Toronto, so I guess it would be around that time.

Gary Pig Gold: John and I went to interview Edgar and it turned out he very wisely arranged for his band to be practicing as we came into the house so that we would get excited, which we did. So he gave us a great interview about the Kinks, but also planted a seed in our heads that we should get his band booked. They'd never played Toronto and by this time they'd already been together four years.

Now, I'd had a bit of experience booking my friend Roy's band the Specs that I'd quit York University to tour Newfoundland with. We weren't your typical bar band though: We did an entire set of early Beatles songs, and even snuck some originals into the act when no one was looking. In fact, in 1976 I'd met Paul Kobak when he came by to check us out; I think he'd just booked Teenage Head to open for Max Webster at a nearby theatre, and we were sort of comparing notes.

Anyways, I loved what I'd heard of Saucer through their kitchen floor while we were waiting to interview Edgar. So when I left House of Saucer that night, I promised I'd try to get them some work in Toronto. I think they'd already been booked for the Rock Shock gig; John might have had something to do with that, though — he was the quote unquote official photographer for that event.

But immediately after that show, realizing how truly good they were onstage as well as in the basement, I definitely started hustling for gigs.

Edgar Breau: We played the Masonic Temple at something called Rock Shock, which was I think one of the first big punk shows there. The promoters who put it on, they came into Hamilton and caught a rehearsal and put us on the bill for that.

Kevin Christoff: It was with Teenage Head and Johnnie Lovesin. We went on first. It was nerve-wracking simply because it was a big venue and a lot of people. To walk onstage and be faced with that ... Saucer didn't really do a lot of gigging in the first phase.

Edgar Breau: I was attracted to all of this for the idea of going onstage trying to blow people away with what you're doing up there. I had a bit of a mischievous temperament, I think. I just wanted to do something that hadn't been done before — *here*, anyway.

When we were playing in Toronto, not many people were really aware of what we had accomplished in the studio, because this stuff was never released. So in a way it was kind of a weird thing. By the time the Toronto punk thing was going on we had already been through our own kind of war.

Len Cramer: I think Saucer got thrown into the punk scene, but they weren't really a punk band. By the time '77 had come around and they had played with a few punk bands, the other clubs in Toronto wouldn't book them because they figured, "Oh, you're punk by association."

But the punks didn't embrace them as much because they weren't as much about the fashion as the music. So they were sort of always the odd men out. They didn't really belong in any genre at the time.

Edgar Breau: When the Toronto punk scene happened we just gravitated to that kind of naturally. After what we had been through we thought, Okay, this is pretty encouraging now that people are opening up there. I mean, we weren't the only band that was not playing strictly hardcore punk. There were the Dishes, so it wasn't just all punk; there were other bands that had other influences and that. It just depended where you played and maybe who was the bill. It was just maybe a little bit early; the support wasn't quite in place at the time. So it was difficult to really make a go of it.

Kevin Christoff: We found ourselves playing a lot of venues and meeting a lot of people who were immersed in the so-called punk scene.

We didn't really fit in musically with that, but we did have a good rock 'n' roll edge, even back in the mid-'70s. I think Lou Reed and the Velvets were a strong influence on us and I think a lot of punk bands were inadvertently influenced by that as well.

Edgar Breau: Our roots were a little different, so we weren't a *perfect* fit. We weren't into safety pins. I mean, I wore a leather jacket, shades and black clothing and that, but I don't know what it was.

The punk thing ... I didn't really buy records like the Damned and Sex Pistols or that stuff. I don't know what it was. There was a certain amount of posing, and I guess I did it, too, but you know the whole punk ethos: If you think of people like the Rat Pack and who those people hung out with, *they* were *real* tough guys.

Johnny Rotten could sing "God save the Queen" and "fascist regime," but did he actually suffer for that? Did he go to jail? You think of people like Thomas More, who went to the gallows, hung for opposing Henry VIII — *those* people went all the way. Your Martin Luther Kings — people like that that really suffered for what they believed in.

It just seemed like the punk thing, there was a softness behind it. A softness of the head. There was hardness of the heart, but a softness of the head, and I think they got it exactly wrong. You should be more hard-headed than soft-hearted in terms of your thinking, like a realist. But the punk thing was exactly the wrong thing. You had to be moronic and hard, and in the end I just couldn't accept that philosophically.

Kevin Christoff: Not to beleaguer the negative, but a lot of people just didn't think we were punky enough, which we weren't. We weren't pretending to be punks; we were just a band trying to find some work so we found ourselves playing in places where a lot of the clientele were into the punk scene and listening to bands like the Ugly. Even the Head, I never considered them a punk band, but we didn't really quite play the same sort of style of music as they did either. So some people got it, some didn't.

10. THE 367 conTinGenT

l-r: Margaret Barnes-DelColle, Gambi Bowker
Lucasta Ross, Nora Currie / photo by Gail Bryck

Margaret Barnes-DelColle: Power Street — that was really the hub of where the whole thing for us and punk rock and the Viletones blossomed.

There were a lot of people that lived in that house and we were very open. On a Friday around six o'clock the phone would just start ringing and there'd be like fifteen phone calls and everybody would be like, "Okay, where are we going tonight? What club is everyone going to, what bar, what bands are we going to see?" Then late at night, because it was a really big house, that would be where everybody would come to crash instead of going back to the suburbs. So it was really a hangout.

Right around the corner from that was where Nora lived, so it was kind of a community. It was great, it was fun, it was really crazy.

I always keep a daily journal. Not like I'm writing my daily thoughts in it, just things like, "Going to see a band on such a night, got a doctor's appointment this day, had to go to school this day, had to work this day," that kind of stuff.

When I went through my journal from 1977 ... Your memory fails you sometimes, and when I went through it I was shocked. I mean, yeah, we did drugs, but I was stunned. I was like, "Oh man, we did *that* many drugs?" It was just incredible. On every page I'm writing what drugs we did, and things like when people OD'd and got taken to the hospital.

I was going to Sheridan College and I took fashion design out there. I graduated in '77 and Nora lived around the corner at 367 Queen Street. She lived in the apartment upstairs, and the downstairs was just this little storefront that was empty. One day we did diet pills or crank or something. And we were just kind of hanging around and she was like, "Yeah, it'd be so cool to open a little punk rock store like Manic Panic in New York." And because we were high I was like, "Yeah! I'll do it!"

So we just started moving stuff into the front store and planning things and getting paint and we got furniture to make a countertop and all this stuff.

Colin Brunton: I started to notice that something new was happening around all of this music when people were dressing differently. I started to notice tons of homemade handbills around the streets. There was a store at John and Queen just east of John, between the Beverley and what's now Starbucks, and it was the first place in Toronto where you could buy black jeans. That was one of the big problems. When this thing started it was like, "Yeah, we've gotta get black jeans." And it's like well, fuck, you can't get them *any*where, you have to order them from New York or something. It was so superficial and vain; it was crazy.

Anya Varda: I remember waiting in the snow at a bus stop in Toronto for an hour wearing open-toed, clear, plastic stilettos with rhinestones in the heels, hopping from one foot to the next. Anything for fashion back then, anything. We walked very quickly. You were slipping and sliding and well, you know, your feet got wet and then they dried out. It was kind of crazy, but as cold as you were you sacrificed *everything* for fashion.

John Hamilton: Blue jeans were verboten. The Ramones got away with it because they were there earlier, but when I joined the Diodes, no blue jeans – verboten. And there was no colour, either. You wore black or you wore red or you wore white and that was it. There was a very strong sort of aesthetic that people would adhere to.

Colin Brunton: I remember the first person I knew with black jeans actually went to the trouble of dying them. I barely knew how to wash my clothes; I wasn't going to try *that*.

You started noticing people chopping their hair off sometimes.

John Hamilton: We used to haunt old clothing stores, that's what we used to do in the day time. Toronto in those days, there were millions of forgotten little cubby-hole places to be discovered, like a shoe store out on Bloor Street somewhere that would still have stock from the 1950s. In those places you would find pointy-toed Beatle boots for cheap, like five bucks. The King Sol place on Bathurst had peg leg black jeans, and there was another near the Beverley, too, Textile Warehouse, that had these fantastic jackets from the '50s that had all kinds of patterns.

Margaret Barnes-DelColle: We must have done speed for a couple of days and a few days later I kind of woke up and went, "Oh my god, what am I doing? What were we thinking?" So it was like, "Okay, okay, I'll do it, but I'll only open the store on Thursday, Friday, Saturday, and Sunday," or something like that; four days a week from twelve to six.

I made up buttons that called us the 367 Contingent, and that was right next door to Teen Agency. They were 369 and it was a little tiny place, too, but bands would come there to see about getting booked and then they would come in my shop and hang out. I had a pinball machine and a jukebox and the guy let me put all my own records on, so it was all punk rock. It was probably the only punk rock jukebox in Toronto – maybe *Canada* – so people would have to put money in to play that.

Freddy Pompeii: All I knew was that you couldn't get this squeaky clean new stuff. You had to wait until Patti Smith recorded on a major label to get anything. She had a couple of singles that she put out as a calling card. And Television had a single, "Little Johnny Jewel," which was like a noise record. Most of these bands did something but it never got out of New York, even if you got news of it.

All of a sudden in '77 you started seeing Sex Pistols. Margaret was gonna have this punk rock store and she decided she was going to carry everything punk, like handmade clothes that people wanted to put in there on consignment, and of course the music. So we had a shelf of all these singles from all over the world that were distributed by this little importing company, I think it was called Jem Imports. It was a key distribution tool for everybody in Toronto. Not only did you get stuff that was distributed by them, but they would also distribute *your* record worldwide.

Margaret Barnes-DelColle: I had a magazine rack where I had fanzines that I started getting from Britain like *Sniffin' Glue*. So over time I just started hooking up with people, and because I was there people would come in who'd made buttons and made T-shirts and slowly it just started to grow.

Captain Crash: I lived above New Rose. That was fuckin' mayhem. That was another place where at the end of the evening there would be two inches of beer on the floor in the store. Oh, and my apartment would get trashed. My stereo system was blown up, the speakers were all fucked. It was mayhem. I had to move out of there because I couldn't take it anymore. I'd be lying there in bed and I'd hear this *ding ding ding ding*. It would be the pinball machine at four o'clock in the morning at New Rose. But it was great fun while I was there.

They opened at twelve. It would usually start at eleven o'clock in the morning, ten thirty in the morning, with kids banging on the door, punkers from California or out of town and of course the place to come is New Rose so they would come and bang on the door. If they wanted to spend a whole bunch of money I would phone Margaret, "Come on, you gotta get up," or I would just tell them to come back later.

It was a place to hang out and became that way almost immediately. It was named after a Damned song and it didn't take long. When the store first opened Margaret made a lot of the stuff so she was in her little workshop around the corner and Fred was doing the cash and Margaret would come over later after she had finished making belts and T-shirts and whatever, buttons. So I think it was because of Fred hanging out there in the beginning that everybody would come by there. Fred was a really amiable character, lots of personality, pretty smart, and really gentle. Too bad he got so fucked up later on.

Margaret Barnes-DelColle: Further down on Queen Street, really close to where Citytv is now, was a record store called Record Peddler. A lot of times people would go there for records and then they would ask where my store was, or sometimes if it was really young girls or something they would say how they were afraid to come to my store. The guys at the Record Peddler would be like, "There's nothing to be afraid of, just go there."

It was more like a party atmosphere, and I think that was more what was scaring these young girls at Record Peddler — "Oh, the *Viletones* are down there."

Freddy Pompeii: Most girls didn't like us too much. We were nasty, we were just nasty. It came with the act. Would you bring a Viletone home to your mother?

There were girls that would, and there were girls that just wouldn't. The same girls that would go and see Cheap Trick or AC/DC, like groupies, wouldn't come and see us or hang around with us. We were too gross. Gross and scary.

We scared the shit out of these girls from Chicago or Detroit. They had one of those hand-done rags called *Gabba Gabba Gazette*, named after a Ramones song. They came to Toronto to interview me and Steven and Mike in the back room of New Rose. I had just shot a whole bunch of Percocets that were made into liquid, so I was throwing up every five minutes. Steven was doing downers and Motor was completely drunk out of his tree. Chris Haight was pretty loaded too. I don't know what he was loaded on but he was always loaded on something.

These were really good girls; they were sweet kind of teenagers who wanted to be punk rockers really bad and they came down to interview us to put us in their magazine. Well, we scared the shit out of them, and not meaning to. But here's this guy you're talking to and every five minutes he's got to lean over the sink and throw up. And Steven was trying to get money out of them and trying to get them to buy beer for us and trying to come on to them. They were *sort of* laughing, but didn't know whether to laugh or cry. It was funny on one hand, but it must have been really scary for these girls who didn't know we were pussycats at heart.

They wrote this article and put it in their magazine, but it was a very negative article. You could tell that they were scared. They were not very good-looking girls, either.

11. united front

The Nerves, Crash'n'Burn, 1977. Jack Lee, Paul Collins, Peter Case / photo by Ralph Alfonso

John Catto: We were kind of riding along and this would have been a Saturday or something and we were getting ready to open the Crash 'n' Burn on Thursday, really this close, right? So we're literally sitting around, kind of rehearsing and kind of putting the thing together, and in walks this guy. He's just wandering in; no one's ever met him before except for Ralph. This is this guy Bob Segarini, and this is his second day in Toronto or something. He's turned up from L.A. and he's kind of hanging around. He goes, "Oh, I found out you're doing this thing." And we're like, "*How*?"

Ralph Alfonso: In the beginning, word got out, and then Bob Segarini had just moved in to Toronto from Montreal and he used to be in this great glam band called the Wackers. I'm from Montreal, I knew who he was, so we hooked up. He wanted to be part of the scene and we're like, "You know, he's a cool guy, but not really cool enough to play." I don't think he was pushing himself as a musician then, but we got him to do sound. So our soundman was Bob Segarini, this respected power pop guy.

Bob Segarini: The guys from the rental company for the PA were a couple of big fat hippies in biker gear smoking pot in the back laughing at the kids, and so I sort of shoved them out of the way and I did the sound. Which in those days was bring down all the instruments, push up all the vocals. That's all you could do because everybody played really loud.

John Catto: And then Bob Segarini goes, "I've got this idea! There are these friends of mine from L.A.," who were touring across America in literally a car and a trailer, this band called the Nerves. And he goes, "Why don't you get them to play? You can open it with this L.A. band." And we went, "Okay." And this is the band that did "Hanging on the Telephone" that Blondie later covered. They were another kind of power pop band with three-piece suits and Rickenbackers.

Peter Case: I knew Bob through Greg Shaw. He hooked us up. I had a band called the Nerves. We went on this national tour and we were out on the road playing shows all around the country, and basically Greg gave us an introduction to different people he knew in every town.

We loved Toronto because it seemed like a very big city. We'd just toured the whole country. We'd been to Chicago. I love Chicago now, but at the time Chicago had no music scene. Cheap Trick was over in Rockford and that was as good as it got in that whole area. There were no bands really playing original material in Chicago in 1977 that would be anything you could fit into that scene we're talking about. There were in Ohio, but that's Cleveland — just a hard-hitting kind of town. When we got up to Toronto there was just this real creative scene and there were just a whole bunch of real cool people. It was a much bigger group of people. It seemed exciting and cosmopolitan.

John Hamilton: When we opened the Crash 'n' Burn, it was like the sun had come out. There was actually a place where we could have fun. We only put a few benches in; we wanted people to stand up and to mingle and to move around, so the only benches we put in there were in case you were ready to fall down, you could have a place to sit. It was sort of the beginning of those big dance clubs, like The Government. It was the first one of those ever in Toronto.

There were no bouncers, so the bouncers weren't gonna beat you up. There must have been some leftover bathtubs from the *Disaster* so we used to fill those up with ice cubes, throw in the beer, and we'd serve it in plastic cups or paper cups because you couldn't have glass. People were into breaking glass from the Colonial Underground because Leckie was into cutting himself with broken glass. We didn't want anybody to get hurt so we threw it into paper cups.

And then people started coming around.

Bob Segarini: I was attracted to the Crash 'n' Burn because it reminded me of San Francisco in '65, '66 and '67. It was like, to me, the *anti*–Summer of Love.

Deborah Harry was a friend of mine from New York, so Deborah had gotten wind of this thing. I had made friends with Paul Robinson and John Catto and John Hamilton, and I just loved these guys.

Gary Pig Gold: My favourite memory of the Crash 'n' Burn was Ralph being the doorman in this Sgt. Pepper–type military uniform with the hat and everything. And he had an old velvet rope, pretending it was Studio 54 even though it was in an alley with garbage and everything.

Ralph Alfonso: Actually it was my old movie usher uniform: Red jacket, white shirt, and black, clip-on bowtie.

Harri Palm: Crash 'n' Burn, that was the catalyst really. All of a sudden all these bands that had been playing basically private parties and funny little off-shoot gigs had a place to play, and that place rocked.

Paul Eknes: We weren't nepotistic; we didn't have rivalries – that's the whole thing. We were helping each other out with ampage or, "You broke a couple strings on your guitar; here, have my guitar because I'm not playing tonight." We were helping each other out because we knew this was an important scenario, not just in Toronto history but in rock 'n' roll history and in our *own* histories. We knew this had to happen because we all loved the same sound, we all loved the same people, we were all sleeping with the same people, ha ha ha, but only because we loved them.

John Hamilton: The one thing that should be remembered about that club is it was a *people's* club. It wasn't promoters *exploiting* people. That's what we were against. The El Mocambo and the Gasworks, where they would give you a dance floor about this big and pour watered-down beer … I played those places and I'll tell you, these people would come down to have a good time, they'd plunk them in chairs, pour them full of shit beer, charge them a fortune at the door, and if anybody even looked like they were having a good time the bouncers would kick the shit out of them and throw them out the door.

When we opened this club, it was like the kids making a club for themselves. It was like Mickey Rooney and Judy Garland saying, "Let's put on a show in dad's barn!" And the thing was we got rid of all the tables and people started to meet each other. At these other clubs, you could spend a night sitting at your table and you'd never see anybody or meet anybody. So that was the best thing about it.

Ralph Alfonso: It was a united front and the bands got 80 or 90 per cent of the door, which was a pretty honkin' deal. As the reputation grew, then the audience expanded beyond the OCA crowd.

Chris Haight: Right off the top there was always a little bit of friction there, because after all, they were art students and we were *us*. There was always that line there.

Paul Robinson: In terms of anything, we were first of all just making music really for ourselves a lot of the time or doing it for friends – a very, very small group of people.

We were a bunch of art students that were trying to make visual art, and we were also really into certain bands and things and were just giving it a go ourselves to make music we liked that wasn't being made, especially in Canada. I think in a lot of ways we were just lucky to have fallen into a time slot that let us create something that was original and both exciting and enjoyable to do. I think that we're really lucky in that respect.

But all of us were trying to do visual art as well and I think that it probably set us completely apart from all of the other Toronto bands at the time, which were the Viletones, who were kind of just rockers and not really artists but were doing something that was exciting as well. Teenage Head were a bunch of working class kids from the Steel Town basically and were on a totally different wavelength, but I will say that Frankie was a great performer and there's no doubt the guy had star quality. So did Steven Leckie. Steven Leckie had immediate magnetism; he was riveting to watch.

We were coming from very different places but we were all able to grasp the same concept and the same idea, which we went ahead and did. I think we were different, but we were also resented. Teenage Head really resented us and said we were a bunch of art students basically. I don't know why that was so negative – "Oh you're a bunch of art students." I don't know what we were supposed to be. Most good bands came from art colleges anyway, traditionally.

Captain Crash: We hated the Diodes, big time. We hated them with a passion. It was just something to do.

They lived around the corner from us. They would invite us over for a party and we'd go over and beat them up and steal all their booze and come back to Power Street and drink their booze and laugh at them. Just stupid things, you know? There wasn't animosity. It was rivalry is what it was. And we wouldn't *really* beat them up. We'd punch them a couple of times and they'd punch us a couple of times. It's not like we were killing the guys. It just wasn't what the scene was all about.

They were too artsy fartsy, that was the thing.

There was a big division there, the guys who all went to OCA and shit and then there were the kids from Yonge Street, the Dog and shit. It was a totally different scene and yet everybody, they were all still friends and they had to support each other and everybody went to each other's gigs and we went to the parties. And yet, we were pretending that we were enemies.

Rodney Bowes: The Dishes and the Diodes were more clever and ultimately disliked for that elitism. I think it's just kind of summed up in that the genre called punk rock supposedly had to revolve around some kind of a street thing, and be kind of a tough thing, where the Diodes weren't.

I remember walking down Queen Street with Ian and I guess John Catto and Steven Leckie and Freddy. Steven was talking about, "You're just little mama's boys" and that kind of crap and then punched Ian in the side of the head as in, "How do you like *that*?" And Ian's like, "You hit me!" And he's like, "Yeah? So hit me back." And Ian's like, "No, I'm not gonna hit you back." And he said, "See?" And I thought that was a great kind of visual interpretation of the divide; that this was all posturing.

Nora Currie: The division between the art scene was a big deal. The group that I was more involved with, they hated that scene. They were very dismissive of that part of the scene.

It was very set up along class lines. These were young people with university educations, with artistic natures, and with privilege, although there is no big privilege in being an artist. The Viletones and the Ugly were working class with no money, and so it was very clearly about what was seen to be privilege versus complete lack of it.

Blair Martin: That seems a bit of a cop-out to assume that anybody, just because they're middle class, may have had a comfortable life. We're all subject to the modern world and we don't all have the same strengths and weaknesses.

Don Pyle: The Crash 'n' Burn was only open on weekends. It was sort of a moving scene. Unless you were already in the art college scene with the Diodes, the Dishes, Drastic Measures, the Cads, then there was the Viletones and Teenage Head who were definitely beyond art scene bands. It took a while for them to start playing shows together and develop a camaraderie. They had separate audiences for a short time until it was like, here, we have a common interest between the art people and the rockers.

Ralph Alfonso: We knew that something was happening. My thing at the time was not only was I part of it, but I was documenting it at the same time. So while I'm running the Crash 'n' Burn I'm also writing about it — "A typical night at the Crash 'n' Burn." It was kind of weird. I was sort of writing about something in the past tense even though it existed in the present. So we knew — well, maybe because it was part of the Diodes coming out of the art background, they knew that documentation and prominence was important, so we tried to stake our claim.

It was like we wanted everybody else in the world to know that we existed; that the Diodes existed, that the Toronto scene existed. Because we realized early on that if you're going to succeed within that genre of music, you can't depend on the Toronto or Canadian infrastructure to prop it up because there is none and inherently it's rejecting you anyway.

Ian Mackay: There was a golden moment where we needed solidarity to survive but there wasn't any commercial value, so there wasn't any opportunity for the scene to fragment. There was still infighting, though, because bands were getting left behind.

I think what happened was when we opened the Crash 'n' Burn, we held the door *and* the keys. Paul wanted to use the opportunity to put us onstage more often if possible. I don't think it was deliberate, it was just, "Hey, we don't have an act to cover, let's open." But I think there was a certain amount of resentment at the fact that the Crash 'n' Burn was becoming *the* place, and we had the leveraged position.

Paul Robinson [CIUT-FM, Greg Dick interview, 2007]: I think I was very democratic, and really thought that all of the major Toronto bands should play there. Even though in a lot of ways we weren't getting along so famously, I insisted that the Viletones and Teenage Head, even though they badmouthed me a lot, should play, and so they got booked in.

If it had continued, *everybody* would have played there because I was incredibly democratic, and I just thought that everybody that was part of the scene originally should play whether I liked them or I didn't like them personally.

Ian Mackay: Other bands with whom we were solid, like the Dishes for example, were complaining that they only got one gig the whole summer. But we were trying to bring in talent partly to legitimize Toronto and partly to legitimize ourselves and the other bands. But everybody got a headlining act. All of the major bands that summer got one shot; I think we got one headlining and two openings, that's all we managed to squeeze out of it.

But I do agree that May, June '77 was the point of complete solidarity, camaraderie. And then it was over and it became competitive.

John Catto, John Hamilton, Steven Leckie, Paul Robinson the day Crash'n'Burn was built, 1977 / photo by Ralph Alfonso

Ralph Alfonso at the door, Crash'n'Burn, 1977 / photo by Tom Robe

The Diodes. Crash'n'Burn opening night / photo by Ralph Alfonso

l-r: Bob Segarini, Steven Leckie, Doug Pringle, Mark Carter, Michaele Jordana, Chris Haight, John Hamilton, 1977, outside the Crash'n'Burn / photo by Ralph Alfonso

Paul Robinson, Gordie Lewis / photo by Ralph Alfonso

Viletones contract, 1977, courtesy Ralph Alfonso

12. down to sane

Mickey Skin: There was this band called the Tools and they were supposed to play at a free school called SEED. It was on Bloor Street and I was going there. This dance teacher, Rolando Romaine, he kind of challenged me and said, "If you get a band together in three weeks you can do our opening set." Jula had been taking guitar lessons and I just went, "Oh yeah, let's do it!"

I had never thought much about being in a band before then. I always wanted to do acting and performing and I was in dance, so the band thing was just sort of a challenge; it was something fun to do. I was always a performer. I wouldn't say it was the music, it was more the performance opportunity.

It was also convenient because my parents were in Europe that summer so we took over the basement. It was like "Oh great, we can practise here." The neighbours put their house up for sale right away. Ha ha ha.

Julia Bourque: It was the spring of '77 and our friend Mickey got it going. She had a friend who was a songwriter who said, "You'd be great in a punk band." I had an instrument.

Mickey Skin: Then I met Freddy Pompeii at a music store. I was sort of doing sound so I was going to clubs a little bit and stuff like that. I said to him, "You gotta hear our band, we're practicing." We were just around the corner so I dragged him down there.

Anna Bourque: We had all worked at summer camp together and that's where Jula and I met Mickey, and Mickey and I became best friends. We were living together in a flat on Major Street when Mickey came home one day with Freddy behind her. He followed her up the stairs and she was saying, "We have a gig! We have a gig!" and we weren't anything. Ha ha ha. And so it was, "Well, what's that mean?" "We're gonna be a band and we have a gig with the Viletones." We just sort of went along with it when she said, "Let's be a band."

"Oh, you're gonna be the singer? Okay."

Jula could play guitar so there were just two choices for me. Linda had been an ex-boyfriend of mine's ex-girlfriend. I was at Ryerson University doing film and I asked her if she'd be in my films and so I just said, "Do you want to be in our band?"

Linda Lee: It was an interesting dynamic because everybody was really different. Jula and Anna came

almost from a heavy-duty feminist attitude. They loved Robert Altman films; they shared all of these major, major common bonds. I felt like I was an interloper, but only for a very, very short time. After playing together, I think after our first rehearsal, it was like we had known each other for centuries and centuries.

Julia Bourque: I was the only one who actually played an instrument, so I showed my sister how to play the bass. And a friend of ours, Linda Lee, she didn't know how to play the drums so we rented a set of drums and she kind of learned how to play. We had a couple of friends who could play instruments so they came over and coached us.

Linda Lee: Jula was the only one that had actually had musical training. I have a degree in music, but my degree is in voice. I guess they needed someone to play drums, so that was it.

"New Wave Music: No-Star Rock," by David Livingstone [*Maclean's*, April 7, 1980]: Patzy Poison was not exactly Keith Moon on drums, but letting drop one of her heavily eyelined lids in a slow-motion wink in the middle of some old '60s boy-girl song, she was living proof that there are other talents besides musical proficiency.

Linda Lee: The first rehearsal, we were practicing in Mickey's basement and the Viletones had heard about us and they came to see us practise. They all came in through the main door except for Steven, who opened the basement window behind me and threw himself in. That was the first time I met the Viletones.

I used to see the Viletones walking around Yonge Street in their leathers with their girlfriends and stuff. My boyfriend and I would look at them and think, Who the fuck are these people? Not only just because they were incredibly interesting looking — some of them were seriously cute — but there was also an air about them that if you looked at them the wrong way they could, through telekinesis, slit your throat.

Anna Bourque: After Mickey met Freddy, the Viletones played at the St. Lawrence Hall, which is a beautiful room. Nobody knew what punk was then so you could book places and nobody would know what a disaster it would turn into for them.

I know that night I sat on Steven's face when he was singing. He walked out into the audience and I don't know whether he fell down, which was highly likely because he was prone to that after copious amounts of whatever it was, and I didn't wear underpants in those days.

But we both got rather a shock because of course no matter where you play, if it's punk, everything's wet. Just suddenly beer's everywhere, *everywhere*. It was fantastic.

We saw them at the Colonial basement downstairs. It used to be the Meat Market. That was the first bar I ever drank in when I was a young teenager with my fake ID. The Viletones played there and Chris fell off the stage backwards but kept on playing, he didn't stop. He was fantastic. And Steven was breaking glasses then. What he did before he'd break the glass, he'd whirl his arms just to get the blood down there so that when he cut himself it was meaty, it really looked good. But he'd also say, "Cover your eyes," so nobody got glass in their eyes. Isn't that the sweetest thing you've ever heard? And then he'd smash the glass or the bottle and he'd cut himself.

Julia Bourque: I saw the Viletones at the Colonial Underground. That's where I first saw Steven Leckie cut himself. It was so gross. Oh gosh. He was just a kid; I'm sure he was younger than I was. The tough guy image was so silly because he wasn't really tough at all, he was actually from a pretty good background and was quite smart.

Mickey Skin: One thing led to another and the Tools heard the Viletones were gonna come to their concert, so they cancelled it because they were so afraid of them. But then the Viletones told us we could open for them at another gig.

Linda Lee: We were supposed to open for Mickey's friend's band called the Tools. It was at a dance studio or something, and they were so terrified of us when they saw us. I don't know why we were so intimidating. Maybe Anna and Mickey were just a little bit too powerful in the way they felt.

Anna Bourque: We lifted all our own equipment and we didn't depend on anybody for anything. We were solid citizens. No fakery, no girl-ery.

*   *   *   *   *

John Hamilton: I remember we had the Crash 'n' Burn open, and this was so long ago in Toronto that you would actually notice a poster on a telephone pole. Literally when the Zoom first started the Colonial Underground, we made posters and put them up downtown, which I think is how Leckie and Lucasta and all those people came to see us. The poles in Toronto were empty; there were no posters on them. So if you put up a poster about your band, people would stop and look at them because it was something that was really different.

Mickey Skin / photo by Ralph Alfonso

So around the time the Crash 'n' Burn was rolling, we were walking down Duncan Street one day and we saw a poster for the Curse. This was a new band; it was a *women's* band. Paul was always the guy to get right on to anything new; Paul and Ralph must have gotten in touch with them and booked them for the Crash 'n' Burn.

Julia Bourque: The Diodes had that space for the whole summer. The Liberal Party was a major tenant there so it was quite a scandal.

It was a great space, though. It was wonderful because it was so dead; the whole area was totally dead. It was just business, there was nothing else down there. On a Friday and Saturday this place opened up and it was just wall-to-wall people, which would have meant about two hundred people. They got it together and filled bathtubs full of beer. It was a booze can; it was great. It was so much fun. It was better than a high school dance.

Did you ever go to camp? You know how close you get with all those people you just met a week ago? It was like that: It was like summer camp, and everybody was your new best friend. I'd never seen anything like it. I was at York University at the time and I'd never seen such freaks in all my life.

Anna Bourque: It was fabulous and terrifying — *terrifying*. I'd picked up the bass three weeks before, I didn't know how to play. I had a book with me that I put on the stage floor that had drawings of the neck and where to put my fingers for each song.

Julia Bourque: We had practised in Mickey's mother's basement on Major Street for three weeks. We wrote about ten songs.

Julia Bourque / photo by Ralph Alfonso

Gail Manning: I think we all had a wonderful, marvelous sense of self, that as women we could do whatever we wanted and certainly didn't want to get put down by anybody. We were as good as the boys.

They were extraordinarily entertaining. Mickey was just a great, great front person. She was really, really funny. Jula and Anna were a solid guitar and bass player. It was just pure entertainment. I can't say to you that it was the greatest music in retrospect that I ever heard, but at the time it captured what a girl punk band was all about. Today would they stand the test of time? I can't say that. But at the time they were just great fun.

Nora Currie: I loved their music. They were not accomplished musicians and that wasn't really necessary in punk; it was kind of one chord music. It was more about performance, which is an essential part of music and the songs and the lyrics and the message. They were feminists in all that true and positive meaning about reclaiming space and asserting the female identity and agency and sexuality. That was a massive shift, so it was very fulfilling. They were *just* as capable of smashing things or getting into a fight.

They would throw assholes off the stage. Johnny Garbagecan actually got his name because the first time they played, he was so offended as a guy — first of all who was already in a music scene — that these women would get up and dare to do that.

Anna Bourque: It was pretty scary. I seem to recall I had nine Newcastle Browns that night and I wasn't anywhere near down to sane. It's an incredible thing to do. Oh, and the sound was terrible, *we* were terrible, and we threw food at the audience. I think the first night we threw birthday cake because it was Linda's birthday, which was kind of fantastic. Because when you're holding a cake in front of an audience, you know what they do? They move like waves. As you sort of aimed the cake they would move away. That's what made it so musical. Ha ha ha.

Mickey Skin: It felt very natural. We were maybe a little bit nervous, but not that much. We were doing it so much in tongue-in-cheek and in fun that I don't think we were thinking of it as, "Oh wow, we're in show biz."

It was just, "All right, this is a big party and we're the leaders of it." And that's kind of how it always was.

"Punk Rock: Toronto's Nasties Create a Style That Goes Beyond Mere Posturing," by Peter Goddard [*Toronto Star,* July 16, 1977]: Six weeks ago the city's first, and so far only, all-female punk band played its first gig. The moment the Curse was onstage they started to tell the men what they thought of them — and it wasn't all that nice.

Nora Currie: Meeting the Curse, watching the Curse play — I'm a feminist and I was at that time, and it certainly wasn't a popular word or place to be at that time. So for me, it was very exciting to see women so sensual in music. In writing it, playing it, and telling men to go fuck themselves in a political and productive forum. That, to me, was the thing that drew me the most to them.

Johnny Garbagecan: I had to have an alias because I was wanted by the police. I couldn't use my name; my name sticks out like a sore thumb. So I threw a garbage can at the Curse. They were playing at the Crash 'n' Burn and there was a garbage can that they put ice and beer in. I threw one at them at the stage and I guess it stuck.

They were terrible. The Curse couldn't even play. They just used to make noise.

Pop Music Beat, by Gerald Levitch [*Toronto Sun*, June, 1977]: Mostly, they perform as if they'd never seen their instruments before.

Nora Currie: They *couldn't* play. But they had an energy and a presence that was so strong and so powerful that their ability to play really well didn't matter; it became part of their performance and their charm and their energy and why we went to see them.

Anyway, Johnny was so offended at the Crash 'n' Burn he threw a garbage can onto the stage. So he was called Johnny Garbagecan as a result, but he became one of the biggest fans of the Curse and was intimately and otherwise involved with them. It sounds so negative, that he threw a garbage can onto the stage.

It's kind of a good example of how punk can inherently be seen as violent. There was an outlaw element to punk and it drew a lot of people from different places, including the criminal element.

Caroline Azar: The Curse were outstanding performers and shock rockers.

Julia Bourque: It was a real train wreck. Total confusion train wreck kind of describes our gigs. And Mickey was so wild. She'd dress up in tutus and throw food at the audience.

Mickey Skin: I don't know how the food came about. I think we did it from the first time. Everything was basically, "How can we have the most fun? How can we taunt the audience and get them going?" Then we started getting creative.

I think at first we had whipped cream, and we did hot dogs, and then Jula started coming up with, "Oh! Let's cook a big pot of spaghetti and we'll throw *that*." It was just, "What's the cheapest food we can cook and throw?" We thought spaghetti was good because it was gooey and sticky and made a big mess.

Jeff Ostofsky: I was working for a rock 'n' roll band. In 1976 the bar scene, the music scene in Toronto was radically different than it would be eight months later. So we're talking about an era that was post-hippie and pre-AIDS, thank God. I thank God every day for how lucky I got to be to not have had to wrap myself in a rubber tire to meet people.

The first band that I worked for before I became a roadie to most of the punk bands was called Hott Roxx, which was a Stones copy band. At the time we would play a week in a bar or three one-nighters. The thing was, we were working constantly doing a circuit in Ontario and at the time we were one of the highest paid bar bands in Ontario. We made about thirty-five hundred dollars a week. But that money went to the massive expense of carting around huge lighting and sound systems and a road crew. It was the more is more theory. So that's what I was doing, only because my best friend was the guitar player. When the band got to the point of needing roadies but couldn't really afford them, the guitar player got his two best friends to do sound and lighting and we both evolved into becoming professionals.

In any case, it was the height of disco and playing Rolling Stones music was just great for people who hated disco. There was a big hook. We exploited that. So I was doing this gig and having the time of my life. I was eighteen, nineteen or whatever and living the cliché life.

It's funny – the bigger the bands get, the less partying and sex you get because you're way too busy and you're way too tired and you're on an airplane. But when you're a band from Toronto and you pull into some little shit fuck town in Northern Ontario, you're immediately identifiable as *different*. So that was way more fun; that was like being a rock star in your own neighbourhood. As I remember it, in the spring of '77 our band went on a tour which took three months. It took us from here to Vancouver and back.

We came back in early summer of that year and I look at a newspaper. Someone picked it up and said, "Look at this, man. *Nazi Dog*? What's that?" It was on the front page of the *Star*. I grabbed the paper and went, "That's not a dog, that's Steve for God's sake!" I had met him when we were kids, like thirteen-ish, and even then he was one of the funniest and smartest, but different, guys I knew at that point in my life.

I loved the guy ... but *this*? I had barely heard of the Ramones let alone cutting yourself onstage and using the word "Nazi." The funny thing is, the last time I saw him before that front page was a few years previous. I ran into him on the street and he was Lou Reed. And then I met him a year or so later and he was David Bowie. Then I didn't see him for all that time and he was Nazi Dog.

So right away I discover that one of my very best friends in life, Anna Bourque, is in the Curse. I said, "Anna, you've never played an instrument in your life. What do you mean I go away for three months and I come back and you're a punk star?" The punk movement was really a whirlwind; like, wow, a lot to absorb in a short period.

Anna Bourque: Those first two shows were fantastic in the way that we were truly horrible. I think you can blame me for most of the badness of our band because I just never got it. I'm just so not musical. I played the viola in junior high school but I just never got it. Everything I did was just by memory, so I never felt that I ever did a good gig because I never felt like I knew what I was doing.

Really, that three weeks between getting the gig and playing was this major education of becoming part of it: The school of becoming a punk band in Toronto.

Ian Mackay, Lucasta, Rhonda Ross, Jeff Ostofsky, CBGB's, 1978 / photo by Ralph Alfonso

13. the boys are back

Crash'n'Burn party, 1977 / photo by Ralph Alfonso

Stiv Bators, Crash'n'Burn party / photo by Ralph Alfonso

"CRASH AND BURN"
ROCK CONCERT SERIES

The NERVES, a new-wave rock band from San Francisco, along with Toronto rockers, the DIODES, will perform at the grand-opening of the "Crash and Burn" spring-summer punk-rock concert series in the basement of The Centre For Experimental Art and Communication (CEAC), 15 Duncan St. (around the corner from the Royal Alex Theatre on King St.), two shows nightly, May-27-28, 8 p.m., $3.

Organized by the DIODES, a new-wave Toronto group, the weekly (Friday and Saturday nights) "Crash and Burn" concert series will be presenting the best of Toronto's underground rock movement in addition to some of the leading groups from the New York scene and elsewhere.

Among the local bands playing will be; the Viletones, the Dishes, Teenage Head, the Poles, the Doncasters, the Cads and the Concords. Negotiations are under way with several New York groups, including:

Crash'Burn press release, 1977

John Hamilton: We worked our asses off, we really did. Running the Crash 'n' Burn, running our club, we'd have to start early in the week, get the Special Occasion Permit, so we'd have to go down and do all the paper work for that. Then we'd have to arrange with a company to get the sound system, so Ian and I would have to rent a truck, go out, rent a couple of big A7 boxes that'll hold sound systems, bring it in and install it. We'd have to go to another company and rent the lights. Run all the lights, run all the cables. Then we'd have to go and buy the beer under a Special Occasion Permit. Then we'd have to go somewhere and buy twenty bags of ice the day before.

John Catto: It was constantly under surveillance by the liquor license people. They were constantly going, "Oh, you have to have crash barriers and you have to have this on the door and you have to have this," you know? Because it was pretty obvious to them that we were pulling more people than the fifteen who used to turn up for quiet little performance art things and buy five beers.

While we were sorting these things out, what we did is we built the bar in the freight elevator with the feeling that if anyone walked in we could hit the button and shoot the thing up to the fourth floor. Ha ha ha. I have no idea whether that would have worked in practice, but it seemed like a good idea at the time.

John Hamilton: And then after we'd play, we'd have to come in the next morning and clean up because it would be a pigpen. We were shovelling it out. We'd shovel it all out and then virtually hose down the floor. We had about four or five mops and we'd have to mop the goddamn floor. So as well as being the stars of the scene, the Diodes were also the janitors of the scene.

We had a lot of help, too. We had this band called the Dents — younger kids who were really good, who were sort of our junior apprentices who came in and helped and worked their butts off. And Jula, my girlfriend from the Curse, would come. I'll never forget seeing Lucasta in her high heels scrubbing the toilet.

Never any of the Viletones; they were useless. They'd drink whatever beer was left over and fall asleep in the corner if you invited them.

Ralph Alfonso: The best night without a doubt was when we had a closed party, the one where all the bands played onstage and in the audience was the Ramones and the Dead Boys and their various managers.

Gary Pig Gold: When Gary Topp brought the Ramones back to town, he couldn't get anyone to come down and write about them.

And I said, "I love those guys! I'll interview them."

Gary hooked me up and after the show they said, "Where do we go to see some music?" And I said, "There's only one place," so we all went there. Except for Tommy, who went out to get pizza. All Joey wanted to do was talk about Herman's Hermits — that's where his vocal style came from. Peter Noone. And Ronnie Spector.

Danny Fields: It was an office building down by the lake in this dreary, abandoned neighbourhood, and it was a cold, dank, dark basement. It was not too professionally equipped with lights and sound and stuff.

I do remember there being an uptake, and I hate the word punk, but in the modern music facilities' capabilities, interest, and stuff the next time we were back — it wasn't like you would play here then you would play there where there's a famous club in each city where you go with this kind of music.

Cheetah Chrome: I think the first time we played Toronto we played the New Yorker with the Ramones.

We thought it was great. Toronto has always been a big party town. A few of us had been up there before. Cleveland is only about six hours away so everybody would go up there and hit Yonge Street and they had cool clothes and things that you didn't get in Cleveland, so a few of us had been there.

For one thing, Toronto was a lot cleaner. I think they had a little more in common with the English kids, being part of the Commonwealth. It's a big city, and it's much more metropolitan than places like Cleveland and Detroit. I think they had a different set of gripes than we'd had in the States. We were never big into politics of any sort back then. We were one of the non-political punk bands. We didn't sing about it because it was kind of boring, we thought.

We were pretty excited and the show was great. It was one of the few places where we really connected with the audience early on; it was really cool. We hung out afterwards and got to meet a lot of people and that was pretty cool. I know we met Steve Leckie and Eva and all those people that night.

Gary Pig Gold: It's like suddenly we're connecting — "Oh, well, you're in New York and this is all happening there, too?" I had been over in London and it was happening *there*, too. It was so much more exciting when you actually had that rapport.

Ian Mackay: We were talking to the U.S. bands in the dressing room after their performances. We were comparing notes on what they were experiencing in the States, and it was a very similar experience. It was tough, tough going.

It wasn't, "Oh you're a breaking act and you're doing something different." Essentially most people thought that it was garbage, and at times we even thought that ourselves. We had a lot of self-doubt, but we were having a lot of fun and we did know that there was a precedent of a return to simplicity and a new form of music emerges from it. We never knew whether that was really gonna happen or not, but it really did, didn't it?

David Clarkson: In '76 and '77, when I was what's called "punk" now, you have to remember that it didn't really even have a name then; there wasn't a particular sound that you had to have, and there was no special dress code. That's what was good about it. It definitely wasn't just about wearing swastikas or dog collars. I always thought that kind of stuff was just pointless and too obvious; just for attention.

I was only interested in having the best band, and writing new kinds of songs that were modern and urban. I didn't care about politics, or provocation even, that much.

Gary Pig Gold: Other people had to call it a movement. But that's for *other* people, not the people who were actually doing it and living it. *We* were not a movement.

None of us, at least me and the people I knew, were aware of creating a scene. We never dressed in what was supposed to be "punk rock." If *my* clothes happened to be torn, it was because I'd been trimming the hedge for my dad or something.

The "movement" came from above and from outside. It was *applied* to the scene.

Ian Mackay: When we were in the middle of it, there wasn't the same sense of history being made that there is now. It just was chaotic, disorganized, stuff would start again, stop again, you'd make some headway in what you believed and the next day you'd be shut down. So it was hard work; you had to have a very thick skin to put up with it in the early days. It paved the way for a lot of bands.

My favourite part was the backstage discussions, talking to Dee Dee Ramone and Stiv Bators.

Cheetah Chrome: Crash 'n' Burn was a complete dump, but it had a great crowd and those nice low ceilings that you can bump your head on when you jump up and down. The crowd, they were just fiends. I think a couple of the guys from Thin Lizzy came down. That's the first time we met them.

There was a lot going on in the crowd. Some of the craziest shows we ever played were in Toronto.

Ian Mackay: I was on bar duty when I wasn't playing, so I would be serving beer all night long. There was a lot of anxiety with the whole thing, too. It was hard to do it every weekend. There was violence. It was the first time I ever really felt stress.

There was total chaos. There were nights when people who knew me from high school came down to see the band and a couple of them left in disgust. They were saying, "This is violent." There were fistfights breaking out. We attracted a very interesting cross-mix in the very early days. It wasn't, "How do you behave?" It was, "What do you do to be an anarchist?"

Pop Music Beat, by Gerald Levitch [*Toronto Sun*, June, 1977]: As for the Viletones, they came out spitting and pouring beer on the audience, which was reciprocated.

Ian Mackay: There were some very wild moments. Steven Leckie used to get beer bottles thrown at him. I even think *I* threw one at him. I remember him saying, "I'll remember that. I'll remember that, Ian!" It definitely had a violent undertone to it in the early days. It was a weird mix; it was about eighteen- and nineteen-year-old thugs from the East End. It was too bad that it was rough at times.

John Catto: Another interesting thing that happened at Crash 'n' Burn is right around the same time, Thin Lizzy were recording *Bad Reputation*. And one night, in walk all the members of Thin Lizzy going, "We're rock stars, let us in." Ha ha ha. And we were like "No, we won't let you in. Who the fuck are you?"

Basically, they eventually paid, or someone broke down or whatever and they ended up hanging out there for the entire duration. I would guess that there was some member of Thin Lizzy at almost every night the Crash 'n' Burn was open. There's loads of stories about Phil Lynott getting into fights with people.

Johnny Pig [*The Pig Paper* no. 5, August 1977]: According to sources unnamed, Mr. Lynott was in town to deliver the keynote address at the annual Irish Immigrant Aid Society Dinner and Dance, but rumours being what they are revealed that he was actually in Toronto for a hush-hush hair transplant to his upper lip. Maybe that's why foul-mouth Phil risked a possible hemorrhage to remark menacingly to the roving Pig lens, and I quote, "Fuck off. FUCK OFF. If you want to keep your film, you better stop takin' pictures."

Paul Eknes: Phil Lynott took a swing at me because he was after Cynthia Ross of the B-Girls and I said, "She's with me." And he goes, "What are you, some little Toronto punk?" And I went, "Kinda." And he goes, "Do you know who I am?" And I go, "Yeah, fucking Thin Lizzy, Phil Lynott. I love ya. Boys are back in town!" And he goes, "Yeah? She's with *me*." He was drunk and took a swing. I ducked and gutted him — not gutted him, I didn't actually take his intestines out, but I gave him a shot in the gut and we were pulled apart. Cynthia said, "What are you doing? You *are* a stupid little Toronto punk! This is Phil Lynott from Thin Lizzy!"

I think Mike Nightmare might have stood up for me. Back in the day I was less buff. All I remember is somebody pulled Phil off me and me off him.

Nora Currie: Mike got into this big fight with the guy from Thin Lizzy. It was brutal. Here's this guy in our country, checking out the scene, and Mike made racist comments to him along the line of being Black Irish, which is ironic. Phil was a black man who was Irish. Mike was Irish and he made really racist remarks to him. It was just such a vicious fuckin' beating.

Steven Leckie: It was a stack deal because Mike Nightmare was a beautiful street fighter, really good boxer, but what he didn't reckon on was that Thin Lizzy had around half a dozen bodyguards that weren't gonna let anything happen to Phil. Mike got his nose all busted but what a brave boy; what a beautiful, brave boy.

Mike Nightmare, punched out by Phil Lynott / photo by Ralph Alfonso

Anna Bourque: The Crash 'n' Burn was these arty types mixed with these thugs; it was a real coming together.

I remember meeting Tony Torcher from the Ugly for the first time there. We were getting beer out of the bathtub or something. I said, "So who are you?" "Tony Torcher," and he spelled it for me: T-O-R-C-H-E-R, because that's how he thought "torture" was spelled. It really shows you the polar opposites. It's this whole arty crowd from OCA and General Idea, and you've got torture being spelled with a C-H-E-R and Tony thinking that that was true.

Ian Mackay: I didn't think that the bands we brought in from outside were all that great compared to what was happening in Toronto. I actually thought the Toronto bands were a lot better and a lot more original.

I think we were bringing in other bands to establish legitimacy for the Toronto scene, but I don't think it was necessary. I thought we were better in a lot of ways.

Ralph Alfonso [Bomp De Bomp column in *StageLife Magazine*, Nov. 1977]: It was certainly one of the most incredible things to have ever happened to the city. To see the mobs of kids dancing frantically around the stage, dripping sweat in the human furnace was a sight bordering on the unbelievable. Better than CBGB's (the Ramones said so) and as good as England's Roxy.

Michaele Jordana / photo by Ross Taylor

14. cn tower

Steven Leckie: It's funny about Toronto in that it does produce some of the greatest cultural gurus of the 20th Century, from Michael Ondaatje to McLuhan to Northrop Frye. There's something in Toronto being what it is, yet having this insight that is unique to us, I think.

Blair Martin: Because of Marshall McLuhan being here, this was probably the intellectual capital of the world. We had this great thinking; this guy who right now, whose studies and concepts and understanding of media are just starting to become current again, he was here in the back of the university. There are a lot of people working in Toronto, writers certainly, who are really understanding of media in a way that people are not in other places. This seems to be a talent for Torontonians. So you have the spirit of Marshall McLuhan there in his garage at the university thinking up all these great media things that'll become current, and still are now.

When I came from the States in 1970, we didn't have cable television. But there was cable television in Toronto. The *Baby Blue Movies*, now that's Moses Znaimer. All of a sudden there's a guy, he opens up this TV station, he has this really sort of racy soap opera from Australia that has female nudity in it, and he starts showing *Baby Blue Movies*. Now what he's actually doing, the way I see and the way I analyze the situation, is he's showing people the future content of things like HBO. And he's also saying, "Hey, look, world! This is Toronto. This is potentially a big market. Toronto will be a great place to experiment with the future of television since we don't have any TV code here." In the States they're governed by a code of certain content and certain things you can't say. Here, there's nothing; there was no code as to what may or may not appear on television, none whatsoever. So hey, man, I can put tits on TV. Whatever it means to somebody, that at least informs you at the back of your mind if you're half intelligent that you live in a place where revolutionary stuff is capable, and that high intellectual and/or artistic activity is also capable.

So not only are we a world class city, somebody's told us we can also be creative, so that all plays in our minds. I think as a group of people we had a sort of a confidence in ourselves, and we were as well informed as people anywhere else.

This is one of the few places David Bowie used to be able to come in North America. There was a time, I guess it would be '72, '73, David Bowie did probably eight gigs in North America. That's it. One of them in Toronto. So we're aware that we're a communication centre.

I think that the intellectual, spiritual confidence to have something like this happen was there where it hadn't happened before. I can say in New York, you'd expect it. In a lot of ways the early punk scene as reflected through somebody like Patti Smith is really just the old New York folk scene filtered through the Andy Warhol looking glass. You put people in small clubs — a small club like CBGB's, although it's got revolutionary content, in terms of New York City it's kind of old hat. Whereas in Toronto, it was actually a *new* thing to have a little fuckin' stinky club where you could go in and actually play original music. That's actually a completely new idea.

Toronto has all of a sudden this action, and this business, too, after the Party Québécois elections in Quebec. All of a sudden all the business moved here. They built Metalworks Studios and Queen came here to record one of their albums. We had all these big things starting to happen that were continually informing us to our own sense of being world class and our right, therefore, to have those kinds of aspirations and expectations artistically, creatively, etcetera. That's the general background, and beyond that then it's the input of the individuals coming out of that.

Michaele Jordana: I am a Canadian painter and this all happened at the convergence of art and music, and I think it's really important for Canada to have a history.

Young women need people who have worked all their lives in art. We were the first new wave punk rock group in this country. It didn't exist before us. We created the look with a lot of other people helping us, a lot of friends who were very creative, and it all just came together beautifully. We created the look and the sound and the language of new wave, which survived. With a small of group people we played Crash 'n' Burn and CBGB's and Max's and all the great places in New York and met everybody. I just think it's very important now to claim a stake in history.

When I came to Toronto, I came out of art school. It's a whole different personality; it's not really an extrovert, but an introverted person who spends a lot of time in her studio. It was a gradual process that created Michaele Jordana. My *real* name is Michaele Berman. It was a transition that went over a period of a few years. Michaele Berman was a force to contend with, but Michaele Jordana became just a huge energy that even shocked me.

I came to Toronto right after I finished art school in the early '70s. I met my partner, Doug Pringle, who was in a band called Syrinx, which was the first electro-pop band, one of the few on the planet.

I had a show of whale paintings in Toronto — huge, super-real paintings of slaughtered whales. I decided to go the Arctic after that and really see for myself what was going on. So I went up and spent a summer living on the ice floes in the high Arctic, practically in the North Pole. That's where the name the Poles came from. And I came back and started doing performance art because really, we were drifting on the ice pans with a few Inuit people, and starving, and they'd caught a whale and it was a most incredible ritual that I was lucky to experience and photograph.

We came back and had a show of photographs called *Carnivore*. I did performance art pieces called "The Rites of Nuliajuk." Performance art at the time was brand new. I wrote "The Manifesto of Performance Art" with a friend of mine who really also was an excellent Canadian performance artist at the time. And we performed this at Innis College and around Ontario. I was performing a re-enactment of what happened on the ice with twenty tons of huge ice blocks, and Douglas was doing music. It was all pre-taped with loops and everything. I was never going to go out and actually use a microphone; I was just a performance artist shaking and taking on the persona of the whale or whatever.

But eventually I started singing. It was at art galleries like A Space. It just grew and grew and grew. We got a cult following that followed us everywhere, so we started getting invited to play larger and larger venues.

Everybody knew my name was Michaele Jordana, but the Poles consisted of rough-and-tumble people. Douglas and myself led it, and the rest of the band were Scarborough guys who came from another place. They brought that street energy into the band.

Doug Pringle: We were a little bit older than the rest of the people in the scene, only by five years or something like that but enough that we were half in and half out. I guess I was probably one of the only musicians that actually had a reputation for having done other things in the music business before, so that sort of put me in position of having a bridge into the rest of music. And I had people say to me, "Why are you doing this three-chord thing, aren't you afraid of wrecking your reputation?" There was really a split between people who got it, and people who *didn't* get punk and new wave. The record companies were really, really slow to pick up on what was happening.

Michaele Jordana: I remember hearing Patti Smith, who was so different from everything that had come before her. She just let things flow and I admired her. I guess we come from the same — we kind of look the same in a very arty way. Put us side by side we wouldn't look the same, but we weren't totally commercial-looking women. You could peg us as artists. There was a tradition there. The whole thing wasn't about being commercial, it was about being wired and on and saying something with your music. It was about communication and it wasn't cheap.

I remember hearing her music and not really even wanting to see her, because as a performance artist I wanted to evolve my own style.

Doug Pringle: Crash 'n' Burn in some ways was a seminal event because it was so outside of the laws and so outside the club scene. It was just a place where people who knew what was happening had to go.

I think we played there the second or third week. The Diodes opened it, then I think it was the Viletones, then the Poles, then Teenage Head. That was the sequence; it was sort of a pecking order that had been established. The Diodes were the ringmasters.

Andrew McGregor: I really credit the Diodes for running that place because I'm sure it wasn't easy. But for one summer that's where the scene was and anybody who was into it was there Friday and Saturday night, or at least one of them. I think I only missed two shows down there; one was a fashion show weekend which I think was really for the OCA crowd. But there were some fantastic shows down there; a lot of experimental stuff down there.

The Poles, their first show down there was I guess you'd have to say really experimental. I think their first show was the best one I ever saw them do. Eventually they kind of turned into a power pop band, but in the beginning you didn't know who these people were or who Michaele Jordana was. She came out all dressed up as a mummy and gradually peeled the bandages away.

John Hamilton: We booked in the Poles with Michaele Jordana, but she was a real pain in the ass. She started immediately demanding a cut of the bar. She had all these fans of hers that wore Birkenstocks. She brought in all the dumpy art people. I liked Doug Pringle; he was a good guy.

We booked her once and we couldn't stand her, so we never booked her again.

Freddy Pompeii: We did maybe two shows with the Poles. They weren't the favourites because they were older. Pringle was in Syrinx.

That was like an instrumental, psychedelic thing with electronic music. It was good stuff, but it wasn't anything like punk rock; the fact that he was already popular and had an album out with those guys sort of made him an outcast in the scene. You sort of had to be brand new and young to have the integrity that was necessary for the kids to like you.

And the kids didn't like them because she was sort of like a Patti Smith imitator to a certain extent, even in the way she wrote songs. What happened is when they would play these shows like the Crash 'n' Burn — we did one with them at the Crash 'n' Burn and I can't remember the other one, it might have been in New York — they had these things, these sticks that they used at the end of the show where they did their finale. It was like they were shooting guns at each other. They were these electronic sticks that they would hold out and run the other hand over top of it back and forth and it would make noise like, *wooooooo woooooo weeee-wooooo*. It really didn't have anything to do with the youth at the time, you know? They had the look down, they wore the right clothes, but it was more like a new wave thing than a punk thing.

I always liked them regardless of their lack of originality. I still like them for having the balls to go out and do what they did and trying to master that thing with the sticks and the way they put their show together. She was just a little too hard to take because she was really high strung. The kids in the audience would throw shit at her, which was sort of what happened at a punk rock show, but she took it to heart. She would come to us after a show and be crying and stuff, "Why are they treating me like this" and whatever.

Ian Mackay: One of my favourite Crash 'n' Burn gigs was the gig by the Poles. It was really genuine; they were just real, genuine people.

Freddy Pompeii: Michaele Jordana and Doug Pringle were really nice people. You could sit down and have an intelligent conversation with them and be informed and educated and entertained all at the same time. They were part of the scene. In fact, they were sort of like the equivalent of the Stranglers in England.

The Stranglers had the same problem. They were older than the punk rockers so they always were out of place at punk rock shows, although their music was just as aggressive and they looked great. But they were considered too old to be in that scene. You know who else fell into that category in Toronto was the Battered Wives; they were all older guys, older than me. They were playing mod music from the '60s like "My Generation" and stuff like that. It definitely bordered on stadium rock.

I saw that happen a lot in different scenes, where there was always an outcast; some band that nobody thought belonged there.

But they worked just as hard as everybody else, you can't take that away from them. They were pretty well set up in the way they worked. Doug Pringle had been around for so long that he could get rehearsal space wherever it was available. He had a lot of connections, being an older guy.

Michaele Jordana: People will say we weren't there, but we were. It was us. There are going to be other people that say, "It wasn't really them, it was me," but it's not true. It just isn't true. There were a few other women around at the time who kind of looked punky, but uh-uh. Their music had nothing to do with it.

Our music was refined because Douglas had been in Syrinx, but it was still loud and hypnotic. People entered trance states. I could see it.

I guess people saw in it what they wanted to. Some people who were at the beginning with us, the artists, they understood it was communication. As it started filtering through, I don't know what other people got from it, and in a way I wasn't really prepared for that because I am an artist. I'm not really meant to be totally commercial. I'm more of a seer.

I think that the whole movement was visionary, and people allowed me that luxury and they allowed me to develop it. I had influences; I had classic influences from Beethoven to even David Bowie. He was such an artist at the time. Great painters. I was constantly referring to all the art that had ever created me. That's how I lived my life.

Steven Leckie: The Viletones did shows with the Poles in '77, and Michaele Jordana and Doug Pringle were at a Mensa level of intellect. They were involved in the theories of Marshall McLuhan in a big way, and that's why they knew the epicness of writing a song like "CN Tower." She was borrowing a little bit from Patti Smith and a little bit from Berlin cabaret but they were highly intelligent, and if people thought they were maybe bandwagon jumping it was only because they were a little older and they didn't come from the pure OCA world. They didn't come from the hard world that we did, the Viletones. Maybe they weren't organic punks the way the Curse and the B-Girls were. They were almost like the translators of the whole thing.

I was good with them. They had a practice space at a boxing club at Pape and Danforth, and she was always really good to me. But I think there was a lot of cattiness around the OCA bands; around the whole deification of Carole Pope. It was bitchy; that gay thing, it's in their nature.

I think the people in that part of the scene were at odds with the fact that this was unfortunately, to them, a masculine, almost misogynist art form and I think it kind of threw them for a bit of a loop. But the Poles I thought were cool. They certainly weren't punk and they weren't new wave, but they had something to say that was intellectual that fit.

Strangely enough, intellectualism always fits in with punk.

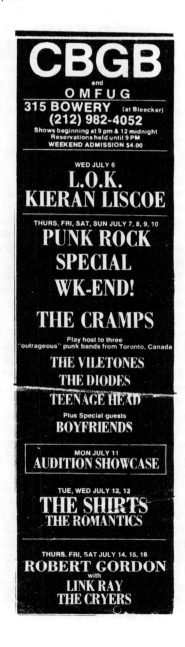

15. canaDian invasion

Paul Kobak: Teenage Head had a fan base in Hamilton and a growing one in Toronto. The next step was to get them into the recording studio.

We recorded some demos at Cosmic Studios in Hamilton that I tried everywhere to pitch. Not the most enthusiastic responses. Getting any kind of gig that paid decent money was difficult, so I'd always had it in mind for them to be recording artists and play concerts and go on tours. In the interim, all we could do was keep playing the Toronto scene until more doors could open.

Dave Rave: I remember going to the studio with them and cutting a version of "Tearin' Me Apart," and they had a song called "Wake Up Shut Up." It's a great song. But there were no singles yet. Nobody was making their own yet; it was still too early for that.

Gary Pig Gold: Teenage Head had a five-song demo at the time which was amazing, and "Picture My Face" I can distinctly remember Paul Kobak playing for me in his car. I said, "Wow, the tambourine is so loud, it's like a Motown record." And he said, "Yeah, we want to get a record deal."

I think that tape probably got Teenage Head into the building. After all, they *did* have career aspirations. That's why the tambourine was so loud. That's why they put "Picture My Face" as the first song on the demo, because that was by far their most commercial song. Like "I Wanna Be Your Boyfriend" was supposed to launch the Ramones — that was the single off their first album and they made a point of, you know, "Let's tone it down a bit for this record."

Stephen Mahon: I remember the first time hearing our song on the radio, on CFNY. They played one song off our demo tape. I can remember sitting in Kobak's car thinking, How can they be playing it? We haven't made a record yet. But I guess Paul had gotten them the demo, so that was really cool to hear that coming out of his car speakers — "Hey, they're playing it! Turn it up! Turn it up!" You know, that clichéd thing when bands hear their song for the first time, which can only happen one time. Paul really did a lot of cool things on the ground level that certainly helped us move forward.

Then we got hooked up with a guy named Jack Morrow. He was connected with another player named John Brower. They did shows in the '70s. They were sort of con men slash music promoters.

I guess it's hard not to be a little bit of a con man in the music business if you're not on the artists' side of the fence.

Paul Kobak: First, I'd like to provide you with a bit of background on them. John came from an Upper Canada College type of wealthy family.

John was hanging around the Yorkville scene when it started and got into concert promotions, notably the Doors at the CNE in 1968, promoter of the Rock Pile, where Led Zeppelin first came to town, John Lennon *Live Peace 1969* at Varsity Stadium — with an amazing lineup — Festival Express 1970, a five-day, across-Canada train trip with Janis Joplin, Grateful Dead, The Band. John is about eight to ten years older than me, so he was doing all this stuff in his young twenties.

Jack was twenty to twenty-five years older than me. He was a street person, a con artist, a hustler who knew the ropes. He'd spent some time in jail around this time, for writing bad cheques.

Stewart Pollock: Jack Morrow. "Jack Tomorrow." His name was Jack T. Morrow. He had so many aliases, that guy.

Paul Kobak: Jack had previously successfully promoted James Brown for a New Year's Eve event but lost his shirt promoting Tanya Tucker at an outdoor event. He moved on to manage Abraham's Children in the early '70s, who'd released an album and had a couple of minor hits on the radio. They broke up after a couple years.

Apparently Jack and John had known each other and collaborated on each other's projects to a limited extent. For whatever reasons, they were the promoters of Norwester '76, an outdoor concert in Oregon. The Hells Angels came, things happened, and they came back to Canada broke.

I suppose a picture could come to focus now of a pair of seasoned buzzards or hungry sharks looking for fresh opportunity.

1977 arrives and everybody is looking for The Next Big Thing in music. The rumblings underlying all point to punk rock, as the Sex Pistols help open the door wide for all the bands that have been in waiting. John and Jack do their reconnaissance, asking everyone who the best band in Toronto is.

Everyone says, "Teenage Head from Hamilton."

Michael Dent: My first introduction to the punk scene was Jack Morrow, who was the manager of Teenage Head. I lived up in the 'burbs, that's where my band was formed, and I somehow met this guy named Jack and he told me about this band called the Dishes, and they were playing at the Beverley Tavern so I decided to go and check them out. I met the band and I really liked them and I thought they were really cool. I'd never heard anything like them before, so I met Steven Davey and I used to hang out at his place. He turned me on to Chris Spedding and Deaf School and Roxy Music; basically the alternatives to the Led Zeppelins and Black Sabbaths.

Barrie Farrell: Michael Dent was a very bizarre little dude in high school, and he hooked up with Bob Ezrin and he told him to produce KISS. He was the guy. And Bob Ezrin said, "Okay," and made a bazillion fuckin' dollars. Michael knew how to sneak his way in and get free tickets to rock shows.

Michael Dent: Jack asked me, "If you had to choose one band for us to manage, who would it be?" So I went, "Teenage Head," and they did and they took off from there. Paul Kobak was still managing Teenage Head at that time, but he took over with John Brower.

I told Jack Morrow to pick them because I thought they were the most musically proficient. They really knew their instruments and how to play, and they had a great stage image. They sounded great. They were Teenage Head.

Stephen Mahon: The story that I heard goes that John Brower got wind of the Sex Pistols making millions of dollars signing to labels in England. That was world-wide news.

Obviously he had his ear to the ground and knew that at that moment punk rock was able to make quick cash deals with labels, and was on the lookout for Canada's Sex Pistols so he could do that and make money. It makes perfect sense to me, that's why I believe it.

John Brower [CBC Television, *Punk Strox '77*]: I think punk rock is the rock 'n' roll of today. It's this new generation's expression of their frustrations and aspirations. I don't think it's a fad. I think it's the beginning of a new approach to music. I think that very shortly we'll see records in the Top 10 in America by punk rock and new wave bands, and after that the floodgates will be open and I think we'll have much more acceptability.

Stephen Mahon: The word just hit the streets, like "What's out there, what's out there, what's out there? Diodes, Viletones, Teenage Head, Teenage Head" – I guess he kept getting vibes back – "Teenage Head, Teenage Head, they're the ones, they're good, you should look into that," so that's how it happened.

Paul Kobak: So I'm laying in bed one morning when I get a phone call from someone named John Brower asking me if I could bring the band to Toronto to a rehearsal space, I think it was somewhere on Danforth, for an audition for he and Jack. I said I'd get back to them concerning the timing and went about to do my own recon. When I found out we could hook up with these guys I thought, Great! Precisely the types of backgrounds with connections needed to get the band into the big leagues.

So I took the most logical steps: I had the band formally sign a two-year contract with me as manager to cover my butt, then we met with them. They were impressed enough that I'd offered to split management with them any way they'd like, and we could technically rearrange things once there's money coming in. For now, we were still at ground zero. I'd agreed to focus on taking care of the band, the gigs and the promotions.

John and Jack were great promoters, and the three of us clicked.

John Brower [*Billboard*, January 14, 1978]: We're in the business to sell records, we're not trying to revolutionize the record business. When this scene pops it's going to happen fast and when it does, I'm going to make damned sure I'm ready to ride the crest with my band.

*   *   *   *   *

Stephen Mahon: At the very same practice space the Viletones were there, too, because I remember talking to Leckie that day and he was talking about how we should all go to CBGB's.

Steven Leckie: Because of my DNA, bravado, the way I was raised, all kinds of different elements, I said "Well, why can't I do this in New York?" So I had no problem getting Nick Stipanitz from Teenage Head and this other ragamuffin, to talk them into driving me down to New York.

The Viletones ethic was infused with a real American attitude because of Freddy and because of my ancestry. We didn't think of, oh, let's get a gig in Peterborough, the way Teenage Head would.

I knew they always had cool cars in Hamilton and I got one of them to drive us down to CBGB's.

Stephen Mahon: What a trip that was. There were six of us in a Duster; it's just like a mid-size car. Six people in a car at any time is tight ... meanwhile, it's ten hours.

We went down; it was me, Gordie, and Leckie – so we were kind of all on the same page – but then the three other people were from Paul Kobak's record store.

This guy Trent, he drove, and then for some reason these two other people just tagged along. Kobak was paying for that trip, oh yeah. You've got to thank him for something like that, give him credit, because me and Gordie didn't have a nickel and neither did Leckie, and for him to set that whole thing up and put gas in the tank and give Trent that money to get us to New York to do that was really cool.

Gordie Lewis: If I could relive one day from that time, it would be going down to New York City. That was it.

The only media that you could find information out, other than radio, was the print media. So basically all we had was magazines and pictures of things; pictures of bands playing at CBGB's, and we knew all about what was going on in New York City. So we just decided we were going to go and see if we could get a gig down there and that was it. We definitely were not sure whether we were going to come back with one or not, but we did. It was great. We found CBGB's, we talked to Hilly Kristal, and he said, "Yeah, you guys can play here," and he put us on a bill with the Cramps.

Steven Leckie: Went right in, middle of the afternoon, right up to Hilly Kristal, showed him a couple of press pieces I had, and he could tell just by my look. You could tell a punk by more his hips; the way he held himself. And I got the gig.

Freddy Pompeii: What happened with the Viletones was something completely out of the ordinary. We were only together a short time and next thing you know, we're playing CBGB's. It just didn't happen that way. You had to wait and wait and wait and wait and work and work and wait and work before something like that happens.

Stephen Mahon: It's funny in retrospect. It probably wasn't necessary to make that trip; we probably could have ended up going and playing anyway had it been set up just on the phone, but I guess it was cool that we just stood right in front of Hilly Kristal and asked him.

The negotiations took five seconds — "Sure you can come, just come and play. You're not going to get paid, but come on down," and that was it. We were just like, "It's that easy?" But it was a fun trip. That was our first time to New York, and Leckie was great because he was always dressed the same as he would onstage.

It was kind of funny. We were sitting in a car for ten hours and he's got this leather necklace with the big pointy studs sticking out of it and the leather pants. It must have been uncomfortable. It was in the summer time. You know, you'd stop for gas, go in for a leak, and here's Steve Leckie dressed like that. That was the difference with me and Gordie.

We always dressed just whatever; street cool. But that was the Viletones. That was their image. They were really punk.

Gordie Lewis: Us and the Viletones were the two Canadian bands on the bill, and then somehow the other bands kind of latched on to it of course. You know, "What do you mean you're going down to New York and playing CBGB's without us?"

"Yeah, sorry, we're the ones who went down and got the gig." Ha ha ha. So the Diodes latched on somehow, and I think the Dents just drove down and hung around outside the door. But it was me, Steve, and Steve Leckie that went down there. We were just looking out for ourselves.

John Hamilton: It was still pretty early. Nobody had a record contract or anything like that, and everybody was watching what everybody else was doing.

Somehow word got out that the Viletones had booked at CBGB's — the first Canadian band that was gonna play there, right? And we couldn't let anybody get ahead of us. We found out that the Viletones had been talking to Hilly Kristal. It was probably Ralph or Paul who got on the blower and said we wanted to play there. Of course, I was living with Jula then so whatever I knew Jula knew, so then the Curse wanted to play there, too. So Hilly Kristal went from booking the Viletones to doing a whole Canadian weekend.

The Viletones of course hated us for doing this because they actually got the idea first, but we all jumped on it as well. It turned out we all played down there — the Viletones, the Diodes, the Curse, Teenage Head, and the Dents.

Mike Anderson: It had turned into this attack on New York City from Toronto. A whole bunch of us went. It was an invasion kind of thing.

Paul Robinson [Crash 'n' Burn press release, June, 1977]: If the Toronto bar scene won't support us, we'll find alternatives. This is perhaps the most significant movement Canada has produced in ten years and the Toronto weekend at CBGB's will only strengthen the credibility of this unique Canadian sound.

Gordie Lewis: It was a great experience just to be able to be involved in something that was happening; this whole punk thing was just starting and at the time it was London and New York and Toronto, so to be able to have New York be so close and be able to actually go down and play and perform was great.

Mike Anderson: It was the first time I'd been to New York and I thought it was quite interesting. I understand New York's changed quite a bit, but it was kind of like going to another planet. It was back when they had graffiti on the subways and all that kind of stuff. It was quite something, like if you take Toronto and amplify it by about twenty. It was like Yonge and Dundas in some areas, particularly where we were staying at Times Square right down there at 42nd Street. It was thick with porn and all that kind of stuff. That's not why we were there; we were just there because it was the hotel that was affordable and all that kind of stuff. It was still kind of a dump, but that's New York for you.

I look back now and I think '77 was one of the best years of my life, that summer of '77: The Summer of Sam. He was still at large then so they were still like, "Watch out for your daughters," and stuff. But I liked it; that was a good year. It was a hot summer, very hot. We went to New York and they opened all the fire hydrants because it was so hot. They just let them go and the kids were running in them.

Well, we got there and booked the hotel, went down to the club and checked it out. I think we did a sound check. We just hung out when we got there.

Chris Haight: In CBGB's I remember they had this one pinball machine called Old Chicago or something I used to play all the time when I was there. I remember the one night just playing this thing and Blondie walked up to me, but I wasn't gonna stop and go, "Wow! How you doing?" You know? I was ignoring her. Ha ha ha. I'm looking at the machine and she's looking in my ear and she goes, "You're the guy that cuts himself." It was so hokey. It was *so* hokey, man. And I figured, I know we're from Toronto but it ain't *that* hick of a city, so right away I knew we had the drop on them. I don't know if I got a charge off of it, but I just remember deliberately avoiding her.

Mike Anderson: We did the sound check, walked around New York, went back and played that evening and there was a lot of people there. There were all these celebs hanging out there, too, like Deborah Harry and Andy Warhol.

Sometimes I would think of punk rock, which was a label we were given at that time, and I didn't really quite feel like a punk. I had a different feeling altogether. I had a more rebellious feeling towards corporate music or whatever, that was my thing, but there it was staring at us in the face. And it was supposed to have shock value, punk rock, and being in New York City I thought, How the hell is *this* shocking anybody? What is the shock value of *us*? Like, how can punk be so shocking in this town compared to just what it was like on the

street? Knife fights right in the middle of the sidewalk and always something going on, everything, crazy people running around.

Anna Bourque: The weekend seemed very ad hoc. I remember I was wearing ripped fishnets and these shorts — at the time they were known as exercise shorts — but they were the cotton ones with the rib around them. Farrah Fawcett I think wore them, but it didn't look the same way on me.

And I really remember how filthy it was. CBGB's was old beer stuck with stuff on top and then beer on top again. It was like the stuff you find old bugs in, amber. That's what it was like, full of ancient sticky.

Linda Lee: I remember being in the washroom at the club, which was really, really — it felt like you'd walked into a subway that somebody had been violently ill in and that was used to piss in for the last twenty years.

I was washing my hands and I felt a presence come in, and it was Bryan Gregory who was the guitar player in the Cramps. There's a rumour going around that he actually was so evil that he was decapitated; he was that bad of a human being. But he walked in and he was probably about my height, really, really, really thin, and he had the most incredible pockmarked skin, like jagged looking. And he had blonde hair and one bit of it was behind his ear and it was long and greasy, and the other strand hung right down here across his face. He was incredibly ghastly looking. He just stood there and took out his comb and admired himself for like two minutes and I was just standing there looking at him, wondering who this guy was.

Julia Bourque: When we played New York it was like we'd made it. These were clubs I'd heard about and read about; they were iconic. It just seemed like, "Now I can stop doing this, I've done what I set out to do." Playing a club in New York seemed very, very important.

Gordie Lewis: It was one of the greatest experiences that I've ever had. It was NEW YORK CITY; it was everything that we read about. It was great just being down where the Ramones were playing and where the New York Dolls came from, because that was our favourite band. And to actually *be* in New York City ...

It was one of the best moves we ever made, to go and do that. And by that time Teenage Head were getting paid, so it was actually kind of like a job. It was great. We were doing gigs and actually making some money at it, and we just kept on doing it and kept on doing it. We were really lucky. We were really lucky to be able to have that whole punk scene start when it started, because we did start a few years earlier than the other bands.

So when the whole thing did start to gel, we were already playing and we already had a whack of original songs.

Janis Cafasso [*New York Rocker*, November/December, 1977]: Frankie Venom from Teenage Head was the first to swing from the pipes at CBGB's with a long line of copiers to follow.

Stephen Mahon: We already knew our set; it was tight. As young, hungry musicians, you give us a full club and almost always people would like us because we just played straight ahead rock 'n' roll. We weren't like a Devo or like an art band; we were just a *fun* band. So you put people in your club like that and give them some beers, and we're going to entertain them.

"The Sound of Tomorrow Alive in Toronto," by David Winter [*Entertainment Weekly*, July 27, 1977]: Frankie Venom is probably about the most penetratingly visual front man without a gold record in the music business today. He evoked screams from the raucous crowd pressed five deep at the CBGB's bar and danced a storm with a writhing crowd of punk rock crazies at the side of the stage. At one point during Teenage Head's frustrated anthem "Disgusteen," Frankie catapulted behind drummer Nick onto the amplifier, then he launched himself Tarzan-style across the stage, swinging from a water pipe, delighting everybody by landing square in front of the microphone on the beat and into the next verse.

Paul Eknes: We played CBGB's and this girl was standing beside Steve Leckie like, "Oh, you think you're so tough," while he's singing, and she takes a cigarette and just puts it out on his loin. He keeps on singing, takes the cigarette, relights it, takes a drag, puts it out on her forehead. And I'm standing in the audience going, "I'm *so* proud to be from Toronto."

That was Steve Leckie. He's kind of my idol. Even though we knew each other for years and years and years, he never ceases to amaze me.

Linda Lee: The Toronto scene was much larger than New York's. Perhaps that's just me, the way I felt about it, but there was a much greater impact here. Of course when you're travelling you see it differently, but you would imagine it would be the opposite way and that New York would appear larger. But it didn't. It really seemed restricted to half a dozen bands that all had lots of money, and then the poor, struggling ones didn't get a chance to play CBGB's.

And there might have been hundreds of little clubs that we just didn't know about but I don't think there was; I don't think it had that familial thing about it.

Margaret Barnes-DelColle: I just remember getting wasted, and that a lot of New York people showed up. A lot of New York bands came to see them because at that point the Viletones had a reputation that was bigger than just Toronto or Canada. So through going down there they met a lot of people that they hooked up with. You know, Johnny Thunders and Cheetah Chrome and Stiv Bators. They just made a lot of connections and put on a really crazy show.

Freddy Pompeii: The first night we played CBGB's on the Canadian weekend Steven cut himself up and he went too far. By the end of the set he was really bleeding bad. I think he might have nicked an artery or something. So he got rushed to the hospital, they bandaged him up and he had some stitches and everything, and he came back.

At the end of the night these Hells Angels were standing in the back of CBGB's where we would unload our equipment and where the bands leave from. You could pull your car into the back. And there were four or five Hells Angels standing back there and sort of blocked Steven's way and they said, "Hey listen, kid, if you like hurtin' yourself we can help ya out." And he said, "Well, what do you mean?" And they said, "Well, if you like cuttin' yourself up we'd be glad to help you out with that." Very, very sinister. Evil. And Steven got so fuckin' nervous and upset about that. It took a trip down to the United States of America for it to sink in that what he was doing wasn't very smart, and that certain things could incite certain things in other people.

Chris Haight: For some reason I don't think the Diodes got an invite, but they decided to go down there anyway. So they were probably the last band to go on because there was no organized time frame for them.

Ian Mackay: When we got there it seemed like we would *never* go on. The place didn't even start filling up until midnight and we were all really, really tired.

We went on around two-thirty a.m. I think we fought or drew straws over who would go on first, second, and third. Then the Cramps came on as the headliner and they didn't go on until four a.m. There were eighty, ninety people — there were enough — but sixty of those people were from Toronto. But we wanted to do it, we wanted to go down there as a contingent and all play.

Chris Haight: They weren't supposed to be there, to make a long story short, and by the time they slid on the stage near the end I remember they were all shook up and just downhearted because nobody hung around to give them the support in New York City. I wonder what they kept picking on them for, the Diodes.

Steve was even worse. He would make up detrimental shit. They sounded okay. I just don't know what it was about them.

Steven Leckie: I never liked Paul Robinson, and that's cool, that doesn't even matter. Looking back on it I could have been nicer because my nature is to be more kind, but I was young, I was loaded and really on fire, and I think I gave people a harder time.

I wasn't sensitive all the time to people who maybe should have been treated with sensitivity. Instead of saying, "Hey, Paul," I'd go, "You fuckin' poseur." So there were rivalries but I'll tell you, it always felt like when a band walked into the Horseshoe you knew they had balls. But when the Viletones walked in you could hear them *clank*. We were so sure of ourselves and our stature because we had the one thing that none of the other ones had, and that was a lot of press. Everyone knew that we were the ones, you know?

John Hamilton: That weekend, there was a lot of competition between us all. It was friendly, but deadly. Everybody knew that maybe one day there would be a record deal.

Variety came down. I think we got some reviews that we were irresponsible because we played so late or something. Ralph actually cut them all out. He actually managed to turn them into positive publicity, because if you're a punk band and *Variety* was saying you're irresponsible ...

New Acts: Teenage Head, by Kirb [*Variety*, July 13, 1977]: In Frankie Venom, the quartet, ages 19–21, who've been at it for about two years, have a solid mobile close-cropped lead singer who spends much of his time on his knees with his back against the floor, making visibility difficult save for standees. When he's visible, he moves constantly, often gyrating, often with his rear to the audience. In one number, he climbs to a platform behind the drums and swings on an overhead pipe, almost knocking a cymbal over as he reaches the stage.

Gordie Lewis: To actually have people come and see us play, and then have media there like *Melody Maker* and *Variety*. The *Globe and Mail* sent a guy down to take a bunch of pictures, and when we came back it was "Punk Pilgrimage to New York City."

It was really cool and it was really exciting. We would have been twenty years old, so at that point it was the whole justification for this crazy idea of trying to make a living out of being in a band.

Freddy Pompeii: Right after our CBGB's show we got a write-up in *Maclean's* magazine. They sent us professional photographers and the whole theme was Punk Rock in Canada From Coast to Coast.

Most of the bands they named in this article were Toronto bands. Of course we were one of the bigger ones that they talked about and it had a great colour photo of the band, a full-page colour photo. Being spotlighted like that is a big thrill. We knew we were making a big noise with stuff like that happening.

"Punk Rock: Toronto's Nasties Create a Style That Goes Beyond Mere Posturing," by Peter Goddard [*Toronto Star*, July 16, 1977]: At CBGB's, the heart of punk, only one question mattered: Is Toronto tough on par with New York tough?

...It was not a matter of making it in the Big Apple; it was one punk centre visiting another.

Ian Mackay: What can you say? It was a good moment of solidarity and we got some great press out of it as The Weekend Toronto Conquered New York.

But the reality was that we showed up, we played, and we left. That was more the case. But we were the *first* Canadian bands down there doing this, which is important.

Stephen Mahon: Look at what went down prior to that. We all know the Ramones did their whole thing there and played there a hundred times, and just walking in the place was awesome for us. Certainly it was a boost.

When we got back to Canada the *Globe and Mail* had that article with the picture of us in it, and that's when the phones started ringing with agents wanting to know who we were simply because we went down and did that. Had the *Globe and Mail* not done that front page story it may have gone under the radar quite a bit, I would think. The underground punk scene may have known about it, but the masses knew about it that weekend when that paper came out. It certainly gave us a boost, definitely.

Even just morally, you just couldn't help but be excited about playing there. It was almost like a downer coming back — not to [Hamilton] or Toronto, but we were starting to play shows where we'd get sent to Ajax or Whitby. It certainly wasn't CBGB's. It was tough. We paid some dues.

Frankie Venom ["Teenage Head: From Hamilton with Energy," by Jim Mason, *Lakehead Living,* February 4, 1981]: We made $11 U.S. on that trip. We came back and threw our manager a $1 bill and told him that was his ten per cent.

*   *   *   *   *

John Brower [CBC Television, *Punk Strox '77*]: I think Teenage Head are on the threshold at this point of making it. They've crystallized the audience here and in New York, they have come through with solid music, and they'll be recording very shortly. And I think from then on, you'll see them as a concert touring act with legitimate recording success.

I think that we're right up there. It's beginning to be big now. It's in Toronto — of course we're the biggest music center in Canada. I think it will spread from here as it receives recognition and airplay.

There's been no commercial exposure so consequently there can't be any big money. Hopefully we'll change that very shortly.

Stephen Mahon: Jack stuck around longer than John. When we didn't sign a million-dollar deal, he was kind of gone. He didn't have any other input other than when we went to his place a couple of times for a photo session. I think he might have given us a hundred dollars between the four of us to go down to Kensington Market to get some stage clothes, but beyond that Jack took us under his wing.

John wanted that quick deal. He did set up a couple of auditions. Capitol Records was one, and he really was more or less looking to take down a huge dollar advance and it wasn't going to happen in Toronto. I don't know why.

Deane Cameron: I worked for an English record company that was involved with a lot of the big punk bands. Whenever I brought a punk band in, it was simply, "We've been there, Deane."

Canada was a little late in. The great punk bands in Britain were late '75, '76, '77. It didn't really take root here until the early '80s.

Stephen Mahon: Maybe they heard about what happened with the Sex Pistols: It wasn't like they left, the company just said, "I don't care if we gave you that money, fuck you." And when you think of something like that happening, obviously the Canadian labels would be hip — "You know what? This could happen to us. We could give Teenage Head a million dollars and they could go on TV and do something slanderous and be in the same position." So John was after the big bucks and it never happened.

"Punk Band Seeks $25 Million Policy," by Peter Goddard [*Toronto Star*, Aug. 9, 1977]: Teenage Head, the Hamilton-based punk rock band, has applied for a $25 million insurance policy.

… "We see it as a necessity," said manager John Brower. "There's so much violence in punk rock you never know what's going to happen."

Paul Kobak: One of their gems occurred when Teenage Head applied for a $60 million insurance policy. We arranged to have a Rolls Royce noticeably present at the signing. The premiums were twenty thou a month or something like that. Well, all we did was apply. But it worked. Sure, it's cheap media attention, but you can't pay for that kind of exposure, and everyone was under the impression we were going to be the next big thing.

Deane Cameron: I really wanted Teenage Head. But my mandate was to find acts out of Canada that attracted globally. Well, in my mind they were of global quality. I felt that. I liked Frankie Venom. I thought he was very charismatic and could be a star.

And there were a couple of tracks I really loved, "Lucy Potato" and "Picture My Face," that I really thought were hit records. Even though they were a punk band and at the time it was thought that punk bands would not get on the radio as it were, to me those two tracks were incredibly commercial. So I felt that was the basis on which, if they could write those two — and I'd seen the show; I don't think it's any coincidence that Teenage Head was probably the biggest of all the punk bands; in my view they were the best — I thought there was potential.

At the time I was stationed here in Toronto working for Capitol Records, EMI of Canada as it was called then, but I in fact reported into the U.S. company. So I would do demos of Canadian acts and would submit them and the A&R team for North America, of which I was one, would vote on the acts that we wanted to sign.

On two occasions I took Teenage Head in and suggested that we sign them, and that would have meant a worldwide deal. And I couldn't get anybody to agree with me, really. Nobody voted along with me to sign. So they never got signed.

Stephen Mahon: I can distinctly remember [John Brower] telling someone from Capitol that the first thing we have to do is relocate the band to L.A. We were all looking at each other like, "What? *What?* We're gonna do *what?*" And looking back in retrospect, wow, what if they'd have said, "You know, you're right. Let's do it." Because then we could have given the L.A. punk scene a good shot in the arm, because that was before much happened there.

So who knows? It never happened. The guy just looked at John like, "As if. You guys aren't even getting a free pizza out of me never mind L.A." He tried, though.

We never did play in England, either. If I had a nickel for every time somebody said, "You guys should go to England, you'll be great there." But that's just Canada. There's a story there. It wasn't meant to be.

Gary Pig Gold: I guess the double-edged sword with Teenage Head is they've always been able to work.

Stephen Mahon: As soon as Jack came in, it was gung-ho. I remember we had a meeting and he had T-shirts and stuff made up. There wasn't really much left for Paul to do except maybe drive us to Toronto. Because when Jack took over, he just started putting a spin on things and we never looked back.

Right away he just started finding us work. Whereas Paul was just this guy from Hamilton who worked at a record store that had his heart in the right place, but he didn't have a black book full of connections.

Gail Manning: Jack was a great manager. Jack was a get-it-done guy. He knew everybody and he knew everything. He had been around for so long. He knew all the record company A&R guys. He knew all the presidents. He knew bankers, he knew lawyers, he knew all the media people. He had great relationships with all the radio station managers, all the top DJs. Jack just had a huge, extensive network of people that he knew.

Gary Pig Gold: The Viletones couldn't go out and get an agent and do a bar tour that early in the game, but Teenage Head could. I don't know if that's good or bad.

But they could be Teenage Head at the Crash 'n' Burn, too.

Dave Rave: I think that when Teenage Head played Crash 'n' Burn they *became* Teenage Head.

Gary Pig Gold: The best show I saw that band ever do was at Crash 'n' Burn. That was when Frankie was climbing across the heat pipes in the ceiling, but *this* was the time the pipe actually broke. It was like a running joke; eventually it's gonna break. Certain people would go across on the pipe. Frankie would always go, and this night it finally broke.

Ralph Alfonso: That was an amazing night, except Frankie smashed a hole in the stage so I had to charge them to fix it. I'm like, "Dude, we just spent a whole day making that stage; you've gotta pay for it." I think I charged them fifty bucks. He rammed his mic stand into the stage, and you can't do that.

Gary Pig Gold: They were just so tight; you could tell they'd been playing together forever in the basement. They had the jump on practically every band, only because they'd been playing that long.

Nora Currie: Teenage Head were much more aligned with the Viletones and the Ugly in their performance, but their music wasn't necessarily. It was more mainstream and more representative of the art scene, but they were accepted in both.

I loved seeing Teenage Head play. They loved what they were doing and they were all so cute and exciting and sexy. Frankie would climb and bend himself into all these shapes. They were all cute little skinny boys that could bring out a combination of desire and danger. Frankie was a bad boy playing in a not-so-bad-boy band. There was Steve Mahon with all this hair and he didn't really dress the scene but he was a great musician and really sexy, so Teenage Head could move through both camps of punk and were also their own thing.

[*Melody Maker*, July 30, 1977]: Frankie Venom is not a bad singer, after all, and when he chooses to get off his rear and or face the audience, he is a resilient and mobile stage performer. During one Troggs-sounding number, he climbed onto a platform behind the drums and swung from an overhead pipe onto the tiny stage area, nearly knocking over the drumkit, like some kind of crazed Tarzan.

Gary Pig Gold: CTV went down and filmed Teenage Head playing C 'n' B, but the camera was on my friend Martin E-Chord all the time, who was rolling around the floor. But that's understandable; that was the great thing about punk, especially in those days. The show was on the floor, too, not just on the stage.

And that's why we started those bands in the first place. It was like, "Well, *we* can do this." There wasn't much pretense, and there *shouldn't* have been any divide between the audience and the stage. Sometimes Frankie would just come down and start dancing in the audience for ten minutes when he should have been playing.

John Hamilton: Frankie Venom was the greatest front man in the history of Canada. If Canada ever had an Elvis Presley, it was Frankie.

Gail Manning: He had a great look. He developed that over the years, but he had charisma onstage. Frankie was just a natural showman.

John Hamilton: At the Crash 'n' Burn he was fantastic. He'd be crawling around on the pipes hanging off the ceiling and he had so much energy and he had a great voice and fantastic stage presence. In some ways he was the best front man I ever saw. In a lot of ways he's one of the greats. He was youth personified when I first saw him. He was the freshest thing.

Ross Taylor: The first time I'd ever seen Teenage Head was at the Crash 'n' Burn. I was really quite impressed with them ... But what was the most amazing thing of all was Steve Leckie in the audience stealing the show.

He was causing trouble; swinging his chain, giving the Nazi salute. It wasn't even a Viletones show, but of course he had to steal the attention. Frankie responded with a salute, too. The Nazi thing was a shocking thing to get people's attention.

Frankie Venom: Oh fuck. Once again, debauchery at its finest. Madness. They had that stupid amyl nitrate. They called it rush. Do a couple sniffs of that, before cocaine was real famous, or infamous, or what have you.

Tony Vincent: To me, when I think of the Crash 'n' Burn, it was this huge fire and all these kids throwing gasoline in it. It was totally out of control and it was like every single kid in that place was drunk. And I mean *really* drunk. There was no boundaries, nothing, you did whatever you liked.

Sometimes it's hard for me to describe it. You just never knew what was gonna happen next. All of a sudden you're talking to somebody then a fight breaks out; someone's throwing shit at the band; one of the guys in the band is attacking someone in the audience, like Cheetah Chrome would do. So it was chaos, it was chaos. It was *fun*, but it was kind of scary at the same time.

Stephen Mahon: Crash 'n' Burn was the best of all those worlds. It was how much fun you could have at a house party, it was how much fun you could have at a club, it was everything. There was no worry about bouncers beating us up. All those people were wanting the same thing: To have that same kind of music and to have the same kind of good time.

Gordie Lewis: I remember we were kind of saying, in a way goodbye, because by that time we were playing colleges and stuff. We were starting to really get some momentum at the time. We had management and I could see things getting kind of bigger, and I could see that we were going to move on.

Crash'n'Burn,
1977
/ photos by
Ross Taylor

16. Rebel unorthodox

Freddy Pompeii: We rehearsed in some of the worst places in the world, like this basement that Steven decided he wanted to live in. The people renting it to us didn't want anybody living down there but Steven lived down there anyway. He had this dog he called Spike and this dog shit all over the fucking place. It was up and down the stairs and all over the floor and outside the place and in the bathroom. If you weren't careful you'd step in it and drag it all over with you.

The landlord showed up and seen the dog and him and all this shit and he threw us out right on the spot. This was always the case; we were always getting thrown out of rehearsal spaces because of Steven. And he thought it was neat.

"Oh, it's neat, man, it's neat getting thrown out."

"Yeah? *You* find the next place then."

Sometimes it was like dealing with a three-year-old, I swear to God.

Mike Anderson: I remember there used to be a rehearsal studio on Queen Street right across from the psychiatric hospital, and they used to leave the door open sometimes so you'd get these people just walking in there. We'd be playing and some of them couldn't handle it; they just couldn't handle it they were so paranoid.

Steven Leckie / photo by Ralph Alfonso

Then there was the old Nash rehearsal studio. It used to be at the corner of King and Sherbourne I believe. There were these old drunken winos, party-all-the-time kind of guys around there. There were rats and the whole thing there. It had everything. Cockroaches. But it had lots of different rooms.

Then we went to Stop 8 up on the Danforth at Coxwell. It's an old music store. Then we had one on Yonge Street above a store at St. Charles. And then after that we didn't rehearse that much. We just played.

Freddy Pompeii: It was all hard with the Viletones. It was all difficult because we were always really poor.

But on the other hand, it was like the best time I've ever had in my life. Everything we did was fun. It was a big rush and it just felt so good.

I had the most freedom I've ever had in any band. All the hard times were worth it. Not having money, not having equipment, getting thrown out of rehearsal spaces, getting thrown out of hotels because of all-night parties in the middle of the winter. There were never any disappointments. It seemed like once it started rolling, everything came to us. We always played good gigs. We never had to play an empty house from the very beginning. The fact that we were so poor was the only thing that made it a drag.

All we wanted to do was play and we couldn't have anybody hold us back. Especially for Steven; he was the most desperate of us all. He was with one girl, and then he wasn't with a girl, and then he was on the street, and then he'd pick up some chick and that chick would take care of him for a while. That's how it was with Steven all the time. Steven was the real thing. The *real* thing. He was quite the sight to behold.

FILE magazine did a whole issue that we were the centre feature of, and *People* magazine also did a punk rock article and one-third of the article was about us. We were written up in Andy Warhol's *Interview*. Our first gig at CBGB's was written up in *Variety*. So it kept snowballing like that. Those things just kept happening and kept happening.

Anya Varda: I think the Punk issue of *FILE* really legitimized the scene here on a real international art level, because there was so much publicity about stuff coming out of London and New York. And Toronto was this little tiny town in Canada.

People tend to sometimes write Canada off as filled with Canadians who are really nice but don't really have an identity of their own; they just kind of are someone's little brother or sister that kind of tags along. And I think it showed to people that we didn't need to be validated by other people; that we really did have our own unique scene happening that was even more fully rounded than it might have been in London or New York. It wasn't just punk rock; it was art, it was fashion, it was all of the cool stuff that I think fattened the pot for us in a way.

Freddy Pompeii: Then we were offered a management deal with a company called Mega Media Productions. We met them as soon as we got back from New York.

What they did is they struck a deal with us. They rented equipment and they rented us a rehearsal space, so we didn't have to worry about that shit, and they paid us each a hundred dollars a week for at least that month. Included in the deal was a record. They put out our first single, which was "Screamin' Fist."

Tibor Takacs: Mega Media was a business partnership between three people who saw themselves as artists — myself, a director; Stephen Zoller, a writer; and Don Jean-Louis, a neon sculptor. The partnership was originally formed as a way to finance the post-production and distribution of our movie *Metal Messiah*. Once the film was finished and met with some success we decided to keep the partnership going to produce more films and branch out into other media: publishing, music, art, theatre, etcetera.

In 1975 Stephen Zoller and myself were producing a rock 'n' roll play. We held open auditions for a band that could be featured in the play. Steven Leckie presented himself as a lead singer with a band. We were impressed with Steven's punk posturing and enthusiasm for the play. We soon realized that the band Steven said he had, had just been hurriedly assembled for an audition and had not played together. We didn't mind this as long as everyone was willing to work hard to create a rock 'n' roll act.

After several auditions/tryouts we felt Steven and his group would be problematic. We gave them a place to rehearse and dropped by every once in a while. They were just not disciplined enough to work within the confines of a professional theatrical production. We loved what we were seeing and hearing, but it was just too raw.

It was Steven in front singing, an Asian guitarist, a Native Indian drummer, and a bass player. We reluctantly decided to go in a different direction.

It would be several years later that we met again. He now had a band, the Viletones, and they were meeting with some success and he was looking for management. I think Steven saw us as serious people who could take an artistic vision or dream and make a plan and carry it to fruition, as we did with *Metal Messiah*. I think he was looking for someone to run or organize this thing he had created and that was growing very quickly.

At first, the Viletones were the only group that had our interest. There was nothing else on the scene that was as innovative, original, and sincere. To me, music always had a cynical, obvious business aspect no matter how cutting edge it was. When I saw the Viletones for the first time, I felt and experienced something new: Pure performance art and raw emotion. They had this explosive performance style that I had not experienced before in any medium. You have to remember Stephen Zoller and I were very interested in the fusion of rock and theatre. Most of our theatre work was concentrated in this area.

The first time I saw them live I think was at the Crash 'n' Burn. They came off not as a bunch of punk kids, which other bands in Toronto were, but as serious, pure rock 'n' rollers with some kind of greaser, beatnik overtones. Other Toronto punk or art scene bands seemed suburban compared to the Viletones. I remember being impressed with how they looked. They wore black. I think Freddy was already losing his hair. He looked very mature to be in a band. They looked serious. They looked like a serious band. They looked beyond their years, so to speak, but they were extremely energetic and very intense and loud — and theatrical, of course.

Besides the show, I liked their sincerity, and Steven's drive for success. The guys in the group were all basically good guys. They were not posers.

They seemed very interested in our offer; at least, Steven did. I'm not sure they knew what it really meant.

Steven Leckie: The Viletones were part of their art scheme. They were smarter and older than us, and they knew that to add a little bit of us into it would help their currency.

Chris Haight: Tibor managed to keep a really close leash on the Dog.

The M&M boys were supposed to be taking care of the shows, but they had a money guy whose name was Don. He was an eccentric millionaire and he would dole out the expenses for the gear, keeping these guys out of jail, stuff like that. That's how it worked, but that didn't last long.

As soon as they made the scene the Dog couldn't run away with the cash box anymore. That was one change, anyway.

Freddy Pompeii: Mega Media was basically a stepping stone for us. The band was already together and playing gigs and we had made a name for ourselves.

They rented decent equipment for us. We got Marshall amps. I got a better guitar; I had an SG, a Gibson SG, but they got me a Les Paul.

The single was part of the deal, the three-song EP. After rehearsing for about three weeks straight we went into the studio.

Mike Anderson: Our first recording was just bang, bang, bang. We went through all the songs we knew. It was an actual studio at a farmhouse somewhere up around northern Ajax or Whitby or someplace.

Freddy Pompeii: The owner was this hippie. He was a typical '60s and '70s musician who was able to get himself a twenty-four-track.

The bulk of the material was written in a way where we would just start playing in a rehearsal space and we'd put a song together right there on the spot. Chris was a very astute songwriter already. With adding Chris to the group, it made it a lot easier for me and Mike to come up with stuff because we had a team going.

Steven never considered himself part of the team that was me, Motor, and Chris as songwriters, because he wanted to be *the* songwriter and he wanted to get the bulk of the writing credits; he wanted to make the money. It was a very greedy kind of attitude.

He was always like, "I came in with the idea. I was the one with the idea." And I would say, "Well, you came on with a couple of words but you had to have a band behind you to write the rest of it, so how do you explain that you were the only one writing this song or that you

were the only one with the idea?" He knew he was wrong so he'd just drop the subject. You could always tell when you had Steven and you were making sense to him, because then he would just stop talking and he'd go and tell someone else, "Oh those guys think that they're writing the songs but I'm writing the songs."

Chris Haight: It was like pulling teeth trying to get these guys together. Steven refused to even rehearse unless there were a couple cases of beer. That was, like, automatic. So he'd just sit in a corner and pout until it showed up.

A lot of crazy tunes were written like that, too. "Screamin' Fist," for example. He'd already consumed halfway through the practice, so he was tits up on the floor, right?

Mike Anderson: Steve was asleep on the floor when we were playing that.

Chris Haight: And they're going "Steve! Steve! Somebody's *paying* for this rehearsal space!"

I figured the only way to get him would be to just turn the bass up full and just hammer out the quickest, mind-boggling throb imaginable; start hammering on the floor where his head was. Sure enough, that was the intro to "Screamin' Fist," and sure enough, about two minutes into it, he just jumped right up off the floor and just started doing it.

Mike Anderson: He got up and started yelling, "Screaming fist! Screaming fist!"

Chris Haight: That's where that song came from.

Freddy Pompeii: In the beginning I had written a few songs of my own on a tape recorder, and I would bring them to Steven and say, "You're gonna be the singer so you write lyrics to these things." Sometimes he didn't know what to do as far as writing lyrics, so I would give him a few ideas and I'd say, "You take it from there."

All the rest of the songs, he could kind of fake them. So what would happen was we would go in a rehearsal space and he'd have an idea, like three or four words put together, and I'd say, "Well, okay, let's try this," and I'd string some chords together. Chris and Mike would follow me into it and we would start throwing ideas in between the three of us, and then Steven would start to get the feel of it and start dancing around and getting ideas. Then he would start writing lyrics. They were always different, though. He never committed anything to paper. Whatever he could remember, that's what he would sing. So it might be completely different the second time and the third time from the first time.

After he started learning how to write with us, then it became a group effort and we could rely on him to come up with something solid.

Ninety per cent of the material was a group effort. "We'll put a chorus here, we'll elongate this part; Steve, this is where you can improvise, you can do your show." There was a lot of improvisation going on, even onstage, because Steven would change things as he went. Not because he wanted to, but because he couldn't remember. But that was one of the strengths of the band, that improvisation; it was something that we were sort of forced to do and learned to do and it worked for us.

Steven Leckie: One of the most personal songs I wrote is "Never Feel Sad." And I'm pretty sure that that's about my mother, because I guess organically I'd like to deny it but I know that all those lyrics and all the misogyny is focused towards her because I didn't have that in real life.

There are times when I'm saying shit that Snoop Dogg hasn't come up with and it has to do with just dealing with, through art, the betrayal of the divorce and being abandoned and then being raised by a ne'er-do-well playboy father who lived in Montreal. He would pay the rent, but I was living virtually alone.

Bob Segarini: The Crash 'n' Burn was below, I believe, the Liberal Party headquarters and next to a place where they parked buses. A big, giant field of buses.

So one night Leckie's there drinking beer and he says, "Come on, we gotta talk." We go outside and he either busted a lock on the chain or we went over the fence to where all the buses are parked. He jimmies open a bus and we go sit in the back of it and we're smoking cigarettes and talking, and Steve is telling me about how nobody understands him and his dad's hard to live up to and all the normal stuff.

This is a guy that I had seen at the Colonial like a week before, rolling around in broken beer bottles.

Steven Leckie: I'm pretty sure that "Richard Speck" and "Screamin' Fist" are just for entertainment. "Never Feel Sad" I've always had this feeling is about my mom, I'm sorry to say. Or maybe happy to say.

You know what I'd love to hear right now? "Walk On the Wild Side." God, I love Lou Reed. I really love Lou Reed. That's fuckin' genius. So that was the most personal one — "From the corner of my eye where the blood drips from/Tears won't come no more." Yeah. Where I transcended feeling sad about it and I needed to observe myself; put myself in the sweepstakes of pop culture. When you throw your heart and your hat into the form of entertainment and art you're also throwing it into the middle of genius and people are thinking, well,

I've heard "Heartbreak Hotel" so it better be good.

I think really, lyrically it came very psychologically with the best insights my teenage brain could come up with. Even listening back to something like "Never Feel Sad" and understanding, "From the corner of my eye where the glass cuts deep/From the corner of my eye where the blood drips from/Tears won't come no more," you know where it came from? It came from pain. Punk, in the Viletones sense, came from pain and loneliness.

Caroline Azar: In punk, people were singing what they were suspicious of, from lint on their jeans to the state of the nation.

Steven Leckie: With the Viletones you had songs about Richard Speck, the serial killer. You had songs like "Possibilities," where you're introducing a new type of guy that doesn't get jealous on the stuff that a guy before would have. You're introducing things like "Screamin' Fist," and that's all coming from agony.

Chris Haight: Steven would be the lyricist, and I loved him because he used to come with some really mental things, right? But they were great. A lot of times he didn't sing the same thing twice, but it didn't matter because it was all interesting to me.

Freddy Pompeii: Steven was the least experienced of all of us, and he had to work the hardest. He would do stuff like, while he was recording the vocals, he would hold his hand out and hold a cigarette lighter underneath to burn himself so his vocals would be more intense. Now, I don't know if that really worked or not. It made him yell a lot, but I don't know.

We did all the songs in one take — "Screamin' Fist," "Possibilities," "Rebel."

Steven Davey had written a song called "Rebel Unorthodox." He brought it over to my place and I called Steven up and I said, "Come on over here. Steven Davey has a song he insists would be for us to record."

So Steven came over and Steven Davey picked up the guitar and played it. It was really faggy. The lyrics were great, but it was real sugary and it rhymed too much and it was too perfect. It was just like Steven Davey; just too perfect. And he says, "This is just for you guys. You guys could do this. It's perfect, it has the perfect title: 'Rebel Unorthodox,' what do you think?" And Steven and I looked at each other and went, "Uhhhh … well, maybe we'll use the idea but we don't think we can do the song the way you showed it to us just now." And he said, "Well, why not? What's wrong with it?" I said, "First of all there's too many chords." Ha ha ha. And he's going, "Oh, well, you could do it your way." I said, "Yeah, we'll do it our way. Of course."

So we kept the title and we wrote a completely different song, and on the record we even put a disclaimer saying, "Thank you Steven Davey," to give him some kind of recognition for the title. It was the third song on the EP and we just called it "Rebel." It has nothing to do with what Steven Davey brought over that day, but ever since then he's been telling everybody that we stole the song from him.

You know he was one of our biggest supporters, he really helped us out a great deal, but he did that with everybody and then he would turn on them after. It was a very faggy kind of thing that he did; just getting real pissed off at us and acting like a thrown-away lover. He's too much. Ha ha ha. He was very feminine in those days onstage. But I guess that was just the Bowie thing. We used to make fun of him to his face; not to get him pissed off or anything, just for a laugh, you know? And he would get very insulted so we knew we couldn't do that to him anymore. It was a drag.

Steven Davey: Did you know that I wrote the B-side of the very first Viletones record, "Rebel Unorthodox"? My name has never appeared on it.

On the first record it says, "Inspired by Stephen Davey." I wrote it at a party. The Cads had a party once and I wrote it for the Viletones on the spot. I came up with the title, of course. It's much too literate for Steven Leckie — the rebel unorthodox? I mean, come on. "I'm the boy born on TV/History's made a martyr of me." He wrote all the part about, "Fuck the FLQ" and all that, you know. I just went, "It's in the key of E."

Freddy Pompeii: The songs for the first EP were produced on twenty-four-tracks but they didn't have to use much because we just had guitar, bass, and drums. Most of the tracks were taken up on the drums and this guy really got our sound down on tape really easy, because we played really loud.

Usually when you play in a studio you don't play that loud. You play at a lower volume and then they crank everything up to make it sound louder, but we only knew how to do what *we* were doing. I played maybe two notches down from ten. I usually played at ten. I put *everything* on ten — the bass and treble. So yeah, it didn't take much time and it felt really complete and it felt really good to all of us when we got done. We were all really happy with it and we couldn't wait to hear what the finished result would be.

And of course Steven had to have a tape so he could run around and brag to everybody that we were recording our first single. He ran around to the bars with a little tape recorder saying, "Here, you wanna hear it? You wanna hear a new Viletones song?"

Because people were always challenging him because they didn't think that there was really a band, ha ha ha, so he always had to prove himself.

Freddy Pompeii / photo by Ross Taylor

Steven Davey, Crash'n'Burn
Scott Davey (Dishes) out of frame / photo by Ralph Alfonso

17. crash and burn

John Hamilton: We booked the Dead Boys because we really liked them. It was just a great summer. It was blisteringly, bloody hot all summer. It had to be ninety degrees all the time.

You would get in that room and there was no acoustic deadening in there. If you make a club with a lot of rugs and carpets and that kind of stuff it sucks up the sound, but if there's a club with no carpets or wood, it's like a concrete bunker; the only thing that sucks up the sound is people's bodies. So the Crash 'n' Burn, when we rehearsed there during the day, was like a big echo chamber. But when it filled up with people at night all of the sound waves must have just penetrated right into those bodies. There was nowhere else for the sound to go; it really got to people.

It was a physical experience being in there. It was boiling hot, people were wearing virtually no clothing and what they were wearing was usually soaked in beer. There was this light green, snotty-looking speed people were doing and it was really energetic and the music and all that complemented it. People would just go crazy; they really would go crazy. It reminded me of Stonehenge or some kind of voodoo ceremony.

The Crash 'n' Burn never could have happened if anybody had really been around in that area. Queen Street West would have been like the Portlands now. There was nobody around except us, so we could go crazy and make as much racket as we wanted. It was deserted. The only thing happening was the Royal Alex [Theatre], and occasionally you'd get one of those horse-drawn carriages that would come by the Crash 'n' Burn with a couple of tourists in it.

Sam Ferrara: Chris Haight kind of closed the place down. Outside there was a horse and carriage and the tourists would go up and down that street. Chris finds all these bags of old, stale buns, so we're on each side of the road. Everyone would just leave when the Diodes played — they'd go outside. It was their place, too. Ha ha ha. So then this bun fight started. We were whipping them at each other, and this horse and buggy came by and we started whipping them at people in the back and the cops came and they got busted.

Gary Pig Gold: Paul Kobak and I got a huge garbage bag full of stale buns. There was a Mafia bakery up on Hamilton Mountain, and he knew where to get all the day-olds out back. We took the ones we didn't eat ourselves on the drive in to the Crash 'n' Burn the night the Dead Boys were playing and just starting throwing them at everyone and everything.

Paul Kobak: I remember going down the alley across the street to behind Ed's Warehouse Restaurant and seeing these huge, clear, plastic bags filled with day-old buns, dragging a couple of them out, and starting a bun fight across the sides of the street. It lasted ten minutes or so and was a lot of fun. There were just a few of us playing around at first but then word spread inside the club and before you knew it, there were a couple dozen of us in the fray.

Gary Pig Gold: The minute Stiv Bators opens his mouth for their first song, he's pelted. But what does he do? Stand and fight back, or *spit* even? Nope. He makes a beeline straight offstage, actually kinda frightened.

True, those buns may have been a bit harder than if they were fresh, but I remember thinking, "Come *on*, Stiv! They're only *buns*. You're supposed to be young, loud and snotty, remember?"

Ian Mackay: When the Dead Boys played, I couldn't believe it. I was gonna be late, I was gonna arrive just before, and I came down to Duncan Street which was an empty, deserted street at night except for the Royal Alex Theatre, and we had a lineup right around the street to get in. We had to turn away *so* many people at the door.

Once they heard about the Crash 'n' Burn, it was like everybody in Toronto wanted to go to it. Then, *boom*, it exploded.

John Hamilton: But then you'd get some really brave people at the Crash 'n' Burn.

Crash 'n' Burn

15 Duncan St, Toronto Ont, Canada, M5H 3H1
(416) 368-4933

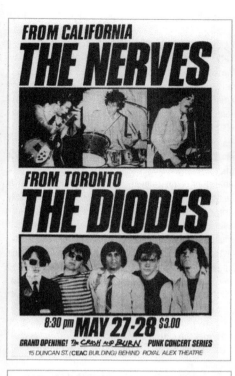

Diodes, Crash'n'Burn / photo by Carol Starr

You'd get some guy who came up tough and is now rich and he'd come with his girlfriend. He'd have on a tuxedo and she'd have on an evening gown and they'd look in the Crash 'n' Burn and say, "Let's check it out." Nobody would give them any flack; it was pretty open. Anybody who wanted to be there was there, so it was okay.

Gordie Lewis: The whole scene started to grow so quickly that now it was becoming a little more international. The Dead Boys played there. When the Ramones came to Toronto to play at the New Yorker they came down to the Crash 'n' Burn, so it was becoming a very hip place to be for the hundred or two hundred people who knew about it.

John Hamilton: The heat in that place in the summer was unbelievable. When the Dead Boys were playing and I think most of the stage lights had gone out, there was one big spot on the stage and the music was throbbing. Everybody was jumping up and down. I was standing back as the club manager, having to sort of still be on top of things, and I wasn't in it, I was *of* it. I was thinking, We've stripped civilization away here, the music and the beer; we've gotten down to the sheer pagan, Dionystic, bacchanalian revelry here.

Ralph Alfonso: The club was only open Friday and Saturday, but there's this whole myth that has grown out of it and none of us have gone out of our way to poke holes in the myth. If people want to think that it was open every day of the week and that Blondie played there, then so be it. Ha ha ha. Once these things take off it's like a train, you can't stop it anymore. But the reality of it was, it was only open on a Friday and Saturday and it was really just a warehouse space.

We had all kinds of people try to get gigs there but I'm glad we were kind of picky about how we wanted that space to be, because towards the end it got a little hairy.

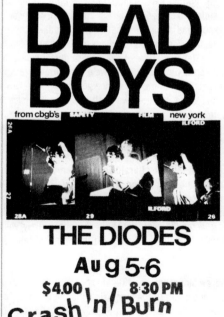

First and last concerts.
Diodes and Dead Boys photos by Ralph Alfonso
/ Nerves poster design by Dean Motter
/ Dead Boys poster design by Ralph Alfonso

As soon as punk got into the media spotlight, then all the hooligans came out.

Rodney Bowes: The media would talk about the violence of punk and the message and how outrageous it was and people urinating in public and fighting and blah, blah, blah, cutting themselves onstage. So it created this super myth.

The Crash 'n' Burn was starting to get out of hand. With the downtown people, there was kind of a code of ethics where this crap didn't really go on. And I remember at the end of the Crash 'n' Burn, all of a sudden it spread out to all the 'burbs. The press had gotten a hold of this and we got all these kids from Scarborough and Mississauga that actually *were* tough kids.

Ralph Alfonso: When we started the Crash 'n' Burn it was a sort of novelty thing and what happened was concurrently, of course, at the same time there was the rise of the Pistols in England. And I remember very clearly when the line was crossed.

There was some sort of airport incident where one of them threw up on somebody and that made all the wire services. Up until this point we all knew who the Pistols were and all that because we got all the English papers every week. We would get *Sounds* and *NME*, so we kind of *knew* what was happening over there. But as soon as the Pistols' misadventures started being carried over the wire services, suddenly this whole other thing happened where the sensationalist side – this whole novelty to punk and the violence and throwing up and *rebellion, man* – started coming across. And we saw in the club the initial audience, which was music people and people from OCA and more artists; suddenly they were getting pushed out by what I call the vicarious people – you know, "Hey, let's go down to the Crash 'n' Burn, beat somebody up; let's go check out these punks."

Gordie Lewis: I knew it was the last time that we'd probably be there. We'd go every Saturday. I remember a bit of forlornness that things were changing and probably for the better for us, but maybe not for this nice, cliquey, cozy little urban scene at the time. We're only talking about a couple hundred people really, and those same hundred people would be there.

But you could tell the suburban kids were all coming in; it was growing and it was kind of like, it's goodbye to this little thing that nobody else knows about. It wasn't a secret anymore, and that's what I kind of remember of the show that we played there.

We knew it was the last time, and it was a great place; it was a great time.

Rodney Bowes: I had a kid pull a knife on me in the club. It just got really weird. We were all like, "Man, this is getting really out of hand, this is actually now getting scary." Because these guys were coming down thinking, "We better bring guns and our knives because this is dangerous." For them, they were going to *downtown* Toronto, which was kind of the myth. It was a much more intellectual thing that was happening there than this brawling, but they came with that mindset.

George Higton: Maybe punk provided density, if you will, musically. It's a musically dense form; there's little separation of instruments, it's like a monochrome. At the time the word minimalist was tossed around wildly, with abandon. I don't know, it was always kind of a suspect aesthetic because as I said, given the sheer density you were not meant to distinguish necessarily anything particular in the sound. It was just a force. Experience it, don't judge it, don't criticize it. It's just a force; it just is. And when the song is over in two minutes the force will be gone from the room until we start the next song.

The mainstream media in fact would goad many of us, and the early performances were just massacred. Outright, savage hostility. So naturally you'd ask yourself, "Why is this universally hated?" But even in a larger mainstream publication, *Rolling Stone* for example, which people read at that point, you would actually read arguments that would say punk is a very interesting phenomenon but musically it doesn't stand up to Stephen Stills. It was these quasi-scholarly, quasi-critical put-downs. So we'd recognize there was some sort of cultural resistance going on here – "This is interesting. How can we push this? Can we force a confrontation?"

Media at the time was universally hostile. Strangely hostile.

Pop Music Beat, by Gerald Levitch [*Toronto Sun*, June, 1977]: Punk Rock seems to have captured the media's fancy more than the public's. Nevertheless, out of a sense of duty, I went to hear the Viletones, Toronto's most notorious contribution to the genre. They were playing in an ad hoc dive called the Crash 'n' Burn on Duncan Street.

Andrew McGregor: I saw Gerald Levitch in the Crash 'n' Burn one night. He was a music critic. He wrote for the *Toronto Telegram*, later the *Toronto Sun*. Well known in the '60s and '70s. He must have been about fifty.

He was there with a photographer and he'd come down to cover this weird punk scene thing. People were hearing about this. Everybody thought murders were going on there or something.

He comes down there and he survives the opening act. Then the Viletones come on. Steven Leckie was still Nazi Dog then, and he gets up there and starts reading the lyrics off a piece of paper. Anything went. So he gets into this tremendous row with the audience and finally he's in the audience and he's brawling with about three guys and I guess he's starting to get hammered. So then the drummer jumps over his drum kit and leaps into the audience, I guess to save the Nazi Dog.

At this point Gerald Levitch runs for the door, banging people out of the way, his photographer flying behind him with all his equipment trailing. That was it; he survived I think about two minutes of the Viletones.

Ralph Alfonso: You got people reading about the Crash 'n' Burn and we got exceptional coverage. The *Toronto Star* would put us in their listings. We got a big breakthrough in the *Globe and Mail*. I think Paul McGrath went to see Moxy, I think they were playing Massey Hall or something, and then he came down to see the Diodes play the Crash 'n' Burn. It was a really positive thing. I don't have the review in front of me now, but it was kind of like, "These young upstarts are going to give bands like Moxy a run for their money." So we could see the audience growing.

In a way, you just tried to feed more into the media to get more press. For Steve Leckie and the Viletones, it was exactly what they wanted — that was their image. So it only makes sense you want to do that even more if that's what it takes to get coverage. But it kind of hurt the scene in a way. On the one hand, it did get people out to your clubs; it did get people out to your gigs. But on the negative side of it, it maybe got the *wrong* people to your gigs and got the *wrong* people interested in what you were doing.

At the Crash 'n' Burn it seemed to exacerbate the violence and the negativity a bit, because now all of a sudden all these people looking to get into a fight started coming out. You were feeding this negative energy, which is not good. And that was the beginning of the end of the original punk scene.

There's only so much cutting up of yourself that you can do. Eventually you're going to run out of blood.

Rodney Bowes: It started getting really weird. Number one, we weren't used to being in clubs where you didn't know every single person there, and all of a sudden the Crash 'n' Burn had hundreds of people; you couldn't move in there, and it was all people we didn't know. So you felt like, "What are all these people doing in my house?" It was like a house party gone wrong.

Ralph Alfonso: At the Crash 'n' Burn there was a side entrance that you had to come in through, but there was also the front side of the building on John Street which was the doorway to the offices. That wasn't our entrance. Our entrance was in the alley. One night some drunken guy smashed his way through the front door and he comes into the club and I'm looking at him and I'm going, "What the hell did you do that for?" And he was like, "Oh man, punk rock!" So I ended up chasing him all the way up to the Rex Hotel and calling the cops on him, and it turns out he was on parole. I'm like, "Oh my god, is this what it's coming to now? We're getting *these* people coming down here?"

It's what happens with every movement, from the beatniks to the hippies; that moment when that crossover from these idyllic beginnings when it's kind of an inside thing where we're all part of a scene and we all know; we're kind of play acting in a way, like, "Yes, we're all looking tough and that but there's no way we're gonna beat each other up." But how do you explain that now to outsiders coming in whose only exposure has been this mass media, third-hand representation of it? So now these guys are coming in and they're looking for fights.

Every night there was a freight elevator that I would have to get to which took me up to the CEAC office, and that's where I would count the money and then I would come back down and take care of stuff. This one night, earlier in the evening, there was this famous guy called Johnny Garbagecan [who] I guess was trying to pick up somebody's girlfriend or something, and these guys were not into that. While I'm upstairs counting the money I heard somebody getting beaten and I'm like, "Oh my god, what's going on," right? So the next morning I sort of got out and walked around and I'm like, "Wow, I wonder what happened here?" And there was bits of this guy's skin around the wall. So somebody had just totally beaten the shit out of him.

John Hamilton: I remember Johnny Garbagecan getting beaten up pretty bad, but he almost went looking for it. He was a weird, masochist kind of guy. We were hosing bits of him out of the gutter one day at the Crash 'n' Burn.

Ralph Alfonso: That fight with Johnny Garbagecan was pretty much the last straw. Because the CEAC people, obviously to make money, rented the bottom half of the building to the Liberal Party of Ontario, who kind of tolerated what we were up to until they walked in Monday morning and there was this skin and blood on the wall.

Linda Lee: People were complaining about all the noise and beer and vomit outside.

Ian Mackay: We got closed by complaints. There were so many people that wanted to get in, they were so frustrated, they started to deface the outside of the building. There were mini riots. People were throwing stuff; people were bringing down their own beer and camping outside; the cops were driving by every night, so as it got more and more popular it became a magnet. Plus, the press started writing about it. You know, "I went to this great club last night and it's the hippest place to be right now in Toronto." That was before any of the local clubs were down there and before Queen Street was anything.

Ralph Alfonso: The Liberal Party wrote this famous letter to CEAC saying the group downstairs has got to go. The legal capacity was only really twenty or sixteen or something, and we were packing it with two hundred people a night. It was just a sweat fest. So of course you've got to fix the toilets, you've got to set up alarm systems and all this stuff — which somebody's got to pay for, so they were kind of going, "Maybe it's time you guys moved to another location."

It certainly wasn't about the money. I really wasn't interested in being a club owner or any of that stuff. Neither were the Diodes. So when it naturally winded down we kind of figured, let somebody else move it forward. We've done our bit.

Bruce Eves: I think it was a mistake in retrospect to close it, because no one anticipated the 1980s. The funding dried up and we were sitting on a cash cow. I mean, there were limousines lining the street. I didn't recognize anybody who was there, but there were rich guys there. I don't know if they were record executives or whether they were rock stars, but there was money and we could have just renegotiated the whole thing and said, "Hey guys, let's turn this into a money-making venture."

Ralph Alfonso: There was a very serious meeting about it and Amerigo Marras gave me the name of a realtor to find another location — actually an empty, small building further down in that laneway. But suddenly it's real money and all that stuff and we weren't really into being club owners. It was bad enough cleaning up after everybody at the Crash 'n' Burn.

And yeah, it was Amerigo pushing that. So it could be a case of Amerigo — he was the money man and owned the building, I think — forcing that. I mean, we weren't paying any rent so if a tenant came a-calling, out we go. Maybe he and Bruce were good cop/bad cop.

We were definitely on the radar of the city inspectors, who started coming in and making us buy exit signs, and bathroom checks and giving us an official capacity of thirty people, I think. Obviously, the crowds we were attracting and maybe using the alley as a public urinal might have gotten any number of people to get the city on our case, who knows? But definitely, the violence — the ex-con on parole who smashed the front door glass on the John Street side of the building was probably the final straw.

There may have been politics going on towards CEAC that we may not have been aware of. They were dependent on arts funding from various levels of government. Who knows?

William Cork: Crash and I, we were thinking that the RCMP ran the Crash 'n' Burn, or actually maybe CSIS to keep an eye on the new bunch of radical kids that were up-and-coming? Oh yeah, the Crash 'n' Burn was a set-up by the Liberal Party. It was the basement of the Liberal Party headquarters. It was no accident that we were there. That was given as a total fucking set-up. It was an undercover operation to watch potential subversive young people. I don't know whether the Diodes were just being suckered.

Ralph Alfonso: When people showed up the next weekend there was a sign I think that said it was over. I cleaned the stuff out and it was over. People knew it was over. We were kicked out and rightly so; it got really stinky there.

The last two weekends got really violent. I can't blame CEAC; they owned the place and one of their main sources of income was through renting the middle floor to the Liberal Party of Ontario and they were paying the rent. And I think everybody was getting really disturbed that the violence was ratcheting up.

Julia Bourque: When the Crash 'n' Burn was over, it was the end of an era. That summer was the best. And then the scene started to change.

Ralph Alfonso: It was very obvious that the tide had turned. It was just very bleak. I remember one girl just started crying that the Crash 'n' Burn ended.

Anna Bourque: The Crash 'n' Burn is a lawyer's office now ... I see the ghosts hanging around that doorway whenever I go by.

Ralph Alfonso: Some people got so deep into it that when the Crash 'n' Burn died it kind of threw a lot of people off kilter because it was like, "*Now* what am I supposed to do?"

Those Friday and Saturday nights were the centre of their scene. It was where you got dressed up to see your friends and you hung out after and you went for drinks at the Beverley or the Black Bull. But as soon as you pull that away there's no rallying cry anywhere, so I could see where it would throw people off balance.

Paul Eknes: I think back in those days, we weren't ready to be smart enough to let this carry on. I mean yeah, there was drugs, there was alcohol, but not lots and lots. We weren't stupid or anything, but any chance we got to make a difference I think we kind of blew it to tell you the truth. Because instead of having some smart people taking care of the finances or security or making sure that, "Okay, everybody drink responsibly"; how can you say that to a 1977 punk — drink responsibly? It's like, "Yeah!" *Bash!* And then things get broken and the cops come.

We just messed up like every other generation does, which is too sad because everyone talks about New York and London, obviously, first-generation punks; L.A., Oakland, Cleveland, second generations. But we were there. And as far as I'm concerned I think we kind of blew it.

Johnny Garbagecan, Nora Currie/
photo by Gail Bryck

Crash'n'Burn; Steve Leckie, Chuck Waxman (original Viletones manager)
/ photo by Ross Taylor

ParT Two: 1977-1978

Diodes sign with CBS, 1977.
Producer Bob Gallo is standing, middle.
Ralph Alfonso (far right) wears a shirt he
found on the floor at the Crash'n'Burn.

18. FRieNDLY BuT DeaDLY

Ralph Alfonso: After the Crash 'n' Burn everybody drifted off, and I sort of drifted off and I went, "I've got to figure out what I'm going to do now."

John Hamilton: When we realized it wasn't going to last as a club we basically thought, Well, we've got to get a record deal because other people are going to get in on this.

Freddy Pompeii: On the surface, as far as the newspapers and entertainment rags were concerned, it seemed that the art crowd and the rest of us were divided. But really the whole scene had a lot of camaraderie and all of the bands worked for each other; everybody was promoting everybody else because the *scene* was the most important thing. It wasn't like, "My band is the best and we're just gonna work for my band," it was like all the bands pushing for each other. That's really what was going on behind the scenes.

That division between art school bands is something that Steven started. He was a genius at getting promotion started, and that's how he promoted the Diodes. It was like the Beatles and the Stones of the punk rock scene. They were the Beatles and we were the Stones, and that way we pushed each other up the ladder. You have to remember, there's no such thing as bad press.

John Hamilton: We almost thought it was a divine right to open up the newspapers and read about ourselves. So you would get this panicked phone call in the morning that the Viletones somehow got in the paper. Or that they were playing CBGB's so you had to be there, too. But we were all friends, too, because we were all against the totally rotten, mafioso music scene that was just the scum of the earth.

So we had rivalry among all the bands. You could count on Steven Leckie to slag the Diodes in an interview. It was sort of like those guys in a boat that gets frozen in the Arctic. You're all there together, but you're getting on each other's nerves so you're fighting.

Steven Leckie: I don't think that division between the OCA bands and everyone else was there in the beginning but I know that me, I wanted to make a line between the two camps consciously. I recognized an opportunity to play off that Beatles/Stones–type thing. I think in the very beginning we co-existed just fine, like the Diodes and the Poles, but then I wanted a division because what was at stake was the audience.

In other words, they struck me as people that were playing for each other. I always thought Martha and the Muffins were playing for their peers at OCA, where I felt that the Viletones needed to perform for the disenfranchised; for the kids in Scarborough that I'd never know. I always looked to give most of my attention to the kid in the back row that I'll never meet. I would hear things, like a guy would tell me that he pawned his stereo to come down to see us and that would really, really, really touch me because I know what that's like. I know what it took me to have to sell as a kid to get tickets to Mott the Hoople or whatever at Massey Hall, so that really touched me that a guy would be that hardcore.

So I created a division and then really wrapped my heart and instinct around the East End bad-boy bands. But because of who I was and the way I was self-taught, I could still shuck and jive and have avocado and shrimp with Steve Davey at the Peter Pan, but really was just as happy having fish and chips at Langley and Logan.

Ralph Alfonso: Just so we destroy this myth once and for all, this is where the Diodes/Viletones rivalry comes from:

It comes from me backstage at the Colonial Underground talking to Steve Leckie about how he wanted me to be his manager. Meanwhile I said, "Well, you know, I'm already talking to the Diodes about managing them," and he's like, "You can manage us both." I go, "Yeah, that'd be cool. We could have the Stones and the Beatles and create this rivalry with you guys, because that's how the Stones and the Beatles did it." So I kind of talked about that and I said, "We can create some tension and get some good press and all that." But ultimately, I'm looking at this guy dripping in blood and I'm thinking . . . maybe not.

And then Steve all of a sudden starts doing all this stuff in the press and I kind of go, "Steve, what the hell are you doing?" When you're starting out, you take that stuff seriously. He goes, "What do you mean? I'm doing what you told me to do." And I go, "Right, ha ha ha, well, I wish you wouldn't because it's kind of a drag. Now we've got to slag *you*, so what's the point of that?"

John Hamilton: The rivalry was friendly but deadly. Up to that point, everybody knew that maybe one day there would be a record deal, and suddenly there was.

John Catto: By the end of the summer the people from CBS were floating around. They kind of appeared the day after the last Crash 'n' Burn gig. I don't think anyone from CBS ever actually made it to a gig there, but they appeared on the scene literally within two or three days of it closing. I remember this distinctly because we hadn't even gotten all our stuff out of there yet.

Paul Robinson [CIUT-FM, Greg Dick interview, 2007]: The Crash 'n' Burn closed on the 6th of August 1977, and I, the following week, was riding my bicycle by Toronto City Hall and heard this band playing. I started talking to this guy who said, "What do you think?" And I said, "They're shit," basically, and they were. He said, "Oh, I manage them," and I said, "Well, I'm sorry for you." I was just giving it back to him.

It was a progressive rock band called Zon, and Zon were signed to CBS. And basically he said, "Well, if you're so good then give me *your* demo." And so I did. And then we got a call.

Ralph Alfonso: It was really funny because no sooner does the Crash 'n' Burn close and we're kind of like, "Now what do we do?" that Paul is walking through Nathan Phillips Square and I guess some girls went up to him and recognized him and said, "Hey Paul, blah blah blah blah blah."

And unbeknownst to him, some managers were there and they saw this.

Paul Robinson [CIUT-FM, Greg Dick interview, 2007]: I can't even remember that. I think that's a complete myth.

Ralph Alfonso [CIUT-FM, Greg Dick interview, 2007]: These two girls came up and said, "Oh, you're Paul from the Diodes" or whatever, and that impressed them.

Paul Robinson [CIUT-FM, Greg Dick interview, 2007]: Okay, I remember some people that I'd never seen. But again, we were starting to get our name around in the press, etcetera, etcetera, and these guys actually saw these two girls come up to me and start being very friendly. Kind of, "Wow, you're in the Diodes!"

Ralph Alfonso: CBS Canada was looking for a punk band because they had all just come back from their convention in London, which was the famous convention where Elvis Costello busked outside of. Anyway, they saw the whole thing that was happening there and the one guy — I guess he's a visionary now, Bob Gallo — came back and goes, "We've got to get ourselves one of these punk bands because this is the future; this is what's happening." And the way it used to work then with record labels is they kind of preferred if one manager took care of all their bands, you know what I mean? They didn't really sign Canadian bands.

Paul Robinson [CIUT-FM, Greg Dick interview, 2007]: Ian and I actually went down there and played the demo tape for them on August the 8th. On August the 12th, CBS said they were interested in signing the Diodes.

Ian Mackay: By the summer of '77 there was a record contract out. CBS had discovered the Boomtown Rats, so CBS had examples of bands that were breaking in England and they were in Toronto. The Toronto-based CBS unit was looking for a band, they wanted somebody, and I think there was a race between Teenage Head and us.

Paul was the guy who was driving us to a conclusion on that contract, so in that respect Paul mixed with the right circles to make something happen and he was doing exactly that. He made it happen.

John Catto: We talked to CBS and they went, "Oh, we're really interested in you." That was it, actually. They came to us and said, "Here you go, this is it."

Ralph Alfonso: I don't know what I expected to happen with the Diodes when I became their manager, because I had never been a manager before so I immediately had all these dos and don'ts of what we should or should not do and stuff like that. But I knew what to do press-wise and I knew what to do promo-wise because literally, I had just graduated from Sheridan in journalism and there was a marketing course. So it was like, "Hey, I just studied all this. You guys can be my guinea pigs into media manipulation."

I'm certainly not a Malcolm McLaren type of person but it was great to put what I had just learned into practice, so I'd be writing proper press releases and things like that. It was all a great learning experience. There was no template, so we didn't know where the goal post was to aim the ball. It was sort of like, okay, well, first things first, let's establish ourselves and then second thing, establish a beachhead into the States and other countries and see where that'll take us.

The goal at the time was see if we can get a record deal. Towards the end we were fixating on that. There was never any thought of doing it ourselves because yeah, you could probably make your own single but then what are you supposed to do with it? The only way out of here, the only way you're going to spread your music and your message forward, is to somehow get a real label involved to give you the medium to disseminate what you're trying to do.

Paul Robinson: We were creating something that really couldn't be compared to anything else because there was nothing to compare it to in Toronto; there were only a few other Toronto bands. When we got signed, we kind of felt we always would. We never thought for a minute that we weren't going to get signed, from the very beginning of forming the band. It was just a completely naïve approach I think to music. We just said, "Well, doesn't *everybody* get signed?"

John Hamilton: I'm not sure exactly how the record deal happened. I think CBS Records had heard about all this punk stuff. Somehow CBS was given the mandate to find a punk band. It was a pretty tight-knit scene and gossip went around incredibly — in a day or so everybody knew everything that was going on.

I think CBS initially was interested in Teenage Head because they were more commercial; they were still a little bit of what CBS liked — they had long hair, or three of them did, anyway. So they were investigating Teenage Head and somehow Teenage Head blew it. I don't know what it was. Something about it didn't go down, something didn't jive, and then we got in there.

Paul Kobak: Nobody could believe it back then, that the Diodes actually got a contract before Teenage Head did.

The '70s was a real transition period in music. We heard a lot of Stampeders, Lighthouse, Edward Bear,

Guess Who and others because the CanCon rules had just come into effect. That meant radio stations had to play one-third Canadian artists. Guess what (not Guess Who)? There weren't enough Canadian recording artists to go around without listeners getting bored of the DJs. So the record labels started to experiment with picking up the wrong end of the stick and beating about the bush with it. That's how the Diodes got signed.

Ian Mackay: I think Teenage Head would probably say we stole their record contract. The manager of Teenage Head at the time, I think he demanded a large sum of money or didn't understand the way CBS operated. Whereas I think what Paul [Robinson] did, he was able to get introduced to the management company that represented a lot of acts for CBS, and so they in turn worked with CBS to introduce us.

Gordie Lewis: They decided on the Diodes, but I knew it would be okay. I just knew we were better and I knew eventually they'd come around. We were serious; we weren't kidding. I knew something else would come our way. Like anything, you feel rejection. But that's the music business.

Stephen Mahon: I remember being a little bit envious, like Wow, look at what they got. What happened to *us*?

Gordie Lewis: Really, at that point I was just glad they'd signed *anybody* because if you think about it, if this was England or the United States, all three bands would have been signed by that time. But they were so scared they thought, Well, we've gotta sign somebody so let's pick the most docile of the three punk bands. Which they did.

The Viletones were a true punk band, they were, but they were great. Teenage Head was a little bit more of a combination of things, a little bit more rock 'n' roll. The Diodes were definitely a little bit more poppier, cleaner, very inoffensive; they wouldn't get in anyone's face at all. So I think they decided to go with the cleanest of the three. But if it was England all three of us would have been signed. But in Canada, no.

Paul Robinson: I know why nobody else got signed at that point.

We were basically up against Teenage Head for the same record deal at CBS, and we got signed because we had management that wanted to play ball with CBS. Teenage Head had management that CBS didn't want to deal with as much, and that's basically the only reason CBS signed us instead of Teenage Head.

Warner Bros. sent about five of their A&R people down see the Viletones. Steven Leckie came out with all this Nazi costuming on and Warner Bros. just freaked and ran out the door. They didn't get it at all. They just went, "Oh my god no," and went running in the opposite direction. That's why the Viletones never got signed.

John Hamilton: Everybody liked the Viletones but it was like, "A hundred thousand dollars in *these* guys?" They were totally out of control. The only time they got together to practise was so they could all chip in on a case of beer.

Freddy Pompeii: CBS was looking to sign us, but the reason they went for the Diodes was that the Diodes were very business-like in their dealings. They were very easy to get along with. They were kind of ass-kissers, you know? The golden boys.

John Hamilton: The Viletones were this band that should never have worked. I don't know if they were ever really musical, but they certainly were morose, sad, kind of weird. Although they were actually musical sometimes, once Chris Haight joined. Freddy Pompeii had been playing the Gasworks as a folk singer, so he was actually a musician but he was a pretty terrible guitar player. He did make an interesting sort of noise and he did have a cool stage presence. Motor could play like one beat on the drums. Chris was a guitar player who was playing the bass. And Steve Leckie was this out-of-control guy who was a fantastic mimic. I remember seeing him do a David Bowie impression once that was so spot on; great actor.

But nobody was going to risk big money on the Viletones, so it came to us. We were well organized, we had the look, we had the music, we rehearsed every day of the week. We did it like a business. We would show up every day — not too early, eleven or twelve, have a couple of coffees, rehearse till about three or four, then go over to the Beverley Tavern.

So we got in pretty fast with CBS and they realized as soon as they met us that we were fairly straight-ahead, hard-headed guys who were a good investment.

CBS Records of Canada [press release, September 22, 1977]: Mr. Terry Lynd, president of CBS Records Canada stated that the work of the Marketing Division will establish the Diodes as the major viable force of commercial new wave music in this country.

Freddy Pompeii: They had everything together. They had all these songs written, they had publishing rights together, everything was copyrighted. Everything that had to be done in a business way was done.

And they had management already.

We were the biggest name, but we were also scary. We were very scary.

Chris Haight: I think they just took one look at us, did a three-sixty, and said, "I don't know, these guys are just too nuts." That's what I think happened. But I'll tell you, ours was a pretty hard show to top. Ha ha ha.

Ralph Alfonso: I doubt they would have signed the Viletones, knowing the A&R guy Bob Gallo, because of the names Viletones and Nazi Dog. CBS is a very straight label. The only game in town was the mainstream label, so if anything about you was un-sellable then you're in trouble.

Freddy Pompeii: Steven was the one with all the scars on his arms from cutting them up, and he always had a tough guy act that he played all the time. He always had this attitude like, "Don't fuck with me because you'll be sorry. You're fuckin' with the wrong guy." And these record executives didn't want to hear about it. It was, "We want a punk band but we want a punk band we can control."

We were never in the running for any kind of big contract with any company. Our reputation was just too fuckin' out of hand, and I wouldn't have had it any other way. I didn't necessarily want to be soaked up by a major label. I would have preferred longevity to being a flash in the pan, and being a flash in the pan is what happened to the Diodes.

Steven Leckie: It didn't matter that they got the deal because we had moneyed management on our own, so it didn't matter. And in the grand scheme of things historically speaking, the record you'd want on your jukebox is "Screamin' Fist," not the Diodes.

That's just the way it is. We were the ones. And that's a beautiful feeling. I sleep very well knowing that. I don't like having to marginalize my thinking on, well, if you had've played it straight you could have an SUV and all of that. But I'm a lifer. I'm a struggling artist and that's the way it is, and that's all fuckin' right. That's all fuckin' right with me.

Ian Mackay: We were immediately set aside. I didn't like it, but it happened.

What was interesting is there were two sides to that. There was the behind-the-back ostracism, you know — "Those fuckers got this contract, they don't deserve it, it should have been us, blah blah blah." But in social circumstances there was some sidling up and wanting to associate or wanting to be a part of this because we were the only band who had this. So people were ambivalent and kind of two-faced about it.

It's funny what happens. It wasn't the money at all; it was more the opportunity of a shot at fame, having something, and being unique. It was exactly the same in the art scene, too. The artists who were breaking big time were getting ostracized, but at the same time people were sidling up to them.

It was a bit of a surprise that it all happened so quickly. We weren't really ready for it, but it happened and we had to deal with it.

Ralph Alfonso: There was jealousy and we were quite hurt by it. I don't know why people are like that. It's not like we went around going, "Hey, we got a record deal!" I don't know where all that stuff came from. It's very bizarre.

But I don't think it separated us from the scene. The band all hung out with everybody. I don't know where that came from. I mean, you reap what you sow. We had the foresight to start the club and we hand-picked the bands that played there; everybody got to play there. I was doing my bit as a writer to put the scene on the map, which I think I did, and it got people to come up and check them out. It was kind of like, we'll give you the canvas and you do what you can, but if you're not going to take advantage of the momentum that maybe we've started, is that *our* fault?

Steven Davey: The Diodes were perceived from day one as bandwagon jumpers. And then especially when the Diodes got the CBS deal they were seeming like careerists.

They never played at the Beverley.

The Diodes seemed to be going, "Hey, we're punk too."

Ralph Alfonso: There's this misconception that the Diodes were a very calculating machine, but we weren't. We were just like everyone else. If thinking about your future is scheming, well ...

Money ruins everything – that's the problem. It's like as soon as there's a perception of success, there's going to be a divisive line.

Paul Robinson: In the beginning everybody supported each other, went to see each other, and everybody hung out together. But a divide really started to come when we got signed, partially because they were so jealous.

I know why we got signed and they didn't. It was a) We found industry people that helped us get signed; b) We were quite intelligent guys that were writing some very, very good music at the time that was very timely.

We had the material, we had a pretty good image, we had reasonable management at the time and that actually helped a great deal. Any band that's out there trying to make it, I would really say that the best way is

to have a good manager. You just cannot do it yourself; you think you can, but you can't.

Ralph Alfonso: The Viletones got more press than the Diodes did. I don't get it. I mean, we've all been aware of the jealousy towards the Diodes. It's been a perplexing thing all these years. Everybody had ample opportunity to take advantage of the scene. It's not like we schemed to get a record deal.

We just worked harder, I guess. We mailed out stuff everywhere. I was just working really hard. We all worked really hard, so if that's a sin so be it.

Freddy Pompeii: The Diodes were the first ones, but they were not a punk band like we were.

There were two completely different styles. We had a very aggressive style. We were fighting with the audience and cursing at them, and they were cursing back and throwing beer bottles at us. Never intending to hurt anyone, of course, just throwing them in between the personnel.

Ralph Alfonso: The Dishes should have had the first deal because they were first, but why didn't they? I don't know. When I interviewed Seymour Stein at CBGB's, he knew all about them.

Tom Williams: I used to go to Larry's Hideaway, I used to go to the Beverley. One of the favourite bands I lusted after was the Dishes, and I don't think they ever got a record out that I can remember. And I loved them. I thought they were a wonderful band, but I can't really remember why nothing ever happened.

Ralph Alfonso [*New York Rocker*, November/December, 1977]: Earlier this year, Sire president Seymour Stein came up to see them rehearse. He offered them the opportunity to play CBGB's with Talking Heads. The Dishes refused.

Steven Davey: The Dishes' manager was the only representative for Island Records of Canada. We couldn't even get *them* to listen to a demo. They said, "Oh, they won't like you, they won't like you." Meanwhile you're going, "Well, they've got Ultravox." The Canadian music industry was so lame back then; they just didn't want to know.

At the same time as this I was a rock critic for the *Toronto Star*. They would send me to review the Lettermen at the Royal York, and I'd totally trash it.

They would send me out to review Triumph, say, and I'd completely kill them in a review, then try to go into the record company with my tape the next day. It was the worst thing that could have happened.

I was just persona non grata in the majority of the Canadian record industry.

But it gave me great pleasure a year later to be able to call these same people up and say, "Remember that band I told you about who opened for me? Well, they're now signed to your label and they have the number six song in England."

We really did open a lot of doors. Somebody had to.

Ralph Alfonso: Yes, Steven Leckie should have had a deal by all rights. He was the right guy in the right place at the right time. But what happened? I don't know what happened. Maybe you shouldn't call yourself Nazi Dog.

I like him, he's a brilliant character, but ...

Jeremy Gluck: Say CBS had signed the Viletones and they'd made some sort of phenomenal debut album. It would have been a great relic now, there's no question about it. But no one in Canada would ever do that. I mean, the Pistols could barely get a deal in a way, much less the Viletones in 1977 Toronto.

Steven Leckie: The fact that we didn't get a big deal on CBS reinforced how fantastic we must be. It's like *The Hustler*, with Paul Newman. He's a pool hustler playing against Jackie Gleason. Jackie Gleason's playing Minnesota Fats, the greatest pool player of all time. Here's the line: Paul Newman's character says to him, "You know, Fats, I'm the best, and even if you beat me I'm still the best." That's that James Dean way of thinking, that because I'm a failure is proof of my greatness. And that's a Viletones logic somehow.

Freddy Pompeii: The Diodes were the good guys and we were the bad guys. The rest of us they didn't want to touch.

Chris Haight: The Diodes were approachable and they were a safe bet. But I defy any of them to say that getting signed didn't change them.

Paul Robinson: I don't think it ever tainted us in any way. We were never pretentious, we were never posing, we were never anything. We just were what we were, and again very lucky to be doing what we were doing when we were doing it. Which is why we got signed and nobody else did.

When we got signed we were off. For Ian and myself it was like going to the next step in terms of almost being a performance artist and in terms of understanding all of the marketing and graphics involved with being in a band.

Ian Mackay: It wasn't until we started picking up guys like John Hamilton — who was in the music business — that we realized this was a very different thing.

I was taking courses at the Ontario College of Art which were heavily influenced by Marshall McLuhan's writings. I remember Dean Motter, who was teaching us; I was asking him if I should do this Diodes or not, and he said, "Think of it as a media probe. You can go and be a rock star, but think all the time that you're probing into the whereabouts of the rock business."

But it didn't happen. It was too much, it was too big; we became part of the business, not us analyzing what was going on inside it. It might have appeared that it started out that way, but it was not that at all. It became something that was bigger than us, and we had to catch it because it was breaking faster than we were.

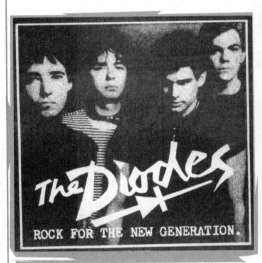

ROCK FOR THE NEW GENERATION.

ABOUT OUR ARTISTS

THE DIODES

Canada's premiere punks came together a year ago at Toronto's Ontario College of Art. In twelve months THE DIODES have built a massive new wave following, have operated "Crash 'n' Burn" - Canada's only punk rock club, have stunned audiences at the celebrated CBGBs in New York, and have signed with CBS Records for world-wide distribution.

"Red Rubber Ball" is their killer debut for CBS, the first single from LP. It's monolithic music delivered in true hard rock brawler style.

THE DIODES deliver pure unadulterated raw power. This is hot.

Mickey Skin, Jimmy The Worm (middle) / photo by Gail Bryck

19. from hell

Freddy Pompeii: Crash 'n' Burn was the place to go. After that there would be a few speakeasies that would have punk rock, but mostly it was bars we had to go to and play, and that limited us to people over twenty-one.

Anna Bourque: Every new venue became, "Maybe this will be the new Crash 'n' Burn." It was in little bits and pieces.

Nora Currie: And for so long after you were trying to get that joy back, to reclaim that moment.

Mickey Skin: There were places that we would get for a few gigs, and when the club owners realized we trashed the place they would never let us play there again. It was like floating.

Mike Anderson: There were some strange things that did happen. There was one night that we played at the Town Hall, of all places. I think it was Jimmy the Worm, Chris's brother, who got us in there. He did a lot of booking with bands back then. He's not alive anymore. He got us a gig there and called it The Postal Employees Annual Springtime Dance or something like that. There was Teenage Head and us playing together.

The place was immaculate, full of antiques and all kinds of things. Behind us on the stage was this great big window with all these nice little panes. There was a crucifix — I don't know where it came from, this big heavy crucifix. Somebody threw it and it broke into a million pieces. I turned back and watched it crash through the window, and the moon was coming through. It was one of those eerie nights with a big moon and everything, and it crashed the window into a million pieces. "*Oooh* ... sacrilegious or what?"

Chris Haight: What's memorable about Toronto is it was honest to play here. Nobody would pad your psyche to make you feel better. If you stunk they told you. And unless you couldn't handle the truth, then I don't know what the hell you were doing. But yeah, I would say it was a pretty honest place to play.

Blair Martin: The first time I saw the Viletones was at Yonge Station and it was okay. But I think around the same time I saw Thin Lizzy and Queen, and I was seeing other concerts that were starting to seem like rip-offs. I was starting to go to these big shows and I would think, Well, you know that drummer in Queen was pretty shit and if the drummer in the Viletones was kind of shit, well, *this* guy was kind of shit, too. Then I realized, of course, if you're the drummer in the Viletones and you're at Yonge Station, that's a much harder gig than being the drummer in Queen and being shit. Because out of that whole crowd of however many people they could squeeze in [Maple Leaf] Gardens in those days, it doesn't matter if you're shit, they don't know.

But if you'd go and see the Viletones or one of those bands, you realize that's a hard time going and playing in a fuckin' bar and being good and giving any kind of illusion.

Freddy Pompeii: We got kicked out of Yonge Station once. Tibor Takacs got us a gig there.

They had the bright idea that they would start booking us in all these mainstream Yonge Street clubs, which hired metal bands, rock bands. So I knew that it wasn't gonna work. I had been through that when I was eighteen with this band I was in that had a recording contract in Philadelphia. I knew the downfalls, the pitfalls, and I knew what not to do. I chose to be a showcase band, which was you put a show on and you leave. You don't go in there and play all night.

So they would book us into these bars where you had to play like three sets, and we didn't have enough material to play all those sets so we had to repeat. Steven was out of his element. There were all these straight people and older people wondering what the fuck he was doing.

"Boogiemen" [*Toronto Sun*, November, 1977]: It seemed the owners of the club warned Nazi Dog... to stop blowing his nose on the front tables of the audience.

Freddy Pompeii: We were booked there for a week. After the second night the lady who owned the place called us downstairs and she says, "I'll pay you guys for the rest of the week but I don't want you playing here anymore."

"Why not?"

"Well, the cursing and the spitting and whatnot."

And Steven said to her, "Well, okay, we won't play here anymore but it's not because you're firing us. It's because we don't like playing here."

Steve didn't do anything to get us kicked out; we got kicked out because of who we were and who the people were in the audience. They were all just drunks. Working class people and drunks who would drink until closing time and basically ignore the band on the stage. The band would play to a full house but with no response, so it wasn't for us. I think Tibor, who was our manager at the time, our caretaker, saw that right away and he stopped trying to book us in those kind of places.

Mike Anderson: Back then you had to make your own venues. It wasn't like it is now. I think it's a lot more diversified now. If you wanted something then, you more or less had to create it yourself.

Chris Houston: The funny thing about the early punk rock gigs is most of them were in failing discos, so you'd have a bunch of people with safety pins through their clothes and ripped up and green hair in shag-carpeted disco-rama land.

Tibor Takacs: David's Disco happened to be one of the locations in our *Metal Messiah* film and we made a deal with Sandy, the owner, to run the place as a punk club during the week.

"Punk Rock: It's Dying in Toronto Before It Was Born," by Don Martin [*Ryerson Review*, September 23, 1977]: "It's just a fad," said Sandy Leblanc, manager of David's, which is open to punk rock groups every night until midnight, when it becomes a gay disco. "I would be very surprised if it lasted another seven months before it fades away completely.

"It can't survive for the simple reason punk rock is not socially acceptable. At the moment, we are the only punk rock club in the city because no other managers will tolerate them."

Freddy Pompeii: It was a gay disco and it was losing a lot of business, so they opened it up to the punk rock scene. It was a really nice place to play because it was our room. We, the Viletones, had our own dressing room there, we could sit in the control room and play whatever records we wanted to, and we could bring in any band that we wanted to but we became the house band.

It became the gathering spot, and everybody had a place to go. It was open seven nights a week and they would have shows. It was the next place after the Crash 'n' Burn that served liquor where bands could come in and play whatever they played. They would book, like, three bands, four bands a night and the scene really blossomed when that started happening.

Wayne Brown: David's I liked. It was kind of small. It was on two levels. It had a staircase in the middle that went around to the second level and a statue of David in the middle of it. The statue of David was two levels high, so when you were on the first level you were at its head and down below, in the pit, that's where the bands played.

Chris Haight: I remember when they first opened up. They had the statue there with the water flowing out and the whole shebang. Everything looked just so brand new.

About twenty minutes later there were cigarette butts in the pond and beer bottles; guys were doing poppers — some kind of shit that they broke and inhaled and got them really, really zonked for like thirty seconds.

Dave Elley: David's was the amyl nitrate capital.

Chris Haight: Plus, David's was that whole gay thing on a larger scale. That aspect had been speckled here and there, but this was the full-blown thing; this was the real deal. There was a restaurant part, too. When I went over there to get something to eat I could see all the gay cops. I thought it was kind of educational for me.

Dog was the DJ there for a while, too. It was like a place to hang out in between gigs.

Gary Pig Gold: I remember hanging at David's after a Saucer show or something, waiting for Imants to drive us back home to the suburbs. I wandered upstairs and on came — at full blast through this really good sound system — "I Feel Love" by Donna Summer, and then "Trans Europe Express" by Kraftwerk. Quite a change of pace from "She's a Dog." But I thought *this* was very, very interesting, too.

I don't think Steven Leckie was manning the turntables that particular night, though.

Ralph Alfonso: There's a whole gay undercurrent which permeates not only Toronto but the entire punk movement. When you realize the punk uniform of that whole leather jacket and jeans and things; that's completely lifted out of the Christopher Street gay scene.

Nip Kicks: There were things like David's that were absolutely typical of the Toronto punk scene. We were on the fringe — as on the fringe as the transvestites, almost.

David's Club was a gay palace, and then there are all these street kids coming in. At midnight there'd be this switchover and what was great about it was everybody was cool. Nobody looked at each other as freaks. There'd be these transvestites that would be having a laugh with us, batting their eyes and bouncing their phony boobs, but it was all in fun, it was all interesting fun. That's what I liked most about the scene, myself, was just seeing that everybody's welcome.

Michael Dent: My mom told me in April if I didn't have a job by June when school ended, I'm out. School ended and she said, "Do you have a job?" I went, "No."

"Out!"

So I was on the streets. I knew nothing about welfare or anything like that. It was very, very bad but a great learning experience. I stayed all over. I even lived in the vaults above David's for about a month. They had a cold storage thing. It used to be for fur coats and stuff, all these vaults. Sandy was always trying to get in our pants. It was a very bizarre time back then. Absolutely bizarre times.

Alex Currie: I never went to the Crash 'n' Burn, but I remember going to David's. That was neat. I'd never really hung around gay people. Punk had a lot of asexuals, transsexuals, and everyone seemed to be getting it on but me. Ha ha ha. I mean, I had this huge red-haired Afro, albino skin, and this goofy high voice. I thought that would work.

Around that time I hit eighteen and I was getting sexually curious, and I just wondered what a dick would taste like. So I tried that. It was salty, that's all I could tell you. It was very salty.

Freddy Pompeii: It was six months after the Viletones had gotten started and we were playing at David's, and I see this kid with this crazy Brian Jones haircut in the audience wearing aviator glasses. I said, "Are you Jackie?" He says, "Yeah, man, I'm Jackie, how you doing, Freddy?"

Then he says, "Aw, man, can I get back into the band? Can I please get back into the band?"

"Sorry Jack, but the position has been filled."

"Oh, really, man? I can play way better than that guy!"

"No, sorry, man, the position's taken."

And that was the end of Jackie. I never saw him after that.

"Punk Rock: It's Dying in Toronto Before It Was Born," by Don Martin [*Ryerson Review*, September 23, 1977]: "Punk is too violent for most clubs because it can incite riotous behavior among its followers, causing considerable damage," (Sandy Leblanc) said. "I am rather strict here. I have a contract with every punk rock group that performs here. They cannot leave the stage to mingle with the audience while performing, and I pay them after the gig and deduct any damages they have caused during it."

Don Pyle: I remember there was this guy that worked there named Mr. Shit who ended up being in a band called the Hate. He was this short little guy from the punk rock scene who was the waiter in this gay bar. He had a T-shirt that said Mr. Shit across the front.

Margaret Barnes-DelColle: *There* was a weird character, Mr. Shit. He would get you to spit in his hand and then he would eat it. Now what was that about? All kinds of stuff like that happened around you all the time.

Freddy Pompeii: Mr. Shit was just this little short guy with a shaved head, or a real short haircut, and he was like a scene maker. He wanted to be in a band so bad; he was always talking about his band this and his band that, but he never had a band.

Mr. Shit would get on his back in front of the stage with his mouth open and Steven would be spitting into his mouth from five feet above. I thought that was gross. Some of the things Steven did I just did not find amusing.

Gerard Pas: The wackiest shit that I saw that really turned my crank because it was so wild and bizarre was at David's. I remember Steven Leckie, or Nazi Dog, pissing off the edge of the stage and there were people dancing under his stream of urine. It was disgusting. Some people with a fetish might say it wasn't that disgusting, but I'd never seen anything like that and it was disgusting. And I liked that. Not because I'm a kinky fetishist, because I'm not, but that was the kind of thing you'd see there.

If you were my daughter I wouldn't want you to have go through such depths of despair to realize your pain had meaning, but there were a lot of people in a lot of pain who were all screaming collectively. It was once described to me by a psychologist that sometimes it's really important as you're developing to realize you're not alone in your pain, and that there are other people that speak that same language and understand it, just by the numbers. So those numbers there conveyed to me that there was this underlying sense of pain, and that my pain had meaning, because I was watching all these other people with similar types of their own various angst or fears. That's what would have titillated me, because of my interest in suffering and trying to understand it.

And Steven Leckie; I mean, he was just totally fucking out of his mind. In fact, I liked that so much that I started hanging out with those guys. I liked his madness enough that he was the kind of person I wanted to get to know better. Go figure.

Nip Kicks: With me, despite where I ended up fitting into the picture, I don't really like blood and gore. It doesn't appeal to me.

I think it was David's Club. There was the buildup of before they came on. The darkness of the club; there was almost a gothic atmosphere in this gay palace but it was all dark when the punks were in there. It was kind of surreal. And I remember the suspense of Steve coming onstage and this almost dread of, "Uh oh, what's going to happen? Is he going to cut himself?" And there was that sense of not wanting him to, but you couldn't not watch. It's a bit like getting ready for a roller coaster ride or something like that.

Wayne Brown: I can remember the second time I saw the Viletones was at David's, and it was like a war. The audience against the band, and at one point Steven was holding a round table like a shield because there were beer bottles flying at him left and right and all I can remember from that night is the sound of breaking beer bottles on that table. They were literally hiding from an audience that wanted to kill them.

He was such an antagonist. He would antagonize people until they just broke. He'd get on somebody or a few people, at almost every show I saw him do in those early days, and just rip into them and make them want to hurt him.

"Punk Rock: It's Dying in Toronto Before It Was Born," by Don Martin [*Ryerson Review*, September 23, 1977]: After only five weeks of allowing punk rock to be performed at David's, Leblanc is beginning to have his doubts.

"Let's face it, I'm in it for the money," he said. "As soon as the groups lose their drawing power or if they get too violent, they're out the door."

Freddy Pompeii: It was a definitive time for us at that point. It was *our* time. It was *our* club, and we were getting more popular by the day.

*   *   *   *   *

Nora Currie: Mike Nightmare went to the same high school that I went to and was friends with my brothers. It was a Catholic school and it was out of the city; we had to travel a fair distance to get there. One morning my brother started to notice there were all these abandoned cars in the parking lot of the high school. Mike had two or three brothers and they were all wild. My brother was like, "What the fuck? What's with all these cars here?"

The Mulroney boys stole a car every morning and drove to school and then just left it there. Ha ha ha. They weren't old enough to be driving, either. You couldn't make that stuff up. They were expelled the same year my brothers were expelled.

So I knew Mike. They formed the Ugly. I guess they saw themselves as the main competition for the Viletones and they were gonna be meaner, badder, and better than the Viletones. And in terms of the nihilism and the rebel bad boy, they won hands down. There was no contest.

They came on the scene later and there wasn't enough space for two bands like that, so there was a competition. They were better musicians but that wasn't an issue in so many ways. It was a very small scene and there just wasn't room for two bands of that nature, so it was competitive.

Tony Vincent: I'm from the East End — that's where I grew up. It was kind of like a slum area. There were a lot of scraps, a lot of kids fighting, gangs and stuff. But anyway, I met Mike Mulroney in St. Dunstan's — that was my Catholic school. The first day I met him he'd just got out of St. John's — that's a reform school. We just started talking. He was a bad kid, too, but he wasn't *that* bad. He'd get in trouble for stealing clothes and things like that. I guess it's the same now. Kids who were bored got into trouble.

Johnny Garbagecan: Mike was a character, I've got to admit. I grew up with him and Tony. Mike had a bunch of brothers and Tony had a bunch of buddies and we all had this little gang out in the East End of Toronto. We were nasty. Actually, we were mostly into drugs. We were all speed freaks for a number of years.

Raymi Mulroney: Growing up in that school, St. Dunstan's, I remember Mike and Tony used to tease each other and that; stand in the corner and laugh at each other if they got in trouble. It was a Catholic school. The only people in there were Italian and Irish and it was run by nuns. That's the kind of upbringing I had.

Mike was the wild one. He had sword fights with the teachers. If a teacher came up with the pointer and slapped it down on the desk, Mike would be doing sword fights and pick up a ruler. Ha ha ha. He was a wild man.

Johnny Garbagecan: Back in the '60s, the little clique we had in the East End used to go down to the Gasworks and get into fights on purpose. We used to hate the mods, and every time we went down to the Gasworks we were basically guys with leather jackets and would get into fistfights with guys who wore that other stuff. It was just something to do, you know? Friday night we'd have enough money to go downtown and get drunk and fight.

Tony Vincent: I started playing in bands when I was like, fifteen, sixteen. My first band was a band called Vacant Lot, then I got into another band called the Praying Mantis. I met Sam Ferrara and we started this band called the Marquees which was all British rock 'n' roll. We were together for five years, we knew one hundred and fifty songs, and we used to play every night from nine till one in bars. We all had black leather jackets, black denim jeans, and this was before the Ramones.

At that time there was bands like Goddo, Rush, Triumph, which we all hated because you needed thousands and thousands of dollars and lighting and a PA – that's the only way you could get into playing the clubs. So what we did was we rebelled against that and we started using our own equipment.

Sam Ferrara: I was in a band called the Marquees; this is way before the punk days. We toured five years straight – Northern Ontario, Southern Ontario – and the drummer and I got really tired of it and started writing our own stuff. We hadn't even heard of punk yet; we just started writing our own stuff behind the other guy's back because we were gonna quit.

Tony Vincent: The lead singer started getting commercial. The music we were playing got lost. We had to play Peter Frampton, Aerosmith.

Johnny Garbagecan: I worked with Sam and Tony for five years. We travelled around on the road with another band. To be honest with you, I was wanted by the police and it was the easiest way to become invisible because I was always moving around.

I knew those guys through drug dealing, Tony, anyways. They had lost their roadie – I think the guy went to jail or something – and they asked me to come along on a tour. I went and didn't come home for five years.

Sam and Tony had been together at that point for seven years, and the Marquees was an excellent band. Except they did very stupid things. The music scene's a very tight scene, and if you get blacklisted in the agencies that hire in these clubs – because that's where the money is when you're first starting to play – you're screwed.

And the lead singer unwittingly picked up a girl one night who was under sixteen. Her father owned the club that we were playing in that night, so the next morning this idiot gets a phone call from this guy going, "Where's my daughter?" Kevin thought it was funny.

Well, they never played again as the Marquees. They had to change their name. They couldn't get a gig. Once you were blacklisted by the unions you were toast. So they changed their name to Lightning, and that didn't go nowhere because by then everything was falling apart.

Sam Ferrara: Before I was into punk I was a rebel. Same with Tony, he was always a rebel. Kevin, our singer, was not; he was more of a square. He broke my nose, too. While I was driving.

We were on our way up to Thunder Bay. It was a pretty icy road, and we'd just finished rolling a truck and I'd landed outside standing up, facing the truck. Johnny Garbagecan was our roadie back then. So we had this other truck on the way to Thunder Bay and Kevin's going, "We're gonna be late to the gig, go faster, faster, faster." And I looked at him and said, "Who's driving here?" And all of a sudden *wango*! The side glass is filled with blood. So I pull over and Tony started driving. That's one of the reasons why I quit that band.

Actually, I quit that band right on the highway. I said, "Pull over, I gotta piss." Went to the back of the van, got my bass out, my suitcase, crossed the highway and got a ride just like that, back to Toronto. And they must have said, "Where the hell did he go?" I was gone. They didn't even see me. I got a ride with the first car, which was great. If you're gonna quit, you gotta quit good.

Johnny Garbagecan: To be honest with you, I was sick and tired of travelling on the road with bands that were going to make it – *next* year. It was always everything's tomorrow. We had an accident, a couple of them, when I was with this band and I just didn't want to travel anymore. We said, "That's it, we're not going north of Bloor Street." So we stuck in Toronto.

Raymi Mulroney: I had the privilege of being born into an Irish Catholic family with Mike Nightmare as a brother, ha ha ha. No, he was great. He was like the backbone of the beginning of the music scene in that era. He was always there for people.

I don't know how to put it. He gave people a chance. He'd give you the shirt off his back – that kind of guy. Mike influenced me to learn how to play guitar. He had bought a guitar and he was writing and that, singing along with the New York Dolls and Iggy and Bowie – the major influences for me as far as big name acts and stuff. Mike really had a lot of things going.

I don't have much education but I've done every-thing, I'm a jack of all trades. And like I said, music is *one* thing – I like to write. I've always liked to write and draw. Our family, we weren't big writers and we didn't have a radio going in the kitchen at all times. I grew up with the old scene, the old Frank Sinatra. My folks influenced me a lot and I'm going, "What the …? How come I ended up in a punk rock band listening to that kind of stuff?" But then I had Mike and I had two other brothers older than me – I'm the youngest of four – and they were all rock 'n' rollers, real into fashion. Put it this way: They could start their own fad. That was the type of brothers I had. Everybody was a good dancer and we were good pool shooters. We're very intuitive people, and Mike, he was a wildcat. He said, "Hey, what's this punk rock scene going on?"

We'd gone to see the Viletones at the Underground. Leckie was doing the whole Iggy thing, cutting himself and smashing bottles off his head and whatever.

It used to be just an old-timer place; drink draft down in the basement of the Colonial. Nazi Dog had a swastika flag hanging off his microphone stand. This old guy walked by and he went to rip it down, because I guess he was part of the war and didn't like it. And he pulls it away and goes into one of his songs, what was it, "Possibilities," ha ha ha. That was pretty heavy.

Right away, Mike turned to me and said, "Let's start a punk band," but he had somebody else in mind for the guitar player. Then Mike introduced me to Nazi Dog.

I remember Mike picked up a chain, about fifteen or sixteen links, a real thick chain. Leckie was wearing it around. He goes, "Hey, check this out," and he puts it on the table. Mike went, "It's cool," and hits him right in the face with it. Picked it up and hit him with the chain. That's how I met Leckie, ha ha ha.

Hey Leckie, if you're hearing this, even though Mike's dead, the battle's going on, the battle of the bands. It was always like that, "Who's the coolest?" But that's what the scene was all about.

Sam Ferrara: Mike Nightmare used to be our roadie in the Marquees, so we just got together and started writing.

Tony Vincent: Mike approached me and says, "Look, let's start a band together. Let's call ourselves the Rotten." I said, "Sure, let's do that."

Raymi Mulroney: Sam came to call on Mike one day. I seen this long-haired, black-haired guy. He goes, "Is Mike coming to rehearsal?" or something like that. He was wicked. It was like wow, who's this freak? Then he cut his hair down a bit for the punk scene.

Then the guitar player quit, Brian Vadders quit, so my brother said, "Hey, I got a guy for ya: My brother. He plays guitar."

Tony Vincent: Raymi probably played guitar for six months before he joined us, and Mike was always on his case about what he should do – "You can't keep up with us, your guitar's out of tune." It was mostly Raymi and Mike arguing; well, you know, two brothers in a band, that's going to happen. Mike was very hard on his kid brother. Me and Sam were okay; we'd played together for a long time so we were pretty tight.

Sam Ferrara: We used to call ourselves "hoodlum rock" way before we started hearing about punk.

Nip Kicks: I think the Ugly were funny because they had a certain respect amongst the scene for their honesty. A lot of people looked at them as being the quintessential … well, we used to call it hoodlum rock, ha ha ha. In the early days we would almost be insulted to be called punk because it had different connotations and the label hadn't really quite stuck yet.

Sam Ferrara: Actually, the Ugly was going to be called Rotten, that was the original name, and then Johnny Rotten came out. So Tony goes, "Fuck it, let's call ourselves the Ugly."

Raymi Mulroney: We rehearsed in the Philips Building and that was a wild, wild place. Hot summer afternoons in this abandoned factory and you're the only ones in there.

Steven Leckie: The Ugly got in there because Mike Nightmare would pay for practices by robbing convenience stores at gunpoint. This is pre–security cameras where you could really get away with it.

Raymi Mulroney: It was a great place for bands. It was a meeting place. It was the Viletones and Ugly, and that's all I remember as far as punk bands rehearsing there.

I was arrested there. What happened was we had a PA the original guitar player had rented. He never took calls about when his next payment's due, so instead of Long & McQuade coming to get the PA, they think we stole it. Because we had moved from one rehearsal studio in the Philips Building to another section of it, they figured we were gone; we'd robbed them. So we were arrested but all the charges were dropped. Ha ha ha. It was funny.

Mike was the only one who wasn't captured that night. He was late for practice, thank God, but he witnessed everything. He was up on the roof watching us get arrested. Ha ha ha.

We rehearsed thirty-nine days straight, this band, and our first gig was I think with Teenage Head. That was August 10 – my birthday. I turned nineteen. That was at Club David's.

We had twenty-two songs on one set and each song was probably about two minutes long, average. The set would be about forty-five minutes, boom. Oh yeah, of course I was nervous; strings were breaking and everything.

Mike was a pusher. He always wanted to rehearse and get better and better and better, but I guess no one took him seriously. The songs were too crazy. Have you listened to the lyrics? They're nuts.

Sam Ferrara: Mike was nuts. He was totally nuts. If you really listen to the lyrics, they're true. They're true stories and the lyrics are weird.

Mike Nightmare: I'm like a psychopath on the run. [lyric from "No Place To Go"]

Freddy Pompeii: Nightmare was kind of like a man about town. He was a real juvenile delinquent, for sure. He was known to pull off B&Es and holdups and all kinds of shit; played around with firearms. He was just a bad guy. Not a bad guy, like if you *knew* him; he was a nice guy, but he was definitely a criminal. A small-time criminal, but a criminal just the same — a thief. They stole all their equipment from different places.

Raymi Mulroney: We were sort of in the background. We were too heavy. Everybody wanted really pop music like the Romantics and Teenage Head — that real three-chord bop stuff. We were like very *underground*-underground.

William Cork: I went to Club David's one night in the laneway off of St. Nicholas Street and I heard this horrendous noise. Well, I started out at the Chimney where Rough Trade were playing. My girlfriend and I lived with Rough Trade and she had sort of cornered me into this obligatory social visit to see her friends there, meaning Rough Trade. Frankly I hated them because they used to back me into a corner there because I listened to Iggy Pop and called me a punk and I had no idea what they were talking about; it pissed me off.

I thought I was going to freak out, that there was nothing left in the world but disco, and I ran out of the Chimney and ran down the laneway off St. Nicholas Street — I didn't even know where I was going — and I heard this horrendous noise coming out of this place. I opened this metal fire door and walked down this pitch-black dark hallway. It was like being in a funhouse at the CNE and I felt my way around to another door and opened it up and the Ugly were playing in there. They had an audience of, like, three people and I think they played thirty-five consecutive nights for five bucks each and I thought they were amazing.

Greg Dick: I always gravitated to the heavy-duty punk stuff. That's always what I liked the best. I liked the loud, loud, crazy stuff.

Nobody could touch Teenage Head for playing. The Ugly had Nightmare and they were heavy, but Nightmare was the real deal. *Nobody* could out-tough that guy. He was so real it was unbelievable.

Nora Currie: Mike was the most beautiful man of all, of any guy you'd ever seen. And you won't find very many women, or men, who wouldn't agree with me.

He's what's called Black Irish: black hair, black eyes, movie-star handsome in that Irish devil way with white, white skin, red mouth, a face that looked like it had been drawn on. He was slim, had a perfect body, fabulous sense of style, and he was also the ultimate bad boy without any construction or planning. He didn't have to be designed; it was already there.

Don Pyle: I think a part of the thing that was exciting to me about the Ugly was that they were scary. They looked like they really were thugs, they looked like they really did just get out of jail, they looked like they were all using drugs, all of which I think turned out to be true. And they were very noisy and aggressive and probably one of the least tuneful of the early bands.

Mike Nightmare was more a shouter than a crooner. He was not a pretty singer at all. He was very aggressive. They had an amazing bass player and drummer. Actually, all three of the Ugly were really fantastic players, as were the original Viletones. You'd see a band like the Curse who were just beginning to learn how to play their instruments but were just as exciting, but you could tell something's not quite the same. They didn't have the power behind them because they weren't as tight, not as experienced.

But the Ugly probably were the most misfit of all the bands that were starting out then. As you got to know people you'd know some of them were putting on this outfit to go to the show, and then they'd go home and go back to their lives and put on a different persona. But the Ugly did seem like they really were what punks were. These were the no-good kids, and the Ugly certainly were.

Tony Vincent: Early on, the Ugly played for five minutes at the Piccadilly Tube and we got thrown out of there. That was one of our first shows. The owner came screaming out of his office going, "This music sounds like it's coming from hell!"

20. No more Beatle

Nip Kicks / photo by Don Pyle

Raymi Mulroney / photo by Gail Bryck

The Ugly / photo by Gail Bryck

Gary Pig Gold: I remember rushing out of David's one afternoon all excited 'cause I'd just gotten Saucer a gig there or something. I run right over to the Toronto Bus Terminal, buy a ticket to Hamilton, and have just enough time to call Saucer House to tell them the good news. And Edgar answers, without saying hello or anything, just says, "Elvis is dead." And stupid me — this is still the summer of '77, right? — I go, "Elvis *Costello*??"

Zero: I think I was turning seventeen; it was '77, Elvis Presley had just died. He died on my birthday. So he's on the news and my mom had gone down to New Rose and she bought me a dog collar.

My friend Gambi was there; we were inseparable for a while there. They gave us champagne. Did you ever drink champagne out of the bottle? It's horrible because it's all fizzy, so if you try and chug it, it goes up your nose, ha ha ha. I remember that because I remember it stinging and laughing and getting a dog collar and Elvis Presley had just died on TV.

He sort of started a lot of it then all of a sudden he dies. Then there are people like me sitting there drinking champagne and wearing a dog collar.

Larry LeBlanc: Lester Bangs goes on my radio show saying, "Son of a bitch should have died after the Army. He hasn't done anything in twenty-five years."

Thanks, Lester. There go the phones ...

Steven Leckie: The day Elvis died I was at Club David's. I was devastated when I got the news that officially he died. I played "Jailhouse Rock" over and over and over. It was constant. I felt vindicated later when one of my heroes, Joe Strummer, was in a documentary saying there were two types of punks: the ones that thought Elvis was a joke, and the ones that were hurt when he died. And I was hurt when he died and I was hurt like Joe, because Elvis Presley is the pinnacle. Elvis Presley *is* Iggy Pop, the MC5, the Sex Pistols, Malcolm McLaren. Elvis Presley was the man who took things that very few could. So the night Elvis died, August 16, 1977, I was a DJ at our club. So that's where I was, thanks for asking. I fuckin' love Elvis with a passion, always will.

Gordie Lewis: It's funny. What I recall, we were rehearsing at Club David's. I forget who came in and told us Elvis had died. It was that day.

And I remember the reason that it was an important day to me is [when, years later] I was doing a lecture.

I was taking this course over at McMaster University about the history of popular music and there was a whole little bit on punk rock. I just offered my services — "I was there, so I could tell you a little bit about punk." The professor took me up on it and I was preparing this thing I had to do. And I was trying to figure out, where are the boundaries here? You know, it's 1977 with the death of Elvis, and probably the end of punk was the death of Sid Vicious in 1979, and without saying the birth of punk — without being right on with the birth of punk and the death of punk — those were the two boundaries that I used to explain what happened in those two years; that those were signposts of the attitude or the outlook as far as music.

At that point, Elvis was the *big* Elvis. He was being ridiculed by the punks, and I never understood that because we always liked Elvis. Elvis and rockabilly actually kind of *saved* us, because that's what gave us one of our first gigs. We had to go into this country bar and we didn't have any country songs but we wanted the gig. So we went, "We can't learn country music, what can we do?" And that's when we picked up on the rockabilly. Which has got a whole lot to do with the punk scene. A lot of these bands were going into that same area, too, but at the same time there was this anti-Elvis thing. The Rebels did "Elvis is Dead." I guess he was becoming a cartoon of himself at the time and the punks picked up on that. But the whole thing was anti-*everything*, though. It was anti-Beatles, anti-Rolling Stones.

That was one of the cries of Steve Leckie — "No more Beatles, no more Stones, we just want the Viletones!" Ha ha ha, he would yell that out at his shows and that was fine by me, it was funny. But we were all thinking, I kind of *like* the Beatles, and I kind of like the Rolling Stones and I kind of like Elvis, too.

So his death, right in 1977 seemed, not ironic, but I don't know what the word would be. Elvis died in 1977. Disco was starting, but then there was this whole punk thing going on at the same time, so his death, to me, did have some sort of boundary on punk starting and where it went to.

Michael Dent: Actually, we played with Teenage Head on the day Elvis died. It was at David's and there was this pail and I said, "Guess what? Elvis —" and I kicked the pail across the dance floor, like, "Elvis kicked the bucket." Ha ha ha.

Rock 'n' roll dies, punk rock starts.

*   *   *   *   *

Joe Sutherland: The media love anything that is different. They love anything that is *radically* different even more. They love to point fingers. They love to stare. You know how your mother says, "Don't stare at that old man?" Well, that's what the media does. So punk became an obvious media event.

The punk scene was definitely something that was totally new at the time and I would say that I'm a chronicler of events, and I just went on down to have a look. I wasn't necessarily even going to bring the camera out until I saw what was going on, and it was interesting enough that out came the camera.

You know, you almost had to have seen the music scene before to realize the change that was happening. And it was a *huge* change. The CBC brass were horrified by punk rock and ordered an early cut containing footage mainly from the New Yorker Theatre destroyed. However, neither Peter Wronski nor I were working for the CBC when we shot it. The footage was shot on reversal stock so they were editing the original footage and when it was destroyed there was no backup. Our agreement with the CBC was that we had only sold the right to use the footage and it was to be returned to us afterward.

If somebody, a fairly straightlaced person from the 1970s, is ordering something destroyed ... If you saw it, I don't think you would find anything all that shocking in it by today's standards. But by those standards it was hugely shocking.

I hate to say it, but I think the Dead Boys were much more dynamic than the Ramones were. It often baffles me that they never achieved the same notoriety. I think that was one of the reasons the CBC threw the footage out. The actual film — which included the Crash 'n' Burn and the footage of the Ramones at the New Yorker — when they were cutting this together of course they went with all the dynamic footage, which was Nazi Dog and the Dead Boys. The Ramones seemed to be nice, calm people. Not exactly what you expected in the punk era, ha ha ha.

Gary Topp: There were instances where people would be going out after a show at night and the cops would bust them and take away their studs. It was a very threatening scene if you were pretty straight, and the city *was* pretty straight.

I'll always say that the punk rock scene in Toronto changed Toronto drastically. Queen Street wouldn't have happened without the punk rock scene. Old ladies wouldn't be wearing black. The architecture, the entrepreneurial undertakings; I think it all had to do with the punk rock scene in Toronto. And as it grew so did the city, which has changed drastically.

I don't think it was the times; I really believe that that scene changed this city. And now it's as boring as it was before.

The media glamorized the violent aspects, and whether it was violence or show biz we'll never know. People couldn't play, as you know, but they were *so* much more interesting, and the energy was a zillion times stronger than anything that was going on. And again, you didn't know what was going to happen. There'd be fights for real or not real. Steven Leckie used to incite riots like crazy. I have a tape of a show where he's just blasting the Diodes. There was band warfare going on. It was very good times.

Gary Pig Gold: You started having the press come down, but they were writing about it for not the right reasons exactly, or talking about the audience. We were going, "Look, this is great *music*, too."

They were talking about it for the wrong reasons.

"Not Them! Not Here!" by Paul McGrath [*Globe and Mail, Fanfare*, May 11, 1977]: The Viletones are not a group of musicians, they are a spectacle, so no talk of music shall enter the argument.

Gary Pig Gold [journal entry, August 26, 1977]: *CBC* Take 30 *taping at David's. Questions asked during set-up: "Do punks have groupies? Can you phone some and have them come over and take their clothes off?" "Will there be any knifings? It'd be great to have a shot of an ambulance arriving." "Why are all punks so skinny?"*

Hana Gartner [CBC TV, *Take 30*]: I have been listening to you [Teenage Head] this evening and to the Viletones, and if I may be honest the only thing I got out of it was a headache.

Gordie Lewis: The media's take on it did bother me a little. I liked the whole fashion idea behind punk; I thought that was great. Because we weren't about violence at all, I knew that was just a shtick, you know?

Yeah, I was disappointed. I didn't think Steve Leckie had to do that to himself. He did get kind of carried away and I just thought, Jeez, Steve, that's unnecessary. But that wasn't us, so if that's you, well ...

I understood a little bit about the rawness because even though we rehearsed and were writing songs, we didn't consider ourselves accomplished musicians. We considered ourselves *learning* musicians. So yeah, okay, we're a little raw right now and we'll get better, and I knew we would. I never lost sight of that.

Stephen Mahon: Fanzines were obviously not as financially sound as *Rolling Stone*, so you knew that when someone came to a gig and said they were from *Sniffin' Glue* or wherever, they were probably going to be more acceptable to what we were doing simply because we were sort of on the same page. They were working for a magazine that wasn't really mainstream, and our band wasn't really mainstream.

We never did get on the cover of *Rolling Stone* — how come?

Gordie Lewis: I think I did have the common sense that I was just glad there was some sort of media attention of *any* kind, because that was important. Again, because I grew up with magazines and things like that, I knew this is where I found out about bands. I found out through the media about a lot of things, so it didn't bother me *that* much. I was just glad somebody was there with a camera doing something. I wished there was more.

Stephen Mahon: I do remember the cameras and the cables and the lights, the bright lights. It would never bother me that [Hana Gartner] said our band gave her a headache. I would just laugh that off. We did what we did and you either liked it or you didn't.

It almost figures; it's CBC. You couldn't think of anything more uncool back then than the CBC, ha ha ha. I kind of remember just thinking what a waste of time that was, but it probably made sense; it wasn't like somebody coming from some punk mindset and interviewing us. I don't know what they were after. They were just jumping on a bandwagon that summer, I guess.

Enzo Petrungaro: There were members from the Viletones and there was Michaele Jordana from the Poles and there was Teenage Head. Everyone was really, really young at the time and they were creating something that was brand new and fresh, and they kind of scared the CBC reporter. She was like, "What the hell is this?"

Joe Sutherland: I think punk was sort of like watching a slow car crash. That's what it was when I started filming it. Nazi Dog, Steven Leckie, was getting drunk and slashing his arms. What do you do for the next performance that's bigger? Slow car crash — there goes the fenders, there goes the hood. I was aware of that even when I first filmed it.

Steven Leckie: Michaele was a very perceptive woman. On the CBC interview Hana Gartner is asking about this Nazi Dog cutting himself. [Michaele]'s going "No, that's life affirming." And that really resonated. It really made me think, fuck, she understood that this wasn't GG Allin; this was to show what procedures need to happen to make the world forget about Fleetwood Mac and Led Zeppelin, and I thought that was mega hip.

Sex, drugs, and rock 'n' roll. The sex is the Dionystic element, the drugs are the chaos, and the rock 'n' roll is the celebratory nature of it. People love themes of sex and violence.

I've been told I've influenced everyone from GG Allin to Sid Vicious to Stiv Bators, who I knew very well before he died, that the idea of doing this was actually an affirmation of life. If you factor in that I'm nineteen at the time doing that that's just being Arthur Rimbaud. That's taking a Patti Smith lyric to the performance level. That's the song "Horses" — "The boy looked at Johnny, Johnny wanted to run, but the movie kept moving as planned, he gets stabbed, stabbed." That's what it is, sort of. And the cultural intake of cinema at the time — you had a whole audience that I knew were very hip in real time to *Clockwork Orange*, *Taxi Driver*, *Apocalypse Now*. They needed their entertainment to be strong. And to usurp things like Led Zeppelin and disco you had to really show your mettle, I think.

But now I'm very aware that if society heard of a singer, or anyone, on a stage cutting themselves up it would be, "Oh, you need mental healthcare." I've got a theory that what used to be hip is now called dysfunctional. If I brooded around like Marlon Brando in *The Wild One* you'd say, "You've obviously had a rough childhood." That's not the fuckin' point. I'm being who I am. I'm kickin' out the jams, motherfucker, meaning the jams are all the societal bullshit that you're supposed to do. Kick them out, they gotta go.

Pre-punk there was a violence, an organized fight against the American government. Mine was just pushing the memory of Ronnie Hawkins out of your fuckin' mind forever. Ronnie was *the* man on Yonge Street for twelve years, he really was. I wanted to make sure those motherfuckers up there knew the future was coming their way and there was nothing they could do about it.

Blair Martin: You ever seen the interview on the CBC? It's very funny because that is [Steven Leckie's] little moment of genius. And if you look at it in a historical context and the framework of everything, it's quite a really remarkable bit of film both personally for him and also historically of things as they might have been. And I'll tell you why I read an awful lot into that.

When I look at how that horrible woman [Gartner] keeps interrupting — I mean, she's really doing a bad job. First of all, it's very interesting because it reflects very accurately how mainstream reacted to punk rock initially. This pop culture thing that had been going on since the Beatles didn't really have something like this where the older folks disapproved. Our parents got a little bit worried with Alice Cooper hanging himself in the middle of the record or killing chickens or whatever the fuck that first crowd of '70s shock stuff was about.

Yeah, it disturbed our parents a little bit but jeez, did they ever react negatively to punk rock. Everybody just *negative, negative, negative.*

"The Viletones: Destructive Punk Rock Masochism," by Steven Davey [*Metropolitan*, April 25, 1977]: Peace and love, the Viletones say, was a scam merchandized by our parents, and they don't buy it. When you put your finger in a light socket, you may get hurt; it may also wake you from your complacency.

Half-boy, half-beast, Nazi Dog goes for the jugular and doesn't let go.

Blair Martin: A thing like Nazi Dog; on the one hand it's a pretty gratuitous invention intended to further a pop music career, and in that sense it's quite satirical in terms of the world.

To what I call the Bob Dylan generation it asks the question, "How fuckin' liberal really *are* you? Can you take the sight of me sticking my tongue out at you singing nyah-nyah-nyah-nyah with a swastika on my arm? Can you really take it?" It asks that question. I don't know if that was ever his intent, though, so it's an interesting thing because nobody's ever asked him about that one. I'm sure to him it's an entertainment device to further an entertainment career. But it's an interesting point that I've never seen anybody ask him. It's very odd. But there you go. They ask him about cutting himself.

They were hostile to it, and that generation, that Bob Dylan generation, was *really* fuckin' hostile to it. So [Gartner]'s hostile, she's bad, she's interruptive. She interrupts him three times before he says something that really, if he had lived in another country — if he had been in England or he had been in the United States, if he had been either part of the New York scene or part of the London scene and said what he said on the CBC that night, I think that would have been enough to change a lot of people like that.

I think [Gartner] asks him at one point, "I'm really trying hard to understand what you're doing here; what is it that you're doing?" And Steve — when I watch it it's really quite a magical moment for me, but maybe I just have an active imagination — Steve wipes his lip, his nose with his cigarette finger, "I'm just trying to, I'm just trying to, I'm just trying to have fun and I'm making money having fun."

He never was making any money; he was making chump change if anything and it probably always had to go on the rehearsal space or some other fucking expenditure. He's full of shit.

And his gaze swings forward and he says to the camera — and he sort of does a contraction, I'm not sure if he's saying "I'd" or "we'd," but it's, "... like to create a generation gap." And I just thought, *That's it*.

He goes on to explain, "My parents like the Beatles and Elton John and Fleetwood Mac." He just explains the theory of this new thing, and I don't remember anybody ever doing that. Can you imagine if it was one of the Ramones on *60 Minutes* actually saying that? People who didn't get it who were otherwise hostile would have clicked in, in a moment.

Steve Leckie / photo by Ross Taylor

"Hey, yeah, man, somebody's playing music for *my* generation for the first time. Why didn't I get it before?" Because that's really what happened with a bunch of people later on.

Right, Steve Leckie's magical moment. That was his real moment of genius and I think really reflective of the way Toronto got missed. There's this guy, his little moment of punk rock genius and oh, it happens on the CBC so everybody missed it.

Enzo Petrungaro: That to me sums up what punk rock really was. It was creating something that you can call your own that wasn't your parents' generation or a couple of generations back.

A lot of guys in that same interview, especially the Teenage Head guys, they were so young and when they were put to the question they couldn't even answer it. They're just out doing what they do. It's like a natural thing to them. This is just what they do. If you were freaked out by it, too bad. It wasn't like they knew, or were even consciously trying to get that reaction from people. It was just like a natural thing and that's why I think it's important to be like that, because that makes that music timeless. I can put that music on today and it's still as relevant to me today as it was on those days, whereas a lot of other music that was created since then I think is very disposable.

David Clarkson: Remember, I was barely twenty years old, and had just grown up in a time when they taught us in school what to do when the atomic bomb dropped: Get under your desk. I just wanted to get on with being who I wanted to be. And that was the whole point, really. We were ignoring the rules that we could — for as long as we could get away with it — and making this freedom to do whatever we wanted. And part of that deal was that you let other people do whatever *they* wanted, too. Inventing new things and being free — to me, that was the whole point. And if anybody is still interested in that after thirty years, well then, good.

And I think that's what pushed some people over the edge, and why we got ambushed at the Colonial: Playing outside the rules like that makes a certain kind of person really nervous and threatened, and they can't take it. I didn't quite realize it at the time just how high the stakes were.

21. the danger light

Mike Nightmare / photo by Gail Bryck

Mike Nightmare [*Shades* no. 3, Winter, 1979]: My mind rambles on and on floating from thought to thought till it pulls the drawers from the filing cabinet of some subconscious primal learning which instinctively directs an imaginative finger tip to a file marked G my memory machine clicks on the danger light the caution bell and the sight of blue metal wrapped in plastic G being for a gun a very simple and direct form of intelligence so easy to point so easy to unload so easy to hide breathing under the floor boards of an unknown location again a regression of shock the white lights passing overhead as one is wheeled down the sterile antiseptic hallway into the metallic elevator comforting faces assure me no harm will be done abrupt stop elevator doors open more wheeling more assuring faces an unconcerned attendant person tightens the straps around my ankles my waist my wrists my chest an audience of bland faces gather about me the big cheese takes command of his flock to tell them the reason I am being treated in such a manner he takes his position behind me the electrodes are attached an evil looking man steps out of the procession of bodies I am injected and destroyed again the danger light the caution light the sight of blue metal no plastic a red flash ...

Sam Ferrara: I used to see Mike just before the Ugly, even. I saw him once on the subway with marks on his head from shock treatment.

William Cork: The 1960s were a pretty weird time. They were actually building concentration camps, detention centres, across the northern States. They built the Northern Interstate at the same time, the idea being, said Spiro Agnew, they could have tanks on that highway anywhere in the continental United States in about forty-five minutes. He publicly advocated locking up everyone with long hair.

When I went to high school, they tried to give me a chemical pre-frontal lobotomy. They called my parents in. I went home that day after school and my dad said, "Nobody's ever gonna touch you but me." And he wound up and broke my nose.

But Mike, he wasn't so lucky. His parents were these well-meaning-but-not-very-smart immigrants from Ireland – first-generation Canadians. He was going to marry this girl in high school and then thought better of it and decided he was going to take off to L.A. and be in the movies. His mother talked him into going to see a psychiatrist with her before he left, and he did it just to placate her. He went in there and when the interview was over he said, "I'll see you later, doc," and the doctor said, "No, I think you'll see me now." Two guys in white coats came and hit him up, and the next thing he knew he woke up on an electro-therapy table.

He was having electrodes glued to his forehead and he looked up and the nurse sticking the electrodes on was his mother-in-law-to-be: *Revenge!* They burned him so bad that for the rest of his life he had scars the size of nickels burnt into each side of his forehead, on his temples.

That song by Lou Reed, "Kill Your Sons," that really meant a lot to him. They had him on these heavy, hypnotic tranquilizers, but bit by bit he started palming them and throwing them away. And slowly, over a two-year period, he started to figure out who he was again and one day he woke up and he was sane.

He was wearing one of those little hospital gowns – you know, with your ass hanging out – and he decided he wanted to get out of there. This was in the Towers in Scarborough, the psychiatric hospital there, and he busted into a locker that had patients' belongings and pulled out these clothes and put them on. They were somebody's that were way smaller than him, and Mike was only five-five. He couldn't do the pants up and they came down to his mid-calf. He couldn't get the shoes on. He didn't care. He took off out of a fire exit that was on an alarm, and so the whole hospital started ringing and ringing and Mike flew.

He got to this house in suburbia, broke into their garage, hot-wired a car and started backing out in it. And standing right behind the car was a police sergeant. It was *his* car.

His parents meant well. They signed him in there but actually the entire thing was illegal – they never had his permission. They wound up letting him go. They had to. Years later, Mike joined part of the class action lawsuit against the psychiatric establishment.

He was part of the lawsuit that was mental patients from McGill University, when the CIA was up here giving people LSD and zapping them on electrotherapy. They ended up dismissing his part of that because they said it was beyond the statute of limitations in Ontario. In Quebec they could pursue it, but because he was from Ontario there was a six-year statute. And I mean, for two of these years, he didn't even know who he was. The actual class action lawsuit didn't surface for some time.

His parents meant well. They were real paranoid in the 1960s. I mean, if you had long hair you couldn't even go to a restaurant here in Toronto. There were signs on all the restaurant doors. If you just went in and sat down somewhere and ordered a drink or food they'd throw you out. They were real scared, real paranoid. People were blowing shit up all over the place. Half the cities in the United States were on fire. It was a whole different world.

Chris Haight: Apparently, once upon a time – this is what Tony Torcher was telling me – Mike was just a straight-on nice guy. And then some institution got a hold of him and did the old shock treatment on him, right? And after that I heard that he just changed into Mike Nightmare. He went from Mulroney to Nightmare. And I remember there was times when he'd go, "Chris, when I go like this, I can hear my brain wobble."

Tony Vincent: Mike Mulroney received shock treatment when he was eighteen, against his will. His parents signed for it and said, "You have to see a doctor, they'll help you." He had no idea he was getting shock treatment. That's where the transformation into Nightmare came from.

Before that he was a sweet, nice kid. When I met him after he had the shock treatment he was gone, he wasn't there anymore.

Chris Haight: But that's when his lyrics really got interesting. They weren't no "I love you" shit, man.

I thought guys like him and Jimmy the Worm didn't get the credit that was due to them. I always said to myself that if I ever had a chance I would make sure that these guys would get their due, and I got that chance. At least he'll live on to a degree. No matter what happened with relationships and stuff like that, he was always okay with me. Straight-up guy all the way. I had to say that.

One-on-one he was a good guy. They wrote some great stuff, they wrote some really good stuff.

*　　*　　*　　　*　　　*

Nip Kicks: The band rivalries were funny. It was really interesting because I didn't really know the Viletones at that time. I knew mostly the Ugly and the Curse and so you know, you'd hear these murmurings here and there and you just didn't really know what to expect. The bands didn't really want to say anything bad about anybody else but sometimes they couldn't help it.

I shy away from talking about individuals negatively, but I'm sure you've heard about different characters, and certainly Steven Leckie was a difficult character to work for, work with. Genius, brilliant manipulator of people, and he'd push and push that envelope.

I have to admit, the guy put on a great show. Steve was a great performer in the "Screamin' Fist" and "Possibilities" days. I wasn't really into him cutting himself, but they put on a hell of a show and they ended up being a pretty good band. But I knew of Leckie's reputation, and he tended to try to use some of the other guys a bit like thugs, especially Motor Mike. He used to pick fights and get somebody like Motor to fight them for him before Motor kind of caught on. I didn't like that at all.

Freddy Pompeii: Within six months the city was flooded with punk bands; kids just started putting together bands left and right. And of course because we were the first we were at the top of the heap, you know? So that was good for us because we could get a lot of people to play gigs for us so we would have some warm-up bands. We just promised ourselves right from the beginning that we would just do headline shows; we wouldn't do any warm-ups or anything, and that's what we did.

The Viletones were on top. The Viletones were Number One and everything was Viletones, Viletones, Viletones. The Ugly, for some reason they couldn't get to first base, or else they thought they couldn't get to first base. But I mean, *we* were Ugly fans. *Everybody* liked the band.

Nip Kicks: Mike always had a bit of a quiet rivalry with the Viletones. Sometimes not so quiet, sometimes quiet.

Mike didn't like to talk about it publicly because he didn't feel that was appropriate and he probably didn't want to stir up shit, which is really funny because Mike was quite an in-your-face kind of guy sometimes. Whether it was a matter of some little bit of code of honour in there somewhere, or whether he just didn't want to be seen as cutting up other people because it didn't look good on him, or whether there was some strategy behind it as far as getting things done or alliances, who knows. It wasn't anything personal; well, sort of personal with Steve, but not so much in the sense with Fred and Mike and Chris. They were all fine. Nobody ever had problems with those guys, it was always Steve.

Steven Leckie: We felt a rivalry only – no, I guess no rivalry, really. I think we surpassed rivalry.

Tony Vincent: There *was* a rivalry there going on. They would badmouth us onstage and we would do the same thing. "Viletones can fuck off," that's what we would say. Steve would criticize. Steve's good at that. He criticized every band. The only band *we* criticized was the Viletones.

Nip Kicks: There was definitely a rivalry. Tony was pretty vocal, but again, he's a pretty much straight-up kind of guy and he wasn't afraid to tell how he feels. But it was rivalry more in the sense of one band wanting to headline more than the other; one wanting to be the better, real thing, more so than any kind of meanness.

I think the Viletones were probably a little bit conscious of the Ugly, too. I think everybody was a little bit conscious of the Ugly. They were the underground threat.

Johnny Garbagecan: I was on the road with a band from Hamilton doing sound, trying to make money to pay the rent, and I heard those guys had a practice hall in Brentwood Studios at Brentwood and Eglinton, where the Viletones used to practise. The Viletones wouldn't practise unless everybody else was out of the building. Steven was always, "They're gonna steal our songs, man, let's wait for everybody to leave."

Raymi Mulroney: Johnny Garbagecan recorded a bunch of our songs at that rehearsal space in October, 1977. It was all live off the floor. On it you can hear Tony talking about the Viletones and Mike's going, "Don't say nothing bad about the Viletones when we're on tape," ha ha ha.

Freddy Pompeii: Steven would really instigate the rivalry because that's just the way he was. He always had to get over on Mike Nightmare and Mike Nightmare really felt it, so they were always doing stuff to out-do each other; you know, stage antics and doing outrageous things on the street and in bars.

Usually Johnny Garbagecan would add to it, instigate it with stuff in *Torrana Punks* – "Mike said this about Steven, and Steven said this about Mike."

Chick Parker: There was a real long-standing rivalry that went before either band was formed, apparently, because the first time Mike and Steve met was they both went down to watch Keith Richards when he was on trial for the whole heroin thing. And so did I, and so did Zero, and pretty much everybody that ended up in the punk scene later was down at that trial to catch the patron saint, as it were.

Mike was always saying that Steve had stolen this idea from him, and I think at one point he even claimed that the name Viletones was his. I don't believe that, and it hardly matters now, Mike being dead and all this having happened thirty years ago, but it was pretty bitter. On the other hand, they were two sides of the same coin, so they kind of got along, too. It was rock 'n' roll stuff.

Sam Ferrara: The Viletones and the Ugly were neck and neck. We even rehearsed at the same building on Brentcliffe.

Steven Leckie: At that period in our development we had Mega Media financing it. We had a practice space in this luxurious kind of Toronto thing that Rush practised at. We would often like to have kids watching us practise and there'd be ten, fifteen kids there. Rush would be there, Honeymoon Suite, it was a real mish-mash but it was a money rehearsal spot. We wouldn't have been able to do it on our own.

My biggest memory of that place is my managers bought me a gold-plated microphone. Thing is a Shure M58 with the ball head, the regular rock mic. Mine was real gold-plated and someone ripped it off.

Also, my memory of Mike Nightmare taking his .38 out of his pants and firing it at the ceiling with Sam and Tony. All that shit's for fuckin' real. That was a whole all other level. That was me without the intellect. You know in *Clockwork Orange* you had Alex; Mike Nightmare was like the dumb one they beat up at the beginning for raping a girl. Mike Nightmare was a guy without a plan, but he had a heart and he never got what he should have.

Chris Haight: The Ugly had a gun, but they had it for different reasons. It was just the allure. Maybe somewhere in one of the shock treatments he emerged as his favourite gangster, I don't know.

Sam Ferrara: Mike came in one night at a rehearsal and he goes, "I got a new gun," and he starts shooting it in the ceiling and the cops came. For some reason Mike did not tell me this bass that I bought was hot. I figured it's five hundred bucks; it can't be hot. I don't know why but the cop looked at the bass, looked at the shield number, and goes, "This is a stolen bass."

I go, "*What?*" So the bass got taken away and I got put away for stolen property, but I didn't know. So I had to pay. The guy got his bass back undamaged, I spent some time in the slammer, paid a big fine, went to court, and now it's on my record. That wasn't very nice of Mike.

Freddy Pompeii: Mike was a real good-looking dude. He was tall and very thin and had a really good stage presence and he was pretty talented, too. He didn't quite have it down like Steven had it down, but he still was different in his own way. And the Ugly were a pretty decent band. They didn't really put out a big sound like we did. It was kind of like a small, fuzzy sound in the beginning, but he would keep adding to the band and firing people in the band. I mean, his brother was in the band with him, and it was Sam Sinatra and Tony.

All of them were small-time hoods and they were all getting locked up for something, all of them except Sam. Sam was the only levelheaded one in the band.

Nip Kicks: I think most people looked at them as being the hardest-core punk band as far as being true to their thing. They *were* the hoodlum rock, and they really were what they were. No pretense; not so much like the Viletones, which had so much more image involved. They got a lot of respect.

*　　*　　*　　　*　　　*

Anna Bourque: Our place was a hangout, the Curse House, as they called it. I remember Frankie from Teenage Head, Steve Mahon was there, too, and a bunch of guys from somewhere. Frankie always had a girl-friend. Frankie was pussy-whipped, always calling his girlfriend – "Yeah, I'm at the Curse House." And nobody cared if the boys were at the Curse House because everybody figured we were dykes or something, so it was okay, the guys could hang around. I'm not sure if it was that night or another night that Steve Mahon peed over our balcony. We actually had a toilet, but he peed over the balcony and Leo, the downstairs neighbour, was outside. He got peed on – did he ever get mad.

We used to have Attic Boys, Mickey and I. One guy was Australian and he'd never seen snow before. He lived in our attic and he did the dishes and did our laundry and that sort of thing. He broke his arm skating at Nathan Phillips Square but he kept doing the dishes, which was good. We had another Attic Boy who was lovely. We'd catch him going to play hockey instead of doing our laundry. Then we had another guy who was gay and very out-there fey.

Mickey Skin: Ralph, he was this gay guy.

Anna Bourque: The Portuguese kids on the street were just murder to him. He didn't stay very long; it was just too hard a neighbourhood to live in if you were really out.

Mickey Skin: We kind of wanted to be female chauvinist pigs, like male chauvinist pigs. So Ralph was our Attic Boy and he was supposed to clean our house and do our laundry and we tried to abuse him as much as we could.

One time the Viletones were over there partying and they got into all his clothes. I remember Nazi Dog blowing his nose into Ralph's pretty, lacy top. They were just so awful. I don't think Ralph was home at the time. Steve Leckie would come down in our bathrobes and would be all dressed up in Ralph's effeminate clothes and would be prancing around.

We trashed that poor apartment. We had water guns filled with Purple Jesus punch we would squirt all over the walls. And we had one party and I swear there had to be three hundred people there. It was jam-packed with people all the way up the stairwell and out the house. You couldn't move; it was nuts. I think we had the promo thing down pretty good. Anna was pretty good at phoning the right people and getting things going.

Tony Vincent: The Curse were kind of weird. You'd go down the hall and they'd be using the toilet and they'd leave the door open. "Can't you close the door?" "No, it's natural." Whatever that means. That's kind of gross.

John Hamilton: At the Curse house, I stayed over with Jula and we were having breakfast in the kitchen. I was playing the guitar and Mickey comes in wearing this little shift or something. She hikes up her shift and sticks her vagina in my face and says, "Have you ever seen a bald pussy before?" She'd had the crabs or something and she'd shaven. I think that was the first time I'd ever met Mickey personally. It was like, "Thanks Mick, it was really nice of you to share that." She was such an exhibitionist.

Linda Lee: It was debauchery. I remember Mickey coming into the kitchen and we were all sitting around the table. Steven was there and Freddy was there, and I think Chris was there. She had a T-shirt on and grabbed a spoon – like a baking spoon, a long thing – and put one leg up on the kitchen table and slowly took the spoon and began inserting it into her bits. There was some debauchery, yeah, absolutely.

Chris Haight: I guess they had a lot of balls for chicks. They sure were a lot of fun to party with, I remember that. It was a chick band but they were pretty off the wall. I think they were one of the first serious girl bands around.

Linda Lee: Steven Leckie couldn't hold a candle to Anna Bourque, no way, shape, or form.

Paul Eknes: Anna was, as far as I remember, one of the first Toronto punks that actually sang about something – feminism and political correctness and "Let's get things done" – while still doing a Slits bass and drums groove. The Curse were fantastic. The Curse House was a communal abode that always allowed any of the Toronto punk bands to hang out and sleep over because we were sometimes homeless.

Linda Lee: I didn't ever spend a night at the Curse House. I went back to my safe British boyfriend on Queen Street, which is where the rumours came from that Patzy Poison doesn't have a vagina, because Patzy Poison doesn't sleep with anybody – although Patzy Poison did end up sleeping with a couple of them.

We were real goofs. We laughed at everybody and in turn weren't the least bit offended when people laughed back at us. There was nothing [Mickey] wouldn't do. Think about how brave you would have to be to walk into a kitchen full of people, put your leg up on a kitchen table, and stand there with a spoon. And she just thought of it as, Well, that's what I'm doing.

These three women were completely and utterly fearless in their sensuousness. As long as you weren't hurting anybody; and hurting anybody meant that you didn't break anybody's heart, that you didn't physically hurt anybody. The first part I don't think any of us managed to succeed because it's impossible not to break hearts, but we were truthful. What you saw was completely what you got. No bullshit, no pretense, no nothing.

Nora Currie: I was in New Rose one day. At that time it was called a newsletter – today it would be called a zine – and the first one that I ever saw was called *Torrana Punks* and it was fantastic. It was cut and pasted together and done on a typewriter with photographs and was Xeroxed and cut out with articles and it was this fabulous collage of a creation. It told you what was going on, what was playing, who'd done what; it was gossipy, very positive and filled with information that wasn't in the mainstream media at all. So Margaret showed it to me and I remember thinking, Oh my god, this is amazing, who is doing this? It was made by someone named Johnny Garbagecan and I said, "I *have* to find him and talk to him."

He was just a lovely guy, full of energy, very knowledgeable. At the time he was unavailable – he was with Anna Bourque. I adored her and I kind of fell in love with him, but I knew he was with someone. So I called her up and she said she was finished with him and I could have him.

So I did. I was with him for a very long time.

"I Accuse You" was a song that Anna wrote. Anna would sing that song and Johnny and I would always be there. The words go, "I accuse you of being an asshole/For hanging out with assholes like him." And Anna would sing it and she would always point to me – "I accuse *you* of being an asshole." She was very mad at Johnny, and she was mad at me because she thought it wasn't a good idea that we were together.

Anna Bourque: I was certainly an aggressive presence, shall we say, because there were people who did want to ruin things. If somebody spit in my direction or threw something, I would step off the stage and the crowd would part. I remember lifting my foot up and pushing people away.

Nora Currie: I remember her throwing someone off the stage. He jumped on the stage and she told him to back off. Anna picked up her foot more than once. And it was also the presence that she projected; it was the toughness of it all. It's not that she wanted to kill anybody, except when she threw Johnny down the stairs.

Anna Bourque: But that wasn't onstage. That was *personal*. He needed that. He was hiding under Nora's bed and I thought he was going to hurt her. I lifted her bed up and there he was, so we got in a fight. I hurt my hand. I thought I'd broken my hand – it started swelling – but I didn't. But it didn't stop him.

Mickey Skin: The Ugly used to stay at our place a lot. We felt that they should pay us rent. So they would go and do what they called "box tricks," which was basically bringing groceries to us by lifting them out of the store.

What they would do, they would put a box in the shopping cart and then they'd go through the aisles at the Dominion on Bloor Street and fill it with expensive stuff like steaks and lobsters and things.

Johnny Garbagecan: Mike taught me to choose all the choice stuff. He'd say, "Put that back," and I'd say, "But it's good." He'd say, "Nah, it's too cheap, man, go for *this* stuff." He had all the caviar and all the really expensive sirloin steaks and everything else.

Mickey Skin: And then they would put it by the edge where the railings are and then go buy one little thing, walk out of the store, lift the box out of the cart and run home with a box full of groceries. So when we ran out of supplies we would always tell them it was time to go do a box trick.

Johnny Garbagecan: We had six to eight people to feed every night. That's how we ate at the Curse House.

One time Mike got busted and the judge said, "Don't tell me this is the first time you've done this, look at the things you stole." The guy had a list and it was all the most expensive things you could find in a grocery store. He started rattling it off. Mike ended up in jail a few times.

Jeff Ostofsky: Mike, I'd never met anyone like him.

It's important to note that the nucleus of punk bands and the scene itself — the important quote unquote people in it — some of them were pushing thirty then. And Mike was, I guess, a kid who grew up doing crime and stuff. But he did see himself as an Iggy Pop-ish type character. And he had this physique that I was in envy of. No weights, no exercise, just this beautiful physique, and this face, to look at it was to read the map of his life. Very expressive face; very dead-end-kid face.

Nip Kicks: Mike was the quintessential hoodlum rocker. Then you had the Curse who, although they were certainly making statements, did it in a much more humourous, light-hearted way. So you had this contrast of this heavy, heavy ugly, pounding banging, and then you had the Curse who were always off the top and a little humourous.

Nora Currie: What's interesting is that the punk scene attracted a lot of guys like Mike and Johnny and Tony and Colin [Fox], who came over from Britain. He played with the Battered Wives. They were like lost boys who turned to low-level crime — and probably would have ended up just being hooligans — who had found this arc, and they were stars. They had that criminal piece, but they were shitty criminals.

Jeff Ostofsky: It was us against the world, and unlike other punk periods, a lot of the guys weren't nineteen and had done jail time and lived. So it was the real deal.

Johnny Garbagecan: I just landed in the punk scene. Like I said, one day I said, "I'm not going north of Bloor Street anymore."

In the '70s all the lampposts were clean, and what drew me to it was the posters. I remember I used to try to peel them off and collect them. That's where I got the idea from for *Toranna Punks*. A lot of the stuff that was coming from England — they were a couple years ahead of us. You could already steal ideas, although I don't think too many people put out a publication with a photocopier.

Whenever I misspelled something and I swore, I'd type that in, too, because I didn't have anything to

erase the ink with. We were pretty poor, man, no wonder we had to do box tricks. I thought it was pretty unique, myself, the box trick. I even did it once later on in years when I was starving. It was so easy.

Mickey Skin: The *Toranna Punks* magazine, Johnny Garbagecan decided he was gonna start doing that in our flat.

Nora Currie: Anna is a writer and she didn't have a typewriter. In addition to being involved in the music scene before, both Johnny and Mike were involved in the robbery scene and were break and enter artists — artists of a different sort. They had been arrested and had done time before. It wasn't all they did, but it was the least glamourous or interesting side of their personalities.

Mike was a second-story man; he would climb buildings and break in. Anna needed a typewriter and no one had any money, so they went out and stole one for her.

Captain Crash: They're already drunk out of their fuckin' minds. So they go and they start breaking into houses. There's a guy sleeping on the couch, but there's a typewriter there. So they fuckin' tiptoe around this guy sleeping, steal his fuckin' typewriter, they get it back, it's fuckin' six o'clock in the morning.

Nora Currie: They brought it home and they were so proud, like a cat bringing in a dead bird and laying it down for its master.

It was Russian. It was a *Russian* typewriter. They were so stupid. It was of no use for her at all, but she thought it was very darling.

Johnny Garbagecan: We stole that out of a place on Spadina beside the church. I never checked the type.

I just brought the typewriter home and when Anna started typing, it was all these weird letters. So we took hammers and smashed it and took pictures of us smashing the typewriter. Yeah, it was me and Mike.

That's pretty funny: I risked my neck for a typewriter that we ended up smashing an hour later. It was useless. Now that I think about it, I was homeless for a few years and I used to walk by that church all the time. No wonder that whenever I walked past it I got these bad vibes. Maybe I need to atone for that.

Anna Bourque: I took pictures while they smashed it with a hammer. It seemed like art at the time.

Mickey Skin: I was like, "Can't you guys just bring it back? Do you know how hard it is to get a Russian typewriter?" No, they had to destroy it. I'll never forget that because I remember feeling bad for the poor guy; the guy was in the room sleeping when they broke into his room. We did all kinds of naughty things like that. When they brought it home I go, "What a bunch of idiots, stealing a Russian typewriter."

I was really naïve, too, because Anna knew that they were going out prowling and breaking and entering and stuff. I had no idea until one night they came tearing through the house screaming, "The cops are after us! Don't let them in!" They came in through the front door and were going over the balcony and over the roof out the back door. We're like, "Oh thanks a lot, guys." Somehow we never did see the cops, so I don't know what happened.

I was like, "What the hell's going on?" And Anna's like, "Mickey, haven't you noticed they wear their shirts up to their necks in black?" I thought that was just the look, ha ha ha, but evidently they were doing B&Es all the time which I was clueless about.

Tony Torcher was sniffing glue. I remember one time he was in my living room high and screaming at me to bring him all my glue — "*Gimmeallyourglue!*" I was like, "I don't have any more glue." "You're ruining everything! I need more glue!" One time he told me he worked for his uncle digging graves to make money — that was his day job. He told me once, "Oh Mickey, I always think of you when I'm digging graves." Like that was a romantic statement.

22. second best

Alex Currie: The show I thought was the funniest was the one when the Dead Boys were playing the New Yorker. Stiv Bators came up to the snack bar and he laid out these tampons and started methodically putting ketchup on them getting ready for the show. I thought, Wow, what a showman.

Colin Brunton: They were really bad boys. They weren't even nice to good people. We thought, Why are you trashing our dressing room, because we're nice and we're treating you fairly?

My memory of them was it was their turn to go onstage and they're just not showing up, so we were like, "Come on guys, you're on now." "Hang on, hang on," and it was like what the fuck? And they come marching up the stairs and I just gave one of them a look like, you know, What's taking so long? What's going on? And he just kind of looks at me with that young, loud, and snotty look on his face and goes, "Aw man, we can't go onstage with hard-ons." So they had to get their blowjobs from — I'm not gonna say who — downstairs before they went onstage. That's my distasteful memory of the Dead Boys.

Cheetah Chrome: We met the B-Girls the first time we played the New Yorker. That's when Stiv met Cynthia.

Cynthia Ross: I was a designer doing windows for the Bay and Holt Renfrew in Montreal, coming back and forth to Toronto. That was during the days when punk was just starting. I was really into music and going to see a lot of bands and was starting to have the feeling that, "You know what? None of these guys can play, anyway, so why don't we start our own band?"

I approached Lucasta. We were in the washroom at the Thin Lizzy concert and I said, "Wait a minute, why are we hanging around all these bands? Why don't we just start our *own* band? You can sing. I've never played bass but I'm sure I can." I'd taken piano as a child so I had a music background.

Lucasta Ross: Okay, it didn't exactly go like that. We were at a Thin Lizzy party at a hotel and the guys were starting to get a little crazy with some of the girls and we didn't want any part of it, so we just took our drinks and locked ourselves in the bathroom. It was in there we started talking about how everybody's getting a band together these days and we could do it.

By the time we unlocked the bathroom door we said, "That's it, we're a band." So that's how we started.

Cynthia Ross: Lucasta said, "Sure, but my best friend has to be in the band," and that was Xenia. I said, "We're gonna need a drummer so my sister will be the drummer," and we started rehearsing in my parents' basement in Thornhill.

I'm a little bit older than the other girls so I grew up with Humble Pie and Led Zeppelin and all these people at very small concerts. I'd gone to England and I knew Ron Wood from the Stones. I had gone to New York fairly regularly in the early '70s, like '71, '72, and was friends with Johnny Thunders from the New York Dolls so I knew about that whole scene. That's sort of where the seed started.

John Catto: The Ross sisters were always around. All these girls I'd been seeing at gigs since I was fourteen or something – all those New York Dolls and Stooges gigs that were in the '73, '74 period – if you went to any gig then you'd see Xenia and you'd see Lucasta and Cynthia and all of them. It's all intricately linked; all these disparate people who were around all got pulled together. The question is how you add that up.

Xenia Splawinski: How did I know everybody? I'm not even really sure. I already had been a real downtown girl, so at a very young age I'd already been hanging out at all the clubs. But that was pre-punk; it was more in the disco club scene. And I don't know if it just naturally morphed itself over. I didn't know the OCA people until the band was starting.

I knew Steven Leckie from public school. Our original drummer was part of the management team for Rush, so there were all these connections through the industry as well.

Lucasta Ross: We had a bunch of the guys from the other bands around that lent us instruments and equipment and taught us how to play them.

Xenia Splawinski: Lucasta had been singing since she was young; her father wrote jingles and she used to do these, so she'd been a professional singer.

We formed the band before we knew how to play, except that we did have a good singer so that was on our side. Actually, John Catto from the Diodes took me to Steve's Music and helped me buy this little, fake Les Paul Junior and taught me my first three chords.

Lucasta Ross: The Diodes were huge in helping the B-Girls. They were just wonderful. They actually came up with our logo, they showed us how to play some of our instruments, and helped us with songs. They were a

Xenia / photo by Ralph Alfonso

Xenia, Cynthia, Lucasta, CBGB's / photo by Ralph Alfonso

Xenia / photo by Ross Taylor

great help; they were really good friends of ours.

Xenia Splawinski: Well, we had all wanted to be in bands, we had hung around bands; it was something we were always interested in. It just became an opportunity; it was the time that you could do that sort of a thing, you didn't have to have it all together before.

I was so excited to be part of that band. It was like a dream come true. It was like everything I had been working towards through all my teenage years. I was around eighteen at that time.

Cynthia Ross: We decided it was easier to write our own songs than to learn other people's songs, because then no one knows if we're making mistakes or not.

Xenia Splawinski: It was just a matter of trying to actually get my fingers to move between these three chords from hours on end with bleeding fingers. We would practise for fourteen hours. We would have these rehearsals just to try to get one song to sound like a song, because nobody knew how to play. And we had gigs; we had gigs before we knew how to play, so we had to really put it into high gear and get it together. We were very diligent, considering. We did practise for very long periods of time in Cynthia's parents' basement. We would get together every day and just keep on trying and trying.

Lucasta Ross: I could sing and I knew my part, but they were still learning how to play their instruments so that part was a bit frustrating. But it didn't really bother me. Then I picked up a guitar, too, so then I was learning as well. It was just so much fun that it made up for the frustration that might have been.

Cynthia Ross: We wrote six songs and learned them and we did our first gig at David's. We played the same songs twice; we did all the things you're not supposed to do, but I think that's what made us endearing. The first song we started, one of us came in on the wrong note so we just stopped and started over again. It got people rooting for us.

Colin Brunton: Their cutest little moment was one of them broke a string and she kind of sheepishly handed the guitar to one of her roadies or friends because she didn't know how to tune it or even put a string back on the guitar. She had to wait, very cute looking, while this guy put the guitar back together for her. It was great.

Lucasta Ross: I wouldn't even want to hear tapes of our first performance but people loved us. Musically, not so hot, but we were having so much fun and we were trying so hard. Everybody knew how hard we tried.

Xenia Splawinski: Cynthia was the leader of the band. She was very good at connecting and talking to people and things like that. And we were likable; we weren't heavy-duty punk, we were more poppy so we weren't gonna destroy everything. And people wanted to give us a chance; they were eager to have girls play.

Lucasta Ross: There were certain bands that incited the crowd more, the Viletones, mainly, and other bands that came to town like the Dead Boys. The B-Girls, if you were just listening to our music, is not punk.

We were in the punk era and at that time there were a lot of bands that were called punk bands, but how do you define the music? How do you compare Patti Smith to the Viletones, yet they were both considered punk? So we fit in there somehow, but our music was not the kind that incited people to start pogoing into each other or smashing beer bottles on each other's heads. We always played gigs that were more melodic, I suppose, so that kind of stuff rarely occurred at our shows.

But I was at a lot of them that did — a *lot*. I did my share of bandaging people. Sometimes people just did it to themselves and other times it was done to them. Lots of blood in those days.

Cynthia Ross: The Curse were like the female version of the Viletones. We were the good girls. I don't think there was a rivalry between us, but I think people tried to create that. We liked them, they liked us, and I think it was good to just see other girls up there doing that. We always supported other girl bands.

Xenia Splawinski: The Curse were in a completely different space than we were in and I'm sure they ran into a lot more problems that way. But also they *provoked* the problems.

We weren't provocative; we weren't going around angry and fighting with everybody and causing big problems. We were assertive, we were aggressive, we got places, we got to do what we wanted to do but we got it more through putting ourselves forward and being pleasant about it and being reasonable about it. And I think that was refreshing to people at the time, too.

There were things happening behind us, but people didn't put it in our faces. We'd hear about the jealousies, we'd hear about the problems and things like that, but because we were so non-aggressive it didn't really come in our lap. It would be more like, "So-and-so's out to get you."

Lucasta Ross: I think what was really important about us was we just wanted to have a very good time. Although we played on the fact that we were all girls, we didn't misuse our sexuality at all, when that's what most of the female bands were doing. We wanted to be completely different. I don't want to say be wholesome, but we just wanted to project an image of just fun and not nastiness or trying to change the world. It was just fun. We really loved the girl groups of the '60s and we wanted to emulate *them*.

Cynthia Ross: I used to knit those sweaters that look like they have holes in them. I made them for everyone in the band. We did all these corny, hokey, Shangri-Las–type things.

Lucasta Ross: You can't say it wasn't just about the music, it wasn't just about the fashion, it wasn't just about hanging out. It was everything combined. Each one was as important a component as the next. Not everyone played an instrument or were in bands, but they'd just be part of the scene because they always came and they always gave you a lot of support. Fashion was huge. You didn't have to be in a band, but you had to look like you were. That got you in the door. And more likely than not, the next day you were *in* a band, that's how quickly they started up.

Xenia Splawinski: Everybody was trying to mold themselves against their heroes, mostly coming from the UK. The New York scene wasn't so big yet. Toronto and New York I think were birthing close.

Toronto was pretty happening and you really have to give the Diodes and the people who started it credit, because they really caught it at the beginning for North America and Toronto had a very well-established punk scene. I would say it was really London, New York and Toronto were the first ones, much to our Canadian surprise. We were all just doing it and being it, but we didn't realize we were actually at the cutting edge of the whole thing. Canadians have such a second-best complex.

23. two devils

Paul Robinson, Wendy O. Williams / photo by Ralph Alfonso

Paul Robinson: When we went down to New York over the summer and we played CBGB's it was really, really crazy. We got back to Toronto and John Corbett said, "Look, I'm quitting the band, I've got to earn a living." So John quit the band at that point and Ian became the bass player because until then we had had two guitarists. Really, John Catto didn't need the extra support of a rhythm guitar in the band; he really could handle all the guitar.

We said, "Okay Ian, you're going to play bass." Within three weeks we were signed. It just happened really quickly after that and we were going in to record as a four-piece.

Ralph Alfonso: CBS at the time was a really strange label. They had local disco bands — they had a band called Crack of Dawn who were actually pretty good — then they had this prog rock band called Zon. It was this real mishmash of stuff. They were all managed by the same company, Franklin House, so it was pretty much if you wanted to sign with them you also have to sign to this management company because "it just makes it easier for us, the label.

Lucasta, Greg Shaw (Bomp), John Catto; Horseshoe Tavern / photo by Ralph Alfonso

We don't want to deal with different managers or people bugging us all the time." Very weird, but you've got to remember, at that time in 1977, Warner Bros. didn't have anybody signed to them. I think they had maybe Fludd, I don't know. Nobody signed bands, so it was this strange thing.

John Catto: It was kind of like, "Oh, you guys have gotta get management. We've got this management company that handle all these bands."

Ralph Alfonso: The Diodes struck their deal with Franklin House before they struck their deal with the label because that was the deal — "You sign with these guys, and *then* we'll sign you." So I guess they cut their deal with two devils.

John Catto: This was, like, the worst thing, but it seemed to be part and parcel of the deal. In fact at the time they seemed to have a piece of the publishing, so it was the strange inter-mechanics of what goes on.

John Hamilton: There was that point when we signed to Franklin House where Ralph was saying, "I guess my job's over now," and I said, "No way, Ralph, are we gonna deliver ourselves into Franklin House carte blanche." There was no way we were ever gonna let Ralph go.

Ralph Alfonso: Even when the Diodes got real management and a real record deal, the companies didn't know what to do. It was an instance of having the right music, but wrong country, and we were ten years ahead. That is the sad legacy of punk from the 1977 era. If the Diodes had been in England or been in New York or even L.A., a lot more would have happened. Actually, *any* of these bands — Viletones or Teenage Head — but that was part of your thinking then. The B-52s, who were kind of coming up at the same time, were based in Athens but they were very smart early on to kind of go, "Hey, we're going to move, get out of Athens, go to New York and spend a lot of time there and build ourselves up." Which is what happened and they got signed to Island.

In hindsight, what I would do now, we would have — we should have — probably moved to New York or moved to England. But that's the only thing that I would do different now. I would seriously go, "We should get out of Canada and establish a base in New York, or at least hang out there for a couple of months and see if we can get some notoriety." That's the sad thing. Sire Records were out there signing up everybody — though they did come to Toronto to check out a few bands.

I think they checked out the Dishes and it wasn't quite right, but they might have come along a little early in the game and didn't come back.

John Hamilton: The Diodes never could have happened without Ralph. He was the fifth Diode. He was the guy who stood in the audience and told us what we were doing wrong. He even gave us a little booklet on how to behave as Diodes. It had our dress code and who we should talk to and what we should say and what we should not say.

You can't underestimate the guy out in front who sees what you're doing. Ralph was as important as any guy in the band, if not more important.

Ralph Alfonso: I think I was kind of resentful at the time because I hadn't been included and next thing I knew it was, "Ralph, you've got to come back, you've got to help us." They worked it into the deal that the label paid me to be their PR guy, which was pretty unusual but it was pretty cool.

John Hamilton: Ralph ended up working for them; they gave him a job. They didn't like it, they resented that, but we knew that he would at least protect our interests. But he could only go so far.

It happened really fast and it was great. It's wonderful to be successful. It's wonderful to actually have a record deal and go into a recording studio and do all the stuff you've been dreaming about doing and having all the technology there and actually being able to buy decent equipment. John Catto had this homemade guitar which was great but it never was quite in tune.

John Catto: When I was about thirteen or something I had some sort of Japanese 335 copy and I wanted a Les Paul, so I kind of built a new body for it and stuck the neck off of the 335 copy on it. That's what I used all the way up to getting a deal; it was the only thing I had.

Ralph Alfonso: Our first choice for a producer was we wanted to get the guys that produced the Sweet, Chinn & Chapman, I think, because they had also done some work with Generation X. So we brought the Generation X single in and we go, "This is what's happening, this amazing pop sound, can you get us these guys?" And they're like, "Well, no, we're CBS Canada, you get Bob Gallo. He'll make it sound like that." But it was good.

Ian Mackay: Maybe by then we were already being pushed into a box by the record company. Some of the raw energy of the band was lost, certainly in the first record. It was, "No, you've got to sound like this and like that," and we were too young and too naïve to know better.

John Catto, though, was the real voice of opposition with respect to our producer on the first record. He had a lot of artistic integrity. He always had a pretty strong vision of the way the band should sound.

I always felt he was leaning toward heavy metal a bit too much, but that's why I thought John Hamilton was a nice foil; he kept us somewhere in the middle.

John Hamilton: I'll give Bob Gallo his due. He was good, but then he was bad, too. He would take each guy apart and say, "You're the best guy in the band and the other guys are no good." He started doing that shit, but I'll give him his due, he was good in the studio. If we made another record I would use him as a producer, but I'd keep him in line this time.

Ricki Landers Friedlander: He never worked up the band members against each other. That's a fiction. Having known Bob for twenty-five years and worked with him with many bands, I can vouch that it is not in his character to stir people up. He is one of the finest and gentlest human beings you would ever meet.

Paul Robinson: We were quite in awe in some ways with Bob. Bob was a great producer who worked with many important people. He worked with Ben E. King, which wasn't at all related to the Diodes but obviously everybody knows about Ben E. King. He also was one of the original Atlantic people. Obviously it would have had a lot more impact on people making soul records or whatever it would have been called during that period, but the thing that really separated Bob for us was that he worked for a band called Question Mark and the Mysterians, who wrote "96 Tears." He pretty well, I think, was behind that record.

John Catto: It's hard to be objective because when we first went into the studio with him we had no idea how to record anything. So it was real influential. He taught me how to tune a guitar, how to string it.

Ralph Alfonso: Because we were the first band signed, we got all this freedom to do whatever the hell we wanted. [Bob Gallo] was pretty open to everything. He goes, "What do you guys want to sound like, what is this whole aesthetic?"

John Hamilton: The Ramones were the big influence on everybody, there's no taking that away from them. When I first saw the Diodes they were really strongly influenced by the Ramones, but you realized the Ramones were this great idea but it wasn't going to expand. It was really powerful and really great but it was kind of locked into what it was. It wasn't going to form a chain.

So we started moving away from that. We liked the fast, the loud, harkening back to the Brill Building sensibility where all the '50s songwriters used to write all the melodic two-minute pop songs. But then we started moving away from *that*. John Catto was really influenced a lot by Tony Iommi from Black Sabbath. His guitar style was very much like that. There aren't too many major chords; there's a lot of consecutive fifths, modal scales; not blues scales. So we all brought different influences there.

We'd been playing a ton and we were really tight, we were playing really well together, and basically we went in and did the first record almost virtually the way we did our stage show. We played live off the floor, all together at the same time, and then we probably over-dubbed some backing vocals later on and a few guitar solos and stuff like that. But the first record is pretty much the way the Diodes sounded live. They gave us carte blanche on the first album because this was the happening thing.

Paul Robinson: The album was written before we got signed to CBS; this was all material that we were currently performing. It was just us and what we had, and I think what Bob realized is that all we wanted to do was get good live performances down.

You've got to remember we went in and did the album in two weeks. That's the way they used to do it in those days. I think maybe they mixed it for three or four days. We were signed to CBS in August or the beginning of September, and that album came out in October or November. By today's standards, it was done extremely fast.

Ralph Alfonso: The first album is the best and most brilliant of the stuff they've done because it's very pure. There's no record company interference in it and the lyrics, which, kind of like the Ramones, work on a very satirical level. John Catto did live in the suburbs and did go out with suburban girls and plastic girls and all that stuff. That was the reality they were dealing with.

Ian Mackay: Paul had kind of an acute sense of class difference, I think, and understood what privilege was and what working people were. And he brought a lot of that into the band, understanding what the haves and the have-nots were about. It was kind of a pastiche of somebody of wealth, but he had a good idea of what was going on in that area.

Paul Robinson: It was my idea to cover "Red Rubber Ball." This is really dating me: My parents took me to see the Beatles when I was eight years old, and the support band for the Beatles was a band called the Cyrkle and they did "Red Rubber Ball." I really loved the song and it stuck with me. When the Diodes formed I said, "Let's do this as a cover," so that's all.

We kind of thought that it was funny to put it out because Paul Simon hated punk so much. But we already were doing the song live when we found out that Paul Simon hated punk, so it was just a coincidence. We've perpetuated the myth for years.

Gary Pig Gold: When I heard "Red Rubber Ball" I thought, Huh, this is really slick, covering a song written by fellow CBS recording artist Paul Simon. This might really get them where they want to go.

in the studio with Bob Gallo / photo by Ralph Alfonso

Paul Robinson: I think the reason that was released as our first single had little to do with us. I think it had a lot to do with the Canadian music industry. They thought, Okay, nobody's heard of the Diodes so of course we couldn't possibly think of releasing one of their own songs. We'll have to release a cover version. Which was typical of the Canadian music industry. And so "Red Rubber Ball" I guess hit the right note for the music industry.

Ian Mackay: The expectations went from zero to a million over night. Suddenly we had to be a band that was going to record an album, we had to be on tour, we had to really be good at what we were doing, we had to do tons of interviews. We were working very hard from about October '77 on. It was non-stop. We almost disappeared from the social scene because we were so busy just trying to make something happen.

Paul Robinson: The reason we could get the album out so quickly was that CBS had its own pressing plant. They recorded the record and did all the marketing and pressed it all at the same location in Scarborough or wherever it was, and that was unusual. That's why it came out so quickly. But it was one of the earliest punk new wave albums to come out. It came out before the Sex Pistols album.

I know we played the Shock Theatre and I remember in the audience, in the front row, was the guy from D.O.A. and he was wearing my jacket. I had sold it to New Rose and they had sold it to him. I thought it was really bizarre looking down at this guy wearing my jacket who I'd never seen before. That was our first gig we did after we got signed by CBS.

It's probably not for me to say that, but it's a definitive record of its time. Obviously we were following in the footsteps of the New York Dolls and Iggy Pop and the Ramones and bands that we really respected, but we still had our own angle as to what we were doing. We weren't copyists. We weren't a cover band. We never did Ramones copies or New York Dolls covers. We just went out and did our own thing basically and that's our interpretation of whatever we felt was happening. We didn't sit down and plan it. It wasn't a calculated, contrived thing. And I'll never compromise, and that's probably why we didn't make zillions of dollars like some of the other bands that actually cashed in on the wave of things. We got in there and we got out. It's a great statement, really. It was all about youth and it was all about expression and it was all about not compromising and not doing what other people were doing. That's why we were original.

There were a handful of bands doing that sort of thing and we were all slightly different but slightly the same. In Toronto, and Canada in general, we were one of the bands doing that, along with the Viletones, Teenage Head, the Curse, the Dishes ... A handful of bands were just doing what they felt and were following their intuition. People from all over the world genuinely respect what we did and really were influenced by us, whether they be in Canada or France or Sweden or wherever. It's great for me to reflect on those things because it makes it all worthwhile.

Don Pyle: With the Diodes, I was much more aware of them being self-conscious about being stars, the perception about them being much more what the established norm of mainstream success was. And that was proven right very early on because they got signed to CBS. They put out their first record on a major label.

But I think that I was also a big supporter of the Diodes because they were hated a lot; it was very competitive between the Diodes and the Viletones, and the Viletones were very verbal about hating the Diodes. I think that I liked the Diodes more at the time *because* they were the underdog, *because* they were hated.

Carmen Bycok: I hated the Diodes because they were another band who were so cocky, saying, "Oooh, we're going to make it big." In my eyes, if you were a punk you never thought like that. You didn't give a care whether you made it big or not or whatever. You were just doing it because you loved doing it and all that. You just did it because you liked doing it for your little crowd and if you made it big, you made it big. They weren't actively seeking to make it.

I don't even think the Viletones ever did that whole, "We're gonna make it big." They had the thing about saying they're the best punk band in Canada. They would have those verbal wars with D.O.A., but I think with the Viletones, it was like they did their thing and then when they didn't want to be doing it anymore they just went ahead and did other stuff. Like it wasn't that they wanted to make it big, and that's what the Diodes were like.

After the Diodes got the deal, it was, "Look at us, we can't talk to you anymore." Ha ha ha. We were at one subway station and John Catto, he was on the subway platform, I was on that subway platform, and he's definitely trying to make it seem, you know, "Aren't you going to recognize me? Don't you know who I am?" Like trying to get that reaction from me? I'm not going to give you the satisfaction. Now I listen to their songs and think, "That's pretty good."

Ralph Alfonso: The only way you're going to find acceptance is among your peers, and the only peers we had were people in England and people in New York and to a smaller degree L.A. – the L.A. scene wasn't as developed then, it was just kind of starting. We were doing the right things but in the wrong country. There was no indie record label to help you; there was nothing.

When we got signed and I was sort of the shadow manager it was like, "How do I pull the levers of the record company?" They weren't thinking globally. A Canadian record label will only think in terms of Canada so it's like, "How do we get all this press in London, Ontario?" I'm going, "Well, that's cool, but how about London, England? How do we get your UK branch to move the band forward?" So that was the frustrating part. It's like a message in a bottle. You're just shooting it out blind and who knows where it will land and who will pick it up and what they will do with it. I can only speak for myself and the Diodes, but we worked really hard to carve some sort of something in the tree of punk. You know, "I WAS HERE IN T.O." written in a big heart carved out with the arrow – just picture that.

We worked really hard.

*   *   *   *   *

John Hamilton: Just before they sent us to Max's Kansas City to play our big debut in front of all of the American show business types, they figured we needed about a week's worth of seasoning. So our management at the time – Ralph was always our manager but there were these guys around from Franklin House – these guys who were our pseudo managers sent us down to some godforsaken club in the middle of nowhere. I think it was in Windsor or somewhere around there. It was this godforsaken hellhole club. We walked through the door and it smelled. The place was a total dump and it was in some boondock sort of area.

John Catto: Every band I think will have some story about being booked into a straight bar and all the stories are bad. All of them are just horrendous.

John Hamilton: It's just one of those weird coincidences about how you can be in the wrong place at the right time.

John Catto: I remember walking into this bar and the first thing you see is this Frigid Pink poster; really proto-garage punk. I've never even heard a Frigid Pink album but everyone has heard that single "House of the Rising Sun." And I'm looking around – it's like Stooges and MC5 and everyone had played this dive and have their agency photos tacked up on the wall in frames.

John Hamilton: So before we played the pinnacle of New York, Max's Kansas City, we did about a week, or at least three or four days, in this terrible club.

It was probably some of the best shows we ever did for some of these dumbfounded yokels and a few people who were actually hip in the town. And I remember Paul was tearing tiles out of the ceiling and throwing them around in the audience.

John Catto: When you start going across Canada and you start doing these things in Thunder Bay, it's seriously weird. There's always these people with blacked-out vans – it's all a little bit *Texas Chainsaw Massacre*. All these gigs would be like that.

John Hamilton: And we went from there to being at the top of the line at Max's Kansas City, playing in front of Blondie and the Dead Boys and the Ramones and all the press in New York City. So we sort of went from one end of the scale to the other. It was such a weird artistic thing. It was supposed to tighten us up as a band. We could make all the mistakes we wanted there as long as we didn't make them in New York.

Paul Robinson: Going to New York and playing Max's Kansas City and CBGB's; I think just being there when something is happening and being a part of it, and feeling like a part of something that was your movement — it was all exciting. There's too much to remember; it was being at the centre of everything.

Max's Kansas City / photo by Ralph Alfonso

Ralph Alfonso: You have this fantasy, even to us at the time, that once you're signed to a label then all this stuff will happen. But you quickly learn that that's not so. Maybe one part of the company knew what to do, but they weren't able to get other parts of it.

They weren't able to coordinate all of the wheels in the car to move forward on us. Like when we were in New York playing Max's Kansas City, we got the word from head office that we should go to the *National Lampoon* office and protest.

John Hamilton: We were supposed to get signs and protest because they'd done some kind of thing about Canada; they had a beaver chopped with an axe or something. We thought, forget it, man, we're not gonna do anything stupid like that. And that's when it started to get problematic, dealing with record company idiots.

Ralph Alfonso: Right after that things went wrong. Because I think somebody at the label wanted to have this provocative "punk band" stirring shit up, which is not what the Diodes were about so it was kind of contrary thinking there. I think that caused some ill will. So you've got the head of "marketing" or "promo" suddenly going, "Well, if these guys aren't that punk band doing what we want, screw 'em."

Ian Mackay: There was a big expectation; there was a lot of buildup from CBS New York and it was a packed house. We were so nervous, and I think there was a mild disappointment in the audience. But mind you, it was the intelligentsia of the punk scene out that night.

A lot of people who were very serious music people.

That was our moment. We had completely blown them away, and we played well that night, but I think we came across as, "Yeah, yeah, yeah, we've seen that, it's kind of like a Clash/Ramones combo thing." New York is looking for something like, "This is totally different, now I'm into it." So we kind of sat in a nice place that was ourselves, but we were somewhere between the British and New York scene. And that was the Toronto sound.

John Hamilton: New York is always chasing its tail. I remember being down there and having Syl Sylvain telling me Devo was the latest thing, but next week it was something else. They're always chasing trends down there. They have the attention span of a flea. So unless you're something they haven't seen before, they're bored, whereas you can go out in Middle America and make a zillion dollars. But New York would be bored shitless.

Ralph Alfonso: Wendy O. Williams was there before she was Wendy O. Williams. She was Wendy O. Williams: Porn Star. Her manager, Rod Swenson, was doing documentaries on a lot of bands so he promoted the show.

John Catto: He certainly knew a mark when he saw one. Our management came along and he goes, "I tell you what. I'll promote the show and I'll film it and we'll do it at Max's. I'll have my P.A., Wendy, introduce them." So we turn up in New York and there's this guy in this gold lamé motorcycle jacket lurking around and Wendy, who was the star of all his little films and his stage shows.

Ralph Alfonso: Wendy was the emcee; she interviewed the band. The Rezillos were there and local luminaries. Lydia Lunch and Brad, the other guy from Teenage Jesus, were there, and all night long they had their heads stuck in the PA stacks just drooling. They loved the Diodes but I'm going, "This is to the extreme, sticking your head in the PA bin. That's pretty messed up."

Lydia Lunch: If I stuck my head in their amp it must've been because they stuck their tongues in my mouth.

Ian Mackay: Unfortunately, our management company turned out to be the worst thing for us. I think they were using the money they were making from us to promote their main band, a Canadian heavy metal band.

They charged a hefty management fee of every advance that we got. So if we got an advance of five thousand dollars, they got a fifteen per cent management fee up front. They would take their fee off the top and keep the amount in their bank account, and they would dole it out to us as we needed it for living expenses and sound expenses.

At the time we weren't keeping a proper account of that money. They nibbled it away like piranhas.

John Catto: Our management basically went off with our advance and went looking for ways to spend it.

John Hamilton: But playing New York was great. We were the real toast of New York during our proverbial fifteen minutes, playing Max's Kansas City and stuff like that.

When we played at Max's or CBGB's we'd say to people, "We're gonna make it. We're really going there." And they'd say, "For sure you are, man. Alice Cooper has been on this stage. And somebody else who's famous has been on this stage here before you." But the thing about Canada is there's this defeatist mentality. You'd say to somebody in Canada, "Our band's going to make it," and they'd say, "You're just getting above yourself. This is just Canada. It's not gonna happen."

The whole time I was in the music business in Toronto it was like that. If you didn't want to play cover songs it was like, "Who do you think you are, the Stones? You think you can play your own music?" I went to England and there it was *assumed* you could play your own music. But Canada? It was such a colonial mentality.

They build condos now and what do they call them — "Marina Del Rey" and "Malibu."

Ralph Alfonso [*New York Rocker*, November 1978]: While punk has become tolerated by Toronto's populace at large, it still must struggle for due recognition as a musical entity. Part of the problem as to why nobody's taken too seriously is because no local band has achieved any substantial success. The Diodes may have come closest with LP sales of 10,000 and European release of their records, but the closest they got to making the charts was #96 with "Red Rubber Ball."

24. the missing piece

Gary Pig Gold: The Loved Ones were put together in early 1977 out of the remnants of the Specs, with Roy and his friend Simon — who later went on to front the Start, for starters.

I wanted us to rehearse near where I was living in Mississauga, but Simon introduced me to Steve Park, who was a great guitarist, had a really great record collection, and as a nice bonus had a *real* comfy basement to rehearse in. Plus he lived right across the street from the McMaster University cafeteria, which I could sneak in to eat at real cheap any time of day or night. So I relocated to Hamilton for a few months 'cause I couldn't afford the daily commute from Port Credit, plus hauling a bass and amp on the train didn't really work. Especially during rush hours.

Stephen Park: Simply Saucer had been around in the Hamilton scene longer than Teenage Head. I think I'd kind of heard of them, and I remember seeing them at a show in Toronto and being pretty impressed.

Gary Pig Gold: Being in Hamilton afforded me extra time to hang out at Star Records, plus keep an eye on Simply Saucer, who I was running material down with in preparation for recording. It was only natural that Simon and then Steve would start following me over to Saucer House after Loved Ones rehearsals, and that Edgar would wonder what I was doing lugging a bass guitar around.

Through hook and by crook, I soon started booking bands at the Hamilton YMCA and YWCA. I'd really hit the big time by now, right? Pretty soon the Loved Ones had enough material to play an opening slot, too, so on October 29, 1977, we played the James Street YMCA with Saucer.

Those guys really, *really* liked us. So much so that they stole Steve right away from us, right after the gig! But no biggie, I was just glad to see him playing; he fit in perfectly — Saucer got better and stronger in no time. And I could still eat at the McMaster cafeteria whenever I wanted to.

Stephen Park: It wasn't like I played with the Loved Ones and went home with Simply Saucer. I don't know exactly how it happened. There was sort of a mutual interest there. I think Simply Saucer were looking at changing their lineup and I think I liked the sense of experience that I saw in the band.

Edgar Breau: When Steve left Teenage Head – or was invited to leave, I don't know which one – he ended up playing in the Loved Ones with a guy named Richard Citroen, who eventually ended up playing with the Diodes. I'd seen them play and we were looking for somebody, and Steve liked what we were doing so he came aboard.

We knew the Loved Ones, but I didn't know *him* very well. He was a fine guitar player, he was a song-writer as well, and we were pretty compatible. He's a pretty bright guy so he fit in really well with us.

Stephen Park: I would have been seventeen, eighteen or something like that and it was like, well, this is a rock 'n' roll house. It was like I'd died and gone to heaven. It was total freedom and lots of comings and goings and the usual kinds of things like women and parties, so that was pretty attractive for young guys who were eighteen and nineteen. I spent a lot of time there and it was a pretty crazy place with some pretty eccentric people.

Mickey [DeSadist] didn't hang around there very much. Chris [Houston] came around a little bit. It wasn't the only place. That whole crowd was a constantly moving party, whether it was at the Saucer House or elsewhere. So I don't think that we distinguished ourselves that way, except that we *did* have this house.

We used to rehearse a lot. I wouldn't say every day, but we probably rehearsed five times in a week. There was kind of an immediate comfort there. I think what I liked about the Saucer was there was this diversity. It's not so much a matter of comparing it with Teenage Head. It's just that I saw in Simply Saucer a kind of musical diversity; a creativeness that I found very appealing. We weren't a punk band, but we weren't anything like the mainstream.

Initially I think we suffered from that, but voilà.

Kevin Christoff: One night we get a knock on our door and it was this guy who turned out to be Alex [Pollington]. He was a guitar player and just like people would on Kenilworth Avenue, he just happened to be passing by. He told us he heard us one time playing and kept on coming back, and would sit outside and actually listen to us until he worked up enough nerve to knock on the door and ask us if we'd be interested in another guitarist. So that's how Alex came into the band.

After Alex left, Sparky – he had a stint with Teenage Head in their early days – I guess he got hold of or met Edgar somewhere and through that Edgar said, "Steve's gonna come down and have a go with us."

I remember that first day very vividly. Steve was right into it, playing his heart out, and it just clicked. It was the missing piece. So we went from that point on.

Stephen Park: I was in Teenage Head for eighteen months, maybe two years. I was kicked out.

First of all, I was younger than the band. That was always kind of a factor in terms of … I don't know really how to characterize it. Frank was maybe five years older than me or something like that. I was sixteen when I started playing in the band. I think that was a factor. We played at my parents' house, which I think was a matter of convenience for them. I'm not sure I would say I was used, but possibly. Certainly you could see it that way.

There was a time when we had good relations. I don't really have any relationship with them now. I've seen them over the years here and there and at this point I don't really care, but at the time it was a big thing in my life. And I think there was a bit of a differ-ence in philosophy, too. When the band got started there were different musical interests that we had, and some of them were shared. At one point we were really focus-ing on a Ramones-like sound, which was great, but there were a lot of other things I was interested in and I think there was a difference in musical direction. I think the age difference may have contributed to that.

Gordie Lewis: He was great. I think we just decided we wanted to be a three-piece with a vocal. We felt that that's what we should do, and actually it probably was a good move because that's when we started playing more.

Chris Houston: The great thing about Simply Saucer and Teenage Head is both their dads were guards at the Barton Street Jail, and both were waiters at the Corktown. And I was warned that if you partied with Frank's dad, you'd wake up in Chicago in a hotel room and try to call your wife in Hamilton and you'd realize the area code wasn't going through and you had no idea how you got there. Ha ha ha.

The bands were total rivals because they were coming from different camps and there *was* a lot of competition. But both their dads worked together at Barton Street. Jail guard kids.

Kevin Christoff: Rivalry? Oh jeez, I don't know. I don't particularly see it, or to me there's no issue about a rivalry. It may have something to do with one of our members in our latter stage, Sparky, was an ex-Teenage Head. Whether or not there was a rivalry because of that, or what the circumstances were, I really have no idea.

Personally, I like Teenage Head. I didn't know them very well. We did a couple of shows with them. I thought they were a hell of a band. I liked their sound and they were a pretty exciting group. Frankie at the time was quite a showman.

Maybe it was just sort of a musical — not jealousy, not that word. Just a musical difference. I mean musically, we were completely different. Really, all I can say is I just got the impression that they didn't like our music very much. I don't know about any other source of rivalry. We came out around the same time. I think we had a couple of years' head start on them. Maybe it's a west end/east end thing, like *West Side Story*, ha ha ha. It could be one of these urban legends that spring up and get perpetuated.

Edgar Breau: How am I gonna put this? We did a few shows with Teenage Head where things would happen to our equipment. Our amplifiers wouldn't work. I think it might have been their roadies getting overzealous or something like that. I know when we played Rock Shock, we went out and everything went off in the whole place. Who did it, I don't know.

They came to see us when Steve Park joined. I think the first gig that he did with us, they all came out to see him and to see the band and everything was fine. I don't know really how to explain it all. It wasn't as cooperative back then between the bands. Today's much better. Maybe because it was kind of a new scene and everybody was really trying to scramble; it seemed like it was gonna be something that would take off, perhaps. There were bands like the Sex Pistols, the Ramones, and a lot of those bands had done really well.

There was just kind of a weird vibe that went on between the bands. There seemed to be some hostility.

Gary Pig Gold: We were planning on interviewing a lot of people for the Kinks *Pig Paper*, but when we started talking to Edgar we realized it should just focus on him. We thought, "This is an odd egg", but the minute we broke his shell and started talking we realized we had a lot in common and had the same sort of view; not just in music, but the same world view.

Edgar would tell us about phoning radio stations under all these assumed names to try to get Kinks records onto AM radio in the '60s in Hamilton. That's what he was doing when he should have been in school studying — he was disguising his voice and phoning up radio station request lines. So once we got our Kinks *Paper* out, we invited Edgar along when we took it down to flog at the Kinks' show in Buffalo.

That afternoon we were all hanging around in the alley behind the theatre, trying to talk our way into the sound check, when Ray Davies pulls up. And while everyone else is going, "Oh Ray, it's so great to meet you. Can you sign this?" Edgar, without saying a word, just pulls his sunglasses down and, like a guided missile, scrunches then launches himself up, onto, and clear 'round Ray's neck, clinging there for a few moments while we were all cheering, then slowly sliding down Ray's torso and landing in a heap at his feet.

That's Edgar to me in a nutshell.

*   *   *   *   *

Len Cramer: Saucer went through different phases. The early stuff was much more Syd Barrett, Velvet Underground influenced. Ed was writing a lot of the same stuff, like "Nazi Apocalypse" and that. They weren't more punky, but they were a lot raunchier and it fit in.

I think when Steve Park joined the band they got a little more of a punk edge as opposed to when they had Alex in the band. But Saucer was always more, because they had the Velvet Underground and the Stooges influence; I think that's why they were more *proto*-punks. They weren't punks like when you think of the late '70s.

Stephen Park: Saucer is a band that's had different phases and some people have said the period that I played with them was sort of the punky phase, which was true to a degree because the theremin dropped out and it was more a guitar-oriented band at that point. But I think the songs, although we used to go off into these sort of long — I don't necessarily mean solos, but we were into this other phase of songwriting that had more dissonance. I think that's really a good word there, because there were combinations of chords that one doesn't usually get in those very structured songs.

Kevin Christoff: By that time there was very little of the vestiges of the days where we would turn the amps on and walk around King Street, ha ha ha. It became song oriented and a little bit faster tempos, I guess.

It wasn't even a change in direction, really, it was a development. Ed's songwriting was developing along a certain line. We didn't really see it as being any kind of abrupt shift in direction; it just all seemed so gradual to us because we were hanging out with each other and getting acquainted with each other and musically [it] started to gel. From say '75, we just started shifting in that direction. It just seemed quite gradual, quite natural.

Stephen Park: When I started playing with Saucer I think there was the impact of being this really young kid playing in Teenage Head. It had a big impact on me. I was listening to a lot of that kind of music before I played with Teenage Head, but they did have a formative influence on me and I think that was part of what I brought to the Saucer. So the sound got a little bit more on the edge at that time.

25. altar boys

Gary Pig Gold: There was a string of shows at David's that I nabbed for them right away, but getting to know Edgar and especially his songwriting, I was thinking more in terms of getting the band on record. But like about a half-dozen other characters in their immediate circle back then, I'd never hesitate to call myself Saucer's manager or even "agent" if it meant getting into peoples' shows for free, nyuk nyuk.

Edgar Breau: We did play the Toronto punk scene in the '70s. We were in there pretty much on the ground floor, playing the same kind of clubs with the Viletones and Teenage Head and the Battered Wives and the Poles and the Dishes and all them. I remember Steve Leckie saying — he was DJ'ing at David's — we did our sound check and he sauntered over and goes, "I really, really like you guys, but you're not a punk band." I thought that was kind of funny.

When we started out it was kind of the Modern Lovers era and the Stooges and eventually Patti Smith and Television. We were considered more of that category of a band.

We could be very, very raw. That was another side to the band, too. It wasn't a perfect fit when we played those clubs.

Gary Pig Gold: There were certain bands who either tolerated them or liked them, and the Battered Wives come to mind. They didn't mind playing with Simply Saucer because the Wives had a definite '60s foundation to them.

But still, it was *so* much fun to watch audiences listen to Simply Saucer, because again, this was the era of the three-minute fast song and swear at the audience and look "provocative." And Edgar would sometimes stop for a minute and recite a poem, or they would play a twenty-minute song with no lyrics, just moaning or something like that. It wasn't so much theatre or anything; it was just ... *Hamilton*. It was like he brought Hamilton to Toronto. Just as he had brought it to Buffalo by the scruff of Ray Davies' neck.

NYC, Blues Brothers hype Viletones on Blues Bar Jukebox
/ photo by Ron Gwynne

Mike Anderson: Because of Dan Aykroyd's place at 505 Queen, we actually got in with a lot of people like Catherine O'Hara and John Candy and those people. We'd go to their parties and word would get around — "Oh, the Viletones are here."

Cynthia Ross: This guy named Marcus O'Hara lived in a storefront down on Queen with Dan Aykroyd, and they used to run these speakeasies once a week to pay their rent. They just used to open the storefront and sell beer. People would get up sometimes and play music. It was kind of just this fertile ground for people to be doing things in the arts and in music, and everything was really connected.

Freddy Pompeii: You'd walk in at any given night and there'd be Belushi hanging out, or Chevy Chase. That's one of the reasons the Viletones got so much attention, because part of that networking was hanging out at Dan's speakeasy. Word spread really fast in the entertainment community. That was a big deal.

Ron Gwynne was Dan Aykroyd's business manager when Dan was on *Saturday Night Live*, and Dan was requesting the Viletones 45 so Ron brought it down to him and put it on the Blues Bar jukebox.

Tibor Takacs: It was easy to book the Viletones into Max's Kansas City because they were notorious in the punk scene, and any punk club would welcome them for at least a night or two. These clubs never really paid well; the band would play for the door and free beer. *Any* punk band that played Toronto would vouch for the Viletones.

Freddy Pompeii: The band looked great all the time because of the talent up there onstage, all working together. And it wasn't a great amount of talent, it was just using the talent you had and working it the right way and letting the band do the rest; letting the magic of the chemistry happen.

Mike Anderson: Even our light show was basically stark: White light and that was it. We didn't have the reds and the blues and twirls. We just had white light. We talked about that because we could've had light shows, but what we did was just white light.

Freddy Pompeii: The centre of the band, the most intricate part of the music, were the drums and the bass. What the drums and the bass did as a rhythm section to fill out the sound was phenomenal. They made a really big sound and you felt like, when you were onstage with Motor, that you were surrounded by this thunderstorm. Like you were standing in the middle of this thunderstorm.

When it came to writing and recording material, Steven's contribution was very little. The songs had to be written with a guitar because it was a guitar band and a guitar sound. Steve's lyrics weren't all that great, but they rang true at that time for kids that age.

But what he was really genius at was promotion.

Chris Haight: I looked at it as everybody had a job to do. Dog was in charge of PR, Freddy was the guy that made sure everyone looked cool, I was the guy that knew how to play, actually, and you need that to keep it together.

Freddy would be like the guy that Steven would take aside if, for example, Steven didn't know if he looked right. He'd say, "Hey Freddy, do I look cool?" He was only, like, eighteen or something at the time and if he got the nod from Fred he'd go out and perform in whatever he happened to be wearing. But he had to get the second opinion from Freddy, who was the oldest guy in the band.

Motor was the guy that always had to try the hardest. He's a hard worker and he's probably the guy with the greatest sense of humour, too. He also saved the Dog's hide on a number of occasions. Sometimes the Dog would get too full of himself and it'd backfire, and he'd be crying, "Motor! Motor!" So Motor would come in and save him. So everybody had their little role to play.

Steven Leckie: It really motivated me, it really fuckin' motivated me, that press thing. It was a way to give a "Fuck you" to my dad who was in PR, and I was getting so much of it.

Freddy Pompeii: For our first gig at Max's Kansas City, the same summer that we did CBGB's, Steven got on the phone before we went down there. He told some of the top journalists and some of the word-of-mouth people he had done everything that he wanted to do and was going to kill himself that night onstage. He *promised* to kill himself.

Steven knew what he was doing as far as promotion was concerned. I always backed him up on that. But the thing is, I had no idea that he had made these phone calls before we got down there.

There was a big piece of graffiti in New York on one of the walls heading west. It was gigantic, like a billboard: VILETONES RULE. It was written on the third story of a building and if you were riding down one of these streets, I think it was Third or Fourth Avenue, you couldn't miss it. So we're in New York and there was an article in *New York Rocker* that Nazi Dog from the Viletones promised to kill himself and it's gonna be the last Viletones show with Steven Leckie.

Chris Haight: Steve would be the guy that would play the press in little serials, little chapters, like, "I'm gonna kill myself before I'm twenty-one," and this and that. People would come just to see how far he would go.

Some nights he would just totally get sucked in his own little world, and the scars are there to prove it. Other times he would tease the audience. But he always had that knack about keeping the interest up. He was perfect for that. It's as if he knew what they wanted to hear and stuff, because they'd love him. They'd love talking about him. Ninety per cent of it was bullshit, but it was *interesting* bullshit.

Freddy Pompeii: That night at Max's everybody was there. The Ramones were there, Debbie Harry was there, the Voidoids, Johnny Thunders and his Heartbreakers, some of the New York Dolls. Everybody who was anybody in the scene; the place was packed.

Chris Haight: Danny Aykroyd showed up. He was in the dressing room and saying hi to us and chatting and this and that.

Freddy Pompeii: The first EP was ready for when we went to New York. We showed up there with record in hand and sold a lot of records and did a show that was more us than the Canadian Scene show.

Steven Leckie: I went on some good verbal tirades at Max's. It was a good opportunity to do that. I remember talking about how square I thought Americans were.

I took it upon myself to think I was the one to inform an audience in Manhattan, and a really hip one. Because that's Park Avenue; that ain't the fuckin' Bowery. You're playing to the moneyed crowd now, so it gives them something to really think about.

I don't know, the only thing I kind of semi-regretted was when I said, "Don't fuckin' forget it, we're a Canadian band, we're from Toronto." I felt the need to tell the world that, and you had an era also where you had a limited forum to do it in. So on the stage I look at, like, maybe there's ten per cent of that audience that can be used as a sounding board for the things you believe in, like people that are connected in various professions that will go back and tell people that they heard us at the show and promote the cause, if that makes sense.

I was thinking the floodgates would open and more bands from here would go down. But they didn't.

Freddy Pompeii: We had a kind of improvisational approach because Steven had problems with arrangements and remembering where he was supposed to come in and where he wasn't coming in. So we would follow him into choruses and verses because he would forget otherwise.

It wouldn't be four measures, it wouldn't be eight measures, it wouldn't be twelve measures. It was whenever he was ready to start singing again, he started singing and then we would follow. So the songs stretched out. Sometimes they were two minutes, sometimes they were five minutes depending on how he felt onstage. That's where his strength was — in the way he performed and the feel he had for connecting with the audience and the feel he had in working for the band. His contribution was large as far as being an entertainer and a front man.

So we start the show and about the first song into the set I get up on Steven's shoulders to play a lead. He's walkin' back and forth across the stage and he's drunk and he'd done some pills. He was, like, really staggering and he was singing really bad that night because he was so fucked up. And I made the mistake of getting up on his shoulders.

Chris Haight: We would go over the edge, and maybe this one gig just kind of pushed us over completely.

We're going along, we're doing just fine and Danny's out there and that. The band's rockin' and Steven's got Freddy on his shoulders. And then it just went, *kaboom*!

Freddy Pompeii: Halfway through the song Steve dumps me off his shoulders. He leans backwards and I fall off his shoulders and I land on the stage and pass out. I had a real heavy Les Paul guitar and *bam*, I'm out for about two minutes, out cold.

Chris Haight: Freddy falls right on his head and he's out like a light. All of a sudden it just stopped. Everything stopped.

Freddy Pompeii: I wake up with everybody around me — "Freddy, you all right? Freddy, you okay?" The curtains close and there's all this noise outside and some people grab me and carry me up to the dressing room and I start to regain consciousness.

Bleecker Bob, who owned the real famous record store in New York and was going to be selling our record, he loved us. He was in the dressing room and he decides he's gonna take care of me. He runs me over to the emergency ward and they look me over and take x-rays and everything.

Chris Haight: Honest to God, maybe they thought we were too mental, because we never saw Danny Aykroyd again. And that was a show to remember.

Mike Anderson: We were booked to play *Saturday Night Live*. But when Dan came down to see us at Max's and saw Freddy get knocked unconscious, he took a look at that and said, "Forget it." That's the last we heard of it.

Chris Haight: It went from, "Hey guys, I love your band!" to, like, "Danny who?"

But Freddy, fortunately, was okay.

Freddy Pompeii: I went back to the hotel after the hospital. They gave me a bunch of Percocets because we had another show at CBGB's the next night. So I decided to get some rest and try to keep the pain down as best as possible.

Bleecker Bob went back to Max's Kansas City and said I was all right. Everybody was asking about me; if I was all right, if I was dead.

Chris Haight: We knew we were kind of headed in the right direction when they kicked the door closed in the dressing room at Max's afterwards. I'm exaggerating this, but you could see all the hands from the outside all around the door jamb — people trying to get in. We knew that we had something going for us.

Freddy Pompeii: What had happened was, Steven wasn't really gonna kill himself; it was all just a ploy, but everybody in New York was calling him on it. He had to do something spectacular, so he threw me off of his shoulders so the show would be stopped so he didn't have to kill himself. I never forgave him for that.

Steven Leckie [*The Pig Paper* no. 8, April 1978]: It was a mistake, but I have no regrets about dropping him. I'm *glad* I did, but I'm sorry I hurt him. I didn't mean to.

I just wanted to show those jerk-offs at Max's that there is such a thing as rock 'n' roll that isn't played by long-hairs who wear black leather jackets day and night and blue jeans and tennis sneakers like the Ramones. And it worked. I was named one of the Top Twenty Punk Rockers in New York City, and I've only played there three times. I think that's an accomplishment. I'm proud of that.

Chris Haight: When we played CBGB's I remember Dee Dee Ramone in the front row throwing syringes onstage. Stupid Dog, he picks the thing up off the ground — you don't know what the hell is in them — and he sat there and he's doing this on the stage. The crowd just thought it was tremendous.

Freddy Pompeii: People gave us incredible stuff. They'd just say, "You guys *rock*. This is for you." We'd always get handed something.

Chris Haight: I thought it was flattering that Dee Dee would be doing that. At the time I thought this was cool, but I didn't want my mom to find out that this guy's throwing syringes onstage. I still had a little bit of altar boy in me. Dog wasn't much of a shooter. He kind of popped pills and drank his face off, basically.

Freddy Pompeii: Steve was a garbage head. He would do everything except heroin, like the girls that used to do everything but. If he caught me doing heroin he'd say, "I'm ashamed, I'm ashamed," and do his real dramatic thing. I'd say "Knock it off, Steve, you've got fuckin' scars all over your arms." He was such a character.

Tibor Takacs: It was hard to make a business plan. Don Jean-Louis had money invested and we had to protect it and turn a profit. Every way we looked at it the money was marginal till there was a record deal, and a lucrative record deal would only come with a fan base.

The single got some pretty good airplay, actually. I never expected *any* airplay, really, because it was a bit weird for the time, but it did.

Steven Leckie: People were freaked out by our single. I have no idea why. It seemed to capture a sensibility of the time. It's so beautiful.

Tibor Takacs: We tried to enforce a discipline and organize the band to be more productive and focused, however we still could not do enough to prove to record companies that they were serious and responsible. Talent is one thing; business savvy and the ability to make money another.

When we played New York we sent out a bunch of promo packages and then you know A&R people started to say they were going to come. So Seymour Stein showed up at CBGB's and was quite serious about the band.

Chris Haight: Mega Media were always there to point out a great idea. Every show was kind of an event, anyway, but *after* every performance they would actually give you a quick analysis. And they were subtle about it, like, "I like what you did there." They never got too high about it; they just told you, like a nice critique. That's how they would do it.

Tibor Takacs: When I asked Steve to cool the Nazi shit when the record company was coming to a gig, he did not. He said he would, but then he would just do whatever he wanted to do anyway. Steven's not stupid. He would think it would be smarter to shock people like that.

Sometimes he was right, other times he was wrong. He just went with the flow; if it was a very intense show and it was really going well, he just went with whatever he felt like doing. He was spontaneous.

Something happened onstage. I don't remember. I want to say the flag got taken out, they had some Nazi flag, but I don't think so, no. It wasn't that intense. I think they sang "Auschwitz Jerk" or something. Which is enough, you know?

Lucasta Ross: When I look back at it, I'm just mortified that I wore Nazi regalia. I'm Jewish on my father's side which technically makes me not Jewish, but emotionally I am half-Jewish. I remember my grandmother, who *is* Jewish, trying to explain to me how horrible this was. And I said, "Yeah, but it doesn't mean that to me," you know. Very flip and very appropriate for my age at the time. Like the world revolves around me and so what if people don't get it?

And later I looked back on that and thought, Oh my god, I can't even imagine what the Jewish people whose ancestors died in Auschwitz thought when we were wearing this crap. I realize the only reason we wore it was for total shock value, but I don't think most of us realized how deep that shock was — the essence of the shock. I feel very bad about that. But that's youth, and youth is stupid generally.

Tibor Takacs: I think Seymour Stein of Sire Records saw one of the shows with some Nazi stuff; some swastika stuff and that kind of cooled them off. There was some talk — it's a bit foggy for me, but I think there was talk about recording without a contract.

And that was something I wasn't really interested in doing. I didn't think it was the right thing to do. But I don't know if that really was the reason why it never happened; that's maybe just one of the reasons.

Steven Leckie: There was a rumour that Malcolm McLaren had paid off Sire because it would possibly usurp the energy of the Pistols. And I have documentation of that, too. That's the way music is behind the scenes – that cutthroat.

Because a song like "Screamin' Fist" … it ain't "Anarchy in the UK" with all that fuckin' money and Chris Thomas producing it, but it's a bitch of a song, especially in real time. It sort of then sounded like "Ace of Spades" by Motorhead; it had that kind of flavour.

The record companies would have felt the obvious agenda: That this was against Sweet and Goddo, and if we get behind what is probably the better product we'll lose two or three others, you know? And that's how I'm positive they thought of it that way.

Freddy Pompeii: We had been eyed up by CBS and if we would have showed a little bit more professionalism we probably would have gotten the contract other than the Diodes, because we had a bigger name than the Diodes. We were always the first ones that people would approach, and it was almost like Steven took great pride in telling people to get lost. It was like, "It's not enough, you don't have enough money for us." That's one particular thing.

And then there was Sire Records in New York. They were interested in us. Again, Steven just told Seymour Stein to forget it, he wasn't interested. I don't know what he wanted. I don't know what he expected. What the Diodes got was a pretty good deal for a new band doing something brand new, something different. I mean, like I said, we could have had that.

Steven Leckie: When you went to a record store and you wanted punk and you saw Viletones you'd say, "I gotta get that one, too." So timing for us, I was so blessed. It had to happen and it had to happen here. Tons of people would say, "Stay here, stay in New York, you're better than the Dead Boys, they're square, they used to be called Frankenstein, they're from Cleveland." But there was something about wanting to knock 'em dead in Toronto. It was hit and miss.

Tibor Takacs: Steven always thought himself more famous than he really was. He believed his own hype. It was too early to act the star. He needed to spend more time rehearsing and writing songs and less time partying.

I had learned that nothing is easy when art meets commerce. I didn't realize at the time how hard it is for people to face success; even a mild success.

Freddy Pompeii: The stage at CBGB's is high enough that a person can sort of stand up and throw his hands forward and rest them on the stage. I think what happened was Steve was going through his stage antics and he sort of struck a pose in one position, and this guy took out a knife and tried to stick his foot to the floor. But I don't recall how it happened or why it happened. It was just one of these crazy things that the audience does sometimes.

It was like a dream. Not being awake, sometimes you just felt like you were along for the ride.

Steven Leckie: I was on the stage and some chick had something in her hand – I didn't quite see it – and she came down and it landed right through my Beatle boot.

That's when the arc really changed. This idea of punk and real, raw *Clockwork Orange* violence – real, serious violence – introduced itself to me. The knife went through, but I was too young and still too strong to think I should go to the hospital over it. But that was a turning point.

Also, in that time the backdrop in New York was really tense with violence because you had Son of Sam and that was a potent thing. All these things to me were really important, so I knew when you're playing CBGB's you're playing to mostly kids from Jersey, and that's why I preferred playing Max's Kansas City because that was the New York kids.

CBGB's was suburban from the beginning. I thought it was incredibly square compared to Toronto. Very, very square, American kids. The Toronto kids looked proper.

It had that kind of reaction, that this broad would stab me. I thought, Wow, what does that mean? That's kind of going past what Iggy did. Iggy was peanut butter and certain mutilation, but when you're getting to the point where the performer could possibly be stabbed, you're introducing other things. You had darker forces come in to the American brand of punk but not the cool, Toronto/English brand. So that's how getting stabbed in New York was. I think it got a little bit of press up here but it was *wildly* talked about down there.

I think a lot of kids partake in a certain kind of private self-mutilation just to feel, and maybe when this girl saw me exhibit it in more of a performance art aspect, meaning in a public display of self-mutilation, it probably was her attempt to actually fuck it; to actually come with it. If I'm reading my Freud right, it doesn't sound like I'm too far wrong.

She'd probably be making a conclusion from her own mutilations to this guy who could do it onstage, get paid for it, and I'm going to be in union with that; she's marrying it. In other words, I never interpreted her act then or now as a negative thing.

Jeremy Gluck: The thing with Steve is he had genuine charisma and that's very, very rare in a front man. And I think that's why people were quite compelled and horrified.

I mean, he was genuinely horrifying in many ways, literal and figurative. He had that potential to be developed, if he'd had proper management and patience and a disinclination to destroy himself rapidly. Look at Iggy — same sort of thing, and that was his role model, obviously. Iggy though, of course, had a rich benefactor and stuff who rescued him, but for the Steve Leckies of this world there's no such person.

Steven Leckie: I think the timing, when I was doing it as a performance art, bringing it to a rock 'n' roll theatre; to put it on a rock thing and to take it one step higher than Iggy meant this is for *real*. Iggy's was a little mythic; there's no witnesses. There's this myth that a case of beer was all cracked up and smashed and torn on the ground and he writhed in it. Realistically you couldn't do that, it would kill you. But what I wanted to show was you could almost *smell* it. And that's nasty, of course, but that's punk.

So of course not everyone was doing it, but there were a lot of disenfranchised people who were in the punk audience. This was the audience that felt alienated from every other form of music. So when you factor that in, when punk came along it gave them a voice.

When you were the lead singer in the Viletones, you were introduced to more shamanistic and demonic things, perhaps just by virtue. Steve Davey's not gonna get stabbed onstage, or Paul Robinson from the Diodes. I will, though, and it wasn't good but I recognize in it that that girl was making a transference without knowing.

Captain Crash: I was disappointed in him when he didn't kill himself when he got to twenty-three. He promised all those years — "I'm gonna kill myself when I get to twenty-three." He lied.

I don't think anybody took him seriously, but the thing was you never knew.

Colin Brunton: With the Viletones, you didn't know what to expect as far as spectacle. I remember him advertising one show on Halloween at David's, and the cutline on the poster was, "It's my party, I'll die if I want to." And the rumour was he was gonna kill himself onstage.

So that was the big difference with bands like the Ugly and the Viletones. With those guys you never knew what to expect. Like, god, is Mike Nightmare going to jump off the stage and pummel somebody to death? Is Steven going to cut himself open? Is he going to kill himself?

Chris Haight: I think that was half the fun. Nobody really knew what to expect, like where it would go or that kind of thing, so there was always some intrigue with every show. It was always, "Hey, we gotta come back next week to see if he really kills himself!"

Margaret Barnes-DelColle: What I'm trying to remember is if he went to the hospital. He swore he wasn't going to live for very long.

Captain Crash: I mean, fuck, he'd slice himself up onstage; *somebody* would take him to the hospital to get stitches.

I forget how many he was up to. He used to count them. "I got seventy-two stitches for you guys," that's what he would say. "For you guys! Lookit, lookit, this is for you!"

No, Dog, this is for *you*.

Freddy Pompeii: I got him back for that night at Max's, though.

When we got back to Toronto we were in New Rose and he kept putting his hand under the counter to grab beers, and there was money under there. I said to him, "Steve, stay away from the money box. Don't go under there, don't go under there." So he just ignored me and kept going under.

I grabbed him in a headlock and I had one of those staple guns, one of the real high-powered ones, and I put it right in the middle of his forehead. I started pushing the handle down so he could feel the pressure of it and he's going, "Fred, no, no, Fred, please don't. Fred, please don't."

I said, "Steve, you remember that night at Max's?"

"Oh, you know I didn't mean that, Freddy, I didn't mean that, you know that, man."

I said, "Well, you remember that night, don't you?"

"Yeah, yeah, yeah, I remember. I'm telling you, I didn't mean it."

I said, "Well, I told you I was gonna get you, remember?"

He started to sweat. He thought I was really gonna do it. There was half a dozen people in the store witnessing this and they were all looking at me like I was really gonna do it. Finally, I let him go.

I said, "You didn't think I was really gonna do that, did you Steve?"

"Ahhh ... Yeah, man, thanks for not doing that, man. Ahhh ..."

He's standing there all sweating and turning red, leaning up against the wall. I scared the shit out of him. Ha ha ha.

26.
an alley cat walkin'

Mickey Skin: One Halloween night I remember dressing up with Nora. I think we'd done acid and it was Halloween. I was wearing a black face with white rings around my eyes and my mouth and I was wearing this cat suit and black and silver glitter and I had a black leather trench coat over it that I think belonged to Mike Nightmare, but I borrowed it.

We were at David's and Nora's jaw locked, so we decided we had to go to the hospital. So we went down to the Women's College Hospital and now it's about midnight and of course we're drunk and high. We go down there and we're waiting in the waiting room and the people were kind of ignoring us or trying to, ha ha ha, and I kept saying, "Come *on.*" Nora couldn't move her jaw, literally. So finally they put us in a treatment room because I'm sure they just wanted to get us out of the lobby.

I decided while we were there that I should get a VD test — "Well, might as well, while I'm here." They were like, "Well, you'll have to come back."

"Well, I'm here now, can't you do it now?"

I was just being loud and obnoxious. Then we were waiting and waiting and we wanted to be partying and I just got so impatient I said, "Nora let me see your jaw," and I just took her mouth and went *rrreeeerr* and fixed it. She said, "Mickey, you fixed it!" And I said, "Good, so let's get the hell out of here."

We went out knocking over chairs and kicking ashtrays and hightailed it out of there. That was just the beginning of the night.

Then we found one of those salt boxes that hadn't been filled with salt yet because it was October and we hid in the box, because we thought they were gonna come after us. So we were sitting, crouched in the box and peeking over the lid and of course we were howling. We were laughing our heads off and finally we climbed out of the box because the coast was clear. Went to some speakeasy on Wellington or Front Street or Adelaide or somewhere. There was a party going but it was practically over because the booze was gone. I managed to steal the last bottle that someone had stashed and we took off with that.

Freddy Pompeii at New Rose / photo by Gail Bryck

Of course everybody was following us because we had the last bottle of booze. Jimmy the Worm and I forget who else, they were all following us but we kept ducking them by going into alleys and stuff.

We ended up over on Queen Street East where New Rose was and Crash lived above the store. So we decided that was a safe place to bring our bottle and finish. They were in the front, they knew we were going there so they were out in the front trying to call us out and we went and climbed the fence and snuck in the back through the back door and he let us in.

We ended our party there and finally got rid of the rest of them. Nora and I, we were so drunk that we were standing in the hall talking to each other up the stairs in this little, tiny flat with crooked floors, and because the floors were so crooked we were leaning over to compensate and we fell over, we were that drunk. We were stupid drunk. It was mostly about getting drunk. Ha ha ha. That's what we did.

David Quinton: I knew Mike [Nightmare] actually fairly well because I used to be around when the Ugly would play. Put it this way: I knew Mike better than any of the other guys in the Ugly, and I used to talk to him a lot at the Philips Building.

He was — how do you describe him? Do you ever know people who have been in jail? Mike had this edge. This thing about him. He felt like a guy who had done time; he talked like a guy who had done time.

Greg Dick: Mike went out with Ruby. I just would stare at her. I never got to know her. I probably would have just stuttered and fell over, I was so in awe of her. She was just so strikingly gorgeous. She had that little china doll face, black, black hair, everything she wore was just so tight and she was so curvy and so cute.

And I probably could have got to meet her because she was Mike Nightmare's girlfriend, but I was just too freaked out by her, that's the truth. Guys like David Quinton and that, he's younger than me, but he was in a band. He was in with all those people, but I wasn't. I was just a little guy from Hamilton.

David Quinton: I met Ruby in '77. In those days, some of the bands really wanted to experiment with the concept of taking people that had no musical experience and putting them in bands. It was really based on the Sid Vicious concept. So when the Androids first got together we were looking for a singer, and our guitar player Bart Lewis really loved the way Ruby looked and he sort of knew her from the scene and asked her if she wanted to come and sing with us. She was pretty good, and pretty interesting, so she was in the band for a while.

She was a very gregarious, kind of sweet girl with a lot of street exposure. I think at that age — when I was sixteen and I was meeting a lot of these people, I really didn't understand where they were from and what their circumstances were because I was a middle class kid, and some of them had come from some pretty rough backgrounds. Even the Androids used to live together in this house and scrape together pennies to buy food. It was really quite bad.

But Ruby was very cheery and fun and always smiling and laughing.

I remember one really funny moment with Mike. I went with my girlfriend to see *The Elephant Man*, the John Hurt/David Lynch movie. As we were walking out, Mike Nightmare was in the lobby with Ruby T's. I said, "Mike, how'd you like the movie?" And he said, "They said it was a horror movie. It wasn't scary at all." That's what he said; I'll never forget that. It was such a heart-wrenching film — this really heartfelt, emotional film about this poor guy, but it was being listed in the newspapers as horror. Can you imagine the absurd irony of that? It was so stupid.

Anyway, that's what he said. I thought it was so funny and it was so Mike Nightmare. That's exactly what he would be like.

Nip Kicks: What surprised me was how some of these guys could treat their women like such shit. Two names that come to mind would be Leckie and Nightmare; both very hard. I mean, I didn't witness any violence, but that constant sort of putting somebody down to build yourself up kind of stuff. That I couldn't handle.

Freddy Pompeii: Steve's biggest problem was striking out against women. When he had girlfriends he was prone to beat them up. You know, slap 'em around. I had to come in between him and Eva, his girlfriend, once at David's. He threw her down a flight of stairs and she landed flat. Luckily she didn't hit her head or anything.

Ruby with The Androids, Shock Theatre / photo by Ralph Alfonso

I said, "Yo, Steve, what the fuck is wrong with you, man?" He says, "Oh she's faking it, don't listen to her." She's down there, she's crying, and she was hurt. I just got in between them and said, "You can't do that, man, you can't do that." He just says, "Don't listen to her, she's always faking it. She just cries to get sympathy."

Talk about sympathy; I mean, he would go off on tangents to get sympathy. His whole thing about mutilating himself was another offshoot of that behaviour because of all the rejections. He wasn't gonna be rejected this time. He was gonna do things that were gonna make people recognize him, remember him.

Tony Vincent: I think Ruby used Mike to get to know people in the scene. She went out with Mike and then she started her own band. I think they opened up for us a couple times. She got to know a lot of people involved in the music industry through Mike. It's kind of mean to say, but to me she seemed like kind of a leech.

Nip Kicks: I look back now and she had this sort of dumb-ish persona. But you don't know what was underneath that dumb-ish persona.

The first time I met Ruby, I was standing in David's Club with Mike Nightmare. She walked up, said hello, Mike grabbed her T-shirt, ripped it in two, ha ha ha, and Ruby walked away and said, "What'd you do that for?" No explanation, no nothing.

That was how I met her. It set a pretty good pace for the way the rest of their relationship might have gone. I always got along with her because I got along with everybody, but she certainly had a real bitchy side. There was a side that, again, you just didn't trust. You couldn't trust her.

Nora Currie: Mike was an amazing front man. He was raw, pure, dangerous energy. He was frightening. I was always a little afraid of him.

I spent a lot of time with him because he and Johnny were best friends. His girlfriend Ruby was on the scene really early. She was from Chatham and she was so pretty. She was really young; a little younger than everybody else. She left home and came to the city and she had no money. Very pretty, really sweet. She grew up on a farm. While she was very sophisticated and lovely, she still had that farm in her; it's a different kind of mentality than a city one.

John Hamilton: I brought Ruby into the scene. She had been singing with a guy that I used to play with in the Daily Planet called Gord. He showed me all these pictures — I think they were trying to be punk or something. They had Ruby posed on bags of garbage and stuff. I thought that was pretty tacky.

Ruby T's / photo by Gail Bryck

She was a defector from disco. She used to hang out at that disco club on Yonge Street, the disco fag club where we used to snort amyl nitrate. It was the Toronto version of Studio 54. She'd been a regular there, but she was looking for something new. So I met her and I dated her; I guess this was before I met Jula. She started hanging around the scene and I said, "You've gotta come to the Crash 'n' Burn and start meeting some people."

She eventually hooked up with Mike Nightmare, which was pretty bad news for her, actually. Mike was a gorgeous guy, handsome bugger, and he had a dick on him like a proverbial baby's arm with an apple in its fist. But he was bad. He was a bad guy. He had a gun and he'd done robberies and she was always running around with a black eye or a fat lip after that.

Nip Kicks: I don't think anybody liked being around that relationship too much. Watching those two having arguments and spats was crazy.

Anna Bourque: The only person who was mean to Ruby was when Mike was her boyfriend.

Nora Currie: She used to pay him to have sex, and he would keep all his sperm and freeze it. If you opened their freezer it was filled with condoms. He was saving parts of himself for the future — cryogenics.

Anna Bourque: Cryogenics in a freezer in Kensington Market.

Nora Currie: He was ahead of his time. And she had to pay him twenty bucks; but yeah, she had to borrow money sometimes.

*   *   *   *   *

Gerard Pas: I was a member of Parallel Gallery. Greg Curnoe and I got to know each other in London, Ontario. Greg was proud of the fact that he'd been thrown out of the Ontario College of Art, and he was proud of the fact that he was a rebel and a member of the Nihilists. So he was a senior artist to me and really influenced me. I just thought he was so cool and I wanted to be a rebel, too. But I realized that I couldn't do it in London and so I actually went to Europe and fucked around there for a while. That's where I came in contact with other people, in Germany, and I had my art with me and I was pounding the concrete.

Because of my interest in punk and so forth I met some German punks who were artists. One thing led to another and I started doing some performance work there and when I came back it really affected a change in my work. I started wanting to make brash, hard images that spoke about my own pain. A lot of pain that was true and real in my life that I wanted to express the only way that I could and I wasn't pursuing music, I was pursuing art.

So when I got to Toronto I went and visited with CEAC and I brought my portfolio with me. I brought these photos, and they could be construed as pornographic, but they were art. CEAC really thought my stuff was pretty interesting. We became friends right away. They offered me a place to stay because they had this huge, giant building at 15 Duncan Street. Having a place to stay at that time in my life as a young man in Toronto was infinitely more exciting to me than London was.

I was very interested in the Curse. First, well, you know — one, I'm a boy, to start with, so that helped in becoming a fan of theirs. And two, the first time I saw them, it had nothing to do with music. I had a kind of resentment to popular music at the time because you'd just go into a disco and they didn't even need dope, they were already in a zombie-like state. Them and their shiny shoes and stuff didn't interest me. I had already gone through that with David Bowie, and David Bowie to me was infinitely much more interesting, so why would I want to be involved with that disco scene? So when I saw the ladies play, they had so much energy and they didn't give a tinker's damn about anything. But somehow it formed itself into music.

Because I was a member of the Forest City Gallery I could affect change in my town. And I wanted to, God forbid. But because there were people like Greg in the Nihilist Spasm Band, I had a certain amount of support from them. So I asked if I could bring the Curse to London and they said, "Yes, please."

Anna Bourque: We were playing a gig at an artists' thing. It was at a gallery in London, Ontario and the guy was a performance artist and gotten us involved in what was really this night of performance art. He had some interesting performance art himself, having to do with his asshole.

Linda Lee: It was at the Forest City Gallery, and it was weird because there was a woman who was doing a performance piece and she had a gun.

Mickey Skin: That was a weird show in London. They heard that we threw food and stuff, so they brought food to throw at us and they threw steaks and eggs and tomatoes. That was pretty bizarre.

Gerard Pas: It was early in London, and London didn't really understand it yet. There hadn't been any punk bands play here before. But it was a marginally good turnout, about fifty to a hundred people.

But what it meant to me — and this is going to sound selfish, but I don't mind — it was also a means for me to create a little bit of counter-culture for myself. I could design the poster, I could have it printed on a silkscreen and go around town and put them up everywhere and make some shocking image about a shocking band that was going to play at the Forest City.

They brought the Ugly with them, and so it turned into two bands for the price of one. And I could feel, *there* was *my* input. I could look at my mentors and say, "See this shit? I did that."

Mickey Skin: Afterwards our drums got repossessed by Long & McQuade because we hadn't paid rent and they were covered in egg. Ha ha ha. I think they looked at them and said, "Never mind."

Gerard Pas: One of the very first punk soirees that I'd been to outside of Canada and outside of New York happened right after in Detroit at a place called the Spiner Diner.

After the London gig I brought the Curse down there and they played with the Romantics. The show was all organized under the auspices of CEAC, and I'd asked if the Curse could come and they said yes.

27. come on, disease

Now whether the Romantics liked the music or not was completely arbitrary, because they were pretty slick guys and they all wore ties or something. And the Curse, they weren't slick at all. They were pretty rough around the edges. I don't know how many of them actually knew how to play an instrument very much before they started to play in a band. I think it was Julia who could. But they managed.

Mickey Skin: We went to Detroit with Gerard, this guy who did this art piece. I don't know what it was, he was sitting on a pyramid butt naked or something. We couldn't get our equipment through the border and we didn't even have a changing room, we had to change in the public bathroom. We were like, "Where's our dressing room? Don't they know who we are?" Ha ha ha.

Gerard Pas: When we got there the girls didn't have a proper PA and they thought that one would be provided. I had met the Romantics somewhere else — I can't remember where, precisely — but we managed to get their phone number and called them, and they loaded up their shit in the van and brought it over so there was a PA for the band.

Anna Bourque: We had to scrabble things together. That night was kind of evil.

Linda Lee: They kept us waiting for so long before we went on, so finally when it was time I filled my mouth with whipped cream and walked out on the stage and spewed it at the audience. And this guy had a gun pointed right at us. In Toronto, things like that didn't happen.

Julia Bourque: Somebody screamed, "Get down! Get down! There's a guy with a gun in the audience."

Mickey Skin: That was scary. This girl cornered us and said, "I have a special treat for you," and she starts singing "Happiness is a warm gun ..." Then she pulls out a real gun and aims it at us, you know, "Bang, bang." We just about shit our pants.

Anna was mad and she peed right on the jukebox. She said, "I'll show them." Ha ha ha.

Anna Bourque: They said they weren't gonna pay us, so before we left I just pulled my pants down and went for it.

Jimmy The Worm, Captain Crash, Chris Haight / photo by Gail Bryck

Captain Crash: It wasn't so much the punk scene that I was attracted to. It was just one band, the original Viletones.

A couple of my friends were in it and they needed a hand, so I gave them a hand. It just mushroomed from there. I became their manager for a while, and the babysitter.

I'd known Chris since before I went to school, actually. We used to talk to each other before we could cross the road. I would sit on this curb and he would sit on the other curb and we'd talk back and forth, waiting for our moms to come out to let us go across the road.

Chris Haight: He was the biggest kid on the block, really. He was another great fan. Crash was right in there; he was an immediate entourage forever and he knew Freddy and the whole shebang.

Captain Crash: The first gig I saw them do, my girlfriend and I went to see them. I think we were late. We only saw the last song or something, and I think we saw Eva kick the shit out of the Dog with her spiked heel. It was a brouhaha. It was just mayhem. There were four inches of beer on the floor and it was jam-packed with kids going crazy, just drinking a lot of beer and having a lot of fun. It ended up being a madhouse in the end. I think they had to clear the place out. There were a lot of fights, I remember. There were like four or five different fights. It was just fun.

Freddy Pompeii: Mega Media were paying us weekly so we were actually able to quit our jobs. And that allowed us to write songs and we practised about six hours a day for a couple of months straight.

From all the practicing they started booking us in Philadelphia, New York, Jersey, wherever they could book us, Montreal, and got us through the winter.

Captain Crash: It gave me a chance to quit working. They were kind of semi-famous in Toronto. They never had problems getting three or four hundred kids out to a gig. We got paid every week. We had money in the bank and we had a management team that paid us. I forget how much, it wasn't a lot of money; it was like seventy-five bucks a week or something. It would be beer money and stuff, you know? It helped out. We were supposed to turn the gig money over to them but we'd tell them to fuck off. We'd just take the money and divvy it up ourselves.

There'd be fistfights onstage and stuff. We'd be on the road and we'd get so fed up with one another because somebody'd show up drunk and be missing all fuckin' day and show up late for the gig and couldn't play a chord, so there'd be fistfights. You have to be somewhat responsible, even if it's punk rock.

We took it fairly seriously for a while until everybody started fighting and nobody gave a fuck anymore.

Chris Haight: I remember in Montreal there was a label called Montreco, right? And this was a great scam, too. I don't know how they pulled this together.

Freddy Pompeii: They licensed out the single "Screamin' Fist," and they put it out on a 12-inch.

Chris Haight: Somebody from our side was negotiating a deal with this outfit. Now these guys, because it was a 12-inch product, thought they were getting an album. And what it really was, what it turned out to be, was three songs.

All the guys were going, "Holy moly, it's only going to cost us this much to get this album together" … until they went home and found out there was only three tunes on it. I can't believe the guys pulled it off, because I think they were paying comparable to LP prices, but it was just a big EP.

That first trip to Montreal, one of the M&M boys quit by the time we got to Kingston. He just jumped out of the van and said, "I can't handle this shit, man."

Freddy Pompeii: Steve Zoller quit. He says, "I can't take this anymore, that guy's fuckin' crazy." Which would happen with everybody that we would come in contact with that wanted to work with us.

Chris Haight: Tibor Takacs, he's the guy that hung in there until the end. But his partner was just pulling his hair out. The guy had a nervous breakdown in Kingston.

He just bailed out. He got too stressed out and he just quit in the middle of going to Montreal.

The last thing I remember was him going, "I don't know, man," and then he just kind of disappeared.

Freddy Pompeii: Some of them were smart enough to stay away. Some of them were crazy enough and knew that there was something there and they did it anyway. No matter how bad Steven would be, they would hang on. We *had* to have people that were like us to manage us. They had to be our age or not too far away from us, because there's just no way they could put up with Steven. He was always throwing fits.

Steve Zoller just decided he couldn't do it anymore because Steven was threatening him with knives.

Chris Haight: So Tibor, he was doing everything now. But the thing about Tibor was he was really smooth, and he was big enough in stature so you couldn't really push him over and talk bad to him like some of the other attempts at management. This guy was a pretty solid guy and you knew that he could handle his shit, so you didn't really think about giving him a rough time.

Tibor Takacs: I remember I was sort of in charge of taking care of the Viletones; that was my job because Steve Leckie was sort of my friend at this point. And I guess Steve Zoller was — *everybody* was — sort of getting fed up with them because they were irresponsible all the time.

Freddy Pompeii: Steve [Leckie] always knows how to remain friends with the right people. He sees what he can get from them in cash and goods and booze or whatever, and when everybody gets disgusted with him they kick him out.

Steven Leckie: Yeah, Steve Zoller quit. It was too much. You can't imagine.

Let's say in I'm in a hotel, I'm open wounds, I've got a girl in the hotel room that looks like a million bucks, but we can't get in the room because she's passed out on Quaaludes. It's beyond the beyond.

Chris Haight: But Tibor, he managed to keep a really close leash on the Dog.

Tibor Takacs: I only remember the fun times. Like the first night at the Montreal gig there was a rival band waiting outside the club to beat up the Tones.

Freddy Pompeii: It kind of was the fault of the promoters. They billed it as a Battle of the Bands, the French against the English, and we *did* have a little fight with them outside. I mean, we were drunk, you know, and Motor was always ready for a fight. Then after that, everybody was friends. It was like we had to fight before we could fuck, you know? Ha ha ha.

These guys couldn't hardly speak English but they were the nicest guys in the world. I mean, they sent us Christmas cards afterwards.

*   *   *   *   *

Chris Haight: The Dog hardly ever brought up his upbringing. I only met his dad [David Leckie] once, at our first gig in Montreal.

I met his dad before the show, and I guess he was some kind of exec. He was well-to-do and was doing just fine for himself. He was quiet, reserved. I guess he wanted to come down and see what his son was up to. Don't forget, a lot of that crazy press preceded every Tones show. It was more an event than a gig.

I met his sister, I met his brother, I think, but he never talked about home life. Just that one time when he said, "This is my dad." That's the only time Steven ever mentioned him.

Steven Leckie: I had a lot of friends, but there was a loneliness surrounding me, too. It was the angst of it all.

Why was Andy Warhol lonely? I mean, he knew everyone in the world, yet he was lonely. Why was John Lennon so lonely? I'd hate to be at that level. I can only imagine the loneliness of an Elvis Presley. And there are varying degrees to it. You live and breathe off of how the audience is going to take it, and it's just a lonely way to live.

I guess it's a yearning. We're unfulfilled from parental acceptance. Our reward doesn't come from, "That was a good job, Wayne, you're a good skater, now try to shoot." It's easy to understand Wayne Gretzky's dad. Now what if you're fuckin' Lou Reed's dad? "Oh son, you've written 'Heroin,' that's really good." That's awfully slippery terrain; that's choppy.

So that's where the loneliness comes from as an artist. If it's real art, it has to be about alienation. It has to be. My father couldn't possibly understand "Screamin' Fist." He understands "Return to Sender" by Elvis, but Elvis was *pleasing* his parents.

Lonely, and that's the price. Some people pay it in different ways than others.

Chris Haight: Our first time in Montreal, the owner is walking around just high as a kite; he feels so good about his brand new club and his brand new four thousand dollar stage. About halfway through the first tune the Dog just grabs the mic stand and starts hammering this big, big hole in this guy's four thousand dollar stage, and there were wood splinters flying and this and that. I'm looking at Fred and I'm looking at the owner and he's losing his marbles.

The next thing I heard he's going, "You guys better just take a hike right now because you're gonna get a knife in the back." It didn't help that the Dog had come on before he even sang a tune and said, "You know what? You guys are nothin' but a bunch of hicks." And then he did the hole in the floor. I mean, I was concerned at times.

Mike Anderson: A fight erupted with the audience. It turned out to be these gangsters. Chris was throwing beer at them and gesturing and this and that. The director was behind the stage in this little room so we went up there. And when we left, there were people waiting for us outside and this altercation started and next thing I know there's glasses breaking and stuff was going on all around us. Then we went back to our hotel and carried on as usual.

We got called in earlier the next night and the owner, this old Mafia-type guy, says, "Don't do that around here. These kids will stick a knife in ya or they'll shoot ya or something. You don't know who that is." It turns out they were these gangsters in Montreal who rob banks and stuff like that. He says, "You go up to that dressing room and lock the door. Just stay there until we tell you it's time." So we did that, came out to do our first set, and things had kind of tamed down that night. The same people came back and they had suits on, nice suits and ties, they were all well-dressed and everything, and were shaking our hands and apologizing.

It was very strange. I guess they couldn't believe that somebody could be that wild and crazy and not be afraid of them or the situation.

Chris Haight: Can you see how your chances diminish with acts like that? I mean, who's gonna take you seriously and sign you?

Tibor Takacs: It was hard to imagine ever making money with it, and it was taking us away from filmmaking and theatre and all that stuff that we [Mega Media] wanted to do.

Chris Haight: I think if we were a little more civilized about everything we would have had a better shot at it, or a longer shot, but that's just the way it was. A lot of the time we were under the influence — mostly booze — and so perhaps we could've had a better choice of words or better behaviour perhaps than we did a lot of times.

I would remember there would be execs coming down from these different labels. Abnormal behaviour is putting it mildly.

I never really looked at it as any longevity kind of a deal. We were just so full of ourselves and we'd close our eyes and it was like another dimension for us. We didn't care about recording or record companies or nothing. I guess we were just too busy expressing ourselves. We were artists in our own right.

I remember they never took us seriously. We always used to get ribbed for it; that maybe if we paid a little more attention to the business end and less time trying to be rogues or whatever. The press had a field day with us. I'll say this much, that for what it was it was ass-kickin' good and it was very sincere, very genuine. It wasn't like we were wannabe punks, or we'd go home and think about what we were gonna say or dress like. It was right on the money. There was a lot of bad stuff, too, but I don't think it could put a dent in all the great times that came out of it.

Freddy Pompeii: We went down and played CBGB's again after Montreal.

Captain Crash: Nobody would stay with the Dog in the hotel rooms. We made sure he got his own room. He was a pig. He was an absolute pig. Nobody wanted to stay with him.

Chris Haight: Down in New York, we were given lunch money and stuff to hang around for whatever the duration was. And they made the mistake of giving this dough to Dog.

So imagine Dog going out and buying leather pants and this and that, so when it came down to, "We're hungry," he just couldn't look us in the eye 'cause we knew he had dough and we were starving to death. Little things like that didn't really help. You don't want to have any extra internal strife because it was already the hottest firecracker, that whole thing. Even Eva, his girlfriend at the time, couldn't even look us in the face.

That was one of the worst times, because it wasn't like all for one, one for all. I didn't like that at all. Nobody did. We're all pulling the same rope here. We were really pissed off. Mostly we had no beer money.

Back then our whole psyche was fueled by the Dog — "I'm not gonna go to practice unless you guys get a case of beer" — that kind of stuff, so it was just an accepted thing after a while, this is how you start practice. You know what? He'll never forget how me and Motor looked in New York when we were looking at him with our fuckin' hands out going, "I'm hungry." He'll remember.

Tibor Takacs: It was just like babysitting. We'd be in New York and they'd want to score some drugs and they'd have to run around, and I'd have to get them together for the gig. It was like being a babysitter, and I didn't want to do that.

We kept them on an allowance and of course they'd spend it, but that wasn't the part that bothered me the most. It was their irresponsibility. They just wanted to live the lifestyle but they didn't want to do the work so to speak, and Steven eventually admitted to that.

Captain Crash: Nobody ever slept; the only time we slept was for a couple hours in the middle of the morning when you drank too much beer and you hadn't had enough to eat. You'd pass out for a couple of hours and then you'd get up and go, "It's New York City!" You'd just get goose bumps going down the street. As soon as you get in the city limits the hair stands up on the back of your neck.

Freddy Pompeii: Of course CBGB's was packed again and by that time we were getting to sound pretty good; we were actually a working band. We would play without having any breaks in between tunes. We'd build the set up in a way that would keep the crowd captivated so they couldn't just walk out.

Steven Leckie: I got stabbed again at CBGB's. I got stabbed there like fuckin' three times. Mary Harron, who was a writer for *Punk* magazine at the time, took me to St. Vincent's Hospital to get stitched up.

Captain Crash: Steve sliced himself onstage with a broken ashtray and beer bottles and shit. I don't know how many stitches he had to get.

The Dog would never travel anywhere by himself. He'd take a taxi everywhere or get a ride, have somebody pick him up. If he had to take the subway — if he *had* to take the subway — he'd travel with an entourage. He'd be afraid. He looked outlandish. He looked fuckin' outlandish.

So after the gig at CBGB's I took him to the hospital. We're happening, right? I'm gonna get laid that night, I've fuckin' got beers lined up on the counter. We're stars, you know? So I drop him off at the hospital; I'm not waiting for him. Ha ha ha.

He goes nuts. He says, "Crash, this is what I pay you for! You *have* to stay." I said, "No, I'm not. We don't come to New York City every weekend. I'm leaving you here and we're going to this loft after the bar's closed. I'll see you later."

I got in a fight with him the next morning. I remember waiting in Washington Square for the Dog and he was really late, but it was still only noontime and I was catching forty winks. Chris and Freddy and Motor took all these newspapers and they put them over top of me, so I was sleeping underneath the newspapers and they put all these empty wine bottles and beer bottles around my head. I hadn't been drinking, but that's what they made me look like. Next thing I know there's two cops kicking me in the ribs and the one cop's saying, "Come on, Disease, get up, the maid wants to change the sheets." Ha ha ha.

Chris Haight: The cop was right on the money, just like that. Disease — ha ha ha. It doesn't get better than that.

Captain Crash: We were going to the Hot Club in Philadelphia. I started fighting with the Dog on the New Jersey Turnpike in the back of the van. It's doing seventy miles an hour down the turnpike and we're fighting because I wouldn't wait for him. I think he fired me, but he couldn't. Ha ha ha.

Chris Haight: The Hot Club in Philadelphia was good stuff. I'm sorry we never made it to Chicago. We only travelled out of the country to the one spot, really, and that was New York. Unfortunately it was too fast, too furious for us and it just burned up, like, in no time.

Freddy Pompeii: We played with extreme energy, really fast and hard, and it affected people in a very violent way. People would start breaking chairs and punching each other out. It was just the way the music affected them. We didn't incite riots or anything like that; it just happened. Not every gig, but eighty-five per cent of the time they were near riots and sometimes real riots, and most of the time we couldn't finish the show. Sometimes we finished the show regardless, while these riots were going on, so it became part of the party.

Something like that happened in Philly. We had to fight with the audience before we could be friends with them. The first night, the first show that night, we ended up in a barroom brawl with the first two rows. Then everything settled down and they loved us after that. They were there for every show. They got thrown out after every show and they had to pay a new fee to get back in again to the next show and they did it. Explain *that* to me. I still don't get it.

I'd say that that Philly show was one of the best shows we've ever played. It was strange because it was the United States, and I'm an American and Philly is my hometown. I think for that reason it was one of our best shows because all of my old friends were there and it was like my triumphant return to Philly. I was nothing when I left Philly and I came back with this big accomplishment, so I guess I was pretty pumped up.

Margaret Barnes-DelColle: Fred's dad went to see them at the Hot Club. His dad was elderly and he took Fred's uncle Dante with him, so it was Uncle Dante and Sammy. Afterwards, I remember Fred telling me they were freaked out because they went to use the men's room at one point and there was a guy in one of the stalls and a girl was in there giving him a blowjob. They were mortified.

Freddy Pompeii: It was a very strange scene. It was like a bacchanal; a big orgy while we were playing. I'm grinding away with the guitar, and I look over my shoulder and here's a couple going at it in the washroom and the door's wide open for all the world to see.

I was always saying that I would love for the Viletones to get people so excited that they would abandon all their inhibitions, take their clothes off, and start having sex in public. That's what I consider a pretty radical vision, ha ha ha, and it actually happened in Philadelphia at the Hot Club. I couldn't believe it. Steven's saying, "Hey, man, you got your wish! You got your wish!"

Steven Leckie, Freddy Pompeii / photo by Gail Bryck

28. this life is . . .

Don Pyle: I remember there was a New Year's Eve show at David's. The Cardboard Brains played, the Ugly played, the Sofisticatos played.

It just felt like chaos.

Sam Ferrara: There was a buffet, and people started throwing baloney at us. So Mike grabs a piece of baloney, folds it in half, bites it, and puts it around his dick. Raymi starts peeing on the crowd, and Anna Bourque, the bass player from the Curse, went down on me. This all happened while we were playing a song.

Raymi Mulroney: My brother would get onstage wearing a voodoo mask singing, the cameras going off, and there was three hundred people there stoned out of their minds. Booze, prizes, five bucks admission, three bands, everybody decked in leathers. It was nuts, it was a fantastic time, and it just got carried away.

Sam was playing bass, I think Tony was on drums, and Freddy Pompeii was singing.

A girl got pulled onstage, her clothes ripped off. I think I went down on her; I might have, I'm not sure. My girlfriend saw it and flipped out and took off on me. It was real raw stuff. It was nuts. The place got torn apart basically.

Don Pyle: I remember the Cramps were also playing at the New Yorker right around the corner. I went to the one show at David's and then went over to see the Cramps, and minutes after I left the place caught on fire and burned to the ground.

Raymi Mulroney: I think by four o'clock it was emptied out and by six o'clock it burnt down. That's what I heard.

Nora Currie: The Curse were supposed to play David's that night and it was cancelled at the last minute. I was with Mickey and she was so upset. We dropped acid and we were roaming the city, cursing David's. We were going around saying, "We're going to fucking burn it down."

In the morning we heard it burned down, so we were waiting for the cops to come knocking on our door. Ha ha ha.

Tony Vincent: That night I stayed over with Cynthia from the B-Girls. Sunday morning someone called and said, "David's burned down, all the equipment's burned." I thought it had to be a joke at first, but it wasn't. So I ran down there that morning.

The fire was so hot that everything just melted. All the equipment, everything. There was nothing left. I think somebody sabotaged it. I don't know why.

We stopped playing; we just stopped playing. So did the Viletones and a lot of the other bands. I don't think it had anything to do with equipment, it was just the whole thing had burnt us out. It was like, "This is the end." That's what it felt like.

Johnny Garbagecan: I heard about the fire at nine o'clock in the morning and I was there at nine-thirty. I jumped out of bed — you've never seen anybody out of bed so fast on New Year's morning. So I got there and they were trying to figure out, How did this fire start?

Chris Haight: It was just some rickety old joint, wood, so when they put a match on that one it just — *shooop* — like a Roman candle. I don't know much about the demise of him [Sandy Leblanc] or the joint, but I think it was pretty heavy. He was tied into some heavy shit.

Freddy Pompeii: The next day we were over there salvaging whatever we could, our amplifiers and drums and everything. Some roadies were dragging stuff out of this burned-out hole and up pulls this van and it's the Misfits. We said, "What are you lookin' for, man?" They said, "We're lookin' for David's, we have a gig there." And we said, "Well, I don't think you have a gig anymore."

Glen Danzig was a real skinny guy at the time with his hair dyed green in streaks and stuff, and they all just stood there completely disillusioned. I felt so bad for them.

There was another room just starting to open up called Shock Theatre. It was run by some friends of mine, we called him Count Bill, and his wife. He sort of looked like a vampire. The Shock Theatre was an old movie theatre right outside of Little Italy around College Street. They started having punk rock shows there. While the Misfits were in town they put them up there because they had living quarters, and they let them do their show there so they were able to make a few bucks so they could get home.

Steven Leckie: Funnily enough, we were the only band who had actual insurance, ha ha ha, so Motor comes out with this drum kit the Stones couldn't afford. It was gorgeous.

Steven Leckie, Freddy Pompeii / photo by Ross Taylor

Tibor Takacs: The fire didn't help anything. It kind of put a damper on things for a little while. All the equipment got burned and there was no more club. It was *the* venue, really. I can't remember, by that point were there other places that were playing? No, that was it.

That was just another chink in the Viletones' coffin. It was too hard to keep it going, and it was too hard to make it into a business venture which our partner was pushing for. Understand we were using his money and we just barely broke even, you know? It was too risky.

The Viletones were not moving on or evolving as much as I wanted them to. They were just doing the same thing they always did. They wouldn't rehearse very much and new songs weren't forthcoming. It was just like they were happy to be drinking beer and playing wherever.

Steven Leckie: The next day, of course, everyone calls me like, "Steve, you won't believe what happened." I was down there at seven or eight in the morning. For me that's really early.

It evokes a sense of possible mystery ...

Freddy Pompeii: Nobody knows why David's burned down.

Steven Leckie: Losing David's held us back, but I always thought that pain was the ticket that you bought to the Viletones. Teenage Head could play the El Mocambo. I knew *we* couldn't.

But I loved that place. It was so wickedly cool, like Studio 54. People were doing blow on the table — "You

mean you could just do it front of everyone?" "Yeah, go ahead." That's the way it was in the '70s. And I was very young but I was going, "Wow, this life is going to be good." And David's gave you that feeling, too. You could do amyl nitrate and drink like banshees for free.

Freddy Pompeii: I think I'd like to go back to the days when we had David's, except know more of what I know now than what I knew then.

That one period; it was maybe a six- or nine-month period of Viletones history. We didn't know how big it was until we started getting press from England and France and press from the United States. When we played CBGB's we were written up in *Variety* the first time we played. To get written up in *Variety* and you're nobody is a pretty big step, but it really didn't seem that way to us because I guess we were in the middle of it. It impressed *other* people, but we were the least impressed. If I could do it again I think maybe I would have worked harder. That's my only regret; I just didn't work hard enough. None of us really worked hard enough. We were just basically coasting; getting through it.

If I was aware of what was really happening on the outside I think I could relive those years even better, fuller.

The time of David's was when we had the most opportunities to choose from.

Forgotten Rebels; Chriss Suicide, Mickey DeSadist, Pete Lotimer / photo by Stephen Burman

29. Just me

Mickey DeSadist: Before punk started, I was just *me*. I was interested in racing motorcycles and I wasn't very good at it; I never got involved in a race. As a kid I was a class clown in every class I was ever in.

I was one of the guys that hung around everywhere, and I heard some music here and there. I was a fan of Slade and Mott the Hoople and David Bowie and the Spiders From Mars and the Stooges and the New York Dolls. I had a band together and it wasn't the Rebels yet, but I kept telling the guys to stop making their guitars cluck like they were in the late '50s or early '60s; stop making these stupid guitars cluck and start making them *roar* like a guitar should roar. I figured out this neat sound that just carried and carried, and I started trying to put songs together and these guys thought the songs were all too radical. So I thought to myself, You know, I don't think these guys are right. Everybody had the same last name in the band except for me. One guy was into jazz. It was just a fucking walking rubbish heap.

When I heard the Sex Pistols' "Anarchy in the UK" I immediately quit that band. I was walking around and I heard some guys jamming in a basement. These guys were rookies; they were starters the same as me. They were playing BTO songs and stuff like that but they were okay, they were a nice bunch of guys. One was into KISS and making spectacles of himself, and the other guy was a good drummer who was in it to have fun.

So I started the Forgotten Rebels with these guys, Carl and Angelo. I remember me and Carl walking across the field deciding to form a band, and that was August '77.

Then we found out there was supposedly a punk rock band around which wasn't really a punk rock band but sounding like the Kinks or whatever. We went and saw these guys and they were pretty good. We thought, We're better than the opening act they have and we would be pretty good with these guys. So we started hanging around the Saucer House because our first gig was opening for them.

Imants Krumins: We're in Simply Saucer's party house and this guy comes around and it's Mickey. We're yapping away and he's got this chain through his nose and all this.

I went a couple days later to get some film developed at Miracle Mart and some guy says "Hey, Imants," and it's him behind the counter in a suit and tie without the dog chains.

Gary Pig Gold: Mickey was just hanging around – I was impressed first by his wardrobe – and he said, "If I get a band together can you give us, like, a gig?" And I said, "Yeah, you can open for Saucer," because we were renting the Y to play.

So he actually got a band together.

Mickey, Frankie Venom, Edgar ... These were punk rockers before there was such a thing. The cool musicians always seem to come from Hamilton, and still do. It's probably just because of the awful water or the Stelco in the air or something.

Bruce Farley Mowat: There is a good argument that the history of rock music in Canada started in Hamilton, because that's where Ronnie Hawkins touched down in 1958. He was invited up by a guy named Dallas Harms, who was a country songwriter. He wrote "Paper Rosie" for Gene Watson. At the time rockabilly and country were kissing cousins in the '50s, so people went back and forth.

The sequence of events was there was a guy named Harold Jenkins who played up here before that. He played at a place called The Flamingo, and he wrote "It's Only Make Believe" on the back of a paper bag there and became Conway Twitty. Now at the time Harold Jenkins was doing rockabilly, and the word got back to Ronnie Hawkins that you could actually play up here for money.

So Hawkins made the initial investigation. He didn't do too well that first night. Dallas Harms put the call out to recruit people to come out and see him and saved Ronnie Hawkins' bacon.

So that's how rock music came to Hamilton, and perhaps in terms of artists' nucleus, because Ronnie Hawkins' school of rock 'n' roll spawned off people like the Band and Crowbar. Crowbar were also from Hamilton. Dave Foster, who produced Celine Dion, was fired by Ronnie Hawkins.

Gary Pig Gold: But all those cool Hamilton musicians always seem to have to go to *Toronto* to play, or even get noticed.

Mickey DeSadist: I knew nothing about what was going on in Toronto at the time. I think maybe Teenage Head had played there. Frank told me the people in the audience were spectacular in comparison with the city here.

"Punk Rock Helps Push City Group Up Ladder," by Doreen Pitkeathly [Hamilton *Spectator*, December 9, 1977]: None of Teenage Head are teenagers. Frankie is twenty-one, Steve is twenty, and Gordon Lewis, guitarist, and Nick Stipanitz, drummer, are twenty. The four live in Hamilton still, with their families, but they find their music doesn't appeal to the hometown crowd.

"Hamilton is just a bed and a stove to us," said Frankie. "We do most of our playing in Toronto — there just isn't a market for our music here."

Gordie Lewis: There just wasn't the venues. Hamilton was a really big blues town, which I only found out later,

so whatever this punk movement was really wasn't accepted by anybody here, even the musicians. There was an isolation factor, and I think it was a lot of them didn't think we were legitimate. You know, "This isn't real music," a bit of closed blinders on. Music snobbish.

Which was really strange because before that Hamilton was, probably more than Toronto, one of the more musical, open cities in Southern Ontario. But the city *did* change. It became very stale. They really decimated the downtown area with that Jackson Square there, the mall. They just bulldozed the majority of the downtown. They took all the life out of the city.

Mickey DeSadist: Because Hamilton was full of rednecks and skids it was a basically useless, stupid scene here and I bet you the city's suffering for it still because the people that were motivated to do anything in the city left.

Gary Pig had this magazine, *The Pig Paper*, which was a self-motivated type of thing and he decided to put a page on us in there. And at this point we hadn't played a gig yet. The first one was at the YWCA in Hamilton across from the Tim Horton's.

Gary Pig Gold: There weren't that many places to play. They were either being shut down, or burning down, so I was trying to promote shows at the Y in Hamilton. And I only got one on before they shut *that* down.

Chris Houston: There was a famous show here at the YWCA with Simply Saucer and Forgotten Rebels. At that point people would rent halls, and the poor people that rented them out had no idea what craziness was going on.

All I remember was that they had terraced floors in it, and Mickey had this Aims amplifier that was so blisteringly loud that the entire audience was concentrated near the back of the room.

I don't think they've had any rock gigs there since.

Joe Csontos: Honestly — and they'll hate me for saying this — when I saw the Forgotten Rebels, I thought they totally blew. Really amateurish. Mickey was great, but the rest of the band just blew.

Mickey had this vision, and I knew Mickey from the old days; he was a glam rocker. He always liked that music. He liked Mott the Hoople the best, and Bowie and T.Rex, so you can connect the dots with these kinds of guys who were into that music.

Len Cramer: Mickey was doing the *Metallic K.O.* album verbatim. People were throwing glass bottles at his head and it was crazy. And Ed Breau's young brother was going to beat up all the Rebels for some reason.

Imants Krumins: All their fans got in a fight with all the Saucer fans. So there was a big brawl going.

Edgar Breau: I think Mickey burned a Canadian flag at that gig. The people who were running the YWCA were not too happy about that and I don't think we played there again after that.

Gary Pig Gold: I got sued by the Y for four hundred dollars after the show for my troubles. Including, and I quote, "Damage to Vegetables (Carrots and Lettuces), $25.00."

I told them, "I'm not a real promoter. I just promised Mickey I'd put his band on." But the Hamilton Downtown Young Men's Christian Association served me with a notice reading, "I would also like to inform you that at no time in the future your group will be allowed to use the facilities." Not exactly grammatically correct, but I got the message and didn't promote another show for three years. And *that* one was in Long Beach, California, just to be on the safe side.

*　　*　　*　　　*　　　　*

Stephen Burman: I met Mickey at Tim Horton's. I said I'd just come back from England, I was at Screen on the Green in Islington, so that's what got him going. I don't think he'd met anyone who had actually been there and seen the punk scene at the time. That got his goat.

Mickey DeSadist: When "God Save the Queen" came out, I honestly thought that was a major statement. A lot of people stopped caring, and I didn't care in the first place. I remember getting scolded in school for asking why we pledge allegiance to the Queen, because if England's so many miles away why do they have something to do with us in that respect? And I got yelled at by the teacher for merely asking a question. The world was run by idiots at that time.

I can remember when a person that was twenty years old wouldn't talk to a person that was thirty, majorly because a thirty-year-old's views at that time were awfully antiquated. And definitely talking between a twenty-year-old and a forty-year-old was out. They'd be complaining about long hair and stuff like that. Whose body *is* it, anyway? How could our parents have been so ridiculous as to tell us how to wear our hair? How could the establishment at that time have been so stupid and useless that they would spend more time telling kids how to wear their hair than to give them an education process?

So I guess if you call that political, I'd say it was a social change. In England, the record industry got so bloated and big that they were creating stars that were rubbish. They failed at innovation. I guess it happened here, too. All the record labels had failed at innovation, but innovation was happening whether they liked it or not. But what it was, was a *social* change. The intelligent people that were seeking to see something were actually noticing it, the same way the artists were noticing new artwork years ago.

The groups that didn't like the punk rockers were always the groups that weren't having as much fun as anybody else was. When they were saying to us that you don't have enough notes or this is too fast or anything like that ... Mozart was quoted as saying it neither has too many nor too few notes, it has the *right* notes to complete the musical idea.

And it was just music to some, and fashion to others. It was an expression. Finally, the rednecks and the skids were no longer popular; their time was up. People stopped caring. Who cares what the redneck says? Who cares what the teachers or the police say? We know what we want for ourselves at this moment. And the morality rubbish that the parents pushed on everybody, it was useless.

The thing about the Royal family and "God Save the Queen," well, there's a prime candidate to pick on, let's pick on that candidate. The sacred cow was no longer sacred, and a lot of people that didn't care for the monarchy got on the bandwagon. They didn't care. They still don't care. They realized that it's not part of something they want to be part of. Other reasons it happened? Social change. The underground seemed more attractive, and it *was* more attractive, than the above ground. The commonplace was as boring then as it is now.

Stephen Burman: We were the first guys to put chains from our ears to our noses. I remember our history teacher in Grade 10 – she was mortified. She must have been a hundred, one of those really old teachers.

Mickey had just started the band. Chriss Suicide was there from the start. He was the first bass player. The original drummer was Italian-Canadian. A nice enough kid; pretty square, a bit of a rocker. It wasn't his scene so he disappeared pretty quickly.

Chris Houston: The Rebels could only rehearse when Tony and Angelo Maddelina's parents were at church.

Mickey DeSadist: There was a party house on Robinson Street and I saw a bunch of guys partying, and I heard them playing Teenage Head. Pete Lotimer lived there.

Pete Lotimer: I was at work and we hired this guy, and him and I kind of started hanging out at work. He started telling me about Iggy Pop and that kind of stuff, and I had no idea what he was talking about because I was not into that at all.

We ended up getting an apartment together and he was right into Iggy and the Ramones, and I had *no* idea what was going on. I kind of hid my albums when I seen that stuff, ha ha ha.

We just started getting into it. We rented a big house, the big Punker House in Hamilton.

Stewart Pollock: Drink, fight, and fuck — a perfect night out in Hamilton. It doesn't matter the order, either.

There's actually great people there. There's nothing to do except drink, do drugs, and I think that's why so many great entertainers, comedians, writers, musicians, actors come out of Hamilton. It's incredible per capita how many people come out of that city that have excelled in Hollywood and the music business, from the Second City crowd to Daniel Lanois.

Everywhere in the world I travel I run into somebody from Hamilton. Usually the loudest person in the bar. I get to talking to them and, "Oh yeah, you're from fuckin' Hamilton, eh? It shows." I think it's the kind of place where if you don't get sentenced to life there, it's okay.

It must be the Hamilton curse. So many people get sentenced to the fuckin' factories there, or just to mundane lives. The people I grew up with are doing the exact same thing now as what they did when I left there twenty-five years ago. They've got a couple kids in the mix and they've got the house, the mortgage, the dog, the factory job or the nine-to-five of some sort. It's kind of sad in a way, their existence, from my perspective.

House parties seem to be a thing there, and that's really where the punk scene in Hamilton grew out of. There was Teenage Head and the West End crowd. The peripheral fans who later became musicians and played in their own bands or whatever had a place called the Punker's House on Robertson Street. This is the kind of place where you'd finish your beer and just throw it at the wall, and there'd be a big pile of fuckin' beer bottles in the corner. The only thing that was played there was Ramones, Stooges and Dolls. That was it; nothing else. It never stopped playing, twenty-four hours a day. Constant party. Lots of acid, lots of booze, lots of bennies. Yeah, people never stopped.

Pete Lotimer: If we wanted to go to the beer store, we'd go a couple houses down and steal a bike because we didn't want to walk. When we came back, we had this alleyway that came up to the side door, we would come flying up that thing with our beer, jump off the bike, and just let it smash into the garage. We had a pile of bikes because we never took the same one out twice, ha ha ha. When we wanted to go again we'd go and steal another bike.

You'd spend your last nickel on a case of beer, and if you didn't have any money you'd run your Visa up to get a case of beer.

I remember one of the guys putting his head through the wall, but that was normal. He'd be sitting in there and he'd just jump up and run across the room. He's lucky he didn't hit any wood. His name was Brian. He needed a place to stay and we had an extra bedroom, so all of a sudden we had this Brian guy living with us who was insane in a different type of way; not in a punk way, but just an insane way.

Teenage Head showed up there all the time and they brought their pretty girls over.

Stephen Mahon: That was a house party that kept going, simply because the guys that lived there, Dave Elley and the Lotimer brothers, these guys somehow had good day jobs so they could rent this house and on weekends have all this money to party. We never had those day jobs, we weren't those kind of guys, so hanging out there was awesome because you always knew there was gonna be beer.

The living room was set up with couches, coffee table, stereo. The hardest thing was making the needle not bounce on the stereo. I think they ended up trying to hang it up from chains in the corner somehow. I don't think that worked, either.

Pete Lotimer: If anybody showed up with records that we didn't like, we'd Frisbee them out the back. "We're not listening to this Boz Scaggs crap, get out of here," and we'd throw it out the window. So we were into it pretty bad.

That had to be around '77, just when it was really starting to click. I jumped in there. I didn't really intend on being in a band. I took drum lessons when I was a kid for about a week like all kids do. But I bought a set of drums and we put them in the front of the house. Dave wanted to be a guitarist. He sucked, and I couldn't drum, but we'd go in there and we'd jam out all these Iggy songs, just the two of us, for a long time.

There wasn't a lot of punk in Hamilton back then. I'm sure Toronto was miles ahead in that department, but there was an underground of people that really liked it. A lot of them were followers of Teenage Head because they considered Teenage Head punk. I guess they were to a certain extent; they weren't as raunchy as some of the other stuff. We followed them everywhere. Everywhere they went, we were there. If they did shows in Toronto, Windsor, we were there. It was pretty quiet but it escalated pretty quick.

Mickey — that's a really weird thing. I kind of remember this because I always thought it was strange. I had this blue set of Pixie drums in the front of the house and I was piddling around with them, but by no means was I a drummer. I got a phone call; I didn't know who this guy was, Mickey from the Forgotten Rebels.

He says, "Is this Pete Lotimer?" "Yeah." And he says, "Are you a drummer?" I looked over at my kit. It was worth about four dollars with the smashed up cymbals. I used to play it and it would slide away from me and I had to chase it on the stool. I says, "Well, I play a little bit." He says, "My drummer lives at home and his mom, she won't let him play out of town." And I was living on my own in this wild party house and I was pretty young, too; I think I was only eighteen or something. He said, "Do you want to play?" "Sure, I guess."

I guess we met for the first time at the rehearsal hall, just me and him and Chriss, practicing above a lawyer's place. We did some Troggs songs, "With A Girl Like You"; mushy stuff Mickey did. I got into that, but I still wasn't a drummer at that time. I had no hi-hat on my kit, just a ride cymbal and I played like that and practised like that for months. Even at shows I didn't have a hi-hat. I just went without one, and you can hear that on the album. That's the reason I joined the band, because his drummer couldn't do shows in Toronto.

Stephen Burman: I wanted to get involved with the Rebels because nobody else was doing this. Every teenager wanted to be anti-establishment and this was a way to be it; to thumb your nose at authority. And I think at the time mainstream music was pretty lame.

I always liked blues. Naturally, most musicians over time look to jazz and blues. They still have their roots, but they gravitate to that. But I think that at the time, other than traditional roots music, the general music scene in '77, '78 kind of sucked. It was like disco or bloated album rock. It was really a very sad time musically. The only thing coming out of that period that really had any consequence was punk. I think it was just because it was different and it pissed off my parents.

Mickey's voice was never great, but I think it was just the lyrics. Nobody was singing anything that was as relevant. He had this off-kilter sense of humour. We both had this similar sense of humour, liked similar things — very unconventional. Also he was very politically aware. Most bands were singing about, "My girlfriend left me, I got no money, I got no car." Mickey was singing about other things, and that was different. Nobody was doing that. The only bands that were doing anything political were the Clash and the Pistols. The Viletones weren't singing about anything political, so I think we were one of the only ones.

I thought we could go really far.

30. shock value

Johnny Garbagecan, Raymi Mulroney / photo by Gail Bryck

Johnny Garbagecan: The Ugly ended up going bankrupt because of the fire at David's. All of our stuff burned in his club, and then we couldn't get the insurance money because the owner, Sandy — his partner screwed off to Detroit. So we lost our gear.

Raymi Mulroney: Sam lost his SVT, Tony lost his Premier drums, we lost microphones. I think I salvaged one of my amps and Sam had a guitar underneath the stage that didn't get burnt. The neck got a little warped from the heat.

It wasn't until I think about two months later before we got all our equipment back and started up again. It was a real struggle.

Johnny Garbagecan: Our equipment was standing there all charred. Can you imagine that some people came in and actually salvaged what was left of the speakers and stuff?

The insurance was gonna give Sandy a hundred grand. He was gonna buy us all new equipment with that, because it would have only cost about twenty at the time.

Tony Vincent: The Viletones' gear burned down that night, too. It was New Year's Eve. I could be wrong because it's so long ago, but I think it was one of the very few times that we actually played together, the Tones and the Ugly.

After that fire it just seemed like everything went dead, totally dead.

Johnny Garbagecan: The music scene, to me, I thought there was money here to be made. It's not that I ever want to be rich, but it's nice to have enough money to eat and live, right? So that was gonna be my thing.

But the fire at David's changed a lot of things in my life. I think I actually did go and get a job after that fire. I had to go get a job. It was terrible.

Raymi Mulroney: I was working at a hospital. I don't know what Sam and Tony were doing. Mike was trying to get things back together, like, "What are we gonna do?" He was writing more songs.

Then I guess he hooked up with Billy.

William Cork: The Ugly sounded like the Stooges. At that point Iggy Pop had disappeared and he was a one-of-a-kind item. To me the Sex Pistols just sounded like banging a couple garbage cans together compared to Iggy.

Up until that time I had been a big Doors fan, but Jim was dead and then there was disco. Iggy was mowing lawns somewhere. It was like the end of the world. And then the Ugly came along.

It was a pleasant surprise. Mike, he was beautiful. There were only a few guys like him, like Alan Vega from Suicide was like Mike and there was a guy, an Oriental guy in San Francisco, Winston Tong. They were about the three guys, and maybe later Stiv Bators. They were the only people worth playing with as singers.

Raymi Mulroney: Billy was awesome. A little mysterious at first because I was a young kid and he was older. It was, "Where did this guy come up with this theatre? Where did he get his dough from?" He seemed to be always in financial straights, but he always managed to get something together.

He did have a coffin in his basement. It was a Civil War coffin or something like that. A pine box, basically. They said they had to move it out one day and the people next door saw them carrying a coffin down the street. Ha ha ha, you think about it, it was 1978, '79, and here they were carrying a coffin down the street. People were just blown away. He's dressed in skull makeup and stuff. He walked around like that. He used to wear makeup all the time and look like a freak. He'd dress in full leather, buckskin and stuff.

William Cork: Jeez, that's just me, you know? My earliest memory is watching Boris Karloff as Frankenstein. When I was a kid my bedroom was covered in personality posters of Peter Fonda wearing an iron cross in those *Wild Angels* movies and shit. So it was a natural evolution, ha ha ha. Especially on top of walking in to see Iggy and the Stooges on a few hits of acid. It all made sense, ha ha ha.

Raymi Mulroney: Like I said, where did this guy come from? All of a sudden, bang, there he is — "I've got this theatre, Shock. Let's do gigs here."

Ralph Alfonso [*StageLife* Magazine, December 1977]: Let's face it, the people behind the established Toronto music scene don't know the first thing about punk rock. They want to make as much money as possible without bothering to assess the music, the groups and, more importantly, what the public wants to hear.

They're all crawling out of their little holes in the dirt; instant punk managers, promoters, club owners and other assorted losers who've sniffed their way out of their graves for the occasion.

Only one place in Toronto has managed to pick up where the Crash 'n' Burn left off and that's the Shock Theatre. It's run by people who care about the music and are encouraging the local scene.

Nora Currie: The Shock Theatre had started booking bands. So there were elements of goth and people who were looking for a scene and experimenting with different places. It was a lovely time because it was possible for that kind of integration to take place with scenes and music and styles and art.

So shows there were fantastic. Johnny [Garbagecan] was booking the Shock Theatre. Some fabulous bands came in who hadn't made it yet, like the Misfits, the Romantics; and again, it was interesting because they incorporated different elements of punk.

They showed horror films at the Shock. Billy was called the Count because he had an infatuation or an obsession with vampires and death and all those things. He used to actually sleep in a casket and when he moved he would move it around with him. He was very good to Fred and Margaret's son Christopher. Christopher was this little boy and Billy was this total freak. He had all the elements of goth but was much more insane in very positive ways, and very creative. He was a child, as many of us were. A lot of the men I think let their little boy personas play themselves out.

Margaret Barnes-DelColle: My son Christopher grew up in that atmosphere.

Sometimes when I think back it must have been not that great, but everybody really loved Chris. He was just a great little kid and people would kind of borrow him because a lot of people around us didn't have kids; it was rare to have a child. So a lot of couples would maybe be like, "Oh, we'll take Chris for the weekend and see what it's like to have a kid," or single women would be like, "We're going to take Chris to the movies or go to the park or something."

So it was really kind of a communal feeling about everything, and because there were a lot of people in the house he heard a lot of the music and was brought up around it. Probably at the age of six he knew every Ramones song.

Christopher Barnes: I was a little punk rock kid, yeah. Nothing drastic with the hair or anything, but my mother went to college for fashion design so she would make me little bondage outfits and stuff like that.

Margaret Barnes-DelColle: And because we were all dressed up really punk rock, and you never want to do what your parents are doing, he got into this whole thing where he would wear suits. So I'd go out and buy him vintage suits and we would go places dressed in torn up T-shirts and Chris would want to wear a suit. He was six years old, seven years old. It was really funny.

For a while he did modelling; he was in a couple TV commercials and when I would take him for auditions, we were not the typical stage mom and kid. I had purple hair and there he'd be in his little '60s suit or something. They would always look at us like, "Oh my god, what's wrong with these people?"

William Cork: I used to live in the Norm Elder Gallery. Norm was Canada's foremost explorer and different people came to live at the house, like Prince Philip. Norm and his brother were Olympic equestrian champions of Canada.

Anyway, he had this great collection of coffins and he gave me one. For a while I was living in this 1966 Valiant station wagon with a coffin and all my shit in it. That's when I moved to New Rose, actually.

Margaret Barnes-DelColle: Christopher was six, seven years old and he absolutely adored Billy because he had this collection of horror comics and robots and all these things that a kid would just think, Who is this adult with all this great stuff? He called himself the Count. Christopher would go over there all the time.

Nora Currie: Billy was just in love with Christopher. So here was this adult who slept in a coffin and wore makeup and black and was just insane, in very positive ways.

The Count at New Rose / photo by Gail Bryck

Christopher Barnes: The Count made a big impression on me because he got me into robots and art and stuff like that, and so did Freddy. I never got into music much. I played the clarinet and the saxophone for a while in school. I picked up a guitar and Freddy taught me "Smoke on the Water," but that was about it.

Yeah, the Count definitely molded some of my tastes. I remember he lived in a storefront on Queen Street and was refinishing his coffin. It was a beautiful old coffin, and I guess some of the neighbours saw through the window that I was in the coffin when Billy was working on it and they called the cops.

William Cork: This buddy of ours, Fred Mamo, had been throwing millions of pot seeds in the backyards. I had been away in San Francisco and unbeknownst to me, I didn't really look, and there were pot plants everywhere. But I dragged this coffin out to the backyard and I was sanding it with little Christopher and this lady next door, Crazy Mary, phoned the police. I wore a lot of eye makeup and had long fingernails and shit and I was wearing this Crime T-shirt. There was knocking at the door and I walked through the store. I threw the lock on the door and started to walk back to the other end again expecting whoever it was to walk in, but still I see this big figure at the door so I go back and throw it open and it's these two cops. They ask if they can come in and I go, "Sure," and I've got three days' worth of melted makeup on and this T-shirt that says Crime across it. They go, "Your next door neighbour has called us." They go out to the backyard and Christopher's there, sanding away, and he looks up at the police and goes, "Hey, we build 'em!" As the cops are standing there I'm looking around the backyard realizing they're standing in this field of pot, right? Ha ha ha, they never noticed, they were so weirded out by this little kid and this coffin and they just left.

Margaret Barnes-DelColle: Christopher was in his glory. He was just like, "Oh, this is cool. This is *so* great — we're fixing the coffin!" Ha ha ha.

I'm sure it wasn't the best upbringing for him, but I just want you to know he's a pretty stable person today. I think he turned out okay in part because everybody loved him, and it was like having this whole group of adults that were always willing to hang out with him. It was almost like they didn't treat him like a kid; they treated him like one of them.

Johnny Garbagecan: Billy's Shock Theatre was going to be all science fiction movies. But Billy smoked too much hash to get anything done so everything was, "Tomorrow, tomorrow, tomorrow."

Elizabeth Aikenhead: It was like a rundown old cinema as far as I can remember, and it always felt like it was half empty and grungy. At times it felt like there was no one in charge.

At that stage there was a happy atmosphere, it was before things got tense or nasty or scary. It wasn't political, it wasn't gangs, it wasn't violent. It was just fun.

Johnny Garbagecan: I went in there and saw the dollar signs. I went, "Oh great, here's a place we can practise." Billy even gave me an office. All of a sudden Shock Theatre was Ugly Headquarters. I had a key to the theatre.

Sam Ferrara: They had a sub-basement there. Tony and I found it. It was this little door and we walked in with our lighters, and there was a little river going down with a little walk space. It just went deeper and deeper and deeper and I said, "Tony, I'm getting out of here, man, I *hear* stuff in here."

Karla Cranley: I was an office girl. Very straightlaced. I had just split up with a boyfriend. This girl I knew wanted to go to the Shock Theatre and she thought I was sitting around moping too much at home. So she talked me into going with her, and that was my first physical exposure to punk.

So I met all the guys. I thought the music was great. It was really a wild, exciting time. It was totally alien to me. Raymi and his brother lived out in Scarborough and they all had to lug equipment, so I told them they could stay at my place.

Raymi never left. That was it.

I don't know what it was that totally fascinated me. I'd been with my boyfriend for four years at that time, so it's very traumatic when you're young and you split up. And prior to that, I came from a very bad background and I was married when I was fifteen. I left my husband when I was twenty-one and I went to Toronto and raised our daughter on my own. I had to work seven days a week to keep a roof over her head, and then for four years I was with a guy who ran around on me constantly, always coming home with doses and everything.

But to me, it was still better than my husband who used to beat me into a pulp. He broke my ribs, cracked my teeth, you know? So when I met Raymi, I mean, yeah, he always had other girls, but at least he didn't bring diseases home and he was honest about it.

Raymi Mulroney: The Ugly had the whole theatre to rehearse in, so that became almost like a rehearsal hall, the Shock Theatre. It was great; Johnny Lugosi was there and Nora was there and Billy and his girlfriend

Barb and there was Ruby T's and Mike and me and Karla and Tony and I forget who he went out with. Everybody had a girlfriend then.

Next thing you know we started getting back our mojo, I guess. Because when you lose everything and you don't have money, it's a kick in the head.

Elizabeth Aikenhead: I think, when I started seeing Tony, very quickly I ended up being his girlfriend and getting his clothes ready for his show or taking his jeans in so they were tighter and ironing his shirts because he liked ironed shirts and starch. So I was very quickly in a role where I wasn't hanging out in the house, and going out with people I didn't know and that kind of thing.

I ended up living in an apartment with a woman called Karla Cranley above the Varsity Restaurant at Bloor and Spadina. There was a massive Player's cigarette sign. I remember I was seeing Tony at the time and sitting behind that sign not knowing which bar he was coming from. So I'd be up there with Karla. She was going out with Raymond Mulroney, Mike's younger brother. She was older and had a child and was a drug addict, so I also ended up looking after her a lot. Very unreliable, and at the same time traditional conservative in some ways. I ended up discovering her in the throes of attempting suicide a couple of times.

Karla Cranley: I became extremely destructive. I couldn't cope with it anymore. I attempted suicide a couple of times. Ruby attempted suicide a few times. It does something to your head to be exposed to that kind of negativity.

Elizabeth Aikenhead: It was a really depressing apartment. You know, bad lighting and low ceilings and grim carpet and grim furniture.

Karla Cranley: I found it a very, very sad time.

You'd walk into a club, there'd be two hundred people there, and nobody wanted to talk to you unless you were one of the band, like the groupies. Like sycophants, you know? Everybody was always posturing and trying to have a prettier girlfriend or a prettier boyfriend or getting more girls or getting a better gig.

Elizabeth Aikenhead: As soon as I was involved with Tony, I felt so much of my role was not about being in the audience having a great time and having fun. It was very anxious.

I didn't know what he was going to do, I didn't know what he was going to say, I didn't know what was going to happen with the audience, what was going to happen with the band, what the dynamics were about.

Tony Vincent: I don't know why, but a lot of girls from Jarvis Collegiate used to come down to our shows. There were so many of them. They would follow us all over the place. If you wanted to meet a girl, all you had to do was play in the Ugly and it was no problem.

*　　*　　*　　*　　*

Chris Houston: The most desperate of all rock bands would always end up at this one place, which was the Turning Point. Ha ha ha. That was really the bottom of everything.

Don Pyle: The Turning Point was a club that was run by this older Irish or Scottish couple who basically seemed to have the bar as their own rec room, because they were both alcoholics and drunk all the time. It was also such a scuzzy bar that it was completely out of the radar of the police, so they would let anybody in.

Barrie Farrell: The people running the Turning Point were just out of it, so. Ha ha ha. The old lady there would get so drunk she would have her head down — she'd puked, and it was all around her head. She looked up one time and there was nobody there. She looked up again and a fraternity had come in and we were playing there. There were thirty, forty guys with toilet bowls over their heads and bits of things they'd stolen from all over the city. Then she looks at that, puts her head down, Nancy would clean her up, she looks up again, the guys are gone. It was a madhouse.

Don Pyle: It had started off as this coffeehouse sort of jazz thing, and when punk rock came people started looking for places downtown where they could play shows, so they started booking punk rock things. The back wall was this big mural of Jose Feliciano, looking off into the distance with his guitars; a real iconic folk image. There was a very tall stage where anybody could play. The Turning Point was the lowest rung on the ladder of the punk rock food chain. Anybody could play there, it didn't matter who you were.

The owner was always trying to get people in. He was like, "You've got to come in on Friday, we've got the Clash playing! Joe Strummer called me and said the Clash were coming!" It was like, "Yeah right." It never happened, but he would do it all the time. He had this list of three or four known bands that he would use to entice people. "You've got to come down this weekend, the Buzzcocks are gonna be here!"

Anne and Joe were the people who ran the Turning Point. They were probably in their sixties. I'm sure they didn't have a clue how this happened, but all of a sudden their club started being busy. By busy, I mean

forty people. The bands that were perceived as being the biggest bands at the time wouldn't attract more than forty people. The scale of things was completely different. It wouldn't be unusual to go to a show and there'd be fifteen people there. And you knew thirteen of them, because it was always the same people at the shows.

Tony Vincent: There were always women around the Ugly. Oh yeah, lots. Don't ask me why.

Suzanne Naughton: Most of the time the bands used to hang out at the women's washroom, because girls were in there. It's where I usually saw Steven Leckie. Only the guys with the biggest balls dared to go in there. It was kind of intimidating, though. You'd go in and see Mike Nightmare or Steven Leckie or Tony Torcher necking with somebody against the sink. And it'd be like, I really need to take a leak. Do I really want to do it next to these guys?

Elizabeth Aikenhead: I remember I was just sitting watching the band at the Turning Point, and this one girl came and pulled me to the ground by my hair. I didn't even know who it was or what it was about. I think they were having a thing maybe.

It really turned; it wasn't fun anymore at all. Even a lot of the songs I wasn't listening to. I didn't know the words anymore. It wasn't the music anymore. It wasn't about hanging out in the scene. I don't even know what the attraction was. It was just hard to get out of. And I didn't like it necessarily. I was just stuck in the role of starching those shirts and taking in the jeans and running out to Long & McQuade to get extra drumsticks.

It wasn't long after that that I realized this is no fun, I've got to get out of this.

Tony Vincent: I guess you could call me No Fixed Address. I didn't have a permanent place to live. I just kept going from place to place. I guess you could call me a user, too. I would use girls to stay at their place. I did that for a long time. I guess I could have gone back to my parents' house but I chose not to.

Karla Cranley: He was a good drummer, and I'm sure he got creative or enjoyed the music, but for him it was more to do a gig to see how many girls he could get afterwards. And I mean, when Tony and Lizzy moved out of our place and tried to make a home, I felt so sorry for Lizzy because Tony was already married and had a wife at home.

Elizabeth Aikenhead: He had two kids who were raised by his parents. I found out about his kids when I was having my hair done with pink and green stripes or something at the Rainbow Room. Michael, the hairdresser, said, "How are Tony's kids?" And by then I'd

Tony Torcher / photo by Gail Bryck

been living with him for a little while. And I said, "Oh, they're great, they're doing well," kind of not knowing that he even had kids. He'd also lied about his age; he was older than he said he was. Which was fine, I didn't care, but it *was* interesting to know that he had two daughters. That was relevant.

He's basically a really good person. As my mother said when she met him — my mum tended to be a bit of a snob — she spent an evening with him and said, "It's got to be physical." Ha ha ha. She couldn't see an intellectual attraction.

I think I saw that he was a good person underneath everything, and I was young enough and naïve enough to think that I could draw that out and save him. You know the syndrome — girls like bad boys, and I think that was a recurring theme throughout the era for a lot of people.

From there, Tony and I got a basement apartment on Brunswick, and it was also kind of grim but we tried to fix it up a little bit. It was a hundred and eighty-five dollars a month, I remember that. We had hideous '70s furniture; whatever we could find on the side of the road.

I think I weighed eighty-five pounds back then. I see pictures of myself and feel disgusted. We were all like that. My waist was like eighteen inches. I thought I was fine.

Tony had an anger management issue at times, I would say. There was one day when our landlords who lived upstairs heard stuff, heard him storm out, waited a while, and then came down and said to me, "You come upstairs."

They poured me a little drink — they were both social workers, I think — and they were young and really nice to me. They said, "You know, you've got to really think about where this relationship is going and if it's right for you."

Raymi Mulroney: I lived above the Varsity Restaurant with Karla. I had my hell, too.

Tony had his Cadillac. Tony always wanted his Cadillac with the suicide doors, Lincoln Continental. We always had to hire somebody to drive our equipment around or get a truck to move the stuff around.

Elizabeth Aikenhead: I remember Tony and I bought a Cadillac convertible from his uncle — I don't know what he was involved in, but I'd say it was something nefarious.

We were driving back from I think Steve and Eva's one night and he was driving. Out of the blue, a car came and smacked us. Because of the angle, our car was totalled, but the guy insisted on calling the police. That's when I discovered that Tony didn't have a driver's license because it had been taken away many, many years earlier. He told me to lie and say I was driving.

It's the only encounter I've ever had with the police. They took us into separate rooms and there was a really kind, older police officer who gave me a real talking to. He said, "This guy is asking you to lie for him. Lying," he said, "is a criminal offence. But he's got a traffic charge, that's not a criminal offence. You're heading towards being a nurse." He said, "Don't do it. We know he was driving."

So they brought Tony back into the room and asked the question again — "Who was driving?" And Tony said, "Well, fine, I'll take the rap." And the police officers nearly lost it. Ha ha ha. And he'd had a couple of beers or whatever. In those days going to court was a two-hundred-and-fifty-dollar fine, it was nothing.

Which reminds me of going to court for Mike and Ruby. Mike was being charged with B&Es or something. I guess it was also the spirit of, "Oh, this is a big adventure." Sort of a novelty. We'd get dressed up and go to court with the boys to support them. We were nineteen-year-olds and we probably looked like freaks. Ha ha ha.

Mike was bad news. There was no real novelty in that.

Johnny Garbagecan: Mike was so drunk he went to a party, but he was at the wrong house. He was making a sandwich in this house and I guess he was probably wondering where everybody was, and the next thing you know the cops were there. He missed the party by a block. He was just making himself a sandwich and I had to get him bailed out because we had all these gigs coming up.

Somebody asked him what made him that way and he said, "If I wasn't into rock 'n' roll, you guys would be laying on the floor right now and I'd be stealing your wallets." It was either he was in a rock band or he was a criminal. It was gonna be one of the two, and sure enough he died a criminal. We did an interview for the CBC at the office at Shock Theatre and it was on the six o'clock news. Mike's mother heard it and she almost had a heart attack.

That was the part that ended up on the radio. So you can imagine his mother — they were Catholic, went to Catholic school and all that business — so really, it was that or the other.

Sam Ferrara: *CREEM* magazine interviewed us at the Shock. Tony went nuts. This person said, "Can I have an interview?" Tony picks up this bottle and just smashed it right beside this person — "Interview *that*, you fuck."

Tony Vincent: The guy in *CREEM* said, "Check out the Ugly — they are truly ugly."

Jeffrey Morgan ["A Consumer Guide To Toronto Punk," *CREEM*, February 1978]: These bunch of nodes are led by Mike Nightmare... Sure, he's tough looking but, then again, who isn't these days? (And, yes, the band members are indeed ugly).

Sam Ferrara: We had a gig at Shock Theatre once and the cops were after Mike at the time, so the poster was him with a leather mask so the cops wouldn't recognize him. It wasn't for a gimmick, it was just to get the cops off his back. Ha ha ha.

Raymi Mulroney: Yeah, we had to hide him under the stage once at a gig. The detectives were looking for him. I don't know what for, so he was under the stage hiding until they left and *then* we started the gig. They knew I was his brother and stuff, "But I don't know where he is. We're doing an instrumental tonight." Ha ha ha.

Tony Vincent: A lot of people knew Mike did B&Es and stuff. It made a lot of people afraid to approach the band. That's a reason why record companies wouldn't touch us. They were kind of cautious about us. They didn't know what would happen if they actually signed us.

Elizabeth Aikenhead: Mike Nightmare was a troubled soul, I would say. He was similar to Steve Leckie in some ways, as the leader of a band, in that he liked to ignite things. He liked to incite trouble if he could. I guess he had a certain charisma; I didn't see it, I didn't get it, but it seemed there were certain guys ...

"Punk Rock: It's Dying in Toronto Before It Was Born," by Don Martin [*Ryerson Review*, September 23, 1977]: Mike Nightmare, lead singer of the Ugly, typifies the male punk rocker. With his black leather jacket, torn T-shirt and chains draped around his neck he claims to be one of the true punk rockers in Toronto. He comes from the street and has no home, but usually ends up sleeping with one of his followers at her place.

"Punk is walking a tightrope," he said. "Everyone in the punk scene is scared because they don't think it will last. But it's up to the punkers to make it last and to make it popular."

Tony Vincent: People considered us better than the Viletones, like a more authentic punk band. We had more power than the Tones. We were louder, more powerful, and more disgusting. Put it this way: the Viletones, we made them look like nuns.

Raymi Mulroney: Diodes never played with us. They wouldn't play with us for some reason. They had that real pop sound and we were just too hellish. And then Arson, a band called Arson, the Hate, the Mods and that. And then of course the Toyz, the Brats. We were all over the place. We were probably the most played band around, but we weren't one of the most recognized bands because our music wasn't commercially acceptable, I guess. So that's what I meant about not being taken seriously. Mike was just too wild. People were just shocked to shit.

Tony Vincent: We didn't want to send any demos to any record company. We didn't want to belong to a record company, we wanted to do it ourselves.

Mike Nightmare ["Punk Rock: It's Dying in Toronto Before It Was Born," by Don Martin, *Ryerson Review*, September 23, 1977]: I don't think it will die out, but I see it getting more sophisticated. There will be some really great punk artists and from there it will get big, really big.

Right now punk is new. People are trying to attract attention so they shove a safety pin through their cheek or they cut themselves. But this doesn't mean that punk has to stay this way. Right now it is an act, nothing else. Someday it will change and become a form of art.

Sam Ferrara
/ photo by Ralph Alfonso

31. LiTTLe Games

Paul Robinson: We were in magazines like *CREEM* and *Circus*. *New York Rocker* did a feature on us. The *Village Voice* quite liked us and reviewed our single. People started hearing about us because we were getting press down there. In fact, we probably got more press in the States than we did in Canada.

We headed out on tour, but it wasn't really a tour as such. We had a lot of dates that were kind of scattered. We wanted to go on tour but to be quite honest no one would book us on a tour. It was very hard to get gigs, even with a record deal. Most of the clubs in Ontario didn't want to book us, they didn't want to know, and internationally we weren't known enough.

John Hamilton: Our Franklin House management took our advance money and went down to New York and hung out with Blondie's manager and hooked us up with some clubs that we were supposed to play down there.

Then I think Ralph probably did the other stuff and got us hooked into some of the good places to play, like the Rat in Boston. I think we might have played the Hot Club in Philly, and then there were these other gigs that Franklin House got us in New Jersey and Washington and stuff like that. The big tour was the snowstorm of '78.

Ralph Alfonso, "Epic Records and the Diodes: Little Games Are For Little Boys" [*Shades* no. 4, Spring, 1979]: It's the worst winter in thirty years and the Diodes are sent on tour.

From the back of some station wagon, stranded in Philadelphia, the band both *Maclean's* and the *Canadian Magazine* have just pronounced most likely to hit the big time in 1978 is wondering why they're here to begin with.

Welcome to America, lead singer Paul Robinson, guitarist John Catto, bassist Ian Mackay and drummer John Hamilton. Arriving into cancerous alien cities only to find first gigs cancelled by mysterious promoters who'd written the plot with a foolish management.

Paul Robinson: It was the worst snowstorm that they'd seen in fifty or a hundred years. We did literally get stranded for a week, and again we missed a lot of our dates and things, which probably harmed the band in the long run because a lot of our dates got cancelled on that tour.

John Hamilton: We went to Boston and the snow drifts were literally nine feet high. There were armed guards roaming the streets, and here we were on tour.

Ralph Alfonso: I had a correspondence with the girls who put out the *Boston Groupie News*. Because of the blizzard there was a curfew on, so we couldn't drive into town and go to the hotel. But they came out and got us and we were able to crash at their house.

People do it a lot now, but that was kind of a punk thing, to sleep on people's floors and stuff. And at the time it was like, "What is happening up north? Come in, we bring you news from our town." You were like messengers. You were trading information. You represented your city — "We're here to plant the flag for those sixteen other Toronto bands who you may or may not ever see, but we're here anyway, and here's what we're up to."

Ian Mackay: We played the Ratskellar in Boston, which is where the Cars were playing at the time — they were just breaking — and we only had seventeen, eighteen people.

John Hamilton: We played the Aragon Ballroom in Chicago. We played with the Ramones and the Runaways, and that was about the only good gig that Franklin House got us. We played to five or six thousand people.

We had another gig in Washington. We drove all the way down and we didn't actually *have* a gig; this was Franklin House's doing. So except for the few that Ralph had booked, it was a bloody fiasco; we did a lot of travelling for nothing. Inevitably we'd be booked into some wrong club where they would expect Aerosmith.

Paul Robinson: We drove down to Washington and our name wasn't even on the marquee, so we just turned around and drove all night until we got back to Toronto. It was one hell of a drive in terrible weather and it's amazing we didn't get killed.

John Hamilton: It was pretty sketchy. We didn't really get a big break in the States.

Paul Robinson: We got back to Toronto and then I think it was just very, very difficult.

Aragon Ballroom, Chicago / photo by Ralph Alfonso

Ian Mackay: There was virtual rejection initially by the buying public. Our first record I think sold seven or eight thousand, which is small. They were expecting at least fifteen or twenty based on our notoriety. Teenage Head, same thing when they got signed.

We hadn't crossed the chasm. And Canada wasn't ready for this. Canada's *never* been ready. Look at any of the other bands that have tried to break out of Canada. It's almost impossible for a Canadian band to break into the States.

For our scene, it was *really* difficult. Even when we toured the States, we were East Coast — Boston, New York, Baltimore, Washington, and on the West Coast it was San Francisco, San Jose, L.A., maybe Seattle, and Vancouver. And that was it. In the very early days there were only ten or twelve clubs.

Ralph Alfonso: We thought it was something better but it wasn't. It was like, yeah, we've got a major label, but it's a label that doesn't know what to do and although they're trying hard, the whole thing is out of their league.

They had all these cover bands they knew what to do with. You stick them into a bar and you just work them. With the Diodes, you can't do that. You can't stick them into a bar because no bar wanted them. So it was like, "Oh my god, what do we do?"

There was that whole high school circuit, but *they* didn't want the band either because there was this whole perception of punk — "We don't want punk here." There was one gig we did in some suburb of Toronto, and we show up and we played the one night. Then the next night we show up, all the equipment had been packed up and shoved into a corner and this cover band was playing. It was like, "*You* guys? We don't want you here."

It's frustrating, but it's a lesson learned.

CHUM FM in early '77 had a whole promo going about how they were going to do a special on punk rock — "CHUM FM Exclusive! We're going to talk about punk rock; we're going to really get into punk rock Friday night at eleven." So we're all excited about it. "Wow, what's going to happen? We're going to actually hear this stuff on the radio!"

So eleven o'clock comes around on Friday night, the big CHUM punk special happens ... and what it is, it's two DJs sitting around and laughing at all the records. "Look at this! Ha ha ha." They're not playing it, they're *scratching* it. And we're like, "Oh god ..."

Tom Williams: I think any establishment industry is threatened by any form of new music. So whether it was punk or disco or rap or house, or heavy metal for that matter, at first they just say, "That's an aberration over there to what's really important, Peggy Lee or whatever." So I guess they might have felt threatened.

Not that it was going to take their jobs away, it's just that they didn't understand it. When you don't understand it you become your parents, you know — "Why are you listening to that crap?" That's what everybody's parents do, and that's what these guys did.

Ralph Alfonso: The irony, of course, is in 1978 the Diodes were the first punk band to do a live-from-the-El-Mo broadcast on CHUM. So we eventually got them.

Paul Robinson: We did this El Mocambo gig where CBS sort of said to CHUM, "You want Elvis Costello, you'll have to take the Diodes as well."

Ian Mackay: He was a CBS act and in fact, as Elvis became popular and recognized there was more attention paid to the Diodes. I think that Teenage Head ended up on CBS as well for a period of time. I think it was Elvis Costello that might have influenced CBS to widen their acts.

Bob Segarini: The El Mo pretty much shied away from that scene for a long time till Elvis Costello. Then the doors were kicked open for the new wave scene and the punk scene. I remember going to see the Knack there and our peers were making fun of these bands, and we knew better. We knew that this was our future.

Colin Brunton: Of course you didn't notice any of this new music on the radio, because that was the big crime in Toronto. The local bands that had some kind of local notoriety, like Goddo, were just starting to push into boredom and these new guys should have taken over. So you didn't notice it on the radio, you noticed it in fashion and in the buzz.

You were so looking forward to new stuff coming out and who's going to come up with what next, and kind of hoping for the locals to pull it off, too, all our favourites. Which no one did.

Steven Davey: In early '78 I went on CFNY, and not only was I the first person to ever play the Sex Pistols and the Clash on CFNY, I also played local stuff for the first time. They were playing Jethro Tull and Emerson Lake and Palmer back then.

I was on their Import Show. There was no radio or support. We would get a mention in the *Toronto Star* and they would always make a joke about our name or something; it was like "The Dishes — Already a Household Name." But still, we weren't taken seriously.

[Martha and] The Muffins were smart. They knew to pitch themselves in England right away. And of course England bit, the first company they went to.

Canada is a marginalized market, no matter what the genre.

Tom Williams: It was hardscrabble. There was no credibility for Canadian talent, so when you released a Canadian album the stations didn't want to play Canadian talent. They had to, but they didn't want to.

Ralph Alfonso: Canadian radio does not want to play Canadian music. They'll play it, but only because it's legislated.

In the January 14, 1978 issue of *Billboard* there was a New Wave Spotlight section with an article on the Canadian scene ("Canada Learns To Pogo") that quotes Jeff Burns, the national promotions director for GRT (he later worked for CBS and signed Loverboy), as saying he was conscious of the street excitement over such acts as the Ramones and local acts such as the Viletones but couldn't see a bottom line profit to the music. In his view, radio play was the key to sales in Canada and radio programmers had told him they didn't want to know about punk.

Blair Martin: Well, it's that idea of, "Why does anybody want to listen to a Canadian band?"

Ralph Alfonso: The reason we were angry at that time is because there was nothing. I mean, give us *something*. Give us a crumb. Just give us a taste of something. It was like us against *everybody*.

Paul Robinson: The El Mocambo didn't even want us in there, let alone doing a live broadcast with CHUM. And CHUM didn't want to do us either, but they wanted Elvis Costello. It was very, very difficult for our kind of music to get any type of attention or airplay or anything. It was a fight and a struggle the whole time.

Ralph Alfonso, "Epic Records and the Diodes: Little Games Are For Little Boys" [*Shades* no. 4, Spring, 1979]: The place was packed. Gord Lewis from Teenage Head is backstage later to get autographs. The Diodes run up a larger CBS bar tab than for Elvis Costello.

On March 4, 1978, the Diodes were the best rock group in Toronto. CBS and Franklin House made sure this particular distinction did not last for long.

The Diodes, El Mocambo / photo by Ralph Alfonso

Paul Robinson, El Mocambo / photo by Ralph Alfonso

32. iF You can Find iT

Edgar Breau / press photo

Edgar Breau: Sometimes I felt like if you were loud – if your songs were short, fast, loud, and ugly – it was a pretty good fit for what was going on. It wasn't as wide open in terms of what genres bands could play within their own set. *Now* I think it's really opened up. Back then, it was just a little bit more narrow. I found that kind of frustrating. There was that faddish element to it, but eventually I think that went by the wayside. Which I think was a good thing, for me, anyway.

Kevin Christoff: Maybe when we found ourselves out in Toronto and playing in front of people like that, it exerted a certain influence on us when we were onstage, or maybe certain aspects of how we presented ourselves onstage. But it didn't seem to manifest in how we approached our music.

We didn't sit down and consciously try to write punk stuff. And a lot of songs that came out of that period, if anybody heard them, probably went right through them if it wasn't their style, or if it wasn't the kind of thing they were wanting to hear.

Gary Pig Gold: By this point I was actually living in Hamilton. This would have been late '77, '78, because we decided then we were gonna record Simply Saucer. You see, I'd been carrying around for years in the back of my mind the first discussion I ever had with Steven Davey in the Beverley:

My staff used to hold our very first *Pig Paper* meetings there back in the day, and one night I noticed a band set up on the stage with an authentic Dave Clark logo painted across the bass drum head. Now, how many people in Toronto in 1976 knew who the Dave Clark Five even *were*, let alone cared enough to immortalize them on their drum kit? So of course I had

to talk to Steve, the drummer, and always would whenever I'd be back in the Bev.

So one momentous night he hands me an advance copy of the first Dishes EP *Fashion Plates* to review. I open up the sleeve, pull out the record, but for some reason I don't see Capitol or Warner Bros. or anything at all like that on the label. Well, it turns out they'd put this record out THEMSELVES. "You mean, you can *do* that? In *Toronto*??" Steven said, "Sure! All you need is a tape, tell them what you want on the label, then you take everything out to this place called World Records in Oshawa," I think it was, "and they'll do the rest."

That definitely put the bug in my ear to start Pig Records someday, someway.

Kevin Christoff: When it came down to choosing the single, "She's a Dog" was a conscious decision with regards to perhaps trying to reach a certain audience. The song was popular in shows. It's memorable in a very simple way. Whenever we'd play a lot of people would call out for it, so it seemed to be a logical choice for a single. I think it's more pop than punk, personally.

Gary Pig Gold: Simply Saucer, and Edgar especially, said, "No, we've been doing this for years already; we're not punk. We're not a trend. But we'll see if we can fit into this little blip, this latest little thing."

We held a charity corn roast up on Hamilton Mountain to raise money to make a single. We were going to go into Grant Avenue, but we couldn't afford it. I guess we didn't sell enough corndogs. So the only other recording studio available in Hamilton was in this guy's basement.

Edgar Breau: I think the guy's name was John Boyd. It was not a great studio at all. It was a mistake to record there.

Gary Pig Gold: The second we start, John's saying "IT'S TOO LOUD!!!" And I said, "Then you just pull the faders down. You've got to capture this. You don't want to turn them down. They're not the Eagles; they're something else." Long battle short, he just barged upstairs at one point and said, "*You* mix the damn record."

Kevin Christoff: It was kind of funny. I guess the guy got supremely disinterested in what we were doing, because he ended up leaving us pretty well in charge. He went up to watch the hockey game or something like that, ha ha ha, which suited us fine.

Ed spent a lot of time getting his solos the way he wanted, and the singing. One thing I remember, you know that thing at the end of "I Can Change My Mind" where he does that really rapid-fire "I can ch-ch-ch-change my mind"? We'd never heard him do that before until that very day in the studio. Obviously it's become a key component of the song, but we were all looking at each other like, "*What?*" That's Eddy for you, though. A spontaneous guy.

Stephen Park: I think the record had a terrible sound to it. I think the songs were okay. But it's unfortunate that other things were not also recorded, let's put it that way. I don't want to put down the single, because that's really not where I'm going. I just feel it was not a representative picture of the band, necessarily.

Gary Pig Gold: I remember taking the tape into Toronto for mastering, and the guy had *no* idea. He said, "This is distorted." I said, "I know." And he reached for some knob — "I'll fix that." And I go, "Well, no, you can't, it's *supposed* to be distorted." He goes, "But you actually have distortion on tape!" I said, "I know. And it took a long time to figure out how to get that, by the way."

There *was* a day when they wouldn't have cared so much. Those first Who and Kinks and even Stones records *still* sound amazing, even though to many people they're such quote unquote terrible recordings.

Chris Houston: They just wanted totally dead drum sounds, and when you hear "She's a Dog" and "I Can Change My Mind" it really lacks the dynamics in the way Bob Lanois captured the band a few years earlier, because he was a little bit more open.

That was kind of disastrous for the band, because everybody really wanted to get their 45. It was so hard then because these people would go into a studio, and they wouldn't *connect* with the studio. So you'd have these horrible records of these great bands, and you *wanted* to love the band ...

David Liss: Edgar Breau, his music was very Floyd-ian, [very] Hawkwind, which was another weird band that I'd never heard anywhere else except from the speed freaks in Hamilton. So Simply Saucer suddenly went from this really spacey, long, jammy improvisational, hyped-up speed freak rock to pumping out two-and-a-half-minute, three-chord punk tunes.

I remember when "She's a Dog" came out I went, "What? *That's* Simply Saucer??"

Gary Pig Gold: When I put out the 45, I knew it would, and obviously could *only* end up alongside singles by the Viletones and the Dishes and the Cads, etcetera, in

New Rose. And in Record Peddler, who by now had grown from my pleading with them a couple of years earlier to take a couple of *Pig Papers* on consignment to actually having the biggest and best DIY and import record section in Toronto.

To help get the word out a bit more, though, I followed the example of vintage Steven Leckie and decided to plaster as much of Toronto as I could with flyers announcing the very first Simply Saucer Pig Record. But I thought I'd be smart and use wallpaper paste instead of staples; that way, our handiwork couldn't get so easily ripped down off all the telephone poles. So I brought along Martin E-Chord, who handled the paste bucket as well as played lookout, and by the time of the first GO Train home in the morning we had the downtown core pretty well covered.

I wasn't all *that* smart though: The Metro Police had already called my house. "You have to come tear all your flyers down." Seems the cops were already pretty familiar with anything "Pig." They knew where I was.

Edgar Breau: Paul Kobak, he threw our 45 across the room or something. It wasn't really cordial between the two bands. I'll just leave it at that.

Paul Kobak: You see what happens when you stay in the basement too long? Your ego swells to the size of a football field and you start believing your own hallucinations.

No, there was absolutely no rivalry between Teenage Head and Simply Saucer. In fact, we helped them out a couple times by letting them open for us. I believe you could count all the gigs Saucer did in the '70s on one hand. I'd say both hands but wouldn't want to potentially exaggerate.

Gary Pig Gold: Teenage Head were like the flip side to Simply Saucer; they were both the Hamilton buzz bands.

Gord Lewis would work at Star Records, which was the cool store — that's where we bought our records. So we would go up to Star and paste each other's picture sleeves together when we got doing our own 45s. We couldn't afford to actually have the sleeves made professionally, but someone taught us — "No, you just have them printed and then cut it, fold it, glue it." So I still have a good memory of taking the first copies of "She's a Dog" in to Star, and Gord was putting together the sleeve for their "Picture My Face" single on the countertop.

It was hard in those days to put out your own record. It took a lot of effort and money to press a thousand 45s. Then mailing them out to all the fanzines and record reviewers and college radio stations, and anyone else you'd tracked down who you thought *might* be interested.

But I did it because it was fun, and because I thought Edgar deserved it. And you know what?

I can remain extremely proud to this day that I was the *only* person who managed to get Saucer onto vinyl at the time. Since then, many, many others thought that maybe they could've done a better job of it, and believe me I would've been right there to help in any way I could if that had happened. But no one else at all stepped up to bat at the time. No one.

John Balogh: A lot of those bands, at the onset, didn't realize they were in the School of Hard on You.

Years ago, we didn't want to create the indie scene. We would have been happy to be prostituted and signed by a major record deal and given a whole bunch of money and not had to do all the shit we had to do, but that wasn't happening.

The big thing that always appealed to me, and the first thing that appealed to me from Simply Saucer, was the differentness. Back then, who would have been some of the bands in early '70s Canadian music? Lighthouse, Edward Bear — don't get me wrong, they were great pop icon–type songs, but they were at the end of the line. Lighthouse, the Crowbars, the Moxys ... and right behind them, right at their ass, nipping away was what today is called punk. Back then it wasn't really called the punk scene, it was just called the *music* scene.

The movement was self-perpetuated. We were only doing that because we needed to eat. We all felt like we were the underdogs, and we *were* typically the underdogs. We were the bands and we were the people that radio didn't play, television didn't show, and we were the unspoken at the dinner table.

Kevin Christoff: We got some good reviews over the single. We got some positive press on that. Some people maybe didn't like it, but you get that, right?

Edgar Breau: It gave us *a* push, and by and large it got good reviews. We probably needed something more than that, but it did give us some momentum.

Stephen Park: It gave us some press. There was interest in the band, but it was making that interest translate into *work*, really. That seemed to be hard to do.

On the one hand, we would be really excited. There was something in the *New Musical Express* that compared us with the Kinks and we just were floored. We couldn't believe it. But that was somewhere in England, and it just seemed so inaccessible. We didn't seem to be able to capitalize on some of the interest that the single was generating.

SINGLE OF THE WEEK [*Record Mirror*, London, UK, July 8, 1978]: We've Saved It To The End ... The Single Of The Week. Simply Saucer: "She's A Dog" (Pig 1). Canadian band sounding a bit "Oooo very approximately the best single this week, reminiscent of the fab four (harmony wise), constructive guitar work, although the lyrics ... err ... woof? If you can find it, buy it ..."

Gary Pig Gold: Cub Koda — remember "Smokin' In The Boy's Room" by Brownsville Station? — he *loved* Saucer. He gave "She's A Dog" an amazing review in *Goldmine*, about how all the "dog, dog, dog"s in the chorus were driving his wife crazy.

But how to make best of all this press that was coming in from literally all over the world? I was just one guy, with a bunch of Sharpie pens and cardboard mailers, working out of the basement.

Tom Williams: But *most* people were like one- and two-men operations. They didn't have the distribution, they didn't have the know-how, there was no support system in terms of national radio, national television; newspapers tended to ignore the local acts, there were no consumer music magazines that meant anything — a couple of trades that didn't mean a lot. It was kind of a baby industry, really.

I mean, it really was a bunch of people playing Let's Make Records, including ourselves, I think. I think we were pretty naïve and we said, "We can do this," and if we'd actually known what the stumbling blocks were we probably wouldn't have. But we did, and I think that's always the way. Because when you're young you can do anything, in theory.

Gary Pig Gold: Jeremy Gluck, who was UK correspondent for *The Pig Paper*, was saying to come over there. I was thinking California, too — Peter Case suggested relocating there.

Jeremy Gluck: I was always obsessed with living in London. Specifically, when I lived in Toronto I used to hang out with a lot of interesting characters and they'd always say, "Why don't you go to New York or L.A.?" And I was always fixated on London, and I felt at home when I got there.

I'd messed around a bit with my brothers trying to form a band, but anyone can be a big fish in a small pond. I guess I saw instinctively what was happening: I'll form a band, I'll play the Masonic Temple or David's, and six months later I'll be working at the post office. And I thought, If I can start a band in London and can cut it, then I could do a lot more.

Stephen Park: I think being stuck in Hamilton — I'm not sure how to characterize what was going on there. We spent a lot of time rehearsing and we didn't have the self-confidence, I suppose. Maybe it's simple as that. We didn't think that we could make a go elsewhere.

I don't think it was discussed a whole lot, to be honest. In retrospect, I think that was unfortunate. I think that could have made a difference.

Edgar Breau: It probably would have been quicker for us if we'd moved to another city. I think it would have been quicker if we were in New York or London or Los Angeles. That's probably where we should have gone.

I think people had pretty high hopes that the Toronto scene would turn into something like those cities, but it was just kind of premature I guess. It took a little while longer for that music scene to develop. It was kind of early maybe.

Jeremy Gluck: I'd fallen in love with London when I'd been there the previous year, anyway, and that was the end for me; I'd decided. I managed to make a fair bit of progress there quite quickly, the kind you just can't make in Toronto. There wasn't the support necessary to sustain a real scene. It was terminal; I did see that it was gonna burn out pretty fast.

You can form a band in Toronto and it's great, but in retrospect I was better off in London, proving the case, in fact, so my instincts were correct.

Jeremy Gluck, London, 1979 / photo by Ralph Alfonso

Edie the Egg Lady / photo by Gail Bryck

33. ViTaL-tones

Gary Cormier: We proceeded to do twenty-odd shows at the New Yorker, but because they encountered difficulties with the lease [we] were turfed out. Well, not necessarily turfed out — they just decided they weren't going to renew the lease.

Gary Topp: Dee Dee, on the Ramones' second album, is wearing our T-shirt. We did Talking Heads, Wayne County, Tom Waits, John Cale, all sorts of people and a very wide range of music. Like the movies, I always booked what I liked. When it came to music, I started booking out of my record collection.

I continued there for a couple of years, lost tons of money, and had a great time. It kind of built up this scene. Then the guy raised the rent on us and we moved.

Gary Cormier: There was tons, *tons* of debt. And I don't know if it was just because I was younger and felt that no matter what happened I would always have the time to recover and pay back, but it never fazed me or bothered me. I never thought for a second that I wasn't gonna be able to pay that money back. I always believed that it was only going to be a matter of time before the rest of the world embraced this stuff.

All the people that we worked with had the same kind of conviction that we did — that all the other stuff was a load of crap, and that this stuff was for *real*.

We wanted to be able to bring bands here that no one had ever heard of or seen, and build them up and continue to grow with them. That was what we were really trying to do. Money never had anything to do with it. Come and look at my house, you'll know.

There are a lot of people who have become more successful financially, but we never did anything that we didn't want to do. We pretty much called the shots. There were bands that people wanted us to do that we knew would be successful and it just wasn't our cup of tea. As my mom says, it's a lot easier to become famous than rich.

Alex Currie: At the New Yorker at one point, they weren't making very much money at all and they asked everyone to work for free for two weeks. Everyone took a partial cut in pay, but that's pretty amazing considering no one was making that much money anyway.

Gary Cormier: I lived at King and John. It was sort of my neighbourhood. I knew the people who ran [the Horseshoe Tavern], who knew that I was involved in doing shows at the New Yorker. Some of the shows that we did they would have been thrilled to do. So when everything came crashing down around us at the New Yorker I suggested to them, "Well, we could go in and do the same thing at the Horseshoe and not pay rent at all, not a cent. We'll have a building, we'll take the door, we'll pay for the sound and lights and the acts and we'll take the bar." So the Horseshoe was thrilled, and Gary and Jeff [Silverman] were thrilled because it took a reasonable amount of pressure off us financially.

Nash the Slash: Unsung hero of the scene? Topper, Topper, and Topper. The brilliance is definitely Gary Topp. The brilliance, the smarts, is in how to put the package together, how to promote something.

It's such a cross-reference of cultures. John Waters was just making his splash with *Pink Flamingos* and *Female Trouble*. Divine is of course famous, but one of his other famous characters is Miss Edie the Egg Lady. And so Gary Topp, the genius that he is, gets wind that Miss Edie, who was sixty-three years old at the time — a crazy little woman from Baltimore — was doing a punk act as Miss Edie the Queen of Punk.

Chris Houston: The punks really embraced Waters' aesthetic. The Garys actually brought in Divine and did a stage play with Carole Pope called *Restless Underwear*. Then one of the great moments in music was Edie the Egg Lady with the Viletones.

John Hamilton [*Blah Blah Woof Woof* no. 1, May 1978]: Playing the Horseshoe came as a surprise to her since she'd heard nothing of the gig until the Horseshoe's management phoned her in Baltimore to ask when she'd be arriving.

Freddy Pompeii: We backed up Edith Massey, Edie the Egg Lady from *Pink Flamingos* fame. Gary Cormier called me and he says, "Listen, Edith Massey's coming to town and she can't bring her band with her and she wants to know if we could get her a band." And he said, "I can't think of anybody better than the Viletones to back her up."

I thought, Yeah, man, no problem. We'll do it.

I told Steven about it and he got really pissed off. "Why do we have to back her up?" I said, "Look, Steve, we're gonna back her up. You're not gonna be onstage so it doesn't matter. This is the way it's gonna go. We're gonna open the set and then she's gonna finish the show with us backing her up."

Margaret Barnes-DelColle: When they met with her, she was crazy. She was just a crazy old lady; very eccentric. She had these big moles on her face.

Edie the Egg Lady / photo by Gail Bryck

Freddy Pompeii: Edie called herself the Grandmother of Punk. We met her at the Horseshoe in the afternoon and jotted down all of her poems that she was gonna do and we put music to them. We wrote eleven songs with her. We wrote the music and she improvised with the lyrics. She had a sort of control over what the band was doing.

Margaret Barnes-DelColle: While she was in town they put her up in a hotel. I somehow got appointed as her guardian, so I hung out with her over the weekend.

She was obsessed with finding black plastic spiders to glue on to her moles, and that was going to be part of her costume for the show. So we started looking all around town for all these little novelty stores where you could buy just whatever. We found one up on Yonge Street near Carlton and we went and got the little black spiders, and she was thrilled to death.

Freddy Pompeii: Margarita was kind of helping her out with her clothes. Gave her real extreme makeup around the eyes and black lipstick, and a pair of boots that went up into her thigh and came down into a really sharp pointed toe and a stiletto heel. But she was WIDE; she was really wide at the hips. She really looked out of proportion, but it was what made her who she was — that crazy shape and her wearing those clothes on purpose.

Nash the Slash: Edie is about four feet tall and the shape of a bowling ball, and she would wear a leather bondage outfit and a beehive hairdo. She had a *Star Wars* laser sword she was waving around. I mean, it was the most hysterical sight in the world. She had these big gaping teeth and a homely face, but she was absolutely the sweetest woman. She was a cool person.

She goes up and did these songs with the Viletones backing her up, and I swear to this day the Viletones never played better. It was one of their best gigs. They were tight and it was great. And she was so funny. She referred to them as the Vital-tones. "These are the Vital-tones and you're not. I'm Miss Edie and you're not."

Freddy Pompeii: It was two nights in a row and two shows per night. She packed the place. It was real successful. She was a star. She did really good, and we actually made money backing her up.

When we were done there were lineups all the way to the back of the bar, just wanting to talk to this lady and get her signature on a piece of paper or one of her records or a photograph. That's how many fans she had.

Steven was pissed off.

Nash the Slash: So I'm chaperoning Miss Edie and I said, "Where do you want to go?" "I want to go to the gay bars," because that's who she hung around with in Baltimore. All her friends were gay, and so we went to the gay bars and they all knew who she was. They were all worshipping her and it was hysterical. She's just this funny little lady out of Baltimore.

She had her own little junk shop and she hated to tour or leave Baltimore because she had all these stray dogs and cats she'd bring in. She always had to make sure a friend was taking care of her critters while she went off to Toronto on a little junket.

Freddy Pompeii: And you know, she would send us cards every Christmas with a picture of her and it would say, "Merry Christmas to everybody. Me and my animals thank you." And there's a picture of her and her animals. Ha ha ha. It was really neat. It was such an honour to be associated with her.

Nash the Slash: Topper putting together Miss Edie and the Viletones, it was magic. Just magic.

34. Just have a Feeling

The Dead Boys, Stiv Bators (left) / photo by Ralph Alfonso

Xenia Splawinski: Cynthia was engaged to Stiv [Bators] for years. Cynthia and I lived together so Stiv would always be there. He was just as crazy offstage as he was onstage. So it was an adventure living with him, because you never knew when he was just going to fly off and act in these kooky ways.

Cynthia Ross: I actually hadn't seen him play when I met him, so I didn't know what his onstage persona was [at first], but he was really bright and really funny, so that attracted me. And he knew a lot about music, all different kinds of music, so he was a fan.

Xenia Splawinski: When he was straight he was totally sweet; he was actually a very sweet, very caring, shy, subdued kind of guy. But once he got into drugs or alcohol he was completely unpredictable. And he had a very self-destructive nature. He was really the only one of the Dead Boys I knew and I wasn't really into their music, it was too noisy for me. I didn't find it had enough melody in the noise for me. When I was in New York I would go to CBGB's to see them play, but I didn't hang out with them that much.

Lucasta Ross: The Dead Boys got involved with Hilly Kristal at CBGB's. He believed in them and he'd let them eat there and gave them beer.

I got involved with the New York bands the first time the Ramones played in Toronto. I think I'd just turned eighteen and I started going out with Arturo Vega, so just a couple months after that he asked me to come to New York.

He lived with Joey Ramone, so I became really good friends with all the Ramones and they introduced me to everybody. So when the New York bands played Toronto I already knew them. Debbie Harry used to love hanging out with the B-Girls because she had an all-boy band. I knew them all through Arturo in New York, so it was just nice to see them again here.

Once the Toronto bands started coming to New York, that was kind of weird. The first time I saw the Viletones playing CBGB's was weird because it was in my home away from home; it was sort of incongruous, almost, to me. But then I got used to it and everybody was just going back and forth and playing. It wasn't weird when the B-Girls came because I was used to being there, and playing CBGB's was really cool.

Cynthia Ross: We played at the Horseshoe with the B-52s, and we also played there with Richard Hell and the Voidoids. Then we started going to New York about once a month and playing there.

Xenia Splawinski: The first time we went to New York, we'd gotten booked into Max's and there was a huge snowstorm. We were playing with the Romantics, before they were famous. The whole city closed down and we were sort of like, "*What*?" There was no snow to us, but to New York it was crazy. People were sleeping in their stores. People had chains on their cars. We were going, "What the hell is going on? This is like a *snowfall*."

Cynthia Ross: All the gigs got cancelled. I went in to see Hilly Kristal who was the owner of CBGB's, and I was going out with Stiv Bators by this time, and he managed them. We used to call him Uncle Hill. I just said to him, "We're not leaving until you give us a gig, so when are we playing?" He just loved the fact that we wouldn't take no for an answer so he gave us a gig opening for somebody on a Saturday night, where usually you have to do this Monday night, new band night thing.

Xenia Splawinski: And we were opening for, of all people, the Poles. That was a bad scene because you could tell it really troubled Michaele Jordana, and I could understand. We just walked in off the street. It was their first gig in New York and they'd been working, working, working for it, and *we* got put on the bill. I remember going to the bathroom and I was nervous. I said to her, "Aren't you nervous?" She said, "I'm an artist. I don't get nervous." I was like, "Oh, okay, well, I guess *I'm* not an *artist*."

Cynthia Ross: People like Andy Warhol would come to our gigs. We did a gig at Peppermint Lounge with Debbie, and we did one gig at CBGB's where it was a benefit for St. Mark's Church.

That's where Allen Ginsberg did all of his poetry readings and it burned down, so a bunch of musicians were doing this free gig at CBGB's to raise money with people like Mink DeVille, Elvis Costello, the Ramones.

Lucasta Ross: They said, "It's going to be late, but we'll call you when you're about an hour from going onstage so you don't have to spend the whole night here if you don't want to." So we showed up in our pajamas and we played the whole set in our pajamas, which they couldn't believe. They thought that was just so funny.

Cynthia Ross: A few years later I ran into Elvis Costello in Toronto and he was like, "I remember you – you were the girls with the flannel pajamas and the cowboy boots. That was awesome!"

Lucasta Ross: There was another night we played New York and I did a ballad, and when I finished I looked at the crowd and nobody was clapping for about three seconds; they were just sitting there with their mouths hanging open. And all of a sudden they really started clapping and howling and going crazy. I remember thinking, Oh shit, I thought they didn't like me. So that was really great.

I remember being in the dressing room and the old guitar player from Alice Cooper's band – and you've got to know this about me, Alice Cooper to Xenia and I when we were kids was like our *god* – so to have a member of their band ask if they could come backstage to talk to us was just such a thrill. It was like, "Oh my god, I can't believe it." We used to finagle our way backstage at *their* shows, and here he is asking if he can come see us to tell us how much he enjoyed us. That was really wonderful.

Hilly was always really nice to us at CBGB's, and Arturo and the rest of the Ramones always made sure that we were all right and that nobody took advantage of us. The Hells Angels were there because their clubhouse was one block over and they used to ask us if we'd come play the clubhouse, which we'd always turn down because we didn't know how good an idea that would be.

Xenia Splawinski: I think it's important to know that we had the idea before we had the band, so it was pure energy. It was really about willpower and the desire to express ourselves.

Our band was very fun loving. We really enjoyed ourselves, and we had a lot of laughter and a lot of fun. Certainly for most of the time in the band it wasn't heavily mixed up with drugs and alcohol, so it wasn't a destructive sort of thing. We brought a lot of light energy.

Our band really wasn't about the art scene, it was more about *not* the art scene, just enthusiasm and non-pretension. It was definitely a courageous thing that we were doing because it was part of breaking that whole scene of girl bands. It did really take a lot of courage to get up there and play some of the gigs that we played.

We were playing in Hamilton — that was weird enough to begin with — and we were doing a Johnny Cash song, "I Walk the Line" or something. This guy got up onstage and did his own variation that had to do with pulling his pants down. He had his own words about this piece of twine holding his pants up, and he did this whole thing until his pants came down while we were still onstage.

Cynthia Ross: At first we couldn't play so a lot of the reviews were "most improved band ever," because as we actually learned to play our instruments we couldn't get worse. I don't know how my parents stood it, actually having us rehearse in their basement all those years.

Lucasta Ross: We were in some magazines and we got tons of fan mail from all over the world. It was just so exciting. We did a CBC show but from what I heard we were so horrible they wouldn't air us, which doesn't surprise me in the least. I know for a fact, Xenia and I grew up with visions of being rock stars in our heads from a very young age, so when there was so much buzz generated about the band we thought this could really happen.

Cynthia Ross: We had a fan club, a B-Girls Fan Club. I remember getting a letter from Charlotte, I forget her last name, before the Go-Go's started, and she wrote me to ask how to go about starting a band. They'd seen us and they liked us and she had a friend who could sort of play. I wrote her back. We wrote back to everyone.

Greg Shaw [letter to *The Pig Paper,* 1978]: Thanks for PP#7. Like it very much. Outside of L.A., Toronto seems to be the most exciting scene in N. America, and I'm very anxious to check it out one of these days. I hope to come there within the next couple months. I've been very impressed with almost all the Toronto groups I've heard. My favorite is the B-Girls, although I haven't heard them. I just have a feeling I'm gonna love 'em.

Cynthia Ross: There was this guy in California called Greg Shaw who ran a label called Bomp Records, and he heard about us through the Ramones and Iggy Pop. He had a magazine called *Bomp!* and we were featured in it regularly. He loved us and promoted the hell out of us.

Larry LeBlanc: The Toronto scene got a push when Greg came up and championed a bunch of bands. And when he did that he gave a bit of validity to the scene here, which was interesting.

Cynthia Ross: He came to Toronto and paid for us to do our first 45 with Bob Segarini producing at this small eight-track studio somewhere up north.

Lucasta Ross: Oh, that was a blast. That was really fun. I was used to recording so it wasn't a new experience for me, but it was really cool to hear it all get put together. I don't remember a lot of specifics except that I think it was at Bob's farm, if I'm not mistaken.

It was kind of grueling for the girls, but it turned out really well.

Cynthia Ross: Bob Segarini was great. He was really talented, he knew the sound we were trying to get and was very encouraging and thought we were good. We had a lot of people trying to convince us to have other people play our instruments instead of us, but no. The Runaways had initially done that.

We didn't have a drummer at the time. My sister left the band. Once we started doing well ... She worked for Ray Daniels, who managed Rush and I don't remember who else, and at first Ray thought it was cool and kind of cute. Then we started playing New York once a month and he basically told her it was her job or the band. So she picked her job.

Then I guess in '78 Lucasta left the band because she wanted to travel and she had a job and all that.

Lucasta Ross: I had left the band before they moved to New York. I had too much going on here to do that. I will not live in some shithole, rat-and roach-infested piece of crap and struggle to make ends meet. I've always liked to make a lot of money and live well, and that was just not for me. I wouldn't even drive to New York. I flew. So I wasn't on the same level as far as that goes.

It was hard toward the end to leave because there was a lot of animosity going on. I resented Xenia quite a bit. I felt like she'd turned her back on me. We'd been best friends and I'm the one who seriously talked Cynthia into allowing Xenia to be in the band; she was against it and I couldn't imagine doing it without her. So I got her in and towards the end they started treating me really shitty.

I would find magazines with my face crossed out, my name blackened out, really rotten shit like that.

They had no idea that there had been a few record companies who wanted to record me but use backup musicians and not use them, and I turned them down saying it was the band or nothing.

And I never told them that. They'd be quite surprised to find that out. So when I started seeing how they were treating me I just thought, You know what? I don't need this crap.

Cynthia Ross: I think it was precipitated by being scheduled to do a show with the Clash — again, this is my memory — and she basically didn't want to do it; she was going to cancel. That was basically the beginning of the series of things like that. She had other commitments.

Things started happening when we started going to New York on a regular basis. She had a job working for her dad who ran a jingle company, and she was reluctant to go. She had other stuff going on.

Lucasta Ross: It was how they were treating me. At the time I had a new boyfriend who I was really into, and I couldn't believe how crap they were treating me and I just didn't want to continue with that.

Cynthia started getting really manipulative. I remember there was one thing — it's really stupid, but this is indicative of what kind of crap she started to stir up. We were going to do a show and we were talking about what to wear. She wanted to get these big sweatshirts and I just said, "Sweatshirts onstage? Do you know how hot it is up there?" And she said, "No, that's what we're gonna do." I said, "Well, you wear sweatshirts, I'm wearing a T-shirt. I'll wear a T-shirt that looks just like the sweatshirt. I'm not wearing a sweatshirt onstage." Then she said, "Well, you know, Lucasta, I don't see why you think you should have any special blah blah blah." And I was like, "I don't want to be special, I just don't want it to be stupid."

After that I was like, "I just don't need this shit," and so I left. I never regretted it. I was in another band years after that called Minutes From Downtown; we were signed to Capitol. We did one western tour and that sort of fell apart, and after that people were coming out of the woodwork for me to sing for them. I was singing jingles like crazy and doing voice-overs and just making a fortune. So I didn't look back and think I made a mistake, that's for sure.

Cynthia Ross: When Lucasta left I think we became more of a collective because we had to work harder. Really, she was the only one that was basically trained in the band, so she was kind of above everyone on a musical level. When she left it was more equal.

So Xenia just moved over and became the singer. We found a guitar player, Renee [Schilhab], who was pretty good. For a little while we had a guy playing drums because we couldn't find a girl drummer. I think we did two gigs with a guy, one at the Colonial and one at the Horseshoe.

At the Horseshoe gig Marcy [Saddy] introduced herself and said, "I'm a drummer. I just moved here from London. I'm working as a waitress at Chris' Steakhouse." That's where Xenia had just quit her job to go on the road, and we had this gig at CBGB's and we had no girl drummer. She had gotten Xenia's job at the restaurant and said, "I'm a musician." And they said, "The waitress that just quit is also a musician, she's playing at the Horseshoe tonight. Maybe you should go and see her."

I said, "Do you think you can play our stuff?" And she said, "Oh yeah, absolutely." We were rehearsing at John MacLeod's studio around the corner from the Beverley Tavern. She came in and she played all of our stuff including all the stops, everything, perfectly the first time through.

Moving to Toronto was a big move for her from London. She'd never been to Toronto, and within a week we had her coming with us to New York to play at CBGB's.

Lucasta / photo by Ralph Alfonso

Cynthia, Xenia / photo by Ross Taylor

35. ugly Pirates

The Ugly / photo by Gail Bryck

Raymi Mulroney: We just did a gig with Suicide, and we went back to a huge party at 101 Niagara Street and said, "Man, we *made it*, it doesn't matter. This is going down in *history*." That's all I'm saying. It's going to be there.

That was '78 at the Horseshoe. And I remember my girlfriend barfing. Karla. I looked at her — I was, oh, six feet away and I went, "You okay, honey?" She goes *ugghh*, and I said, "Yeah, we made it. This is going down in history." I just knew it. It was like it had to be.

Karla Cranley: And you know what happened that night? I left the gig and I went home and I overdosed.

I think Blondie was there that night, Deborah Harry. I started taking pills at the hotel and I knew I was gonna nod off. So I took a taxi home. I left because I didn't wanna pass out at the hotel. And Raymi told Mike afterwards, "Oh yeah, Karla was doing a bunch of pills. She was starting to nod off." And Mike somehow made it up to the apartment and found me unconscious.

Mike left the party and all Raymi could think about … Raymi and Ruby could walk over a bleeding person on the sidewalk and leave them there. They didn't see beyond themselves, and Mike could. I mean, Mike had a lot of anger and he could do some crappy stuff when he was mad, but he had heart for other people. He didn't intentionally cause pain. And I don't think it was that Raymi intentionally caused pain. He just wasn't capable of seeing outside of himself, you know what I'm saying?

Mike found me at home, unconscious, and took me to the hospital. I was in for two months. I hated Mike for a long time afterwards for that. I was in a wheelchair. I was a total vegetable. I had so much brain damage when I came out of it, I couldn't walk or anything. I lost all my hair. I was on intravenous. I had to learn how to walk all over again to learn to use my muscles. It was horrible. So Raymi thought that was the epitome of everything, eh?

Raymi Mulroney: You know what? Rock 'n' roll is all I believe in.

Karla Cranley: He loved going into bars and have people fawn all over him and buy him drinks, you know what I'm saying? And the more attention he got, the more he loved it. It could be the worst night in the world, and if Raymi went to a bar and five people offered to buy him a drink and told him he was great, he'd be in heaven. He really took the adulation seriously. To him it was his drug, and that's the part of the scene that I couldn't handle.

There'd be twenty girls all in front of the stage that would walk into the change room. These women were just vicious. The orgies and everything. It was really sick. I mean, that's part of the rock scene, it's par for the course, and the women that are involved with it learn to live with it. But I never got involved because I wasn't a groupie. To me, it was never how many notches I could get in my belt. I think if I would have gone into the punk scene with that as a motive, it wouldn't have been so emotionally draining for me. But I met him and I fell in love with him, and I wanted to help him.

*　　*　　*　　　*　　　*

Raymi Mulroney: We had a song, "Murderous Adventure," and one of the lines is, "My life's like living on a pirate ship/You never know when it's gonna get raided."

Ross Taylor: Bands would always have this habit of pirating sets. The first band would play and then they would take a break. As soon as they left the stage another band would jump on the stage, plug in their instruments, and start playing. They'd get into these huge fights over it.

Johnny Garbagecan: How the Ugly originally started playing was they attacked the stage, grabbed the equipment, and just started playing. We were gonna call the band the Ugly Pirates, and they were just going to go around and do pirated sets. It was pretty unique, actually. It was one way to make a name, know what I mean? That's all that really mattered was making noise.

Raymi Mulroney: We did it any chance we were around, I guess. Whenever all four of us were out there at a special gig or some new band was starting out, we'd pirate their set. We were the Ugly and that was it. We'd do anything.

Freddy Pompeii: I think '78 was the best year. That's when they had the Restricted show at the Masonic Temple. One was called Outrage and one was called Restricted, and that included all the punk bands in Toronto on a really big stage, a big venue.

Tony Vincent: Pirating was Mike's idea. We did that at what used to be called the Rock Pile. It's called the Concert Hall now, right on Yonge and Dupont across from Canadian Tire. That's where it started.

It was called Outrage, and I think it was Teenage Head's manager who put on that show. We were supposed to play with the Viletones, Teenage Head, the Curse, all the punk bands, and they dropped us out of it. Mike was determined to play that night, so we just went onstage.

"Natzee Dog: Still King of the Kennel," by Kevin Kennedy [University of Toronto *Varsity*, September 23, 1977]: The Viletones were a much rougher and harder-edged act, led by the most flamboyant person on the scene, Natzee Dog. Their music is tight, tense and fraught with violence lurking not too far below the surface. The Dog has developed a new way of ending their songs by choking his bass player with his chain or throwing his lead guitarist to the ground. The Dog has a tortured, animal-like style of moving as befits his name, and a gravelly, commanding way of singing so that you want to stomp your jackboots at the abrupt end of each song. Predictably he cut himself, then flourished a burning guitar and closed his encore by smearing his blood over his face and chest. Clearly a man who understands both image and product.

Then the Ugly jumped the stage intending to do a pirate set. Instead a brawl ensued, worsening the atmosphere and sabotaging the Concordes' set.

Nip Kicks: The Ugly and their pirate sets, of course, ha ha ha. That was a lot of fun, going to a concert that you're specifically barred from playing and deciding you're going to play.

Chris Haight: Pirating the stage wasn't a new thing; it was happening all the time. But I guess the promoters in this situation, because it was one of the bigger venues and somebody had dropped a few bucks to get the thing happening, I guess they were just trying to protect their interests. They weren't gonna have any of this little tit bat shit that was happening in a small little venue.

It's a fairly big joint. Guys like Led Zeppelin played in this venue; it wasn't like a hole in the wall. So Nightmare figures, well, this is one of the best opportunities he's ever had to pirate a stage that's gonna mean anything.

Tony Vincent: I said, "Mike, forget it, there's bouncers here and stuff." Mike went up to the mic and said, "We're fuckin' playing," or something like that, and the bouncers came out and beat the shit out of him.

Chris Haight: It just happened so fast. Something triggered something off, and there's at least two or three minutes of the security just wailing the tar out of poor old Mike Nightmare.

Sam Ferrara: Raymi and I just had this idea to throw this burning guitar onstage and then take over, ha ha ha.

Raymi Mulroney: We filled a guitar full of gasoline and set it on fire, threw it in front of the Viletones. You know, pirates swing on ropes and they're flaming, so Mike threw a flaming guitar onstage and then we jumped on and got kicked off within a minute. Yeah, then I smashed a few guitars.

Sam Ferrara: There was chaos, and we all got up and got up there and started playing. This is what we do. We pirate. Then Mike and John Brower got in this big huge fight and Freddy's guitar got broken.

Gary Pig Gold [*The Pig Paper* no. 6, October 1977]: As the Viletones completed a final encore, their protégés the Ugly began to take the stage, to the delight of the crowd, for a surprise set. I didn't mind (the Ugly were pretty enjoyable doing their Damned imitation at Club David's awhile back); not many Concordes minded either. But guess who *did* mind? No sooner had The Ugly Singer taken the mike from (Nazi) Dog than John Brower sprinted for his rear stage door yelling "No No No" or words to that effect. The Ugly Singer rebutted with his best Cid Dishes scowl, earning him a spirited clip across the ear from his assailant. Meanwhile, The Ugly Bass Player was already into the opening number, only to find himself ruthlessly floored by one of John Brower's Vagabondian goons.

ALL HELL BROKE. The juicers saw their chance and leapt into the brawl now in full swing at centre stage, busting Freddy Pompeii's guitar en route. (Dry those womble tears, Freddy: We're holding a Pigathon to buy you a brand new one). A chorus of Boo's and raised fists came from those in the cheap seats. From my vantage point in the balcony, the whole thing reeked of Altamont: Even my cries of "Who's fighting and what for" passed unheeded.

Nip Kicks: They went up, "Give me your instrument," okay ... I don't even know if they got a chord before the security and John Brower and Teenage Head's manager rushed the stage. I remember Mike Nightmare doing his

Roger Daltrey microphone spin and letting go and *boof*, hitting John right in the chest. I think they broke somebody's guitar and threw Raymi down the stairs.

Captain Crash: I remember Mike Nightmare was down on all fours when John Brower, the guy who had put the gig together, came running up behind and kicked him right in the stones. Mike just fucking fell flat.

That was totally stupid. They should have let them play. It's no big fucking deal. They thought that they should have been invited — I think that's how they felt — and they figured they were as good as anybody that was onstage, which they were. But it's a crazy punk mentality: A few beers and away we go.

Tony Vincent: So that's how that started, if that makes any sense. It's kind of stupid. Like, you're not supposed to be playing and you're going onstage and on other people's equipment and you start playing. I didn't like it, but Mike thought it was an adventure. He liked to cause shit.

I was in the band, so I didn't want to abandon him. I did it, but I didn't like it. That's the piracy of it all.

Gary Pig Gold [*The Pig Paper* no. 6, October 1977]: Soon the goons outnumbered the juicers and everyone willingly returned to their corners. The Ugly Bass Player lay in a crumpled heap beneath the PA; John Brower was pacing backstage holding a hankie to his lip. I ventured down into the melee and gathered up all the Pigs I could find so we could scurry home to the suburbs. (Nazi) Dog asked us to help him assassinate John Brower. Steve Mahon of Teenage Head seemed unperturbed: Apparently his manager does this sort of thing all the time. The Concordes tried to play. The Ugly went into a menacing huddle outside. The film crews got the blood they had come for.

Paul Eknes: Our bass player Mark Gamage, rest in peace, his father had a little bit of money and was interested in the whole punk movement, so we put on Restricted. It was April 8, 1978, at the Masonic Temple. I believe the Viletones were headlining. The Curse were on, the Dents were on.

The Wads opened. It was my first time on a big stage. Our fourth song was "Brain Damage," and the ending is, "Brain damage! Brain damage! Brain *damaaaage!*" Sold out, two thousand five hundred people, and some guy in the back threw a full bottle of beer right over the entire audience. "Brain *damaaaage!* — POW." So I went down. Got up I guess a couple minutes later and I'm looking at the audience and they're all covered in blood, jumping up and down, and I'm going, How cool is *that*?

The bass player's mother was in the audience. She was a nurse, so she grabbed me and threw me in an ambulance. Ambulance guy said, "Are you the guy who fell off the third floor?" I'm going, "No, I'm the guy who got hit with a beer bottle." But I did actually end up getting to sing a couple more songs.

There was a newspaper called *Shades*, and it said this is the spirit of true punk and roll: Being hit with a bottle, suffering a mini coma, and getting up and singing two more songs. I ended up having eighteen stitches or something.

I got stitched up and then we played the Colonial Tavern. The B-Girls, the Wads, and I forget who else headlined. But my stitches burst because I was trying to hit a high note. It was pretty gross. Pretty punk, but pretty gross. I've got pictures. And after that I was a little bit remiss and shy about appearing onstage because I hated bleeding on people. This is before AIDS and stuff, but you still don't want to bleed on people, especially if they've come to see you. But Steve Leckie's still the best.

Raymi Mulroney: There's a picture of [Paul] and blood pouring down like he blew his head off. That was awesome. He had guts; he went on with the gig.

I always liked the flaming guitar, Leckie trying to break it, falling on his ass, and then he finally doused it with beer because he couldn't break the guitar. We jumped on and got thrown off. I went off into the crowd, Mike went into a fistfight with somebody, Tony was getting dragged off the drums, Sam's getting pushed away. I think we got one beat in there, ha ha ha. And in the paper the next day was, "Oh no, they ruined the atmosphere for the concert and blah blah blah." Aw, no, we're the pirates.

Actually, I *saved* the Masonic Temple. What happened was after we doused that guitar in gasoline I swear to God, we set it on fire and walked behind the curtain. We didn't know that some of the gas was on fire underneath the big huge coat rack, and I went back and went, "Oh shit," and I doused it. No, that would have been a fire starter. There was nobody back there, that place would have went up in flames, the coat rack and everything, then you've got two thousand people. I've always remembered that. I saved that damn place.

I know what it was! I had a bag of pot in my shirt and Mike went, "Hey look, more punk," and ripped the shirt and the bag of pot went. So *that's* what I went back for. I went, "Oh, there it is," the flames are going — oh shit! — and that's when I went back. I lost my bag of pot. I went back for that just as we were ready to throw the flaming guitar onstage.

I remember it like it was yesterday.

Paul Eknes gets first aid from Bent Rasmussen (G-Rays drummer) Masonic Temple, Outrage show. Chick Parker, guitar / photo by Ralph Alfonso

36. rock bottom

"The Curse: Girls Have Got it Covered," by Sheila Wawanash [*Shades* no. 2, 1978]: When Mickey Skin made an appearance she didn't look or act much like anyone I'd seen yet there, or anywhere. She was wearing a pink beret over a short, dark crop (later, she changed it for a helmet in the same shade). There was a pink wool glove on one hand and another pinned to her chest. Predominantly she was attired in a vastly different perversion of classic white on black than the one the bassist had assembled. Mickey's was topped by a sort of grubby tutu.

From the first I was mesmerized, awed, overwhelmed. From time to time I jumped up and down; sometimes I sat with a distinct chill tensing my spine; most often I found myself laughing. Here indeed it was at last, something I'd hoped for and never quite seen before. I wasn't sure what it was I expected after feminism, or what I was going to think and say about it. I still wasn't sure watching these women. I felt a little like Alice after the looking glass. But whatever it was I was sure they had, and induced for others, an astonishing range of arresting ideas.

Linda Lee: We were not all what we looked like.

We weren't mean. We weren't tough. For some unbeknownst reason, I think the actual massiveness of Anna's chest at that time was just such a powerful, powerful presence. She's extraordinarily creative, and strap a bass on that and have her actually play it … well, that's a really, really frightening, fearful thing to a lot of people. Anna could just look at someone and the waters would part, but she was a big, big sweetheart. It's amazing how a physical presence determines everything about you to the person who's looking at you, when in actual fact it doesn't mean anything.

The Hotel Isabella would have punk shows, but rather infrequently. The bands would go in and cause a mess and they'd go, "Okay, no more." Then the money would dry up again and they'd go, "Okay, you can come back again."

Alex Currie: I worked at the Hotel Isabella for a year as a busboy. That was a really great place. It had three bars — in the basement, second floor, and third floor. Third floor was for showcase bands, usually the Cameo Blues Band. In the basement they'd have strippers in the daytime and bands playing at night. I had just come back from college and needed a summer job.

Steven Leckie, Outrage concert / photo by Ross Taylor

Mike Nightmare, Outrage concert / photo by Ralph Alfonso

Anna Bourque, Hotel Isabella / photo by Ralph Alfonso

The Curse / photo by Gail Bryck

My job was to walk up and down Yonge Street with a sandwich board on me, and on the board it would go GIRLS, GIRLS, GIRLS, and on the back it would go GIRLS, GIRLS, GIRLS.

And it gets better. What I'd have to do is hand out these fake hundred dollar bills that you'd open up and they'd say to "Go To The Hotel Isabella." I think I did that for two months. One of the managers, Joe, was a complete dickhead about it. He'd go, "I'm gonna be out there watchin' ya, so I don't wanna see you sitting in a Coffee Time or something like that. I wanna see you walking up and down." A bunch of people I knew that had just graduated – I dropped out of Grade 13 to start working – and there they are, walking down the street, graduates. And I'm walking down the street with GIRLS, GIRLS, GIRLS written on me.

Anna Bourque: We opened for Tom [Robinson] – an English band, gay guy, openly gay – that was really fun. But it might have been really fun because the El Mocambo wanted to put us in this basement dirt floor dressing room and he basically said, "No, no, no, come on upstairs with us, don't be stupid." And he and his band were so lovely that it was just such a pleasure. So many bands of course were so misogynistic, right?

Girls were a certain thing and in a certain place and for a certain thing, and we just weren't that. We probably got treated equally in many ways, but also guys – musicians who are into the sex, drugs, and rock 'n' roll, which, who isn't? – we were … *ugh*. We just weren't gonna blow our way to the top *or* the bottom.

Julia Bourque: I don't recall us being outwardly ambitious. We sort of happened upon it. In that kind of way, we weren't studied at all. We weren't trying to copy anybody we'd seen, because we hadn't seen anybody.

As the scene got bigger and bigger with more and more hangers on it became less friendly, and I met people who I couldn't believe existed. I'd grown up in such a liberal household that I couldn't believe that people had these archaic ideas that girls were girly, or girls were hanging off a man. I always thought that was absurd – Go make your *own* million dollars! It was a funny attitude. I thought that attitude was long gone by the time I was a teenager. I guess it wasn't.

Mickey Skin: At one of the clubs we played, they actually made us stop our set and clean.

We were playing, and when I started throwing the food they got mad and brought out the mops and the brooms. Of course, that became part of the performance, too; that just added to the fun. I didn't care. Of course, the other bands would get upset because when you squish a wiener, the stage was slippery for the next guy. They used to get mad at us. Anything we did to piss people off made us happy.

Captain Crash: One time the Curse opened for the Viletones and Mickey did this thing with wieners on the stage. I kind of forget what she was doing, but the whole stage was covered in broken wieners and Dog stepped on the wieners and he's slipping all over in this fuckin' wiener grease. Oh was he ever mad. He wouldn't play until it was cleaned up.

Mickey Skin: I just jumped around a lot. I was outrageous. I think I had a lot of nerve. At the Masonic Temple – most big gigs, actually – I would dive into the audience and just trust that they would catch me. And they always did. People would pass me around and put me back on the stage. I did guy things – climbed up the speakers and jumped down.

Jula did one of the wildest things when she decided to drill her guitar. She planned it; she checked out her guitar that day and figured out where she could drill without getting electrocuted. Then she turned her amps up full, she had the Black & Decker power drill, and she's drilling the guitar while it's feeding back full-blast.

My parents came to all my gigs, and one time I could tell there was a fight about to break out. It was getting crazy, my parents were sitting in the front row, and people were starting to throw bottles at each other. I remember grabbing onto those pipes overhead and I swung out, stood on the first table, and said, "Okay, if you're gonna fight, I wanna see *blooooood*!" And everybody stopped. Ha ha ha. Meanwhile, my father had dunked my mother under the table for protection.

Somebody got glass in their head, it was still crazy, but it wasn't nearly as bad as it would have been if I hadn't have done that.

Linda Lee: Mickey would get pissed off and walk across tables and throw beer in people's faces. She would pee in a Sunlight detergent bottle and squirt it at people. Jula took a chainsaw to her guitar once. They would smack guys, but they *wanted* to be smacked. These were sixteen- and seventeen-year-old little boys.

Ralph Alfonso [*New York Rocker*, November/December, 1977]: Musical inadequacies are more than made up for by the grossness of some of the material and singer Mickey Skin's repartee of insults with the audience. Lately, even their soundman, Johnny Garbagecan, has gotten into the act with shouts of "You're making me horny, so play some music!" coming from behind the board.

Mickey Skin: I think we got in a fight once in Guelph. That was weird. I took a guy's beer and dumped it on him and he got irate. They just didn't know how the punk thing worked. He should have been so honoured that I actually blessed him with his own beer.

But I never felt intimidated. Never. Isn't that stupid? I never felt uncomfortable or intimidated. After the Curse, I played in other bands where I felt more intimidated. I guess I felt there was more expected of me musically, but with the Curse we were just having a ball. One time the Diodes took a shag rug and rolled it up and sprayed red on it to make a gigantic tampon. They winged it up at us onstage. Ha ha ha.

The punk scene didn't really get ugly until after we were in it. Nazi Dog did all his razorblade stuff, but it wasn't really that big a deal. So what, he cuts himself, you know?

*　　*　　*　　　　*　　　　*

"Shoeshine Boy, 12, Found Slain," by Gwyn "Jocko" Thomas [*Toronto Star*, August 1, 1977]: Police today found the body of 12-year-old shoeshine boy Manuel Jacques (sic) on the roof of a sex shop and body rub parlor 100 yards from where he disappeared on the Yonge St. strip four days ago.

Julia Bourque: There were kids who were supposedly shining shoes on Yonge Street. And I guess they were doing a bit more than shining shoes. They were turning tricks, these thirteen- and fourteen-year-old kids.

In August of '77, this twelve-year-old shoeshine boy, Emanuel Jacques, was killed above a massage parlour. So it seemed like there were these kids getting into things over their heads, and nobody was looking out for them.

We wrote these totally provocative songs, John Hamilton and I. And really, what a nerve. Nineteen-year-olds accusing parents of not looking after their kids till they go out and make a living turning tricks at twelve. We thought we were being so smart, but we were just idiots. Totally offensive. So that was basically the song — "Shoeshine boy/Is that your pay/How'd you make a hundred bucks today?"

That doesn't seem like much anymore, does it?

Anya Varda: I do remember when we were all very young, still teenagers, there was a little boy murdered on the rooftop next to the General Idea building on Yonge Street. That was huge, and he literally was right next door.

We were up on our rooftop taking photographs and it wasn't until a couple days later that we realized that little boy was lying dead not twenty, thirty feet from us that whole day. Just really horrifying.

That kind of stuff did not happen in Toronto at all. It was a terrible, terrible thing. It was very sad.

It wasn't Toronto. It was like things changed that day. Like the outside was starting to creep in.

Nora Currie: There was an incredible response to the murder. You could talk about it as a loss of innocence. We didn't know about our children being murdered before that.

Bruce Eves: It fueled anti-gay everything. It was really awful. It was like, "Well, round up all the fags." There was one very similar event in New York not long after that, and it was exactly the same reaction: Round them all up and send them to concentration camps.

Steven Leckie: Yonge Street was quite unbelievable. Every other door would have massage parlours, strippers, models for hire. It was everywhere until the Shoeshine Boy killing, and then boom.

Blair Martin: From Rosedale to Avenue Road and down Yonge Street, from Wellesley to Dundas, was all body rub parlours. Just marvelously sleazy; a great place to walk around high out of your mind on acid all night as a fifteen-year-old. And people didn't like that.

The Shoeshine Boy murder really put a stop to that whole Wellesley to Dundas area. That scene that started there — the early disco glitter era — people didn't like any of this, and the Shoeshine Boy murder was an excuse to get rid of it.

Anya Varda: I think it changed everybody, really. It sobered a lot of people up. It was a pall of depression, because it was a little boy. It wasn't a grown-up; it was a little boy.

There was all sorts of innuendo as to what he was doing with these guys. As far as I was concerned, that was neither here nor there. It was a little boy that had been murdered. God knows what he was doing or why he was doing it. I don't know and I don't care, and I think a lot of people felt that way, too. It wasn't like he was asking for it. He was a little boy and he got murdered.

It kind of hung over us like a really dark cloud, and it wasn't cool. I think it took the fun off that summer, it really did. It was just hanging over us like a really bad smell.

Fred Mamo: That's when you had the '60s sexual liberation movement and the hippie movement and the free love all come to a head in the so-called Toronto the Good, where in those days you couldn't get a drink on a Sunday come hell or high water. Toronto being the good Scottish Presbyterians that they were did everything

behind closed doors. Then you had this Shoeshine Boy. It was a turning point.

They used to close Yonge Street off; there was no traffic those days in the summer time. They'd have walking streets, like in Europe. After that, they closed down all the massage parlours. That's right. Then it went onto the streets. The sex went back onto the streets when they got them out of the massage parlours, which is an example of how these things backfire.

Anna Bourque: Mickey and I got in a fight on a bus coming back from New York City with these girls who were going back to their reform school in New York State. They wanted our bottle of Southern Comfort. I woke up and they were confronting Mickey. It all turned into terror and I got a black eye.

I have an uncle who is a lawyer, so he encouraged us to sue the bus company, so we did. We sued the bus company for failure to control their passengers, and without going to court they settled for ten thousand dollars. He took half, we took half, and we made a record.

Linda Lee: Our first recording was a 45 with "Killer Bees" and "Shoeshine Boy," and I think it was done at a nine-track studio. There was nothing to it. I just remember hearing it and thinking it was phenomenal. I couldn't figure out how my arms could move that quickly. We really got good.

Gerard Pas: "Shoeshine Boy" was not only expressive and full of energy, it had a social phenomenon. It was talking about something that was applicable to anyone in Toronto who walked down Yonge Street and saw what the fuck was going on there.

What was not to like about that? It was everything I wanted in music. It was vital and it was true and it was speaking about something in our society, as opposed to just sort of being in a trance. So for that reason alone I realized what they were doing was of critical importance to our community in Toronto, and subsequently in Canada at the time.

Julia Bourque: I think we gained a lot of political credibility for women in rock 'n' roll, and I guess a lot of it was really about the whole idea that you could bring music back to the people.

The music back then that was everywhere was really over-produced, orchestra-behind-them kind of stuff. This was a complete rejection of that. We thought music should go back to its roots. There was ideology behind it in a way.

Steven Leckie: The Curse, oh shit, all bets were off. They had songs like "If It Tastes So Good Swallow It Yourself" and "Shoeshine Boy." They were topical.

From the three cities — here, New York, and London — there were strong women in rock 'n' roll. You had X-Ray Spex, here you had the B-Girls, the Curse, Michaele Jordana. Off to the side you had Carole Pope, you had Martha and the Muffins. It was almost fuckin' fifty-fifty when I look at it, and that bodes well for how punk gave liberation across the board where women really probably didn't think of being in a rock band. Women thought if it's going to be musical, it would be more Motown or more of a singing outfit. But to play their own instruments, I think punk entitled that.

Mickey Skin: Then we had our record release party.

Nora Currie: It was their most outrageous performance, I swear to God. Linda Lee, she was very thin, very tall, like a model, and she wore three Kotex pads, one here, one here, and one here.

There was Purple Jesus punch and we put tampons in it so that when you scooped your drink, you would get this red wine soaked tampon in your cup. People were so freaked out. People were gagging. It's gag inducing when you think about it. People were vomiting all over the place, it was fabulous, and we were laughing and laughing.

Mickey Skin: We were winging the tampons at everybody.

Nora Currie: That year the federal government — I think the [finance] minister was Frank McKenna — put a tax on tampons. So Anna and I mailed him used tampons with a message — "Tax *this*."

To tax women's blood was outrageous. Tampons are a necessity of life and that the government should be taking a tax on this was completely unacceptable, so that was part of our protest. Today you'd be arrested. They'd get your DNA and they'd be at your door, kicking it in, for putting obscenities in the mail.

Anna Bourque: When "Shoeshine Boy" came out, of course his parents wanted to kill us, but they hadn't heard the song.

Here's this poor little boy, but what is he doing shining shoes at midnight on Yonge Street, Yonge and Dundas? What parent would let their twelve-year-old do that? It's just not right. Essentially, that's what we were saying: Be a parent, know what your kids are doing. There are horrible people in the world and you're letting him out there to mix with them? Are you out of your minds? You don't need the hundred bucks. Terrible, terrible, terrible.

"Not Entertained By This Music" [letter to the *Hamilton Spectator*]: In disgust, I heaved a record which is supposedly today's music into the fireplace and watched it melt away. Unfortunately, the words and the memories that they conjure up cannot be destroyed. With the thought of provoking citizenship action I must quote a few of the lyrics from this tune:

"Shoeshine Boy, is that your pay? How'd ya earn a hundred dollars today. They'll beat you, Mistreat you! They'll find you — wrapped in a plastic bag."

To make things even worse the name of the shoeshine boy used in this song is Emanuel.

The ink is not yet dry on the judge's orders to commit some criminals to prison for the heinous killing of a 12-year-old shoeshine boy. The ink is not yet dry on the eight weeks of the most nauseating disgorge of garbage that we read in all of the daily newspapers. And here today, people, if we can even call them that, are using this sad, pitiful and brutal murder as a means to fill their coffers with blood money.

What is our direction? Where is our society going? How can so-called, "honourable businessmen" allow this type of music to be published? How can we as parents and citizens of the upcoming generation permit our children to have their minds brainwashed with this drivel in the name of music?

Anna Bourque: I remember Mark Bonokoski was writing for the *Sun* and he came to our record release party. In the article was a picture of Raymond Perkins, our then manager, sucking on a tampon. The little cutline was "Four Punks Hit Rock Bottom," and here's Mark Bonokoski talking about how awful we are and that awful song. He interviewed Jula and everything Jula said was totally reasonable and thought out, and Mark kept trying to wind it all up. It was a lot of brouhaha.

Mickey Skin: We were really surprised. The way that it was written — they said we were exploiting the Shoeshine Boy — but we felt like the *media* was exploiting the Shoeshine Boy.

We were trying to draw attention to the fact that Hey, look at these shoeshine boys, they shouldn't even be out there. They're not shining shoes, you idiots. They were just ignoring the problem, and that's what the whole song was about. We were not making fun of the Shoeshine Boy, we were saying, "Is that your pay? How'd you make a hundred bucks today?" His parents weren't paying attention to him. Everyone was like, "Oh my, it's so terrible," but it's like, yeah, it's going on all the time. So we didn't really expect that kind of a backlash.

But it was good publicity.

Anna Bourque: I just went, "Oh wow." That's how I learned to read a newspaper. That's when I discovered that everything is wrong — that ninety per cent of what you read is just a lie, they just make it up, or they take it so completely out of context.

Linda Lee: The Portuguese community was gunning for our heads after "Shoeshine Boy" came out, because they thought we were profiting from this. We got death threats, big time.

Anna Bourque: We were conscious of what we were doing with the song, absolutely. And also being young and naïve, you thought it was obvious. But of course you don't realize that everybody takes things the wrong way.

Linda Lee: The intent was completely honourable. If you want it to mean something detrimental, *anything* can be taken like that. Look at the Viletones stuff — "Swastika Girl," "Heinrich Himmler Was My Dad" — it's a *song*. It's goofy twenty-year-old kids; the boys are seeing how many girls they can pull and the girls are seeing how much money the boys that are pulling them are going to spend on them. *That's* what it was about. I think anybody who was looking to read anything else into it was barking up the wrong tree.

Julia Bourque: The Portuguese community was greatly offended. The Catholic Church was greatly offended. I think we had a little write-up in *The Vatican News* saying we were the spawn of the devil.

But there were *tons* of articles about punk in the paper frightening everybody. It was the default subject when there wasn't enough news. They'd throw in something about punks.

Anna Bourque: But we were hounds. The whole scene was always, "You guys were in the paper this week!" No matter how bad it was. It wasn't like they were gonna ruin our reputations or anything.

Gail Manning: At that time the scene was so small and it was so grassroots. It was to get as much publicity as you possibly could, obviously, as many gigs as you could possibly play, and hopefully get that ever-elusive record deal.

Anna Bourque: Things have a moment and then they're gone. You can't hold on to it and protect it. I don't know if anyone cared what the newspapers were doing, unless of course you were a real musician and wanted to have a career. Ha ha ha.

With punk, though, it wasn't about the music. So what if the newspapers are going, "Four punks hit rock bottom"?

Steven Leckie / photo by Edie Steiner

37. there's no hope For me

Steven Leckie [*The Pig Paper* no. 8, April 1978]: We're moving to England on May 3, 1978. The whole crew, and we're just gonna do it there. I can't believe some of the bands over there — so much shit! We've heard some rumours of the Clash's manager wanting us and Stiff Records are interested in us. We may not even have to pay to get over there! We're gonna come back to Toronto as "From England: The Viletones." We're too ahead of our time for Toronto, like the Stooges in Detroit in 1969. There's nothing in New York — we've been there a lot. There's nobody else in Toronto who could do this. The only band that I think could stand a novelty chance of making it is the Curse. We've inspired them all though.

"Requiem for Some Heavyweights: Punk Goes (not so) Shocking Pink," by Sheila Wawanash [*Shades* no. 2, 1978]: I discovered that two of the best bands with a strong local following are presently engaged in projects that will take them pretty far a field in the immediate future. The Poles have already finished recording an EP in New York with prestigious John Cale producing.

It will be released in June. After that will come a tour, an album, maybe another tour all the way to Europe. This summer, the Viletones are releasing a new single that should, like their first, hit the charts strongly in England. This time they'll be there to follow up with the live performances right in the heart of punk's green and sometimes pleasant land.

So I started to ask myself what would be left for a summer of dancing in the streets with these two out of town. Of course, there would be enough local dinosaurs left to fill a few bills: the Curse, Teenage Head, the Ugly … But what else was there going to be? And what was it going to look and sound like?

Steven Leckie ["The Viletones: Now and Then, and When?" by Lola Michael, *Impulse,* 1978]: I hate Americans anyway and I want it to be people from England we play to so I can see if they like us. I want to live in whatever area we like the most in London. We support the East End so maybe we'll find like a football team to support and we will be that team so there will be enemies and supporters and we will always have a battle. I fight almost every time I go out – I like to fight – I know that I really can't lose.

*   *   *   *   *

Steven Leckie: Eva was my first girlfriend. She was a beautiful girl. We met at the Gasworks when I was sixteen. I fell in love with her smile; she smiled at me. She treated me with utter kindness from when I was sixteen to twenty, maybe even twenty-one. I wouldn't have been able to have really survived without her.

She was one of the coolest girls I ever met in my life. She was very jealous, but she should have been. She caught me lots of times and forgave me every time. There was a couple times I caught her and wasn't so kind. And she was an incredible seamstress, so she would make all my clothes. She was a good cook. I tried to be good and I cared about her and I stayed with her

Steven Leckie / photo by Gail Bryck

a long time and we went through a lot together. Without that chemistry of her, my life wouldn't have been the same.

Most of the guys I knew had extremely chaotic girls. I think if you're going to be attracted to those kinds of boys you're a crazy kind of girl, which is groovy. Eva was definitely attracted to the penultimate of those kinds of boys, but had so much compassion. When I bled she took me to the hospital. Not all the girls would. A lot of them would pull real drama trips. I would see other guys with their girlfriends and the girl would be screaming at the top of her lungs.

When I got the band, her thing was, "I always knew you could do this." And I was always impressed, because once the band had a profile it was, "Wow, am I ever popular," not realizing it was just people vampirizing. But no matter how crazy things got, I knew in the back of my brain I could go back to Eva and it would be all right.

Freddy Pompeii: He never had a place to live when we had the band. He would live with Eva's parents for a while and they would have a fight and he would get kicked out. Then he would live with this prostitute that we knew named Vickie, she would keep him for about three or four weeks, and then he would meet one of her girlfriends and he would stay with her. Then he would burn his bridges, they would give him his walking papers, so he would have to stay somewhere else. He would contact me or Motor – "I just need to stay at your place for one night," so one of us would say, "Sure, man."

I always made sure he didn't bring anybody with him when he stayed at my place, because I had a kid in the house and I didn't want any hanky panky going on. And Steven was capable of breaking shit. He'd get drunk and fall on shit. "Oh, I'm sorry, man." I had this guitar, a Vox Teardrop, and he smashed that thing to splinters. He wanted to pick it up and pretend he was playing it at David's. So he started strumming on it, then went crazy and started pounding it on the stage while we were playing. Of course I couldn't do anything during the show so I let him do whatever he was doing, but he cracked it right down the middle. I never could get it fixed, so that was that. And that was a real expensive guitar – a collector's item. So he would break things that easily in your house. I wouldn't stay mad for long, but when you can't afford to replace these things …

When we'd get a rehearsal space he would try to live in it and would get us kicked out. It was that real adolescent kind of stuff that he did and he didn't know what the outcome would be, or he didn't stop to think about the outcome. It would be like, "Steve, you've got a place now, be nice to this girl that you're staying with so you don't get kicked out again."

"I can't be nice, I don't want to be nice."

Mike Anderson: We almost moved to England. We were planning to move to London. We were on our way to doing that. We were serious. A lot of things could have happened and a lot of things were going to happen, I think, if we'd stuck at it.

It's unfortunate that in Toronto you have to relocate.

Steven Leckie: Mega Media were going to take us there and I thought that would have been a real mind fuck. That would have been a really great thing. The Dead Boys in England failed, they didn't dig, but our shtick was better than what the Dead Boys were doing.

Freddy Pompeii: What happened there is Steven never got his passport together, and people had given him money to do that which he spent recklessly.

We were all excited about doing it. Things were going good, we had press in England, the record was selling there, the stage was set. We even had a guy that would provide us with bookings before we even got there, so we were all preparing to do it. I had gone as far as to come down to Philly on a two-day trip in order to get my passport and I pulled it off. And I was pretty broke at the time but you know, I did it. And Chris got his, and Mike got his, and Captain Crash, our roadie, he got his. And we were all ready to do it and when we brought it up it was like, "Aw, I don't wanna go to England. I can't do it." "Why not?" "Naw, I just can't do it."

He wouldn't tell us that he couldn't get his passport — or couldn't get it together to *get* his passport — so the whole thing never happened.

Captain Crash: It's like, Come *on*! We've got the tickets, we've got the dough to get there, let's just get your passport. But no, it's that Canadian fear of success. It is. When it comes to an important moment in so many Canadian artists' lives, they just fuck it up in a million different ways. They fuck it up somehow.

Tom Williams: I do think in general Canadians tend to be cautious, so they would tend to say it can't be done rather than just going out and doing it.

Steven Leckie: It was probably because of my youth and inexperience that we didn't go. If I had have been older I would have went, "Look, let's get really serious and let's go to England."

Chris Haight: Maybe he was suffering from the big fish/little pond syndrome. It wasn't like he was gang-busting with confidence. He would still look to Fred about how he looked and stuff like that.

That's too bad; I know we would have made a splash over there for sure.

Freddy Pompeii: It was a big disappointment, and it was one of the many things that made us reconsider having the band in the first place. It was like, if this guy can't get it together to make the next step, then what's the point of being with him? He would tell everybody it was his band and it was his idea to go to England, you know, but I think he was afraid and he sort of created a way not to go. I think he was so afraid of going there and failing.

He used to do that a lot, especially on trips down to New York. Going out of the country, he was always scared. He had to get real drunk before he went onstage. And we always did good whenever we went out of the country; it was even better than in Canada. But for some reason he thought that we would be exposed as fakes.

I don't know what he thought, but we certainly weren't fakes. We were the real thing. I mean, he was on the streets since he was fifteen years old. With credentials like that, how can you think you're a fake? He was just so scared to go to where the Sex Pistols were. And quite frankly, I thought that we would blow them off the stage. I thought that we would blow *anybody* off the stage the way that we were.

Mike Anderson: I think one of the biggest mistakes was not going to Britain. We did very well in the *NME*. And you know what? We were big in Sweden, believe it or not. We got record sales in Sweden. We should have gone to England to see what was going on.

It's easy to say now, "Oh we should have done this and done that." Then again, maybe we wouldn't have happened. We'll never know for sure.

Marty Thau, the Ramones guy, was supposed to come up and see us play and he never showed up; he cancelled. We always got *so* close. People were driving to pick him up at the airport and then he didn't follow through.

Marty Thau: I was curious more than interested.

I had been working with a number of groups in New York. At that time I think I had about five artists signed to the label, of which only two had had albums released at that point. It was a small company, Red Star. It was self-financed and we didn't really have very much money, so I really couldn't have taken on anyone else at that point, anyway.

There was some contact. It probably was through a representative of theirs, and I might have read something about them here or there. They were known to some degree. All the punk groups to some degree were aware of each other all around the world. But like I said, I couldn't have signed them even if I wanted to at that point, being as small as I was.

Mike Anderson: There was supposed to be further workings, like we were gonna go to Los Angeles. There were all these specific plans; we were gonna get a house and this and that.

Freddy Pompeii: Eventually Don Jean-Louis saw that he wasn't gonna make any money out of this and he dropped the whole project. And he couldn't stand Steven. Him and Steven didn't get along. Steven was always insulting him, and to his face.

Tibor Takacs: After the first year of our contract, there was an out clause for us and we didn't want to continue. It involved too much babysitting. Steven was intense, much like a problematic actor, and you put up with it and indulge to a point because he was talented and his posturing was like method acting.

Freddy Pompeii: Steven would show up at practice and he'd be terribly miserable and snapping at everybody and being contrary to everything. By the time he got a few beers in him he was, you know, Mr. Good Times, and then he would reach a point where he would become a nasty drunk. So it was like three or four changes throughout the day. He was difficult to work with most of the time because of that.

Margaret Barnes-DelColle: The Viletones could have been *so* much bigger than what they were. They were like the Sex Pistols of London. In Toronto, they were The Viletones. They could have had much more success and they could have made money, but I think that Steven manipulated people to the point where he ruined it. And they recognized that.

I remember him and Fred used to have arguments where Fred would say, "Man, you'll settle for a case of beer. You'll settle for somebody buying you a drink or getting you high rather than going for the record deal or the contract or the tour. You'll settle for so little when we could be doing so much better."

Tibor Takacs: I always felt it was an esoteric venture that may have achieved cult status. I never predicted, or could see, how punk would be co-opted or appropriated by the mainstream like other rock movements. It was not commercial enough.

But the breaking point that made Mega Media split from the Viletones was that no one in Mega Media wanted to devote more time to babysitting the band.

Freddy Pompeii: We were with Mega Media for about a year and then we changed management. Good things still kept happening, but I'm not saying it wasn't a rocky road.

With Steven, he was a very hard guy to get along with on a daily basis because he had such a large ego. He wanted to be the boss, but he was in a band with three other guys who also had big egos. It was always competition between me and him, like who was the guy who was talked about the most and the most photographed and that kind of thing. He was very jealous of me because I was the guitar hero. But I mean, he got his share. He was definitely the face; he had that look.

We recognized punk as a way to set things into motion for ourselves. The time was right and what we were doing was exactly what everybody else was doing in the punk rock scene. It was almost like it was a psychic thing; everybody was thinking the same thing at the same time. It happened. It wasn't like a commercial thing, it was something that was very anti-commercial and that's what made it so appealing. And still, punk rock has never really made it; what they call punk rock [today] isn't really punk.

Making money was the furthest thing from my mind. Steven was the only one trying to make money but it wasn't happening. We were only making money on our live shows. As far as making money selling records, it wasn't happening. I knew at that point – and I even told Steven – I said, "This is going to be a cult band. This is not going to be a band that's going to be a flash in the pan, we're not gonna get real famous and put out gold records or anything. This is going to be a cult band that's gonna last a long time. It's gonna be around for a long time. People will be talking about it, but we're never gonna make it." And he says, "Yeah, I think you're right."

It's nice to be right once in a while.

Margaret Barnes-DelColle: And after the fact, looking back on it, the other problem was that so many songs were about Nazis, and who could take that and really promote this band? They would never get airplay.

"No More Nazi Dog: Punk-Rock Singer Says Militant Jews Threatened Bombing," by Paul Mann [*Toronto Sun*, October 1, 1978]: Leckie also gave away Nazi war medals at each concert and frequently made the absurd boast that he was related to former S.S. chief Heydrich Himmler.

Margaret Barnes-DelColle: Really, they could have written so much more about music, about anything – *please* – except for Nazis. And Steven, who was so into that in the beginning just as some attention-getter, later had this revelation about some show he saw on TV and started saying, "Oh my god, I didn't know what that was all about, I'm so sorry, I don't approve of that, I don't want to be associated with that."

Well, it was too late, really. You had your shot, buddy, and all the songs were "Himmler Was My Dad" and "Swastika Girl." Where are you going to take that?

Freddy Pompeii: We were just taking what the Ramones did a little further. You know, AC/DC had their logo to look like a Nazi symbol, and KISS had the SS in their name. It was just a trend at the time, so we just took it a step further and he was the one that really pushed the Nazi thing. He really liked the whole Nazi army thing with the uniforms and the style of it.

Chris Haight: There were some tracks that at the time I thought were real attention-getters, but we weren't bigots or anything; it wasn't like we set out to put anybody down. It's just the way that the tunes turned out.

It was pretty, you know, ballsy. And I think that was part of our own demise.

"No More Nazi Dog: Punk-Rock Singer Says Militant Jews Threatened Bombing," by Paul Mann [*Toronto Sun,* October 1, 1978]: Nazi Dog, lead singer of Canada's most infamous punk band the Viletones, has dropped his name and the Nazi theme from the band's act because of alleged bomb threats from the ultra-militant Jewish Defense League.

In New York last night, JDL national president Simon Greenstein confirmed that there are league agents in Toronto that could have made the threats on their "own initiative."

"If the JDL doesn't take care of this kind of thing, who will?" he asked. "Kids are impressionable, they can easily swallow that Nazi hate stuff and think it's cool to hate Jews. We can't afford to ignore anything, no matter how small it seems. The Nazi party started with nine members and grew into the Holocaust."

Leckie says that after a local concert two weeks ago he was approached by a man who warned him to drop the name Nazi Dog and cut the Nazism out of his act or his house would be bombed.

"I thought he was just trying to scare me," Leckie said. "We get some weird people at our shows. But this guy meant it, I made some inquiries and he has a record.

"I've been threatened before, usually by flakes, and they don't bother me. But I'm taking this one seriously."

Ross Taylor: Steve would tell everybody he was getting hate letters from the Jewish Defense League, and it was all nonsense. Some reporter actually checked out his story and they said they didn't know anything about it. Ha ha ha.

"No More Nazi Dog: Punk-Rock Singer Says Militant Jews Threatened Bombing," by Paul Mann [*Toronto Sun*, October 1, 1978]: Leckie himself has had a total of 138 stitches to close self-inflicted cuts while onstage. His arms and chest are laced with scar tissue.

He has frequently incited punk fans to fight with each other for the Nazi medals he gives away at shows.

While he has dropped the Nazi theme and announces at each show that he no longer answers to the Nazi Dog name, he still lives the punk life to the hilt and boasts openly of turning his 15-year-old sister into a punk groupie.

But there's one big difference in his life today — he never leaves the house without a bodyguard.

"Violence has always been part of punk," he says. "But some people don't know when to leave it onstage."

Steven Leckie: Eva was German and lived with her parents in the East End, Main and Danforth, and loved me so much. I didn't live anywhere and she let me live with her parents.

They couldn't speak very much English at all but respected their daughter. We didn't sleep in the same bed, but they were okay with it. They were through the war and that's a fascinating thing with her family: Her grandmother, *oma*, got me real hip to a lot of things I was reading about World War II and her adulation for Hitler, being an older German woman. She lived through the incredible depression — I'm talking about eating a shoe, a potato peel, anything you could find — and then how Hitler made it great for Berliners for a short time. And then of course she hates what happened later, but the real inner Berliners didn't know. And she would tell me all these things, translated through Eva.

Caroline Azar: One thing that was really confusing for me in punk was the Nazi thing. The only person who I think nailed the swastika issue was Sid Vicious, because he was a clown. He was the biggest fool of them all. The rest attached intelligence to it, and that's where it gets dangerous.

If you want to incorporate that imagery, you should be as stupid as the Nazis were. Because once a Jew is gone, the next will be a woman or a black person. It doesn't stop. Genocide in motion is an addictive property.

At the same time, I don't believe in censorship. If someone has to say something ugly, I think they should be allowed to. It's good to know who hates you. If you hate me, then at least I know to stay away from you.

"My Viletones Article," by George Dean Higton
[*Shades* no. 2, 1978]: Not so long ago, at the Existers' Too Good To Be True Party (you should've been there), Nazi Dog, surrounded by a retinue of acquaintances and fans, was telling us he was considering changing his name (his chosen and troublesome one) following a recent change of heart. Was he talking about a humanist conversion?

"I can't really talk about it. It's too personal," he said.

"What are you gonna call yourself," Dr. Bourque asked him, standing near by, 'Comrade Dog?'"

taken. We passed this store that was vacant and asked the landlord if we could take it instead. We weren't dressed punk that day and she said "Well, okay." I think it was a hundred and ninety-five dollars a month.

Gambi and I were both getting welfare and Ashley, the other girl sharing the place, was I think getting money from her mother. But we still couldn't afford it. So we thought, Let's make it a speak because there's nothing to destroy here, just bare walls. Johnny Garbagecan lent us money and we bought ten cases of beer. We made ourselves a little bar, Gambi was behind it, and I would walk around and drink a lot.

Susie Mew / photo by Gail Bryck

38. punk rut

Kerry Wade: I used to go to Toronto all the time and stay with Gambi and Zero. And Zero was like the toughest chick on the scene. Nobody ever bothered us because we were with Zero.

Zero [*Shades* no. 11, 1980]: I'd kind of moved in with Gambi on Main Street and we threw this party and really destroyed the place. So we had to move. We checked out this apartment near New Rose — it was a hundred and fifty dollars, really cheap — but it was

It was great. There was never a bust; never cops in there. They'd come to the door every night, two, three times a night, but they never came in. As soon as they showed the word would come back to the kitchen and the bar would be thrown against the wall, everybody would act like it was just a party. It was organized. I think that's why we had so many people coming all the time.

Once it took me a half hour to get from the front door to the kitchen door, which is not very far. And if you had to go to the bathroom — forget it. Gambi walked into the can once, she really had to go and there's this guy in there getting a blow job.

She says, "Do you mind? Finish it outside, okay? This is a washroom." I remember seeing Frankie Venom passed out in a pile of garbage out back. It was just a great party hole.

Tony Brighton [*Shades* no. 11, 1980]: I remember waking up on the floor once and being stuck on it.

Zero [*Shades* no. 11, 1980]: You couldn't (live in it). I used to go to my mom's for a shower or a bath. The place reeked of beer. You had to put your shoes on before you could get out of bed. You could have washed the floors twenty times and it wouldn't have come clean.

I came home from a visit to Montreal and found the TV and stereo stolen. We had a few more speaks after that, but it was over. We were getting blamed for a lot of things just because we were there.

Wayne Brown: Late at night whenever Zero would have people back to her place, there were usually some Blake Street Boys there.

Elizabeth Aikenhead: I think there were two things that marked a shift in the punk scene. One was when my boyfriend Tony was going home to see his parents late one night in Scarborough, and he was dressed in the usual black leather or whatever. And he was just jumped by some guys who did not like the way he was dressed. Attacked with a two-by-four, beaten up, and had his collarbone broken. He still went onstage, by the way, and played his drums. Until we realized it was a broken collarbone.

And I think the other big change was a gang called the Blake Street Boys. They would show up at various shows and just cause havoc. Steve Leckie from the Viletones would often incite and encourage them.

You could feel things brewing; there would be fights and violence. It started to attract people who seemed to think the whole thing was about toughness and violence and anarchy and making trouble. It took the fun out of it.

Nip Kicks: I'm sure you've heard about the Blake Street Boys and that influx into the scene. They bring up some pretty strong opinions from people.

Chris Houston: Those guys were nuts. They hurt people. What would happen at these gigs was there'd be these guys who'd just go out on the weekend and get into fights.

Gambi Bowker: I think Zero and I were the ones who introduced them to the scene.

When I met Zero I was living with this guy at this penthouse way out somewhere at the end of Eglinton or something like that. I think Zero was seeing one of the other guys that shared it with us, and that's how I met Zero. And we met Ally, who was one of the Blake Street Boys, at that same flat with the group of people we were hanging out with at the time.

I ended up breaking up with that guy because he threw my Sex Pistols album out the window. They were all heavy metal freaks or something.

Zero: The Blake Street Boys were friends of mine. They started hanging out at this place that I used to hang out, and I got to know Ally. I actually went out with Ally for a while.

Ally lived around the corner from my place, so if I was too hammered to go home and I didn't want to get in trouble I knew where the keys were and would just sneak into their house. I knew where everything was. I knew their grandmother, I knew their parents. I used to just go and crash in one of their rooms.

Gambi Bowker: We got to know Ally. He was from Blake Street, but I don't think at that particular time he was really hardcore in the gang yet. Maybe because he was a bit younger than the rest of them — sixteen or seventeen, eighteen maybe. We introduced them into the punk scene — we stayed friends with him after I moved out of the penthouse — and then he was the one who brought the Blake Street Boys into the scene. He probably said something like, "There's a lot of wild women on this scene. You guys should come to these bars," or something.

Ally was a really nice guy. He was really sweet and he was a good friend to both of us. I just think he knew some unfortunate people and was in an unfortunate neighbourhood.

Nip Kicks: I understood that they came from a pretty shitty neighbourhood. Sports facilities? Nah. Opportunity? Not great. There really wasn't a lot to be proud of in that neighbourhood, and you could sort of see where the only thing they had to fall back on was the fact that they were tougher than the *next* neighbourhood. "This block is tougher than that block": That was their sense of pride.

So when they came into the punk scene, that was their prestige; that was their image. Or that was their persona. Or that was their safety net. I think they came in thinking that's what they had to do to establish themselves, and what would make them accepted was that they were tough.

Tony Vincent: A lot of them had committed murders. When they would come into the club, the fun was gone. You could feel the tension, the paranoia. I didn't like them.

Gambi Bowker: Being a punk is sort of living outside the law; not by legal constraints, but by living outside the constraints of conventional society. The Blake Street Boys were living outside the constraints of normal, conventional society. In a funny way it should have been a perfect meeting, except for the fact that they had a propensity for mindless violence.

Nip Kicks: Scratch once told us about one of his first incidents with the punk scene here in Toronto. He went to the Turning Point; I don't remember what band was playing. He went into the washroom to go to take a piss; he's standing at the urinal. Another guy comes in beside him, takes a cleaver out of his pocket, lays it on top of the urinal, and does his business. Scratch is looking over — and he'd just done some hallucinogenics — and he's looking at this guy with this cleaver and he's going, "Oh god." The other guy — I won't name his name but I do know who he is, he was from a band — said, "Don't worry, it's not for you," ha ha ha. So Scratch is going, "Okay, uh-huh."

He goes back out there and he's sitting at his table, and a couple minutes later he sees that guy with that cleaver lunging past him and attacking. It was probably one of the guys from Blake Street.

And the blood's flying everywhere.

Kerry Wade: Somebody tried to steal the cash box at the end of the night. I remember Mike Nightmare in the parking lot with the cash box, bashing this guy in the head with it. I thought he was gonna kill the guy. A couple of Blake Street guys grabbed him off this guy and they all took off in a van. That guy was pulverized and that scared the shit out of me.

Gambi Bowker: Colin [Brunton] was saying that Cheetah Chrome tells him he thought Toronto was more violent than New York. That was really about that time when the Blake Street Boys came into the scene, because it wasn't there before.

I don't remember at the tail end of 1977 ever feeling that kind of fear. By '78, when Zero and I were running 404, one of the most horrible things that I've ever heard in my life happened, which was a bouncer came over from the Horseshoe and the Blake Street Boys were there. Now apparently he'd had a hassle with some of them the week before and he'd thrown a couple of them out and twisted one of the guys' hands in doing it, twisted it behind his back.

He didn't break it or anything. Well, the Blake Street Boys were at 404 and they took him down to the basement and they literally — *literally* — held him down, one of them picked up his arm, and broke it across the knee. And I'd never heard the sound of a bone crack in my life before, or since. That's when I started thinking, Wow, things are getting a bit out of control here now, and I really put it down to them.

Zero: I remember one night, this was wild, it was my birthday, probably my eighteenth, I guess, and actually they threw two parties for me — you know, back then my birthday kind of lasted two weeks, or sometimes longer, so there were more than one party, so sometimes it's the same year but they were all different parties. There was one party that was thrown on Blake Street and at that one I think it was Sam that was getting the shit kicked out of him outside.

Sam Ferrara: I am so glad they liked me, but then again Tony got punched out one night by those guys. He was supposed to bring some beer over to Blake Street from the Turning Point.

Zero: A lot of stuff was just intense at times. It was like a lot of stuff happened in a very short amount of time, you know? It's like you did so much every single day. Everything was kind of an adventure.

I remember we would all go hang out at the Turning Point and nobody had any money, so we would drink and then you ran out and somebody else would buy you drinks and so on and so forth. So by the end of the night nobody had any money left so somebody would be chosen — it was usually the same couple of guys doing it, anyways — and they would go to the washroom at the Turning Point and instead of just stopping there they would keep going to the back and that's where they kept all the beer. We all drank Black Label so they would pick up the Black Label and go down the stairs and then put it at the back where the fire escape was, so then we would leave and go around and get the beer. Then Joe [from the Turning Point], after a while, must have figured, "Why am I always running out of Black Label?" Almost every night we would leave there with a two-four, almost every night. But we drank it, anyways, inside, so it was like they owed it to us, right? Ha ha ha.

Sam Ferrara: So Tony stole all this beer from the Turning Point, put it in the trunk of his car, and the cops pull him over for something. I don't know, maybe Joe called the cops, I don't know — "Those punks stole my beer." The cops confiscate all the beer. We get to the party and Joe Millie's going, "Where's the beer, man, where's the beer?"

"Aw fuck, we got pulled over by the cops and they took it."

Tony gets to Blake Street empty-handed. Joe Millie's just killing him. I had a broken leg and I'm hobbling up the street, trying to get a cop to stop this. So yeah, he got his lights punched out.

Yeah, I remember hobbling up the street because Tony was getting his fuckin' brains kicked in. I was hobbling up the street trying to find a cop to stop this, and I couldn't find a cop. Finally I went back and they'd all stopped and Tony and I just grabbed a cab and went home, but he was all beaten up.

Zero: All I could see was his head bobbing. I was like, "Aw, man!" So I was standing, it's my birthday, it's my party, and Tony Torcher was there and I just sort of looked and I remember I just looked at Joe and Joe was, like, kicking him in the head and I just said, "You're a goof." And that was like a thing — you don't call Blake Street Boys goofs. And Joe Millie turned around and punched me right in the face and I just looked at him and went, "No, sorry Joe, you're not a goof. You're a *fuckin'* goof!" Ha ha ha.

Sam Ferrara: And once that guy starts fighting you can't stop him.

Zero: Then all hell broke loose. A huge fight broke out, *huge* fight. Everybody came out, everybody was fighting everybody, the cops came, people got arrested. It was just total mayhem.

Nip Kicks: Zero's birthday party wasn't the worst of it, that was the beginning of it.

*　　*　　*　　　*　　　　*

Don Pyle: I remember there being a lot of fights at Viletones shows and a feeling of violence; like things could erupt at any time.

I think the fights came later in their career. I think earlier on it was much more implied that the music sounded violent, the scene felt violent, the singer's name is Nazi Dog, he's slashing his chest.

Freddy Pompeii: The Blake Street Boys became Viletones fans. One came to our gig one night and next thing you know all of 'em started coming. They were very violent kids. They were like skinheads, but they weren't skinheads.

They basically came downtown to fight with the punk rockers because they weren't really included in it. But Steven befriended them somehow and got them to carry equipment, and got them into bars for free.

He could manipulate these kids without any problem at all. They were under the drinking age but somehow he would get them in, and they were in paradise. They could get as drunk as they wanted and they could beat up people and get themselves beat up. It was like being in heaven for them.

Chris Haight: I think they identified with the destruction of it all. Yeah, that's right. That's absolutely right. Although I think the press played out the violence thing, I think they went a little overboard.

Mike Anderson: Half of them ended up serving time for murdering people and all that kind of stuff. They were vicious. They were really vicious. They almost killed a security guard with a knife.

Johnny Garbagecan: Ally, he had about four or five buddies who used to come to the gigs, and every time somebody ended up bloody in an ambulance.

I ended up ripping Ally's jacket and got into a fight with them. I got my jaw broken. They were kicking a guy's teeth out of his mouth. I went and stood in the middle and just started swinging a chair. It actually happened at the Horseshoe.

Mike Anderson: Leckie was catering to them, wearing the Blake Street shirt and all that. It was a low rental subsidized housing project in the East End. They had shirts made up and Leckie was wearing one.

Freddy Pompeii: Steve would wear a T-shirt with "Blake Street" written on it and these kids, they loved us. But they had no loyalties. They'd go from one band to the next band. Whoever bought the beer were their friends. I remember one night specifically he incited a riot inside the Horseshoe and these kids just went wild.

Steven Leckie: I learned that trick from Alice Cooper at Maple Leaf Gardens. He liked inciting a little bit of a riot. I learned from a master there, and a lot of times we couldn't finish the set because it was that pandemonious.

That stuff doesn't bug me. It's that Saturday Night's All Right For A Fight idea.

Freddy Pompeii: Steven got the Blake Street Boys to kick the shit out of this big, fat, hippie-looking guy who wasn't a hippie; he was a punk rocker with long hair, which was the norm in the United States but not in Canada.

Mike Anderson: Long-haired hippies were *not* part of it back then.

It looks like I have a goatee on that first EP. It's actually a shadow. That bothered me a lot. You weren't supposed to have beards back then; it was really important not to. You'd see these bands with long hair and beards acting like a bunch of slobs and you didn't want to be one of them.

Don Pyle: I remember Steven Leckie, at many shows, doing tirades against hippies, and at the Horseshoe basically commanding the audience to destroy the place and kill the hippies. "Kill the hippies" was a common phrase then, and people who had long hair were getting beaten up at the show.

Mike Anderson: By this time there was a little bit of animosity in the band and Steven was getting a little bit big on himself — big in the head, I don't know why; just not being agreeable. In one of his glorious moments he shouted out, "Kill the hippies! Kill the hippies! Kill the hippies!"

Chris Haight: When or if I ever heard that crap, I'd just be going "Come on Steve, fuck, get *with it*." To me, I'd already gone through that crap in high school and it was the same old fuckin' deal. It was a nothing thing; anything to stir up the cauldron, that's what it was, if anything.

Alex Koch: I grew up in Calgary and in about '78 I went for a trip out to Toronto and met Don Pyle. We went to the Horseshoe and saw a big gig with the Curse, the Mods, and the Viletones.

I remember at one point Leckie told the crowd, "Everybody pick up a chair." There was a gang called the Blake Street Boys that used to follow them around to all their gigs. He said, "Anybody who's got hair passed their shoulders, crash them." So all of a sudden right next to us this guy just gets a chair smashed over his head. I'm going to Don, "Oh no, I'm from Calgary. My hair's too long." Don's got really short hair and he's going, "No no, you're okay." And I'm going, "Well, how will *they* know if it's okay or not?"

Jeff Ostofsky: Even though it was cool to pooh-pooh big rock bands and the establishment, I still kept my hair very long and I dressed and I identified more as a rock 'n' roll person. I never got into that whole look. It just wasn't me.

I came very close to getting really badly hurt because fuckin' Steven Nazi Dog was in the process of inciting one of his riots; I think it was one of the "Death to hippies" events. I had really long hair, and even though I was doing lights for the band I felt real naked. Nothing ever happened but I was scared, I was really scared.

It was like one of those Wild West saloon brawls. I know as soon as I'm noticed, I'm dead. So I just crouched down by my light board, put my back to the wall, and waited. And waited and waited.

I wasn't harmed. And afterwards I talked to Leckie, because I'd known him a lot before that. I said, "You know what, man? I'm so with you on everything, but you almost got some people really badly hurt. It's okay if you want to do it yourself, but most people don't."

I was scared; very, very scared. It was carnage.

Freddy Pompeii: I remember me and Mike getting off the stage and running out the back door for our lives, because these kids were beating up everybody, including the band. And Steven's up there saying, "Get him! Get that hippie! Kill him! *Kill the hippie!*" And this guy's on the floor on his hands and knees and these kids are putting the boots to him all over the place, all over his face, and there's blood spurting out everywhere.

It got to me. It really got to me in such a way.

Well, first of all we couldn't finish the show, which wasn't really important. What *was* important was there was a kid getting beaten up for no reason. He did nothing. He was a fan that had come to all our shows from the very beginning, and Steven had found this opportunity and went for it. He was trying to get newspaper coverage. He wanted us written up as a band that would start riots, and he'd go out of his way to do that.

He was trying to get headlines, no doubt about it — this thing was incited by him, and he used this gang of kids from Blake Street to carry it out. Nothing ever came of it in the papers; maybe a little corner article about two inches long. It was very embarrassing for me and the guys in the band because people saw him inciting it.

We were safe outside, but in the bar it was like all hell had broken loose. People didn't even know whose side they were on and people got hurt, especially this poor guy who they centred out. They really crippled him.

I don't recall ever seeing him at any shows after that. I think he was scared to come to them.

*   *   *   *   *

Steven Leckie: I'm haunted sometimes in the three a.m. of the soul, as Scott Fitzgerald talked about, that I could have been kinder. Baudelaire talked about wearing the same face at all times, be who you are all the time, and I took that to such a Rimbaudian degree that I viewed my role as, "I'm gonna be the biggest rock 'n' roll prick you ever probably met."

I was okay with girls, and I've reflected on it a lot and I wasn't bad, but there were a few guys that got a cold-cock shot out of nowhere.

I was just so on fire, and when I felt that something wasn't as honest as it could be, you deserved a shot in the head.

Freddy Pompeii: Steven always thought that we were against him, that we didn't like him and were just hanging on to him because he was the star. That was his take on it, and he said so many times.

He tried to get into the entertainment business, he had a gift, but it wasn't honed and he got rejected a lot. He would get into a band and then because of his inexperience and his foolishness and his inability to mix with people and get along with people, he would get rejected and kicked out. There was a lot of those things with him.

He talked a lot about bands that he was in. It was, "Oh I was in this band, I was in that band," but he never got onstage with any of those bands. It was always just rejection after rejection after rejection, and I didn't think he had the foresight to think that maybe his time was gonna come.

I always felt sorry for him because he was so insecure, and he always put on this real tough exterior to try to make everybody think that he was really tough and that he didn't care.

Chris Haight: He went to school with people the likes of Lucasta and stuff, and some of it bordered on private schooling kind of shit. He *is* well educated, and I think a lot of the times he'd just kind of come on with a moronic attitude as a way of trying to protect this confidential side that he maybe wasn't too crazy about anybody knowing about.

Nora Currie: Leckie epitomized all the bad boy, sexist, fuck-all-the-guys, fight-with-everyone kind of romance or characterization of the lead singer. He constructed that; it was very deliberate.

He was a brilliant performer. He was a brilliant front man, and he loved it. He was very charismatic, he was very smart, so he had all those elements going. He also had a self-destructiveness and an external propensity to be disruptive that stopped him from realizing the sort of fame that lesser front men have realized.

Steven Leckie ["The Viletones: Now and Then, and When?" by Lola Michael, *Impulse*, 1978]: I want people to hate us or love us and I will do anything to get that kind of reaction. If I see some guy talking to his girl-friend when we're playing, that means he isn't paying any attention. So I will go down and punch him in the face. Then he'll probably hate us. He had a chance — he could have loved us.

Freddy Pompeii: He was very insecure. I mean, I could see why. His mother left him when he was a kid and he left home when he was fifteen. He was always considered a loser and no good.

He went through a lot of rejection in Yorkville. In the hippie days he used to hang around the scene with people, but he was so wild and trying to get attention for himself all the time that people would just shun him. And he was really bitter about that; that's why he hated hippies so much, that hippie ethic. He was so anti-that because they wouldn't accept him.

Don Pyle: The heart of the original punk rock thing really started to end for me when this gang started hanging out with the Viletones. It created a lot of tension and alienation amongst people and a lot of unpleasant situations. It was feeling like things are different here.

Early on there was a lot of cartoon violence, or people acting in cartoonish violent ways — slam dancing, pretending to strangle each other. But it was all very respectful and fun and mutually agreed upon.

There wasn't this camaraderie happening in the scene, there was much more protectionism with Steven Leckie securing a place.

Things definitely started to turn ugly.

Mike Anderson: I think there was definitely a resentment towards the violence we brought. I know there was, especially from the other bands.

Johnny and the G-Rays had a song that said they believed we're truly evil. Most definitely, I could tell there was animosity for sure. It was an "Us and Them" kind of thing.

It got to a point where we couldn't even play anymore. It was unnecessary violence. Punk rock was a little bit violent, but that was a different kind of violence. That was almost like bullying. I never believed in bullying. There was no reason for it.

Johnny Garbagecan: When people get enough beer in them they get violent and they get stupid, and the violence just follows. With the punk scene, it was like it seemed the bands did cause this frenzy. Tibor and I called it the Punk Rut.

Really, it was from getting too much of that noise all at once. We used to have five bands play in a row. Nobody ever did that; it was always either two bands or maybe three, but never five. Especially with bands that didn't know how to play, all they did was turn it up really loud so your ears hurt. So you got what was called the punk rut, but really it was like a frenzy. The dancing was bizarre.

The pogo, that was like put on your gloves — really. The dance floor used to be dangerous. I don't know what it's like now, but back then it was dangerous.

Freddy Pompeii: We had lost a lot of our core audience because of that. Instead of coming because of the excitement, a lot of the intelligent people who came to see us and really loved us stopped coming.

Steven just thought that was wonderful. He wanted to have an audience full of the Blake Street Boys. And they were nothing but young kids. They were just bums, they didn't go to school, they didn't work, they didn't do nothing. Carrying on a conversation with any of them was impossible because they couldn't put a sentence together, that's how stupid they were. So that's the kind of stuff Steven liked to do.

I used to wish they would just go away.

Mike Anderson: Steven burned a lot of bridges. You can do that a little bit, but don't wreck everything. You still need people out there. You don't want to get hardcore fans that are all pyromaniacs or something.

Steven Leckie: Maybe I assumed that there was a collective, combustive energy out there and I felt that this had to be released. I felt it was combustible in *me*, therefore I assumed it was within a segment of the audience. So I felt that an explosion of violence is like the flip side of sex. If I could create a certain language that would make certain boys react a certain way, it was almost a sexual experience somehow.

I can't think of a time when the band was less than noble; we gave it everything we had.

William Cork: The Blake Street Boys were something Nazi Dog had dug up. They were just his little army of goons.

Don Pyle: Steven Leckie wasn't a fighter — that's why he had all these people around him. He would pick fights, and then ...

William Cork: This hippie kid's eyes got stabbed out in front of the stage at the Viletones one night, and Fred got back to the house here on Power Street, phoned me up said, "That's it, man, I'm never talking to those fucking assholes again. Bill, these are the most uncool fuckin' people of any scene, and I've seen it all."

Freddy Pompeii: We warned [Steven] at that point. We had a band meeting and said, "Listen, man, we are the Viletones. We have a reputation, we all know that, but we're well known now and we're getting more well known.

We don't need that kind of stuff; you don't have to go out of your way to beat people up."

And he would just walk away saying, "You motherfucker, you don't know what you're doing. You don't know what I did for this band." It was him spouting off again.

Then it was maybe two or three gigs after that is when we finally broke up.

Steven Leckie / photo by Ross Taylor

39. die TRYiNG

Mickey Skin / photo by Gail Bryck

John Catto: We eventually ended up rehearsing on Queen Street; John used to run a speakeasy in there. We ran a lot of parties for people like Richard Hell. It was all organic to the period.

The funny thing is, you look back on that period and it's an endless stream of speakeasies. The Toronto nightlife of that time was speakeasy central.

Julia Bourque: It was definitely chaotic; just like a big party, a constant party. You made enough money to carry on going to school, but generally people's incomes were pretty low. We didn't have full-time jobs, very few of us, so there was a lot of time to hang around and meet up with people. You spent a lot of time pasting flyers up on poles. We did run booze cans; that's how we supported our practice space.

Anna Bourque: The night of a speak, you'd just sort of put the word out at clubs and whatever bands were in town, Blondie or the Ramones — or Talking Heads, who were pretty snooty — would show up. They were really fun, just impromptu. And it was sort of like, party all the time, party all the time. There was always something. I don't know if I stayed home for four years.

The place above the furniture store — Cooper's Used Furniture, where the Gap store is now on Queen Street — I think Jula and John Hamilton found it. We shared that space with the Diodes. It was a hundred and fifty dollars a month and we had to run a speak in order to pay for it. Pretty much there was no one living around there, so there was never a problem with the cops, which was good. It was a great place.

It moved a lot. There were speaks all over the place. It was just something you had to do.

Zero: That was a nice hangout. You used to crawl through the window and go hang out on the rooftop.

Linda Lee: One night the back roof caved in. We were having a barbeque combination booze can. Actually, we had another rehearsal space up on Lansdowne Avenue, and our last rehearsal space was above the barbershop on York Street. So the booze cans were at Cooper's Furniture, and they were exactly that.

There were booze cans all over the city, and this particular booze can was just cheaper. It was all our bandmates, but of little interest to me because I didn't drink. I have since made up for that a million-fold, big time.

Julia Bourque: It was a total dump. It was three flights up and the police would shuffle up two flights, but wouldn't come up the third flight; it was too much work for them. They'd huff and puff and then they'd give up and go back down. The Talking Heads would come by after their gig, and the Ramones. People did that quite often. It was just a way to carry the party on. We weren't making out like bandits, that's for sure. It was just a dollar a beer, a dollar to get in.

Tank, who worked for the Viletones, eating glass was his shtick. Because Steven would cut himself, he ended up with cuts inside his mouth. I'm sure they healed; I bet he's fine now. It didn't kill him; I didn't hear about him being hospitalized.

Martha Johnson: There was this party that Mark and his roommate had and there was this guy named Tank.

Mark Gane: He was this huge guy and I'll never forget watching him eat a beer glass.

Martha Johnson: Then he had to go the hospital.

Mark Gane: He passed out at the bottom of the stairs and the ambulance came.

Chris Haight, Tank / photo by Gail Bryck

Julia Bourque: You'd say, "Don't do that. You'll wreck your teeth." I just couldn't believe that people were prepared to do that; suffer for your art. "Well, this too shall pass. One day you'll have to put on a tie and get a job."

It was really a preparation to have fun or die trying. It was this total, self-involved, all-about-me fun and excitement.

Anna Bourque: When we moved our space above a barbershop on York Street, that was around tall buildings and when we played or had bands play the cops knew about it. One night we wouldn't let some guy in because he couldn't afford the two-dollar cover — "If you can't afford the cover you can't afford the beer, so go home." That made him mad so he put his fist through the barbershop window downstairs.

I don't know how you put your fist through that kind of window, but he did. He was down on the street bleeding. I ran down and tourniqueted his arm, stopped a car and said, "Take him to the hospital." And that's the night the cops busted us. The cops were sitting in the barber chairs downstairs. I sort of got them to let everybody go. And they're all, "You know, oh, I just need a blow job," just making all these crude remarks.

One time when we were practicing two cops came to the door. And one of them was a guy I'd gone to school with in Grade 9. He was a pants-rubber when we were in school; rubbed the corduroy off his thighs, that kind of guy. He either would become a doctor or ... who knew he would become a cop? That sort of embarrassed him so much that here's this evil punk woman calling him by his name and remembering him in Grade 9, so he just said, "Well, keep it down, okay?" And they left.

*   *   *   *   *

Linda Lee: I remember Jula and I having a conversation in the dressing room at the Horseshoe one night. Jula said, "I really want to do this. I want to be a rock and roll star." I said, "Me too."

Julia Bourque: We played some fairly big venues. We played at the Danforth Music Hall. We played with Teenage Jesus and the Jerks in New York. The peak for us would have been opening for the Clash. They weren't particularly nice. They were quite to the manor born and very snooty. But their road crew were all Welsh and *they* were very nice. The Clash were total prima donnas.

We had what we called the Curse World Tour in '78. We thought, Yeah, we're getting somewhere. Then you realize, nah, it just didn't happen. It took a lot of energy to maintain playing in a band. It's very time consuming.

Our singer, Mickey, flipped out. Went absolutely off the rails in the summer of '78. She sort of thought she was the star, and so she became less and less involved. We had to carry her things around for her and she just became an incredible prima donna.

Mickey Skin: We didn't really fight with each other until the end, when I got all fucked up on drugs and they hated me. Really, it was my fault that we had this falling out.

I was dating Crash, and we got this manager, Gail. She was Crash's ex-girlfriend. And really, we did much better without Gail. Suddenly she was there — this person telling us what to do. And I didn't like her. She was the ex-girlfriend of the guy I was dating. Anna was the one who really liked Crash first of all, but he really wanted me and I ended up being his girlfriend and there was this rift.

Gail Manning: I know I had seen them at a bunch of different venues, but I met them for the first time at a speakeasy. *Everybody* was in a band, and I can't play and I can't sing and everybody was doing something, and *I* wanted to do something. So I was walking around going, "Can I be your manager?"

And that was it, ha ha ha. I became their manager.

Linda Lee: Gail was a very short-lived excursion into the wonderful world of why women should never be managers of a women's band.

There was a lot of hanging on to the Curse's coattails by women as well as boys. I'm sure it was very sincere, but I think she was more of a groupie than she was a manager. I think she was so much of a fan and kind of fell into this manager role. God knows why we needed a manager. We had a van, we had the keys, so let's just *go*.

Gail Manning: I organized their tour to the States where we went to New York and had a gig at CBGB's and Max's, and then we were going on to Boston. We had no money; I borrowed two thousand dollars from a friend to back the trip. The band had no money to even rent equipment. I had to rent drums from Long & McQuade in my name.

John Hamilton: The Diodes had this gig to play Johnny Lombardi's CHIN Picnic on [Toronto] Island. And I said, "This is it, guys, you're losing it. I'm not playing no fuckin' CHIN Picnic on the Island in the daytime in the summer." I was playing keyboard and sax in the Curse at that time. I said, "I'm going to Max's and I'm playing with the Curse. I'm not playing this CHIN Picnic." So they got Bent Rasmussen to do it.

But anyway, I played Max's and the Curse were right at the top of their form. The Curse could have made a zillion dollars.

But the Curse were fighting with each other as only four women could fight. Mickey couldn't even come down in the van with the rest of us, they were fighting so much. She came down on a plane.

Gail Manning: We had absolute disaster in New York City.

Anna Bourque: Max's Kansas City in New York was the worst gig we ever did. We'd gotten to New York that day — we'd driven all night, Jula and Linda and me — and we brought a couple people with us. Mickey had decided the day before that her boyfriend was buying her a ticket to fly, so she didn't help us do anything — loading up, doing anything. So we drive for twelve hours — I did the driving because no one else had a license — get to Max's, set up, do the sound check, and there's no Mickey, no Mickey, no Mickey.

Then we got a call at Max's from the Toronto airport. They weren't letting her leave. *We* got in with all our equipment because we had a letter from Max's Kansas City saying we were going down to audition and no money would change hands. *She* gets up to customs and they ask, "What are you going to New York for?" And she answers, "I'm a star, I'm playing in a band." So they weren't gonna let her because she didn't have a work permit, right? We had to get the guys at Max's to fax a letter — or I think it was telegrams in those days, I don't even know if we had faxes yet — to the airport, so that she could get on a plane and come down and play the gig in a couple hours. And then she got to Max's, stormed up the stairs of the club, and demanded that we pay her taxi fare from the airport! Her taxi fare cost more than it cost us to drive down from Toronto.

Then she accused *us* of being mean to *her*.

Mickey Skin: I guess maybe there was some jealousy. You know, I was *Mickey Skin*. They were the band, but I was the front person. They said I was star-struck and I was acting like a prima donna, but I probably was to a certain extent. It's part of the whole deal.

Linda Lee: I think the demise did have to do with the falling out of Mickey and Anna. I remember the gut

feeling that I had came across with such severity that it probably is still there now.

The problem with Mickey was she was a performer. She wasn't a singer. She couldn't sing. Mickey was amazing to watch, but if you closed your eyes and listened to her sing, it wasn't the same thing.

The other problem with Mickey is your ego begins to become really, really saturated after a while and I think she began thinking — not incorrectly — that she was the biggest part of the band. But when you begin believing your own press, you alienate everybody else. And you've got all kinds of shit happening if your best friend happens to be the bass player. You've got to be really, really careful when egos begin to take over friendships and I think that's what happened to Mickey, along with the drugs and being tired.

I would imagine if it was that reason, it would be very difficult to be onstage and have it come across as being as fun and as sincere as it was at one time, if that kind of shit's happening. You can't hide that. It's very clear when people don't get along in their personal lives when they're playing together.

Jeff Ostofsky: Long before the band started, Anna and Mickey were best friends. At any given time in their relationship they could be at war over something. To me, there was always friction. But they'd kiss and make up, and that was the way it was.

Captain Crash: I know exactly what happened. Mickey and I were in the throes of fuckin' smack, and it just got real bad. I had more money than brains. I was selling shit and I needed Mickey's help in the equation.

The girls were playing fuckin' New York City so I said, "Mick, you want to hang around and help me out here? You can stay here and I'll fly you down." Meanwhile, the rest of the band are travelling in a fuckin' van. They're roughing it. I was sending Mickey down there and then she had to come right home again; get on a plane and come back — "Oh, I'm flying to New York City and I'm staying at the best of everything." The other girls were ticked off.

Jeff Ostofsky: She became a prima donna.

Captain Crash: Yeah, that's what they thought. Mickey should have been there, but you know we were fuckin' drug addicts at the time and we had more money than you could imagine. "Mickey, this is your responsibility, we have to count this fuckin' money, we have to count this fuckin' hundred and fifty thousand dollars." It takes hours to do that. "We've got pounds of pot to unload in the next three days," and she took it on.

John Hamilton: They loved the Curse in New York. Mickey was walking around on tables and pouring beer on people's heads and doing all this crazy stuff with rubber toys.

Anna Bourque: She was quite fabulously crazy. She reminded me of Lux Interior from the Cramps at that gig, walking on the tables and everything. Then she dumped an ashtray on some guy's head and it was amazing he didn't hit her.

Mickey Skin: I had a lot of dance training. I had done tap and jazz and flamenco dancing for years so I had a good sense of balance, but I don't know how I walked on tables without falling. I think I kept it together pretty good for the gigs. It was afterwards I'd get really messed up.

Linda Lee: Something was happening with Mickey. She actually became almost sullen and mean-spirited that night.

She walked herself off the stage by walking over the tables of the people who were watching us and was being really quite mean. It was really hard to tell with Mickey sometimes whether she was doing it because she was pissed off or whether she was having fun with people. But that night, she'd had it. There was a definite difference in her tone and a meanness in the way she was performing.

And then, she was gone. She just disappeared.

John Hamilton: They got a standing ovation from the crowd. There was Blondie and the Dead Boys and Richard Hell, and it was packed.

And then they immediately broke up. And really, they could have been on the cover of *Time* magazine and the toast of New York. If anybody blew it big time it was the Curse, because they *had* New York. They never would have made a million record sales, but they could have blown away the Cramps and probably all met rich guys and married them.

Anna Bourque: It was just sort of great for that gig to be over. But that was the end of us. That was the last night we ever played together as the Curse. Mickey left.

Linda Lee: It's funny. When you think back to that stuff and try and remember why exactly Mickey did leave, I really don't know. I think she was tired. I also think she was delving into some very interesting drugs.

Mickey Skin: I didn't exactly think of leaving, I just quit. It was an impulsive thing. I was very impulsive. It was like, okay, I've had it with this.

I think we could have worked it out maybe if I hadn't been so messed up, but it just fell apart.

Linda Lee: Right after, my drums were stolen out of the van in New York.

Anna Bourque: Gail had gone to Brooklyn with her boyfriend and the van was broken into and the drums were stolen.

Julia Bourque: So we had to borrow drums and then we carried on. Mickey left in the middle of the night and we had a gig in Boston. We had to do it or we'd be penalized. So we drove to Boston and we didn't have any equipment, so we called up the Romantics who were our friends. They loaned us all their equipment. It was a shambles.

Gail Manning: Boston was a pretty desperate place. The hotel we stayed at was so sleazy, the hookers outside were telling us to get off their turf and find another corner to go hook on. Ha ha ha. We were dressed pretty provocatively — crazy young ladies — and it's like the girls that run the streets are running *us* off.

Anna Bourque: Mickey flew home. She'd been doing drugs and we didn't know. Her boyfriend was a junkie and he turned her on, and it makes people crazy when you do too much of anything.

Mickey Skin: I became really irresponsible, which is what happens when you get strung out. I was not showing up and not remembering the words. And I guess they wanted to do it more seriously and I wasn't taking it serious enough.

I got really messed up after that. I went as low as you can go, headfirst, and immersed myself in drugs completely. It sort of carries you away. And people would give me stuff. They wanted my friendship so they gave me drugs. I never went looking for them; they found *me*, unfortunately. Now we know you're not supposed to do that, but back then it was kind of like, "Oh let's try this, let's try that, why not," you know?

Caroline Azar: We did everything we could to get them back together in the '80s. We even gave them $500.

There was a show going on with lots of women bands. Mickey Skin could not get the Curse together, but got other musicians to play Curse songs. It was slicker, but definitely without that *je ne sais quoi*. Mickey called it Mickey Skin and My 500 Bucks. Ha ha ha.

Linda Lee: When we put this band together I actually had breasts. Like, *breasts*. And I think by the time it fell apart they were literally non-existent because I danced my tits off.

We just had so much fun that I'm wondering what people who weren't coming to the clubs and hanging out were doing, because they were missing out on this wonderful, wonderful scene. There never, ever will be another scene like this one again, no matter how much they try to regurgitate it.

*   *   *   *   *

Gail Manning: Things obviously changed, and the band evolved when Mickey quit. It became a softer, more new wave–type band rather than a punk band, so to speak. The material really changed and became a lot more melodious and more girly.

Mickey Skin: Gail had all these ideas, which, looking back on it, if we had done what she wanted we probably could have made it and blah, blah.

She wanted to call the band True Confessions, which I thought was too girly and cutesy. I liked the rawness of the Curse. So when they started to change and tell me to be more this and more that I was like, "Fuck you, I'm not doing that."

John Hamilton: They couldn't get along with Mickey. Mickey could get as crazy as Steven Leckie. They called themselves the Curse at first, but then they changed it to True Confessions.

Julia Bourque: It became True Confessions pretty quickly after Mickey exploded in New York. We came back and we had a practice space to pay for. I guess we knew that Ruby had a nice voice.

Gail Manning: I would call her a Betty Boop brought to life. She had a great little act and she could do "Give Him a Great Big Kiss" and "Locomotion" and kill that cover with the best of them.

John Hamilton: When the Curse fell apart I said, "Why don't you use Ruby? Because she looks good and she can sing." And they had Alina [Solina], too. They were trying to go power pop by then.

Linda Lee: When Alina joined the band … When your punk band gets a keyboard player, you know your ship has sunk. You just know.

Anna Bourque: So we thought, Let's just keep going and play the songs. It was always the case of who was willing and who was around; who wasn't doing anything.

Linda Lee: We had very unique relationships with each other. I had a boyfriend for most of it so I would go home

to my little life. They lived the life much more than I lived the life initially, but after a year I fell into it as well. We were a little cannibalistic; I think boys thought that we would eat them alive if they came near us. And we shared; we were extraordinarily gratuitous because we shared the same ones. Some of the same ones, anyways.

I loved them. I felt very, very safe when they were around me and it changed completely when Mickey left. Ruby was a far needier person than any of us were.

The Curse was like the family I didn't have. When you look back with a real grain of salt and a lot of perspective, you just think how trivial and how silly any of the hardships we suffered then compared to what came out of it. You're not entitled to have that much fun in your life. You'd walk down the street and have people yelling at you from their cars. Every now and then you'd get, "I'd really like to be your bicycle seat!" Boys being goofy. It was a little piece of celebrity you could have without the bucks to back it up.

I think the most money we ever made was fifty bucks. It's good for three years' work. It certainly wasn't a way to make any money.

People would yell our names. And to this day, funnily enough, people still yell.

Julia Bourque: The period when we were doing things and hanging around was quite brief; the big summer was '77. Then other people got involved, people started to go a bit more mainstream, some people got more successful than others. And after a little while you became more ambitious about it. You want to make it, and you think, Maybe I *could* have a career in music.

So it just got diluted and less focused, and by '79 it didn't exist anymore.

Linda Lee: I think if you took the first two years of the scene, that would have been the pinnacle. Even after the first year there were members of bands that had left, and I think we were one of the few that hung on before the change came.

Julia Bourque: It was over by the end of the summer of '78. Anna had stopped playing. We had a record deal and we changed our name and it was a totally different band, really. Mickey, yeah, she should have stayed, but its time had come and gone anyway. It was kind of done.

Anna Bourque: The scene wasn't The Scene anymore. It's like anything: If you're not hanging around, then people don't know who you are. So we had this golden time that was really fun, and the scene fell apart.

There was no entrepreneurial sort of mastermind anymore. People would try and do some things, but the scene was done. It didn't go on that long. Some people kept on playing and doing stuff, and I'm sure they would say that the scene went on. Some things become same old, same old — probably most things — so you do them for a certain amount of time and then you're just repeating yourself.

I was working at Nelvana at the time, and Nelvana was a great place to work. And *that* became my scene. So I made up my mind to be a filmmaker.

Jula reformed True Confessions with other people and they made other records after that. It all exploded and there you go. It was all perfect, really, although I might have stayed in it a little too long, maybe. I was never going to be any good.

Julia Bourque: I can't recall a single moment, but it did seem that, okay, people have moved on. This music isn't going to be as successful as we thought it would be. It had to become more palatable and more mainstream, and that's reasonable. It had to appeal to more people, have better musicians, be less loud and awful.

John Hamilton: I think Jula was getting too influenced by the B-Girls. Actually at one point Jula was thinking of joining the B-Girls, and I remember them rehearsing in our living room. Anna not so much, but Jula wanted to go in that direction. But it didn't pay off; it wasn't really their style. Although the True Confessions album I think has a few good tunes on it. I remember I did some drum overdubs on that.

Linda Lee: When we started looking for another singer, Ruby really wanted to be in the band. She was a great performer, but she was a tough nut to crack and she hated women. She had a very hard time with Mike being in a band. I had to literally hold her around her waist because she would have everything going — arms, legs — just trying to kill these women, big time. And I remember saying to her, "Honey, I'm so glad I'm your friend, because *danger, danger.*"

It changed things, and I think most of us spent a lot of the time just babysitting Ruby and making sure that she wouldn't flip on somebody or murder somebody.

Karla Cranley: Ruby was a very beautiful girl, and she thought she was the ugliest thing in the world. She hated me with a passion because Mike always liked my shape.

Ruby was very petite and tiny and had no butt. She had the shape I wanted; I was kind of curvy and voluptuous looking. And I don't know if he did it just to cause shit, but Mike used to say, "Jeez, I wish you had an ass like Karla's."

Well, as soon as he'd pull one like that, the next time I'd run into Ruby I mean, she was so cruel. You just wanted to crawl into the ground.

Linda Lee: We had a huge, huge coming out party when Ruby joined the band. I remember having all the press there and the photographers there and standing with her at her mic stand with my arms around her neck, just feeling so happy that my best friend is in my band now. And hearing a little voice in me warning that, "*This is not going to work.*"

We weren't an art band. You can't make a Martha and the Muffins out of a Curse. And as soon as we got signed they wanted to make us into the Go-Go's.

John Hamilton: They did a single originally which Chris Haight and I played bass and drums on, which I didn't like doing. Chris didn't want to do it at all and he was mad at me for getting him into it, but we went in and did the bass and drum part on the single.

Linda Lee: It was a very unhappy experience because they didn't want Ruby to sing. It made me feel very, very uncomfortable and it made me feel frightened. I didn't play drums, John played the drums, so I sang.

Nora Currie: Ruby didn't sing that well. Mickey didn't really sing; she just screamed. Ruby could probably sing well but she didn't have the volume.

Julia Bourque: I guess she just sang so much better than Mickey.

Linda Lee: She actually *could* sing as time went on, a little bit. I think that's why there was relief with the three of us with Mickey gone, because Ruby could sing better. Imitation is the sincerest form of flattery, but as much as everybody wanted it to work, it didn't.

Karla Cranley: When she really wanted to — when she was in a good mood — when she was onstage you were *riveted*. You couldn't take your eyes off her. She just had this presence. Any recordings I ever heard of Ruby, I never liked. But to watch her onstage …

Anna Bourque: Well, the only one in the band who could sing was Linda. We'd get her to go up and sing at the Turning Point. We'd yell out to the crowd, "Is there a drummer in the house," and always there would be.

Linda Lee: I think we were pissed off at each other. It wasn't going where I wanted it to go. I didn't have any interest in being a drummer anymore. I really would have liked to have sung, but the kind of stuff we were doing wasn't stuff that I could see myself singing.

When the single came out — this is when things were getting extraordinarily hairy — they rang me up and said, "Rodney Bowes is shooting the cover today, this is where we'll be." And I went and they'd already shot it without me, so I'm not on the cover. There's a space and it says, "Special thanks Linda Lee." It doesn't even have me as being part of the band. It's Ruby in a bathing suit trying to look very sultry.

Gail Manning: They put out that single with Ruby kissing Jonathan Gross on the front, and I think that's when the band jumped the shark.

Linda Lee: It was just absolutely poppy bubblegum and they wouldn't let Ruby sing on it. They asked *me* to sing on it, and Ruby wanted to beat the crap out of me for doing it.

Bomb Records [*Bomb Blast!* newsletter, January 1979]: Kissing has never gone out of style. How many of you remember the Shangri-La's tune "Give Him A Great Big Kiss"? The New York Dolls recorded the same song on their LP. Well get ready for "The" one version that will have you puckerin' till ya pass out. BOMB's first Chick band, True Confessions have a killer rendition of I Walked Right Up to Him, and I Gave Him A Great Big Kiss. Anyone for a little lip service?

Linda Lee: I think out of the whole scene, the two that managed to get the point across — and God knows what the point ever was; I think it was simply to have fun and dance your tits off and drink as much beer as you could

and get laid as much as you could — it was the Curse and the Viletones. Teenage Head were great, though. They were really fun to dance to but they were much more poppish. They were exactly what Bomb Records wanted True Confessions to be.

It would be interesting to have a tape of a gig with the original [Curse], and then a tape of a gig playing the exact same music with Ruby and Alina. Because I'm sure you would hear something had dipped in it.

I remember playing behind Ruby and just thinking, I *think* I'm still enjoying this. And when you begin questioning yourself, it's like, "I don't know if I want to do this anymore."

Anna, Ruby T's, True Confessions / photo by Ralph Alfonso

Gail Manning, Steven Davey, Ruby T's, Patzy Poison (Linda Lee) / photo by Gail Bryck

40. THirD Homosexual muRDeR

"Disco manager slain 100 stab wounds found" [*Toronto Star*, September 21, 1978]: A discotheque manager was stabbed more than 100 times in his downtown apartment last night . . . [Alex "Sandy"] Leblanc's body was found...by three friends who kicked in the door of his apartment when he didn't answer their knocks or their phone calls.

Mr. Shit: Well, my first thought was not to touch anything. It was evidence. Raymi and I found the body. I don't even know if they caught the guy who did it. But he knew he was gonna die. He told me once, "I'm an ex-con with a record. I'm gay and a drug addict. No way I'm gonna collect my pension." So he knew he had too much going against him.

Johnny Garbagecan: I learned of Sandy's murder when I was sitting in an unemployment office down on Mutual Street, so that's how I knew we weren't even gonna get our insurance money.

When they murdered him, I was helping Sandy. They were gonna put David's back together. I actually worked for him cleaning the place out, him and his partner, some guy from Detroit. They owned all that together.

Raymi Mulroney: It was, "Let's renovate the club, let's tear it apart, gut it again," but then the owner got killed. Sandy got killed.

Actually, it was Nora that told me. I was working at a restaurant and she walked in and she said, "Sandy got killed, oh my god."

William Cork: I remember wandering around in David's and all the ashtrays had Club Bookie's written on the bottom of them. The Tones played there and the Ugly played there. They were sort of sister clubs who shared some kind of mutual investment.

Steven Leckie: It's treacherous.

David's burned down because Sandy, who owned it, was in bed, metaphorically speaking, with some cats in Detroit. It's funny, when you went into David's the ashtrays were Clutch Cargo's, which was their punk club, and we used to have the Romantics up *here* all the time. Like every few weeks, it was weird; these Detroit bands were trying to break. And then I got hip to that this isn't about the bands.

There's some managerial thing going on. It dovetails with the Shoeshine Boy murder. What went on is Sandy was late on a payment.

He was part of these homosexual overkill murders that occurred in Toronto after Emanuel Jacques and none of them were solved. Which tells you the cops know who did it but they didn't bust him. Now the thing is, Sandy was Mob'd up and we knew that, and I thought that's cool; I love that kind of shit. But after we played this big New Year's Eve show, the place was set on fire. It was arson, and very soon after that Sandy was murdered. So you've got to make a conclusion there if you're smart enough: Here's a guy who's connected with Detroit, Mob, punk rock, Emanuel Jacques, so there's a motive – revenge could be a motive – and then all our shit was set on fire.

But mostly, the thing with David's is just the way it all ended: In arson, and the owner murdered. When you're stabbed seventy times, that's pretty hardcore.

Nip Kicks: Who knows what Sandy owed and to who, and what it took to be able to live his lifestyle.

Raymi Mulroney: We did a gig in Detroit, at Bookie's, and I'm not kidding you, we were supposed to go on tour and go to all these little places.

Tony Vincent: I'd never been to Detroit before. Back then it was like a ghost town.

Nip Kicks: My dad was pretty cool. He lent Sam his Alfa Romeo. We took two carloads down. It was Raymi and his girlfriend Karla, Carmela, our friend Doris, there was a bunch of us. I remember in one car I was with Doris and Carm and Raymi's girlfriend, I think. I had no problem – I'm a dual citizen – but everybody else got turned back. So we ended up all staying in a little hotel in Windsor and then sneaking across the next day by bus.

Raymi Mulroney: It took us until eleven o'clock at night to get across the border. We set up, no sound check, and blasted. People had their hands over their ears because of the noise.

Sam Ferrara: Detroit, at Bookie's, that was weird. This was after the owner of David's got murdered. And I walk in and I see David's ashtrays everywhere.

The people that owned the place were very gangster-looking so I didn't ask any questions about the David's ashtrays, because there was a connection there.

Nip Kicks: I remember one of the funniest things was the bartender there who was a knockout gorgeous, six-foot-something blond, who by the end of the day had a five o'clock shadow, ha ha ha.

Tony Vincent: On the second night we played, Mike's girlfriend Ruby was holding on to our pay and she got mugged in the parking lot. Lost all our money.

    Sometimes I think maybe she didn't get mugged, maybe she *stole* the money. I don't know; it just seemed like too much of a coincidence — as soon as we get paid, bang, the money's gone. I never trusted her.

Sam Ferrara: Well, I think Ruby and Mike ripped us off. I'm going, "Where's our pay, Mike?" And he goes, "I gave it to Ruby." So I said, "Ruby where's our pay?" She goes, "I had it down here" — in her shirt — "I was dancing with this black guy, and he just reached in and took it and left." Raymi and I are looking at each other going, "Assholes …"

Raymi Mulroney: Ruby was carrying the money. She got robbed. Someone pick-pocketed her right off the dance floor; ran out with six hundred bucks. And then she was getting in a car to tie her shoe, put her purse down, got in the car, left her purse there with a hundred and fifty of her own money.

Nip Kicks: I don't know what Mike and Ruby's habits were or what was going on outside there, but it was a definite drag; just that fact of not being able to trust them.

Raymi Mulroney: Bookie's was all right, other than the fact that we got robbed. We had no money so we had to cancel. I forget where we were booked, Cleveland or something; the guy had all these bookings that we couldn't get to because we had no dough. That was our big tour.

Sam Ferrara: The next day Raymi and I were just so pissed off. I had an Alfa Romeo, the whole back seat was filled with Schlitz beer and we were just drinking and driving really fast. I was going a hundred and forty miles an hour for about a half an hour, just so pissed off. We were just passing cars. The rearview mirrors were bending and you couldn't hear the radio anymore.

    We never saw a penny. Like, *come on*, some guy reaches into your bra, conveniently? She could have come up with something better; more convincing.

Raymi Mulroney: We got back in three and a half hours — which normally takes five — with a twelve pack, cookin', drinkin' beer, going, "Shit, man." Ha ha ha. It was one out-of-state gig, Bookie's, and it ends right there because we got ripped off.

Steven Leckie, Horseshoe Tavern / photo by Ross Taylor

41. the winning side

Mike Anderson: Steven would always come up to me and say, "We're gonna get rid of Fred." And I'd say, "I'm not into that, we should keep Fred. Why?" He always thought someone would look better, or this or that. Then I'd find out he'd be behind *my* back going to Tony.

    That was part of the reason I didn't feel comfortable in the band anymore. We weren't getting along, really. Steve was always disagreeing with everybody, you know? "I'm the leader/founder of this band" and all this stuff. Well, so what? Leader/founder, what is this? The Communist Party of Canada or something, Steve?

Freddy Pompeii: He tried to do that with all the guys in the band. He'd get Chris and me together and say, "We gotta get rid of Motor, he's just not a good drummer." Fuck you, man. And he would do the same thing with me and the same thing with Chris. "Oh, Chris is too old and he's starting to get fat and he doesn't dress right." No, Steve. This is it, this is the band, get used to it.

    It would go on all the time, it never stopped. If he couldn't get what he wanted from one person he would go to the next person.

Margaret Barnes-DelColle: You know, Steven's like an old woman. He loved to pit people against each other. He loved that.

Freddy Pompeii: It was a lack of a certain amount of talent, and he had to cling to certain people in order to make it happen.

I always told Steven, "Don't worry, man, I'm not looking at you judgmentally or anything." He couldn't fuckin' sing to save his ass, and I really had to push him to practise. He always had an attitude because he was so insecure that he tried to make up for it by belittling me. He'd say, "You can't play guitar, you don't know how to play guitar, we need another guitar player."

Chris Haight: The one thing Steve had to realize, and I think he did realize this, was that the Tones were the Tones for a special reason. You can call it metabolism or I don't know what the hell, but there was just a magic about it. It was a magical experience and maybe we took it for granted how lucky we were to have that going for us at the time. There was more to it than the one or two chords that the songs were basically written on. There was something magical about it. I believe that to this very day. It just happened to take that form.

Freddy Pompeii: What he was sitting on was a really good band. It was almost a miracle, that kind of chemistry. Once in a lifetime. What happened with the Viletones was something completely out of the ordinary. I'm not saying we were the greatest band in the world or anything. We were just one of those exceptions. The four people got together right out of the blue. It wasn't a coincidence; it was meant to happen. It all snowballed for us, but Steven I don't think ever realized how important the band was and what he had.

The magic that was happening between the three of us — well, the four of us, actually, but the between three instrumentalists — was an extraordinary thing. There was this energy there. It was a really good formula and, like I said, it couldn't be duplicated.

*   *   *   *   *

Sam Ferrara: Mike robbed a lot of places. Some of the stuff he did was really bad. He'd break in and rape someone.

There's a song, "They're gonna burn me in hell/These are my sins/These are my confessions," and he's saying all this stuff. He robbed a Becker's store and made the owner get down on his hands and knees and made him bark like a dog. I'm not sure what made him like that. It was just a crazy lifestyle he had. But he was a great front man. He had a way better voice than Steve Leckie; he could carry way more of a tune.

I thought the Ugly wasn't getting really anywhere. The Viletones were getting more ahead than anyone. Steve Leckie used to DJ at David's, and play there, and

he'd always send these little notes — "Join the winning side." So finally I did.

I don't know if it was the *winning* side, though.

Margaret Barnes-DelColle: Steve brought Sam Sinatra into the band. He's a great guy; he's a great musician. Everybody loved him. But Steven would always try and make trouble. He would always try to hook up the guys in the band with other women, break up couples, or get in the way. One time he was pretending to hit on me and came and sat next to me. I got along with him okay, but I always found him to be very childish and I knew how manipulative he could be. So the fact that he would even sit next me meant that he wanted something. He would get real close to me and then he said, "Oh my god, I can't even do it, you're like my sister or something." Not that I ever would have been interested, but he always manipulated things and always liked the drama.

So when he could no longer create or get a rise out of anybody in the band, he brought Sam in. Because he knew nobody wanted that.

It changed everything, it really pissed everybody off, and he got his way in the sense of, Now I have more drama and I can use Sam. And Sam was totally naïve about it. He's kind of innocent in a way. I don't think he knew that Steven manipulated people like that.

Sam Ferrara: I was trying out for the Viletones on top of Tuxedo Junction on Yonge Street. Steve goes to me, "If you can play 'Screamin' Fist' you're in the band." It's two chords, but the hard part about playing "Screamin' Fist" is it's all downbeat; it's really quick and constant.

But we were making too much noise or something. The cops came in and Crash was there. He was dealing pot and stuff; there's an ounce of pot on the table. So we're like, "Oh shit." Then Chris started playing "Blackbird," very nice and quiet, the cops are going, "Oh that's beautiful," and didn't even notice the bag of pot. They just said, "Well, keep it down boys." Ha ha ha.

Mike got really pissed off when I quit the Ugly. I made sure he didn't have his gun. He called me a traitor and all this shit.

I'd kind of had it with the Ugly. But then again, if we probably would have stayed together things would have been different. Maybe. Maybe Mike would still be alive. He'd be in jail, but he'd still be alive. But you never know.

Freddy Pompeii: When he wanted to bring Sam in as bass player and we moved Chris Haight to lead guitar, all of a sudden we became a Chuck Berry clone. Which is something I didn't like, and nobody else in the band liked it either.

Chris Haight: I liked Motor's style, but even with him doing what he was doing there still really wasn't a pegged backbeat, which is what they really needed for what was going on; power chords and shit. So that's why that happened.

Freddy Pompeii: I thought that the band was fine the way it was. We put out a sound that was original and it didn't sound like anybody else. As soon as you added that second guitar, it smoothed it out so much.

Sam Sinatra is a really good bass player, but it wasn't the Viletones anymore. It was something else. It wasn't a nice direction that we were going in. It took all the edge off of it. Everybody in the band knew that, but Steven always had to be the guy making the decisions and he always was trying to make everybody in the band feel like he was superior to them in all ways, right from the start.

I never said anything to him to make him feel insecure. In fact, I did everything to empower him to get better. Even if he was terrible, I would say, "That was great Steve, you're doing fine, just keep doing that."

Raymi Mulroney: I was surprised when Sam left. I thought he was gonna stay for a while, but he understood where I was coming from. We were starving; nothing was really going on. He had seen it coming and I had seen it coming. We were crazy.

William Cork: Mike had always been a criminal, always. His briefcase that he always carried to meetings had a couple of *Mad* magazines in it, a 45 by Question Mark and the Mysterians, a .38, and a little tape recorder. He was constantly badgering me to be his partner in crime, but that ain't me. He needed somebody to bail him out of jail pretty consistently, so ...

Raymi Mulroney: We went through a year of hell. It was a year of hell, but the Ugly was the Ugly. It was a great band. When we were on, we were on. We had great times, great rehearsals. I remember a lot more pros than cons about that band.

Nip Kicks: If I'm not mistaken, Steve had sort of been soliciting Sam and Tony for a while. It was weird, because I think it was Sam who wanted to leave first. I remember one trying to talk the other into it. I think Tony was torn between his loyalties, to Mike and Sam. Same thing when they left the Viletones, actually. I think that was a tough decision for them both. They spent a lot of time thinking about it.

Raymi Mulroney: I don't know if Mike was upset when Sam left. I wasn't around. I left first. I think Sam and I

almost left at the same time, or close to it. Sam didn't stick around much longer and I remember Tony Torcher saying to me, "Good luck with your new venture." He was disappointed, but he understood. Because Sam and Tony played together for so long they sort of missed each other. Those guys were like brothers almost as far as they played together so long, you know? They were always there.

Tony Vincent: I knew Sam and Steve were planning that out. Steve was trying to get him to join them when he was playing with us, so when he did leave I wasn't surprised.

We were so tight; we played together for so many years. It was like I lost half of my body or one of my legs or something. When we were playing a song, he knew exactly when I was gonna do something. He followed me to a different part of the song, I would follow him – we knew our moves perfectly. We were like one mind. I was just sad because we played together for so long. People used to say we were the best rhythm section in the city.

Nip Kicks: I remember going for walks with Raymi and I remember going for walks with Mike, and of course I was hanging out with Sam more than anybody else, and Tony. I remember hearing them both complain about each other, each in a very different way. But I think the day that things really changed was the day that Mike threw a knife at Raymi in the rehearsal hall. That was probably the day that sealed their fate.

Raymi Mulroney: Two Irish guys and two Italian guys in the same band – "I'll fight with my eyes closed." There were fights. I remember going onstage about three times with a black eye. I'd say, "No, I want it to go like this," and Tony and Sam would go, "Hey Mike, yeah, let's do it that way," and Mike would get jealous because I got my way; the younger brother got his way. So he'd go, "Come here, I wanna talk to ya." *Bang!* Sucker punch right in the face, ha ha ha. It's true.

But hey, he loved me.

Nip Kicks: I think one of the things I learned from Mike was to walk down the middle of the road instead of the shadows. I don't have any other way to put it. He had a strut that let you know he was coming. From Mike there was a projection of confidence, and I think I picked up on the way people related to him that way. I mean, he was a tough guy. He would use whatever means necessary – whatever it took – and in those days, certainly, he wasn't lurking in the shadows. He was larger than life. He was right there, and take it or leave it, that's the way it was.

I was really lucky. I never had any problems with him in any violent way, I never had any confrontations with him. I'd been a fighter all my life, too, but in my mind I was the less experienced guy. I was the younger guy, the rookie, but maybe I still had that little bit of mystique. But I think that more than anything else, I learned that. That whole pirating concept; that brazenness.

Elizabeth Aikenhead: I remember one time Mike was onstage at the Horseshoe, I believe, and he had a condom full of semen that he threw into the audience. He was a bit of a scary character.

Raymi Mulroney: The punk scene in Toronto wasn't happening fast enough. We wanted to get into the mainstream of music, and nobody took it seriously. We had a manager — what'd they call him, Captain Kangaroo, I can't remember his name now; he ran the campus bookstore up on Bloor Street. He's the one that set up the tour we got robbed at.

We figured after a year we'd be big rock stars. I guess we were being a little selfish in that way, but I don't know. It just got too cutthroat — who's who and who wants fame and all that stuff. The whole thing was fame. We didn't think that way. We just thought, Let's play, let's play, let's play. But when you're starving you can't. You've got to go get a job. That's what I was relying on, actually. That's all I was doing, playing music and trying to rely on that.

Yeah, we wanted things to happen too fast. We were expecting too much too quickly. We were playing everywhere, so if we stuck around like some of these other bands like Teenage Head, if we had have done that ... But we didn't. It was a great rock scene, I guess you could call it. It was awesome, but like I said, it didn't happen fast enough. We were thinking, "Where's all these promoters? Where's all these people?"

I didn't have money coming in, and the only job I could get was at nighttime so I sort of faded out from the band. I can't make it to rehearsals; I got to pay the bills or I'd end up on the street. What good would that be? So there's my girlfriend and I struggling to get by and I gave my notice to the band. That was it. I said, "This ain't going nowhere. I'm not making any dough." I was being selfish, I guess. I could say I was selfish that way. I wanted things to happen a lot faster.

Zero: Raymi was pretty well gone in '78. I don't even think he was around in '79. He kind of disappeared almost as quick as he came.

Tony Vincent: That wasn't the end of the Ugly. We got another bass player. Raymi quit, too, so it was just me and Mike left. We got another guitar player, Chick, and

this other guy, Frank, so it was a totally different sounding Ugly. That's when we made the first record.

Chick Parker: They got another guitar player but Tony didn't like him because he was Italian, even though Tony's Italian — "He looks like a wop." "Uh, Tony ...?" And he had seen me play and thought I looked incredibly cool, so he basically asked me to join to boost the cool factor. So I joined the Ugly because Tony thought I looked cool, not because of any sort of playing ability or anything, which back then was probably good ...

*   *   *   *   *

Steven Leckie: ["Please Call Us Punks Again Leader of Viletones Says," by Peter Goddard [*Toronto Star,* September 2, 1978]: "I just called myself Nazi Dog to propel my name ahead. It worked. I'm famous enough. What I don't understand is why we haven't gotten a major recording contract yet."

Freddy Pompeii: There were companies besides Mega Media that were interested in us. Teenage Head's management wanted us, but we ended up not getting it because of Steven insulting John Brower. Other people would come down the line, like the people that did the Battered Wives. The Battered Wives weren't even a punk band; they were a rock band and we could have had the money that backed them up and put the albums out and handled tours for them. They weren't better than us; in fact, they were older and kind of imitative. But they were professional and they got from Point A to Point B to Point C. Same with Joey Shithead in D.O.A. They got pretty famous.

All of that was handed to us, and we never got it. We never took the offers. Steven turned them down, time after time after time. Steven was like a hand grenade with the pin pulled out, throwing it around — "I don't want it! *You* can have it!" These people would come to us — "Oh, you guys are great, I've never seen anything like this onstage, where'd you get that sound?" They'd come to us with all this praise and then Steven would just tell them to get lost and insult them, so many times. It was really disillusioning.

Larry LeBlanc: The Toronto bands were reluctant. Some of them didn't know what to do, so they just took a belligerent attitude because they really were unsure on how to approach it.

You see, one of the problems is they wanted to have nothing to do with the music industry. Well, that's a cute theory. But you have to interact with *somebody* at some point. It would have probably been thought of, I would imagine, as part of the establishment, I would think.

Don't kid yourself: the industry here wasn't waiting for them with open arms.

Freddy Pompeii: But they still came. Roger Mayne's deal on Razor Records, that was pretty good.

Mike Anderson: Roger was just out there looking around to record some music. He was a personal friend of my father's, actually. He used to go to parties that my father and mother had, and he used to play guitar. And then he had a business that made duplications of videotapes.

I invited him down when we played at the Underground. I don't know why he showed up. Maybe I really sold him. He was really high about the whole idea of what we were doing. We were going to open up for Burton Cummings and all that shit, ha ha ha, at one time. That would have been really weird — *really* weird.

Freddy Pompeii: Roger and Razor Records wanted to be involved in promoting the Viletones. So they were basically our second record company, but they weren't our management company. They didn't do the same thing for us that Mega Media did. And yeah, it was Motor's connection, basically.

Mike Anderson: I never asked Roger to come out and start recording with us; somebody else did. I guess he liked music and kind of missed what he was doing. He was basically into the same type of thing back in the Yorkville days.

Freddy Pompeii: Roger Mayne was in the Ugly Ducklings and he was a real veteran of the studio; he knew what he was doing. Which I don't think worked for us. I think the second EP was weak compared to the first one.

For instance, he made me record with a different guitar than my Les Paul. Chris Haight played lead guitar, I played rhythm guitar, and we had Sam Sinatra playing bass. It was the first time, with very little rehearsal, that we were playing with an extra guy; with Chris playing guitar instead of bass. For me, I was unhappy playing a guitar I wasn't used to; a guitar that didn't sound like a Viletones guitar.

Mike Anderson: We went to Masters Workshop or something like that out in the north part of Toronto. There was a little more time allotted, and we actually did things in steps and made sure our timing was together. We did the bed tracks and then we did the overdubs and more vocals at Sounds Interchange, which was a big studio. It was a little more refined.

Freddy Pompeii: On the first EP, it almost sounded like we had to bridle our sound because it was getting away from us. On the second one, it didn't sound like that at all. It was a little *too* professional. It was a little too reminiscent of early '70s pop music. Maybe trying to sound like the Ramones too much. To me, it just didn't cut the mustard.

Chris Haight: I remember Rod Stewart was waiting for us to finish mixing at the studio. We're making him wait. And the guy says, "C'mon, Rod Stewart's out there." And the Dog says, "Well, make him wait some more."

Freddy Pompeii: Roger Mayne wanted to dominate the sound on the record and produce it and make it sound clean or — I don't know what the fuck he had on his mind. We were Viletones. It's all in the name: *Vile*-tones. We didn't want to sound nice. We wanted to sound mean and vile, just like the first record.

I guess all artists have regrets and if I could repeat anything, *that's* the time I'd like to repeat and make better decisions.

Chris Haight: It was tough enough for us to actually throw the show together and keep it together without killing ourselves. When we weren't fighting other bands or crowds, we'd be fighting amongst ourselves.

Freddy Pompeii: We were getting really sick of Steven's shit at that point, you know, the whole thing of bringing in Sam and adding another guy to the band when we really didn't need it, and keeping us off the [*Look Back In Anger*] record cover and just putting himself on. He really was like, "This is *my* band, and I call the shots."

At that point he shouldn't have been doing that. He should have been on top of things because we had made leaps and bounds towards being professionals. But he was making the slowest progress of all of us, which led him to do more outrageous things to draw attention to himself.

Chris Haight: For example, we just finished the second EP, right? We went up to the Red Lion to celebrate and I guess we were there ten, fifteen minutes and, I don't know what was said or what happened, we started throwing forks and knives at each other.

Mike Anderson: A big fight erupted. We were all getting drunk, Chris and the Dog and I, and Steve started going off — "I write everything! I write all that stuff. I did it all!" It's like, "*Excuse me?*" I threw some cutlery at Steve, a fork. It stuck in the wall, too. Ha ha ha. I guess Roger didn't think too highly of that.

Chris Haight: We all get the heave-ho. The food didn't even come. Honest to God, I don't even know what the hell it was about. But I mean, you can't blame the guys. They were seething; they wanted to kill us. They had just spent all this time and dough doing this little second EP five tune thing, and they had expectations and they had plans. And the whole thing just fell apart. The band couldn't keep it straight.

After their time and effort, just to have it go down the tubes. I don't know why, I still don't know why. But that was the beginning of the end for us.

42. keeping secrets

Chris Haight, Freddy Pompeii / photo by Gail Bryck

John Hamilton: In the beginning, everybody was rebelling against the same thing. But after about a year, a year and a half, people started moving in their own directions, so you could see there was a bit of a fragmentation. The bands' sounds started diverging a bit more. A lot more clubs were opening up. A lot more bands were flooding in.

The other thing was, originally the people involved were all pretty smart and realized that this was sort of an artistic thing we were doing; it was kind of fashionable. It was a pose like the Dadaists and Marionetti and the Futurists, because we were doing this to get attention. We exaggerated a little bit but we

were pretty well grounded. We had this sort of tough-person pose.

But then you started getting people coming in who were kind of stupid and really weren't pretending to be dumb; they *were* dumb. And you got these guys, the Blake Street Boys, who were following the Viletones around and at every gig they would just beat the crap out of everybody in the audience. It wasn't fun anymore.

Freddy Pompeii: Steven was just getting too big for his britches and making too many demands. Me and Chris Haight and Motor X were rehearsing this new band called the Secrets, and John Hamilton was involved in that. We promised each other that if he starts in with his antics again we were just gonna quit and go on as the Secrets. So the whole thing was a secret … that's why we called ourselves the Secrets. We did it on the sly. We had a full-blown band while the Viletones were still going.

How it got started was John Hamilton from the Diodes and Chris were friends for years and years. The Viletones weren't rehearsing enough to keep everybody busy and I was getting bored, and Chris was getting bored. Just by accident I found out that him and John Hamilton were jamming; they weren't planning on doing any shows or anything, they were just getting together because that's what they did. And they were doing some of the old songs and writing some new songs and making plans of maybe putting a record out.

It was John Hamilton I believe that approached me and said, "Hey Freddy, why don't you come over and jam with us sometime?" I said, "What would I do?" And they said, "Well, you could sing." I said, "Okay, I'll give that a try."

Steven would never let me sing because I sang too good. He didn't even want me singing background vocals, afraid that I would show him up. That was all right. I let him have the stage and I was the guitar hero. But I missed singing.

I knew a whole bunch of songs from the past, and they knew a whole bunch of songs that I had never heard of, so it was a real fresh and exciting experience for me and for them. It got to the point where we had learned so many songs. Somebody said to us, "Listen, we need a backup band, why don't you guys open for us?" We said, "All right, we'll do that," and it was at the Isabella Tavern and there was me and this other guy who was singing.

We did some Animals songs and some Rolling Stones songs and some David Clayton-Thomas songs, and we had some originals that we threw together. We called it the Secrets Revue. And we called it Revue because there were so many different people that played with us, and we would bring on different people throughout the set.

I would maybe only play eighty per cent of the set and then there would be other singers, and girls from the Curse and girls from the B-Girls. All the personalities would be able to come up and do songs and we'd back them up.

After a while we started getting a reputation. People were coming to see us because they were enjoying what we were doing. And like I said, this band became pretty solid but we kept it a secret. We never said it was a band; it was just like a bunch of people jamming. And Steven never figured out what was going on because he wouldn't come to shows.

He *did* find out at one point and we said, "Don't worry, man, it's just a bunch of friends getting together." "Oh, it's gonna hurt this band and you shouldn't do it." It was like, "Don't worry about it, man, it's cool." Because the Viletones were so strong, we were getting hired to open rooms. They'd pay us two or three thousand dollars for two sets and first thing you know, these people have a money-making room. That's what was happening with the Viletones at that point. The whole scene was revolving around these new rooms opening up and every one we played was packed.

It was really going to Steve's head because he was making money for a change and he was really getting big-headed – "Oh, this is it, we're gonna put another record out." He was always dreaming.

John Hamilton: One of the reasons that Freddy and Chris and Motor quit the Viletones and started the Secrets was because the Viletones just deteriorated into a brawl every night. So that was one of the negative things. When these things happen, if you don't get above it you're gonna get drowned in it. Because the first four bands have it figured out, but in a week there's eight bands, and then in six months there's ten bands, and then there's a hundred bands and then there's three hundred bands and they've all got plans. It just gets diluted.

So the thing that was lucky for the Diodes and Teenage Head and the Curse and the Viletones was they got a bit above it. Whereas you had all these people flooding in like Martha and the Muffins and the Mods and these come-latelies, so it just gets watered down. Not that some good stuff doesn't come out of that.

Freddy Pompeii: Steve wanted to go with the rockabilly trend. I didn't want to do trends. We'd been establishing ourselves and I didn't think it was a good idea to start imitating other bands. He didn't see any problem with that. He didn't see the short-term and long-term consequences of doing that. It would be so transparent. You'd give yourself away.

He saw those hairdos and just wanted to be that way. We weren't about to follow him down that road.

*   *   *   *   *

Crazy Cavan, Steven Leckie / photo by Ross Taylor

Sam Ferrara: My first gig with the Viletones was at the Isabella. We played about three songs.

Freddy Pompeii: We had just released our EP *Look Back in Anger* and it was our record release party at the Isabella. We played, like, four songs with Sam Sinatra and it sounded good, but it was a little too smooth for a Viletones show. But it was still good; the place was packed.

Margaret Barnes-DelColle: They had this basement bar that was so tiny that every time I saw a band there I thought, I know I'm gonna die in this place. They would just pack people in and you would just think to yourself, There's gonna be a fire in here and there's gonna be no way out. There's only the one entrance and they're going to stampede it. And then you'd get really drunk so you just didn't have to think about it.

Freddy Pompeii: We got up and we're showing off the new band and the new sound and this bartender started yelling at Steven, heckling him, and Steven was doing downers and drinking so he was off the deep end.

He gets up and jumps over the bar and jumps on this guy. I don't know what happened because all the action dropped to the floor.

Captain Crash, our roadie, followed him right over the bar and next thing I know there was this brawl going on.

Sam Ferrara: Then it calmed down a little bit, we did a couple songs, and then Crash picked up this guy who was bugging Mickey Skin and he throws him right over the bar. Then all hell broke loose.

Freddy Pompeii: They closed the doors immediately so nobody else could get in and there was just this big fight that ensued.

I got my guitar out of there because I didn't want it to get broken and escaped through the back door to our dressing room. Steven came up afterwards doing his little Cockney accent — you know, "Oi! Oi!" — and he was covered with blood and complaining that we could never do a show without it getting interrupted with violence. And then the very next thing he asked was, "How much money did I make?" I said, "Steve, we didn't even play, man, what makes you think we're gonna get any money?" He's like, "I'm playin' or I'm quittin'!" It was one of the many times he quit the group. He quit the group every week.

We got paid anyway. The guy was glad to hand us the money. And of course we had a couple of backup bands, we had to pay for a PA system, so we really didn't make any money. I think we walked away with a hundred bucks apiece for the night. Steven was completely insulted and he was drunk out of his mind and he had already been in a big fight. I think he was speeding or something, and we're all standing there and he said, "Is that all you got? Is this all I'm gettin'? I want more than this."

And we said, "Well, that's all you're getting, man, sorry. It's a democracy, you know." And he said, "Come on, Eva, let's get out of here, I quit this fuckin' band." And he walked out. Me and Motor and Chris were all there looking at each other and we thought to ourselves, Well, shit, he just quit the band. I guess it's time for the Secrets to be a band, and that's what happened.

Tank: That was probably the night that I really lost faith in, well, Leckie. Basically what happened is he took the revenue from the door, was in a room with a girl upstairs, and that was the end of them. They just were tired of his bullshit. It was mounting. It was a circle they just finally broke and said, "That's it." They'd play a gig, Leckie would take the money, say, "I'll pay you," and the money would be gone.

Sam Ferrara: I passed out on Steve's couch that night and next morning I had this *Toronto Sun* on my head and saw that we were in there. That was my first experience in the Viletones.

Freddy Pompeii: Steve came crying to us after saying, "Well, I'm okay now, I don't want to quit anymore."

After the Isabella, we did another gig that ended up in a riot. Steven quit and we just said, "This is the last time he's quitting." And lo and behold he calls me the next day, "Oh, I didn't really quit." I said, "Well, we quit."

Mike Anderson: The *secret* became reality. I never really liked the name that much, but it stuck.

By that time in Toronto everything was rockabilly, rockabilly, and Steven Leckie was starting to wear a cowboy hat and combing his hair back.

Freddy Pompeii: We changed the name to the Secrets instead of Secrets Revue and started playing shows. Steven, we didn't contact him or anything. We just said he quit; there's no more Viletones. And that's when he called me up and said, "Look, man, come with me and we'll get rid of those other two losers and we'll get Sam and Tony Torcher." I said, "They're idiots, man."

Sam Ferrara: Tony and I used to steal all of Freddy's glue. Ha ha ha. He had this thing you put around your neck and put your lighter in, but instead he'd always put a tube of glue in there. Tony and I would just take it out and go to the back and just sniff some glue. So Freddy would be like, "Fuck, guys, now I have to replace the glue."

Freddy Pompeii: Sam was a nice guy and he's not an idiot, but he was kind of a follower. And Tony, he would follow anybody and do whatever they told him to do. I said, "I don't want anything to do with those guys. Either it's the Viletones the way it is, or forget it." After we hung up I called Chris and I said, "We might as well start solidifying things with the Secrets because I just told Steven to take a hike." So we started rehearsing in earnest and things started to happen for us right away.

He took it bad. From then on it was like he hated us. We had a band where the music spoke for itself, the entertainment was there, and we were making like two thousand dollars a night.

If it's not broken, don't fix it. That's just the way I look at things. That was a big problem with Steven.

Steven Leckie: I was wild. I was extremely crazy and unpredictable and I could see they were going, "Man, I don't know how long we can go with Leckie." It hurt like a ton of bricks when they left. Chris Haight was the one that they laid the responsibility on to say, "We're ending, who does everyone want to go with?" Everyone chose the Secrets except Sam, who chose me, and that made me feel better.

But it really devastated me. And if those cunts had have stayed together just one more lousy year, they would have been fuckin' household names, Chris Haight and Freddy Pompeii. They threw in the towel way too soon.

Freddy Pompeii: He was very upset. He hasn't forgiven us yet. He hates us because of it. He's just very jealous and very territorial. He holds a grudge a long time, and against a lot of people, too.

I still love the guy. From what we did together, you can't help but have affection for people you have that experience with. He's just got an uncontrollable ego and he can't help it.

It was us against the world when we were the Viletones, and he still holds it against me that I left him in the lurch. But we just couldn't do it anymore. He was just too much. The other two guys felt the same way; they had just had it up to their throats. He was plotting against us after the second EP to bring another member into the band and keep us off the record cover and just put himself on the cover. That was one of the other many reasons that we left him, because he kept doing shit like that.

Steven Leckie: I allowed the success of the band to fall through out of sheer belief and passion in punk. For the industry, it was something you could lick but you couldn't kiss. Like, you can't really have us. Not the real ones. And me and Eva and my little crowd really luxuriated ourselves in the notion that, shit, if you can say the Viletones in the same sentence as the Clash and the Pistols and the Ramones who have heavy record financing, and we're really truly independent, then *we're* the real thing. We're so real, and that was part of the art form. We didn't have Virgin or Columbia Records, but we were up there. So that just showed that idea of even if you beat me, I'm still the best.

Chris Haight: I don't know how many memorable moments there are in his life, but I'll bet the farm that that whole two years with the Tones was probably one of the best and most exciting things that ever happened to him. And for him to not follow it up on another level or a different approach ... Maybe his failure or lack of willingness to do so has made him resort to grasping straws from the past.

I don't want to say this, but it's always in the back of my mind: His whole thinking, he *was* the Viletones, all on his own. If that's so, why isn't he in Hollywood, then?

Freddy Pompeii: Steve learned a few things from me, and he sort of looked up to me because I'd been in jail and shit. He considered that as some kind of a badge of being an outsider. I think he went out of his way a few times to get arrested because now he can say, "Yeah, I've been to jail," like it's a big deal.

Steven Leckie: When the first Viletones, Chris, Freddy, and Motor, secretly had a plan to get their own thing, the Secrets, the heart went out of me, and it really *was* that much of a secret. But I then got the generally regarded two best rhythm players, Sam and Tony. I got the best guys from the Ugly. Sam especially. He was courted by Stiv Bators for months to join what would become the Lords of the New Church. Sam was in London at the time because he had a girlfriend who was a model, and he said "No, I'm in the Viletones, man." Because in real time, why *not* us next? We had the chops, there was an act there, it was worth the ten bucks, you know? It was worth it.

Freddy Pompeii: After we left the band, he formed a new Viletones. He was playing rockabilly. He combed his hair in a pompadour and tried to imitate Elvis Presley. Because that was the thing; that was the next trend. So instead of sticking to his guns and being Nazi Dog and building on what he already started, he changed direction and started playing rockabilly so he could be on top of the trend.

He was missing the point completely.

Ralph Alfonso: It culminated at a certain point for the Viletones where the band quit en masse, they all left, and then that's when you've got the Viletones Mark Two, which was a much more focused and mercenary version of the Viletones.

Whereas the original Viletones Steve got together under his vision, the second Viletones were Steve's *friends*. I could see it coming, because the beautiful thing about the Crash 'n' Burn club was it was a real social gathering place for everybody and I remember there were lots of nights where I'd close up, walk out, and there'd be Steven and Tony Torcher still sitting there on the street, just sort of scheming. You could see that something was about to happen; something was going on. And eventually when the original band left, Tony Torcher's in there, and Sam, and it was almost like the nucleus of it. So it went from musicians to people who were way more in tune to what Steve Leckie's Viletones vision was. Which was a nihilistic view of things. Which is great. In his prime, that's what he was. He was the focal point for all the angry outsiders, I guess.

Chick Parker: Honestly, I thought it would pretty much burn really hot and burn out really quick. I couldn't see that kind of intensity, especially Mike's and to a lesser extent Tony, lasting for any period of time.

But also, it looked like it would be a lot of fun in a very weird way while it lasted. Like the whole scene I thought would sort of burn out, you know, very brightly. And then, *gone.*

Are you familiar with my stage name? Okay, one of the things I didn't like about the whole thing is everybody had to have a tough sounding name, like Johnny Rotten, Sid Vicious, Mike Nightmare, and when I joined the Ugly, Mike said, "You have to have a tough guy name." And I said, "No, absolutely not." And he said, "Well, when I introduce you, what am I gonna call you?" I said, "Call me by my name. You can drop the last name, but don't do anything cute."

So he introduced everybody — "Tony Brighton, Tony Torcher, Frankie Fury, and Chick Cunt." I'm like, "I beg your pardon? That is not how I wanna go down in history."

For the record, they came up with a creative spelling, Kunte, but I mean, my mom saw the record and she knew.

I tried to get them to change it to Charlie Twatts; same thing, but much more humourous, you know — Charlie Watts, Charlie Twatts, but it never happened. That's my legacy. Thank you, Mike. I'm amazed I don't hold more ill will than I do. Because Ugly fans were fairly vocal and terrifically loyal, and I'd be walking along Yonge Street with my girlfriend and, "Yo! Cunt!"

Raymi Mulroney: The record is all the new members. Tony's arm was cut out of the picture sleeve because he quit the band before it was released. So all you see is his arm over someone's shoulder on the cover. Mike was cutthroat. They never sold the records. He didn't like the recording at all. They just sat in a box.

Steven Leckie: Then two days later, after the Viletones broke up, Sam's over at my place going, "Who's gonna drum?" We thought Tony was out of the question because Mike Nightmare kept you there at gunpoint and Tony called and said, "Do you still need a drummer?"

Sam Ferrara: I snagged Tony back. Mike was totally pissed.

Tank: I was surprised when Sam and Tony actually joined the group after that. But I mean there was always rumours going around, and Leckie was very good at manipulating people. He was a very good talker. He could talk people into doing things. That's probably the main reason *I* got started with them.

Tony Vincent: I joined the Viletones because Sam asked me to join. I didn't want to play with Mike and I didn't want to play with Steve. I never liked Steve. But I left the Ugly because we started to stagnate; we started to get

stale. So I said to myself, "Sam wants me to play with him and it's a chance for us to get back together again."

I didn't want to leave, because me and Mike started that band together and we vowed to stay together for life. But I kind of got tired of Mike's antics. He started to get worse. He was doing a lot of crime. I didn't like it. That's when I joined Sam.

Freddy Pompeii: We used to call them Leckie's Lackeys after we left and he put the new Viletones together. The band just wasn't capable of doing what we were doing and, basically, he could lead them around because of what they thought he was. He'd make the decisions and they would have to go by it.

Johnny Garbagecan: All of a sudden, guys from one band would all be in another one. From one week to the next I was scratching my head going, What are we doing this week? I had no idea Sam was leaving. Him and Tony leaving freaked me right out.

The Ugly could have done really well. If Mike hadn't have talked the way he did between songs … You know what? WEA were looking at the Ugly and they came to the first gig at the Shock Theatre. WEA is Warner Bros. They wanted to talk to Mike and he told the guys, "Go fuck yourself, I don't talk to goofs, go talk to my manager." And the guys left. That was a really stupid thing to say and do. It was really stupid. Mike wouldn't have been where he ended up if he had not said that.

That was what stopped us from going somewhere, seriously. I don't often think about it, but the fact that those people actually came out to the Shock Theatre to see the band and they waited to talk to him says something. They must have liked the band. And Sam and Tony and Raymi were a few of the only people who could actually play — I mean to the point where they were really real musicians, not just people who picked up an instrument and started making noise. That's why I thought, Okay, all we've gotta do is make a name and somebody's gonna come along and pick them up.

I didn't even know about it until the next day. He asked me, he says, "Hey Johnny, did you talk to those guys from WEA Records," and I went, "*What?*" After he told me what he said to them.

Nip Kicks: I went with Sam and Tony. I didn't really like the idea of going to the Viletones either, to tell you the truth, because nobody liked Steve. Nobody trusted Steve.

Tony Vincent: It's not that I didn't want to play with Steve. I never *trusted* him. He had good showmanship. It had nothing to do with musical values; it was like a personality thing. He'd be friendly one night and then all of a sudden the next night he's on his high horse.

I didn't know the Viletones had been fighting, I really didn't. I guess you can say I was naïve. I saw it as a way to get back with my old friend Sam and play together again. Maybe I was stupid to do that, I don't know. I don't think so. What's meant to be is meant to be, you know?

Nip Kicks: You're dealing with Mike on one hand and Steve on the other, but at the same time the Viletones were the band that was happening and that was probably the best opportunity to do what they wanted to do. It was a hard call.

And I wonder, in some little way, if Sam might have been digging a little bit in his choice of the Viletones because he knew how Mike felt about the rivalry, ha ha ha. I didn't really think about it before, but there's always that little possibility that he chose them for a reason.

Sam Ferrara: The Viletones and the Ugly were neck and neck, and me leaving was like, "Oh, there's one dead soldier."

Nip Kicks: It was interesting the way things got. There was a certain morality to the scene and I think that's what happened when things broke up, because those lines were being dropped. Things began to break down in a way. People weren't there to just play music. People were cutting each other up and that sort of stuff; the competition. And again, maybe there were little internal rip-offs. There was lots of suspicion of course about Mike Nightmare stealing Sam's basses at one point. Sam lost a couple of Hofners and there was some suspicion that Mike took 'em. That was around the time that Sam had left the Ugly, ha ha ha. It was too bad, but again, I think a lot of that was maybe drugs we didn't know about were coming into the scene already.

Chick Parker: My first impression of Mike Nightmare? That he's nuts. That was also my last impression of him. And it's pretty much everybody's impression. Like, I *liked* him, but Mike was ... oh dear, Mike, Mike, Mike — he had electroshock therapy when he was very young and it definitely scrambled his brains, and his big dream, he wanted to be a rock 'n' roll star. Failing that, he wanted to go out in a gun fight with the police. And he genuinely pursued his goals.

Zero: Tony [Brighton] used to say that sometimes they would show up for rehearsal and Mike would have this gun. And he'd fire it just to get everyone's attention, or just to keep everyone on their toes.

Chick Parker: You never knew at an Ugly gig if you were going to go off to applause or have to fight your way backstage. Because we attracted, next to the Viletones, probably the most violent. Like the Blake Street Boys. They followed the Viletones, and they *really* followed the Ugly.

One night we were playing the Turning Point and the Blakes got in a fight — big surprise — at the front of the stage. Mike said, "Hey, you're knocking over the speakers, you know, go fight somewhere else." And one guy goes, "Fuck you, Nightmare," and like *that* Mike picks up the mic stand and drives it. The guy's head exploded; there was blood everywhere. Well, that was it. They just charged the stage, I'm hitting guys with my guitar and trying to get behind the amps, and somehow we escaped. But we still had to play the next night, and these guys are grudge bearers to say the least.

But we showed up, and they showed up, and somehow we talked it out because they've all got this weird criminal mentality and they operate on a level of respect: I don't care if you stab me as long as you *respect* me. You know the mentality I'm talking about.

And so it worked out, but you could never tell with Mike if everything would be lovely. And he owned guns. One time at sound check he got in a fight with Johnny Garbagecan, our road manager, and they ended up in the middle of Bloor Street just beating the shit out of each other at the height of rush hour. Very entertaining, good by me, but we've got a gig to do here, guys? And the cops, oddly enough, pulled up, arrested them both, and I went down there and said, "I don't want to be difficult, but could we have our singer?" He says, "No you can't, your singer's going to jail." "Well, the guy he was fighting is with us, too; it's a family." Anyway, they got out and we did the gig, but he just — Mike was unpredictable, to say the least.

I liked him. I found him vastly entertaining, but he was nuts. In every sense of the word, he was nuts. But a great front man, and always willing to take all his clothes off onstage. I have no idea why, but he did.

Nip Kicks: There was a romance in a way, this almost gang-ish romance to do with the inner city punk bands.

Chick Parker: You never knew what was gonna happen; it was the real thing. They were punks. They were real street punks. They were criminals. They were street fighters. They were genuine. And they wanted their music from the same — they wanted it really hard and loud and mean, and we gave it to them. We cranked it up and I would just get totally over the top.

Mike Nightmare / photo by Ross Taylor

Mike Nightmare, Tony Brighton / photo by Ross Taylor

Viletones go rockabilly / photo by Edie Steiner

Nip Kicks: In a weird way, a lot of the punks had that almost gang mentality in that we all stick together and you fight for what you believe in. I think some of the guys, Mike for instance, kind of got into that whole image and tried to make that crossover. The problem with Mike is, on one hand he had this image and this sense of that hoodlum sort of thing, but he didn't share the same ethics that the rest of us might have, and so he would rip the other guy off and he would do stupid things.

And Mike burnt bridges. He made a lot of enemies over the years. And drugs: Drugs, drugs, drugs. And that was sort of disappointing, because he started doing little drug rip-offs, much like the Ruby thing. Whether it was because he had habits he had to support or whether it was in his nature to try to take advantage I don't know, but he just buried himself further and further into the ground.

Then he started doing *really* stupid things. We used to laugh about the Swiss cheese incident where he walked into somebody's house and made himself a sandwich and got busted. I don't know if you ever heard of him getting stuck in a chimney.

Sam Ferrara: It was the wrong place. It was a burger place, and he was trying to rob the place next door. So the next day this guy's cooking burgers and Mike's stuck in there; all the smoke is going up to him. The cook heard something and the task force had to come and smash the bricks and get him out. They handcuffed him and put in jail. He was thinking he was going into a jewelry store.

Wrong chimney. Ha ha ha.

Chick Parker: And even the cops were going, "You are the most useless criminal ever."

Nip Kicks: It was really sad because he was a clever, smart guy. What could make him do such stupid things?

Raymi Mulroney
Outrage concert
/ photo by Ralph Alfonso

43. boY Girl stuff

John Hamilton: If you focus yourself too much in a scene, the scene is gonna die. Scenes always die. Yorkville died. Frisco died. Be-bop jazz died. The French cinema died. If you get above it and establish your role, *then* you survive.

We realized pretty early on that we can't just be identified with the scene because it's gonna spread out, it's gonna weaken, it's gonna diversify. So we have to get above it and become the Diodes on our own. That's why, by the second album, we were actually moving away from the really hard punk sound. We were trying to be more melodic and more musical. And we wanted to get established in the States.

We were pretty well received, but we couldn't break against being Canadian, and America's a pretty protectionist place. You take a Canadian album down to them and they say, "Why should we put these Canadian boys up ahead of our American boys?" I think most of the first album sales of the Diodes' stuff went to Europe. I think we sold a hell of a lot more in Europe because the second album, the Americans turned it down. They figured they had enough of their own, or they wanted real hardcore punk and we were trying to be a little more melodic.

Ian Mackay: We did have a lot of walls that we came up against. There was a lot of frustration. It was very hard. And the critical assessment of the Diodes was polarized; *The Sun* and *The Star* thought we walked on water. *The Globe* hated us.

You were creating notoriety which was getting you press, it was getting you notice, but it was *negative* press. Conservative Canada saw it as being okay to be a bad boy in the UK — it was almost preferred — but in Toronto ... Toronto was still very conservative back then. Even my parents were going, "What are you doing, Ian? This is crazy, look at all this bad press you're getting." My younger brothers said, "Why are you doing this? I don't understand, why don't you just play some good jazz like your father?"

In fact, other artists were the hardest on us because they were high artists, and they thought we were doing really lowbrow stuff. So we were ostracized from the art scene. It was an interesting thing that we were ostracized because we were doing that culturally lowbrow pop stuff, and the East End punk scene like the Viletones saw us as the art students. So we were sitting in the middle, feeling the pressure from both sides, and yet we had this record contract to manipulate and make success out of. So we had a lot of pressure to succeed.

John Hamilton: We'd moved away from the hardcore punk stuff by then anyway because a lot of really stupid people had come into it. It went from art students discussing aesthetics to seeing who could pull the biggest booger out of their nose.

There is an inevitable evolutionary pattern. It always works the same way. A lot of people who don't like the way something is — like the initial punk thing was people who didn't like disco and didn't like hippie stuff — as it gets established and gets bigger, it becomes more fragmented. With the punk scene, some people wanted to go in a real hardcore direction like the Tones, and with the Diodes we were moving in a more power pop, harmony-type direction, and I guess other bands were going other ways as well. So it started to fragment.

And jealousies, too. Somebody starts getting successful and it's, "Why them and not me?"

Ian Mackay: It was almost like we were the chosen prodigy — "Now, if you fall flat in any way, you're going to fall flat big because everybody will say, 'I told you so' for their various reasons." We had a modest success despite all of that, but we never broke; we were too early by about three years, I think.

John Hamilton: By the second album we were really under the gun. It was, "Come up with this hit single or you're toast," so that record was done under a lot of pressure. We really were trying to come up with a good pop hit single but not sell out.

Ralph Alfonso: The record company put a lot of pressure to be successful, so the lyrics were tampered with in a way. They were told to dumb it down; it's got to be boy/girl stuff. So some really intelligent songs, higher-level satirical songs, got watered down.

John Catto: For the second album we had a different studio, different crew. We knew a little bit more; in a sense we still didn't know enough, ha ha ha.

Really different studios, because the first one was done at Manta, which was a very big studio with big rooms that you could put an orchestra into. Eastern Sound, where we did the second album, is quite a small studio, like a little room. So you tend to do stuff a little bit differently.

John Hamilton: It gave us a more sophisticated sound, but in a lot of ways it sucked the real Diodes sound out of it, too.

John Catto: We were one album along, so we had more experience. By the time we did the second album we had time to be influenced by people, so you get all these ideas in your head about how you do things.

John Hamilton: We really went overboard. We wanted to do everything; I know I did particularly. I'd been wanting to get into a big recording studio for years. I wanted to use all the gimmicks and try all the tricks and do all the overdubs and put all the extra instruments on and all that kind of stuff. So we probably overdid it a little bit, although some of the songs still hold up pretty well.

John Catto: It's a little more experimental, obviously. If you listen to the first album, it's pretty straight. It's kind of a bunch of guitar stuff and some overdubs, but there are no tracks like the second album where it's got piano and acoustic guitar and vocal experiments. It's a very, very different sort of album; I mean really dramatically different.

I think Bob [Gallo] kind of went in there thinking we would do exactly the same as the first album, and we came in with all these other things. So he was caught by surprise. There was stuff that we played a lot at the time that we never used. We probably recorded "Nowhere Fast"; we definitely recorded "Headache." They're not on the album because Bob didn't like them for whatever reason, usually because the subject matter wasn't girls and cars. He kind of liked girls and cars songs. He didn't care much for songs about suicide. That was a part of it he never really got his head around.

John Hamilton: There's some neat stuff like "Jenny's In A Sleep World," and Ian's song, "Photographs From Mars," although they made us change the lyrics on that. The original words were supposed to be "I want to touch your feelers/I want to feel your touches." They made us change it to, "I want to touch your feelings/I want to feel your touchings," or something. They thought it would be more commercial, so we did it.

Ralph Alfonso: The original version of that song is so brilliant. That was the one the producer didn't get. He's like, "I don't get this, what are you talking about? Can't it be just a boy and a girl falling in love?"

But you know, I should have been a bit more … I had a day job then so I had to be at work all the time, so I couldn't be at the studio. I always have some guilt on that because I wasn't there to be the conscience, I guess.

John Hamilton: We made some compromises on that album for sure. The other thing was even though they wanted us to do this big studio production kind of record, they didn't give us enough time to do it in. So you'll notice some of the tracks are really well produced, like "Jenny" and "Photogs from Mars." A great song that could have been our big hit was "Weekend." It just didn't get the work that it needed. "Dead on Arrival" never got properly finished; the third verse should have been re-done — the lyrics don't quite work.

John Catto: Bob would either care for stuff the way it was or he wouldn't, so there wasn't a whole load of going in and rearranging and editing it to death. The only thing we edited in any way was "Tired," which was slightly changed from the original.

Gary Pig Gold: "Tired of Waking Up Tired" remains to this day one of my favourite records. That is an incredible track, so good for them.

Ken Barnes [*New York Rocker*, September 1978]: "Tired of Waking Up Tired" … is probably producer Bob Gallo's best record since the You Know Who Group's "My Love (Roses Are Red)" in 1964.

John Hamilton: The fact that "Tired" came out as well as it did … We were doing the final mix between eight and nine in the morning. I think Paul and I were there; Ian and Catto didn't show up because nobody could get up at that time or whatever.

We literally had from eight to nine in the morning to mix this goddamn single, and Liona Boyd was in the other room coming in with a thirty-piece orchestra. You've got from eight to nine and then you're out of here, whatever it is. At ten to nine we still didn't have it. This was the worst nightmare of my life.

The engineer finally got a single-edge razorblade and cut the middle part of the single out, which was the solo. Literally cut it out, three-and-a-half feet of tape, put it in at the beginning, and to disguise the cut he put his hand on the wheel and started it up and it gave it that drag, you get that *vroooooooom*. That's what that zoom is; it's not a bass slide, it's disguising the cut. We never played it that way. We had to go back and learn how to play it from the way we mixed it.

That was a lucky accident that it all came together.

*　　*　　*　　　*　　　*

"The Whole Toronto Punk Catalogue" [*The City*, February 12, 1978]: We said we'd never touch punk rock in this magazine, and you can be sure we'll never do it again, but with the local punk bandwagon grinding to a premature and welcome halt, we thought we'd get our hands dirty just this once.

Ralph Alfonso: We were doing the second album. Now we're trying to be a pop band, or I don't know what; it all got messed up.

You've got to keep up the pretense that you're on a major label and things are going great, but the reality is they're *not* going great because all the forward motion that had happened up till that point suddenly stopped. And the biggest obstacle is your own label. They don't know what to do, and even if they *did* know what to do, the music industry at the time didn't *want* to know.

There was a guy called Derek Steed and the *Steed Report.* He used to do a newsletter for Top 40 radio in Canada, and he just dismissed the Diodes album and single. He goes, "What's this junk? How about the new Gino Vannelli?" There were *some* trade papers on board. *Record Week* put Steve Leckie on the cover and we, the Diodes, wrote a punk column called "Black Listed" and tried to put gossip in there. So the industry was aware of what was happening. We did our best to infiltrate some of their media, but they ultimately did not want to know.

The general prevailing attitude was that punk was a sort of circus sideshow. It's good for a few laughs, or it's good for a funny aside for a columnist to write, "I went to the world of punk and this is what I saw," or, "Oh my god, look what they're doing now, smashing and stomping on each other, there's a guy called Nazi Dog doing this and that." It was this sort of superficial coverage. Nobody talked about the music. It was all very dismissive and/or lifestyle-oriented: What is it about these kids that's making them do this? Where did their parents go wrong? It was '50s juvenile delinquent stuff.

"Punk Rock!" by Ron Proulx [Ryerson University *Eye*, September 29, 1977]: In the early '50s there were two major street gangs in England: The Skinheads and the Teddy Boys. During the early '60s there were the Mods and the Rockers. Now in the '70s it's the Punks and the Teddy's. The two groups, like their predecessors, clash regularly in street fights and other confrontations. The Punks, unlike the earlier English gangs, came about as a result of political rebellion rather than social differences. In America, the economic factors that have made Punk such a violent movement in England are less severe. Instead, Punkers here are more concerned with the fashion of the movement.

The Punk music industry in Toronto is nothing more than a search for stardom, an exploitation of a trend, and the stage acts show they will do almost anything to gain attraction. As for North American record companies, they are aware of its potential but have adopted a "wait and see" attitude.

Ralph Alfonso: You've got to remember, a major label, all they want is sales and they want hit singles, so they're not there to propagate a lifestyle and/or your philosophy. They're there to make money, so you're always going to go with the sure bet. So if the Diodes were the sure bet, then they placed all their bets on that.

They just came back from England so they saw all this stuff happening. Unfortunately, what they didn't realize was, England was different. There was media acceptance, there was radio acceptance, everything was in place.

Okay, so now we've got our punk band. We've got surefire hit singles; let's go to the bank. Then you find out that Canadian radio doesn't want to know. It's like, "That's cool, but we don't want to play it."

Then you find out record stores don't really want to sell it. Then it's like, "Uh-oh, what have we done? Where do we take this now?" Then you find out you can't get any gigs. There are no gigs to play. The clubs don't want you because there was no such thing as one-night stands. You had to do Monday to Wednesday or Thursday to Saturday. Then you find out your management can't do anything for you because they're not plugged into the punk world.

There were supposed to be all these tours that never happened. There was supposed to be a tour with Robert Gordon that never happened. The only thing that *did* happen was we opened for the Ramones and the Runaways in Chicago, we got an encore, and there was a big write-up in the *Chicago Sun Times*. We made a lot of friends there, but that's all.

John Hamilton: The other thing, too, is the fact that CBS in Canada ever even signed a band that produced anything in Canada was a bloody miracle, because in those days all the record companies here were distribution for American product. So that they actually did an album of a Canadian band was pretty amazing. It was unbelievable. The fact that the Diodes made *any* records was unbelievable, especially by a major record company.

Tom Williams: Although they paid attention to foreign relations more, I think Canadian record companies were reluctant to sign any local punk acts because there was no real market.

The punks drew very little. Larry's Hideaway probably held three hundred people. The Beverley probably held less than a hundred. You know, they looked like they were really hot, but how many people were they playing to? There was a small club market, but I don't think there was a huge market for it.

I guess if you look at the bands that came out of that scene, not many survived. They didn't make it because they didn't appeal to enough people. So consequently, how did they stack up to the rest of the world? I really can't tell you, because not many of them lasted long enough to have a career.

John Hamilton: The second album didn't get released in the States, and that was a big blow. At that point it seemed like we weren't gonna break through. People like Elvis Costello and the Police were breaking through, who were basically just jumping on the bandwagon. They were just old hippie groups who had shaved off their beards.

I was getting disillusioned by that point. I realized we'd gone as far as we could go and it wasn't gonna break through; it wasn't gonna go all the way.

So at that point I left.

Paul Robinson: John Hamilton thought he could go out and just make it on his own. He formed a band with some of the Viletones called the Secrets and he didn't tell us about it. We recorded our second album and then he quit, which partially led to CBS dropping us but maybe that was just an excuse. Then we found Mike Lengyell after that.

John Hamilton: I didn't want to play the bar circuit with the Diodes because I knew there was a dead end there. At that point Chris Haight and I, we'd been making some tracks from our old Zoom days and we were approached by Bomb Records who said, "We'll give you guys a record contract."

Chris wanted to quit the Viletones because he couldn't take all the fighting — Steven Leckie can be hard to handle and he was fed up with all that. Then when Chris quit, Freddy and Motor quit, too, because they couldn't take Leckie either. They said they wanted to play with us, and that kind of changed the dynamic of everything. So we started the Secrets with Freddy and Motor and put the Zoom stuff on the side. There was a chance we could play Danny Aykroyd's club in New York — Freddy knew him really well — and we figured that might be a big break, because it looked like nothing else was happening. They were even talking about putting us on *Saturday Night Live*.

Paul Robinson: My attitude was always that drumming is a skill, and even though John was a songwriter and is credited with writing some of the songs, we didn't necessarily want that from that stage onwards. We just wanted somebody who wanted to drum and didn't want to give us attitude.

Ian Mackay: I don't know, maybe he had some artistic differences with Paul. I know that's ultimately why John Hamilton left, which was a big blow to the band. With John Hamilton and John Catto, we had two great songwriters and we had a synergy in its modest way; the sum of the two influences was greater.

John Hamilton: I don't think I ever felt in place, to be perfectly honest. For one thing, I was about a generation older than all of them. I was twenty-six when I started joining the Diodes, and they were all between twenty and twenty-one. People like Chris Haight and I, we'd actually been playing around Toronto as full-time musicians since about 1969.

Ian Mackay: I didn't think of John as an outsider. He wasn't part of OCA; he didn't participate in the breaking art of the time like John Catto and Paul did, but he was by no means an outsider.

John Hamilton: It *was* a different world. They were the Thornhill art school crowd and Chris Haight and I were Scarborough guys. There was a class difference there.

Ian Mackay: John Hamilton was a great songwriter, too. Paul and I contributed some; not as much. I would say that John Catto had a lot of the lyrical development already worked out when he brought a song to the table. Paul did a lot of editing and maybe added a verse or two. My songwriting skills were minimal, really. I was so interested in other things at the same time I wrote maybe three songs, one per album.

John Hamilton: I was kind of getting frustrated being the drummer, and there were too many songwriters, and all the record company stuff — at that point CBS had said they weren't gonna release the second album. The whole thing looked like it was falling apart. We'd made a big mistake, actually: We'd taken a couple of months off. Which was bad because we lost the cohesiveness, and I started hanging out more with Chris Haight.

I probably should have stayed. I regret it now. But the thing is, when it isn't happening it's like a relationship; you start fighting amongst yourselves. So when everything was going and we were really pushing hard, it was happy, it was great. Then we hit this brick wall. We weren't gonna get into the States.

Really, what we should have done was packed up and moved to L.A. But it's all water under the bridge now. The Diodes carried on, they put out another album that I thought was quite good, but basically they never captured that initial momentum. They played the bar circuit for a while. But the moment had passed.

It's true that I knew when it was going to happen. But I also knew when it *wasn't* going to happen.

44. Tomorrow Belongs To Us

Pete Lotimer: We had the party house in Hamilton. We would have thirty people in that house wrecking it, just trashing it, and it was never-ending beer.

I couldn't stay home if I was gonna relax. Home was worse than anywhere. That was the Punker House on Robinson Street.

Gambi Bowker: That place is still condemned, eh? I remember they had an orange shag rug and we lost some drugs in it and we were all crawling around trying to find them, ha ha ha. And they had that floor in the kitchen that was sort of slanted, and you had to be wary of where you were standing on it.

Kerry Wade: One guy wouldn't walk on the floor; he would just go from the couch to the coffee table and then he'd jump over to the chair.

Dave Elley: Or he'd put his head through the wall and crazy shit like that. People would come over every night. Whether you wanted them to or not, they just would. So it was non-stop.

Kerry Wade: There used to be a gang of guys there called the Scurvy Knaves. They used to go there all the time and sort of protect them, and sort of boss them around at the same time.

Dave Elley: They were like psychos, right? They liked us 'cause we were punks, I guess, and they kind of thought that was cool. But they could have just killed us in an instant.

Pete Lotimer: We would get drunk and take our equipment out on the front yard on a Saturday afternoon and start jamming and the cops would show up. "What are you *doing?*"

We were standing in court and they were reading out the complaint against us, and it was fourteen renditions of the Monkees' "I'm a Believer" on the front lawn, ha ha ha. Guilty, you know? Right in the courtroom.

The judge threw it out. He was laughing his ass off.

Greg Dick: There was one of the most fascinating characters that I ever saw in my life, and he turned out to be one of my best friends. He's actually on the back of the second Dream Dates seven-inch. His name was Crazee Harry, and he was just insane.

Crazee Harry really deserved to be called Crazee Harry. He was the real shit, and he would come to Toronto. He was a huge Dead Boys fanatic. Harry was crazy; he was just nuts. He drank so much booze and he would just do things.

Joe Csontos: He once said, "Joe, look at this." Carved in his arms was *Season's Greetings*. He goes, "Merry Christmas!"

He already carved it, but there was still blood dripping out. He goes, "Check this out, that's punk." I go, "That's stupid." He goes, "It doesn't hurt."

Harry was right there from the beginning.

Greg Dick: His mother had a hair salon in Hamilton, and I remember one time she was gone away for the weekend. We just went crazy in his mother's salon. He started colouring people's hair different colours and he ended up, unfortunately, smashing the shit out of the place. Harry was like an uncaged animal. You had to see him. He was nuts.

Joe Csontos: I was with my girlfriend and her best friend at the Punker House. I ended up in the bathroom with my girlfriend's best friend. I didn't realize she was in there, because they didn't have a lock on the door. We kind of looked at each other and went, "Oh my god," and started making out. And then we were like, "This is bad." But it was like, "We need to be together."

We were in there for I guess a long time; too long for Harry. I've got my foot against the door and — knock, knock, knock — "Come on," "Just a minute, just a minute." Knock, knock, knock, "I gotta get in there." "Just a minute!" I've got my heel against the door so they can't push it open and all of a sudden, literally, a chainsaw comes through the door. He chainsawed the door in half and he goes, "How's it goin'?" We just said, "What are you doing, are you *crazy*?" "Yeah! I'm Crazee Harry."

All of a sudden it stalls and he tries to start it up, and then there's smoke in the Punker House everywhere. I go, "What are you doing?" And he goes, "Bad mixture. Oil and gas, bad mixture, smoke everywhere."

Dave Elley: He walked around the house — *brrrrr, rrrrr* — and there was so much smoke you couldn't even see.

He was a crazy guy. Heart of gold, but he was just crazy.

Kerry Wade: We used to hitchhike from Hamilton to Toronto two or three times a week; go to the Horseshoe or the Turning Point, go see bands all the time. Crazee Harry worked in a glass furnace so he made a ridiculous amount of money — "Do you guys want to go to Toronto and see a show?" "Sure." There'd be ten of us sitting at their place and he'd go, "Okay, let's go." We'd all take a bus there, he'd pay for us, all our beer, everything. I remember taking cabs home from Toronto with him.

Dave Elley: He used to carry bacon around in his wallet. That's the kind of guy he was.

Kerry Wade: He was really odd — like, *really* odd. The first time I went to a Teenage Head show at Kilroy's — I swear to God this happened — some guy, one of the Scurvy Knaves probably, walked over and shoved a safety pin through Harry's ear, and he didn't do anything.

There used to be the 99 Cent Delta; it was all-night movies and they'd play *Dawn of the Dead* and all the horror movies. He'd bring a chainsaw to go see *Texas Chainsaw Massacre* and run around. Then he made a skateboard out of his chainsaw.

Stewart Pollock: Most of us didn't have jobs at that point. It was as much fun as we could have. That's '79, '80, somewhere in there.

Yeah, this whole scene sort of grew out of that, with Teenage Head on the up-rise. There's a scene in *24 Hour Party People* and you heard it repeated again in the Ramones' *End of the Century*: You'd go see a band like Teenage Head, there's this room of forty people, and all those forty people went on to be something, or

started their own bands. Out of the Teenage Head crowd were all these bands like the Forgotten Rebels, the Loudmouths, Mad Daddys; everybody was a musician, basically.

Pete Lotimer: We were living on our own; it was Dave and I, in this huge house. It was beautiful — velvet wallpaper, and it was a brand new frickin' place. It was unbelievable. We might as well have burned it down, ha ha ha.

Oh man, the things that happened in that house. I don't know why, but everybody came to that house. It wasn't the Rebels so much, but all the punk rock people would come back to our place. Very seldomly did Mickey and those guys come by. Everybody else came.

Mickey DeSadist: The band was a three-piece and I had to play guitar as well as sing. The easiest thing to deal with as a three-piece was the fact that there wasn't four people arguing. There was only three people.

But those two guys, Pete Lotimer and Carl [Chriss Suicide], they basically had the right idea. So I supplied the songs and they made them sound good. I can't find Carl anywhere. But bless his heart, I'm glad he was around because he was good for the start of the band and he's one of the reasons the band stuck around, in getting off the ground and being around for a long time. He was a guy that helped complete songs, that's why you'd see my name and his together in the songwriting.

Pete was there to party. That was his main goal with anything to do with music. He was there to party, and party he did. And Carl partied a lot, too, so that's fine. I basically had to keep my sanity about myself because even though he was a hard partier, Carl was a great guy. He was a roller skating instructor, you know. A great place to pick up teenage girls, ha ha ha.

Pete Lotimer: Mickey's a go-getter and it wasn't long before he was saying, "Let's do a show." We rehearsed for a little bit and it was, "Let's do a show." "A show? Christ, what are you talking about?" Ha ha ha.

Mickey DeSadist: Out first gig in Toronto was at the Isabella Hotel opening for the Battered Wives. Yeah, it was a fun gig, as any gigs could be.

Paul Eknes: The first time they played the Turning Point, Mickey DeSadist actually safety-pinned his bell-bottom pants because he was from Hamilton. He safety-pinned them to make them skin-tight.

Chris Houston: What we used to do was you couldn't buy straight legs, so you'd get your mom to take in your bell bottoms.

Some kids actually would have to move out because their parents didn't want them wearing straight-legged pants. So they would sew them back up normal when they went home.

I got beat up because I had straight-legged pants, standing on my parents' corner. A guy jumped out of his car and punched me in the face.

Paul Eknes: Mickey wore a Canadian flag upside down attached to his leather jacket on the back and I just thought, Dude, you're so sick *and* cool at the same time. He was playing to like eighteen people and he's saying, "I know you hate me. I know you hate me because when you go home and sleep with your girlfriends they're going to be yelling, 'Mickey, Mickey, Mickey!'" Ha ha ha.

I thought, You're a seventeen-year-old ugly guy with safety-pinned pants and an upside down Canadian flag. How cool are you? I was already like twenty-one at that point and I just thought, Hats off, Mickey, you are the best.

Mike Anderson: Forgotten Rebels, they were always younger and sort of outside; somewhere over here.

Greg Dick: My favourite version of the Rebels was the very first version. In the beginning, Chriss Suicide, he was almost like a Mike Nightmare; he was a real evil motherfucker. And Pete Lotimer was just a scruffy drummer; he was like a Hamilton guy. The Hamilton guys didn't really give a fuck about being pretty. If you look at the record, Suicide's got a mustache and his hair's parted in the centre. But he was tough. He was a fuckin' tough guy.

People in Toronto didn't like them. Toronto was very cliquey and it was hard for them to get in. And people really weren't ready for Mickey. He has a very unique style of singing, and it almost comes across as he's a bit of a comedian. But he's a very clever songwriter; his songs are catchy. He eventually started revealing that he was really inspired by Ian Hunter and David Bowie and people like that, but in the beginning he could write good songs.

I think it was his personality. He had no problem being himself, and he liked it when people didn't like him; it didn't intimidate him at all. I give him credit for all those years of going out and doing that stuff, and one thing that I realized years ago was Mickey *really* believes in what he's doing. It's a joke, he has a sense of humour, but he's serious. *That's* the real Mickey. He's not putting on an act. If you go and talk to him when he's coming off of work, he's still the same guy you'll see on the stage at Lee's Palace.

But in the early days, I think he just rubbed people the wrong way. They were just like, "Who the fuck do these guys from Hamilton think they are?"

Bob Bryden: The desire to dismiss the Rebels, I really think it's a part of the Toronto vs. Hamilton thing. That rivalry seems quite real — being a native of neither but a sometime inhabitant of both gives me some objectivity to the phenomenon, I think. And I do know for a fact that the Rebels sold out or near-packed every single show they did in Toronto. It was a given. So people are jealous and develop selective memory.

Mickey DeSadist: If there was resistance from Toronto I didn't feel it. I heard that people in Toronto were saying how bad Hamilton was at the time, but if they bothered to take the time and play here, they'd realize how good it really was. It was a scene that was started by Teenage Head and additionalized by us, and it was actually a good scene.

We were like the end of the first wave. The first wave of punk was the people who bought a copy of "Blank Generation" by Richard Hell. And I don't remember what number my copy is, but I think I'm within the first five thousand. That was the pivot point for punk rock, that 45. That's what would qualify somebody as first generation. Yeah, I would say we were first generation because of that.

The reason we sound *second* wave is because Teenage Head made it [to Toronto] first, because they had a lift to get there and stuff. And we actually formed *after* Teenage Head. Frank was the one who introduced me to the New York Dolls, and I saw them on TV very quickly after Frank told me about them. I thought they were a cool band and I bought the record, but I was more into glam than anything else. I liked the live Mott the Hoople album and the Stooges' *Raw Power*. Those were the two albums. I didn't particularly like the first and second Stooges albums all that much, but I liked *Raw Power* and I liked *Mott the Hoople Live*. And coincidentally, that's what the Sex Pistols listened to, and so I would have ended up having a similar sound.

Pete Lotimer: We started doing shows all the time. Mickey would say, "We've got a show this week," and back then it was three of four nights. You'd go to the Turning Point and come home and I'd go to work with no sleep on Wednesday, Thursday, Friday, Saturday night.

I was baked and drunk. We'd do a show and we'd drive back, and they liked to drive around the graveyard. I'd be in the back seat going, "Can we go home?" Ha ha ha. He had a Mr. Submarine in Toronto that he always had to go to after the show and I'd just be going, "Oh my god."

You just had to go along with it because it was Mickey. And that voice of his — "Let's go down to the graveyard." "Okay." Down we'd go, drunk and smoked up at the graveyard and fucking walk around reading graves, I guess. I don't know why he wanted to do that, though. It was always the same Mr. Sub and then off to the graveyard and then he'd drop you off at five in the morning. I had to get up at seven. We had a lot of energy back then, though, so it was fun.

First it was a few shows, and the next thing you know it was, "Do you wanna make an album?" I still couldn't play. I could go and bash the drums behind those guys and make a lot of noise, but then it was an album. He was non-stop, always busy driving around and rehearsing and always getting shows. Sometimes the rehearsal was just a piss-up, but we were always there every weekend. He had good ideas; good writing ideas.

Mickey DeSadist: I didn't really have to work on it very much. I always had a sense of humour, and I just put my sarcasm to work. Some people were offended and some people thought it was really funny, and I noticed the intelligence between the people that were offended and the people that realized that I was being silly. And I wanted to exploit the newspapers just for the sake of getting publicity that we wouldn't have to pay for, like the other guys in the disco groups did.

Pete Lotimer: I helped write some of the stuff like "Angry," but it was really Mickey that did the other stuff like "National Unity." I put a drumbeat to it, but the song was already there. "Third Homosexual Murder," again, I threw a beat to it but I didn't share.

Nothing made me uncomfortable back then. I was comfortable playing the songs, and I was comfortable thinking that people were gonna come beat us up. Sure, come down, beat me up, I'll be drunk anyways, ha ha ha. I liked it to a certain extent, and I still think back and think we made a mark because of Mickey, really.

I was happy to go and drum in a bar. Mickey wasn't. Mickey wanted to play, but he wanted that controversy. And the more he got, the more he loved it. You could tell he loved it. He was in the limelight and he loved it. I enjoyed watching Mickey do that. He was the leader, and I just loved playing the drums.

I'm back here knocking my cymbals over and the drum kit's taking off on me; I didn't know how to stop it. Some of the stuff when I think back now I wonder, how stupid was I? I just let the cymbals float away. The stands were worth a buck and a half, so they would teeter back away from me. By the time I was done a set, the drums were nowhere near me, ha ha ha.

Stephen Burman: I financed — me and Mickey financed — the first EP. We did the cassette demos, and we sold a bunch of those.

Imants Krumins: I know they put out a demo, and I remember Mickey had it at the Saucer House. I gave him ten bucks. He said it was four, but he didn't have any change. So I said, "Keep it, put it towards your record or something." He may deny all this, but I remember. Ha ha ha.

Gary Pig Gold: Late one night in the summer of '78 I took Mickey and his crew over to CFMU at McMaster for their World Radio Debut. They played this little cassette, *Burn The Flag*, that Mickey kept apologizing for — "It was just done on a Radio Shack mixer," he'd laugh, but I thought it sounded great.

But even better was the *interview*. He was a natural. Part Johnny Rotten, part Don Rickles. Talking about the mayor of Hamilton being in the Mob, and how Pierre Trudeau's brains were leaking out his bald spot. Before long the phones were lighting up like a Christmas tree, as they say in radioland.

So I took a cassette of *that* immediately over to Gary Topp, who wanted to start booking Mickey as a monologuist. Years before Henry Rollins, of course. And we were gonna put out a special Pig spoken-word album called *An Evening with Mickey DeSadist*. But Mickey, heart of gold, wouldn't go for it. "I'm not a solo act," he told me. Those Hamilton boys are loyal if nothing else.

Stephen Burman: The Viletones had done a seven-inch single, but there weren't too many people at the time who had done a four-song EP, so it was kind of different. I mean, the cost was the same as doing an album … But obviously when you're producing it yourself, you have to pay for all the recording.

Pete Lotimer: I remember we were going to do the recording; I think it was a Saturday morning. I was out just getting hammered the night before. Of course in the morning I had a quart of chocolate milk and half a pizza or something, trying to make myself feel better, I guess, and a beer probably.

We were driving down the Queen Elizabeth Way, I'll never forget this, and I was feeling sick from that milk and all that crap. I rolled my window down, whipped the friggin' milk; I feel sick, right? And two minutes later up comes this Ontario Provincial Police car with the wipers going, frickin' milk coming off it. Pulls us over, huge ticket for littering, and that was our start to the frickin' recording.

The funniest thing I ever seen was that car pulling up with the milk flying off, ha ha ha. Frickin' Mickey — "Dammit, I can't take you anywhere."

Then when we did the recording, those guys mixed it and I basically just sat in the corner, ripped. I had a few beers, relaxed as hell.

Mickey DeSadist: We didn't know what we were doing and we didn't know what the hell was going on. You can tell that we didn't. It makes for an uncomfortable situation no matter how much you want to be there.

Pete Lotimer: I took the hi-hat off the kit and went and put it in the corner, and the guy says, "What are you doing?" I says, "I don't know how to use that," like, "Get it *away* from me, ha ha ha. I don't know what it is. It's got a foot pedal on it and stuff and I don't want to deal with that. I have foot pedals enough over here," ha ha ha.

Mickey DeSadist: See, the thing is ... okay, I'll just tell you the truth. I got the title from the Alex Harvey album *Tomorrow Belongs to Me*, and I thought *Tomorrow Belongs To Us* was a good title.

The Sensational Alex Harvey Band was a fairly unusual band. Imagine Alice Cooper with a Scottish accent right around the "School's Out" era — that's what they were like. And he had a weird sense of humour, too. He got arrested for drunk driving in the United States and had Al Jolson makeup on. You know, the cop pulls him over and it's this Scotsman wearing Al Jolson ... Once he ran up onstage in England dressed as Hitler screaming, "I've been framed! I've been framed!" Ha ha ha.

That was one of my influences back then.

And there was bands like Sparks and stuff. It might not be the most exciting music when you listen to it now. I jammed on my guitar to myself all the time, and I thought that playing the way the majority of commercial bands were playing at that time was really not that great. Like the good commercial bands, Boston and stuff, you still hear them. But for every band that you remember a million years from now, there's always a guy you also remember like Neil Sedaka. You're always gonna remember that guy. So there's always a lousy, lousy, lousy something for every great something that happens.

I guess for every Sex Pistols there's a Neil Sedaka.

45. shooting it

Jeff Ostofsky: One thread that runs through the whole story you're telling, and is in fact a commonality, is heroin. Some of us did it more than others, to the point where it was a detriment, including myself. In the interest of accuracy, it needs to be mentioned.

The scene — there's a line of junk that runs right through it. It was a factor. It lasted a lot longer than the music, that's for sure.

"Punk Rock: It's Dying in Toronto Before It Was Born," by Don Martin [*Ryerson Review*, September 23, 1977]: "I think dope and booze are intricate parts of the punk rocker's make-up," said Mike Nightmare. "They need it. It feeds them.

"If I'm a little too high, then I drink a bit of beer to bring me down. If I'm down, then I use a little speed to pick me up. The amount of energy you use up on that stage is unreal. You just have to be high or else you cannot expand to your full potential," he says.

Freddy Pompeii: I remember I was more involved with it in the Secrets than in the Viletones. In fact, in the Viletones I remember being high once onstage and thinking afterwards, Jesus Christ, I just didn't have any fun. It was like having a blanket over my head while I was playing. There was no showmanship.

And I had promised myself after that, "No more heroin for shows, and make sure I stay away from it. As long as we're playing gigs I'm not gonna mess around with it. And no heroin for sex," because it was horrible for sex.

So that's basically how I stayed away from it for so long, because it was *everywhere*; everybody was handing it to us.

Steven Leckie: Well, I hate to tell you this, but the Viletones were the biggest proponents of smack, even though me and Motor didn't do it. We were happy with beer. But heroin came up hard, and it was probably through the Viletones.

Captain Crash: It was only a factor in the last few months of the original Viletones, I think.

Well, everybody was familiar with drugs. Everybody had a bit of a drug history. But when the Viletones first got together everybody was straight, everybody was normal. We drank beer, smoked dope, fucked the chicks. That was sort of the motto: Fuck the chicks, smoke the joints, and drink the beers.

Then the fighting started, and drugs came into effect. People changed. People's lives changed.

It totally fucked it up, absolutely without a doubt.

Freddy Pompeii / photo by Gail Bryck

These guys used to have such a great, high-performance show. Then they started doing smack and they'd get up onstage and they just thought they were so cool, they were so into themselves. And yet it was taking them twenty minutes to tune a guitar. They would just stand there looking at themselves, looking at their hands playing the guitar, all fucked up.

When it started out, the Viletones were basically a gang. They were a troop that hung around together twenty-four hours a day. Later on with all the infighting, and especially when the smack came in, it wrecked everything. Wrecked it big time.

Steven Leckie: Freddy was very connected with where to cop and everything. It wasn't anything at all part of my world or you would have heard about it, but those guys were all on heroin, Freddy and Tony.

Chris Haight: We got into worse trouble. The dark end of the street got darker for us.

At that time the whole scene was geared to that. If you weren't into somebody's wheelhouse as far as certain drugs and shit like that, they would look at you as an outsider. There was an inner clique when it came to that kind of bullshit. The no-good scoundrels that we hung around with, I mean, *everybody* was into that kind of thing.

Gambi Bowker: The scene dissipated at the same time the heroin started coming in. People who didn't get involved themselves stepped away from the scene because of it. They were saying, "This isn't how it started out. I just want to play good music. This isn't supposed to be that dark."

Heroin is a really dark drug.

Freddy Pompeii: Friendships started to fall apart. There were people that didn't do it, and there were people that did do it, and it quickly became the ones that did it were always hanging around together or were in contact with each other. The ones that didn't do it were really not welcome; they didn't have anything to offer.

You sort of lose your desire to go out and play; you don't want to go out on the road because you're not gonna be able to get any heroin. You don't want to leave town.

Most of the bands were getting into it. The Ugly were definitely getting into it. Everybody. Everybody started getting into it. Your hygiene falls off. You don't want to get washed anymore because your skin feels weird when you take a shower. Everything goes haywire.

Nip Kicks: Heroin threatened to break up the Ugly. Sam didn't use, he wasn't into it, and Tony was and jeez ... Heroin was all over the scene. Tony, I mean, wow, the heroin was a problem.

Margaret Barnes-DelColle: The weird thing about the whole scene that was different than other scenes that had happened in my life was that everybody was very, very open and accepting of everybody. Nobody really knew that somebody came from a poor background or a rich background, because the clothing was such that it made everybody equal. And in the style and the fashion, it also made everybody creative whether you really, truly were a creative person or not. You could kind of just do your own thing and show up at a club and be very accepted for the way you ripped your T-shirt, or the vintage clothing that you wore, or whatever you did.

More and more of that seemed to spark and encourage people to form bands, with people who had absolutely no skill, no talent, no nothing. Even though they were bands which would go out and try to get gigs, they really were, I think for the most part, about being a group of people banding together.

It just always seemed to me then, and even now, that the level of dysfunction was really high. So many people came from such dysfunctional backgrounds, and none of that mattered. Where maybe at a different time and place, your dysfunction would show and you would be the odd man out. But in punk rock, you *weren't* the odd man out; your dysfunction was just part of everybody else's dysfunction. It wasn't something that was discussed; it wasn't like a twelve-step program where you would say, "My father beat me," or, "My mother was an alcoholic." Because there were so many crazy people that were on all different levels there.

And that's the other thing: So many people are dead.

William Cork: It's the ultimate time bomb. It did the same thing in that scene that it did in the scene before it and the scene before that.

In the Beat scene, the same thing happened. I don't know how William Burroughs lived as long as he did. A lot of people didn't. There aren't many of these people left from that scene that you're looking into now.

Margaret Barnes-DelColle: The pot thing, there were some people that saw that more as a hippie thing and so they didn't want to have any part of that. So it was heavy drinking and a lot of people would pop pills, too. Quaaludes, and Mandrax — we'd do just about anything. Mescaline, people dropped acid a lot.

You felt back then like you could trust people. Nowadays, nobody trusts each other.

You would never really go out nowadays and buy drugs in some bar from some stranger, but back then, man, you had no problem. You somehow thought that they wouldn't hurt you; that everybody was there for the same reason — to get high. So there were a lot of drugs. Coke, people couldn't really afford so much, so it would be diet pills and speed.

And then slowly it started changing. I remember, for Fred and I, we were really afraid of the whole idea of heroin. Anything else we would do pretty much, but heroin really scared us. Chris Haight's brother was doing heroin, Jimmy the Worm, and he would come over to Power Street all the time. He would be like, "You guys should do this, it's really cool," all this bullshit. So Fred would snort it.

Freddy Pompeii: Chris was already a [heroin] user when he was younger. I hadn't had any experiences with it. I just started becoming aware of it towards the beginning of the third year we were together. It was basically fans that would turn us on to it, and I just figured if it's this widespread and this many people are doing it, then might as well give it a try.

I didn't get hooked all at once. It took a while. But then I started noticing it more and more. People in the audience were coming into the dressing room and saying, "You wanna do a little of this," snorting it and stuff. And then shooting it came later on.

Margaret Barnes-DelColle: It just sounds like *Reefer Madness*, "Once you start, then you can't stop," but it really was like that. Fred would tell me that he had snorted heroin and I would be like, "Oh my god, you're going to be addicted." I was just freaked out and horrified. And he would be like, "No no no, I'm okay, I'm just snorting a little and it's kind of fun."

Freddy Pompeii: It was almost impossible to get completely hooked [at] that time anyway, because there wasn't enough in Toronto. It would be there and then it wouldn't be there. So you would suffer a little bit of sickness, then it would go away and you wouldn't see it for six months, then somebody would come back from Europe with a whole batch of it. They were basically young kids whose parents were really rich and they happened to be able to buy the shit, and they would hand it out for free until somebody got hooked. Then they'd start charging them money for it. It's the nature of the beast.

Margaret Barnes-DelColle: Then one time — which I will never forget because it changed my whole life — Jimmy came over and he said, "No, you can't have any unless you shoot it."

So Fred let Jimmy shoot him up with heroin. I was like, "Oh my god, this is it. We're all gonna die." I was freaked out about it. And then it was like, "Oh, he's okay," and time passes.

One day I'm down there hanging out with them in the kitchen and they're like, "Just snort a little line." I'm like, "Oh, okay, can't hurt." I don't know if you've ever done heroin, but it feels great. Before you know it, Fred's like, "You'll be okay, I'll shoot you up and you'll see what it's like. You're going to love the rush and it's gonna be great."

So then each time your resistance wears down. You don't see anybody dying and you don't seem to see any adverse affects; you just see them having a good time. So I did it.

Then you want to do it more, and before you know you start finding reasons to do it, like, "Oh, today's a sunny day, let's go score some heroin." Or, "Today's a snowy day, let's go score some heroin."

I think people become psychologically addicted before they become physically addicted. Then, before you know it, you're in. I know that's what happened with us, and I know that's what happened with a lot of people.

Johnny Garbagecan: I got strung out myself. I didn't even know these guys were doing junk.

One time we were going to play in the United States somewhere, and we were supposed to meet at Freddy's house at midnight on a Saturday. I walked in and Freddy was just mixing up his shot for the road and I grabbed it off the table and said, "Give me that," and did it myself.

I didn't wake up until we were in New York City. I hadn't done it for about five years — not heroin, anyway. I had gotten away from it, and then I walked into Freddy's and like I said, he was just putting it away — I didn't even know he was into it — and that got me started again.

Christopher Barnes: I was about six months old when Freddy met my mother. I was six, seven years old in '76, '77 — that's when I guess the Viletones were happening. I just remember going to gigs with them, and them dressing me up and just hanging out.

There was all kinds of stuff going on. I remember guys from Second City TV hanging out — the Aykroyds and that whole crew. And I remember going to Dan and Peter's speakeasy up the street from us on Queen; they had a pinball machine there that I would always play while they hung out and smoked pot and did whatever they did. A lot of drugs were around. I got to see a lot of that.

There were big parties. Needles were involved, but I probably didn't know exactly what it was until much later.

Freddy Pompeii: After we had the Secrets I started hanging around with Chris Haight more and his brother. We had more time to ourselves; nobody was paying us like Mega Media, so there were long periods before we started getting gigs and things like that. There was a lot of free time, and that was time that we ended up doing dope to kill the boredom.

Then I started noticing I was getting sick when I stopped. And that's when I realized that I had gotten a habit. Because I was doing it every day because I wasn't doing music every day. I guess it was around the beginning of '79 that that started happening. And *everything* was about that afterwards. Our whole lives were dominated by that. Who had it, who was selling it.

Margaret Barnes-DelColle: I always made a connection between Anne Rice's vampire books and doing heroin. Like a secret kind of underground nighttime culture; like being a vampire. It was like a secret club, and you had an attitude about it. Psychologically you just convinced yourself that you were truly hip now, and nobody else knew how to really be hip.

Then it was reinforced by Johnny Thunders. I used to sell drugs to Johnny Thunders when he would come to town. I sold drugs to Wayne Kramer from the MC5 when he came to town. I sold drugs to Willy DeVille. All these people are from the States, and they have records and they're famous, so you become part of that circle. Meanwhile, you're all sinking fast, but you certainly don't think about that. You think you're really, really hip and you belong to a special club, and that's how you convince yourself. And then slowly, of course, you can't work your job and you can't pay your bills and one day you're just like, "Maybe this isn't so hip."

Or you die.

Freddy Pompeii: We all took turns selling it and being customers. It was like the way it was.

If you knew somebody who came back from Europe with a bunch, then all of a sudden you were the guy selling it and you had a built-in clientele. That's all you wanted to do was get high. Sell it and get high on it, and the next day you wake up and you had to get high again because you're sick; a vicious cycle.

Everybody we knew were getting into it, and the people that weren't getting into it stopped coming around. So it was like basically everyone we knew became junkies, or were junkies, and it was really bad. It was horrible. It was one of the most horrible experiences of my life that I can look back on and say I wish that never happened.

I curse the day that I even tried it, as wonderful as it is. It's just a wonderful high. It kills every pain that you have. If you're depressed, it takes the depression away. It's a really great substance. Better than anything else; better than speed, better than coke, better than marijuana. It becomes the first thing that you think of when you wake up in the morning and the last thing you think of when you go to sleep.

Chris Haight: Now you've go to keep this in mind: When I said the dark end of the street got darker, that whole thing just consumed every idea or whatever you had. It just kind of took over.

Originally [Freddy's] was a neat place to hang out. A lot of the bands that would come in from the States, especially, they'd have to make it down just to say hi and this and that. But because of the scene we were in, when the Heartbreakers would come to town they would spend a whole weekend at Fred's. Up all night, and doing this and doing that. Some of it, no honour among thieves.

Things didn't pan out as we hoped they would, but that was the place. Freddy's was the place for the hardcore artists.

Chris and Freddy, New Rose / photo by Gail Bryck

Teenage Head / photo by Ross Taylor

46. until it bleeds

Paul Kobak: It was tough getting the first recording contract. I mean, I could see how the Diodes did it. They're such politicians – "Oh, that guy there, he's head of A&R." Next thing you know, the four them just lock in on the guy and start talking. "Oh, we're the greatest band, blah blah blah." They were talking dollars and cents in business-like approaches that most bands are clueless about, and that's probably why CBS took a shine to them. They were well managed from within.

And we had problems, like I've said before, because of John and Jack. They had their pros and their cons, but we were sort of blacklisted as a result of that from the other companies. Too many burnt bridges. You know, people talk to each other, and next thing you know everyone says, "Stay away from that guy."

We really tried with Capitol a number of times, and MCA. No one was biting. But there was the bonus of having IGM as a distributor for CBS, so we'll just go with the smaller label and still get the distribution.

Stephen Mahon: The chain of command was our manager Jack Morrow knew Gary Salter. He was, I guess, in charge of Inter Global Music. They were both kind of like con men–type shysters. And it just made sense that if Jack had a band, who would he go to, to try and get a record? He would go to someone he would know first, so that's what he did.

I think Gary Salter also owned or partially owned Thunder Sound studios, which is where our first album was recorded. So that's how our record deal happened.

As to when or how, I'm sure it probably went through Paul Kobak – "Good news, you guys have a record deal," and there was never anything formal because those guys would never have done anything really formal. Like, *legitimate*, that's what I mean by formal.

Dave Rave: At that time record company deals were so rare and so odd that I don't know how that all happened. I know that Jack Morrow had a lot to do with the deal through IGM. That was all shady stuff, wasn't it? It might have been.

I just thought Teenage Head were so unique and so interesting that why *wouldn't* they get a deal? But I think a single like the one the Diodes had wouldn't have hurt. I think it was very successful, too. I remember hearing it all over.

Who else had deals? How could you not sign more? Compared to Britain and America, there was no Seymour Stein, no Malcolm McLaren. So even though Hamilton was bad with its infrastructure, at least we had Paul. And in Toronto there was Ralph and a few people, but look at how much was missed. And that's a shame.

Stephen Mahon: We were just older teenagers and, "Yahoo! We're gonna make an album," and we would never have questioned any kind of legalities as to how it was gonna happen and how it was gonna get paid for. We just knew that at a certain day, show up at this recording studio and start making your album.

Frankie Venom [*Shades* no. 4, Spring, 1979]: It's what we wanted to do for three years and after rehearsing and playing ... and after changing from record company to record company, here we are. Overall, though, we had a good time. There was this one guy who wanted to make us a new *Abbey Road*, you know, Bible reading and all that stuff, but we just told him off.

Things have been getting better, there's been more girls, and they're getting all uglier, too. But I like the ugly ones, at least they're chicks, before we only got guys. But we're happy with how things are going. It's been our dream for a long time and it's here.

Stewart Pollock: I originally met Teenage Head in a very odd sort of way. I was managing Roots Shoes in Hamilton. I was about seventeen or something at the time. At that point, I was collecting pogey *and* welfare *and* working. It was before all the systems were linked together. It was a pretty good time, actually. And selling drugs, too, probably. I had to keep the addictions going, you know?

I worked in Roots during the day from ten till six or whatever, and then I'd go across the hall, change my clothes and everything and work at Mankind Shoes, which was this kind of upscale, Florsheim, alligator shoes and shit like that. Actually, my very first shoe sale ever was to Liberace in that spot. They'd just gone from the negative heels into these Beatle boots and stuff like that; purple Joe Jackson shoes.

This guy named Dave DesRoches came in and bought a pair. I'd heard from a few people that this band Teenage Head was playing at Kilroy's, which was a pub in the west end of Hamilton. So I was telling him about it. "You should go check the band out. I hear they're really good. If you're into these kind of shoes, you should be into that kind of night."

So I go there that night, and Dave's onstage with them! He didn't tell me at the time. I started talking to them afterwards, and ended up working for them the next day. It just seemed to work, whatever the reason was. We got along great. And they needed people at that time, too. They were just starting to make some headway and break through a little bit, you know, playing more bars and starting to get some attention.

I worked for them for quite a few years after that, everything from lighting to road manager, merchandising, professional babysitter. And it's great fun, no money, you stay pissed and high, it's all good.

Dave Rave: I remember seeing Teenage Head play a bar in downtown Hamilton at the time. They had pictures of Marilyn Monroe and the American flag up in there and they were doing a matinee, and everybody hated it. But you know, I've always had an instinct about that: Everything that's against something is the reason why it's going to happen. And as long as you have the strength and the firm belief of your conviction, it's going to happen. And I knew that. We weren't fortune tellers, but we had trust in the future. I just remember thinking that eventually, something's going to happen to these guys.

Stephen Mahon: That's probably the most important thing Jack did for us, was get us into the studio.

Dave Rave: "Picture My Face," not the album version but the single version, I remember going, "Wow, this is

fabulous." I was playing it for my friends and they're all like, "This is so simple," and I was like, "Don't worry about the simplicity." "But the chords are simple chords!" "Who cares!"

There was still that thing going on; that resistance. But forget that, listen to what's going on *underneath*. And that's how I think punk rock influenced everybody. Eventually Bruce Cockburn got a leather jacket. That's what these renegade gods did; they opened the door for something new and concise and clean – *Boom*, you know?

Stewart Pollock: Shortly after I met them we all sat around and glued the picture sleeve together for the first single, which was "Picture My Face."

Bob Bryden: We were gluing it together like an assembly line.

Gordie Lewis ["Teenage Head ... and How to Get Some," by Cameron Gordon, *The Nerve Magazine*, October 2006]: It was basically a vehicle to help support our gigs. It was a picture sleeve, which we ended up designing ourselves. The idea was to keep up with all the cool releases coming out of the UK at that time but in the typical Canadian way, that was deemed too expensive by the label so we had to improvise on our own.

Paul Kobak: When Teenage Head first had "Picture My Face" released as a 45, I drove to B.C. and back hitting every radio station I could to give a personal pitch.

Jack and I had ulterior motives. Back then, a Toronto radio station wouldn't playlist you unless someone else did first. Jack was between a grey-to-a-black area around much of the music establishment for a number of reasons, but had previously worked with a guy on an outdoor concert and the guy was owed money still. Only a couple hundred bucks, but the guy was now the program director for CFOX in Vancouver. So that was my mission: Hit every station you can on the way to B.C. and bribe the guy with two-hundred dollars to playlist Teenage Head.

It worked. I got back to Ontario and found that CFOX had put "Picture My Face" on medium rotation. At that point, Jack and I were able to really make things happen in Ontario.

Gordie Lewis [*Blitz* Magazine, March/April 1982]: The "Picture My Face" single came out when the punk thing was going strong. The Sex Pistols were making news at the time by puking in the airports. That sort of thing had an unfortunate effect on the playlist possibilities of certain Ontario AM stations.

Since then, CKOC has come to understand how the music has evolved. They and the stations like them are much less likely going to notice the sensationalism that the newspapers blab at everyone.

Paul Kobak: The first single got picked up in Germany of all places. We kept trying to break the States so many times, but there just wasn't enough cooperation. That's why I kept wanting them to tour. Keep hitting New York City until it bleeds. Hit Detroit, hit Chicago, hit Boston. Get some of the rep up in the papers, and then that way the record companies will fall more into place.

But things were fairly chaotic back then.

Frankie Venom, Gord Lewis / photo by Ross Taylor

47. and now, live FRom toronto

Gary Cormier: At the Horseshoe, there was a lot of pressure on us in terms of being able to come up with something all the time to present. So we did that for a while and then money circumstances came up; we hit a bump in the road with Jeffrey [Silverman] who just realized that this was not for him.

Eventually it turned out that Gary and I were going to forge out on our own. At that point we were probably fifty thousand dollars in debt. All I've ever done my whole life is backed things I believed in.

Then we did this little band called the Police. When they strode out onstage Gary and I just took a look at each other and said, "Holy fuck, this is for real."

By that time, the Horseshoe had told us that they were sick of punk rock and that they were going to go back to a country and western policy.

Gary Topp: We once had a woman come in from Capitol Records, because we complained that we couldn't get any of their artists. They were all going to the El Mocambo, which just didn't really fit. She said, "Well, you don't have carpet on the floor, so there's no way you're going to get our artists."

The Horseshoe was a country bar, initially. Stompin' Tom used to play there. But then it was kind of dying and we were invited there. Just before we had been there somebody had produced the Hank Williams show, *The Show He Never Gave.* It was a very successful show and played across Canada.

We weren't making money at the Horseshoe. We weren't making money, period. But you just keep plodding on. So if we weren't making money, *they* weren't making money.

We were just starting to make money, and he said he wanted to go back to country music. He threw us out, so our last swan song was with all our favourite bands from Toronto.

Gary Cormier: We had decided we were going to do two big shows to end it all; one was going to be called The Last Pogo, the other was going to be called The Last Bound Up.

Colin Brunton: I had perhaps — *perhaps* — smoked some marijuana that night, and I may have allegedly drank a number of beers and I may have been really inebriated and hammered. And I heard Andy Paterson mention to Gary Topp about The Last Pogo. I said, "What's that about, Gary?" He says, "Oh you know, bands were thinking of putting on this show because we're getting kicked out of the Horseshoe, and we're going to do this big thing."

I had taken this little two-week filmmaking course, and in my allegedly inebriated state I just blurted out, "Fuck, that sounds like a great idea. I'm gonna make a film about this!" And then I went home and when I got up the next morning, really clear-headed, I thought, That actually still sounds like a good idea. I've had many late-night, drunken, inebriated thoughts that the next day just don't pan out, but I thought, This sounds really cool.

So the guy who *really* pulled it together is this teacher, Patrick Lee, who taught me my little film course. We shot a little punk film called *Bollocks* together — a three-minute thing just learning how to operate a camera and edit and stuff.

With tons and tons of help from him we managed to somehow get some film stock and equipment and then just set it up. I contacted the bands. We were originally going to do both nights, but of all the bands that played that weekend the only single person that did not want to be filmed was Carole Pope. I thought, Okay, whatever, if I can't get the whole second night there's no point in doing the second night; I'll just focus on the first night.

Then I went to all the bands and I said, "Okay, guys, I have so little stock, pick one song you want me to film." And they all picked the right song. The Scenics, because they're so avant-garde and weird, picked their shortest song.

Andy Ramesh Meyers: We [Scenics] were definitely outsiders in that scene.

Colin Brunton: The Ugly, because they were so not avant-garde and just wanted more screen time, picked their longest song. So there you go.

Then we got the thing done and the rest is history.

Margaret Barnes-DelColle: I remember at the time we were all a little bit aggravated about it. People were misinterpreting that, even though everybody was looking forward to the gig and doing it. But Fred and I would always talk about, "Last Pogo — last *what*?"

Sally Cato: In my opinion, it changed after Crash 'n' Burn. That is when — they didn't know it then, of course — everyone was forced to go pro. Everyone went into factions and it became about survival. The Last Pogo was the last nail in the coffin of an already-dead scene.

Rodney Bowes: I think the *real* last pogo occurred before that. As far as I'm concerned, it ended with the Crash 'n' Burn. We had moved on.

Drugs factored into it every point of the way. What were we doing? Coke, smoking dope, and alcohol. I remember we were doing valiums and tranquilizers and stuff like that with beer. But we weren't really using it; it wasn't really fucking our lives up. It was a much more recreational thing.

With guys like the Ugly it just started to creep up, and all of a sudden we started becoming aware that Freddy Pompeii was a junkie, and that there were a *lot* of people that became junkies. And it changed it. It just made it a different deal. Band members were stealing each other's equipment. It became kind of nasty. Yeah, I'd say pretty well that The Last Pogo was the *last* pogo.

Nip Kicks: At that point, people had started not going to see the bands so much as going to find out where the parties were. The speakeasies were getting bigger and more popular, so people were going to those things more than the gigs after a while. And more and more of the various drug cultures were getting involved. People were just getting wilder.

William Cork: It was already a done deal by then. It just left a bad taste in my mouth. I didn't want to be here anymore. It was in the air.

Quite frankly, there will never be anything like Yorkville. Period. End of story. Everything else has been a pale attempt to get something together, and it never happened. And *now* look at Toronto. It's destroyed. It's become completely victimized by a City Hall whose constant game is to sell out to the nearest big real estate baron. That's what it's all about here now.

Toronto used to be really fucking cool. There were all of these Tudor houses everywhere and millions of fucking freaks and tons of the best dope in the world. Yorkville used to be a line from Avenue Road to Bay Street of Harley Davidsons with every kind of dope and fucking shit ever known to man, and it was really groovy. Never for a minute did we think that something as demented as punk rock was ever ...

I mean, Freddy [and I] were pretty much horrified by how quickly the scene went down like a bullet, and how really shitty it was at its root.

Zero: Everything was coming to a boil.

The Last Pogo — everyone keeps saying, "Were you there?" I don't remember if I was there. I remember being totally anti–Last Pogo because I didn't like the fact that somebody was saying, "It's ending, here's the end, it's the last pogo, that's it." I didn't like that whole idea of somebody almost dictating what was going to happen, how it was going to happen, and when it was going to happen. So I was really anti–Last Pogo because it was our hangout; that's what we did every night. What do you mean it's going to end? Where are we going to *go*, for Chrissakes?

Andrew McGregor: As soon as it became cool to be punk, it was no longer a viable scene. The original people were genuine hipsters; they were the beatniks of their era and totally anti-commercial.

Sometimes it was bad enough that people were making records. People were angry about that sometimes. And of course, that's always the way it is with the true believers: This kind of thing can never last. Just like the folkies. Eventually Bob Dylan comes out there one day with an electric band, and that's the end of your folk scene. This was the same thing; it just kind of came to an end. The scene was over, and you had the school kids coming down to Queen Street looking for what was hip.

Greg Dick: When you were at The Last Pogo, there were a lot of straight people there. It wasn't all cliquey. You had corners of the bar that were cool and you had a lot of onlookers. I remember that's when Leckie would be famous for coming in and picking out the people he thought were hippies and starting trouble with them. It was always quite entertaining to see him do that.

I think The Last Pogo was the turning point of punk becoming a very exclusive society.

David Quinton: I remember the *Toronto Star* being out. There wasn't usually a lot of media coverage for punk. They took a picture of all of us onstage; all the bands. Kind of interesting.

Nip Kicks: The whole thing did not work out well. Just about every jerk who was ever attracted to the scene probably showed up.

I remember not being real impressed. We didn't feel that everybody was as well represented as they could have been.

David Quinton: The Mods did The Last Pogo three months after I joined. I was seventeen years old. I remember there was a lot of talk of what it meant, this sort of Last Pogo. Are we pronouncing the end of something? And I think to a certain degree, there was this feeling of the end of punk and now it's becoming new wave; it's becoming something else.

"Above Us, the Wave: Jack's Guide to a New Kind of, ahem, Music," by Jack Batten [*The Canadian*, November 4, 1978]: You've heard of Punk Rock? The raw stuff that's played by guys with swell names like Johnny Rotten and Nazi Dog? The music that's dumb on purpose? Featuring singers who are given to baying at the moon? Got it? Punk Rock?

OK, now forget it. Punk Rock is already out of style. What's in current vogue is something called New Wave.

David Quinton: I always lamented the fact that the original version of the Ugly wasn't on the [Last Pogo] bill, because to me they were one of the defining bands on our scene. I thought it was too bad that the Diodes weren't there.

Gary Topp: I never liked the Diodes. We never booked the Diodes.

First of all, you're in that era of punk rock. I mean, I've always had attitude. I do what I believe. I never thought the Diodes were very good. They were very cartoony, but I always thought they were poppy and wanting to be like the Ramones. I'm not saying they didn't play well, but I could never take them seriously.

Colin Brunton: Let me tell you, if Gary didn't like somebody, he had a really good reason.

I think a lot of it was jealousy with some people. Who knows how many bands there were *really* in the city

after that Ramones concert, but of course everyone wanted to play at the New Yorker and then the Horseshoe. So Gary can't book everybody, and he's not gonna book just anybody.

I remember one night at the Horseshoe we booked Jesse Winchester. The place was jam-packed; they made a fortune. [But] the guy was so fuckin' boring that Gary said there's no way. Never again.

David Quinton: I thought it was too bad that the original Viletones weren't playing. Those are the only things that sort bugged me about it at the time; some of the bands on the bills were questionable and weird, and I didn't understand why they were there. Nothing personal against them, I just didn't get it.

Mickey DeSadist: Well, there was a lot of favouritism going on there and it was obvious that Teenage Head, the Viletones, the Mods, and us were the best bands. See, the Ugly played The Last Pogo. I didn't think we needed to, but I wish we did, anyway.

Us and the Ugly opened up for the Dead Boys and we both laid a real big impression on the audience, and later the Garys had us open for Iggy Pop and the Cramps. So it shows you what the promoters actually thought of us. And maybe it had something to do with some band's management not wanting us to play; their hands may have been tied, because some of the bands that played The Last Pogo shouldn't have been there. I'm not going to be pointing out people and saying that they stunk, but I mean the Cardboard Brains and the Everglades were not exactly the main, great bands of the time. Johnny and the G-Rays should have been on that; I don't even remember if they were. They weren't even a punk band, but they were an important band at that time.

David Quinton: Johnny MacLeod got a raw fuckin' deal. He was way better than his treatment.

You know what, though? A lot of people can say that, and you've got to sort of deal with it. I always say there are a lot of Beatles and Rolling Stones in basements around the world that we'll never hear. It's always tragic when talent doesn't shine through, or people don't recognize it.

Greg Trinier: At that time, we had established ourselves as a pretty good band so we didn't show up three hours before the gig; we'd show up twenty minutes before the gig.

I walked in there, I looked down the long corridor towards the stage, and there were so many people smoking that you couldn't even see the lights, that's how much smoke was in the room. I went, "Oh my god, this place is *packed*."

Mark Dixon: I think that was only our fourth time playing the Horseshoe, so we were pretty new still. We knew it was going to be just jammed, which it was. Hot and jammed, just as it looks in the pictures. All these people outside; you don't know how many they're gonna let in, you don't know really what's gonna happen, how calm everyone's gonna be. You figure it's gonna get out of hand; I think we probably knew that.

Scott Marks: The carnival atmosphere was definitely there. But there was a nasty kind of a — I don't know, there was just not a real good feel there.

Mark Dixon: The Viletones weren't supposed to play and they talked Gary into letting them up after we played.

Freddy Pompeii: [Steven] insisted on being on that show. He talked Gary Cormier into being in it. He said, "We were the first band, and I should be up there with everybody else and you better let me do it or else I'm gonna get my boys to jump you." Gary thought it was a good idea to let him do it to get him off their backs.

Gary Topp: Steve Leckie didn't want to at the beginning, but then I guess he felt left out so he got in. It wasn't the original Viletones, but it was still very exciting. Nobody really knew they were gonna play so it was an added treat. He accomplished what he wanted to.

Greg Dick: I think why the Viletones probably didn't want to play at The Last Pogo was they weren't going to be the featured attraction. But at that point punk had started to become more manufactured; there was "new wave," and people in the suburbs were getting into it.

I'm sure the Garys liked it, because that's when they started booking the odd Danforth Music Hall show and stuff.

Steven Leckie: Even the very day of the thing I just said to Topp, "Okay, I guess we'll play." I asked the guys, "Are you up for this?" Also, I think I might have been a bit uncertain because I'd just gotten yet another new guitar player, so we probably weren't one hundred per cent sure on how that would go. But he ended up being an awesome player, Cam.

Richard Citroen: At The Last Pogo he debuted the new Viletones with his guitar player du jour, and Sam and Tony on the bass and drums. They were great, just great. I thought to myself, finally Dog's got a band that's as good as he is.

Freddy Pompeii: We broke up about a month before The Last Pogo. That was what he *called* the Viletones at that point. But you can see that it's an imitation of what came before. If you ever saw the Viletones ...

Tony Vincent: I don't remember much of it because I was on valiums. All I know is Steve had a broken arm and Sam had a broken foot. It wasn't a very good show, but they filmed it.

I didn't like the way we played. I don't know, maybe it was my fault. Valium was the drug back then; valiums and booze. Can you believe that? I don't know how we even managed to stand up and walk to the show.

Steven Leckie: Sam had to use Steve Mahon's bass, which is upside down and it's left-handed. He did, after awhile, figure it out.

Sam Ferrara: We weren't really booked for that, but we played anyway. It was a little bit of a pirate; not much, not like the Ugly. That was when Johnny [Garbagecan] got his jaw broken. Or was that another time?

Steven Leckie: The way, I think, it was set up, the bands were fairly lightweight. I think they wanted to give a good representation, but something like the Cardboard Brains and the Ugly are coming from another world. Then by the time we did our thing — and I had my hand all bandaged because I'd just put it through a clock a few days before — we were at a good point in things, so the kids just went nuts.

Colin Brunton: What I'm hearing is that it was pretty much the Blake Street Boys getting out of hand, although that may not be true either. One guy I talked to said, "Man, that was one of the most memorable slash unmemorable nights of my life. I was so drunk I can barely remember what happened, but I *do* remember smashing tables and chairs."

Gary Cormier: See, the Horseshoe was sort of an after-hours place where the cops would hang out and drink. In those days the bars were only open until one o'clock in the morning. When the cops came off shift they would come down and drink all night and leave at four or five in the morning. So they hated when we came in there and took over. They felt completely alienated. This is the only thing that stands out in my mind.

When it all did come to an end, they created the problem by saying we were over-crowded and coming in with this big show of force. There was no reason for it other than they were thumping their chests, saying, "You guys are out of here, we're taking it back now."

Gary Topp: The cops were in the place as plainclothes, off-duty, sitting at the bar drinking. Teenage Head were a big draw. They were pretty popular. The Viletones weren't scheduled to be on the show because Steven was playing one of his games that we weren't worthy, but they did play.

Then Teenage Head were about to come on and the cops told us to close the show down. There were too many people in the place, it was unruly, whatever. So I got up and said that, and all of a sudden there was a huge riot.

Captain Crash: I was in the dressing room, behind stage, and I was looking out the door and it was just total mayhem. I'd seen it umpteen times before so it was like, "I'm going back downstairs again," you know? And then when we left it was like, "Okay, the fight's coming and it's now down the stairwell," so we just went out the back door.

Sam Ferrara: Everyone was going to the back, towards the stage, and I just kind of followed Motor Mike. I was right outside in the laneway and Mike was at the door — he's a big guy — and anyone who was trying to get through he'd go *boom*, knock 'em down, *boom*, knock 'em down. I'm not a big guy, so I'm not into fighting. Even if I was a big guy I'm not into fighting.

Dave Elley: We were supposed to play, actually, because Teenage Head was the last band of the night. They said we could play before them or something, as if that would have ever happened, but we were there anyway.

I remember sitting downstairs and the people upstairs were just freaking out. I was down there thinking, Wow, we've got to get out of here. We thought the floor was going to cave in. Those people were just nuts, so we got out of there. It was pretty scary.

Gordie Lewis: I remember arriving late for that picture they took at the beginning, and I was pissed off because that was my girlfriend's fault — I did have a girlfriend by that time.

But what I remember the most was just being downstairs, waiting to go on and play, and just hearing this rumble and bumbling, like a hurricane going on upstairs. All this *bang, boom, bang, bang,* and not thinking anything about it, just sitting there having beer with Frank and not even caring. Ha ha ha.

Slash Booze: You could hear it going on. My mind is fogged and I kind of recall thinking, There's no way in hell I'm going up there. Something bad's happening.

Stewart Pollock: Teenage Head were just walking onstage to play their set. The undercovers realized, Stop this before they go on because there's gonna be a problem in here. They didn't want them to go any longer because they wanted to kick everybody out.

So Steve's asking the cop, "Please, just one song, *one song,*" and everybody's bitching at the cops, "Come on, *one song*, that's all."

Stephen Mahon: To be truthful, I got there late because I was drinking all day. I didn't make a habit of that, but for some reason I had met this girl I knew and we hooked up with the guy who produced our first album. I guess I knew I had that show that night, and that's why I was in Toronto with her hanging out. It was one of those days where you sort of start around noon and you're young and you're foolish. And at some point someone was saying, "Steve, don't you have to get down to the Horseshoe for something?"

So we get in a cab and we get to the front door of the Horseshoe and it's jammed. I was just perfectly drunk enough where I knew this was gonna be fun. I just remember crunching through the whole Horseshoe to get to the dressing room. That was like swimming upstream. I probably got there just prior to us having to play, and I remember arguing with a cop because they weren't gonna let us play. They let everybody else play, and then there's urban legend as to why those cops were there in the first place.

Chris Houston: We were all downstairs in that little dressing room and Leckie called in the fire marshal and Frank punched him out or something. He came up from the side and announced it to everybody and Frank was right there. He had figured how long the cops would take to get there and close it down so he called this right in before the Viletones set. He had it timed, but Teenage Head got to do a couple songs before they closed it down.

Stephen Mahon: Anyway, they were there, right beside me, and stupid me, drunk, was arguing with him. I probably didn't even put together that he was an undercover cop. He was somebody that was obviously allowed onstage and was trying to tell us we couldn't play, and I was kind of like, "I've got the power because I know all the people in front of us *want* us to play." That's probably what gave me the nerve to even talk back to him.

I believe that's why we were allowed to play two songs, because I think we were already standing onstage ready to start. So I think the wisdom there was what can it hurt, let them play a couple of songs. Then it was over — literally over.

Frankie Venom: We opened up with "Picture My Face," and the fire marshals came in and grabbed Steve's guitar — "*Stop!*"

The whole place went nuts. Tables were flying, chairs were flying, and fighting, blah, blah, blah, blah.

Stewart Pollock: They tried to break into a second song but the cops were like, "I don't think so." The people in the audience didn't catch the play with the cops, because they were undercover. They didn't realize what had happened so they just thought, You fucks. We've waited all night for this and you don't even come out and play.

They destroyed the place. There was a wrought iron fence that was twisted. Wrought iron does not twist easily. Chairs broke and tables overturned. They really messed up the place.

Joe Csontos: I got there about midnight and I jumped up on a table because everyone was at the front. I was hanging onto the ceiling and I saw Teenage Head were up there. There are chairs flying and skinheads are here and it was, "Who's gonna get killed?"

Another thing I always remember is that Canadian punk was a big drink culture as opposed to getting high culture. This was all about getting a pint and getting pissed, or doing bennies and drinking beer. That might explain the violence. Everybody's speeded up and drinking. They weren't mellow by any means.

Colin Brunton: It's the mob mentality, right? It's like it's chaotic, there's a lot of crazy music, it's jam-packed, so when someone does something it just leads on. At that point we weren't even filming so they weren't doing it for the camera for sure, but yeah, it was kind of weird.

Gary Topp: There was one guy, Evan, who had come to the show dressed as Dr. Strangelove in a wheelchair. He would not get out of his wheelchair when this riot started.

Colin Brunton: Evan Siegel had a band back then called the Swollen Members. He'd come to The Last Pogo in character as this faux Dr. Strangelove and wouldn't get out of character, even when tables and chairs and bottles were being thrown around him. He just kept wheeling around avoiding stuff.

Gary Topp: I remember him waiting for somebody to help him down the stairs and these people were throwing tables and chairs, smashing chairs. And he was just staying calm in his wheelchair. It was great.

Colin Brunton: But no one expected a riot. Although I've heard that people think the Ugly phoned it in and said,

"There's a big problem here, you should shut this place down," because they wanted to be the last band on that night. Which I wouldn't put past them, but who knows.

John Kancer: I remember being in the aisle and bodies were flying.

David Quinton: It ended like that. Rather than with a big explosion, it ended with Teenage Head being thrown offstage.

Dave Rave: That was a scary night for me. I remember getting everybody in the car, running out the back door and grabbing Gord. That was an intense night. It was a *negative* night.

Gary Topp: I believe in spontaneity. I think people were into this underground scene and I don't know what audiences thought, but I always thought you never knew what was going to happen two hours later. You never knew what the band members were gonna do onstage. That's what rock 'n' roll is about, and it was true rock 'n' roll in the purest sense.

Everybody wants to be a rock star and it was a time when they could put on a guitar and play, and the energy and excitement of the performance made up for maybe a lack of playing skills.

At The Last Pogo the cops closed the show down and I got on the mic from the mixing console and said something like, "We have to close the show down, the cops think it's unruly and unsafe so please just leave like they want you to." Then I put on "Anarchy in the UK," and it sounded like a thousand lumberjacks cutting down trees because they were swinging wooden chairs against these bar tables all around you. It was incredible.

Chris Houston: There was nothing that resembled a bar. It was just mountains of wood and tables.

Gary Topp: The next day we did the second show, and the kitchen was *filled* with broken chairs and tables.

Andrew McGregor: People were just going crazy. They had I think every paddy wagon in the city parked outside. I don't know if they had a SWAT squad back then, but all the heavies were there.

I never really understood what happened that night, or why the police showed up in force. I know there was a bit of the punk hysteria going on, but considering it was the last night of this club, and not the first night, I'm not sure what they were trying to accomplish.

I mean, the whole thing's funny. If they'd have just waited another hour everybody would have left.

Rodney Bowes: It was like we'd created a monster.

I'd been out of it, I'd been out of those clubs, and then all of a sudden we had this show to do. It's like this excuse to go nuts.

It was over, really. It was just a mess. The whole thing kind of disintegrated. A lot of people were doing heroin. The whole thing was a mess, a real mess.

Wayne Brown: It was an unpredictable, bloody mess, ha ha ha.

You know what? I didn't really see any of the bands play. I *heard* them. The place was so packed – *so* packed. I had this stupid attitude to begin with that I knew all these bands, I'd seen all these bands, I'd played with most of these bands, and why did I need to be up front and personal with these people at this point, at The Last Pogo? I'd seen them so many times.

So I stayed at the bar the whole night long and drank my face off, and the next thing I knew the place was being flipped upside down and people were being hurt and tables and chairs were flying back and forth. And then I can remember it almost being silent. Like this burst of anger had just been unleashed, and then it just shut off.

Greg Trinier, The Mods / photo by Ross Taylor

Edie Steiner: The Last Pogo was weird because of the whole ending to it, where the police came and chairs were flying in the air and tables and everything sort of exploded. It seemed like an apropos finale to that era.

Wayne Brown: I already had it in my mind that I was leaving here. At the time of The Last Pogo, I didn't really feel like it meant much to me. I just knew that I was going to New York and I was gonna put a band together, and I was just gonna carry on.

Carmen Bycok: I hid behind the bar with Wayne Brown. Chairs were flying, glass all over the place, and we managed to sneak our way out the front door.

It was so funny because once the cops came and all that, we were standing across the street. You could see the cop cars and all the crowd in front of the Horseshoe. We were across the street looking at that and then we said, "So what do we do now? Know of any parties?"

Zero / photo by Ross Taylor

48.
THe music Business

Gordie Lewis: The thing I remember most about The Last Pogo was, as a band, we were given a real taste of reality the next day.

Paul Kobak: Jack felt the way to go was to constantly be playing bars, high schools, small venues. Abraham's Children had taken in two hundred and fifty thousand dollars one year just doing that, so he was hooked on that idea.

Stephen Mahon: We started playing high schools and I don't think we would have been asked, or allowed, to play those if our music wasn't so beyond the standard punk sound. It was in your face, but something was catchy about it. There was a melody there that most people tend to like more than, say, a badly written dark song with bad chord progressions and more yelling than singing. It just makes more sense to me that that's what people would like more, and that's what we did.

I'd look into the kids' eyes at the front of the stage, and I knew it was the first time they ever saw a band. And I remember that feeling myself; how magical it was to see a rock band and hear them. And that's the same look I got in those kids' faces when we did those high schools. I knew for a lot of them it was the first time they were allowed to go to the school dance and of all the bands, they get to see Teenage Head — their first band — and they loved it. You're so impressionable when you're young. And they'd all hang around afterwards and want to get your autograph and stuff.

Inter Global Music [press release]: Teenage Head are without a doubt the tightest, toughest Rock 'n' Roll group in Canada today. Having started over two years ago in "the pits" of Toronto, they have out-lived and out-played virtually every new wave group to come along and are now playing the college circuit to packed houses everywhere they play.

Gordie Lewis: We got really used to playing for people at colleges and universities and everybody loving us, and that probably was us getting a little cocky.

Stephen Mahon: The Last Pogo was a successful, cool gig packed with people and we were the last band on. The next day, we had to go to New Brunswick. This was like going from a high to a low.

Our first Canadian tour, to the East Coast. I'm sure you've heard from Gordie and Frank how dreadful it was.

Gordie Lewis: Steve drove. Me and Frank and Nick took the train. We were going to Oromocto, New Brunswick. We were going there for a week. And then we were going to Fredericton for another week. And then we were going to another place, Richibucto, New Brunswick, for another week.

We had to walk out of this really big train station in Montreal to the *old* Montreal train station, and it was just this desolate walk. Nobody else was going to this other train except us, and it was all dark. And as we keep on going, more and more people are getting off, so by the time we get to Fredericton Station it's a ghost train; we're the only ones on it, and this is like six in the morning. We got our taste of reality: The music business.

We get dropped off at this nowheresland in New Brunswick somewhere outside of Fredericton; we don't even know where we are. We wind up hitching a ride with some guy in a pickup truck. And I remember him dropping us off at this place — the Luna Pizza Pub in Oromocto, New Brunswick — and nobody was there to greet us. It was just a restaurant. We sat there and waited, and finally Steve came with the truck with the equipment. I guess we set up the equipment. I remember sleeping on the stage when we got there.

Oromocto is an army base camp, and the Luna Pizza Pub is where they all came to hang out.

They hated our guts. They didn't want to hear "Lucy Potato." They wanted to kill us.

Stephen Mahon: It wasn't just one-nighters we were doing, either. You played a *week* — how awful. It's bad enough that people don't want to come for one night, now you've got to try and go for *six*?

Gordie Lewis: We did one set, and some of the army guys took us outside to get us away from the people because they hated us. So therefore, we were fired. But we weren't *really* fired.

Stephen Mahon: The first week, we got paid to *not* play. We had to sit on the stage — isn't that crazy? I guess the club owner was committed to paying through the agency that booked. He couldn't just say, "You're fired, fuck off," so the worst that he could do was make us still show up because he knew he had to pay us.

Gordie Lewis: What he made us do, to keep our money, was that we had to show up every single night at the club for the rest of the week, and sit there and not play. We had to come at nine o'clock and eat pizza or whatever till one o'clock, and then we could go back.

We had to do that for six nights to get paid.

And where they kept us for accommodations was a trailer park. No TV; I think there was electricity, so we had a radio. There was no tape deck, nothing like that, so all we had was a radio. We all just stayed in this trailer, and all we did was play cards. That's all we did. It was horrible, and we did that for a week.

Stephen Mahon: This is still when we had no pocket money at all; no one had jobs, so there was that whole starving thing. Starving artists. That's what we were doing: We were a starving punk band, and there were still two weeks to go. "Oh my god, how bad can this get?"

The next week was Fredericton, which is the capital of New Brunswick, so that was a little bit better. We didn't get fired; we got to play every night so that wasn't too bad, but I think between me and Frank somebody got sick from, um, being with somebody, ha ha ha, and the mood was just no good.

The *third* week, they were supposed to be shipping us out to a place called Richibucto, which is another four hours' drive away from home for another week. The place was called the Bear's Den.

Gordie Lewis: At the end of the Saturday we decided, "We're not going to Richibucto, we might get killed. Remember what happened in Oromocto? *Richibucto*? That's even further north."

So we just left. We just said, "We're going home."

Stephen Mahon: Nick was our spokesman. Nick made the call back; I don't know if he called Jack or if he called the agency, but he more or less said, "Don't expect the band to show up there, because we're coming home." So the third week never happened.

Frank went to the hospital and got his cure, ha ha ha, and Jack actually flew down and I remember looking at all the test strip negatives of the pictures we took for the first album. So that was kind of an upbeat thing, Jack showing up and here's all the pictures from the photo shoot because we knew our album was going to come out the next year. But it was a huge step down from the Pogo to the realities of being in a bar where there isn't even one person that knows who you are or cares. And even if you *do* play, they're going to hate you anyways.

Gordie Lewis: So that was a real awakening; that it's not all downtown Toronto, a filled Horseshoe of people loving you. It can be a pretty rough business.

Stephen Mahon: Good call to not go to that third week because I'm sure it would have been awful. It was right before Christmas, too, and I guess we were all getting a little homesick kind of. How old were we, twenty, nineteen? I can remember feeling really down, sort of depressed.

It wasn't the fact that we were starving. It was just that we're banging our heads out here. *Why?* That was just something Jack did because he thought, "I got them three weeks of work, what could be better?" But he wasn't the one who had to go up onstage, ha ha ha. So we came back after two weeks, and I remember just feeling so good about heading home.

Gordie Lewis: Oh yeah, we were threatened — "You'll never work again," all that crap. We left, we went home, and of course nothing happened.

The wildest thing is, I sell sports memorabilia and this guy comes and starts talking about Oromocto and I said, "Oromocto, I know where Oromocto is." And he says, "Oh yeah?" Then I started telling him I was in a band and we played there and they hated us and we nearly got killed.

And he says, "That was *you?*" Ha ha ha. He says, "I'm one of the guys that got you out of there alive!" He's a great big army guy with tattoos; he was in Bosnia, and he says, "You're right, they did hate you and they did want to kill you." And we didn't know; we were really naïve: "What's going on here? Why are we here? Why don't they like us? Why?"

It wasn't fun. Not at all. That brought me down to earth.

We still talk about it. I remember the drive home was the fastest drive home. I don't remember it taking any time at all. It seemed like driving from Hamilton to Toronto.

Yeah, what I remember about The Last Pogo is Oromocto, New Brunswick.

Nick, Stephen, Gord / photo by Ralph Alfonso

ParT THree:
1979-1981

49. somewHere else

B-Girls / photo by Ross Taylor

Gary Topp: With The Last Pogo, Moses Znaimer walked in the night of the second show and wanted to have a meeting with us. This is just when people started to take it seriously, so he wanted to be first and shoot our shows for broadcast on Citytv.

We basically said, "You're a little late. Where have you been for the last eight months?" He always stole everybody else's ideas as far as music went, anyway. But that's the way it was. People just didn't take it seriously.

Greg Dick: I guess around '79 when things really started dying down, it seemed all the really cool girls I'd seen turned into New Romantic girls, and a lot of the guys either went rockabilly or New Romantic. There was a place called the Voodoo Club on St. Joseph's Street, but I couldn't get into it. I just started hanging on to the remnants of what was left of the punk scene and started my own band, the Dream Dates. It was still pretty cool, but it wasn't the same as the first couple years. Punk lasted for two years. It really did.

James Bredin: I mean, it's unsustainable anyway. What's going to happen? Is the whole world going to start wearing leather jackets and everyone will be punk?

Nip Kicks: It's like anywhere; when things are close-knit you can really pick who you hang out with. But then as the circle grows, and somebody becomes a friend of a friend or a friend of a friend of a friend, they don't know you as well, you don't know them as well, you don't trust each other and you might not be *able* to trust each other. And so that camaraderie wasn't there anymore; it became people trying to divide and conquer. And it's funny because some of the people who were in the scene at the beginning, people like Steve Leckie, were

great at that, at just separating people and making people not like each other.

Zero: People broke up with each other that had been with each other for a long time — bands, couples, everything really started shifting and changing. So that was '79, where the massive criss-crossing and blending occurred. A lot of switching; a lot of lost puppies looking for their ways. So things had changed, and they changed pretty quickly.

A lot of different types of music kind of blended in at that point. The Blake Street Boys weren't really hanging out much anymore, not after the Horseshoe, really.

Mike Anderson: Yeah, there was a big time there when nothing much was happening. I don't think it was the end, but something did change. All those people like the Police and Elvis Costello and all that, they were still going on. All they were doing was climbing up the ladder of rock 'n' roll success.

Zero: Things were dying down around that time, and The Last Pogo had a huge effect because everything came to a stop. Then everyone started hanging out at the Turning Point, which was kind of okay when it was an alternative, but not when it became the *only* place.

And then it was the Edge, bringing in big bands and bringing in other people that were not just us. And there was a cover charge. Zro4 had a bit of a feud going with the Garys, so they wouldn't let us in for free most of the time. Everything changed. It was just totally different. It was almost like not as much fun.

Carmela Morra: For me, what marked the change was the opening of the Edge. Adam and the Ants and that whole thing was happening; that was shit. It was from the Ramones and that whole thing to something more bigger.

Gary Cormier: We went to England for a couple of weeks and met with Miles Copeland, whose brother managed the Police and also had a number of little record companies and bands that he worked with. He'd been in the business for ten or fifteen years prior, and the scene that he'd originally nurtured had sort of dropped off. I guess he was scanning the horizon looking for something new and got involved in this punk thing, because of the energy and the conviction of the people involved.

I think if you ask Gary and if you ask me, the thing that we looked for the most in whatever we wanted to present at that time was, "Make me believe it." Whatever it is, if it's Hinduism or if it's rock 'n' roll, just make me believe it and we're there. So we hooked up with the Copelands.

There were nineteen people for two nights at the Horseshoe to see the Police and one of them was a friend of mine, Ron Caplan, who ran a place called Edgerton's, which was a little old house at the corner of Church and Gerrard. He was coming to these outrageous punk shows we were doing at the Horseshoe and quickly sensed what was going on and appreciated the energy that was going down.

When the Horseshoe all came to an end he said, "Why don't you guys come and do what you're doing at Edgerton's?" Most people that we bounced this idea off of were reluctant because the Edge was a little room; held about two hundred people. It was known for promoting folk music, which was a far cry from punk music. Gary and I discussed it, and we were kind of relieved in a way that the Horseshoe had come to an end because it was a lot of pressure booking a room six nights a week.

But we also knew we were on the cusp of something. Having seen the Police, we thought something was gonna happen there, and it would be worth being around when the whole thing does come to fruition.

Cynthia Ross: I think that what I would say is probably no different than what people would say now in film and theatre, which is that in order for people in Toronto to support you, you really have to go somewhere else. Then you'd come back and everybody was on side. But Torontonians don't tend to support their own artists; it's always better somewhere else. We experienced that.

We had a lot of support from the Garys, and we were kind of the house band at the Edge for a while. It became like our second home. We played there once a month and they let us rehearse upstairs for free.

We started bringing people that we played with in New York, like the Boyfriends and Levi and the Rockats, up to play at the Edge. It started to feel like the New York scene was more of a family to us than the Toronto scene.

Everything here was a little more disconnected. It wasn't really one common scene. There were the art bands, and the Ugly and the Viletones, and then you had a bunch of splinter bands like the Dents and the Denteens; they were more poppy. Whereas in New York, music was different, but it was one scene and everybody supported each other. You'd go to a show and everybody would be there.

I just think in Toronto people are much more cautious. I think Toronto is just too uptight.

Xenia Splawinski: Going to New York all the time gave me something to compare Toronto to. There, you had two things going on: You had lots of clubs, so there were quite a few different venues you could play. Then you had the international scene coming through; all these big people coming through, all these opportunities. David Bowie would come to our gig. We weren't his cup of tea was what he said.

In Toronto it was limited. The scene was limited, and the people after a while became a limited group. It was a small grouping of bands, and you went through the same dramas and the same scenes with people enough times. But in New York, there were more options. More options per drama, more options for people, so it was really a much broader place for us to connect.

Why *wouldn't* you leave if the big thing was to be in New York? We were playing in New York all the time, travelling back and forth, back and forth, so we said, "Let's just go."

Cynthia Ross: It was just a really positive time, where it seemed like art and music and poetry and writing were all connected and everybody supported each other. We all went to each other's gigs; we would all stand there and scream for each other. It was a very good scene at the time.

We started playing at CBGB's regularly, about once a month, and we decided we were going to move to New York.

Xenia Splawinski: And to be in New York in those days was amazing. It was *so* much fun. To hang out at CBGB's and everybody was there — the Ramones, Blondie, Talking Heads, the Dead Boys. To be there at that point before their careers took off was such an awesome experience. And then once their careers took off, to see what was happening with the different groupings of people was so much fun; it was so alive. And it definitely had more options, it had more possibilities.

That's where we hooked up with the Clash; that's where we hooked up with Blondie.

Cynthia Ross: The Clash happened to wander into CBGB's one night because they were recording in New York. Mick Jones and Joe Strummer came up and introduced themselves to me, because I was the band's manager. They said, "We really like you girls, we want you to open for us." I thought, Yeah, sure, nice line, but it'll never happen.

They actually had their manager get in touch with me, and we were supposed to tour with them.

Xenia Splawinski: They asked us to come and tour in England.

Cynthia Ross: We had gotten our passports, they were paying our tickets, and we were gonna use their equipment. Two days before we were supposed to leave, I got a telegram that their drummer had broken his arm, so the tour was cancelled. It was really disappointing. Then I got a call from Mick Jones saying they would make it up to us and have us on their next American tour. So I thought, Okay, that's pretty cool, we'll see if it happens.

And it did. Their record company tried to get them to use an opening act that already had a recording deal and was on their label, but they insisted — and they did this with other bands as well — they always had bands that they supported opening for them.

Xenia Splawinski: The Clash were really about the underdogs, and supporting people that are just actually really trying. You could tell that was exactly why they supported us. It wasn't because we were fabulous musicians, because we weren't — we were still at the beginning of our career — but we had spirit, and we were really trying, and that was what they supported in us.

Cynthia Ross: So we ended up opening for them a couple times in Toronto, once at O'Keefe Centre.

Henry Martinuk: That was just great. It was the B-Girls, Undertones, and the Clash. Three bands on different levels of talent and songwriting, but everybody proficient in their own right. The B-Girls were great.

What really pissed me off is that everybody that I knew was *downstairs*, in the bar. That was typical for us. Everybody was getting drunk off their asses, which I thought was kind of a betrayal to the hometown crowd. I thought, You assholes, how come you're not supporting the home band? You've got to have a good attitude any time the bands are playing, and this is a great opportunity for the B-Girls.

Cynthia Ross: It was the last rock show at O'Keefe Centre because the audience tore the chairs out.

John Kancer: There were all these busted chairs, ha ha ha. That's where we were sitting. Not only that, our good friend Paul ended up doing damage to the washroom and it was that that cut the O'Keefe; that was it.

Joe Csontos: I remember Kosmo Vinyl going, "*There's* a rock 'n' roll fan, *there's* a rock 'n' roll fan," and he's pointing to the seats; these two rows of destruction that was left over after.

Xenia Splawinski: The Clash took us on tour twice, in Canada and then on the eastern part of their North American tour. We couldn't afford equipment. We had our own guitars and instruments but we didn't have amps, we didn't have drums, we couldn't afford to rent the vehicle to be able to do this. They said, "Just come, use our equipment, come on the bus with us." They really took care of us. They were great to us.

The best show was the Fillmore East. It just had such a magic to it. You have to understand that when we toured with the Clash they were doing their *London Calling* tour, which to me was the most magical thing I'd ever seen. To me, that was the Clash at their greatest and their show was so incredible — the energy of it, the buzz around it, and what it was giving people. The places were big, but not too big. It felt like history. It felt like we were a part of history doing those gigs.

Cynthia Ross: We didn't get paid very much. I think it was three hundred and fifty dollars a show but we didn't care, it was just the thing of doing it.

They actually watched all of our shows. They stood on the side of the stage while we played.

Deborah Harry was a big supporter of ours. She produced a couple songs for us and really was sort of a mentor. She gave us a lot of advice and came and did sound at some of our gigs. It was at the height of her fame, so she used to do things like wear ridiculous costumes so no one knew who she was. One time she wore a frog mask.

Xenia Splawinski: So we had all these things that were happening that seemed way over our heads sometimes, and we kept rising to the occasion and just kept it fun.

I think that we brought to people the idea that first of all it could be fun, that the punk scene didn't have to be heavy all the time, and that you could do it if you wanted to. And I think in many ways that's what our mission was.

Cynthia Ross: Another interesting thing happened. We were playing at CBGB's one night and these two Hispanic guys came up and said, "We saw you with the Clash, we think you're really good, we want to give you free rehearsal time." So I said, "Well, that sounds good."

Then I said, "Where did you see us with the Clash?" They said, "We saw you at the Palladium because our friend lives under the stage." And I said, "What?" They said, "Yeah." And I said, "Does security know?" They said, "Oh yeah, they know. He lives there. He has a bed under the stage and we watched the show from under the stage." I thought, Thank God we don't wear dresses.

They were squatters. They had a building at Avenue B and 6th Street and they were running electricity in from a neighbouring building, and they ran this recording and rehearsal studio there. They gave us free time the whole time we lived in New York. They became our roadies.

We were pretty corny, actually. Before we moved to New York, Xenia and I lived at Sherbourne and Bloor off of Bleecker Street. So because there was Bleecker Street in New York, we decided we were going to change *our* corner to be Bleecker and Bowery, because that was near CBGB's. So we made this street sign to say The Bowery and she climbed on top of my shoulders to cover the real street sign. She was standing on my shoulders taping this sign on top of the street sign and these cops came cruising down the road and I thought, Oh my god. It was about two o'clock in the morning. They stopped and said, "What are you doing?" We were like, "Nothing." And they couldn't figure it out. The sign was there for about a week before it came down. We always did silly things like that.

I think at the time it was much better to be a band from somewhere else than to be a band from Canada, so in order to make it here you had to go somewhere else. We became really big here once we had moved to New York and were playing there regularly, so when we came back we would get much bigger crowds and lots of media attention.

Peter Goddard from *The Star* was quite infatuated with us. Somehow he got *The Star* to pay me to write two stories about living in New York and sleeping on floors. I think I did two, and I think I got a hundred dollars each article or something like that.

He wrote a number of articles about us, comparing us to Sandra Dee and stuff like that. When he wrote a review of the Rolling Stones album *Some Girls*, he included in his review — "Would sound good in between sets by the B-Girls."

Xenia Splawinski: The Toronto scene became very limited. There were so few venues. When Crash 'n' Burn was over, there was the Edge. And again, that was the great place for the B-Girls. They took us under their protection, they managed us, and gave us rehearsal space upstairs. We were really one of their headlining acts. We would sell the place out the most. But it was a very small place, and once it closed things got really, really limited in the city. It became harder and harder.

Crash 'n' Burn was it. After that, nothing had the same energy again. None of the other places ever had that kind of energy to them.

But in New York, CBGB's maintained that energy all the way through. It was able to be maintained in New York, where Toronto's clubs were more like the kind of place where you'd sit in a chair and watch the band. There wasn't the room to get up and to act out and to have some space to do that in.

You didn't really think you could be successful in New York. We were so surprised that we were welcomed into that scene. And not only welcomed, but we were so *honoured* in that scene.

To be able to be successful in New York was the big thing.

John Hamilton, Xenia; backstage, Max's Kansas City, New York / photo by Ralph Alfonso

50. a LiTTLe Dream come TRue

Steve Koch: I wasn't born in Calgary but more or less grew up there, so it was kind of a hometown. I was going to university there and was a pretty alienated young guy.

I opted out of pop culture, I think. In the early '70s I kind of gave up on popular music. I was listening to other stuff, jazz and blues and stuff like that. In university I was basically getting a degree in anarchism, which really came in handy later. I didn't have a whole lot of friends.

I was also real interested in playing guitar, but I was learning blues style and country style guitar because, like I said, I wasn't really into the early '70s rock music. Being the age I am I loved the '60s pop music — the stuff the Ramones later covered — but I was a little kid then.

My younger brother and I started a band, and basically I had to learn how to play rock guitar because that's what they were doing. So he kind of introduced me back into some of the cooler '70s stuff that I missed, like New York Dolls. So I started becoming aware of it but I still wasn't that keen on it.

I heard the Patti Smith album and the gates were starting to creak a little, like something exciting was happening. I loved her Rimbaud allusions — I was into the French symbolist poetry and stuff; I was reading that at the time as well. I got the first Ramones album, and the floodgates opened. It was like all this frustration and anger and feeling of powerlessness, and they just came along and said, "Hey, you can do this." I thought, Wow, that's amazing. I *could* do that.

So I bought into it. I got the dog collar. The only punk in all of Calgary, for sure.

In the fall of '77 I saved up all my money and went to England for a couple of months and listened to some bands. I saw *everybody*.

Then I came back, still had a half-year of university to finish, so I finished it, and I saved up a bunch of money with the object of getting out of there, because by that point I really kind of hated Calgary.

By the time I got back from England my brother had joined up with Buick McKane. They were a local bar band in Calgary. That was Reid Diamond, Brian Connelly, my brother and another guy who was the singer. They were pretty cool. They were kind of fellow travellers with me. I sometimes think I mortified my brother because I would show up at his gigs all crazy looking, and he's younger than me so he was probably really embarrassed. But he never said that so maybe he wasn't.

I was certainly the only punk rocker that they had ever seen. They were kind of on the same page a little bit, but they couldn't really come out of the closet exactly. I remember being at the Airliner Tavern, which is a pretty heavy duty tavern there, and they'd say, "Okay, here's a Rolling Stones song you probably don't know," and they'd play a Dead Boys song. Nobody but me would get it. Calgary wasn't really ready for it. My brother got beat up. Everyone was getting beat up all the time. It was a real homogenous kind of society; homogenous in a way that people probably can't understand now. Everybody listened to the same music, everybody dressed the same, and if you were different it was pretty weird.

I didn't have much awareness of the Toronto scene until I got back from England. I saw at a local bookstore they had a copy of *FILE* magazine, and I was fascinated because I had no idea that this was going on in Canada. I thought I was all alone in the world and would have to move to England or New York. Then I saw the magazine and was thrilled and fascinated because I saw pictures of the Viletones and stuff.

Viletones, Tony, Sam, Steven, Steve / photo by Ross Taylor

Right away I wrote a fan letter addressing it to New Rose, and asked them if I could buy a copy of the Viletones single. They not only sent one back, but they pinned my letter up on their board. It was probably the only fan letter they ever got. Steve Leckie carried it around for years. Even when I was in the band, he thought he had something on me because he finally figured out it was me.

I'm really glad I did that, because Don Pyle responded to my fan letter.

Don Pyle: When I was fifteen or sixteen I was going to Calgary to visit my brother.

Freddy and Margarita were both very, very nice to me; almost parental with me. They were like protectors in some ways, and encouragers and supporters. I was in [New Rose] and told them I was going to be going to Calgary. Freddy told me that they got this fan letter from Calgary and said, "There's a punk in Calgary. You should write to him and make friends with him before you go there." So he gave me this guy's address, and it turned out to be Steve Koch.

Steve Koch: I was in Calgary, still living at my parents' house, and this letter drops down. It's addressed to John Koch and my mom says, "Well, that's not for us, there's no John Koch here." We left it there for like two days on my stoop. Finally one day I held it up to the light and could see the letter inside was folded up like a paper airplane. And I thought, This has *got* to be for me. So I open it up and it was from Don Pyle. He got my name wrong and he said, "I'm coming to Calgary and I'm a punk too and you're into the Viletones, I'm into the Viletones, let's meet up."

Don Pyle: He wrote back and said, "Don't come to Calgary, there's nothing happening here, it's dead, I hate it here, I hate everybody." Then he said, "The only thing close to a punk rock band in town is my brother's band, Buick McKane." So Steve and I were actual pen pals, and then Alex started writing to me. So when I went out to Calgary they were going to be playing, so they invited me to come to one of their rehearsals.

Steve Koch: He actually came to my house, which was weird. I'd been to England so I'd seen those kinds of punks. So I had this idea that this Don Pyle is going to be this crazy, extreme guy.

He shows up at my door and he's a regular guy. I'm going, "This is not what I was expecting." But as it turns out we got along great, and he got along really great with my brother, too.

Don Pyle: I went to the basement of Brian or Reid's parents, listened to their band rehearse, and ended up hanging out with them and being friends with them. We remained pen pals over the next little while, and I think it was not long after that Steve moved to town.

Steve Koch: He's the first guy we went and saw when I showed up in Toronto. I saved up my cash, and me and a friend just drove for three days solid and wrote poetry all the way.

Early on when I went into New Rose, Margarita Passion was really talking up this great new band [The Demics] that she'd just heard about from London, Ontario. They were gonna open for the Dead Boys and they're gonna be amazing. So everybody was all excited — "Oh, *another* cool new band" — and they were fantastic. The Dead Boys were fantastic, too.

We saw a lot of bands in those early days, but a lot of it was local stuff. If it wasn't local it was probably up from New York. Once in a while you'd get somebody over from England. Not a lot of cross-Canada stuff going on because there was three thousand miles of nothing in between.

Don and I formed a band when I first got here. We called it Crash Kills Nine and it was me, Don, Eddy from the Dents on drums, and this guy named Boring Bill from a band called the Plastic Bags. We rehearsed up a bunch of songs, wrote a bunch of songs, played one show. We'd never played before, but we figured we can do "Blitzkrieg Bop" and the Viletones song "Rebel." We got up onstage and we did fine, so we said, "Hey, we can really do this!"

Don Pyle: He quit the band we had together to join the Viletones, which hurt me at the time.

Sam Ferrara: We went through a lot of guitar players and then Steve Koch came in. Steve Koch was the one that worked out.

Steve Koch: Actually, when I left Calgary I jokingly said, "I'm going to Toronto to join the Viletones." I might have as well said, "I'm going to Toronto to join the Rolling Stones." I didn't really mean it, but it was kind of a crazy thing to say; in a certain sense it was like a dream. When the opportunity came I thought, This is just perfect. So it was like a little dream come true.

Steven Leckie: Steve said to me that he moved here from Alberta to join the Viletones. I knew that he wrote us a couple times at New Rose, and he knew roughly where I lived and kept going to this convenience store and sure enough, Tony asked him, "You wanna be in a band?" And he said yeah, because he knew who it was, so that's probably the reason why.

Captain Crash: Steve Koch from Calgary did this cross out of razorblades and sent it to the Dog with this great big fan letter and wanting to play. That letter was so impressive that they said, "Let's give this guy an audition." I think he was too clean cut, but he was really talented and good-looking. He was just too nice.

Steven Leckie: We just frightened all the other guitar players. Because I *hate* musicians, I really do. I like being with artists, but *musicians*? Who cares?

Think about it — fuck 'em. Musicians? Show me what I've never seen before. It seems like I can name ten albums and who's surpassed that? You put on a record like *The Rise and Fall of Ziggy Stardust* and man, these boys are geniuses, they're not just musicians. Or a Doors record. It's more like hearing Arthur Rimbaud singing in English than it is just a rock singer. I like that visionary aspect.

Axl Rose is a musician. He's lousy, but he's not an artist. So that's my personal thing on that.

Steve Koch: At that point it's December '78 and they're looking for somebody. I was hanging around in the Edge with a couple people I knew, Siren and Verlana, and Tony was there and he must have been talking to them and lamenting the fact that they had no guitar player. The girls had seen me play with Crash Kills Nine at our single gig and they said, "You should check this guy out." So Tony looked at me and he said, "You don't really play guitar, do you?" I said, "No really, I do." He said, "Okay, I'll try you out."

He wasn't prepared to introduce me to the band but he said, "You just come down to the rehearsal hall and we'll see." So it was just me and him and I played "Sonic Reducer" and "Search and Destroy." He said, "Oh, so you really *can* play, okay."

He told me to learn all the Viletones songs from the singles, and he was prepared to introduce me to the band for a tryout.

Steven Leckie: He was stunning, like just *visually*. I loved his seriousness, and he was just a fucking killer player. He's one of the best now. So those are three pretty good things to like about a guy in a rock 'n' roll band: Great looking, my sort of temperament — like he was serious and quiet — and a killer player.

So yeah, he did end up staying a couple years. It was awesome, just awesome. I always got a bit shy in the beginning of the practice just walking into the room and seeing the three of them. I never stopped being a certain fan of Sam and Tony. They were that good; that unique. They just thought way out of the thing. Still, I've never seen anyone fuckin' pick up a Hofner. Him and Paul McCartney are the only two that come to mind.

Steve Koch: I had to go through this big hazing ritual. We had to punch each other out and stuff, and Tony was warning me about Sam. You know, "He's a mean guy." Sam's looking at me and says, "So you think you're a tough guy, eh? Let's see you put out a cigarette out on your finger." I said, "Let's see *you*," and he looks me in the eye with those little beady eyes and so we did it. You didn't want any wimpy guys in the Viletones.

Sam Ferrara: Oh, it was stupid. We were upstairs at Lee's [Palace] and he wanted to be a Viletone. So I'm looking at his fingers and I said to him, "Okay, put this cigarette out right there and I'll do it with you." So we both do it and we looked at each other and went, "How stupid. You're in." That was dumb.

Steve Koch: Our first gig was at the Turning Point in January '79. Sam and Tony were giving me pressure to do well, but we'd rehearsed and I knew the songs so I was okay with that. But everybody else in the audience were wondering, "Who's this new guy? We don't even know him. He wasn't here in '77." So there was some pressure, but I didn't really let it bug me.

Steven Leckie: He was a very, very mysterious kind of guy. Very intriguing; very private. He must have had an incredible constitution, too, because he had some straight job. Our schedule would be off the board and he'd never miss anything, ever. What I'm getting at is, I couldn't have partied to six in the morning and went to a square job at nine a.m. I don't know how he did. So he had that going for him, too. That's why he would want to stay.

Steve Koch: As soon as I got in the band I found out that Steve and Tony had run up an eighteen hundred dollar bar tab at the Turning Point, so we had to play the next three gigs for free. I'm going, "Well, that's just great. There's no way I can drink enough to catch up with you guys."

Steven Leckie: We had a good groove, the four of us. I think we were pretty well on the same page. And I wrote so much. There was good songwriting with that period with Koch.

Steve Koch: We used to do "Disgusteen" by Teenage Head and say that we wrote it. Mostly we did original stuff; it was kind of fifty-fifty. It was the older Viletones stuff from the single and new stuff that Sam and Steve had written.

Sam Ferrara: With the Viletones, when it became a five-piece I started writing a lot for them.

Chris Haight and Freddy Pompeii wrote, too, and Steve [Leckie] would write lyrics. He wouldn't write music but he still claims he does.

Freddy Pompeii: Today he'll swear that he wrote those songs, but all the music was done by me and the rest of the guys in the bands.You can't just write a song by waving your arms around.

Sam Ferrara: I came up with the whole concept of "The Last Guy in Town." I said to him, "Here's my bass. Play it." He couldn't play. He finally admitted to me, "Okay, you wrote 'Last Guy In Town'."

I even had to remind him what the song was about. We wrote it upstairs at Lee's Palace. The lyrics are written in a booth in magic marker, dated and signed. It was about one of the waitresses at the Turning Point. We'd heard she'd been with every guy in town except for us, and it was "The Last Guy In Town."

They reupholstered that seat. If they've left the old one there, I bet you if you cut it it's probably still there.

Steve Koch: The sound of the band changed a lot. I think it was musically a better band.

The thing you have to keep in mind about the original band was it wasn't actually so much about the music, it was more of a performance art. It was violent theatre. The fact that they happened to make good music now and again was cool, but it wasn't necessarily the main point. But the '79 Viletones was probably musically a better band, but maybe a little less of the theatrics.

Steve never really cut himself onstage while I was in the band, and he lost all the Nazi paraphernalia. Which is good, because I wouldn't have put up with that.

Freddy Pompeii: He hurt himself pretty bad in New York; he hit an artery. But most of the time it was just cuts and he ended up with really bad scars, which he used to brag about and show people. You know, "Look at this one and look at this one," but even he got sick of that after a while. I think you'd agree that that's just a psychological thing to cover up his insecurity.

Steven Leckie: It was maturity and no place left to cut, and it hurt like hell.

It hurt my brother. I didn't know that. It hurt his feelings. After a while you go, "For four hundred bucks, is that what I'm doing?" I knew it was getting a hell of a lot of press and it was part of the greater good, but the art of doing that wasn't necessary anymore. The powder keg had been lit, the people that saw it, and the aftershock was something I knew everyone would hear.

Peter Goddard once told me it was the idea of ruined beauty, which is a Shakespearian theme. GG Allin was physically unattractive, and he's doing it and he's shitting in a bag. But imagine Bowie doing it compared to the singer in AC/DC, it's saying something very, very different.

So I didn't need to keep doing it anymore and it became kind of a shtick; something expected and tired. But mostly it just hurt and it was stupid.

I'm glad I did it, but it was something to get over. I stopped after Sid died in '78. Here's a boy who's carving in his chest GIVE ME A FIX; that's punk, man, that's hardcore. Walking that wire of self-sabotage; in the hands of another band that would have been sure rock 'n' roll suicide.

In the hands of the Viletones it adds to success, so what does that tell you about culture? Why is it that made us more successful and talked about and glamorized, but if another band did it, it would have floored them?

It only gave *us* more gigs, more attention. So it's tantalizing.

Viletones; Steve, Steven, Tony, Sam / photo by Ross Taylor

Steven Leckie, Steve Koch / photo by Ross Taylor

51. punk city

Bob Bryden: Hamilton is the first and last steaming bastion of punk.

I've kept journals my whole life. Sometimes a month will go by without writing anything, but there are time periods in my life where I'm very disciplined about it, out of need more than anything else. So I have tons of journals from that whole period, from 1977 to 1983.

From 1968 to 1977 I had been involved in my own kind of independent music scene. Bands called Reign Ghost, Christmas; I recorded about ten albums back in that time period. Now they're all being bootlegged, which is very flattering. Anyway, it was pretty dark stuff, pretty introverted stuff. Very, very underground, very anti–the system. One of my quintessential stories is Christmas released an album in 1975 and I remember hearing CHUM FM play the darkest, heaviest piece on the album at about two a.m. The next day "Sweet City Woman" by the Stampeders was released, and they never played our album again. So I consider "Sweet City Woman" single-handedly responsible for the death of the potential of serious music on Canadian radio. I loathe and despise that song.

Cut to the chase: '75, Christmas broke up. Then I spent two years just meandering and travelling, literally guitar-on-the-back, all over the place. I was really floundering. I got into theatre at that time because I thought maybe I'll try my hand at acting. I ended up in B.C., came back to Ontario in December of '76, and I spent two years floundering here.

All the time I was floundering, though, my good buddy Mike Shulga owns and runs Star Records in Oshawa. They were even just slightly ahead of Records On Wheels in terms of being an alternative record outlet. I consider Star Records the original, especially in Canada, alternative music outlet. I would pop in there all the time and he and I would talk about music and stuff and he would always say, "I would like you to manage a store for me one day." Clearly, he could see that I was floundering.

So one time I went in there, August of 1978, and he was on the phone arguing with somebody. There was an intense exchange going on. And he put his hand over the phone, looked at me and said, "Bob, would you like to go to Hamilton and manage a record store?" I had just popped into Oshawa for the afternoon; I was fed up with downtown Toronto and said, "I'll go to Oshawa and hang out." Walk in and that's what I get.

I said, "You know, Mike, I've gotta go to Hamilton this Saturday. Why don't I check out the store while I'm there?" He said, "Perfect, perfect."

So I went downtown to the corner of King and James to Star Records. I walked upstairs above the United Cigar store at the corner there and I walked into this very, very strange place; this crazy, strange situation. I could tell it was just chaos. It was a mess. It was a wreck. His cousin was the official owner of the store but had mismanaged it to the point of insanity. What he *really* wanted to do was manage Teenage Head.

Paul Kobak: I wanted Teenage Head to be playing concerts, recording, and touring. I didn't want them to burn themselves out and lose their creativity. Unfortunately, the band was constantly harping about lack of money. The guys would often end up coming home with twenty to fifty dollars each after a night's gig. Constantly renting equipment and vans took a big chunk out. That's pretty disheartening for a group of budding rock stars, especially with all the constant praise and crowd responses they'd received.

So we approached the booking agencies. Back then, there was the Music Shoppe and The Agency and several small independents. That was it. They controlled the bars and high schools. We approached them all, and slowly began working with The Agency. I think this was some months before Teenage Head recorded their first album. In the meantime, we kept trying to get a foothold in the States. These were all loss-leaders financially and I used monies coming into my record store to always make up differences.

I'm not sure of exactly when; I'm guessing it was 1978 when Bob Bryden came into the picture. My time had been increasingly consumed with Teenage Head. I was having problems with my employees at my store. I'd increasingly become taken advantage of and needed an honest, reliable store manager. My cousin Mike finally helped out by sending me Bob Bryden.

I could tell within minutes of speaking to him that he'd be good for my store. I let go of my staff and let him hire his own. That finally freed me up more so I'd be able to work with the band more.

Bob Bryden: He had been taking money out of the till and pouring it into Teenage Head. If Gordie Lewis said he wanted a Gibson Les Paul, Paul Kobak would reach into the till – this was the rumour – and take five hundred dollars from Saturday's sales and go out and buy him his Les Paul. I'm not kidding. That was the way the store was being run; it was rock 'n' roll. Classic stuff, really.

When I went back to Oshawa I told Mike Shulga, "You know what? It's chaos in there, but I'll take it, I'll take the job." This would have been Saturday — it was really fast — and basically he said, "Monday, go to Hamilton and take over."

So on Monday I arrived in Hamilton. I started sleeping in the back of the store, the whole bit. I just took over, and I was the most unpopular guy in Hamilton at the time. This punk-run record store got taken over by the pseudo hippie and that was very, very unpopular. Paul Kobak had no boundaries; he was just like, "Come on in and be part of my world." This had become a real haven for all these street punks and kids and bikers; it was just insanity. I was like a marshal coming in to clean up the old town. It was right out of the movies.

One day I get a phone call from both Mike *and* Paul, each one telling me to don't listen to the other and blow what they say out of their ass. As an aside, when I first got to Star Records, Teenage Head were just releasing their first single. They were practicing in the store, money was being channelled to them that shouldn't have been, and all kinds of stuff.

Stephen Mahon: I don't know, I always thought that Paul had control of the store. I really did. I know Bob worked there, but it's possible that he was given the reins and maybe things were just getting too stupid. Ha ha ha. We didn't burn the store down or anything.

Bob Bryden: So I take over and I kick them out; they can't practise at the store anymore, so that made me really popular. So just at the point when I seem like I'm the anti-punk — though I'm not really, as I am into what is radical and edgy; I'm not very popular with the Teenage Head gang — into the store comes Mike Grelecki, who is Mickey DeSadist, of the Forgotten Rebels. They start to come in and hang around the store. And because they see that I'm not in the Teenage Head camp, the Rebels camp moves in and I'm really popular with *them*.

I start to hear songs and I start to talk to them and I start to get a sense of them — especially Mickey — being writers. See, the thing with me is, Hamilton is punk city, and it's glam rock city, too. But it's also a drink-beer-and-talk-about-cars city, and that's what bugs me. Because I'm into lyrics; I've always been into lyrics, and I've fought the fight of my life through, "Well, I don't listen to the words" — well, I say I'm not interested. Because if you don't listen to the words, you don't know where people are coming from. You don't know what the band's philosophy is if you don't listen to their lyrics. So I'm really into lyrics and writing, and my modus operandi of life is, as Shakespeare said, "The play is the thing."

Well, when it comes to music, the *song* is the thing.

And the funny thing is — and this is almost verbatim what happened — Mickey DeSadist comes in one day and says to me, "Bob, you're the only guy we know who's ever been near a studio. We made a record and it sounds like shit. Will you help us?"

Mickey DeSadist: Bob Bryden worked at Star Records. He was the guy that knew something that was going on. We didn't know what was going on ourselves in the studio. We knew nothing. He was a big help. He's also a very honest guy. We knew he was honest and sincere and everything.

Bob Bryden: So I became the Rebels' producer, just like that. I said, "You've already recorded it?" "Yeah, it sounds terrible. We need help." So I go into the studio with them and I would call it *salvaging* more than producing. I remix and fix and add effects and touch up these four songs they'd recorded, which then becomes their first EP and they give me a credit as producer. So that was my indoctrination into producing punk. It sort of happened by accident, but everything I do happens by accident.

That was cool, that was interesting. I had my name on this record, and I hadn't had my name on an album in four years. So I went, "Oh, I guess I'm back."

Pete Lotimer: I look at the photos from that EP now and that was a big piss-up, too. Ha ha ha. I don't remember a lot of that, but wasn't that guy dressed like a girl? Wasn't it Burman we were beating up?

Stephen Burman: I did all the photo sessions for the album. They got a bad rap with the gay community over "Third Homosexual Murder."

Pete Lotimer: Again, the pictures, all arranged by Mickey. It must have been "Third Homosexual Murder." We were trying to promote it or something, ha ha ha. Mickey just kept at it and at it and at it. There always has to be someone in the band doing it.

Greg Dick: The Rebels — the first band was always the one that knocked me over. That first EP was just heavy duty. I can put that on right now and crank it up on the stereo and it's as loud as anything I can crank on. If I want to piss off my neighbour, I can *still* put on that 12-inch single. Wow, that's heavy.

They took a lot of flack, and I know that Steve Leckie didn't like them. He still has a little bit of a venomous sort of attitude towards them and I appreciate that; I understand where he's coming from. Mickey's a real shit disturber — "Third Homosexual Murder"? Nazis?

When "Third Homosexual Murder" came out there was a gig at the Turning Point where all these big leather guys tried to get in to beat the shit out of him, and Mickey had to escape. So they were very controversial.

Mickey DeSadist: I don't know if that's true. I really don't remember if it's true or I made it up. I've never had a problem with the gay community, and they've never had a problem with me. But getting them all excited and upset to get them to phone the newspaper? Well, I've got no problem with that. They can do that now if they want and I'll send them my approval. I'm all for same-sex marriage, especially if the chicks are hot, ha ha ha.

Stephen Burman: You have to take the Nazi stuff tongue in cheek, but some people just don't get that. That didn't help the Rebels' reputation … but of course it didn't help that Steven Leckie was calling himself Nazi Dog.

Mickey DeSadist: You know what? The important thing about that EP was that it got so much publicity for nothing. People like bad news, so we just decided to give a pile of bad news and laugh at them. That's all it was. There was never any real Nazi-*anything* behind the band.

You ever took a dog turd and put it in a paper bag, put it in front of somebody's house, set the bag on fire, and knock on the door? That's basically what we were trying to do.

We did that, too, eh? Took dog turds, put them in bags, and … I'm serious. We did that. We picked a random house because there was this nice bush across the road that we could all hide behind. We meant to throw it at the guy when he came out.

So that's what we were doing; we were bugging this guy simply because of the observation we could make when he came out. Back then there was no such thing as portable phones, so what we do was phone a whole pile of pizza places and then hide behind the bush and watch the guy's expression every time somebody would deliver a pizza to his house. And every five minutes somebody would come over, ha ha ha.

Stephen Burman: That EP, it added credibility. But because we didn't have a record company behind us there were a lot of uphill battles. We got screwed by one company who went bankrupt and took half of our records.

Pete Lotimer: I didn't know what was going on with the money and I didn't care. The way we operated, you weren't gonna make a lot of money. You just went and played. Unorganized chaos. It was punk rock.

But nothing could go wrong back then.

Everybody was happy, everybody was drunk, the shows were great no matter what happened. If Carl didn't show up because he was late, me and Mickey would go up there and he'd play weird songs and I'd drum to them. We could do that for an hour and people would love it. Drive around the graveyard at four in the morning? I had no problem with that.

Stephen Burman: We got banned from a number of bars for our antics in hotel rooms, throwing TVs out the window. The Isabella Hotel, we used to play there a lot but we got banned for a while for destruction to the rooms and stuff.

Pete Lotimer: I never had a bad time in the Forgotten Rebels. It was a blast. Mickey makes you laugh; his attitude, the way he dressed, the way he talked, everything. He always had a cigarette. He never smoked it, hardly, but he was always holding a cigarette.

If somebody said something dumb, that was gonna be a song. Or if something happened in the papers he'd call you up — "Let's write about that!" I'm going, "*Nooo!*" Ha ha ha.

I remember the car broke down on the way back from one gig once, and my girlfriend Trudy and I were literally sitting on the side of the highway with the drums because I didn't want to leave them in the car. We're all punked out, makeup all running down because I just did a show and my eyes were bleeding black. Some guy in a pickup truck came by. "You okay?" "Yup." "Get in," and he's drinking, right? "Have a beer." Back then everybody did it. But that was fun; even *that* was fun, standing out on the side of the highway because it's all part of this wild spree we were on. I can't believe Mickey's still going on with that.

Stephen Burman: Mickey never really got wrecked before a show. He might get wrecked *after*, but he was always pretty conservative before a show. That's probably why he still has his brain as opposed to so many of the others who just crashed and burned.

Pete Lotimer: I think that record gave Mickey the push he was looking for. The time was right, and Mickey *knew* the time was right. And it was. It gave us a push, but, I left shortly after it came out, I think. I don't know how long; I couldn't even tell you. But I could see that they were getting busy and starting to write other songs, political songs. I could see that if I didn't get off this train now, I'm gonna be on it for a while. I could see that. That's not a *bad* thing, but when you're looking for something else, it's not a good thing.

I don't know what he was planning, or if he waited for a certain time to do it. I know he was adamant about doing it, and he wanted to do it.

And he went and did it.

52. fashion victim

Steven Leckie / photo by Edie Steiner

Freddy Pompeii: Another reason we wanted to disband the Viletones was Steve wanted to go into the next big thing, which was rockabilly. He wanted the Viletones to be a rockabilly band, which I thought was kind of stupid. What you're doing is you're jumping on every trend that comes down the pipe, so obviously you're *never* gonna get out of Toronto.

I knew even when I was a teenager not to follow trends too closely and to just be yourself, and eventually something's going to come to you. There was no trend to speak of when we put this band together. The Ramones had long hair. It was our own thing; it just so happened that the Sex Pistols beat us to the press.

But he's definitely a fashion victim. That's one of his biggest drawbacks. He changed with the trends on cue and it's not a good way to be, especially if you're in rock 'n' roll. You've gotta stick to your guns.

When the Clash came out he wanted to be the Clash, when the Pistols came out he wanted to be Johnny Rotten. All of them. Every band that was coming out that was considered underground, he wanted to be. He would just change weekly. Change his whole stage persona, which *kind* of worked out for him because he started to become known as an improviser.

But people just didn't know he was stealing it from everyone else, because word didn't travel on this kind of thing too quickly.

He ripped off a whole song from the Jam. It's called "Girl Won't You Let Me," but it's actually a song by the Jam called "Away From the Numbers," on the very first album. He says, "Let's do this Jam song just to prove we could do it." So I learned it and we taught the band and we did it. And he changed the lyrics and told everybody *he* wrote the song, which is a big copyright breach. You just can't do that. Eventually somebody's gonna sue you. He tried that a few times where he would come in and say, "I've got this real neat riff," but it was something that he got from somebody else. We would find out and then we would nix the song.

But just because he read something in a magazine like *New Musical Express* and *Melody Maker*, which came to the United States and Canada a short time after they were published, that news never got to the mainstream press for months. So he would find out what the latest trend was in England and then put his own spin on it to make it look like *he* came up with the idea, and it worked for him for a while. Until he got with people who were looking at the same stuff he was looking at.

It was real childish; he was always doing that stuff. That's why I say he was definitely a punk rocker. He wasn't sophisticated in any way, shape, or form.

Ross Taylor: I would go with Steve to see all sorts of shows. Steve Martin, the comedian, came to town. It was when he was big on *Saturday Night Live*. For some strange reason Steve wanted to go, and he and I went and sat in the fifth row. The article in *The Star* the next day talked about how Steve Leckie was at the show. It was quite amusing.

Gary Topp: The good thing that came out of that punk scene and the developing new wave or whatever you want to call it, was, as opposed to kids now, that specific generation had the benefit of hearing the music of the '60s and music of the '50s and even earlier. That generation of kids were open to all forms of music, so you'd get bands like the Stray Cats, bands like the Pogues, Sun Ra.

So those kids who started out sort of punky or totally alternative in the true sense were infusing all this different music that they had heard or were interested in learning about into *their* music. That was a great part of those days in promoting music. You could bring a rockabilly group totally unknown from England. We were promoting that way, anyway. So all that infusion of different music was what I think kept that particular music alive and developing.

Steven Leckie was totally into rockabilly. It was a big, major influence on his music and his look.

Andrew McGregor: There wasn't a lot of rockabilly in Toronto. I remember Jack Scott played at the Horseshoe one night. The Cramps really re-introduced rockabilly here and they did some fantastic shows at the Edge, and that kind of got people into rockabilly in this area.

Ross Taylor: Steve had a very wide range of musical tastes. He loved rock music, but he also loved a lot of the old '50s stuff.

Then he got into rockabilly. When I would go over to his house he would always play these old rockabilly albums, and he was into Elvis like you wouldn't believe. He was a closeted Elvis fanatic. I think it was the showmanship and the whole lifestyle.

Freddy Pompeii: He did a version of "Blue Moon of Kentucky." Somebody was turning him on to Elvis records and he wanted to sing like Elvis, but he was not capable of singing like that. Ha ha ha.

Mike Anderson: He never talked to me about that. I had no idea that was going on. I guess that was a trend that started happening with Handsome Ned.

Freddy Pompeii: There was *no way* I was gonna play rockabilly. It was like country music compared to what we were playing.

Ross Taylor: But as the band changed, especially when Steve Koch joined, this rockabilly movement going on in the UK at the time was a scene Steve was particularly attracted to. When Crazy Cavan came to Toronto, Steve was just like, "That's it. I'm really going to start working on this style of music and start playing it."

Steven Leckie: It was time to make a decision. The Pistols were finished. The Clash were kind of going reggae, which of course we wouldn't do. But the rockabilly thing — and there's a certain way to play it, like English rockabilly, that's really, really glittery — it's really cool, and that's the area we were more focused on.

Captain Crash: The Dog had unbelievable insight. I remember we'd argue as a band. We were trying to figure out a path to take. Where to play, where to go, who to talk to. And the Dog would say, "No, we gotta go this way." And the four of us would say, "No, man, no, lookit, we gotta go *this* way."

The Dog would argue until he was blue in the face and a year and a half later, the fucker was right. He had that insight.

Blair Martin: When Steve put out his first record, they knew they weren't going to be playing like this forever. You changed every couple of years. Nothing is going to stick around. You weren't going to be doing this five years from now.

None of us were punk rockers, really, except for the two days, in Steve Leckie's case, it took him to get his fuckin' picture in the paper. And after that, he was an aspiring rock 'n' roll singer.

Jim Masyk, Steven Leckie, Handsome Ned / photo by Ross Taylor

Ross Taylor: During that period we met a fellow called Handsome Ned. He wasn't Handsome Ned at the time, he was Robin Masyk and his brother was Jim. They were in a band called the Velours at the time.

We were watching Crazy Cavan at the Edge and Steve Leckie's sitting here, Robin was sitting here, and his brother was on the other side. And every time Crazy Cavan finished a song, Robin would give me an elbow and say, "*We* do that! *We* do that song!" I was getting fed up. He was in Mr. Green Jean coveralls and a straw cowboy hat and he looked like he just fell off the turnip truck. I said, "So who the hell are you?" after he was doing this all night, and he said, "We're the Velours."

Steve and Robin started talking and we found out that yeah, they were playing around and they were doing a show that week at the Ontario College of Art. So we went to see them, and sure enough this guy could sing. He had a voice that was unbelievable; he just floored us. The band was so-so, but when Robin sang he did have a voice like Elvis. It was deep and rich and powerful. Steve was actually quite taken with him and started having those guys open. This fusion — they were really a rockabilly band with country influences; Robin had spent time down in Texas and was unbelievably influenced by Texas music — that style of music started creeping into the parties we would go to and the scene we hung out in.

Tony Vincent: I went along with it because I was in the band, so it was either I quit or keep playing.

I did it because Sam was in the band.

We played a lot of covers, rockabilly covers. It was Steve's idea to do it. He was wearing smoking jackets and sideburns and sparkle socks and he had a waterfall [hairstyle]. We called him Squiggy from *Laverne and Shirley* because that's what he looked like. We got away with it. I don't know why.

Sam Ferrara: There was a lot of energy. Tony and I had been playing together since I was sixteen. We knew what we were gonna do next without even looking at each other, it was so tight. And Koch on guitar just topped it right off.

The rockabilly stuff was powerful. We didn't get a good hello for that; I think we started it too soon, because no one was really listening to rockabilly at that time. People were throwing stuff at us, yelling out for old Viletones songs.

Steve Koch: The big gig, the Gang of Four / Viletones / Buzzcocks gig, a lot of people had bad memories about that. But I thought we played well and presented our rockabilly-Viletones thing well.

I know people threw bottles at Steve. It was a test of wills, kind of. Steve had basically decided that it was time to wrench the Viletones out of doing the same songs over and over again and we needed to do something different; we were getting stagnant. He wanted to do some rockabilly and some country stuff, but pump it up because obviously Sam and Tony are like the Who, so whatever they do is gonna be loud and fast. We'd been gradually working these songs in, but this was the big presentation of those songs to a big audience and people were just not prepared to go for that. It was not his time.

But hats off to him. When Steve Leckie said, "I'm gonna do a Hank Williams song," that was probably the most punk thing he did the whole time I was in the band. That was very courageous, and rather than muddle along with the same old crap over and over again, let's take on a challenge.

But his audience was not prepared to go along with him.

Blair Martin: The guitar was still on a Marshall amp, but it was still rockabilly. It was like finding a way to grow up; find new interests.

Wayne Brown: I remember one of the nicest Viletones shows I've ever seen — ha ha ha, "nice" — one of the *best* Viletones shows I've ever seen was at Convocation Hall with Steve, Sam and Tony. At the time they were experimenting with a bit of a punkabilly sound, and it was good. It was really good.

It was probably one of the biggest shows Steve had ever done, and I think because they were playing Convocation Hall they were all on really good behaviour, probably for a few days before, and they really shined on that show. And they looked great. They looked *so* amazing. They had a little bit of that rockabilly look to them. Yeah, they looked really hot at that time.

Ross Taylor: Steve Koch was fortunately a proficient-enough guitar player that he could actually come up with the things required to play that kind of music, which wasn't just the flat three-chord thing like it had been prior to that.

But it didn't go over so well with the fans, initially. It was a big show; huge sellout, thousands of people there. Steve Leckie comes onstage wearing pink pants and a gold smoking jacket doing the Elvis Presley moves. The fans were booing them and everything else. I remember at one point Sam screaming at Steve onstage, "Let's do 'Screamin' Fist'!" Steve stuck to his guns through the whole thing.

Steven Leckie: I think the people that loved us for the "Screamin' Fist" type thing really hated it, but it seemed to be the smart thing to do. I mean, they didn't really know how to take it because the first time we showed it, it was at a show with the Buzzcocks and Gang of Four and everything so they were expecting us to be ...

But I came out in all haute couture rockabilly clothes that Eva made me; devastatingly great fitting, I mean really dead accurate, true '50s stuff. Elvis would have worn this. And that's how I came out, in the whole nine yards. But after a while I think people kind of, they kind of dug it I think. And Handsome Ned was coming up by then, too, so it created an atmosphere.

"Viletones Play Punkabilly for Puny PCH Crowd," by Geoff Gordon [University of Guelph *At Guelph*, 1979]: The group that at one time was banned from playing in New York for promoting bar-wrecking brawls made an appearance at Peter Clark Hall last Wednesday night.

People seeing the Viletones for the first time were in for a major disappointment. The band under Steven Leckie's (formerly Nazi Dog) tyrannical guidance has moved from extreme punk into something mellower called "punk-billy."

Throughout the band's violent early days, Leckie would go home to his Gene Pitney albums and get down to his early rockabilly favourites. It is in this direction that the Viletones are moving. As much as Leckie may enjoy listening to rockabilly, the Viletones are just not suited to this kind of music.

Close to one half of the first set was devoted to rockabilly. As much as the audience seemed to enjoy the music, the group did not seem to be as relaxed as they were when punk was played. The second extremely short set, though interrupted by a broken guitar cord, was much more fun, possibly because more punk was played.

Perhaps the reason the Viletones didn't go over too well was due to the fact that Peter Clark Hall witnessed the sparsest crowd of the year. Also, Bobby Lewis, Viletones' guitarist, was playing his first show with the band after spending some time with the Androids.

The best examples of the Viletones' rustiness occurred when they were playing some of their older tunes such as "Possibilities" and "Dirty Feelin'." Even so, the band has the talent and ability to go places. They sure could use a better drummer, as the present one is pretty talentless.

To illustrate what a wipe-out the night was for the band, they simply knocked over the drum kit and threw their guitars on the ground at the end of the show. Maybe some night with a larger, more responsive audience, they could show the people of Guelph a little more of what punk was, and reveal how commercialized their rivals, Teenage Head, have become.

Editor's Note: Due to poor attendance of the Viletones pub, the Rex Chainbelt pub, scheduled for Wednesday night in PCH has been cancelled.

Tony Vincent: There was a write-up in the paper about the Viletones playing rockabilly. Steve's really into press. He doesn't care if he's lousy, he doesn't care if people pay him, as long as he gets press. That's all that Steve cares about is the press. He loves having his picture in the paper, which I don't care much about. I just want to play music. I don't want to be a rock star. I don't want to have a write-up about me in the paper or a picture of me in the paper. I don't care for that stuff. I've never, ever wanted to be a rock star. I just wanted to be a musician.

*　　*　　*　　　*　　　　*

Steve Koch: I think we got Crash to drive us down when we played Hurrah's. It wasn't a real memorable gig. It was more memorable as an experience just to play New York City.

Sam Ferrara: I met Woody Allen there. I didn't know it was Woody Allen, though. We came in and we had all the equipment and stuff, and there's this guy sitting at this table with a big lineup of people. I wanted to know where the bathroom was so I figured this guy looks important, so I go up to him, "You know where the bathroom is?" He just looks at me and points.

I come out of the bathroom and Steve Leckie goes, "Don't you know who that was?" I go, "The guy who knew where the bathroom was." "That was Woody Allen!" "Oh, I don't like him much, anyway."

New York was fun. Steve almost got us killed, though. We were in this restaurant, really late at night, and he picks a fight. He doesn't know that this guy is friends with the whole restaurant and I'm going to Steve, "Shut up, will ya?" And the guy just looked at us and handed us some crosses and said, "Leave." "Let's go!" That was creepy.

Steve Koch: And we had a ton of fun playing in Montreal. We got in lots of trouble. Lots of fights and trouble.

Nip Kicks: We played a bar there, the Hotel Nelson, and the bar itself was one of those suspicious bars. Rumour was it was run by the Dubois brothers, who had kicked the Italian syndicate out of Montreal. And when we got to town I remember one of the people there said, "Don't worry about anything, everything's taken care of, have a great time." And the implications seemed to be that basically you could do whatever you want, and don't worry about repercussions. They basically gave us almost whatever you wanted, and for Tony that meant smack. And that was a bad weekend for a lot of reasons.

Steve Koch: The band that opened for us was called the Electric Vomit. So if that was an example of the scene, there *was* no scene.

Rick Trembles: The Viletones were violent. Steve was violent. The band that I was in opened up for them. The Electric Vomit. We were all sixteen or something. We were kids. We hardly knew how to play.

We did our set and they come and they had their beers on their amps. Just the volume they were playing at would make the beers fall down and roll around on the floor. We were right in front and our drummer would pick up the beers and put them near him with the intention of saving the beers and giving them back to the band after.

Nazi Dog takes the mic stand and just shoves it really hard into our drummer's face. I was right next to him, and the mic stand shattered my beer that I was still holding. So I'm left standing there with a broken bottle, and our drummer took off because he was in shock. It was the first punk rock show he'd ever been to, and I was contemplating tossing my broken beer right at Nazi Dog because I was so pissed off; you know, the adrenaline starts going when you're attacked. He thought we were stealing his beers, apparently.

So I look around and there's all these fans that came in with the Viletones; either fans or bodyguards or roadies, I don't know what, but they were really pumped up and getting into this potential confrontation. One of them looked like a body builder and all decked out in leather and he was just looking at me, smiling and making fists. He looked like he was going to tear into me if I did anything, and enjoy it. He looked way bigger than me.

So I just threw the bottle onto the floor and took off. It was a three-night gig and we had to open for them the next night, and our drummer didn't want to do it anymore. He chickened out, he was so pissed off. He said, "If this is punk rock I'm outta here," so we had to get a drummer at the last minute.

We did the show and our singer ran after [Steve] the next night and demanded to know what happened, and demanded an apology. Our singer used to stutter, so it must have been really funny. We hardly knew how to play and we looked like a bunch of nerdy kids, and these guys were trying to look really tough and they had this badass reputation. They must have thought it was hilarious to have this singer come up stuttering, "W-w-why d-d-did you d-d-do that?" Anyway, he apologized, finally. He just said, "Sorry, I thought you were stealing our beers." Which doesn't really excuse it much, but ...

It was that drummer's first punk rock show and he was trying to be nice.

Steve Koch: What else? We're walking down the street and a bunch of us get into a fight with a local guy. Somebody threw a tire at us. I'll never forget that. Why are you throwing a *tire* at us? That must be really hard. And then he ran away.

Sam got run over while he was in a cab. A bunch of people are piling in the cab and he's the skinniest guy in the world and he's not completely in the cab and the cab goes and his foot goes — *foop* — around the tire of the cab and it breaks his foot. So he got run over by the cab he was in. He went to the hospital and they said it was just sprained. He gets back home and it's not sprained, it's broken.

He's always got a broken foot. There's a million pictures of Sam with a broken foot. He's fragile.

Nip Kicks: Sam actually got his foot run over by the cab he was in, ha ha ha. It was one of the most bizarre things I've ever seen in my life. But that was another case where, I'm not even sure of the chronological order because it was the first and last time I did smack.

I could appreciate all of a sudden, in that moment, how dangerous it was because it felt so good. I have to admit, I didn't care about anything for that short period of time.

Luckily, being a control freak, I didn't want anything to do with that anymore.

But I'm also pretty sure that weekend we had Tony in the shower and he'd OD'd. That was a bad scene.

Tony Vincent: Heroin started to come in right after the rockabilly stuff.

I OD'd three times. The first was in Montreal and someone took a picture of it. I saw it, and my face was purple. Someone threw me in the shower and I started coming back. Then another time I was with my friend Jeff, and he started dragging me around. Someone saw it and said, "Man, what are you *doing*? You've got to call an ambulance." All I remember is being with Jeff, and then I woke up in the hospital with this bracelet that said "Mr. X." I didn't have I.D. or anything on me. Another time I OD'd a girl punched me in the heart and brought me back. It was the drug of choice then, yeah. A lot of people were doing it in the scene. It's like peer pressure.

Steven Leckie: Tony Vincent, in that era of the Viletones, wakes up in Montreal and the girl beside him has overdosed and died. She's swallowed her vomit. Montreal homicide squad, the whole nine yards, it's very self-evident it wasn't a murder, we see what it is. That was just a day in the life. When you have that kind of speed, it would have made anyone in Guns n' Roses blush.

I'm surprised all eight of us are alive, but I guess what kept us alive was the intellect; the knowledge that we're dealing in art here.

Elizabeth Aikenhead: I think one of the first times I realized heroin was around was at Freddy and Margaret's store.

It was a Sunday afternoon. We were hanging out there and I think Tony and some people had gone upstairs. And I remember being totally freaked out and really disturbed by the image of a belt around an arm and the end of that belt in his mouth. The guys were almost panting over the extended arm. That image really, really disgusted me and horrified me and disturbed me. That was crossing the line.

Then I remember hearing about the next incident at the Hotel Nelson in Montreal. One of the guys overdosed and they had to walk him in the shower and do all that stuff, and I heard about this later. So that was very upsetting again.

And then hearing about people compromising their values and their integrity to buy drugs. And often it would be a one-time thing — "An old, old friend from Scarborough came to town, got something, it was on the table ..." There was no resistance, even if it had been months, years; that allure was so powerful.

I just loathed that. I found it almost physically repulsive. And seeing that with Karla as well, completely together and then getting into speed and compromising everything that you say you believe in and all the responsibilities that you go on about; throwing it all up in the air and hurting so many people.

So I just said, "Okay, that's it." There was no hope, that's it. I think as a young woman who somehow felt a role and a need to be needed, or a role in being useful and helpful to people, that's when I realized there was no point. You can give as much as you can, and then there's no point.

Gambi Bowker: I think a lot of people were just thinking, This is the new drug this year, and those were the people who unfortunately ended up having severe problems with it or died.

There was an old-school crew in Toronto that were involved; they were the older ones on the scene, but it was kept quiet. It wasn't something that everybody knew, and you didn't have people shooting up in toilets at the Horseshoe or the Cameron House. The people doing it were doing it for themselves, and that was it. It wasn't part of the scene.

Unfortunately, a lot of people who got involved with it thought, "Because those guys are functioning, they've been junkies for years, I can just have *fun* with this." And it's not a drug to have fun with.

Elizabeth Aikenhead: [Our neighbours] Ellen and Raymond came over and they gave me this little cat that we called Ringo. I used to joke that the cat was such good company I didn't really need Tony around. So we lived together with this cute little tabby in the basement. The biggest piece of furniture was Tony's drum kit in the bedroom. It was massive.

Before long Ellen and Raymond had a friend who was moving out of her great apartment on Avenue Road. It was a nice second floor with two bay windows, so I moved into there and was trying to break up with Tony at the time. Before long we did, which was great, but it was very difficult once and for all to say it. As one friend used to say, "You guys were up and down like a toilet seat." Tony had really tried to clean up his act and be together and be the good person that he is, but it wasn't meant to be at all.

So I moved into that apartment. It was fantastic. I tried to make it home and Tony helped fix it up, but we were over. There were some drug issues that I wasn't prepared to accept at all, so I found a real strength and was able to say, "That's it." Sam Ferrara was instrumental in helping me out on a couple of occasions with Tony, because Tony trusted him and loved him and so was able to accept Sam's support and leadership in that situation. So I'm forever grateful to Sam.

Nip Kicks: There was a lot of trials and tribulations going on there, especially with Sam, who loved Tony dearly but was having a real struggle with the heroin. And again, I was lucky because that was my one taste and that was it. When I came back I think I slept for three days after the Montreal trip.

At that time not too many other people in the scene were doing heroin and it hadn't really invaded things at all, but boy oh boy, it hit large later. In the early days it was all bennies more than anything else; bennies and beer. For the most part that was the stalwart as far as drugs go. Coke hadn't really made its big influence yet.

But people weren't there for the drugs, they were there for the music, and that's the difference. In the early days you'd go and see all the flyers you could find on who was playing where and where your friends would be, and there were only two or three joints you could go to. Then I started seeing that people were going out looking for the parties, not the concerts anymore. It became the *parties*, and that was a switchover.

Sam Ferrara: I think the audience was more violent than the bands. There were times like backing up Iggy Pop in Montreal, I had a beer can right in the head, a full one.

Yeah. They totally sabotaged that gig. I doubt it was Iggy Pop who did it; he's a nice guy.

Steven Leckie: I was playing with him in the St. Denis Theatre in Montreal. He's pretty hip. He knew what I was up to, and the Dead Boys. And I guess that's pretty well all there was on the horizon: Two younger bands that were trying to go for the specific crown of Iggy himself.

They did [sabotage that gig], absolutely. Yeah, you know what they did? It was sold out of course and while we were on the stage, the house lights still on, they open the doors and the kids are running down to get their seats. And the reason was because the crew at the St. Denis Theatre turned out to be the same crew that worked at a big bar in Montreal that I played in with the other Viletones, with Chris and Freddy, and that bar got closed down after us. That's why it was sabotaged.

Sam Ferrara: We go on and nothing is miked except for Steve's microphone, house lights are still on, and we must have sounded like a little transistor radio on this big stage.

Rick Trembles: It was really hideous. The music seemed to have degraded even more. Everybody was hyped for Iggy Pop, and the Viletones come on.

Sam Ferrara: So people started throwing shit. I think we got through maybe three songs, not even, and we said, "Fuck this."

Rick Trembles: For one thing, probably the audience figured it's Montreal, how come there wasn't a Montreal band opening? If you have the Viletones, they're not that great. You could've given a Montreal band a break.

The audience tore into the Viletones; they just despised it. It was non-stop booing. I remember they had some guy who looked like a throwback from the mid-'70s with platforms on; he looked like a clown. Everyone was booing them and being brutal.

Steven Leckie: They let the kids in. They wanted them to see behind the curtain and not let us have any magic. And then they wouldn't give us the full effect of the sound and lights, and that would be a direct result more I think of a managerial decision on Iggy's part. I wouldn't do that. It would be my best interest to hype up the opening band, I think. But in those days, the way to defend yourself would be to make sure, especially the Viletones and Dead Boys, couldn't come close to what Iggy was doing.

He's a real fuckin' prima donna; he's just a bit of a prick that way. I would have been worried, too.

Rick Trembles: A couple years after the Viletones there was a movie – I'm not sure if it's *Crash 'n' Burn* – about early Toronto punk in black and white playing in Montreal. I brought along a small mickey of Southern Comfort; I thought I was going to end up partying the same night after the movie, but I really wasn't used to hard alcohol. I was kind of young still. I got wasted and went to the movie, and as soon as the Viletones came on I remembered that episode with the mic stand in the face and I got all pissed off and I was yelling at the screen, trying to get payback for what Nazi Dog did.

Everything started spinning and I found myself rolling in the aisles yelling and yelling and yelling, "FUCK YOU, VILETONES!"

The next thing I know, the cops are escorting me out of the theatre and I end up in the drunk tank overnight. I wake up the next morning with puke all over my shoulder and the cops just said, "Goodbye, you're free to leave." Go back home to my parents' where I was still living, all covered in puke.

So I got back with the Viletones. We're even now.

53. waking up fired

Mike Lengyell, John Catto, Ian Mackay, Paul Robinson /
photo by Michael Gray

"The Diodes Modulate Energy," by Mandy Harper [McMaster University *Silhouette*, December 6, 1978]: A new drummer has joined the Diodes in recent months, whose name is Mike Legyell [sic]. Apparently Mike "dropped out of the sky" and it was love at first sight. Mike is not as involved in the writing or theatrical aspects of the band but provides and nurtures his own creative inputs. With musical influences such as Buddy Rich and the Jimi Hendrix Experience, Mike provides the Diodes with solid rhythm. "I like to play hard, strong and rhythmically." His technique is effective.

Mike Lengyell: I moved to Toronto from London [Ont.]. I kind of wanted to make a career out of it, so I thought, I'll move to the big city and play for recording bands. So basically, that's what I did.

I just happened to pick up the newspaper when I moved to Toronto and saw an ad for a CBS recording act and said, "Well, I've got to answer this ad." It turned out it was the Diodes.

I was slightly different than the other guys in the band. They were all art students at OCA and I was kind of a journeyman musician. I'd been playing in bars since I was seventeen, just playing in cover bands, getting your chops together; it's a slightly different approach to those guys, which was the art scene thing. They just kind of picked up instruments as an extension to their performance art.

My first impression was these guys obviously had to have something on the ball. They seemed very intelligent and artistic in their own way and I was pretty intrigued by them.

272 treat me like dirt

It was a whole new scene that I was getting involved in; a complete change from what I had been used to. They seemed like they wanted to just blaze their own path.

Obviously, they had a record deal.

Paul Robinson: The second album was supposed to come out at Christmas. We didn't get a Christmas card from CBS, and then the next thing I know they'd sent us a letter saying we were dropped from the label. I don't know if it had anything to do with it, but they canned our album immediately after John left. That probably wasn't the reason they canned the album. Record companies are notorious for doing that sort of thing.

Bob Gallo ["Swan Song for Punk Rock's Diodes," by Steven Davey, *Toronto Star*, January 25, 1979]: We felt that the Diodes would start as punk and then . . . end up a good straight rock band. The only way we could make the Diodes' music more palatable was to go more pop. When I played CBS in the States the new tapes, they thought the Diodes sounded like the Bay City Rollers! They wanted heavy rock or disco and the Diodes died right there.

John Hamilton: After they didn't release the second album in the States, CBS dropped the Diodes.

Ralph Alfonso: We got the record deal completely by fluke and then we lost it a year later and I'm sure people said, "Well, there you go, how did they blow that one?" And it's easy. It's *so* easy. I wouldn't wish that on anyone, what we went through.

It's all the stuff that nobody knows about or cares about. It's all, "They got a record deal first when I should have got one." Whatever. The same thing would have happened to you. What makes you think it would have been any different?

Ultimately what it comes down to, and this is the thing which I've realized because I've actually stayed within the industry and now I understand the mechanics of it: We were in the wrong country. We were in a country that does not support its own. You would think they do, but they don't.

Canadian radio really doesn't want to play Canadian music. There's a reason why Neil Young left and Joni Mitchell and all those people. Canada didn't want *them* either. Leonard Cohen had to go the U.S. to get a record deal.

I mean, the punk scene ran into it. Every other scene ran into it after that. Nothing's changed. This is the one sad aspect; the one un-talked-about aspect of all of this: The only reason a lot of major labels sign Canadian acts is because they're legislated to do so by the government.

Tom Williams: I was in Warner, and I was so frustrated by our lack of signing Canadian acts that that was one of the reasons that Al [Mair] and I started Attic.

The major companies weren't really signing Canadian acts. Some of them made a reasonably good attempt, but a lot of it was all for show. They had to do it as part of their commitment to the government — not really to the government, but they felt they had to do it. They did it because they *had* to, not so much because they *wanted* to.

Ralph Alfonso: It kind of happened more in the '80s when all these mergers happened. The government would not approve your merger unless you guaranteed them you were investing in Canadian culture, so the record labels never talked about it. I didn't even know until I was working at Warner Canada, and every couple of months I had to count the roster because they had to have a certain percentage of Canadian acts. And now I'm able to look at things, having that knowledge now, where certain major labels sign acts and the acts only ascend to a certain degree of success and then they get dropped. Or they get two albums and then they're gone, because if you get to a third album you have to pay way more money. So it's almost a pattern like, "Hey, man, we tried. It didn't happen. Now go away and leave us alone."

John Catto: It was this thing that went on at the time. CBS Canada really didn't have much faith. They were really aware of being this backwater thing, so they'd always be riding on whether or not CBS America would release stuff. And CBS America looked at the first album. They never put it out. It got carried into America on import and then we recorded the second one, which would be the summer of '78. We finished it off at Eastern Sound and CBS went, "Oh, we're not even gonna put it out because we've spoken to America and America said, 'No, not really interested'." So because America weren't interested, CBS Canada just weren't interested in putting it out.

Ian Mackay: I was angry because I thought that it was better than the first album.

I think the first album was more authentic; the second album was a much more exploratory album. We started to try different things. It might not have been the best album to listen to, but it had a few really good songs. It was a period of artistic growth; reaching out and trying to find different areas to move musically. So in that respect it was a better album, but it may not have been a better package for the listener.

John Catto: CBS America did a refusal on *everyone's* album. They did a refusal on the Clash's album, too, so it wasn't any huge surprise.

Ralph Alfonso: We tried to play the game. Like I've said before, you've got a record deal one minute and the next minute you're out on the street and you're a bum. Welcome to the record industry.

But it was good. We were the only band that got a legitimate deal. Teenage Head got one of these weird deals where they were signed to this sort of dodgy disco label that had a distribution deal with Sony a little bit after the Diodes. By the time Teenage Head got their deal the Diodes had come and gone.

Freddy Pompeii: [The Diodes] just got chewed up by a record company and spit out and that was it for them. It's hard to keep going once you have that level of success and then you don't have it anymore, like a child star.

Ralph Alfonso: The drag is, Toronto was an incredible epicentre. We were in a brilliant position because we were in the middle of New York and England, and then you took the Canadian sensibility which always leans more towards the British.

And people would come here, like the Dead Boys were just freaking out at how amazing our scene was. And Greg Shaw flew up wanting to sign up Toronto bands. And, typically Canadian, a lot of the bands didn't want to sign. But he ended up doing stuff with the B-Girls, so the word *is* there. But Canada being what Canada is and not having the infrastructure … We didn't have *NME*, we didn't have the *Village Voice*, we didn't have *Sounds* magazine. We didn't have people like Nick Kent and Charles Shaar Murray to romanticize our scene.

John Catto: We carried on for a bit. It was like the life wasn't in it. So what basically happened was we broke up. I think we broke up to shed our management, you know? If it wasn't literally the truth I think it was the unspoken truth, because they kept trying to put us into these regular bar scene gigs.

It was just horrible. You couldn't play anywhere. You couldn't play at the college gigs; we did something at one of them and it was just awful. Regular bar gigs were like a nightmare.

Joe Owens ["Record Hassles Breaking Up The Diodes," by Katherine Gilday, *Globe and Mail*, January 12, 1979]: We just don't feel the band has lived up to its potential in terms of the market we'd originally envisioned for it in this country. We invested a great deal of money in them, and now we're just trying to cut our losses.

Ralph Alfonso ["Record Hassles Breaking Up The Diodes," by Katherine Gilday, *Globe and Mail*, January 12, 1979]: When it was all set to go, CBS marketing had no idea what to do with us. A bunch of them got together to discuss it, and the best they could come up with was that the Diodes should go out and promote seal hunting. We were disgusted with the idea and refused.

John Catto: We just kind of broke up and that lasted for eight months, nine months.

Ralph Alfonso: We had our farewell gig at the OCA and I came out and did a rant about CBS, evil empire and blah blah blah, and the band pretty much disappeared.

John Hamilton had left and we had a whole new drummer and everybody disappeared and we were kind of on our way.

Paul Robinson ["Swan Song for Punk Rock's Diodes," by Steven Davey, *Toronto Star*, January 25, 1979]: We're tired of the way we've been treated by our record company, our management and the radio stations. They've never known what to do with the Diodes and never will. We're terminating all our contracts. We don't want to be the Diodes anymore.

Ian Mackay: I went back to school and finished at OCA, and then I started going to U of T doing computer science.

Mike Lengyell: I just wanted to keep playing, so when the band broke up the first time I played with Michaele Jordana and the Poles for a little while, and I guess a few other local new wave bands; they all had record deals. I played with Stanley Frank for a while, he was a Canadian guy. I think he was from Montreal. He had a record deal. Who else did I play with? I played with Handsome Ned for a while. Johnny MacLeod. Who else? There was somebody else, but basically that sort of Queen Street new wave scene.

John Catto: I put together a little solo band that played around Toronto and had all these songs that are basically two-thirds of the third Diodes album. We did a bunch of shows at the Beverley and we did a thing at the Palais Royale, which was a fairly big show.

Then right in the middle of this, when it's all sort of going hunky dory, I get a phone call from Jula and it's like, "Oh, I heard this rumour that CBS are gonna put your stuff out." And it's like, "Oh *really?*"

Ralph Alfonso: There was an album called *Permanent Wave* that Epic Records U.S. put out.

They felt so bad because they weren't releasing any of this punk stuff, so somebody got the bright idea to do a compilation and test out all these bands that they had ignored. The Only Ones were on there, the Diodes' "Red Rubber Ball," and what happened is the album came out and started getting airplay on all these AOR radio stations in the States. By which time, of course, the Diodes didn't exist anymore.

I was working at Attic Records at that time and was getting all the American trade papers and I'm like, "Holy shit, what's going on here?" It looked like "Red Rubber Ball" was going to become an American FM hit.

Paul Robinson: CBS said, "Oh my god, what have we done?"

John Catto: In Toronto, the guys went, "Oh, look at this record. Isn't this one of ours?" And someone from across the office goes, "Yeah, we've still got one of their albums in the can."

They said, "Let's get them back in here and sign with them."

Ralph Alfonso: There was a new guy, Bob Muir, who had just started at CBS Canada and he was seeing all these trade papers and said, "Don't we have an unreleased album by these guys in the can? We should put it out." So they decided because "Red Rubber Ball" was getting all this American airplay they were gonna stick that on the second album on the off-chance that maybe it was gonna be a hit, and then they tried to re-sign the band.

It was a really strange paradox. We ended up helping them promote this album, but we weren't signed to this label.

Ian Mackay: I think it was Dean Motter who had a big influence on that; the guy who told me to go do a McLuhanist probe. He had moved on from OCA and had become an album cover designer at CBS Records. He told some of the A&R people there, "Don't you realize what you have in the vault? This is a fantastic record. You should think about getting it out there."

By then the scene was already starting to break so they said, "Hey, we've got this done, maybe we should release it." We encouraged it heavily, of course, so it came out and we wanted to get back together on the strength of that album release, to see if we could make a go of it.

Paul Robinson: CBS wrote to us and said, "Look, we've dropped you but we want to release the album. Do you want to sign back with us again?" That was only so that in case the album did really well, they would have us signed to them. We said, "Release the album and yes, we'll consider signing with you."

John Catto: And we're going, "What's to make us think it isn't going to be just exactly the same again?"

Ralph Alfonso: Of course they need our help to get it going. So we come in and go, "Hey, that's fine, we'll help you go out and promote it for you, too." Because we thought this was a way for us to parlay into getting a real deal with somebody else.

It created this really funny thing in the press. I think Jonathan Gross who was with *The Sun* at the time goes, "I just had the weirdest thing. I was up at CBS and I'm being offered toast and tea and the Diodes were there; the very same band that slagged this record label a few months ago, and now they're all buddies again."

And we were all, "Yeah, whatever. Whatever gets the music out."

Paul Robinson: They released the album, and about two minutes later we signed to RCA. We just went, "Well, sod you. You dropped us once." So we just signed another deal for the third album.

Ian Mackay: I think that all the political dust settled and we kind of got a second chance, and re-established our contacts as a band that had been. So the second time around was a lot easier for us. We had more of a groundswell of local support, of scene support; we were much better musically at what we were doing, but some of the critics just didn't like us.

It was tough.

Ian Mackay / photo by Ralph Alfonso

54. national unity

photos by Steve Burman

Caroline Azar: Trudeau was the Prime Minister at the time, and it was funny that you have the laid-back Liberals in power and this punk explosion happens. Then Reagan comes in and you have hardcore. There's nothing more tuneless. It's the sound of the disarray of society. The unravelling of western culture is what that music is.

Pete Lotimer: The one show that stands out for me was when we were at the Armories. I don't know how Mickey does it: He lined up a show and we were backing up Pierre Trudeau.

Stephen Burman: My dad was the treasurer for the Liberal Party and Trudeau was giving some speech, so we got them a gig there.

Bob Segarini: The Liberals had to blink back the tears. Ha ha ha.

Pete Lotimer: They said, when we got there, they knew who we were. But they said, "You can't play," I think it was "National Unity." But it could have been "Third Homosexual Murder." Who knows, because those people didn't like *any* of that stuff. They didn't want us to play it. Mickey agreed to it.

Well, the first song? "NATIONAL UNITY!" he screams, and away we go, and they pulled the plug. I was howling. It was all for nothing. Off we go. Mickey knew it was gonna happen. I'm like, "I lugged my drums up here for that bullshit?"

But that was a fun show. We just stayed there and got drunk. That was the first show I ever had the plug pulled.

David Liss: While they were there they had a copy of their EP, and they kept following Pierre Trudeau around and sticking the EP in his hands with a photographer trying to take a picture of him. Somebody kept going through the crowd sticking this EP in his hand, and he kept handing it off. And I don't know how many efforts they took — these days nobody can get that close to a politician — but in *one* photograph of him handing it away [Trudeau] appears to be holding the album, ha ha ha.

Bob Bryden: Literally, the picture is him handing it over to his Secret Service guys.

Mickey DeSadist: We got one of the band members' girlfriends to walk up to him and hand it to him. Because we figured if you send a guy, a guy looks like an aggression. You send a girl, a girl always comes across as innocent.

David Liss: That caused them a lot of trouble, and I think the show I went to after that was D.O.A. and the Forgotten Rebels opening at the Delta in Hamilton. It was maybe a three hundred seat theatre, it smelled like piss, and there were maybe under a hundred people; a lot of punk rockers and probably a lot of people from Toronto.

Chris Houston: The Delta Theatre was a real rundown vaudeville house that used to host the Marx Brothers and stuff. Parts of the plaster had fallen off and this place was, like, from the land that time had forgotten. They had punk rock shows there and that was kind of fun. The audience would just be steel workers stoned on acid drinking way too much beer, and the bouncers would be putting the boots to everybody in the parking lot. We'd be wondering if people were going to be alive or whatever.

David Liss: I think D.O.A. was part of the way through their set and through the back doors came dozens of guys in plaid jackets, baseball hats and baseball bats, and uniformed police. And they just started running around wailing on people and chased everyone out.

Never a news item, interestingly. That's one thing I remember from the idyllic punk rock days.

Pete Lotimer: Another time we played a place — I think it was Exile on Main Street — and I had a girlfriend back then, Trudy Trouble her name was.

We ended up going in somebody's pickup truck. We were sitting with the drums in the back of it on the way to Toronto, smokin' and drinkin'. She asked me if I wanted to some do some acid. I'm on my way to a show and I'm going, "I don't think it's a good idea ... ah, what the hell."

I walked into that show and that friggin' acid kicked in. We were backing up this band and this poor kid had a brand new set of drums. Well, here comes Pete Treason high on acid and drunk. I destroyed the poor guy's kit. And I couldn't play. I was a mess. Trudy was at the back of the bar laughing her head off at me. I was up there knocking cymbals over.

I'll never forget that show. I was so goddamn high. I shouldn't have been back there. Mickey's turned around going, "What the hell's he doing back there? It sounds like he's building a shed." That was funny, because you could get away with that back then. People still loved us. They'd be going, "You played *great*," and I got cuts all over my hands from the cymbals, my sticks were broken in half, Trudy's still back there laughing at me. But they liked it. You could be bombed out of your mind, as long as you went back there behind those two guys and you made noise, they loved it. They loved Mickey. He had the personality and he jumped around. Chriss Suicide was nuts and made faces and they liked it.

We never made any money. Maybe Mickey did, but I never saw any money. I didn't want to, really. With any of the bands I've been in I never thought about money. It's just fun for me.

The Turning Point, we played some great shows there, but the Blake Street Boys were always coming down to beat us up. Every time we played we heard they were coming down to beat us up. And I'm going, "Why am I gonna get beat up? I didn't do anything." I don't know why. I guess it was just 'cause of Mickey and his attitude. He used to slur people or whatever he wanted to do. At the end of the show it was, "Grab your kit, quick!" And we'd run down the back stairs and fuck off.

When we played two or three nights there I would stay at a motel overnight with Trudy, and the next day we'd wake up at noon and go across the street — there was a big park across the street — and just drink sangria on a blanket all afternoon and show up at the show just pissed. And I think back now and I could have been a single guy in a pretty big band, but I always had a girlfriend. Maybe I was scared to be a single guy in a big band, ha ha ha. I had the same girlfriend the whole time. She went with me everywhere. She came to see the shows. If I played three nights in a row, she came every night. I had no money, so the rooms we got were pathetic. You'd wake up in the morning and make all this noise before you turned the light on so all the cockroaches would fuck off, ha ha ha. If it wasn't so bad, you only saw a couple thousand instead of a million, ha ha ha. She never complained.

We didn't eat much back then. You had to stay awake so you'd be doing bennies and beer and acid and all this shit, so we didn't eat much. We were skinny; we were terrible eaters. We drank like mad and didn't eat. That's what you're not supposed to do, right?

We drove all the time. "Impaired? What's that? Who cares?" You'd lose your license and keep driving. "Who cares? Let them catch me again." They didn't throw you in jail back then, so it was okay. How I was gonna make it to thirty, I don't know. I don't know how we didn't die in car crashes because we were pissed all the time, weaving around and friggin' too drunk to even be driving. But we never got in an accident. Nothing ever happened. But yeah, the amount of drinking that went on, my boss back then swore I wouldn't make thirty, and when I turned thirty he was just shaking his head going, "How'd you do it?" Then I made forty and I'm *still* going. I quit drinking a few years ago; that's probably helped, ha ha ha.

I was glad I left when I did. And they did well, but I don't think I had the drumming potential to take them as far as they went at that time. So I left and I was happy I left, but I kept playing and I got better.

When I was in the band, I might have maybe become accustomed to liking that shock thing a little bit. Some guys were just out playing bars, but *we* were backing up Pierre Trudeau and got unplugged. People talk about that. They don't talk about the show we did at the Turning Point, they talk about Mickey going, "I'm gonna play that song. The Prime Minister ain't telling me that I can't play that song."

But in another way, I didn't share the desire to go on doing it. It was a lot of political stuff, and that's mainly why I left the band. I just wanted to rock 'n' roll and he wanted to sing about, you know, bombing the boats, and I don't know why I left because of that but it just wasn't what I wanted.

If I hadn't have quit the Rebels my life would probably be different. I think so because if I would have got better and released those albums that they did ... they did a lot of touring. I never did that.

I left before all that started. Which is probably a good thing because I only had one change of clothes back then, ha ha ha. I wasn't ready to tour.

*   *   *   *   **

Bob Bryden: I had forgotten how much fun and friendship Chris Houston and I shared before he was in the Rebels. He was one of the kids who used to come in and hang out at Star all the time.

I [remember] Chris and I travelling to Toronto together to see the Rebels at the Turning Point and being denied entry 'cause of it being sold out. How's that: The producer and the next bassist can't get in to see the band.

Chris Houston: It was Bob that really turned me on to Mickey. He had a picture up behind him at Star Records and he'd point to Mickey's picture with his Flying V and his hair. And it was kind of Bob pointing out the qualities of Mike that really made me think, Okay, I've gotta work with this guy.

Mickey DeSadist: Houston was a student at the same school I went to. I ran into him outside the school. I don't know what he was doing there, because I was already finished. I don't know what I was doing there, even.

Houston, he sold Gord Lewis a guitar and he was bragging about it. And I don't know if Houston knew anything about anything at that time, but he seemed to know something about something, anyways. So I talked to him and he learned to play bass and he was a guy that kind of had a lot of wacky ideas and they sounded fun, so I hung out with Houston.

Chris Houston: He used to work at I think Woolco or something, and he'd get the new employees to charge up all the electric drills, the cordless ones, and put them in the kids department. When you have kind of a backward town, people like Mickey can have a lot of fun.

One thing about Mickey is that he's always been a really great player. He knows his music really well and he takes it seriously. When we first started out in punk rock they said we couldn't play, our music was shit, blah, blah, blah. Because of that, you'd really work hard at making your music legit. The bands that lasted were very serious about their music when they weren't perceived as being musical people.

I was in a band called Middle Class Noise with Dan Jones, who was an author. Middle Class Noise were pretty hilarious, then I was in a band called Rich And Bored. Then I really wanted to be in a *real* band. Mickey hung out at the Westdale Tim Horton's donuts, so in order to get into Forgotten Rebels I'd have to hang out at Tim Horton's and talk to Mickey to prove myself to be in the band. He held court there. That's where he kind of ruled. Ha ha ha.

The first gig I did with the Forgotten Rebels was at the Turning Point. It was a fabulous bar. You could be six years old and get served there. I borrowed the Westdale [High School] drum kit to go do this gig, I was driving with the Rebels, and it was my first gig at a bar.

There was a set of teeth removed from somebody's head. Mickey kept one as a memento. There were six broken arms, three broken legs, I think two people had their rib cages collapse, I'm onstage trying to play and I'm looking out there going, "Wow, this is what bars are like?"

There were all sorts of people who had emotional problems who would break beer glasses and roll around in them trying to be Iggy. There was I'm sure a lot of future schizophrenics of Canada who were at those early gigs, because they had found other people that were kind of wacky. Some people really took it seriously, and for other people it was just to dress up.

Throughout all that time period there were horrible acts of violence. I'll hopefully never witness anything like that again in my life.

Mickey DeSadist: The sobriety was kind of important to me. If you could get through a show with your instruments playing, I was happy. Otherwise I wasn't happy. Some people would party too much. Pete liked to party and Carl liked to party. I'll never forget the time Carl, holding his bass, turns to Houston and goes, "Chris, can you tune this for me? It keeps melting in my hands," ha ha ha.

Chris Houston: I think on that gig we rented three separate PA systems; *one* of them made it to the club. We laughed when we went by this car on the highway. We went, "That looks like the car with the PA in it," and it was. Everything that could go wrong ...

Chris Houston, Mickey DeSadist / photo by Ric Taylor

55. (OFF) white WEDDING

Margaret Barnes-DelColle: Fred and I decided to get married. We'd been together for like, ten years. So we just got married at City Hall. Next door was Teen Agency, where Gail Manning and the guy that ran it with her, Paul Kobak, had a motorcycle. I think he gave us a motorcycle escort down to City Hall.

Fred had dyed his hair black and wore black leather pants and a black shirt with this sequined thing across the yoke. I wore a beige spandex dress that I made with a leopard skin chiffon over top kind of thing, and I made Nora's dress for the wedding.

Captain Crash: And the ten-year-old kid, ha ha ha.

Margaret Barnes-DelColle: Christopher wore his little suit.

Freddy Pompeii: It was a real freaky wedding. It was a leather wedding. It was the most different wedding I ever saw. There were all these freaks that filed into City Hall. It was really neat. A wedding to remember.

Captain Crash: Nellica had the reception at her place on Maitland. She had this great big two- or three-bedroom apartment. It was quite lovely. She got all the flowers and decorated the house, but where she got them from was from Mount Pleasant Cemetery the night before, so there were all these funeral arrangements all over the apartment, ha ha ha.

Freddy Pompeii: I remember sitting there looking around me and seeing all these fuckin' freaks, ha ha ha. It was a mixture of fans and friends that were there.

That was the first part of the party. Then the second part was the Secrets played at the Edge. We did a little Viletones reunion and Steven got up with me and Chris and Motor and we played "Screamin' Fist" and a couple other tunes. Somebody in the audience said, "*Viletones!*" And Steven said, "This is the Secrets, this isn't the Viletones!" Ha ha ha. He got all hot under the collar.

Mike Anderson: That was a real drink-up. Ha ha ha. The family was all there. It was pretty crowded and it's all a blur to me. I just remember picking up my bass drum and lifting it over my head.

Freddy Pompeii: I go into the bathroom at one point and there's everybody in there trying to mainline and mix up their dope and it's like, "Awww, Jesus Christ, keep this door closed. I don't want my parents or Margaret's parents coming in here. Do it *later*, you know? Don't do it here."

And I remember my dad sitting there, and he's looking at me and looking at all the people with different-coloured hair and spiky hairdos and tight clothes and leather and tattoos and stuff and he says, "Ever since those mop top guys from England, you kids have never been the same." I'm thinking to myself, What's he talking about? Then I realized he meant the Beatles. Ha ha ha, "You kids have never been the same."

It was a pretty rowdy wedding.

Margaret Barnes-DelColle: Fred's parents showed up at the last minute and they were completely mortified. They were good Catholics and it was this punk rock wedding. They were like, "What is going on?" They were pissed off the whole time.

They gave us money; people had taken a collection. As crazy as it was, it was so sweet. They pulled that all together. We had no clue. It was a big surprise and everybody was just so great.

Freddy Pompeii: We had a limo waiting outside for us, and Crash had bought us a honeymoon in Niagara Falls.

We had a nice suite that was overlooking the falls. It wasn't open season yet. It wasn't the tourist season yet. Crash got a pretty good price so he got us a really nice suite. It was like the main suite in the hotel. That was kind of neat.

Margaret Barnes-DelColle: It was May, and we got there and it was unseasonably cold, really cold, and the hotel had turned off the heat. We were freezing every night and we were like, "Can we get extra blankets?" Because we were on the side of the falls, so the wind was blowing up against the windows and we were freezing.

Freddy Pompeii: The marriage lasted a pretty long time. Me and Margaret were together for twenty-three years before we split up, and neither of us regretted it. It was a good time.

The only bad time was the heroin time. That was the really sad part, but once we got out of that shit we were doing fine again.

56. DanGer Boy

Nip Kicks: I think one of the turning points with the violence in the scene was when one of the Blake Street Boys, Tony, was murdered. He was stabbed seventeen times. Although it didn't happen at a punk gig it struck some of us home, because the guy was eighteen years old. One of the nicest guys on Blake Street; one of the most innocent guys. The kind of guy who would never pick a fight, but would finish it.

Steven Leckie: We had two real hotshot London roadies, Gary Vortex and Scratch, and they were real, for real fighters, Scratch especially. There'd be these brawls that looked like scenes out of *Raging Bull* with Scratch taking on, I swear to God, like three of the Blake Street Boys. You could see Scratch, with like ... He should get his nose fixed. I got mine broken then, too; you can sometimes see it. He got his smashed in; never got it fixed, though.

Steve Koch: It was almost typical that there would be a fight at a Turning Point gig. Big fights; sometimes the whole bar would erupt.

There was a bunch of Millie brothers, a whole bunch of them, east-end Irish kids: Relatively poor, feisty, looking for trouble. I kind of befriended Tim Millie and I remember him telling me one time, "I'll fight anybody. I'll fight any two guys. I don't care." And I'm thinking, Fight any *two* guys? I don't even want to fight *one* guy.

But fighting for him was a way of life, and it was just fine. He'd fight any two guys right now. I remember seeing Joe Millie walk by once in a full body cast from his belt line up to his neck, arms out like this with pins along his neck holding his head up.

Steven Leckie: Lots of them are dead now, like the Millies. For the most part, they were pretty good. And lastly, they were a certain kind of bodyguard system.

That was part of the thing. When you went to a punk show you could sort of smell the blood, literally. I mean it. It does have a certain odour, with an earthy thickness to it.

I'm really lucky I got to do all that. Like I got to feel what people write about. Really, really, there's a loneliness to it, but it's a magnificent quest that only leads in a circle, ultimately. Because for some reason I never gave a shit about money, and I guess I kind of knew what I would and wouldn't get from this life. So Blake Street Boys are tied in with that. I understood these guys. I understood that you're the ones that aren't gonna get a lot of the stuff in life, but you can get *this*. So I think that's what their attraction was — that it was a for real thing. We had things that they could relate to, that they were doing. Yeah, that's what they were attracted to, just the *truth* of it. We got a payoff, too. Having them around was a good buffer.

Sam Ferrara: Those guys used to follow us around to every gig and start shit. Well, Steve would instigate it, too. There was a point where we couldn't play anywhere, hardly, because the bar was just like, "No, those boys will show up."

Captain Crash: It was scary then, Blake Street Boys and stuff, eh? They all went to jail for murder, every single one of them, over the course of about seven, eight years.

Steven Leckie / photo by Gail Bryck

Captain Crash: They killed people on Pape Avenue, they killed people on the Danforth, they killed people in the projects. One at a time, they went to jail.

Barrie Farrell: I was at one of the big wahoos at the Turning Point one time and I'll tell ya, the first two guys to run out of there were Steve Leckie and Tank. For all his bravado and eating glass, they were the first out the door, man, ha ha ha.

Anna Bourque: Steven was such a shit disturber. He'd go, "Fight! Fight!" He'd push people to it, and he'd sneak to the back and have a few drinks and never get involved.

Nip Kicks: It would be funny to hear Steve's take on the Blake Street Boys because his intent, or much of it, was to use them as his thugs, and it didn't work out. It didn't work out at all, because they saw through him as much as everybody else did.

They didn't like the idea of being used, either. He would try to sic them on people.

Steven Leckie: Blake Street's way different now, the whole city is, but they grew up together since they were little kids and they totally loved the Viletones, and I totally loved them. Because they were the ones that never get lionized, they were the disenfranchised, they were the Bowery Boys, and I had a, still do, soft spot for that — "I'm going to be your band," and they'd be like, wow ...

My main focus is the kid I'll never meet in the back that it was not easy coming up with the fifteen bucks, probably can't buy a T-shirt and drinks. That's where my heart lies. Not to the guy who's got a Hummer and Rolex sitting over there with a pretty good table. I hate that. So Blake Street would have represented the antithesis to that. Something like the Dishes was a very moneyed, very homosexual, pro-business kind of crowd, and we weren't that. So I wanted to take it even further and actually let them know they could really hang with us.

*   *   *   *   *

Nip Kicks: Scratch made the headlines a couple of times. The first time was at a soccer game.

Ross Taylor: Scratch was a guy from England, a huge Chelsea football fan who for whatever reason had to come over here; family something or other. He didn't really want to be here but was, and started exploring the punk scene and hooked up with the Viletones and became their roadie.

His second day here he sees a poster advertising a football game. So he goes to Varsity Stadium to see a football game. Of course, "football" to him was *soccer*, right? He sees these guys lining up and goes, "What the hell is going on here?" He gets drunk and goes to the field and climbs up the goal post. His picture made it into the *Sun*, hanging from the top of the goal post. The next picture was of the cops carrying him away. Ha ha ha.

Nip Kicks: The other time he made the news was when Scratch was arrested for wearing a dog collar. It was funny because I gave him the dog collar, he got arrested for a prohibited weapon kind of thing, and he fought it.

"Punkjunk: Glitter vs Criminal Code," by Lorrie Goldstein [*Toronto Sun*, April 4, 1979]: Nick "Scratch" Bartlett...is to appear in court May 14 on a charge of carrying a prohibited weapon — a $25 spiked dog collar.

Margaret Barnes-DelColle: I think the law at the time was that it was illegal to have a spiked collar on your *dog*. They didn't perceive that people were going to put it on their own necks or their own wrists.

At one point the police came in to New Rose and said I couldn't sell that stuff because there was a law against it. I got a couple radio interviews and I got a write-up in the paper. But I still sold them.

The sales did increase, but I had to keep them behind the counter. They became kind of like contraband.

I'm sure there were fights where people got hit across the head with a bracelet, but they were truly a fashion thing.

Lucasta Ross: Lots of people got ripped to shreds with those pointy, pointy studs. They *did* use them as weapons, and sometimes not even on purpose. But you're getting passionate with somebody and suddenly it's like, "You've just gored me." People would stick pins and things in themselves and if there was a fight or they were just dancing crazy they got ripped out of people's faces. It was disgusting.

Freddy Pompeii: Certain kinds of spikes were illegal. We wore the highly illegal ones. We had to be real careful wearing them on the street because the cops would take them away from you. So in order not to be hassled all the time, there was certain stuff we could wear for show and then there's certain stuff we would wear as the legal version on the street. But that was one of the things the cops jumped on right away.

It was sort of like a porcupine's defense mechanism. Most punk rockers weren't tough guys. They were mostly kids that were rejected in their neighbourhoods and their towns.

There would be one or two or three in each town and they would gather in Toronto, and they wore all this stuff to single themselves out so they could make friends of like character. They didn't start wearing that stuff for violent intentions, but it sort of got that way after a while. A small guy could be a little bit more dangerous if he had studs around his neck. If a guy grabbed him by his dog collar, he was gonna get a two-inch spike in his hand. All a little guy would have to do was start swinging his arms around and if you got near him, you were gonna get cut. So they became a symbol of "don't touch me."

In the beginning they were wearing them because they didn't want to wear turquoise bracelets or whatever else we were wearing in the '60s anymore.

Nip Kicks: And it was Scratch who made it basically legal to wear a dog collar. They tried to have him arrested as it being a spiked wristband, but he fought it in court and he won. It was a little victory, because that's when people could start wearing things that were not offensively spiked and get away with it. I remember that was kind of funny.

Paul Robinson: People used to just scream, "Hey Elvis!" at us all the time. We thought that was funny. Nobody had really seen people wearing black leather jackets and kind of looking rock 'n' roll. All the other bands were hippies, so you'd walk down the street and they'd scream, "Hey, Elvis!" Or we'd be driving in the middle of the night up in the Rockies or something, and people would undo their pickup windows and point their shotgun at us. It was very strange. We were not normal by their standards.

I think I'd be more scared of it now than I was when I was twenty, though.

Michael Dent: It was pretty scary back then until it became safe, thanks to bands like the Police and Elvis Costello, and FM radio. People looked at you and they just didn't understand, and because they didn't understand they wanted to beat the fuck out of you.

Mark Gane: You'd walk up Spadina and guys from Scarborough would go, "*Fag!*" And you'd go, "What?" If you were dressing a certain way, you were automatically some sort of fag. And they would throw that word like you were supposed to get into some fight with them. They were inviting you to get pounded out.

That was supposed to be really insulting, to be gay. And you'd go, "Who cares? Go back to Scarborough."

Suzanne Naughton: I had things happen to me that were so weird. I was standing at the corner of College and Yonge, waiting for the streetcar, and this guy threw a beer can in my face. I got spit on all the time because I was wearing a leather jacket.

Nip Kicks: It's so funny when you think about the persecution the punks had at the time. Some days it was scary to walk down the street. That's when the headbangers and the disco folks, before they co-opted our clothing, beat us up for it, or they'd try. So even walking down Yonge Street was a risk. They'd attack almost anybody, even our girlfriends.

Suzanne Naughton: One time a guy threatened he was going to bash my head in with a brick. We were wearing leather and stuff and these two guys were backing out of a parking lot and didn't check behind them. So I smacked my hand down on the back of his car and said, "Watch where you're going." And he got out and he said, "Don't you hit my fucking car," and I said, "Oh grow up," and walked away.

So they followed us in their car and cornered us where Dundas Square is now. They pulled up on the sidewalk, came out, one had a tire iron, the other one picked up a brick and said, "Fuckin' dykes, we'll kill you. We'll bash your fuckin' head in." They were so stupid. It was ridiculous.

I talked him out of it. There were a few times like that. A lot of ugly things like that happened. People got punched in the face for no reason; girls, guys, whatever. You had to learn to run on stiletto heels.

Wayne Brown: We had a big blowout at the Turning Point one night when the Viletones were playing. These kids from a dance club down the street all came to the show with baseball bats and they did some serious harm.

Nip Kicks: Johnny Garbagecan and maybe Ruby T's had gotten in a confrontation with a couple of the guys from the King Cole Room, which was one door over, ha ha ha. I think one of the disco guys had gotten cut, I heard with his own knife, and this whole scene had started.

One poor guy came running into the Turning Point where the Viletones were playing, all bruised up, and said, "There's a hundred people out there!" And there were. They had come back with their uncles, nephews, cousins; there was like three hundred disco people out there and they just filled the whole of Bloor Street.

Suzanne Naughton: I forget who came up to me; it might have been Tank. He said, "Don't say anything, just get up and follow me. There's a hundred Italian guys waiting outside with baseball bats." So we followed him and went out the back entrance.

Of course Steven hears this and he's right down the stairs.

Nip Kicks: In the club Steve rallied all the troops — "Danger Boy" — and he went down the *back*, ha ha ha, and everybody else went down the front. Maybe a hundred and fifty or so, whoever was in the club that could fight, went out front and there was a huge brawl all the way up and down Bloor Street from Philosopher's Walk from Avenue Road to Bedford.

Wayne Brown: They hurt quite a few of us, enough that a few of us went to the hospital. That was a pretty scary scene. I always escaped, ha ha ha. I always escaped. I'm not a fighter. I will fight, but I'm not a fighter.

But it's funny, because who did I escape with? Steven Leckie, ha ha ha, who started it all. He wasn't much of a fighter either. He was an instigator. Yeah, I escaped with him in a cab. All I can remember is looking through the back window and there were people swinging bats on Bloor Street, and people going down. It was just like a small mob scene outside of the Turning Point. It was such a mess.

Ross Taylor: When they were doing the Turning Point shows, there was a gang of Italians that dominated that neighbourhood that would hassle them all the time. Leckie and the Viletones and a bunch of other people, they decide they're gonna have this Punk March down Bloor Street, right through the heart of this neighbourhood, to proclaim their rights.

James Bredin: It was this anemic march down Yonge Street with about five cops. They actually weren't sure what was going to happen so a whole bunch of cops showed up at first, and they sort of sized it up and most of them left.

John Kancer: Everybody was giving punks a hard time, and this march turned out to be a bloody mess.

Sam Ferrara: I think Scratch is the one that started it. He mouthed off to one of the Portuguese or Italian guys and hit them or something, and all of a sudden all these people came. The whole neighbourhood attacked us. But the whole march was about, "Can't I just walk down the street?" Just because you looked a bit different you'd get hassled. I was gonna get a T-shirt that said "I'm Italian Too," ha ha ha.

Ross Taylor: They had a banner with them, and in no time flat they're descended upon by this bunch of Italians and get in this huge fight.

Sam Ferrara: I had this big motorcycle belt thing, and there were five guys on me and I was swinging it around. Nip got his head punched in, and Scratch did, and a few other people did, too. But we made it, ha ha ha.

Nip Kicks: It was interesting how much prejudice was imposed upon us, and yet we're one of the most open, welcoming groups around and quite self-policing. We didn't like bullies and bullies soon found themselves taken care of, ha ha ha.

It's funny to see how that worked. There was that diversity where you would be able to have long hair, short hair, no hair, blue hair, green hair. Every sexual orientation, every colour; I thought that was such a cool thing, and yet how close-knit a community it could be because of that.

Suzanne Naughton: We were iconoclasts. That's basically it. When you are, you have to expect the consequences of your actions and we were quite prepared for that. I don't ever remember backing down from a fight.

Nip Kicks: Again, it doesn't really matter who's getting hurt, you've got to do something. Part of the whole punk scene thing is you don't stand by and watch.

All those incidents, though, they brought people closer together. They bonded people in some ways, just like anything else. Like a tough hardship. It was a lot of fun — crazy, but fun.

Punk March / photos by Ross Taylor

57. Take Today

Steven Davey: The best party I ever had was a cocktail party for the B-52s when they first played at the Horseshoe. It was when I lived on Yonge Street over Art Metropole. Everybody used to drink like fish back then.

It started at five o'clock and people were told not to bring anything. All we had was gin and vodka. I went and rented martini glasses for seventy-five cents apiece and we had pickled onions and stuff. The last person fell down the stairs an hour and a half after it started. It was it like a whirlwind microcosm. This was a beer-drinking crowd, so they're like "Wow, you can have *ten* of these." And then, "Oh my god." People were just drinking straight vodka, straight gin, and dancing all over the place.

The cool thing about the fourth floor of the building was this huge semi-circular window looking right over Yonge Street, and the windows actually opened over the street. Frankie Venom of Teenage Head climbed out on this beam from the roof and swung four stories over the street.

Gordie Lewis: At the time he would do crazy things like that. He did crazy things like that onstage, too, like climbing up the rafters. Pretty dangerous things, really. He had a tendency to be like that.

We had a great front man. We had somebody who could command an audience. He's got that ability, and he had it tenfold when he was twenty-two years old.

Captain Crash: Toby Swann from the Battered Wives had a speakeasy, and upstairs there – it was getting late into the night – Nazi Dog and Frankie have a bet to see who can drink the most rush. Rush is amyl nitrate; you used to buy it in the tenderloin district. It was liquid and you could inhale it.

They drank the rush. There was a fuckin' L-shaped stairway with a window on the landing. Fuckin' Frankie did a somersault in the air, never touched the stairs, and his fuckin' legs went through the window and he almost went down to the fuckin' pavement. He was a story and a half up but he got caught in the fuckin' window.

Frankie stayed at my place that night. I lived at Jane and Bloor; I used to take the Expressway, but I had to take the fuckin' side streets because Frankie had to puke every thirty seconds. I never saw anybody sicker in my life from drinking rush.

He did that twenty-four hours a day; that's how he lived his life.

Frankie Venom [*Shades* no. 4, "Teenage Head: Them Again" by Angie Baldassarre]: We couldn't get along with our producer, Alan Caddy, who only cost us money and time. We were constantly quarrelling, everyday, until the album was mixed and ready to go.

We went into the studio and when we heard it we said, "Fuck you, no way." He kept telling us that that's the way it's gotta be, and we told him that he was full of shit. So he said, "Fuck it, I'm packing it in," and now it's all up to us. Which is great, 'cause who can tell us what we wanna hear, it's our band, it's our sound.

Paul Kobak: From day one, when we were in the studio, their first album was a nightmare. Largely because of Alan Caddy, and other guys like Keith Elshaw that thought he was a producer. The guy had a real tin ear.

Stephen Mahon: Alan Caddy had control over that first album. He just didn't nail a sound down that we would have wanted. He had another band, the only one I can think of on the same label, called Silver Connection and they had that song, "More, more, more, how you like it, how you like it." It was disco, so it was really like a three-sixty for him to take this punk band and put that on his label. But he did. Jack would have gotten the studio time, a deal was struck, and we went and did it.

Gordie Lewis: We did it in bits. It was okay. We had done some recording in Hamilton at a tiny studio, so again we weren't totally foreign to the recording process. But it was difficult.

Dave Rave: I was doing session work over at Grant Avenue and I was working with Danny [Lanois] all through '76, '77. So I remember going to Gord and talking about how Grant Avenue is a place we should go to. And Jack, it didn't make any sense to him, recording an album in Hamilton. "Are you kidding? We've got to work in Toronto."

So I brought him down and introduced him to Danny.

Gordie Lewis ["Teenage Head ... and How to Get Some," by Cameron Gordon, *The Nerve Magazine*, October 2006]: When we recorded the "Top Down" single, it was actually Daniel Lanois who engineered that session.

I guess we used him because he was a local, still living in Hamilton at that time, but also because our management company didn't want to give the job to a rookie. Daniel ended up singing backup and playing keyboards with us in the studio but again, that's just an example of how collaborative and how tight the scene was back then — it was a small number of people but there was a lot of overlap between everybody involved.

Bob Lanois: We were not doing a lot of punk and when those guys came in, I remember we were kind of scared. But we never looked back, and it was a great time. I remember wildness and lots of shoving and really loud voices and some falling down. And lots of great music.

"Take Today with Teenage Head," by John Mars [*Blitz* Magazine, March/April 1980]: Recently, the group went into Hamilton's Grant Avenue Studios to re-record "Top Down" for release as their new single. Grant Avenue has a relaxing atmosphere, and on the new 45 it sounds as if they have been able to devote a lot more time and attention. As a result, the new version of "Top Down" sounds more like a pop tune, the sort of thing that might get them the airplay they need.

Not likely, though, as most Canadian AM stations are more likely to play the latest Dan Hill record.

Gary Pig Gold: Why that "Top Down" single was not a huge worldwide hit, or at least got covered by the Ramones or even Beach Boys — *anyone!* — I'll never know ...

Gordie Lewis: Again, the beginning of the whole punk rock thing, we were considered undesirables by the recording industry. We were considered undesirables by the engineers, by the producers; it wasn't real music, it wasn't real musicians, it was this, it was that.

Dave Rave: The engineer was putting his hands over his ears.

Gordie Lewis: So there was definitely an animosity that we could feel amongst the people we were working with. Which I don't understand, because when I listen back to that first album, for a bunch of nineteen-year-old kids there's some really interesting musical things going on there, and I think that's why it still survives today. But we had to deal with that the whole time.

Stephen Mahon: We really felt like we were on the outside. We were just four punks that got let into the studio to do our thing and do it kind of quickly, you know, like a couple of weeks maybe and then that was it.

Alan Caddy was hired to work in that studio on a day-to-day basis, so, "What am I doing today? A soap commercial," You know? "Yeah, okay, today it's a rock band, okay, great," that kind of thing. So it was never easy to do that; that's why we never did like the sound of that record. We wanted our stuff to sound really hot, like the Pistols and Ramones, and ours sounded kind of weird, if weird's a good enough word to use, I guess.

We weren't allowed to be there during the mixing, although we did end up making a beef at one point and did go in and were allowed to sort of sit by the soundboard and make comments. Whether they really listened to us or not, I don't know, ha ha ha.

Gordie Lewis: And the Sex Pistols didn't help. All these punk bands that were coming out were considered commercial failures. The New York Dolls, the Sex Pistols; their first albums did not sell when they first came out, therefore this genre was not considered a money-making form of music. So the industry people weren't that crazy about working with us because they weren't seeing money at the end of the tunnel.

But that was just the attitude of the time, and all it did was make us fight harder. Because we knew what we were doing, and we knew we really liked it.

Stephen Mahon: I always compared it to the Pistols album, because that was just such an in-your-face onslaught. You could turn the Sex Pistols album on and it was just great.

Our album was a bit more thin. You could turn it up and it was okay, but it just didn't have that shine, and I think that's because we didn't have a producer that was thinking what we were thinking. Whereas the Pistols had somebody that was right there, cutting edge, and knew how to record guitars and bass and drums and make it sound like it's *kicking*. We didn't have that. This guy didn't know punk from shit, so that was unfortunate. That was just Canada — Welcome to Canada. You're getting an album, there's a tape recorder, it's recording; it's always kind of bush league a little bit.

It sort of regressed. I always thought that was kind of weird because the five-song demo was good, and I thought it should be at least as good as when we do our album, but it didn't work that way.

But it had a cool cover. I always loved the cover.

*　　*　　*　　　*　　　*

Frankie Venom / photo by Ross Taylor

"Teenage Head: Them Again," by Angie Baldassarre [*Shades* no. 4, Spring 1979]: "The band's not happy with the label at all, there's just no relationship with the company. Look at us, the stage is fucking shit, there's no money, the same fucking clothes, we're not satisfied with the gigs we're getting, we're not satisfied with anything right now. We hate it. I'm seriously thinking of getting into professional soccer or something, it just depends on how the album goes: If it dies, the band'll die."

This was Frankie Venom speaking for Teenage Head in an interview at the Mad Mechanic regarding the release of their long-awaited debut album. At the time their depression and feelings of frustration showed that obviously their patience had long since worn threadbare.

It's an expectable attitude, though, for a Toronto band fairly green in a studio. While major record companies usually tend to nurse their artists in their expectations of sound and style, only rarely can these artists really achieve in their discs the product they want.

The making of *Teenage Head* appears, from the outside, anyway, to have been a period of much turmoil. Venom himself concurs, in the same interview, by noting just one of the pressures of the product from the internal hierarchy of Inter Global Music ...

"I think it's going to be a good Canadian [album]. By that I mean that, although Toronto has done well financially with bands like Goddo and Hellfield, ours is going to be a good representation of Canada, it's going to turn other people's heads in other countries towards our direction."

Stephen Mahon: I can only speak for myself, I guess, but we never looked ahead at stuff. We would just take one day at a time, and every time we would reach a plateau of success it was just amazing. In other words, I never felt in my heart, "Wow, one day I'll get a gold record."

You often hear people say that they know they're going to be successful. That sounds phony when people say that. We just did what we wanted to do. Our gut feeling was the way we dressed, the way our songs came out, the artwork we picked, that was just us being us. In other words, it was never contrived, which a lot of bands were.

We were trying to do stuff like what the Dolls and the Stooges were doing. If anything we copied them a bit, but we didn't do that because we thought it would make us millions. Those bands were never successful, anyways. We always knew the Dolls weren't successful. They were successful to *us*, but we knew that they weren't mainstream at all, and it didn't matter. That's what we liked; that's how we wanted to sound.

So thinking about how fast it would go now, it was just "take one day at a time." We were super lucky; even if we only just made one album it would be, "Wow, what an accomplishment." To think that not long before that first album we were just kids from high school jamming in a basement, with dreams of being rock stars.

Gordie Lewis: The Viletones and the Diodes would have been our biggest competition, but everybody was. We would look at some of the bands that were playing before the punk scene, like say, Goddo, a generation older than us, and we *had* to be totally different than them. We *had* to be cooler than them. It was just mandatory. We had to be better.

And I remember thinking as a kid, too, I couldn't understand why cool bands couldn't come from Canada. Why can't a New York Dolls come from Canada? And there weren't any. It was all Burton Cummings, it was Goddo, David Wilcox. Nothing wrong with the bands, but why can't we have something really cool and unique coming out of this country? That motivated me. I wanted to be that band; I really did.

Stephen Mahon: I'm sure a lot of people didn't know if we were just a flash in the pan or what, but getting an album back then meant something.

It was just so great to have it all happening, to see the cover, to be holding it in your hand finally. It was a big thing for us. It was an accomplishment.

I know from the get-go when we heard our mixes we were bummed out, but we didn't let that dampen our spirits. We knew there was nothing we could do about it. Go back and re-record? I don't think so. We just swallowed the pill. The fans weren't thinking what we were thinking. They finally had an album of the songs that they heard when they came and saw us play. They weren't critiquing it like us.

Other than the production, the only drag we hated was we were hoping to get the thing released in the States or England, because we knew that was key. Canada's a small, little fish in a big ocean. You know how many times people said, "You should go to England"? I wish I had a penny for every time someone said that, oh my god, and they're right. We probably would have done great there, but it just never happened. No one had the brains or smarts to get us on a plane and hook something up over there.

You look back and you think what if, what if? That's the big "what if" when you watch the Titanic story: What if there were enough lifeboats? What if there were enough life jackets?

*   *   *   *   *

Stewart Pollock: We toured a lot, basically playing every shithole in Canada that could take them.

Stephen Mahon: When the first album came out we went the other way: We went out *west*, and that was pretty cool. Things got easier. CBS was distributing that album, which was a major player. So in every city, like Winnipeg and Calgary and Edmonton, there were reps there from CBS that would meet us and maybe take us out for a dinner, and make sure the club had promo and radio stations were booked with interviews.

Stewart Pollock: A lot of travelling in vans, pretty trying, but we were basically drunk the whole time. You just stayed drunk, and those were the days when you could jump behind the wheel of your vehicle and nobody really cared.

It was a lot of fun because we were breaking new ground everywhere we went, in a way. The manager had this slogan — "We'll Bring a Party to Your Town," and that's how we sold the premise of Teenage Head, as this party band, and it really worked. The music was fun. Every gig was great. There's something about that band; they *still* kick ass. They've had their ups and downs, they've had their problems, but I really think they should have got a lot bigger than they did.

Stephen Mahon: We ended up in Vancouver and there was trouble out there. That's when Frank did swear on the radio.

David Liss: During a simulcast in Vancouver on a radio station — there were no alternative radio stations back then — they were warned, "It's a live broadcast. Try and behave yourselves."

Well, Frank, very specifically, that's *not* the thing to tell him. Because he went on a rampage.

He basically, and loudly, and with much profanity, made disparaging remarks about the club, about the radio station, about women, about everything he could think of between songs — "They told me not to swear — well, fuck you." No delay. This was actually national news. So they were forewarned the next night in Edmonton. It was the same thing, different radio station, different broadcast — "Do not do that, do not do that."

They did it.

Stephen Mahon: They had to stop the whole broadcast halfway through and it was really bad news. It was like, "Well, you guys just ended your career, basically, because this radio station is an organization of several stations right across the country. Maybe all over North America. And you just offended them greatly by doing that, you stupid punkers."

We kind of went back to Toronto like, "Oh shit, what did we do?" Basically, what did *Frank* do? Because the star treatment — the radio and record company people there waiting for us and doing interviews and taking us out to dinner and stuff — as soon as that happened, it was just "Forget it. Forget these guys. They're off the list of people to help," kind of thing.

*   *   *   *   *

Chris Houston: Then there was the delightful Larry's Hideaway.

Ross Taylor: There'd be these big, wooden posts with cockroaches crawling all over them. You wouldn't put your beer down because roaches would crawl in the bottles.

Kerry Wade: I remember going home and finding a cockroach in the sleeve of my coat from being there.

Chris Houston: Fred Chagpar, the manager, was a real piece of work. He was a unique personality.

Fred Chagpar: I wasn't famous, so to speak, but if I went on the street people would say, "Oh, here comes the punk guy." I had nothing to do with it, but yeah, I went along with it because we were the only club doing it.

There were other clubs that wanted to do it but couldn't, only because they didn't take a lot of the risks that I did. I took a lot of risks, and Larry's was really successful; extremely successful.

Chris Houston: Larry's actually had an hourly room rate on the wall. When you went upstairs — fuck, it was so scuzzy — Larry's had a deal with the Don Jail that all of their [inmates] just out of jail could live there, but they had to work there and spend all their money there. So the staff were just the most delightful people in the world. And the rooms had shared toilets. So you'd go up into the band room and immediately you'd open up your suitcase on top of things so you wouldn't bring bugs back to your house, and you'd open up the door to the toilet and there'd be two guys sodomizing each other. Ha ha ha.

Fred Chagpar: Larry's Hideaway had a bad reputation in all phases of that business. Why? Because Larry's Hideaway was a hotel, so to speak. We had one hundred and one rooms.

We had three lounges downstairs. A pub, a dining room — which was then gone because nobody wanted to dine there, so to speak — and the lounge where punk bands and clone bands came in.

We had three floors. The first floor was for welfare recipients, and the other two floors you would not find travellers coming there to live or stay overnight. I mean, yeah, they would come, but they wouldn't like it because it was filthy, dirty.

Chris Houston: They had stalactites growing from the water deposits, so you'd see the big stalactites growing off the ceiling. Kind of a cool room, but it definitely had a sordid edge to it.

Fred Chagpar: It was known for two things: Punk bands and hookers.

Did we know the hookers were coming? Hard to say. If a guy comes in and rents a room, how do we know who follows? People would say, "Well, you're running hookers." Listen, we didn't promote it, so to speak.

My immediate family, which is my wife and I had a young daughter at the time, they were not too happy. They didn't know what I was doing. So every time my wife said, "How was your day?"

I'd say, "I had a great day."

"What did you do?"

"I booked some bands."

Booked some bands? What did I know about bands?

Chris Houston: Fred was like, "I don't care if you get on the stage and shit in the bucket. If you draw people, you're good to me. If you don't, get out of here." He was fantastic.

Fred Chagpar: I remember a local band I really liked was the Battered Wives. My favourite band. They were clean, but punk. Decent, mature crowd. Was it a punk band? I don't think so.

The second band I really loved was the Forgotten Rebels. Very innocent before they went on the stage, and as soon as they got on stage it was all over. They started to spit. They would, say, keep a case of beer onstage and they spit it out everywhere. I didn't mind. Not everybody wanted to do it because it would ruin your place.

So, getting back to how I would describe Larry's: It had a reputation. Was it a good reputation? Well, in the band scene, the bands were happy. The had a place to play. Nobody would give them a chance, and I did. The people who lived there and got their cheques through the government, they were happy because if their cheques were late or they needed extra money I would hold their rent off.

But apart from that, did I know who was following a guy or a woman? I don't know. I'm not a policeman.

Suzanne Naughton: The punk clubs were the only place you were safe from yuppies. Yuppies, to me, were like a cancer on the face of Toronto. There were too many of them. I remember being at Larry's and these two yuppies came in and they were like, "*Eww*, it's kind of dirty in here."

Fred Chagpar: It wasn't the King Edward Hotel, so to speak.

Suzanne Naughton: And I'm thinking, Fuck, this is *my* space. You're in my living room. So we started heckling them and saying, "Go back to Scarborough" — mind you, all the guys I was with were from Scarborough, but we were giving them a hard time. She mouthed off to me and I'd just got a brand new beer. I shook it up and I sprayed her from head to toe and soaked her eight-hundred-dollar outfit, because she was in my space. And they left, and that's what I wanted. Mission accomplished. Felt no guilt, no remorse, and if it had developed into a fight, it would have been a fight.

We had very little turf, and what turf we did was very jealously guarded and we were very, very protective of each other. If we saw anybody in a fight, that's it. Whoever you were with piled on top, because there weren't very many of us.

Fred Chagpar: If a stranger would walk in on a busy night and see these punks bouncing from a stage on top of each other, they would say, "Oh my god, they're fighting."

They're not. They're having fun. It was fun.

Chris Houston: Larry's Hideaway was such a strange establishment. You were just lucky to get out of that room alive. Either the bouncers would kill you, or there were strange people coming and going from the rooms.

Fred Chagpar: We had bouncers. There were fights. There were big fights. Did I want those fights? No. I didn't give them swords and tell them to *start* fighting.

Chris Houston: It was big; it'd be packed there all the time.

Suzanne Naughton: People used to go mental. Somebody would take his shirt off and dive off an amp for no reason, just weird things like that. And then it became what I referred to as choreographed, where certain kinds of pogoing were done en masse. And then the whole mosh pit thing started happening.

I got trapped once at Larry's Headspace. We were sitting stage left and everything filled up behind and started pushing us into the corner. Tables were being pushed and we were being crushed. We all had to stand on the table because we were being pushed against the stage, and we actually got handed out over the crowd. That was my first experience being dragged across a crowd to get to the back. I was starting to really worry because I actually really damaged my hip; somebody cracked a table against my hip. People were acting like assholes.

It got right out of hand. That's when it started getting weird; it wasn't fun anymore. The element of potential danger had become like grievous bodily harm.

Chris Houston: They called it Headspace for a while because Teenage Head was the head band there.

Alex Koch: When they were at their peak that was their place, pretty much.

Gail Manning: Paul had to sink a lot of money into the band initially. It was his band and so they were at the forefront; obviously the focus. They were breaking through and were a lot more popular at the time than some of the other bands, so they were easier to get bookings for.

Paul Kobak: Larry's Hideaway became known as the Headspace. I wasn't too crazy about that name, but that was all Jack [Morrow]. Everyone knew that.

Stephen Mahon: He had a certain style about the way he was gonna try and sell the band. For example, the very first T-shirt that was ever made, Jack made it, and it's the one that said "Blow My Jets, I'm a Teenage Header." That's him. He came up with that.

It's kind of funny today, but it wasn't our idea. Because the whole thing was never sexual anyway. It was always the [Flamin'] Groovies, and someone like Jack would never get that. He just totally got the whole sex side of it, so that's what he was trying to sell.

Gail Manning: They had already released their self-titled album. They had the most potential to get a record deal. They were really focused. It would be phoning around to labels; it would be phoning the newspaper columnists, sending out press releases to them, inviting them to come to gigs — really trying to get a media groundswell going, and that really kicked into high gear when Jack took over the band.

Paul Kobak: Jack had increasingly wanted to distance me from Teenage Head. He'd thought it the best if I branched out by opening my own booking agency, utilizing Larry's as a home base and booking two to three bands a night, seven days a week.

Stewart Pollock: Paul started Teen Agency.

Gail Manning: It was named Teen Agency after Teenage Head.

Stewart Pollock: He had this big, huge Thunderbird car; it was a really nice luxury car, and it ended up getting impounded. Crash was keeping his stash in there, so nobody could afford to get the car out. There was eight ounces of fuckin' junk in it. Ha ha ha.

Paul Kobak: Freddy and Margaret were kind of notorious that way. I was right beside them. Right beside them. That's where I had my agency on Queen Street there.

Margaret had her store on the other side of me. And yeah, sometimes spontaneously after a gig I'd invite forty, fifty people back to my place, which could barely hold over twenty. And do you think they'd bring their own booze? No. But there used to be a lot of after-hours things going on. There were speakeasies happening around the east end of Toronto, right around that area. We'd go pop in, three in the morning, there's some instrument onstage and we'd just jam around. Not that I played an instrument. All I ever played was manager and agent.

Back then most of these bands didn't have any form of management, and the first thing a radio station or a record company does is scrutinize the management.

I knew I could help these bands out, being not just an agent but sort of an interim manager for some gigs here or there, and I did help out a lot of bands. I'd be sending bands to Ottawa, London, all around Southern Ontario more and more. But once again, when you're an agent, what's ten per cent of nothing? You know these bands would be getting paid a hundred and fifty bucks for a night. What are they gonna do, slip me fifteen bucks? That's okay, I've got a store, I'll pass on that.

Gail Manning: I wasn't at Teen Agency too terribly long. I left and became the sole booking agent for Larry's Hideaway. I was booking all the bands in there I guess six nights a week and I had a little office and my office got broken into. The whole thing got trashed and all my demo 45s and posters and all the stuff I had got stolen, and at that time Jack had kept begging me to come to work for him. They really didn't want me to be alone upstairs in the office at Larry's because that's where all the hookers were — it was a pretty seedy crowd — so the owner was saying, "You better go work with Jack at his office."

So I just booked all the bands from Jack's office but became terribly much more involved with Teenage Head doing all their publicity for them, and that's how that happened. Jack's company was called Frenetic ABC, but everybody called his office Teenage Headquarters. Paul was pretty much out of the picture by that time.

Paul Kobak: In '79 I was booking Larry's Hideaway. They'd just invested into a brand new PA system which at the time I think was about twenty thousand. Which is about two million right now, it seems. It was a nice enough room, and once again I never got paid for anything there because it was a strange arrangement. Jack knew the guy that owned the building, and one way or another I never got paid diddly for anything I did there. But for a year I booked the room solid, seven days a week, and I'd usually have two bands a night. So that gave a lot of leeway to all the local groups that never had exposure.

I was trying to help the Mods out. We drove down to Chicago and other places.

Stewart Pollock: I got into the States a little bit with them. We [Teenage Head] toured with the Mods down through New York and Detroit and I can't remember where else. Philadelphia, Cleveland. But mostly it was Canada.

Bob Bryden: Ha ha ha, the Tour de Cleveland. They just basically said to me "Yeah, we're going to Cleveland, do you want to come?" It was only for three or four days. I said yes.

I've got to be careful because this is another one of those things where I'm really a stranger in a strange land. I was older than them by five or six years and not really into the party hearty scene. I never have been. I've always been thinking too much to get into that.

In one sense, it's the antithesis of everything I believe. It's just nihilistic and destructive. It was basically a drunken bash for four days. I'm talking about silly things like driving down the highway on the way to Cleveland, drinking beer, and throwing the cans out the window. That wasn't my scene then and it's not my scene now. They were just so messed up in that way.

Stephen Mahon: I don't even know where we played in New York. It was either Max's or the Mudd Club. It was kind of downhill from there. Philadelphia might have been okay, but Cleveland there was *nobody*. I think that was where only the Mods played; it was so bad and so empty that we didn't even play.

Bob Bryden: I was really proud of them, that Canadian bands were down there. This was before Teenage Head had any sort of rep, so nobody was really in the audience. Maybe ten to twenty people.

Stephen Mahon: I mean, here's these bands going down trying to play off this whole punk movement. But when you hit those towns, if the people have never heard of you, why go? The whole trip back then was if you were from England. That's why everybody went to the Edge when the Garys did shows. All you had to do was say you were from England and the place was packed. Seriously, that's the mentality of Canadian people back then, and I'm sure American people felt the same way.

Bob Bryden: Drunken bash from beginning to end pretty much sums it up, for Teenage Head, at least. The Mods would have all been in the same vehicles, but my main memories are just of Teenage Head swearing their heads off and throwing beer bottles down the highways all the way there and back.

Greg Trinier: Well, they're like rock 'n' roll. They play hard and they party hard and they're fun. But you've gotta be young to keep up with them. I can't imagine ever, *ever* trying to keep up with them past the age of twenty-five. You'd never do it.

Stephen Mahon: Back at the motel we'd get a case of beer. The Mods were fun to be with. They had the Jam and Who mentality. I think they were into trashing rooms.

Stewart Pollock: The Mods destroyed a hotel room down in Detroit and had to replace all this shit in one of the rooms. We stayed up doing acid all night and we totally trashed the rooms; levelled them. So the dressers and everything were flat, and that didn't really go over well.

David Quinton: A bunch of us got involved in this phone book fight so we were ripping pages out of the phone book, crunching them up, and throwing them at each other. It seems innocent enough, except you know how many pages are in a phone book. When you start ripping them all out and crunching them into little balls and throwing them at each other, pretty soon the whole room fills up with paper, so it was like as high as the top of the bed. There was phone book paper everywhere.

And then of course it degenerated into a wrestling match and Greg's brother, who was our roadie, got thrown into this heavy drapery by our soundman and behind the drapery was this basically floor-to-ceiling window. The window smashed to the ground and made a sound that you can't believe, it was like World War Three, and as you can imagine we weren't staying in the fuckin' Hyatt House. We were staying in a pretty bad part of town in a bad motor hotel, and the guy that ran the place came out with a shotgun.

I immediately ran to the bathroom because I was terrified, and I locked myself in there. He just demanded money on the spot; money we didn't have. So we ran to Teenage Head, who were staying also at the same place.

Stewart Pollock: We hadn't gotten paid yet – that was the big mistake. Word to the wise to bands: Get paid before you trash things.

Greg Trinier: When we went down to the States – they weren't really well known down there, as well known as they are up here. In Ontario they're like gods and down in the States they had no promotion, no one knew who they were. I think it was an experiment just to see what the reaction would be like. But we played places where there weren't many people so we just had fun. There were different pockets. In Cleveland and Chicago there was nobody there. I shouldn't say *nobody*, but the places weren't that packed.

Scott Marks: I remember we played our show in Cleveland, got in the car, and started driving to Chicago. About midway through the night we stopped at a restaurant on the road, one of those twenty-four-hour road restaurants. We were all tired. I remember Frankie causing a scene and then the State Trooper showed up. He's complaining about his hot dog not being cooked right or something.

At three o'clock in the morning, halfway between Cleveland and Chicago, dressed like a bunch of punks, this isn't what I want to get into, you know? If you want to make a statement, make it somewhere where it's gonna count.

Greg Trinier: We didn't make much money going down there. We would get half the gate and they would get half the gate, and there was no gate at a lot of places so we didn't have money. So we would all put our money together and buy a couple of hot dogs and split them between our band.

That was probably the most memorable thing, not having anything to eat for days. We were pretty hungry. Mind you, the bartender would usually give you beers if you were playing so that was okay, but you've got to have some food at some point. Beer is not food, although to some people it might be.

Mark Dixon: That was the only time I ever wanted for something to eat. I think David had a credit card he didn't tell anyone about. He'd sneak off every now and then and come back looking pretty happy.

I hate to admit to this story, but one night at the bar we took a tip off the table. Me and Scott were just sitting there and there's the bartender's tip, but at that point he looked fatter than us. So we took it and went and bought some hot dogs or something. We had to eat, so we stole the bartender's tip. That's the lowest of the low, but we were in Chicago and there was no end in sight. And David wasn't coming across with the credit card at that point. I don't think he was allowed. He did later, when he heard about how we were starving. He took us all out ... "But we're gonna have to pay my dad back."

Gordie Lewis: I guess that's why I kind of felt bad, because I probably knew that it was a big deal for them. It was a big deal for us, too, but somehow I knew we'd be okay. And it wasn't that bad, but I'd say it was like a fifty-fifty thing.

Again, it's not just something you can go and do. There's got to be some sort of plan to it, and that's why the first New York trip worked so well. There was a plan to it. You can't just hop out of nowhere and make it work, like we're gonna be the punks from Toronto and play these clubs and drive down and just hope for the best. It just doesn't work that way.

Again, it just taught us that it's not going to all be easy.

58. winding down

Joe Csontos: I had started hanging around at the Simply Saucer House on Steve Park's invite and got to know them, and saw a couple gigs. I saw them at Pere Ubu at the Horseshoe and I was blown away and became a big fan.

I had some friends at Guelph University and I said, "You *gotta* book this band, they're great." The single had just come out, "She's a Dog." On the strength of that, I think two gigs, this would be '78 I think or '79, one at a bar close to the university ... It was kind of a disaster.

Namely it was a disaster because, in my mind anyway, they were not of the fashion. They had been a band since '74 so they grew up kind of like a Velvet Underground, Stooges thing. Just by the virtue of being around, they *sort* of melded into the punk rock scene. I used to tell them they were way ahead of their time. Or behind their time. They didn't wear the accoutrements of punk rock at the time, so it was either one or the other.

Edgar Breau: We weren't wearing safety pins and the fashion things that were driving it. So at times we didn't really know where we fit in. Maybe we were in the wrong place at the wrong time.

Joe Csontos: For the people that really liked punk at the time, it was, "You have to be *this* way." So a lot of people didn't like them because they *weren't* that way. They were melodic. If the Only Ones had been a Hamilton band, that's kind of how they were. They didn't really worry about prescribing to any ideology.

Kevin Christoff: I didn't live at the House until '79, just as the band was breaking up.

Edgar and Don [Cramer] lived there. We still practised every night and sometimes it was a closed practice, but quite often we had somebody there. We had our own little scene going on. We partied a lot. It was a place where people could come. There would be beer and if there wasn't, we'd get some.

The band would be downstairs and we'd do our thing. That's always an attraction, isn't it? Somebody playing loud music. And of course you'd make friends and form alliances and bonds, and it becomes the place to go. That's basically it, and it stayed that way for the duration.

Edgar Breau: That's all I knew from the beginning to the end. I always lived in the rehearsal places and it was usually a lot of people hanging out which was okay at first, some of them became friends and that, but in the end it seemed ... With a band, there had to be a lot of drugs and drunkenness all the time. It was a way of life everybody was living, and it seemed to take precedent over the music after a while. And that's not how I had started out, or the band.

By the end of the decade I just couldn't handle much more of it.

Kevin Christoff: And maybe towards the end it became, more than anything, I think, a boredom thing. After a while the work dried up, and instead of channelling our energy into something more constructive like trying to get some money together and going into the studio again, it became a party hangout.

Edgar Breau: Things were deteriorating onstage as well. We weren't sober onstage. I guess some people can do it — heavily drink and play well — but the people I was playing with couldn't do it, and I couldn't do it. You begin wondering why you're doing what you're doing; what was the whole rationale of doing this in the first place, to spend all that time and then have everything just degenerate like it did.

I punched somebody. We played in Guelph and I was really drunk. Somebody started heckling us. I invited them onstage and I punched them in the head. I felt really ashamed afterwards. I thought, There's something really wrong going on. We didn't last much longer.

Kevin Christoff: The last show we played was a place called the Mississauga Belle. It was in a strip mall just off the highway in Mississauga. I really don't recall too much about it. It was a pretty dark, dank sort of place.

It was after that gig that Sparky announced he was gonna leave the band.

Stephen Park: There was a level of discouragement that was sort of settling into the band, and I guess I just started wondering where it was going to go. There didn't seem to be anything indicating that it was going to progress for us. I just felt that I wanted to pull out, which I don't regret. Life's like that.

But you see, I think the funny thing is, you don't have a good sense of time when you're very young.

You don't realize actually how much time you have, and in retrospect I think it's unfortunate that we didn't stay together and that we didn't move somewhere and try to shake things up and give ourselves a chance.

Kevin Christoff: Nobody talked openly about what they were feeling or thinking. Not to my knowledge, anyway. Maybe Edgar was talking about trying something different, but I don't think so.

I'm starting to remember now that Sparky maybe mentioned something to me just prior to the show. He didn't say anything about that he was intending on leaving after the show, as I recall. He just said he was getting a little dissatisfied with the way things were going, and he wanted to make a change in his life and go into a different direction. I was kind of trying to say, "Don't do it now, don't leave the band unless you absolutely feel that that's what you want to do." I guess he did.

Stephen Park: When I told them I was leaving, I don't think it came out as a surprise, put it that way. The mood had sort of degenerated for a time and so I think it was more, rather than an abrupt announcement, something that was kind of broken and then it fell apart.

Kevin Christoff: After Sparky left it became, "Well, let's get another guy," and there just didn't seem to be the fire anymore. It was at that point, maybe a week or so after that I kind of handed in my notice. I think Ed and Don already had another guy lined up on guitar, and I think they were intending on trying to find another guy on bass and making another stab at it. But for whatever reason that was not to happen, and that was the end of the band.

It just kind of wound down. That's the saddest thing about it. Maybe if we'd had a big blow-up onstage or something it would have been memorable, but it just kind of worked its way down. We were all kind of hanging on to the fact that this band could not break up, that we can't die, but there just seemed, in the air, a sense of just going through the motions. And a lot of it was boredom.

Stephen Park: It would have been interesting to see where the band would have gone had we stayed together. I personally think I was too egotistical, and that's why I felt I wanted to leave the band. I had my own issues in terms of what I was bringing to the band as a songwriter and so on.

I think now in retrospect, I have such high regard for Ed's songwriting. I really think he's got tremendous talent, so I see it as a privilege to play with those guys even though it didn't really, in the commercial / successful sense, go very far.

Edgar Breau: The band broke up in '79. We weren't a hardcore black-paintbrush-on-a-black-canvas kind of a band. And that was maybe one of the problems with us. I don't know.

It was hard to keep the thing afloat, and I'd been doing that really from about 1972 on to '79. Living a pretty wild life. It was hard living that lifestyle by 1979. I didn't want to go over the edge into oblivion.

Chris Houston: Someone committed suicide in the front room at Saucer House. A lot of drugs going on there.

Imants Krumins: It was one of our friends that lived there. It was nothing to do with punk rock or the band, but he just blew his head off. That's sort of when that era ended. At that point, I think everybody decided it's time to kill this and get out of that house.

Edgar Breau: The band was out of control in some respects. There was a lot of substance abuse going on. There were a couple of guys who were pretty strung out on heroin. It was just turning into one kind of crazy party, and the focus had shifted away from the music into more of a lifestyle thing. So we weren't really able to make that kind of jump we probably needed to make. We weren't very focused in getting the business end of things right. There were just too many crazy personal things going on in our lives.

Kevin Christoff: So much has been said about the various substance abuse issues. I don't buy that. We were no different than any other band. We drank, we partied, we did various other things. That was a factor, a contributing factor, but it wasn't *the* reason.

The reason was just boredom: Boredom of not being able to get a lot of work, to reach a larger audience, to see an LP come out, whatever. Just not being able to seal the deal, I guess. And then it did start manifesting itself in the fact that around this time Ed wasn't bringing in a lot of new songs — nobody was, for that matter. You know, there just seemed to be this sad winding-down period. The watch had run down.

Stephen Park: I don't think we were at the point where we were not creative or productive in terms of musicianship, but I think in terms of life, goal orientation, we didn't have enough focus. We were lacking that a lot, and that's where you need good management. We didn't have any, really.

Len Cramer: That was always Saucer's problem, lack of management. It wasn't so much do-it-yourself back then like it is now. They didn't have a clue what they were doing.

That's where Teenage Head had the advantage. They had the good management and the money behind them.

Stephen Park: I think the whole music business is a tough business in the best of circumstance. I do think we were very withdrawn and isolated from the rest of the scene, and that was not a good thing. It definitely didn't help at all. But would that have actually made the difference? Maybe. It would be a *maybe*.

Kevin Christoff: Ed and I have talked about this on many an occasion, when we say "what if."

We both seem to concur that we can pinpoint where we kind of went wrong and let things unravel as opposed to refocusing. What would have been better was, "Let's get into a studio and let's get these tracks recorded." To get some of the tracks down of tunes we were working on at the time that weren't like the old Saucer. They weren't something that you heard on the radio; they weren't something that you heard other bands at the time do on the stage. They were uniquely Ed's and, accordingly, uniquely ours.

But at the time finances were non-existent and we didn't have anybody who was backing us, so it wasn't meant to be. But yeah, with the benefit of hindsight that would be number one. That's the thing that leaps out more than anything, to try to salvage the band. If we'd have done things differently in that capacity, who knows? Maybe we would have gotten some more press; some recognition at the time. If we had tried to make a stamp of that time, get something preserved from that era of the band, that would have been good.

Stephen Park: I think it must have been hard after I left, the look backs and the what ifs. But you have to either go back to it or move on, and I think Ed's done a bit of both.

Edgar Breau [CIUT-FM, Greg Dick interview, 2007]: There were scary people coming into our lives at the house. Some really scary kind of criminal elements. I remember one night we got broken into, we were held up, and I had a machete on my neck; this guy threatening to kill me.

All I wanted was to get away from it at the end. It was kind of a release for me in one sense when the band broke up, because I could live a semi-normal life and continue to play music.

I sold all my stuff and I bought an acoustic guitar, I was really into John Fahey and people like that, and I decided I was gonna try to re-tool and learn to play acoustic guitar on my own.

Kevin Christoff: Everybody's got influences and they do factor in, but Ed seems to be able to channel those influences and make songs uniquely his own. He just seems to be able to cut right through to the heart and meat of a song, both lyrically and musically.

I hold him in very high regard as a songwriter. I've been fortunate enough to witness his development over the decades, and he's honed his craft and he practises and he works and he never ceases to amaze me. He always comes up with something really, really good.

I think at this point, what drives him is simply the fact that that's what he is, he's a songwriter. Wherever the germ of the idea comes through or what suggests a song to him, he's able to block out the everyday distractions of work and kids and everything like that and make that thing happen. So he can do it.

He has this inherent talent. I think he's one of the greats. I think he's one of the best songwriters out there, and I'm including some real great names, too.

Edgar Breau: Chris Stigliano had a fanzine called *Black To Comm*, which I think he named after an MC5 song. Chris has been putting out this fanzine for twenty-odd years now. Chris was really encouraging, and he had a lot to do with the eventual critical acclaim that the band got. So everything kind of happened after the fact. When the band broke up all we had recorded was a 45. The music that is on *Cyborgs Revisited* had never really been heard in the late '70s.

Gary Pig Gold: I was always very, very conscious while doing *The Pig Paper* that I wanted to cover music, and interview musicians, who wouldn't be irrelevant or gone altogether a few months later, when Punk became New Wave became Rockabilly became New Romantic or whatever. That's why a typical *Pig Paper* may have John Lydon on the cover, but he'd be right up against Buddy Holly or the Ugly Ducklings on the inside. Maybe that's why I suppose Freddy Pompeii was absolutely correct when he famously said at the time that *The Pig Paper* was the best science fiction mag he'd ever read.

But at least it's allowed me to continue publishing to this day. And I guess that's one of the things that first attracted me to Simply Saucer as well. They'd also staked out their turf years before "punk" came along, and as a result their music has never been specifically bound to that particular era. So their recordings have always remained available, somewhere in the world, for over thirty years, always sought-after and revered, and in many ways I believe Edgar and the band are actually just hitting their stride *now*.

In fact, a Saucer concert I saw in the summer of 2007 was just as powerful, in many ways more so, than the ones I saw in 1977. So there!

59.
You Take
TomoRRow

John Balogh: Unfortunately, when I started to book hotels and bigger venues, some of the bands were already vaporizing because the of the lack of momentum or nucleus behind them. Simply Saucer was one of them.

At the end, when it was free flowing and coming to a point when it was starting to be commercially melded, and steered in a direction where guys like Jack Morrow took control, *then* bands were getting paid. I can remember those bands getting paid five, ten grand a night. Now I'm sure the bands never saw any of that because the agent was probably fifteen per cent and the manager's end would have been twenty-five per cent, so there's thirty-five sucked up into the world. And then there would have been some pariah wart like me as the promoter who would have wanted at least ten per cent to do it. So out of ten grand, which sounds like a lot of money to a blue collar worker even today, it's *not* a lot of money. Because by the time you pay sound and lights and roadies and trucks and food, you know what? Out of ten grand there's probably fifteen hundred or two grand left. It's eaten up by costs to get you there, and create the illusion if you will.

I think it's credible to those days that those nucleus guys were half asshole, half human being. The guys like Jack Morrow. Probably if you talked to Gordie he'd have mixed feelings about that guy, from half asshole to half human being. The guy had some great attributes but was a thief. You can't really forgive one from the other.

He needed to have some humanizing skills. That's what should be offered in the music business; some lessons in humanistics, if you will. Because I find a lot of the guys at the top, they inherit this disease. It's called Shit On Everybody. And they seem to forget that everybody starts at the bottom and works their way up. There's only two people in the world that don't. One of them's a ditch digger.

Paul Kobak: I told you what kind of hustlers Jack and John [Brower] were. See, Jack was just waiting for my contract to expire in 1979, and when it did he locked up the band with an iron-clad contract, and things just weren't the same from there on. He wanted to get rid of me because I was too close to the band. Trouble is, the band wasn't listening to me. I really wanted for Teenage Head to go the concert route instead of playing bars, because that'll just knock you out and then you don't get creative and write songs anymore.

I just wasn't able to do enough on my own. I was too much of a rookie and didn't have the old-boy connections that these guys did. I thought it would be a great blend. It's just that no one could get along with each other.

I went to a lawyer, who unfortunately wasn't a music lawyer, and he just drafted something up on a couple of sheets of paper and that was in the middle of '77. So my contract ran out in the middle of '79. But Jack by that time had already steered me on to doing stuff with other bands. I was helping to manage the Mods, the Secrets; I was being called on by a number of bands periodically just for advice, I guess. The Viletones, Steve Leckie asked me to manage them. The Androids, there was a bunch of them.

I don't think there's much more you can say, really. The scene was just starting to open up, and that's why I felt that the timing was right to do something like that. On the one hand, I was already being edged out with Teenage Head by Jack and I don't know, I could yell at the guys in the band, but what's the use? They became indifferent and just too wrapped up in their own situations and they didn't pay attention to what was happening. And I found out later Jack was badmouthing me about this and that and the other thing to them, so that didn't help my ego much either.

Teenage Head, Crash'n'Burn, 1977 / photo by Ross Taylor

Stewart Pollock: They used to call him Buckle Flaps and Cash Kobak. He had all kinds of names. Frank was just so abusive to him — "Come on you fat fuck, give me some fuckin' money." "Kobak, go get some fuckin' beer." He'd just order him around and abuse him.

Stephen Mahon: From what I remember, Jack tried to keep Paul around. He knew we had a bond with him. But Paul wasn't going to be second fiddle to anyone, that's the impression I got.

At the same time, I remember him being excited because of John Brower's history. He had put on shows and things like that, and he knew that for a new band it was important to make connections like that. But I guess he didn't realize where it would lead to.

Gordie Lewis: Our management people got rid of Paul, which happens in the music business. Every band, I'd say every single band that has any success at all, has somebody that was there in the beginning, they've moved up the ladder, organized management has come in, and it's just the cutthroat way of the business. It's, "See ya later, no longer need ya." And it's cruel, but you know, it happens. All the time.

And we were no different, and that's what happened to Paul. I remember saying — I could see what was going on — I said, "Paul, really, you're not our manager anymore, *these* guys are, and you're the one who introduced us to these guys and they're pretty strong guys. You can obviously see that they're motivated; they're moving. You can be *something* in the band, like be somebody else, whatever."

He didn't want to. He wanted to be, "*I'm* the manager of the band." But there was no way; it was not gonna happen. At that point I just shrugged my shoulders and said, "I can't help it anymore because I want to keep on moving forward and I can't stay here. None of us can. We've got to keep going."

That's not one of the most pleasant things. I've got to live with that. It's unfortunate, but Paul couldn't do it anymore. He couldn't take us to the next level. He just didn't have the ability to progress.

Dave Rave: Rock 'n' roll takes casualties; you have to do something to make it, and unfortunately there are winners and losers. I think eventually maybe it does even out, maybe not, but you don't know. You just want to go, "Okay, right now somebody's going to help us out, let's go, we'll do it." And meanwhile the other guy is thinking something else; he's got *his* view of it and it doesn't fall in with your view. Then other people start stepping in and going, "Leave this guy behind, *I'll* take you here." And you go, "Okay," not thinking that maybe you hurt that guy badly.

You're just thinking, Oh good, we want to keep going.

I don't think it's done maliciously. It appears to be, but I think it's just we're all dumb. Everybody's dumb, and everybody wants to move forward. It's the grand prize. I think that's just business in the long run.

Paul Kobak: I believed in them. But, I don't know, they lost it. They became oblivious to me. I don't know how to explain that better. Jack, if you ever sat down with the guy, you'd be pretty amazed. He's got the gift of gab, better than I do. Well, *had*. He's dead now.

You know, I never made a penny from them, 1977–80. In fact, by December 1979 I'd relinquished my store to my cousin, as I'd accrued twenty-five thousand dollars in debt with my main distributor, Records On Wheels. In 1980 I had a briefcase jammed with receipts totalling thirty thousand dollars attributable solely to Teenage Head. Gary Cormier suggested a good lawyer to me. I paid the two hundred and fifty dollars for the visit, showed him my contract and receipts but when he looked me in the eyes and asked, "Do you really want to go ahead and sue these guys?" I thought about it and said no. I'm not sure what I was thinking. Probably just all the time and energy we shared together for "the cause." I felt like a woman who didn't want to take her husband to court.

It was always, "Give me the money this week." Gord was really bad for that. Nick was no slouch. Frankie, he just wanted to make sure he always had lots of money in his pockets so he could get drunk every day, which I think he still does. I taught him everything he knows.

Stewart Pollock: Frank was the one that everybody liked. As loud and as arrogant as he was, and as rude as he could be, people really liked Frank. Everybody wanted to be his buddy, and Frank loved it. Everybody he knew that came around, "Got any blow? Got any money? Buy me a couple of beers," he'd lay into them right away and set the tone right from the beginning of the relationship — "*You're* paying for everything. It doesn't matter if I've got money in my pocket or not, you're paying for it."

Paul Kobak: "Taken advantage of" — everybody that knows has reflected that expression on me at one time or another. "Oh, you used to manage Teenage Head. They did a number on you, didn't they?" It was semi-common knowledge. *Semi*. It's not something I agree with, but I don't know, it's got to be attributed to my own foolishness.

I fucked up. I trusted them. I've been shafted by enough people throughout the years, but usually it's at the very initial stages. I figure okay, I've known this person for a little while.

What's he need? Two hundred bucks? Five hundred bucks to get some kind of thing happening? And meanwhile, he's talking about projects down the road that we're talking fifteen, a hundred thousand bucks about. So you figure out by that point how for real the person is. You cut them some slack. If they don't pay you back or do things timely as per agreed, then you know that you could have lost a heck of a lot more with them down the road than you just did.

John Balogh: The other thing you have to remember about the bands is no matter how talented you thought they were, the thing that projected them to the next level was a nucleus of people behind them: Their management company.

Teenage Head were a great example. Their manager was an asshole: Jack Morrow. Everybody in that band would tell you that. He robbed them blind, but you know what? As a manager went, man, he was an in-your-face, sixty-five-year-old man who was dealing with a bunch of young punks, who kept them in order, and would go out and rob the places of as much money as he could.

I know, because I was a promoter. I would hire the band. That fuckin' guy would be at the door with me two hours before the band showed up. He'd make you empty all your pockets so you didn't have a dime in your pocket, so at the end of the night when he frisked you, if there was any money in there you stole it from the door. That's how tight that guy was. And you know what? For many years I saw Gordie's brother come up and go "Oh, I'm Gord's brother," and the guy would go, "Good. Fuckin' pay here and get the ten bucks back off of Gord." And he would. The brother would have to pay.

Gail Manning: He knew how to put the machinery in place to get the backers, to get the money, to get things done to dangle a band in front of a record label and get a deal. He was really great, I thought.

Paul Kobak: Once he had gotten his own management contract and I got left out in the cold, I remember Gary Cormier verbally berating me about that.

I mean, as manager, mine was for ten per cent, his was for twenty. So he'd take twenty per cent right off the top. That's how he paid his rent and his car bills and everything. But it's not like he never told the band what he was doing. And it's not like he probably didn't remind them that, "Is that your signature right there? Uh-uh. Well, this is what it says." I spoiled them by never referring to *my* contract.

Stewart Pollock: Teenage Head had great riders. It was booze galore. It was a full page: Two bottles of Jack Daniels, two boxes of Blue, two boxes of Heineken, a bottle of Kahlua, two bottles of vodka. It was an incredible amount of booze they gave us every night.

I think the manager really wanted it that way because it basically kept the band pickled, and they didn't ask about the money and they didn't ask about all the other business parts of things. Just keep them on the road and keep them drunk.

Paul Kobak: I would like to say I would have dropped out sooner from Teenage Head to save my record store from all the incurred debts. But at the same token, I learned so much invaluable experience dealing with people and working with all these other bands as well that that's a really tough one. I wouldn't know where to draw the line on that.

Gordie Lewis: We never said thank you to Paul Kobak. That's one of the things you lose control of, and certain things you just don't think of. But yeah, Paul Kobak really helped us out in the beginning.

Paul Kobak: They went as far as striking my name off the album credits after the first pressing of their first LP.

60. orchestrated chaos

Viletones / photo by Ross Taylor

Steve Koch: We played Welland twice. It was the New Dexter Hotel. Weird, weird, *weird* place. We got rooms upstairs. It was an old Ontario kind of hotel. All the rooms were painted green and they had those beds that were just like springs; little mattresses that were three inches thick. It was a place where derelicts lived. And the band.

There was a guy there we called Crab Man. He couldn't walk; he could just kind of crawl down the hall and stuff. Sad people. There was a little guy who had Nazi regalia. He was about a hundred years old. Weird, weird people there. So we played one gig there. It was fine. We stayed in the weird rooms and had some fun. I seem to recall Nip painting a gigantic rising sun with spray paint on one of the walls inside the room and nobody cared. It was probably still there the next time we were there.

Sam Ferrara: I think when we first drove up, somebody put up a bed sheet that said "The Viletones" and there was a big swastika. So we were fucked right from the start.

Steve Koch: The next time we were there, we had to bring our own PA. Sam drove; Sam had a broken foot at the time as I recall. We had to rent a PA, we went down there, set up the PA, we're ready to play, the PA is too small. It's barely working.

Nip Kicks: As I remember, we were in a one-horse town with one, maybe two bars, and this was the bar. The people, especially with "Nazi Dog" on the marquee, were coming there looking for a bit of a spoil.

Steve Koch: We're playing, we're too loud, nobody can hear Steve, he gets frustrated, he says, "Screw this, I'm not gonna do it."

So Sam and Tony and I keep playing "No Fun" or something for a while and then we said, "Well, this is just dumb," so we go offstage, too. We're just milling about. There's all these Welland guys, local hoodlums basically, and now they're getting a little restless because they came here to see the Viletones and they're hoping to get their fill of whatever they read about in the paper that punks do. It wasn't happening, and they were getting a little grouchy.

Sam Ferrara: I had a broken leg then again, too. Ha ha ha. There was biker guys there, and actually Steve Koch sort of instigated something. I was going, "What are you doing, Steve? These guys have a lot of friends, and they're *big*."

Steve Koch: Sam will say that I started it because there was one guy that said, "I thought you were a girl," or something, so I say something smarmy back to him and he goes all sullen back to his table. Then he comes back and he basically says, "Let's fight." I'm going, "Well, I don't wanna, sorry. I don't wanna fight." So we're having a little tête-à-tête, a staring contest, and he's way bigger than me. They're all big, those farm boys. But nothing happens. He sits down again, I sit down again, and then some of his other friends decide that it's just not good enough that there was no fight tonight, so they start fighting with Tony or something.

Pretty soon, all of us are there and we're way outnumbered. There's twenty of them and there's us and Scratch and Nip. Scratch comes downstairs, hears there's a big to-do, and he's always up for that. He's got his baseball bat.

Nip Kicks: There was no room to swing a bat in that bar. It was taken away immediately. He had a cane broken across his wrist and it broke his arm.

Steve Koch: I certainly remember that cry. So he's useless.

Nip's never useless in a fight, but he's sensible. Nip could probably take them all out if he had to because he's a martial arts expert, but literally there was twenty of them. So he's backing us all up saying, "Let's make our way to the upstairs and lock the door."

Nip Kicks: We got back to the hotel okay. The band was still intact. Everybody took off back to Toronto and they left myself, Scratch, who was on morphine and all bashed up, Gary who had a bad ankle, and his girlfriend Deirdre who was fighting with him. We're stuck in this hotel and we can't even go down into the bar because all the patrons are still there. The drum equipment's there; all the equipment's still set up.

Steve Koch: All night long these guys got nothing better to do than hang around the Dexter Hotel. Literally, five in the morning, they're still there just walking around. They figure we've got to come out sometime.

Nip Kicks: The next day we sent Deirdre out for coffee and as she's going out, the crowds start to gather. Next thing you know they've got lawn chairs out there. They've got their coolers. They've got cars coming around, dropping people off, picking people up. Meanwhile, I'm calling Toronto. We're all calling our friends around Toronto. I'm calling bikers and I'm calling guys from Blake Street. I'm calling everybody I can think of to try to organize a party to come down and get us out.

Tony Vincent: We were inside the hotel room just shitting ourselves saying, "We're dead, we're dead, we've gotta *do* something." I think Steve came up with the brainstorm — "Phone the police." "Yeah, that's not a bad idea!" Ha ha ha.

Nip Kicks: But it never, ever occurred to me in those days to call the cops. I never thought of *that*. But after being barricaded in this hotel for about forty-eight hours, Roger from Razor Records came down with the Ontario Provincial Police commissioner and a couple squad cars, and all we did was leave.

Steve Koch: The police give us an escort out of town. We left our gear there, actually, so the next day Sam and I rent another van — he's still got his broken foot, he's got no license — and we drive into Welland with Nip. We pull up in front of the hotel, in about one minute flat load our stuff into the van, and squeal out of there again.

Nip Kicks: I remember being barricaded in that room and looking out and not knowing what was going to happen, with this flimsy little corridor between us and them, ha ha ha. And I'm the only healthy one there. It was pretty scary.

And the whole thing started when the PA didn't work properly. If the band had have been smart, and Steve [Leckie] hadn't have been prima donna-ish and kept the crowd happy, settle them down for a little bit, it would have been all right.

Steve Koch: Just another day in the life.

Nip Kicks: I quit working for the Viletones. I was always there to make sure nobody got hurt, but if somebody picks a fight, I'm sorry, you're gonna fight it. And there came a point when I think Steve [Leckie] wanted Scratch and I to be more henchmen than security. Fight his fight. And we weren't into that. Neither of us were into that.

We had a bit of a scene — I think it was in London, Ontario — when he was having a heckle-fest with one of the crowd, but he had started it. And then when we didn't intervene, Steve turned on *us*. He turned on me specifically and said some interesting things into the mic, and we had a little shouting match ourselves to the point where the bar security said, "Hey, leave him alone," ha ha ha. But I remember he got me so pissed off, *really* pissed off, and I was so mad I was shaking and I was trying really hard not to explode. I was like a little pressure cooker.

I said to Tony and Sam, "Listen, that's it, it's done. I'm finished, it's over, I'm out of here, because I'm gonna fucking kill this guy."

We're going back upstairs and Steven says to me, "I wanna talk to ya," and I smile, thinking, Yeah, I wanna talk to you, too, ha ha ha. And we got in a room together and I'm thinking, This is it, and he turns around and pulled a beautiful move. Says, "Nip, man, I really love you, brother." And I'm dying inside because I'm just ready to tear this guy, I was just was so mad, and he just knew how to push those buttons to get you to second-think what you were gonna do.

I still quit after that show, but I couldn't hit him, ha ha ha. But I have to say, I certainly thought about it.

Steve Koch: For me and the Viletones, it ended in probably November or December of '79.

Why did I leave? I wonder about that. I think I was discouraged by the fact that there never seemed to be any new songs. It seemed like it was falling apart at that point because of how badly Steve had been snubbed by the rockabilly thing. He was in a bit of a funk, it seemed like it was going nowhere, and he was getting into a bit of a tailspin. I guess I just felt that it wasn't fun anymore, and it's got to be fun.

I'd seen the Demics, of course. I probably first spoke with Keith and J.D. Demic at the Buzzcocks show. We met them at the Black Swan across the street, we were sitting over there drinking and talking, and they talked us into getting them into the show for free.

I think I was later approached by Iain Atkinson. They had moved to Toronto around that time and their guitar player, Rob Brent, had decided to stay in London.

*　　*　　*　　　*　　　*

Demics / photo by Ross Taylor

Dan Husband [http://londonpunkrock.kicks-ass.org]: It's the summer of 1976. In select major cities the early punk rock scene is starting to shift into second gear. Keith Whittaker travelled to England that summer and returned to London Ontario all revved up about the so-called pub rock groups such as Dr. Feelgood, Graham Parker and so on. During the winter of 1976, a Toronto band called Rough Trade started a week's residency at a bar in London. On the first night Keith Whittaker and Mike Niederman bump into each other. Keith has the idea of the Demics or at least that type of band in his mind, Mike will be instrumental in helping it see the light of day.

In late Spring 1977, Keith and friend Lyndon Andrews are in Victoria Park (located in the center of the city) having a "kick around" with a soccer ball. Iain Atkinson happened to be walking through the park at the time and they recruited him on the spot for a band.

Keith Whittaker [*Shades* no. 14, November/December 1980]: Me and the bass player Iain Atkinson started it about two and a half years ago. I'd just come back from England where I'd seen some of the punk bands — Damned, X-Ray Spex, Vibrators, Motors — and I was really excited by the energy of that situation. The kids were nuts, they scared me at first. I went to this club in Croydon and the kids were going mad, jumping all over the place. Anyway, I picked up a few records and brought them back. It was just starting to happen here; Toronto had the Crash 'n' Burn club but in London [Ontario] there was nothing. So me and Iain just got together with some friends, held some auditions and got a band happening.

Iain Atkinson: Keith, I'd gone to high school with, and Jimmy, when I was trying to learn how to play I met his brother and found out he played the drums. So he used to come over to my house and play in the basement a couple of times with some other guys. And then Rob had an advert up in a music store saying, "Does somebody want to play punk rock?"

I phoned him up and said, "Sure, let's have a go."

And then he said, "I've met this guy," and it turned out to be Mike Niederman, and *he* knew some guy who wanted to be in a punk rock band as a singer. That person happened to be Keith, who I'd also talked to independently of that just from hanging around.

And so one day we all met over at Mike Niederman's with a different guy playing drums. He was a friend of Keith's called Nick Perry. Nick wasn't really up to the job; the first gig we did it was blatantly obvious to me that he wasn't going to cut the mustard. Then I started trying to find other people. The first other person we tried was Marcy Saddy. She came out and it wasn't really quite right. Then I got Jim to come down and it was good from day one, so that's what I went with.

That's how it really worked, no matter what anybody says.

Dan Husband [http://londonpunkrock.kicks-ass.org]: November 1977, Eddie and the Hot Rods play for three nights at London's premiere rock club, Fryfogles. Rob Brent sits at Mike Niederman's table. At the same time, the downtown London loft scene is inhabited by artists, printers, eccentrics and nut cases. Clothes and drainpipe jeans began to crop up amid the prevailing flairs and long hair. Pot and psychedelics give way to bennies and alcohol. The members of the Demics have first met in this milieu. Rob Brent joins the band as guitarist. Keith Whittaker was from Manchester, England and Iain from Cambridge, while Rob and Nick were natives of London, Ontario. Keith already had the name for the band, a Manchester slang insult meaning "loser," "dork," or "wanker." The Demics speedily assembled a repertoire of covers and originals, still rehearsing at Niederman's loft. A short six weeks later they are asked by Mike to play a Christmas party there. The Demics make their first public appearance at a "private" loft party for two hundred and fifty people on December 23, 1977. They are the first of many bands to form in London, and they have a crazed audience right from the start.

Iain Atkinson: London, Ontario in the '70s – I guess you would call it dull. There was nothing. London is a funny town in a way. There's a whole sort of arts community there, but when I first got into this stuff I had no idea it even existed.

You do the usual shit. You go to high school and do these same things that everybody does when they're in high school. Then you get out of high school and think about, hmm, what am I going to do now? So that became the thing that I did then.

In terms of being in a band it was, to a degree, a whim. There was no ideological element to it at all.

I hadn't played for longer than six months or maybe a year before that. I sort of wanted to be in a band so I thought, Well, I'll try this because it's supposedly about having a go. So you have a go and find similar, like-minded people.

In the Demics, nobody had really done anything before except for Jimmy the drummer who'd played in country western bands since he was fifteen, being dragged around, underage, sitting in the back there, falling off his stool piss drunk. He started early, I guess.

As soon as we started the band, a large percentage of the people who were in the local arts community — supposedly they were famous, I didn't really know about that, they were sort of on the periphery — were a little bit involved. Certainly supportive. That might have been part of what made it go over so well; the fact that this whole arty-farty thing that goes on was there. I guess we just tapped into it or something.

Gerard Pas: I had a really close hand with them. By that time I had already brought the Curse and the Ugly [to London] and was a member of a gallery and showing internationally with CEAC. I still had my home in London as well. I had a studio downtown there, a couple of my friends had studios downtown, and we wanted to see a change. We wanted to have something to do. There was sweet fuck all to do, and if Toronto had nothing to do you can *imagine* what it was like here. They were selling tickets to watch paint dry, for fuck's sake.

Andy Crosbie: There was crazy shit going on, like people putting meat under glass and letting it sit there for a couple of weeks and then inviting everybody to an art gallery and smashing it open.

Gerard Pas: So we wanted to try to do something and we met Keith Whittaker. I'd known him already as a teenager, a smoking-pot-at-the-park sort of guy, but he was hanging out downtown as well as drinking beer at the York, which is where we would often go. We got to talking and he said he really wanted to do something, so we got together and put up some ads looking for other musicians and we hooked all that shit up. They met at my friend's studio and we formed a little group of friends and started helping them.

Iain Atkinson: Gerry Pas? He wanted to be our manager and to a degree, I guess maybe for a month or two, he sort of was. He was trying and doing whatever he could do to get it some attention. I'm not sure whether it was effective or not. I don't really know. I was probably in a drugged-out haze at the time. That's actually not really true, but I was young. You don't really know. He was certainly involved and again, he would be a guy

from the art scene and that would be part of the crossover.

Really, in the beginning there was a whole lot of the art thing involved with punk. Certainly Rob Brent was the intellectual of the group, so it was all about art to him. It was supposed to be very orchestrated. As much as there may be a huge amount of chaos involved, it was supposed to be *orchestrated* chaos from his standpoint.

I think that Gerry's heart was probably in the right place. It's not impossible that he made Rob think about certain things, but he certainly wouldn't have made Keith think about anything at all because he wouldn't care. He'd just say he was a fuckin' wanker and that'd be it.

Did he do anything? I'm trying to remember, and trying to say something positive. Because my claim is *I* did, and Mike Niederman. It was just some sheer fluke that everything just kind of fell into place. Pure chance.

Gerard Pas: The Nihilist Spasm Band had just been given a big grant and bought a big PA system. As a kid, when you're seventeen, if you don't ask then they won't say no, so I took all that shit over to Mike's. We invited all our friends and had a party and the Demics played. They didn't even have a drummer at that point. Back and forth between studios is how it started.

Keith Whittaker [*Shades* no. 14, November/December 1980]: The first gig we played was in this studio that belonged to the town punk and he handed out free invitations. We knew ten songs and two hundred and fifty people turned up.

Dan Husband [http://londonpunkrock.kicks-ass.org]: The result of that show was a near riot. It sent the crowd into an electrified frenzy that spilled onto the rooftop and street and culminated with damaged cars, fights, and a couple of blocks of broken windows. Nick Perry now recalls that evening as "absolutely electrifying." It was truly the birth of punk in London.

Iain Atkinson: I'd say to some degree Mike Niederman was a catalyst for that thing at the beginning. He provided us a place to play and to rehearse. We sort of outgrew it to a degree within a very short period, on top of the fact that he's not going to want to have a million people in his loft every two or three weeks because it was where he lived. So we started playing in bars.

Keith Whittaker [*Shades* no. 14, November/December 1980]: We went to a club owner and asked him to let us play. He wasn't sure about this punk rock stuff, but he let us play one night and it was a success. We kept playing there and the club owner sold a lot of beer and retired to the Bahamas. Gradually we developed a scene in London which is now quite large.

Gerard Pas: We introduced them to all the other young people involved in that art scene in London, so then they had a core of people who were interested in them. And it was *fun*. They weren't doing, like, the Nazi Dog stuff; they still had a little bit of melody in their music, and some of the covers they were doing were Iggy Pop's "I Wanna Be Your Dog." That was very attractive, and London really needed it. And within a question of short months, they were packing that place every night they played there.

Iain Atkinson: Maybe there was some kind of subculture thing that was going on then that I didn't know about. Because from day one, it seemed to me like the reaction was incredible.

I don't think that we expected for one second to get that favourable of a reception. I think we kind of expected to get, "Oh fuck off, play some *proper* music." But it didn't go like that. From the very first time, people went kind of berserk. It was almost like in the comic books. You would never dream that it would go that way but it did, and it just kind of *kept* going like that.

Dan Husband [http://londonpunkrock.kicks-ass.org]: In the true street-level punk fashion, the band was launched outside of the established music-biz structures of the time, including licensed clubs, agents and managers. Yet, despite their notorious nature, club owners at the time were all too glad to book the Demics. After their explosive debut show, word spread quickly about the band. The owners of the York Hotel, which normally booked contemporary acts like jazz, blues and country, took a chance with the Demics and after the owners saw the crowd they drew and how much they drank, they were made the house band.

Iain Atkinson: It could have been hundreds of people. Anywhere we would play would invariably be packed. The York Tavern was basically on the verge of going belly up. But when we played there the whole place was literally packed to the ceiling. It was totally weird. That was within the first five gigs.

Dan Husband [http://londonpunkrock.kicks-ass.org]: Within months, the Demics and others like NFG would permanently change the face of London's musical landscape. Nick Perry, no stranger to reckless behaviour, ventured on to further pursue the wild side of youth and the law. The band rehearsed for a month with Marcy Saddy, later of Toronto's B-Girls, on drums, until drummer Jimmy Weatherstone joined, completing the lineup.

The son of a London police officer, he had played professionally in country and western bands as a teenager and was the only experienced musician in the band.

Jimmy Weatherstone [*Shades* no. 14, November/ December 1980]: I'm from London; I knew Iain before. We'd been jamming and he said, "Come down and try out, we need a drummer." I'd never heard of punk rock or new wave. I was into heavy metal.

Iain Atkinson: But once he had done it a couple times, he was in. Because I don't think he really wanted to do country and western.

And thank God he had been playing for a long time, because that was a really good underpinning for the whole thing to sit. To me, it's the drummer that is really an absolutely critical part of the whole thing. If that person can't keep time, you're screwed, and he could certainly do that.

We were hearing about Teenage Head, and getting their record and covering "Picture My Face." I think we just did it for fun because it was really good. And also listening to the Flamin' Groovies, which is where a lot of their stuff comes out of. I remember them playing at the Cedar Lounge.

I don't think we knew much about Hamilton, really. I think I might have seen the Forgotten Rebels once for ten minutes.

Dan Husband [http://londonpunkrock.kicks-ass.org]: Over the next two years the Demics played at least one weekend a month to packed audiences of downtown artsy-types, punk rockers, factory workers and students. A few audience members formed their own bands and were soon playing opening sets (NFG, Regulators etc). Toronto bands and fans also found their way to the Cedar Lounge as a punk rock circuit of seedy downtown bars began to form in London, Hamilton and Toronto. As the local newspaper put in the headline of a story on The Demics in May 1978, "New Wave Band Floods Hotels' Coiffeurs, Sells Tide of Beer."

The Demics met the Viletones a few times socially in Toronto, and Tones guitarist Freddy Pompeii got the band their first Toronto gig, opening for the Viletones at the Horseshoe Tavern.

Iain Atkinson: Freddy Pompeii gave us our first gig, yeah. Rob I think would have been most likely the guy he talked to. Freddy was a really nice guy, but I don't know how Rob would have met him. That might have been Gerard; he maybe knew them, that's possible. So he *did* do something.

I knew that I immediately didn't like Steve Leckie. I thought he was a fuckin' twat.

We were opening for them and he came on acting like some prima donna rock star. I think he's a pretentious twat, really. I don't think he was the genuine article. I think he *plays* the part, but I don't think he's the real McCoy the way I think Keith was the Real McCoy.

Keith Whittaker [*Shades* no. 14, November/December 1980]: We played with the Viletones at the Horseshoe. I was blind drunk and shit-scared and tripped on that little stairway up to the stage, did a somersault, and jumped in the air. The audience mostly thought I did it purposely; people were saying it was a great entrance.

Iain Atkinson: You kind of get used to the unpredictability of someone like Keith, and you just get pissed off, and you just do whatever is required to get around it. Say, okay, we're having a rehearsal and the guy comes in completely pissed from the get-go, you'd get ticked off. But you just kind of get over it because you also know he's the front man. He has much more of a burden than you do. He was the focal point.

I think that pressure did weigh on him. Maybe in retrospect he was far more nervous about doing it than certainly I ever was. That's not to say you don't get stage fright, but I think he was far more scared than we were. That explains his getting completely pissed, completely fucked up before shows, and falling on his face. To us it was embarrassing, but to people in the audience they thought it was just great and authentic. It'd be part of the shtick.

But that's also part of the whole thing about why I think he was the genuine article. He wasn't that selfish. Even though there's all this bravado that's going on while you're playing, some of it's a little bit made up.

Dan Husband [http://londonpunkrock.kicks-ass.org]: Through constant live playing the band added new original songs and covers ranging from rockabilly to '60s garage psychedelia to punk, building a repertoire of short, fast, loud, punked-out pop songs about boredom, anger and frustration, all laced with Keith's sarcastic wit. High energy music, by and for the pissed off.

By early 1979, all of the members of the band had moved to Toronto.

Keith Whittaker [*Shades* no. 14, November/December 1980]: We're sort of revered and hated. They're pissed off at us because we left, as if we ditched them. Which isn't true.

Iain Atkinson: I think we got kind of wrapped up with being here. Maybe we were too big for our boots, there is that possibility, but we did go back to London and play from time to time.

There was no sense of nostalgia, of, "I want to go back and play my hometown."

It's not that I didn't like the people; I was really appreciative of the people who came out and enjoyed it. I can't fault that. And you would certainly want to go back and play for those people, but not in terms of the town or anything. I *still* don't even like going there.

Keith Whittaker [*Shades* no. 14, November/December 1980]: There was no money, no manager, no incentive. I don't think we really believed in ourselves. We were waiting for someone to come along and do it all for us. We were spoiled, I guess. And we moved from London to Toronto at that point, which was a big thing to us.

But I'm glad we moved.

Dan Husband [http://londonpunkrock.kicks-ass.org]: The Demics returned to London for gigs throughout 1979. New bands were entering the fray and claiming their turf in the scene. At some point in 1979, many fans were startled to hear of the pending breakup of the original lineup.

Iain Atkinson: We hated each other's guts — on some days. You know, I'm not really sure why Rob left. There was definitely always antagonism between Keith and Rob. That's totally understandable. They come from, in some ways, two different sides of the fence. One person is all primal; the other person, it's all in their brain,

Demics; Jimmy Weatherstone, Iain Atkinson, Rob Brent, Keith Whittaker
/ photo by Mike Hannay, courtesy of Ready Records

everything's an intellectual exercise. And that's Rob. Everything had to be planned. It was organized chaos. I think his goal was he would be able to control Keith and kind of direct him to some place.

Sure. That's really going to happen. Keith was not a controllable person, even though he might, to a degree, would have wanted to be controlling other people.

Maybe he realized that Keith was completely uncontrollable and so he just didn't want to do it anymore. I don't think it was antagonism to the point of, "I hate your bloody guts," or anything like that. There was very little fisticuffs involved.

He did another band afterwards called Mettle, and it was a vastly different thing; a vastly intellectual pursuit.

Mike Niederman [http://londonpunkrock.kicks-ass.org]: Rob was always interested in a wider range of music than what The Demics were about. For instance, he organized with a few of us a performance of a Stockhausen piece involving four shortwave radios. No audience — just us performers. He was also very interested in Lamonte Young's musical theory, which Rob pursued in the band Mettle. Keith, of course, was more into alcohol.

Iain Atkinson: I got Steve [Koch] to come and do it instead.

Was there animosity? There might have been a bit. I think he was sort of angry about it to a degree, which is unfortunate. I think [Rob] was angry because I didn't quit, too.

Steve Koch: Almost at the same time that they were looking for a guitar player, I was looking for a job, so it was good timing for us. They invited me to their rehearsal spot down on Baldwin Street.

We rehearsed a few things. It was a whole different style of music. Viletones is very free, feeling-based stuff. If the song went four verses or five verses it didn't really matter. If you have a thirteen-bar solo or a nineteen-bar solo it didn't matter, you know, we'll get back in when it feels good. But Iain and J.D. were more structured musicians, so I had to lose some of my bad habits to get into their group.

Iain Atkinson: If we were going to be rock stars and get a record deal, then we figured we needed to go to Toronto. Even though we'd already done the thing in London, I guess we had delusions of grandeur.

61. The daily rebel

"I don't want no foreign pricks
          to take my job away from me
My tax dollars paid their ransom,
          would they do the same for me?
I don't, I don't want them in my home"

- "Bomb the Boats and Feed the Fish," Forgotten Rebels

Mickey DeSadist: The band broke up, and Houston asked me if I wanted to reform the band with him.

Chris Houston: That lineup kind of splintered and they brought Alan Smolak — Al Mocambo — to play guitar with Mickey, and I came back in on bass. I don't know who we had on drums.

[Chriss] Suicide was kind of nice. After I replaced him in the band he used to call death threats when he found out my parents were away. So in a big empty house, "I'm gonna kill you, I'm gonna *kill* you."

I'm not sure if he meant it. He went on to Slander and he uttered the immortal line, "Now that we have the record deal we can afford to pay for the damages."

Carl [Johnson] had a gun, I remember that. I remember seeing *Dawn of the Dead* and *The Hills Have Eyes*. He was so drunk his gun kept falling out of his pocket next to me, and that scared the bejesus out of me. I can understand why my father wasn't too enamoured by him.

My parents weren't too happy about me being in a band to begin with, you know? They've always been very supportive of me and whatever wacky endeavours. They see it as something to be creative. When you're in high school and you're packing the Horseshoe, or you're playing stadiums at Centennial Arena in Burlington, at least you're out there *doing* stuff.

With me, it's always been my dream, and people know that. When I was a kid, I used to pretend that the tennis rackets were guitars. I lived in Toronto at that time period and my mom took me to the Leaside Crippled Civilians sale and I got a guitar. It took me a year and a half to realize that the low notes were at the bottom of the neck and the high notes were at the top, because I thought they were back and forth. I would just wail on it.

You always have these dreams and stuff.

Mickey DeSadist: Me and Steve Burman were delivering pizzas at McMaster University and we heard a guy playing a Sex Pistols tune with his guitar through a door. We knocked on the door to see who this guy was, and it was Al. And I figured this guy sounds pretty good — he actually plays guitar better than me — and I asked him to join the band, almost right then and there.

Chris Houston: Then somehow this chick knew this drummer, Larry, who was a total jazz-fusion drummer but was desperate for a legitimate rock gig.

And that's how the *In Love With the System* band came together.

Larry Potvin: I went to a rehearsal. Instantly clicked. We had a good time. I liked them because of their energy, and they liked me because I could actually play.

Mickey DeSadist: The difference with this new lineup was you could depend on everybody to be sober for the show.

Larry Potvin: I really loved the music. It was raw and exciting. I knew all the songs and played them, verses and choruses and three chords. It wasn't too complicated because before that I was playing jazz-fusion.

As soon as my jazz buddies found out I'd joined the Forgotten Rebels, they looked at me like I was an idiot and disowned me. But in the meantime, they were making fifty dollars for playing all night and I'm making three to six hundred dollars for playing two hours and having a real good time, ha ha ha. To me, music is music. I wasn't closed-minded. I would play anything that had energy and entertained people.

Chris Houston: On the back of *In Love With the System* he had "jazz" spelled backwards on his shirt. God, he was a great drummer though, as far as I was concerned. Having a super-duper drummer opened up those doors to be heavy, and I think that's when the Rebels became a real entity. I think the other versions have their charms, but ...

Mickey DeSadist: We were a bunch of class clowns that knew we could do touchy subjects and get in newspapers, and we enjoyed writing songs together and having a laugh. We were fun for the sake of fun. We at one point thought we might make a lot of money for it ...

Chris Houston: We tried to be the most obnoxious people as possible. Our ideas of fun would be to go see horror movies and cheer every time the zombies killed someone. The steel workers would turn around going, "This is disgusting." There's nothing better than going to see *Dawn of the Dead* with Mickey.

I kind of pushed Mickey to be more himself because I saw that he had the ability to come up with those ideas on his own. Mickey could get away with saying the most disgusting things, whereas a lot of stuff I was just too fresh-faced to get away with, ha ha ha.

Bob Bryden: Star Records goes on selling records, going on being the alternative record store in town. The Rebels progress, and they continue writing; they're writing all the time.

I went through my journals, and it was very troubling in a way to read them and see I have a philosophical problem with the punk movement. I'm constantly saying, "You know, I'm really into the music side of it, but I'm really not into the nihilism, the self-destruction. They're so anti–the '60s, but that's cool because how many hippies are now pushing pens in offices and all their ideals have gone out the window? And I can understand why you'd be angry, so that's cool. But at the same time, why go to the other extreme? Why are you so self-destructive?"

And it's just an appearance, true, the *appearance* of nihilism. But at the same time I said, "You guys are shit kickers when it comes to music. You're putting life back into music, and you're back into believing in the *song* again." And I'm listening to the Rebels all the time, and Mickey is really becoming a writer.

Mickey DeSadist: We didn't want punk songs to be punk. We were just writing songs about touchy subjects to be silly.

Bob Bryden: I don't agree with two-thirds of the stuff he writes about, but I think he's a brilliant writer anyway. What do I have to agree with it for? I *don't* have to agree with it, I just have to acknowledge it. The guy's a writer.

I mean, "To hell with the Beatles reunion," "Bomb the boats and feed their fucking flesh to the fish." These are not sentiments I agree with, but I have to hand it to him for being able to translate those things into songs and make it fun.

But there's one song that really blows me away. It's called "Elvis is Dead."

Mickey DeSadist: After he died, all the world had left was me, ha ha ha.

Gary Pig Gold: There was this great record from Holland by a band called Tits that I distributed called "We're So Glad Elvis Is Dead." I left a copy of that at Saucer House, and I bet any money it immediately ended up in Mickey's collection. And then, by "osmosis," in the Rebels' repertoire ...

Bob Bryden: "Elvis is Dead, the big fat goof is dead, dead, dead." That song just came down the chute at a practice and I went, "This song has got to be preserved for posterity. The world must have this song. This song *must* be recorded." Those were my exact thoughts.

I phoned up Mike Shulga in Oshawa and said, "Why don't we foot the bill to make an album for the Rebels? Why don't we become a label?"

So Michael comes down. The Rebels were practicing above a restaurant in downtown Hamilton. We heard ten or twelve songs and Mike said, "Yup, it's a go, let's do it." So we got the money together. We weren't quite as irresponsible as the previous Star Records regime back then. We weren't just taking it out of the till; we were making an investment and we were doing it right.

I can bluntly say that I coordinated the whole thing from top to bottom. Everything from the phone calls to the studio to meeting with the band, going over the songs, working out the arrangements, right on through the recording, and I even coordinated the packaging.

Larry Potvin: We were working on *In Love With the System* immediately. We were playing the songs in the nightclubs and concert halls and then we just went into the studio and recorded them all, right off the floor, just *bang*. Done.

Bob Bryden: I called it a guerilla raid. Most of the album was done on one weekend in twenty-four hours.

Chris Houston: Because Bob Bryden had made records with Christmas and with Reign Ghost, he really worked us hard in terms of pre-production.

I got a week's detention, with Bob staring at me to play better, but what made that record really strong was that the players were good. You cannot have a great rock band without a great drummer, and Larry was a great drummer. Very intricate; dead perfect metre.

Bob Bryden: Then I think we went back a few days after and did some touch-ups.

Chris Houston: I'm still mad at Bryden for editing a lot of the stuff out on the record, even though I love Bob. But you need a good producer to translate records, and make them sound good. I think that's what made the difference.

Bob Bryden: I opted for some things that were a little bit different in punk. I wasn't gonna have it mixed in such a way that you would not hear the melody line, and I made sure. And Mickey was all for this. Mickey is a musician, really, and he wanted the melodies, the harmonies.

I okayed the project *because* these guys had melodic songs. They might have been stupid, naïve politics and reactionary politics, but they were really good songs.

With a whole other set of lyrics, they *still* would have been great songs.

Chris Houston: The funny thing is, when we made *In Love With the System* we kind of realized that we'd done a good record.

The actual budget is one thousand eight hundred and forty-six dollars. That was how much the record cost, and some of that stuff is first take. We played it once and Bob said, "Don't play it again."

Bob Bryden: I know it sounds like I'm taking a lot of credit for it, but I'm only taking credit for the superficials; the music is *them*.

If you see the original album which has the picture of Mickey with the cigarette butts and the inner sleeve with a foldout newspaper called *The Daily Rebel*, there's an actual picture of Pierre Elliott Trudeau holding the Rebels' first EP in his hand. So I even coordinated the inner sleeve, and I designed the label, too. Everything. Because nobody else knew what they were doing, and I had some experience.

Three of the biggest printing companies in Toronto refused to print the album. They wouldn't print the cover because it had the song "Fuck Me Dead" on it, the anthem for necromancy.

Mickey DeSadist / photo by Steve Burman

Chris Houston: The song "Fuck Me Dead" was given to us in the toilet at a bar called Marco Polo's. A bunch of high school kids had written the lyrics and they handed them to us. Mickey said, "This is disgusting."

We wrote "Elvis is Dead" at that same gig because Al broke a guitar string and we didn't have a second guitar, so he had to go find a guitar string and do all that stuff. I felt so bad that I started playing a walking bass line, trying to make up some song on the spot. So that's how that song came together.

That's the same gig that Mickey made some stupid gesture to some cops. There were some undercovers there, so the cops came after *me* with their badges off and I had to leave the gig laying flat on the floor of the van with a tarp over me. They were gonna kill us there, but that cop died three weeks later. That kind of relieved me.

Bob Bryden: So they wouldn't print the cover and our record plant was freaking out. If you look at the original album, you see it is actually blacked out on the back cover because that was the only way we could get it printed. But if you look at it now, I think the new version — of course because the world is so much looser now — it's got it on there.

Mickey DeSadist: When that happened I thought, Okay, it's regular, it's run by the same stupid old assholes that are teachers in my school and the same type of stupid assholes that are just going to antiquate themselves anyway. Their time was coming.

People in the '70s weren't into making a mark, they were just into carrying the same crap that was going on. And not even the *good* crap; just the manipulatable crap. And a lot of people that *were* making innovations were really imbalanced; they could do one thing but they couldn't do another. Like the Dolls in the early '70s. If those guys had any brains at the time, they would have actually been a very big band if they didn't have drugs. People didn't think.

Chris Houston: For promotion, Bryden got Kelly Jay — remember the singer from that band Crowbar? — they made a giant *In Love With the System* template version of the album cover. It was about ten feet tall, and Kelly Jay painted it. He said, "I listened to this record and I disagree with everything on it. I'm reduced to doing murals for you assholes." Ha ha ha.

But it took about a year and a half after we made that record for it to kind of materialize in audience appeal, if you know what I mean. I try to stress that with kids: When you make a record, you think it's really cool, but it takes the world a long time to really pick up on it.

62. RIOT in CHinatow

Ian Mackay: Ralph was helping out but he was working at Attic Records, so on a day-to-day basis I was doing a lot of the booking of gigs, managing our relationship with The Agency. They had acts like Goddo and Loverboy, all of the mega bar bands that were playing two, three, four-thousand-seat halls. Bands like Goddo, probably everybody's forgotten about, but at the time they were doing six- or seven-hundred-seat houses, and we did some opening for them.

The Diodes / photo by George Whiteside

were not there. At some point they could see that they couldn't really get above a certain level. But, I guess in the late '70s maybe, early '80s, they were one of the top — I hate to use the word bar band — but they were one of the bigger draws on the Ontario circuit at that time.

Mike Lengyell: In order to try and take it to the next step we did end up playing a lot more. I was used to playing a lot, and I *wanted* to play a lot. Unfortunately, there weren't a lot of concerts that we could do back then, so it did end up being a lot of bars.

John Catto: You still couldn't play anywhere. This is the thing everyone forgets now: There was *nowhere* to play. You could promote gigs; the bar scene just didn't want to know, there were always these nightmare gigs.

It's very strange. There was our club in the basement and the Colonial Underground and all of those things, then everyone hit a brick wall. Because at that point — and it's a very specific point, around 1977 till '79 — no one would book any band from that particular scene into a straight club. In fact, you couldn't even play colleges and stuff.

We did a college in Etobicoke and it was just like a ridiculous violence fest with people throwing bottles and stuff. It just didn't work at all. This is where our management got freaked out.

Ian Mackay: We did very well at Toronto high schools. The kids just *came* to us; we had hundreds and hundreds of kids no matter where we went and they liked the music.

I think we appealed to sixteen-year-olds at the time. We had some interesting lyrics and some interesting musical elements, but a lot of it was a return to basics and I think fifteen and sixteen-year-olds appreciated that because they were just learning musically themselves.

John Catto: We were playing a gig in some little town just outside of Toronto. I think we were supposed to play two nights there, and we played one night. It was one of these funny things where one half of the audience is into you, and one half is really not. So the side that was not into us started chucking stuff. I'm playing away and I've got these white jeans and I look down and there's this huge shard of glass sticking in my leg and blood pouring everywhere. So I stop playing and make a big fuss about the thing and it's like, "Who the fuck threw that?" and this and that and we walk off.

We're sitting in the dressing room and all these guys come in and go, "We know who threw the glasses." We're like, "Uh-uh." So we take off. We turn up the next night and our sign's off the board.

Ralph Alfonso: We ended up getting a deal with Orient Records, which is again a disco label, distributed by RCA. I kind of got more into the background because by this point my career had actually taken off fairly well. I was head of promo at Attic Records and I could only guide the Diodes at arm's length instead of kind of sitting down with them. By this time they had real booking agents, they had a real road crew, they were opening for U2 and all this stuff.

They were really going for it; but again, just a little too early. A lot of things we take for granted now

What happened apparently after we left was basically one side of the tavern erupted in a fight with the other; just a total messy, bad barroom brawl. So that was the end of us.

Mike Lengyell: I know the other guys weren't really used to that. They weren't really expecting that kind of path, and I don't think they liked it that much. Not that I blame them. I didn't really like playing in bars all the time. If I had my choice I'd rather play concerts. But see, if the choice is either playing or *not* playing, it's probably going to be the Ontario bar circuit.

Ian Mackay: Actually, the *worst* thing we could have done was to get on to the Ontario bar circuit for a while; it was just a killer.

In the early days, we were doing all kinds of great concerts. We opened for the Ramones in Chicago, Ultravox in Montreal or Quebec City, Gary Numan in Calgary; we had a lot of good opening gigs, and a lot of good gigs ourselves. We opened for U2's first concert in Canada in 1980 at the Maple Leaf Ballroom on St. Clair West, which was a bingo hall. The guy who runs Concert Productions International gave us a break. He said, "Let the Diodes do it," and it was packed to the rafters — but it was only about four hundred seats. So we had two firsts: the Talking Heads and U2, and in some ways they were almost like bookends in our career, because it was near the end.

John Catto: Touring in Canada is a different experience than someone who's on the road in England or something. The distances are bigger; the scale of the thing is more out of control. It's a really silly thing to do.

Tom Williams: You only have ten cities to play. After you've played those ten cities, where do you go? It's a population thing. It's obvious. You can only do one tour a year, so what do you do after you finish the ten or fifteen reasonably major cities? Sit on your ass?

I mean, you really have to go somewhere else, because you can't go back down to the club level and play fifty-two weeks a year in clubs. So consequently, if you want your career to progress you have to go *somewhere*, whether it's Britain or Europe or Australia.

John Catto: Touring across Canada involves climbing in a van and going, "Next stop is Thunder Bay." Then you stop at Thunder Bay and you can't drive any further; you have to get around the Great Lakes. Then it's Saskatoon and Calgary and all this, and you're just covering so much ground. The distances are *so* big. We did it a few times. Some people did it dozens of times. This used to be the makeup of what being a Canadian band was.

Ian Mackay: We were really pioneering out west. Remember, at this point one band had preceded us out west, and that was Martha and the Muffins — they were with the same agency — and new wave punk was, "The next big thing from Britain and New York, and we've got our own Canadian bands, and let's push them through the west coast and see if we can't pick up a few fans and a few dollars." It was a real groundbreaking scene.

Paul Robinson: We loved playing Edmonton. You just wouldn't believe that Edmonton had this great scene but it did, and I think they were just desperate for something that was different.

We had a really good gig in Calgary once. That was amazing. It was just this club that was absolutely packed; you could not move.

John Catto [CIUT-FM, Greg Dick interview, 2007]: It's just a long, long, thin bar, right? It holds, legitimately, a hundred and fifty people or something like this. So they start letting people in and they start letting people in and they start letting people in. And at some point someone goes, "You better do a head count," and there were up to something like nine hundred or a thousand people jammed into this bar that held two hundred. And it was just insane.

Paul Robinson: I think I ended up crawling up into the ceiling, one of those suspended ceilings, and was just crawling along poking my head in the middle of this massive room that had this huge suspended ceiling. I think part of the ceiling fell down at one point.

John Catto: They ripped the entire suspended ceiling of the club out, from the back to the front of the stage. And when we were playing, people were telling me you could listen to the jukebox at the back of the room clearly because there were so many bodies in there it just blocked the sound past about halfway. Just an insane, insane gig. Wild.

Paul Robinson: I don't think we could hear anything we were playing. I think the audience was deafened by it because it was so loud. It just had one of those great atmospheres that you never could repeat.

I think the next time we played Calgary we were the support band for Gary Numan's "Cars" tour. It was a twenty-thousand-seat auditorium in some hockey arena or something and it was really strange. I must say, I preferred the other gig in the bar. I think we probably worked better on a small stage, because we never had the flash that it takes to do a big stage show because we never had the money to do it.

Ian Mackay: We started to fight a lot near the end. It was tough for us. We had artistic differences I think.

What's ironic is that a lot of the material we did very late that never got recorded was our best, and yet we were diverging in different directions. I was personally going in a *very* different direction. I was getting so interested in computer software that I would be spending all my time doing that. So we'd be on tour in Winnipeg in the middle of a wintry night and nothing to do in our hotel room. The other guys would go out to a bar looking for chicks or something like that, and I remember a few times — I guess I *am* a geek — going to the local Radio Shack and buying some resistors and some capacitors for my next project. I got over it, though. But by about 1980, '81, I was pretty into the computing thing in a big way.

Mike Lengyell: Creative people are generally kind of forceful, you know what I mean? Like you sort of have your own identity, your own thoughts, your own views, and you want to get it out there and sometimes that can create conflict in a group. And of course, just being people, you have your bad times and your good times and your up times and down times, and that happens.

And of course you'd see conflict. If somebody's in a bad mood they lash out, and it may be because they're just in a bad mood or it may something deeper than that. You just never know.

Ian Mackay: I think Paul was single-minded and ambitious, and because of that he didn't have a natural kind of grace about his behaviour and the way he socially interacted. He was very purposeful about the people he met; who he associated with. One might say he was a social climber, but his relationships with whoever he was interested in were genuine. He wasn't a user of people as far as I can tell. He had genuine interests; it's just that he preferred the company of other up-and-comers to people who weren't.

But Paul had a jarring side to him. He and I got into some doozies of arguments. We had a *very* vicious argument in Winnipeg. One bar owner booked all four of us in a single room. We were very pissed off at that. Five guys — the sound guy was there — in a single room sharing two double beds; one guy's sleeping on the floor. By the end of that week we did there, we were ready to tear each other's heads off.

Paul and I got in a terrible fight over — I think it was about, "Your bag's beside my bag and it's too close." It was one of those ridiculous fights. I remember he threw a lot of my stuff down the toilet or something, and I took his bag and threw it out into the snow.

But when we left, since I was good at electronics and John was good at electronics, we went around and disconnected every electrical receptacle in the hotel room and every light bulb, tied it up with electrician's tape, and put it all back together. So everything looked like it worked, except you turn on the light and the light wouldn't go on. Every single receptacle was disconnected, all the overhead lights were disconnected, and the only way they'd be able to reconnect them would be to hire an electrician, open up the boxes, and go in and reconnect them. That was because they booked us into the wrong room.

Mike Lengyell: I think we were kind of optimistic that that tour was going to turn the page for us, or give us a chance to take a step forward. I think we were all really excited about it. I remember that I really enjoyed playing, and I seem to remember that there might have been a little frustration with everybody that things maybe might not work out and that maybe we weren't going to get the break that we sort of expected or maybe deserved.

Tom Williams: You have to have some other markets to tour in. I think also at that time you needed some success *elsewhere* for people in Canada to look at you.

I'm pretty sure if your record started taking off in the States or Britain, then Canadian radio looked at you totally differently. They started seeing you in the trades internationally and saying, "Oh, I better pay attention to this band," whereas before it was just another friggin' Canadian thing they had to play.

John Catto: We were originally supposed to go out and do the west coast of America with Tuff Darts, which was Robert Gordon's old thing, and then that fell apart; they broke up or whatever. Then we were supposed to go on tour with the Dead Boys, but *that* fell apart when Johnny Blitz got knifed in New York. So these things kept almost happening and never occurring.

Ian Mackay: I was too busy working on the day-to-day activities for the band, making sure those things happened, but I remember Paul talking about that Dead Boys tour. I personally don't think that there was ever a tour in the works. I think that's actually a lot of bull. I don't have any recollection that there was a Dead Boys tour lined up.

Besides, I don't think we were particularly suited to the Dead Boys. Those guys were aggressive, nasty little punks. They were really rough guys. They would have been better with the Viletones. I wanted to open for the Clash.

John Catto: We had a very abortive thing about the west coast in America. We were booked so many times to do it. You'd never get out there.

Finally, *finally*, we took it upon ourselves. We went, "We want to play out there and we've never done it, so let's do it on a small scale." We were touring back and forth across Canada making money and had a bit of disposable income so we could afford to pay for some plane flights. We started out in San Francisco and went down to L.A., which is where all these things linked together. In San Francisco in the Mabuhay and also at the Back Door, which was run by the Flamin' Groovies.

When we played Mabuhay, there were people at this gig who hadn't been to a gig in, like, three years. It was really packed, totally rammed. All these people are really into it and you go, "How does this happen?" We'd never had a domestic release. All these people know the records!

Gary Pig Gold: When I moved to L.A. in '79, '80 and said I was from Toronto, they weren't asking me about Teenage Head or the Viletones first, they were asking about the Diodes.

Remember, they got the record deal first in Toronto. They'll always be first, they stuck the flag in the moon, and that's down in history now whether you like it or not. And I *know* those records were available, and were being played, in the States.

So once you get out of the little cliquey thing of Toronto and talked about the Diodes in the bedrooms of Orange County, California, those people don't know, or *care*, that they're from an art college, or that Steven Leckie tries to kill himself or that Teenage Head wanted to play since they were six. They've just heard the records and liked them, and that's all that ultimately counts. Toronto punk, for a lot people, is the Diodes.

Ralph Alfonso: Basically, I walked into The Agency one night and asked if I could use their phones. Two hours later, I had a whole California tour booked. Their booking agent there, Michael White, couldn't believe it. "How did you do that?" I just said, "It's punk."

John Catto: When we turn up in L.A. we're playing the Whisky A Go Go, and we go out on the first night we're in town. We went out to the Starwood and turn up at the door and say, "We're in such-and-such band, we're playing at the Whisky." And the girl goes, "Oh, wait a second. Let me just go off and get the management." We're going, "Huh?" Next thing we know we're raced into the VIP lounge, taken up to the office, and all over the walls of the office of the Starwood are all of our posters. The biggest club in L.A. and they're going, "Why aren't you playing *here*?" And we're going, "Oh, we never thought to." They're going, "Oh, we're *huge* fans."

It's this really odd thing. Unknown amounts of records got shipped into America. Probably a lot in the south, like Texas and so on, a lot in Seattle, San Francisco, L.A., loads out there, and of course none of them were accounted for. It's an unknown quantity; no one knows. When we spoke to Sony about the doing the CD reissue it was like, "Um, we just don't have any record of any imports going on at all."

Paul Robinson: CBS completely ripped us off. CBS decided to export us through a company called Jem in the States, and they exported about thirty thousand Diodes albums to the States which we never, ever got accredited for selling.

They kind of went "missing." They pressed them up and they exported them and they never went on the sheet. So we never, ever got paid for those records, nor did we ever chart in Canada nor get billed with platinum albums, although it's possible that we went gold.

John Catto: I can go, "We sold X amount of records in Canada," but I have no idea whether we sold double that in America. Never know, which is a little alarming but it seems to be par for the course with this whole thing.

The industry trades would have the Top Import charts. All through that '77 period, especially in the December period, we were always Number Two after the Clash's first album, which of course wasn't released in America at that time. So we had this unknown quantity of records going into America. I still meet people all the time in places like Texas over the years who go, "Oh! You were in the *Diodes*." All these people knew about us.

Paul Robinson: Every single time we went to the States, there were thousands of records out. There were more records, in fact, out in America than there were in Canada *ever* on the Diodes. We'd go to Baltimore and they'd have fifty on the racks. It was just incredible, and we never knew what was going on; we never knew about any of this until twenty years later when it all came to a head and people discovered what CBS had been doing. Eventually, they got sued by their bands.

CBS had its own pressing plant, which was unusual in those days, so they pressed records for other record companies as well as CBS; just pressing them up and exporting them and they went under the table. So there was absolutely no accountability for record sales. We never did anything about it because we didn't sell millions of records, but that's what CBS did in those days, and that is a well-known fact.

John Catto: One of my favourite subjects is that "Tired of Waking Up Tired" has never been played on Canadian radio, which is what I get told from SOCAN [Society of

Composers, Authors and Music Publishers of Canada]. And I know for a fact that it got played every morning on every major radio station in the country from 1978, when it came out, until fifteen years later. If you'd turn on CHUM, you'd turn on CFNY, they'd be playing it in the morning.

Because Canadian radio was always based on the sampling system, where they'd pay rights based on samples taken at particular times during the day, it basically never showed up. It doesn't exist. As far as SOCAN is concerned, it's never been played. It's mystery accounting. Who knows?

Paul Robinson: As far as I know, Rodney Bingenheimer in L.A. was playing us all the time. We were getting loads of airplay. We were selling loads and loads of albums in Los Angeles, and they were shipping loads of them out there. We had playlistings in Los Angeles, playlistings in New York, playlistings in Boston. We were on all kinds of playlists all over the States — which is really difficult for a Canadian band that had no distribution other than Jem.

And yet we never, ever got a penny from those albums and we never, ever knew how many of those albums were pressed.

"Record Hassles Breaking Up The Diodes," by Katherine Gilday [*Globe and Mail*, January 12, 1979]: The biggest irony of the Diodes' dilemma...is..."Tired Of Waking Up Tired." ... is currently 17th on the Top 100 chart of KSJO-FM in Los Angeles.

John Catto: What else happened in L.A.? We're being taken around by the barmaid from the Starwood, and she takes us down to this place and goes, "Oh guys, you've *got* to meet Kim Fowley!" Kim Fowley had just come out of this underage place that we were just heading in to. This is late '70s.

We stayed next door to the Only Ones in the hotel. I went out with the Dead Kennedys' manager. That's probably not repeatable.

The other thing of course that happened was the riot. We played at a place called the Hong Kong Café with the Circle Jerks and Agent Orange. It was just this really strange gig.

Mike Lengyell: Somebody came up on the stage and started hassling John or Paul, and they wouldn't stop. It wasn't like, "Hey, I'm having a good time! Hey look at me, I'm jumping up with the band." We'd get that all the time; people jumping up on the stage, they'd dance around for a minute and slap Paul or John on the back and go, "You guys are great," and then sort of stumble off into the crowd.

But *this* person was kind of taking it the wrong way I think, and doing a bit of hassling.

We were wondering, Where are the bouncers? This guy's obviously hassling the band. Why don't they just drag this guy off the stage?

They didn't come, so I think John kind of said, "Look, I've had enough of this guy," took off his guitar, and hit him with it.

John Catto: I pull my guitar off and I go, *Whack!* Ian's almost pulling me away, really pissed off at me, going, "You can't do that!" And I'm like, "I just did," and the guy gets hold of my guitar and then I'm *really* pissed off. I'm whacking this guy; he's on angel dust or something. By this point our soundman's behind the guy holding him and I'm hearing bones breaking and it's really, really bad.

Mike Lengyell: The bouncers I guess finally came up and dragged the guy off. Then it kind of started to get a little out of hand.

John Catto: The bouncers wrestle the guy down and they kick him down the stairs. He comes crawling back up and starts pulling apart the PA. Then the bouncers lay into him again. And then they kick him down the stairs again. He crawls up *again*.

Mike Lengyell: And then, of course, if you're at a bar with a bunch of your friends and you see your friend getting dragged off by the bouncer — even though the guy might be in the wrong — you still want to go and back him up a bit. So I think a slight melee started.

John Catto: Finally they toss him down the stairs, he goes straight for the plate glass window, and the entire contents of the club go raving around Chinatown in L.A. smashing things. It actually made the wire services — "Riot In Chinatown!" "Punk Rock Riot!"

But the one thing I'm remembering is the girl from CBS was at that gig. So there's this poor girl from L.A. hiding out in the dressing room where all this mayhem's going on.

It was just one of those things: How to make a really good impression.

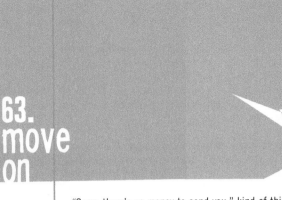

63.
move
on

Stephen Mahon: I've often thought how much I love the first Rolling Stones album and the first Beatles album. There can only be one first album, and first albums can be great because the band has had their whole career to come up with it.

But the quicker the label needs that *second* album, the less time you have to come up with the stuff.

Tom Williams: We knew [Teenage Head's] work from their first album. To be honest with you, I can't remember if the tape came first or the performance came first, but we were totally impressed and we wanted to steal them away from CBS, no question about that. We went all-out to steal them. We wooed them.

We could turn on a dime, and we did.

Stephen Mahon: We started working on *Frantic City* pretty soon after the first one. That's how the industry worked. You did an album and it obviously got our foot in the door, so our manager was probably very aware of the fact that okay, there's a certain time frame, boom boom boom, let's do it.

Stewart Pollock: I remember their first advance was thirty-five thousand bucks to record the album. They spent ten thousand or eleven thousand to produce the record, and that was it, the money was gone. So out of thirty-five thousand they got eleven thousand that went into the record ... and their manager Jack was driving a brand new Saab. I said to the guys, "You might want to ask him where he got the Saab from because they're about fifteen thousand bucks at this point."

So when they confronted him, it all came back in my face. The manager just said, "That's it. Sever him away from the band." He cut me off from the tour right away

Gordie Lewis / photo by Ralph Alfonso

— "Sorry, there's no money to send you," kind of thing. He was pretty calculated in what he did, but what are you gonna do? You can't go against it. It's a machine that's in motion.

Gordie Lewis [*Blitz* Magazine, March/April 1982]: They were rushing us to get *Frantic City* ready for release. The cover art was rushed, and looks like shit. We were shown the proofs and said we didn't like them. But they said, "Too bad. We've got to get the album out!"

Stephen Mahon: We were lucky that some of the songs, like "Disgusteen," we had written for the first album, so we had some spillover songs that were ready to go for our second album. So yeah, I would say within months the wheels started turning: How are we gonna do this, who's gonna produce it, and where are we gonna do it?

Gordie Lewis: And that's where Slash Booze kind of enters the picture. He's the one who played us the Eddie Cochran records — "Okay, we can learn *that.*" So we learned a whole bunch of Eddie Cochran songs, we learned a whole bunch of Gene Vincent songs, we learned Elvis songs. And so that got us our rockabilly influence, which really shows up on *Frantic City.*

We've got "Brand New Cadillac" on there, we have "Wild One," the Jerry Lee Lewis song, but more importantly, this gave me a whole new perspective on my guitar playing. I didn't know Eddie Cochran. I wasn't interested in Eddie Cochran. I was interested in New York Dolls and Iggy and the Stooges. Glam rock; David Bowie, Mott the Hoople, that's what I was into.

I started researching into what the Dolls were about and then realizing they were doing a lot of cover songs, like Bo Diddley's "Pills." It was like, this is really cool! The Dolls went back and did this, and now we're doing it, too. So let's investigate this type of music even more. It helped us grow.

Stephen Mahon: The second album turned out a little bit better. Thank God that turned out a little bit better.

That had Stacy Heydon producing; that's a huge difference, because there was sort of a respect. Stacy had played with Iggy and Bowie and he could handle Frank. He was a musician so he knew where we were coming from, so he got really good sounds right off the get-go. It just made the whole environment really comfortable.

Dave Rave: All cylinders started firing.

Gordie Lewis ["Teenage Head ... and How to Get Some," by Cameron Gordon, *The Nerve Magazine*, October 2006]: Really, Teenage Head didn't have a proper radio single until "Let's Shake" and some of the tunes from *Frantic City* came out. We were a live band, first and foremost.

Stephen Mahon: Q107 really got behind our first album and played "Top Down" all the time. I think Q107 had only been on the air for a year; they were like this infant station. There was this programmer there, Bob Mackowycz, who just simply really liked us. That was a huge plus to have our song being played on Q107 all the time.

Larry LeBlanc: I had a show on Q107 called *Backstage Pass*. It was kind of a mixed show because I would have anything from punk to surf music to rockabilly. I would put somebody like Link Wray on with Elvis Costello and Eddie and the Hot Rods or something like that. I played certainly everything that came out of here that was around at the time, like the Viletones, Dishes, anything like that. But a lot of stuff that was considered punk, wasn't. Like Teenage Head I never really considered a punk band.

Stephen Mahon: So by *Frantic City*, things were starting to get played even more. "Let's Shake" was even starting to get played on AM, so it was certainly looking great when you think of just playing at the Colonial and the Crash 'n' Burn, and then you would look at a chart and there's Genesis and Pink Floyd ... and Teenage Head. It wasn't happening all over the world, but it was something. It was looking really good.

Greg Dick [CIUT-FM, interview with Teenage Head, 2007]: When Q107 compiled its 107 Top Songs of the 1970s, "Top Down" slid in at number sixty-eight, just behind "Long Time" by Boston and "It's Only Rock 'n' Roll" by the Rolling Stones. That was quite an accomplishment. I mean, to get up there on a corporate station like that.

Andrew McGregor: It was a funny thing. It was like you'd sold out if you made a record on a proper label.

Greg Dick [CIUT-FM, interview with Teenage Head, 2007]: Some people would say it's selling out, but I think it was more like [Teenage Head] were invading a station that played a lot of shit music.

Andrew McGregor: *Frantic City* broke the band in the wrong place, on Q107. If you were into the punk scene, the *last* thing you were listening to was Q107.

I'll give Q107 credit: They did some live recordings with Teenage Head that actually got some of their proper sound out there.

Gordie Lewis: We were starting to get these people on our side; important people that did have some clout that believed in us, and so that helped us gain momentum. You get those people on your side and you're laughing. You can't buy that.

Stephen Mahon: Yeah, that was just a really good time for us. When radio starts helping you, back then that really mattered. That was important. There was no Much Music or MTV, so that more or less was a good indicator of, "You guys are on your way."

Bruce Farley Mowat: I saw the *Frantic City* release party. March 20, 1980. It was brilliant. You could see that they were on the ascendance.

Larry LeBlanc: By that point they became almost mainstream. They had "Let's Shake" and "Something on My Mind" and all that kind of stuff.

Tom Williams: Attic wanted to be a full-line commercial label, and we wanted to have music of pretty much every genre. We were very busy with our mainstream acts, being the Triumphs and the George Thorogoods.

You know, Teenage Head to us were pretty mainstream, although they were pretty punk, too, at the same time.

Stephen Mahon: "Something on My Mind" was getting played on AM radio. That was really, really approachable by radio stations and it still is to this day, because it's just a nice ballad; nice acoustic guitars.

Frantic City was just really successful. Within a few months of its release it was gold, and then a few months later it was platinum.

I have a picture of us giving our record to the mayor, right in front of City Hall. He looks like Bob Barker. That was probably the record company's idea.

Gordie Lewis: That was just a management promo, publicity, yeah.

Actually, you know what? It's one of the only cool publicity things that Jack Morrow ever did. He was a real cornball. He'd be the carnival guy — "Step right up!" type of thing.

Gold Album presentation, Hamilton City Hall / photo by Ralph Alfonso

Stephen Mahon: It's too bad it got stolen off the wall at City Hall two months later. Oh well, that's Hamilton for ya, ha ha ha.

Gordie Lewis: We had a vision and it took some time, but eventually the industry came around. But it wasn't easy because there definitely was that animosity, and it's taken thirty years — it took Green Day to really make everyone realize this music *does* sell; people really do like this stuff.

Frantic City was released in 1980 and went platinum. Again, I'm blowing my own horn here, but we more or less opened the doors for this genre. At the time it was all just Burton Cummings, Tom Cochrane, Red Rider — just look at the Juno Awards, the winners, and you'll get a sense of what music was like.

Julia Bourque: There was this collective ideal that you shouldn't sell out, as though it was a real cause.

Stephen Mahon: We had fans before we had made a record, and there were people that thought we sold out when our *Frantic City* album came out because it got played on the radio. You know, like, "Time to move on now, people are starting to like these guys."

People think like that. It's almost like they only like you when you're an underdog. They like to think that you're *their* band — "No one really likes these guys, but *we* know about them." And when we started becoming more popular, these people would sort of be jealous of all these other people showing up at shows, ha ha ha. "I knew these guys before *you*," kind of thing.

So what? What we're trying to do is be successful and have fans and be popular, and have people buy your records because they like it and enjoy it.

And then to say you suck because you've reached the masses, I don't know why it's such a negative thing.

Gail Manning: The president of the fan club, she'd phone the radio stations like fifty times a day saying, "*Play Teenage Head, play Teenage Head.*" I mean, we had more posters, more paraphernalia than probably any other band.

I personally phoned every radio station in the Toronto area every day, the record companies following up, talk to the news media on a weekly basis, all the columnists, invited them out everywhere ...

Gordie Lewis: The big machine was rolling. We had managers, agents, lawyers, and stuff ... You get lost in that; it just becomes too big. The music tends to take a background to everything, and it did. At that point it was more just making it to shows, and maybe partying was a bit too much.

1980 was really strange. It was a really strange time to be in the music business because at the time people were going to consulting agencies. Instead of using A&R guys and their ears as far as what would be the next single, they would go to an agency, and the *agency* would tell you what would be the next single by doing their marketing and their surveys and all this stuff.

"New Wave Music: No-Star Rock," by David Livingstone [*Maclean's*, April 7, 1980]: Citing medical studies, Hilly Leopold of Joint Communications, a Toronto research firm that advises radio stations on programming policies, explains: "Disco really was an electronic Valium because of its inherent frequencies which induce a transfer of energy to the legs. New wave, with its mid-to-higher frequencies, induces a neurological transfer, not a muscular transfer. Instead of moving in a trance-like way, people are more apt to jump up and down."

Gordie Lewis: So what they did was they said, "You know what your next 45 should be? It should be 'Let's Shake'." But we said, "Well, no, we just released 'Let's Shake.' It was the B-side to 'Something On My Mind'." They said, "No, you need to re-release 'Let's Shake,' only change some of the words and make it a little bit more listener friendly." And if you listen to the two versions, you'll see what I mean. You'll hear the difference in the lyrics.

It was the stupidest thing anyone could have possibly done. The radio stations just *totally* rejected it. They said "You're crazy, this stinks." But meanwhile, we had to pay for it as a band; you had to pay for all the costs.

So the record label went and hired this consulting agency to tell them what should be the next 45, they did, we made the changes to it, released it, then it flopped. So who gets the blame? We do. It's, "Oh, sorry pal, your next single didn't quite make it."

So we had to pay someone to tell us to release this 45 that was a piece of junk and it got rejected by all the radio stations.

"Top 100 Canadian Albums Of All Time" Frantic City by James Moore [*Chart* Magazine, February 2000]: "Kiss me where it stinks, so I drove her to Hamilton . . ." Steve, Frank, Gord and Nick made up Steeltown's finest, and one of Canada's, best bands.

While I was growing up in rural Nova Scotia, Teenage Head was constantly on my turntable. Without a doubt, *Frantic City* was the band's supreme moment. There should have been a movement headed by these guys in the United States, right up there with Ramones, the Sex Pistols . . .

Stephen Mahon: We just did our thing. We were proud of it, even if it didn't mean much worldwide.

We always kind of knew that if we could have gotten to England or the States, that would have been *so* much more important than having an album go gold in Canada. I'm not knocking it, it's a great thing to have happen, but we always knew that there was a whole world out there. And we always knew the Ramones were going to England and Australia and Japan and stuff, why weren't we?

We were lucky to just do Buffalo.

Platinum Album presentation, Attic Records.
l-r: Al Mair (Attic), Frankie Venom, Gord Lewis, Steve Mahon, Nick Stipanitz, Tom Williams (Attic)
Jack Morrow, front row, kneeling / photo by Ralph Alfonso

64.
Like radar

Captain Crash: When the punk scene first happened, there was this union that we stuck together by. We would lie through our teeth for each other. No matter how big the lie was, we would back it up. If it was for a member of the band, we would back it up. It was unbelievable how you would stick by somebody.

And then all of a sudden that started to fall apart. People stared arguing more. People lost sight of the goal. People didn't give a fuck what your buddy fuckin' did. So it changed big time. But why, I have no idea, because the intensity was really the same for the music. But it was just people's personalities. They got to know each other too well. Maybe they were hanging around each other too much, fuckin' breaking each other's stereos.

Chris Haight: The Secrets were like the seasoned veterans of all that scene and attitude. They were seasoned veterans who knew just how to work with everything from eccentrics to new-kid-on-the-block artists. They'd hardly give anybody a rough time except themselves. I think they took their frustrations out on each other.

John Hamilton: The Secrets turned out to be a pretty good little band, actually, but it was more of an R&B band. The scene was kind of moving in that direction a little bit; Elvis Costello and Joe Jackson were coming out really strong then and the punk thing seemed to be fading away.

Julia Bourque: John always said, "You've got to latch on to it; it only happens in a city every fifteen years." He said it's a small window, and then it will close. And it certainly did.

John Hamilton: Nobody had really broken through in Toronto, so we thought we might be able to sneak in through this door if the other one's closing.

We played a lot. We played in New York, we played Max's, the Mudd Club, CBGB's, the Hot Club in Philly. We played in Buffalo, we played a lot in Ottawa, we played in Montreal; we played all over the place.

Mike Anderson: The Secrets was more of a fun thing I think more than anything. It was that cult-y kind of thing. There was more adoration towards women; it was more a girl band than a guy band, and less destructive. It was a little more easygoing.

Freddy Pompeii: We were gigging all the time. We even bought ourselves a van. No chaos, no fights, no riots.

It was a whole different attack than with the Viletones. Everybody brought something to the table. There were songs that Chris wrote, there were songs that I wrote, there were songs that we all wrote together and everybody got credit; nobody was stabbing anybody in the back. It was a really nice experience. It was refreshing after what we had been through with Steven, and all the uncertainty that was always surrounding it.

But we all missed the Viletones. Chris Haight was the only one that would say, "I don't miss it," but I know he missed it like the rest of us did. It just wasn't meant to be anymore.

The Secrets wasn't as popular as the Viletones on a national level. The Secrets were more of a local thing. We were big in Toronto, but hardly anywhere else. We got a recording contract with Bomb Records, who the Battered Wives were with. We always had a rehearsal space and we always had places to play. So we stuck with that until I left town.

John Hamilton: Eventually we did make an album with Bomb Records, which is the old story: Big company, big crooks; little company, *all* crooks.

Freddy Pompeii [*Shades* no. 5, August 1979]: Bomb ran out of money. There were several groups they approached on the same basis as us, offers of a demo, "We're going to make you a big group," and all that shit, and they were not really ready to follow through on any of that stuff. They were really soliciting and getting people interested in case the Wives album or the Segarini album sold.

John Hamilton: Then, of course, bad things happened.

Andrew McGregor: There was a real junk scene on Queen Street in the early '80s. It was probably underground before that, but by the '80s you could see a lot of the guys sitting around in the bars just waiting for their man to drop by.

That was probably another thing that hurt the punk music. There were probably too many people that thought, To be a proper punk I should also be a junkie, and their idea of what it was to be a junkie might have been informed by reading a William Burroughs novel or two and it seemed like a cool scene. And of course, it destroyed them musically, and it destroyed them.

Elizabeth Aikenhead: I think that whole scene, that whole period, really taught me the meaning of the expression, "There but for the grace of God go I."

It could have happened to any of us. It could have so easily happened. You're going left, and all of a sudden you're going right. You're going north and *bang*, you're going south. You think you're dabbling in something and you'll get out of it. Some didn't, and lots of people died.

William Cork: Heroin did the same thing to that scene that it did to the hippie scene, that it did to the Beat scene, that it did to the jazz scene, whether it was Billie Holiday, or ...

Andrew McGregor: It hurt a lot of bands, and broke up a lot of bands. But it was all part of the "No Future" thing: Why *not* be a junkie? We're all going to be dead in three years. That's what people were talking about at the time; it's all coming to an end very soon. They were apocalyptic times and that music didn't exist without that attitude; that understanding and perception of the world.

John Hamilton: Both Freddy and Chris started doing it. Both of them got addicted, and they were heroin addicts by the end of the Secrets. Freddy had always been a drug dealer. That's how he made his living.

Christopher Barnes: I remember my dad ... The house was raided once and I was out in the front yard playing in the dirt, and the cops came with their guns drawn. That's a strong memory.

Chris Haight: There were some real good parts to the Secrets, and some real bad parts, too. That album was really rushed. Two reasons: The guy that was producing it was Russian, and the guys that were flipping the bill ran out of dough.

I think we should be lucky that somebody even took the time to put it together considering what the hell they were working with, and that's us included. I'm talking about the whole situation right off the hop. The focus shifted from what you really wanted to do, to, "I gotta do some drugs." It just wasn't real.

I didn't love what I was fuckin' doing and I needed something to *remind* me of why I was doing it, and that's a big fuckin' difference. A lot of that had to do with the demise, as far as we were concerned. Because where do you cut the line from being a virtuoso and you knock 'em dead to, "Well, fuck, I know I can play it. I ain't feeling too hot. I'm going to make a phone call."

I always loved the shit; I think it's your only anchor-hold to going from there to fuckin' nowheresville, bottom of the barrel, dark end of the street. You're hanging on to that, and it just becomes a ball of confusion.

It took me years to straighten myself out.

Mike Anderson: I was the first one to leave. This guy Rudy from Arson was coming around and I was talking to him and he was trying to ask me, "You wanna play in Arson? We're looking for a drummer." I thought about it, and then I did.

Freddy Pompeii: Motor couldn't really play the kind of music we were doing. His improvisational style was too loose; it demanded a lot more skill.

Mike Anderson: I kind of wanted to get out of the R&B kind of thing, too, and I wasn't too happy with the travelling arrangements when we were on the road.

We almost got rubbed out in Detroit and blacklisted. We never had any money. The manager was supposed to come through with this and that and we were stranded. Back then I didn't have the capabilities of jumping on a flight or something any time I wanted, so I was stuck.

I remember running into Teenage Head in Chicago and I said, "Jack, can you give me a lift back to Toronto?" "No, I can't do that."

Thanks a lot, Jack.

With Arson, we went to New York a couple times and to the Midwest — Detroit, Chicago, Milwaukee. That was different. Then I just kind of got sick of all of that. That's when I got into the film business.

John Hamilton: We were crossing borders and Freddy had fifty hits of acid that fell out of his passport that he'd forgotten about or something. It looked like stickers little kids have, so the border guard never said anything. So we'd play New York and Freddy would go and deal fifty hits of acid. Freddy was dealing a lot.

Junkies know each other like radar. We'd walk into a town and Freddy and Chris would meet all the junkies: Like magnets and iron filings, they could tell by looking at each other immediately. They became pals with Johnny Thunders so we started getting into the whole junkie scene, which I didn't really want to be a part of. I didn't want to go that way.

Chris Haight: I think it bothered him terribly so. Just as a person, when he went to fuckin' *high school* he was serious. Drum lessons — "I'm serious. I wanna be a writer, journalist, blah blah," the most serious guy of all.

A pretty smart cookie, too. He was probably going, "What am I gonna do now? Look at these fuckin' guys. This is supposed to be my band."

John Hamilton: We played Ottawa one time, and there was a lot of heroin in Ottawa because of course the diplomats have immunity — diplomatic pouches. So Ottawa was full of heroin.

You could feel the narcs breathing down your neck. There were these guys in the Rotters Club where we were playing, and you could just *smell* the bust coming. I was terrified. Finally we finished that gig, we got out of town, and I was just going, "Man, that we didn't get busted there was amazing." Then Freddy goes back a couple of days later to do some more dealing and got busted.

He eventually had to skip Canada because of that. We were supposed to play the Beverley that weekend. When Freddy got busted it all just went to pieces. Drugs killed that band.

Freddy Pompeii: We would have been the top band in Toronto if we had have stayed together because we were making those kinds of connections; getting recording contracts and recording offers and stuff like that. So because of that I really regretted having to leave, and I really felt like I let the band down, too. But that was it, I had to leave. I *had* to.

I had to go because Crash got busted in Ottawa. We were trying to get some gigs together and staying at a hotel. And Crash was doing a morphine deal while we were there. We had no idea what was going on with him.

While we were getting ready to leave the RCMP came crashing through the door and busted all of us. I had two hundred and fifty hits of LSD that I had in my wallet for about two years. It wasn't really good shit. Crash had given it to me and said, "Try to sell this," and I couldn't sell it. So it was basically notepads in my wallet. I would jot down notes on it and everything.

Well, they found that in my wallet and said, "Oh, LSD," and I said, "Oh my god." I mean, how many times had I been over the border and back going to gigs with that in my wallet, never even thinking about it? But they laid a blanket charge on us, all of us, for morphine and LSD, and then finally the LSD was laid on me and the morphine was laid on Crash.

But before that happened I was going down for morphine just as equal to Crash, so it was either go to jail again — like, turn on my friend and roll over on him and say, "It's all Crash's" — or not show up for court and just leave the country. Those were my choices. So I decided I'm gonna get out of the country, stop doing these fuckin' drugs, and get out of these bad situations. And that's what I ended up doing.

I didn't want to roll over on Crash — that was out of the question. So it was better that I left and he handled his legal problems for himself without having any difficulties of someone having to say, "Well, it's not mine, it's his." That's basically why we really left, because of the court dates and not being able to afford a lawyer and not wanting to turn over on Crash.

That's the situation that was happening then. I couldn't stay in Canada any longer. I couldn't do it.

I had a pretty good ten-year stay, though. A lot of good things happened.

Captain Crash: Fred didn't want to go back to jail. Fred had already been in jail. He got caught with fifty-two pounds of pot and they jerked him around. Although he got a light sentence they made him do the *whole* sentence, and he didn't have fun in jail. So he decided he wasn't going to go back.

The heroin charges were all dropped, the morphine charges were all dropped, but he had this acid in his pocket that he had to account for, so he just decided to split.

One of the things I feel sorriest about is I encouraged him. I said, "What the fuck? What are you gonna go to jail for? Go to Philadelphia."

Margaret Barnes-DelColle: He was in his late thirties, he had to be by then, and he'd never smoked cigarettes. And that's when he started smoking cigarettes, in jail.

He'd gone to jail before for dealing pot and he was like, "I'll definitely end up going to jail again and I *can't*. I just can't do it." So he was like, "We need to move to Philadelphia."

Meanwhile, his dad was starting to have heart problems; his parents were getting old. You don't know where your life's going to take you, but I wish I'd never left, really.

Freddy Pompeii: Up until the point I left Toronto with Margaret and Christopher, we were heavy into heroin. Really heavy into it. We were all into shooting it.

Johnny Thunders came to town with Gang War, Wayne Kramer of the MC5, and the first person he came to see was me so he could get some dope. It got like that. Gary Cormier called me one day because Nico from the Velvet Underground was coming to do a show at the Edge and he wanted to know if I could get some morphine or some heroin for her. I was the person they would call. It was either me or Chris or whoever else was able to get something. It's a bad position to be in because everybody figures, "We know where to get it. We'll call Freddy."

Me and Margaret were locked into it until we left Toronto and came to Philly, and then we finally got free of it. It was a pretty nasty addiction. I don't know if I could even explain to you what being sick is like. It's like the worst sickness you could possibly imagine.

I didn't want to leave, and neither did she. Because things were so bad with drugs, I knew that if I came to Philly I wouldn't have any connections so I'd be forced to clean up. And that's what worked for us.

Christopher Barnes: I definitely didn't want to leave because I had my friends there and my family, my mother's family. And Philadelphia — we were going to another country.

And the whole moving thing was kind of weird, too. My mother and my aunt and her boyfriend were going to drive down, but my aunt's boyfriend had felonies so they turned us around at the border. I remember that being very upsetting. Eventually, we flew down or something.

I think they probably said we were moving for work, so Freddy could get a better job. I do remember going to some hearing about him getting deported at some point. I was up on the stand saying, "Don't send my daddy away." Later, my mother told me he was kind of running away from something.

Margaret Barnes-DelColle: We moved to Philadelphia in 1980, so that kind of just abruptly ended Power Street. I don't know where everybody went after that, but at that point the scene was still going pretty strong.

At the time I didn't really think about leaving Toronto so much. I didn't think about it long term. At the time it was necessary. I was with him, so I moved. I love Philadelphia now, but still, when I come back to Toronto I think I shouldn't have done that. Because I'm a very proud Canadian, and I loved Toronto.

But then on the other hand, if I hadn't have left I might be dead now. I might have just kept doing the drugs. I always say to people, too, if I didn't have Christopher I'm pretty sure I would have been dead. There wouldn't have been anything to stop me.

I was a little bit reserved because I had a son. So I always feel like he kept me from going completely berserk.

Rosy Ruin [*Shades* no. 11, June 1980]: Margarita and Freddy were as vital as anyone to what began here when it was best. They were hardly unsung but they probably weren't understood or appreciated for all they were worth. Soon they'll both be gone — Freddy left a long time ago — but we will be absorbing their impact and influence here for a long time. If we're lucky and things yet turn out at all well.

Captain Crash: It left a huge vacuum. New Rose closed.

Freddy was instrumental on the music scene. A lot of people respected him. His kitchen was like Yonge and Bloor, I'm telling you. From eleven o'clock in the morning till three o'clock at night, there was nothing but people coming through there banging on the fuckin' door. It was just unbelievable. There could be sometimes fifteen people just hanging around the living room who just dropped by.

Yeah, when they left it was a huge hole. Not only from my standpoint of friends missing – I saw them every day pretty well – but in the music scene, and in New Rose going. People really liked those two people. Freddy was an icon. People really respected him. He thought things out real well and wasn't frivolous with what he said. He had some really interesting views, and was always friends with people and complimented people.

It's too bad; the city missed him.

*   *   *   *   *

Margaret Barnes-DelColle: When we moved down here Fred started this band called Thee Immaculate Hearts. They did a lot of gigs in New York and they did one at this little tiny club called Downtown Beirut. It had a long bar on one side of the place and we were all kind of hanging out.

There wasn't that many people that showed up. The guy was supposed to give them two cases of beer and X amount of dollars. So he gave them the beer and they did their show, and then they went to get their money at the end of the show and the guy said, "No no, you're not getting any money. You really didn't draw. There wasn't any money." And they said, "The deal wasn't like we got the door. The deal was a flat rate that you were gonna give us." And the guy absolutely refused.

We were all standing there and everybody was getting really pissed off. So Fred said to me, "Okay, get ready. As soon as you see what's going on, then *quick*, the car's out front, get in the driver's seat." Somebody had brought the car around. They had put all their equipment in the car.

They picked up the bar stools and started throwing them over the bar, breaking the mirrors and the glasses and the bottles and they were like, "Fuck you!" And then they all started yelling, "RUN!" So I'm in front, I run, I get in the car and everybody piles into the car and they're like, "Fucking drive, drive, *drive!*" Ha ha ha. They destroyed the bar because they wouldn't pay them. It was great.

Just because we moved to Philadelphia didn't mean the insanity stopped. It was supposed to, but it didn't. It just kept going.

Sally Cato, Androids / photo by Ross Taylor

Freddy and Chris / photo by Gail Bryck

65.
a GooD
emPLoYee

Chris Houston: I had to get a bass to play in the Rebels, then I had to learn how to *play* bass. Al Smolak had played in Rush cover bands, and it took me a while to really become proficient on my instrument.

What I would do is everyday I'd walk home from Westdale, go sit on my bed, and play *In Love With the System* and practise my bass along with it until my mom called me for dinner. And that's how I became a good bass player. You've got to be bad a whole lot before you're good.

We rehearsed at this place called Bull's Gym, which was a former boxing club.

Mickey DeSadist: Bull Johnson was a real bad wrestler. You know those guys that get beat up every week on television? He's one of those guys that lost to everybody. He was also The Mysterian, the guy in the mask that *won* all his matches, ha ha ha. It was his place. We ended the '70s at that place.

Chris Houston: Somehow we took over the lease and decided on New Year's Eve 1979–1980 that we'd throw our own New Year's gig and make all the money. Basically, that's when the Rebels came into their own.

So I guess we oversold the room, so much that the audience kept falling on the band and all the booze spilled down onto the machine shop downstairs. The cops came and the great thing is that Smolak, rest in peace, convinced them that he lived there.

There was this dog's bed there that was covered with these brown spots. When you don't touch blankets for a couple years they turn brown. He said that was his bed, so the cops left in utter revulsion because they felt he had to be some strange person to live that way, thus leaving us alone.

Bob Bryden: My favourite Rebels story is the great Ramones debacle. The Ramones were coming to town and were actually going to do a concert in Burlington.

CFNY I think were putting it on. Oh – you have to understand that CFNY loathed and despised the Forgotten Rebels. They *still* don't play them. They hated them then, and they still seem to hate them now. The Rebels were anathema to CFNY, the so-called bastion of new music, the so-called "this is where it's supposed to happen."

Not with "The third homosexual murder and the fourth one might be you" on the first EP. Need I say more?

Chris Houston: Well, I think Mickey let it be known that "Third Homosexual Murder" was about the guy that owned David's.

Bob Bryden: There were very specific political interests at CFNY who didn't like that song. But just about every song the Rebels ever made was designed to make *somebody* not like it, so nobody was getting the joke. That's fine, but they wouldn't play it.

Chris Houston: Yeah, there were certain lyrical things that they didn't like about the Rebels. They only picked that stuff up way later. I mean, sometimes it took a lot of these bands five years of being popular and being part of the fabric of people's listening before they would actually play them on CFNY. If you greased the palms of CFNY, they would kind of get behind you. Although they were like the big independent music thing; payola really did exist in those days and *still* exists.

Most of our airplay was college radio and a lot of people, because of the content of the Rebels stuff, had their college radio stations taken away for playing certain Rebels songs. It was kind of like a suicide mission when you played the Rebels on the radio because you know the station manager's going to call you in the office and you'd no longer have a radio show. I know a few people who did that.

Forgotten Rebels / photo by Steve Burman

There was something about the obnoxiousness of the record that tested a lot of boundaries. Mickey's sense of humour is definitely misconstrued by a lot of people, which is okay because they would kind of extrapolate on it and you'd realize that their imaginations were way more perverse than ours. Ha ha ha.

Bob Bryden: CFNY were against the Rebels; they would have done anything to shut them down. But through a strange series of circumstances, we managed to get the Rebels on a bill with the Ramones. The show was in Burlington, so that was cool; that was handy. The Ramones were coming to Star Records. It was a Wednesday, I think, too, so this was a really weird Wednesday.

They got the gig on an unwritten condition that they would not play —

Chris Houston: I'm not allowed to mention the song. It's a great song, though. Mickey swore me to secrecy. You have to get me really drunk at the bar.

Bob Bryden: — "I Wanna Be a Nazi." It was pretty funny; they could do the gig if they *didn't* play that song. And I believe CFNY had something to do with it because CFNY were involved with the production and promotion.

Of course, about three or four tunes into their set — and there were about two thousand kids at this concert; it was packed — Mickey says, "We're not supposed to do this song but we're gonna do it anyway. One-two-three-four!" Boom — they do "I Wanna Be a Nazi." And I'm just sitting there going "Oh no, there's gonna be trouble."

But I didn't anticipate the depth of the trouble. I had *no idea* how big this was gonna go.

Chris Houston: It was beyond *anything*, and that's all I can say. When we played it, boy, you could feel them against the walls.

Mickey DeSadist: Some members of the audience were intelligent enough to know we were goofing off. Like, I mean, there's two Polish guys in the band. We wouldn't actually make it in the Nazi Party, would we? And we did that for a joke only because we knew it was a sore thumb. People were being freaked out that I would talk so casually about guys like Dolf and the boys. So they took everything the wrong way.

Chris Houston: It was more immaturity. I think that when you hear the lyrics to that song it's pretty obvious. There's a disclaimer in the last verse.

Mickey just kind of liked the outrage of it.

Anything that could get people's attention, he would test people with it. When you're charged with inciting a riot three times before you're twenty, that's a good career.

Mickey DeSadist: I had this theory that if they take everything the wrong way, I'll get a good laugh out of it and I don't care. Which was a pretty dumb idea.

Have you seen the original version of *The Producers*, with Zero Mostel and Gene Wilder? I remember being fourteen, me and this guy were watching this movie laughing our heads off, and people thought there was nothing funny about it. That shows you a lot of stuff behind the early Rebels. It shows you exactly our idea.

Larry Potvin: It was only a little *after* the band I started paying attention more to the lyrics and what was going on. Back then, it was just the music, man, and a guy screaming onstage in plastic pants. I couldn't care less about what the lyrics were about.

Chris Houston: The Ramones didn't play that well that night, and the Rebels played *really* well. So it was kind of our night. It was cool.

The stage was huge! I couldn't hear the other band members. All I could hear was my bass amp in this huge place. But it was hilarious, because they just trashed the place.

Before the punks got into that Burlington arena, it was brand new. They ripped off all the letters that said "Centennial Arena." Like, it'd been open for a week, and they were destroying the place before they even got in.

Then there was a riot. So when we left, there was nothing but the rubble of all these brand new chairs in the middle. We got charged with inciting a riot. That was kind of great. Mickey had the great line — "Don't stand there, *wreck* something!"

Bob Bryden: Within a few days I get a phone call from the Office of the Attorney General, and I get a phone call from the Burlington Police Department, and I believe I got a call from the man himself who was offended, I'm trying to remember that.

Anyway, I got a bunch of calls that related to the fact that there had been a man there at the concert who had lost his family in the Holocaust and was just horrified and outraged at this song. So he just blew the whistle.

Larry Potvin: Don't take them seriously, because there's nothing serious to say.

With that band, the only thing I really agreed with was "Elvis is dead, the big fat guy's dead, dead, dead, spend your money on our records instead."

I believed that.

I didn't believe in bombing the boats and feeding their flesh to the fish, but as a young person I didn't understand the implications of what was happening there: People escaping communism; ruthless governments that would kill anything and everybody that would disagree with them. Of course these people were getting on boats and getting the hell out of there. I would, too.

Back then I had just a total ignorance of the whole thing. I didn't really go with the flow in terms of that song. I just was into the music.

Bob Bryden: I guess this was the beginning of the period where hate crime and all that stuff was coming up. It was really serious; they're calling Star Records because we were the band's record label.

So I eventually ended up going to — I'll never forget this meeting — the Burlington Police Department. And I kid you not, I sat in a little grey room, all the walls were grey, with a little table and a lamp on it and two chairs over there and one chair over here. I didn't know they did that; I thought they only did that in the movies. I thought they were going to shine a lamp in my face. And these two detectives came in and what was really ironic is they had the Rebels album with the lyric sheet and everything. *Not* the EP though, the one that has "I Wanna Be a Nazi" on it. They had the album, because even at that time the EP was hard to get.

So they put the album down on the table, and I'm staring at them, and I'm staring at the album. What I had to do was ensure, or assure, the detectives of the Burlington Police who were representing the complainer and the Office of the Attorney General in this investigation that the Forgotten Rebels were not a neo-Nazi organization bent on overthrowing the government and taking over the world. I literally had to convince them of that, and I did in those exact words.

I said, "They are a bunch of kids who are total reactionaries who will do anything to shock you. If you say yes they'll say no, if you say go they'll say stop. They will do anything to shock you." And I said, "Clearly, you have fallen into their trap."

And it was really funny because these guys, at that statement, just folded it up and said "Okay," and that was that.

But I've been forced to think this through. I've had to come to terms with this and say, "What was I thinking when I let them put my name on 'I Wanna Be a Nazi'? I don't agree with that at all." But this is one of Mickey's classics: He says, "Bob, that song's not about being a Nazi. People aren't hearing the verses — there's a line in there that says you've gotta be quite an idiot to believe in this." Ha ha ha. Talk about fine print.

Mickey DeSadist: Better Bob to deal with it than me.

I got a good laugh out of it. Supposedly the RCMP sat there and asked if these guys were involved in any idiotic activity and Bob goes, "No, these guys are just doing it for publicity; they don't know what they're talking about." And the guy from the RCMP goes, "That's exactly what I thought, too."

What really disappointed me is that the only song that ever reflected anything about us was that we were necrophiliacs — "Fuck Me Dead." We all had a secret desire to go to the morgue when nobody was looking.

I'm only kidding, in case anybody else is stupid enough to think I'm telling the truth. Why didn't they accuse us of *that*? Why didn't they accuse us of being necrophiliacs?

I thought they would have got the joke. It was just bait for the newspapers. The newspapers at that time were condemning Smurfs for being satanic, so you know what that was like for us to do that.

Steve Leckie was always an intelligent guy when it came to getting publicity. He knew how to do it. I'm sure he had a few problems in his time that made him lose momentum, because I wanted to see him succeed. I mean, I wanted to see me succeed more, but I wanted to see the Viletones, Teenage Head, the Rebels succeed really well, and Simply Saucer. We all needed each other.

Chris Houston: Then there was our famous gig at Toronto City Hall where it was supposed to be Rock Against Radiation. Then Leckie decided he was going to go *pro*-radiation, so they screwed us around on the bill.

We introduced winos as our parents.

Mickey DeSadist: All I remember is we thought, This is a great place to really stir up a bees nest, ha ha ha. Basically all we did was try to get publicity by just disturbing the show; any slogans we'd shout out was just for the sake of disturbance.

We were just having fun; we were wearing military gear at the most anti-military place, ha ha ha. I remember we had signs — it was Houston, it was all his idea to put the "Pray For War" signs up. Pray for war, ha ha ha.

Chris Houston: That was a great gig. It made the front page of the *Toronto Star* and the *Globe and Mail*. "Disgusting Punk Rock Takes Over City Hall." It was my birthday, too. I turned legal drinking age.

*   *   *   *   *

Larry Potvin: It was looking good for us, and I was hoping that this thing would get bigger.

Chris Houston: It took a while for the industry to really embrace punk and make it easy to get. I think that the initial burst of stuff, because it took six months or a year for things that would happen in London to hit over here, there was a time delay on the record releases and the touring. And after the initial burst of really creative stuff, most of those bands became total drug addicts and were sitting high in apartments all the time. So the scene kind of floundered.

Rock critics said it was going to take over the world, but it took until Kurt Cobain for it to take over North America. That Cobain kid single-handedly made punk rock legit in North America, but that's decades after it happened. *Then* it became mainstream.

Larry Potvin: After *In Love With the System,* I thought we should keep up the same show, the same energy, but just start changing the songs. An original band is nothing without songs, so you have to write songs. Without the songwriting you're nothing; you're just a copy band.

I saw music and bands as a business, a company, a factory out-putting, and I've always felt it had to be treated that way, even back then. Because even as an apprentice electrician, I saw how the foreman has his job and the general foremen have their jobs, and the superintendent has his job and they go to these meetings and they do their planning, this structural planning.

I don't know if Mickey was interested in that. I never felt that he was. We never communicated enough.

I can't remember the things I said, but I remember the feeling I had back then that we had to become more structured and think about what we were doing more.

Chris Houston: Here, by the early '80s, the more *career* punk rock people kind of moved in. Everybody knew the record and what you were supposed to sound like. And everybody wanted to be the fastest band in the world, or the hardest band in the world. So it was less exotic. Music suffered, because people were just trying to go for these certain ... Everybody had the same delusions simultaneously.

Larry Potvin: It might have maybe been a six-month thing for the album to really take off after it was released, but people *were* buying it; it was moving.

Chris Houston: When I realized that the album was finally getting the kind of attention I wanted it to was one of the Horseshoe gigs we did. I mean, there were hundreds of kids waiting for us in the afternoon when we showed up from Hamilton. At that point we started going, "Wow."

Larry Potvin: I remember feeling that we had to become more focused and start talking more about what we were going to do.

Basically we would rehearse, make sure we knew the songs, put a set list together, go onstage, play the songs and Mickey would do his thing. Now today, in order to become more successful, I know that you can't just go along with that innocence. You have to put some thought behind it. Bigger places mean different dynamics; how you move around onstage, how you play to a thousand people rather than a hundred. Everything changes with bigger audiences.

That's one thing I do remember, that I was thinking more towards songs and what the band would do to play the bigger audiences. But of course it never happened.

Chris Houston: Larry was always a fish out of water because he was essentially a jazz-fusion drummer. He had serious drumming chops. He also had a gigger mentality; that was he wanted to be paid, that we should be making more money. And somehow that just didn't jive with Mickey's thing.

I always loved his drumming — as a bass player, I don't really give a shit about a personality. If you're a great drummer, you're a great drummer and I'll want to stick with you. But I knew that he wasn't going to last long in the group. He didn't have a high regard for the music that we were doing, which rubbed other elements in the band the wrong way, ha ha ha.

Larry Potvin: The next album was going to be "Surfin' On Heroin," songs like that, and that was just when the president was doing this Say No To Drugs campaign. And I objected to songs like "Surfin' on Heroin." I remember saying, "I don't know if we should be playing that," because I felt to become successful ...

I remember the Ontario Provincial Police breaking down my door thinking there were tons of drugs. We didn't have anything. We weren't drug dealers. I was rooming with a guy who was a member of that Legalize Marijuana society. But they broke down our door, searched all our pockets ...

So society was changing, and punk, I could see that it was starting to change into something else.

Stephen Burman: People remember Mickey because he's funny onstage. He's got a personality. The Rebels performing live are very different from the Rebels recorded. Going to see a Rebels show, you get to see Mickey's antics and snippets of his performance as a character; there's as much that as there is music.

I remember Gary Topp said he loved Mickey live. He was indifferent to the recorded music, but he kept wanting to put Mickey on any day of the week as a solo act rather than with the Rebels. He offered me all these shows for Mickey as a solo artist, even back then, and Mickey just wanted to do the Rebels thing.

Gary Pig Gold: I would always be mentioning the Rebels to Gary, but he'd say, "I don't know whether I should book these guys." So I'd go, "Then just book Mickey, the singer. Have him just come down and *talk*."

Stephen Burman: So there was definitely interest in Mickey as an individual more so than in the band, because everybody knew the Rebels were Mickey. And if you talk to the young kids at the shows, you'll see that they're starting to realize that they go to see Mickey as much as the music.

Mickey DeSadist: I wanted to work in a team with a band, because I thought that four brains were always better than one.

In London, yeah, I remember somebody offered me — and this was a *lot* of money for that time — a hundred thousand dollars to quit the Rebels and join a band of their choice. It would be a list of musicians that I would pick from that they would put together. And I said for a hundred thousand dollars — and this was a five-year contract — I says to the guy for a hundred thousand dollars, like right now I'm working at Otis Elevator like I was at the time, and I was making twenty-five thousand bucks a year. That's five thousand less a year than this contract I would sign. Then I'm playing in a band making a few more dollars. And then I said, "If you want me to write songs while I play with the Rebels and you can have my songs first, I'll do *that* for a hundred thousand dollars, but I'm not into going on any tours." And I said, "If you want me to join a band of your choice, I would probably want two hundred thousand dollars, but one hundred thousand of it in cash advance," because that was almost enough to retire on so that would have kept me out of the day job thing. And I said, "And I would play locally. For two hundred and *fifty* thousand bucks, which I would have fifty to two hundred thousand in the bank, I will go on *tour* with a band of your choice."

Because see, what I wanted to do, I wanted to just play in a band and party. But I didn't want to have the insecurity of not coming home to a bankroll.

See, if you look at it, if that was 1982, 1983, money doubles itself. I took economics in school, so I understood that if money doubles itself every nine years, by the time 1992 rolled around, that two hundred thousand, which I wouldn't have spent, would have become four hundred thousand. By the time 2001 rolled around that would have been eight hundred thousand. This year it would have been around a million bucks,

and I wouldn't have spent that because I would have it all locked in everywhere. See, I would have had financial security and still been earning from playing, so I would have been able to live for all those years without ever having a straight day job.

I was trying to avoid having a straight day job at all costs, but for some reason every time I applied for a job I was hired. Because I was a good employee at every place I worked, my downfall was that every time I applied for a straight day job I got it, and I got one very quickly.

But then again, I'm not the kind of guy that doesn't like my toys.

Bob Bryden: Well, I can let the cat out of the bag. I was vocal about it then, and he might dislike me for saying this, but we used to say Mickey is a complete paradox. I'm not saying he was a lie; he was a paradox.

You would literally see him go to the foot of the stage and hork up a bunch of phlegm, and I've actually seen this happen — why am I shocked? And he would spit into another punk's mouth and it'd be like they'd died and gone to heaven. So the same guy who would do that and would be up on the stage spewing profanity, if you knocked on his door he would answer in his plush bathrobe, probably silk, with slippers and his pipe, sitting in his armchair with a snifter of brandy. It was legendary around Hamilton.

I'm exaggerating a little bit here, but I'm illustrating that he was actually a pussycat, and that's an absolute fact.

Mickey DeSadist: What really embarrasses me is when people call me a nice guy when I was trying to make a big deal about coming across as a nasty character. Too many people got that point — that I wasn't that nasty, I was just trying to be silly and smirking at everything myself.

Bob Bryden: He wouldn't hurt a fly. He's one of the most conscientious people I've ever met. In all of these years, he's always had a day job. And he's fastidious. He's really disciplined — yeah, Mickey DeSadist is one of the most disciplined people I've ever met in a very straight, normal way. It's show business.

Gary Pig Gold: He never quit his day job — "You need something to fall back on. You know the music business …" I'd tell them to go down to L.A. and play the Whisky and the Roxy, and Mickey would go, "But I gotta be back by eight o'clock Monday to go to work."

Paul Kobak: I had planned a western trip for the Forgotten Rebels, and pretty much had six or eight dates firmed up; it made sense. At which point Mickey says, "Well, if the Forgotten Rebels want to go out west, they can go there without me," because he was still working at Otis Elevator here in Hamilton painting garbage cans. He didn't want to lose his job.

Ahhh, what price, stardom.

Chris Houston: I hate working. No way am I like Mike in that way.

I think Mike had to support himself. See, I lived at home. I *still* live at home. But Mike, because he wanted to pursue his thing in life, he had to pay rent, he had to buy food ... and I don't think his old man was going to bring over food.

Things like rehearsal spaces, usually that was from the band fund. When you played gigs that money would go towards rehearsal. Smolak always took care of that stuff. Al was very good with numbers. The guitar player from the Forgotten Rebels' *In Love With the System* record went on to set up the GST system in Australia ...

A lot of the bands in Hamilton, you could drop out of high school and go on to make fifteen dollars an hour at Stelco. So you'd work for six months and then you'd go on [Employment Insurance] and you'd get enough to buy a Les Paul or Marshall. EI was a lot different then. You could run it for a long period, so most of the musicians would work, because you could always get a job, and then go on EI until that ran out and start up again.

A lot of the bands had T-shirts that said, "Unemployment Insurance Drinking Program." It was, "Meet you at the beer store, we'll discuss our career."

Mickey DeSadist: I always had to have a job. I'm not going to live with inconvenience, being a starving artist. The art stands for itself; the music stands for itself. I'm not going to go around making some stupid record company a ton of money and not getting a major portion towards me. I recognize being in that position is just as ridiculous as having a lousy job.

*   *   *   *   *

Chris Houston: I went to art school in 1980, '81. I had to take off to the big city of Toronto and hang out with the Dishes, ha ha ha. It was a big thing when members of the Diodes would say hi to you. I got accepted. Those were big bands and they did big numbers at the Horseshoe, so these were your idols.

When I moved, we were trying to keep it going. I would come back for certain gigs. Everything was kind of in flux.

Mickey DeSadist: Our last show together was somewhere in London.

Chris Houston: London, Ontario was the first time the Rebels could go away and be rock stars somewhere. We'd come into town and see our names spray-painted on walls and stuff, and we realized that none of *us* had spray-painted it; we had fans with spray guns.

And they treated us really well there. There was something magical about going to London, which is a small city and it had nice air because there wasn't a lot of industry. I mean, when you're from Hamilton ...

Larry Potvin: The last fight – it wasn't a fight I guess, but it sort of was a fight – basically broke up the band.

I was using my van to move all our stuff, so therefore the guitarist believed we should all take part in the maintenance; if anything happens to the van, the band has to pay for it.

Sure enough, the guitar player was driving and saw a truck coming up, so he put it in gear and drove but the transmission didn't like it so it broke. So we only had second and third gear.

We eventually got to the gig, but Mickey was the most upset about having to pay for the transmission, which was like seven hundred bucks. Which was most of the money for the gig we'd just played in London. Mickey really didn't like it. And basically, he's the band. If the band moves, he's the one who's moving the band.

I can't remember what happened; how the band broke up. I think Mickey just decided to drop everybody and move on to the next group of musicians, because he *is* the show.

So it was kind of disheartening. It was just all of a sudden, no more gigs. That was it.

I was hoping we were going to keep going. It was too bad, because I really enjoyed playing in that band. I was hoping it was going to go somewhere.

Chris Houston: My favourite part of being in Hamilton is going to Tim Horton's with Mickey, then driving around and him pointing out all these people on the street. He knows a story on every street person, and they all have bizarre stories. When he does these monologues it's just sheer genius.

He likes characters; he's a character himself. But there's a reason I used to tell people, "There's not room for two Hitlers in one band."

Mickey DeSadist: Chris, he didn't wanna play anymore. He was being too much of a boss, you know, and I'm not going to put up with that, you know? It's one thing when a person wants to work in a team, but it's another thing when they wanna act like my boss.

Houston, what can I say about Houston? Yeah, Houston left. We were pissed off at each other. He kept giving me orders and being a boss, so I didn't wanna put up with it.

Larry Potvin: The hardest time was coming home from London, after the anti-climax gig. It was like, "The band's gonna break up." That was basically it. We were all in the van together.

The guitarist held the money because he was the economics major at Mac [McMaster University], so the economics major made sure that I got reimbursed for fixing my transmission. I paid some of it, the band paid some of it, and that was basically it. It's unfortunate that something like that would break up a band, but ...

Mickey DeSadist: With Al and Larry, it was an argument over a truck transmission or something. It was a silly argument, but for what it was worth it was there. I don't know what to say.

Larry Potvin: I think there are other factors in there that I wasn't quite aware of that were breaking up the band.

I think Mickey was maybe getting a little disheart-ened; maybe he wanted to have more control over the whole thing. It seemed like that's what was happening because he *is* the show; he *is* the personality of the band.

I wasn't thinking of it in terms of one person having all the power and everybody doing what that one person says. I thought we were all a team. Everybody was together in the band. He had his job; we all had our jobs. Those questions never got raised, who's the boss of the band or who does what.

I don't even remember quitting. It was just, "That's it." We met at Jackson Square Mall at a restaurant, and that was it. I don't remember what was talked about.

Between us, it was more of a working relationship, because after the band broke up we didn't see each other anymore. So I was kind of upset, but I went on to the next band.

Al was intelligent, sensible, easygoing. We got along great. He laughed at our jokes. I liked him, but he went his own way. After the band broke up he got his degree in economics and moved on to start his career, and I think he got totally into that. I almost think he even left music all behind and went in another direction, whereas I remained doing the same thing: Tried to play in good bands and finish off my apprenticeship, which I absolutely hated.

Chris Houston: I think Al had to go back to school or something like that.

I remember CHCH-TV videotaped us with D.O.A. at the Delta Theatre, and he went down and did the interview when he was no longer in the band. And I remember calling up CH going, "Well, come on, he's not even in the band anymore, why do you have him on TV?" Al went wearing a business jacket and a suit and tie – "Oh, it's this little lark I did."

You know, we were all very young and very immature, and getting fame and success when you've always wanted it all your life, that kind of sets you off to do lots of stupid things that in hindsight you go, "Why?"

Larry Potvin: It wasn't until my fifth-year apprenticeship where I started making real money. I was a full-time musician for five years, but I gave it till the age of thirty. Because that's what I enjoyed the most, being in a good band, and having fun, making great music, and getting paid for it. I had no interest in being ten per cent successful. I wanted to be one hundred per cent successful, or do it part-time.

And that's what happened. Age thirty came around, and I became a full-time electrician.

Chris Houston, Mickey DeSadist / photo by Ric Taylor

66. THE BiG TiME

Frankie Venom / photo by Ross Taylor

Chris Houston: As much as these bands like Simply Saucer or Teenage Head seemed like they were out in Pluto, there is a real musical knowledge and discipline that's involved with them. It kind of separates them.

Teenage Head whipped all the fuckin' bands in Toronto at the beginning because they had been together for a few years and could really play. And, at the height of their fame, they drank in the woods. While everybody's hanging out in these ritzy clubs with all these millionaires' kids, with Teenage Head you'd go out to Coot's Paradise, drop some acid, and drink a case of beer in the woods.

Dave Rave: From '76 to '79 is Teenage Head's vintage period. They came alive in '77; '78 and '79 were the peak years of that original band, then in '80 the next level happened with *Frantic City*. That's when they became a bigger band; beyond just a rock band. They became a band that could play arenas. And to me, Frank, believe it or not, started losing interest in some bloody weird way.

He enjoyed the energy of those punk rooms. When we started playing the big arenas, I think he lost a little bit of that edge. Not personally on the stage, but in his interest of it. I think part of him missed those rooms where he could be more casual.

He would complain to me. He never talked too much because he was a private guy; he would more grumble. I remember once in a while we'd be sitting here and he'd be going, "Why can't we just get up there and play? Every night has got to be the same songs. We just can't rip out 'Your Generation' by Generation X." They would always do a great version of that, or "Born to Lose" by the Heartbreakers. You could always pull that shit out. Now you had to do "Disgusteen," and people were paying big money to hear that.

There was pressure to it, and it was getting to him.

Gordie Lewis: But there was still an innocence, too. We were still very young. *Frantic City* was in 1980, so we were twenty-two years old. There was a total innocence to the whole thing.

Even the Ontario Place riot that we had in 1980; there were ten thousand, fifteen thousand people there. I didn't really think that much about it, you know?

Gail Manning: We really courted the publicity and the fans. I mean, before the riot at Ontario Place, we hired a float and went down Yonge Street with girls dressed up in crazy costumes handing out buttons and streamers saying, "Come to Ontario Place!"

And it really worked.

Gordie Lewis: My take on the whole thing was they were putting bands in there every week or so and it was free — I'm pretty sure it was free. You paid three bucks to get on the grounds or something like that, and the concert was free. I just got the feeling that even though it was 1980, the industry still hadn't pricked up their ears to what was going on. Even though we were selling records, their attitude was still, "What would we need extra security for? What would we need this for? It's just going to be an average show."

I took the subway down. It wasn't like we were in limos or anything like that. I just got on the subway with my guitar, got off the subway and onto the streetcar, and then was walking off looking for the dressing room. No one even told me where that was, that's how low-key it was. But I noticed there were all these people sitting in the stands, and I couldn't figure out why. It was four o'clock in the afternoon; why are there all these people here? The equipment's not even set up yet, and that was my first indication without even knowing it that there were going to be a lot of people.

It was kind of neat, actually. "Why are they here?"

"Well, they're here to see the band. They're getting here early." I can still remember to this day getting off the streetcar and walking through there, getting this vibe that something's going to happen tonight.

"Tales of the Head," by Glenn Nott [*Hamilton Spectator*, May 8, 1999]: Event officials decided to close the park gates when the venue was bursting full, leaving about fifteen hundred revved up fans on the outs. Police had already filled almost five fifty-gallon drums with confiscated alcohol.

Some angry fans began scaling the fences and attempting to swim the moat that surrounded the facility. Police on horseback were called in, cruisers, too, from as far away as Burlington and Whitby.

Frankie Venom: It was packed; sold out. I think they had that stage that turned around. It was stuffed. People were swimming across the moats. We were oblivious to it because we were onstage.

Stephen Mahon: There was no reason to expect people that couldn't get in would try and swim across or fight with cops. We weren't really expecting it to be that busy.

We didn't know there was trouble outside. It was just really cool *inside*, because there were no empty seats and the grass was all full.

"Tales of the Head," by Glenn Nott [*Hamilton Spectator*, May 8, 1999]: Metro Toronto and Ontario Provincial Police boats were summoned from Toronto Island, and ended up getting pelted with debris. Lake Shore Boulevard was closed.

The throng fed off itself and soon rocks and bottles were flying. An OPP police cruiser was completely destroyed and several others damaged by heavy rocks pulled from the Lake Ontario's breakwater.

Gordie Lewis: I guess it caught everybody by surprise. They had no idea what was going on — and neither did we — with the popularity of the band. They just did not have everything in place to take care of all the people that were there. They didn't have the ticket takers, they didn't have the security, they didn't have the police, they didn't have *anything* to deal with these people. And it just got out of hand because there was nobody to control it.

Frankie Venom: Well, we shut that place down for a summer, but we made headlines right across Canada — "Teenage Head Closes Ontario Place" — BLAH!

In one week literally we sold ten thousand albums. So that was the best show, Ontario Place.

Joe Csontos: I don't remember much because I was already there. I had a ticket, and I just remember there was commotion but I didn't know what it was. I thought maybe there were fights.

"Tales of the Head," by Glenn Nott [*Hamilton Spectator*, May 8, 1999]: Police on horseback rushed the mob, swinging riot sticks. Riot control officers moved in behind them. The crowd was chanting "fight, fight, fight," and "flip the car, flip the car."

When it was over three hours later, ten police officers and many fans were injured and a total of fifty-eight charges laid. There were about two dozen arrests.

Nash the Slash: I was there. And I was even at a better one, a week before that.

Everybody remembers Teenage Head because there was a big riot and the fans even rolled a police car of all things into the lagoon. Well, everyone seems to forget *this* one: A week before, I opened for Goddo at Ontario Place and all hell broke loose.

This is an outdoor amphitheatre, for those who don't know. Sound check was at seven o'clock. There was still lots of daylight. So I'm sound checking and a roll of toilet paper comes flying through the air and bounces off my violin, thank you very much. I said to one of the security guys, "You know, these people, they're really kind of drunk and wasted. I think they've been hanging around the bars. You better be careful. It's going to be a long night."

Well, the gig goes off and went fine. There was no problem with the audience. I went down a storm, Goddo went down a storm. Now it's eleven thirty at night and everybody's leaving. There's six-thousand-, eight-thousand-whatever kids leaving Ontario Place — all these drunken Goddo fans. Well, they get on the streetcar to go to the subway and one of the kids knocks out the window on the streetcar, just as another streetcar coming the opposite direction goes by. So the southbound streetcar knocks out the window on the northbound streetcar. Both streetcars stop and now we have an "accident." Now there are no streetcars going to Ontario Place. Everybody's stuck. So you have a horde of drunken angry people leaving Ontario Place being told that they can't take the streetcars and have to walk all the way up to Bloor Street, which is about three miles, before they can get on the subway.

Then they get on the subway, and they *rioted* on the subway. There was rioting the whole damn time. They were smashing shit. This is all *after* the gig.

The next day the front page of the *Toronto Star* says, "Fifteen hundred Nash the Slash fans went crazy on the subway last night."

Goddo phones me and goes, "Nash, what do they mean, Nash the Slash fans? They were *my* fans!" I'm going, "I know, Goddo. I get all the notoriety though, remember?"

I got banned from Ontario Place, Goddo got banned from Ontario Place, and a week later Teenage Head comes in and basically nukes the joint. Their fans completely took it over the top, and that's when *all* bands got banned. But we were the first. Goddo and I were the first. And nothing happened *at* the gig — the gig was great. But at seven o'clock, I predicted it.

These are great events in the history of music in Toronto.

Gary Pig Gold: I'm not so sure about Teenage Head or even Goddo closing down Ontario Place for all rock bands, because a month *after* both those shows I saw a Jan and Dean concert at the very same venue. It was packed from four in the afternoon on, too, with hundreds and hundreds of kids all over the place. Nobody rioting exactly, though I do remember someone tossed a Frisbee into the lake.

Maybe Jan and Dean aren't considered a "rock" act? I guess they aren't punk. But they were almost as loud as Teenage Head. Almost.

Slash Booze: I remember when they showed the picture in the *Globe and Mail*, they showed the wrong band. It was Bob Segarini or something and they captioned it, "Teenage Head Caused a Riot."

Gordie Lewis: I just thought it was another show until I woke up in the morning and it was on the front page of the *Globe and Mail*. So there was that sense of innocence which was really cool, you know? I'd love to go back to that again, where we still weren't jaded by anything and the momentum was there, there's no doubt about it.

Stephen Mahon: Of course the whole next day was the media — "Guess what happened last night at Ontario Place?" Then pictures of smashed windows and cop cars and stuff.

There was never anything really said about how great our show was. That was totally pushed to the back. There wasn't even a picture of us playing. All it was, was pictures of the devastation. Like it was our fault.

That was inevitable. But all we really did was draw more people than the place held.

Dave Rave: That was the peak of the big-time Teenage Head. It was phenomenal. And I don't think anybody in this country ever created that kind of excitement.

Tragically Hip create excitement, but they don't incite riots.

There was something going on that has not been witnessed in this country before or since. It was the real deal, unbridled, and against the odds of everything. Fifty thousand fans bought that record. I know.

David Liss: That was, in a sense, the beginning of the end for them and punk rock.

I would say that by the time you get fifty thousand showing up for a Teenage Head concert at Ontario Place and people are running wild, that's not punk rock.

Us in Hamilton, we were happy for our friends' success but we were going at that point, "Ontario Place? Teenage Head? And it's being advertised on Q107? Eww … it's so *over*."

Gail Manning: There was a huge amount of publicity behind them, which I think really attributes to their success. They just had *so* much effort put into them, whereas a lot of bands didn't have that. And that made a huge difference.

Stephen Mahon: I think we were sort of figured as sellouts. Maybe not the first album, but by *Frantic City* the punks at the time, they'd kind of written us off. Like, "Fuck that, you're not real anymore." The Demics was where it was at for them.

I remember one girl thinking that. She was totally into the Demics and she just went, "You guys have gone pop. *Forget* it. You're making money now, people are paying to buy your album and come to your shows. You've sold out, man. That goes against the punk creed. You're supposed to be starving and have no money." Which was never what I was into, so be it. Ha ha ha.

Dave Rave: I remember a guy burning *Frantic City* when it came out at Star Records, because the Forgotten Rebels were now "it" because Teenage Head were big. And I always thought that was a bit of a symbolic moment. I remember coming up the stairs there and thinking, Hmm, there's a bit of a jealousy factor.

Slash Booze: How much of a friend are you if you don't want to see somebody do well? Maybe somebody *was* jealous.

They didn't "sell out." You want to make money at what you're doing, don't you? You want to get recognized, don't you? And as far as selling out, they're recording songs that nobody else would touch. So what's the sellout?

Let's look at England for a second: Generation X and Sex Pistols. You can bet when they started to get commercial success there were people yelling,

"Sellout!" That first Sex Pistols record, there's no sell-out there. That's totally different, totally great, and should have turned the world on its heels. And what degree of success did they really have? They were in the same boat as Teenage Head. They had to sue to get their lives back.

People are silly, aren't they? I don't know what's wrong with people. They're just stupid.

I'm smart, they're stupid, remember that. *Frantic City* is a great record.

Stephen Mahon: Even though the album sold well, the cost of making it wasn't really offset. It wasn't like there was enough money where you could buy a Lear jet like John Travolta. There was never a lot of radio money coming in, because Canada's a small little fish. In the States, a million seller really *means* something.

Gordie Lewis [CIUT-FM, Greg Dick interview, 2007]: Steve found out that the first *(Teenage Head)* album was deleted June 2, 1980, the day that we had the riot at Ontario Place. So here's the label — it had already sold twenty thousand copies, which isn't too bad. They were punching a hole in it the day that we had a riot at Ontario Place with five thousand, seven thousand people there. So there's again the insanity of the recording industry, and the industry's perception of this type of music. We had to knock down a lot of walls.

Joe Csontos: I think I've seen Teenage Head literally a hundred times. In my mind they were the quintessential — and I'm biased, because I'm from Hamilton — but I thought, out of anybody, they were the best punk rock band in Canada.

Dave Rave: By the time *Frantic City* came out, it was exploding. "Something on My Mind" and "Let's Shake" were on the radio.

"Something On My Mind," at the time I remember was embarrassing to play. Like, "Do we *have* to play it?" Frank didn't want to play it. Think about it: A hit record, and they didn't want to play it.

And then it all changed.

"Tales of the Head," by Glenn Nott [*Hamilton Spectator,* May 8, 1999]: The members of Teenage Head were to fly to New York for a huge industry roll-out, set up partially by another radio guru from the Big Apple who'd seen the Ontario Place show and was "blown away." They were to play three keys gigs at major New York venues. They were on the brink.

Attic Records had spent $10,000 in setting up the gigs, inviting hundreds of agents, celebrities and press, including wags from *Trouser Press* and *Rolling Stone.*

One of the gigs was to be a live radio broadcast. It was strut time, and the timing was perfect.

Too bad they never made it.

It was about two a.m. Lewis and Mahon piled into a van that was headed for home. Kerr, who had just bought a new car, elected to drive the new wheels to the gig that night.

Lewis has never talked publicly about the ensuing crash, mostly because no one's ever asked him.

"I remember a lot more than I should about that," he says. "I know we were going way too fast. You could feel it inside the van."

On a country road outside Kitchener, the van slammed hard into a tree. Mahon, who was in the passenger seat, was flung forward into the windshield, opening a wide gash on his head.

Lewis, in the back seat behind the driver — an acquaintance of the band — was wearing a lap seatbelt. The force of impact broke his back and some ribs.

"When I saw the car, I couldn't believe they got out alive," says Kerr. "It was mangled. There was blood all over. Someone was looking after them that day."

Lewis and Mahon were rushed to hospital in Kitchener, where Lewis would stay for a month. Kerr shuddered when he saw his friend.

"Gord was in a body cast, and was all suspended and they had to flip him over. I couldn't stand to see him that way."

There was serious doubt that Lewis would ever walk again, never mind stand onstage and play guitar. It was a nightmare, but everyone was wide awake and feeling all of it.

Dave Rave: I get the phone call from Slash Booze. Remember, this is Hamilton and we have that sense of humour, so I thought he was joking when he said, "Hey, did you hear about Lew? Busted spine." And I was like, "Yeah, yeah, right, he must have really busted his spine last night." "No, there was an accident and he really busted his spine." And I remember at that moment time stood still.

It was an amorphous moment in our lives until we found out he was alive, and he was gonna live, and he wasn't gonna be crippled or any of that stuff. But we didn't know that first day what was gonna happen.

The gigs were cancelled and I remember we got a call; this record store asked us [the Shakers] to play. And I remember just taking a pile of pills that night, bennies, and we just played so fast and there was this sad energy, like it was over. The bell rang in a weird way. We played our hearts out for him. I remember we played so fast for him, our buddy who's debilitated.

That's the way you do it when you're a young lad. You don't cry, you just play really hard and fast.

Stephen Mahon: It sort of sounds like a time machine: It would be fun to play Ontario Place again and play Mosport again and go down to CBGB's again; all the highlights. But if I could change one thing, certainly I wouldn't have wanted Gordie to get hurt in that accident. Health is always first and foremost when everybody has three wishes. Your first wish is usually — should be — good health, so yeah, that would have been certainly very cool to have avoided that accident.

Who knows what would have happened? Obviously Gord's back wouldn't have been broken, that would have been pretty cool, but as far as the band goes, who knows? We were all set to try for that American deal, try to break through. Whether or not we would have, who knows? Nirvana still hadn't happened and Green Day hadn't happened, and the Ramones and the Dolls and the Pistols, they were never successful either.

You look back now and you realize what a wall we were up against as far as trying to break through commercially in the States, god. When you figure how the Ramones never did, and look how great *they* were, you know ...

Johnny MacLeod: It was really dead in the early '80s. It was unbelievable. It was as if the whole thing just hadn't made it.

Then there was that terrible situation with Gord Lewis. The guy broke his back in a car accident. Being out somewhere like London, Ontario in a motel room and turning on the news and learning that our dear friend maybe wasn't going to walk again, it was very sobering.

They were basically going to break through at that point. That riot at Ontario Place: Of course the music business don't think, "How awful." The next day the producer got a hundred calls from everybody he knew — "Hey, who *is* this band, man? We want them down in the States if they can get that kind of reaction!" So it was like that for Teenage Head, and overnight it all changed.

David Quinton: Those kinds of accidents can change you forever. I think everybody sort of thought, But for the grace of God, because all of us travelled that way. All of us were in vans with equipment, and every time the van hit a snow drift or skidded funny, you always got scared that something was gonna happen. And I think Teenage Head, in those days especially, were on the road so much that it just increases your odds of something happening.

Andrew McGregor: That was the band I think most people thought was going to make it out of the original scene. Gord Lewis had the accident and that threw everything off track.

They should have been the next AC/DC. They were on their way, they had it down, and they just never seemed to recover from that and wound up on the suburban bar circuit, which was too bad. But hey, you're a musician, you've got to make the money.

But for a brief moment it was all right in front of them, and they missed it.

Joe Csontos: They would have been superstars had that not happened, I think. Because their live shows were just, "What's Frank going to do?!" There was that unpredictability factor. Nazi Dog, he had his moments, but he was never Frank. Frank was the shit; Frank was the guy. He really had it all: witty, irreverent, had the audience from the minute he stepped on the stage.

Stephen Mahon: See, people think because we were all set to do this showcase in New York at this club where the Ramones and the New York Dolls had played, and there was all this American interest and blah, blah, blah ... But I don't think American radio was ready for us anyway. The Ramones were not on the radio. So I don't care who in the States was into signing the band and what had happened.

Maybe we would have ended up having something happen in the States, but I don't think it was the way everybody's portraying it now, where "There was their brass ring — Shit, they never grabbed it." I don't personally think it would have been like that. I think it would have been a good move to do New York, and if we hadn't have got in the accident we certainly would have still been in a great position. We were ahead of our time.

We got back on our feet and still did our thing.

Slash Booze: They had to keep the machine rolling. There were people's incomes depending on them, especially Jack's, so they kept the machine rolling.

Worse have made it; better haven't.

John Balogh: Out of any of the bands from Hamilton, Teenage Head probably had the best nucleus behind them, and that's why the affordable public perception of success was there. Whereas other bands like Simply Saucer or the Forgotten Rebels had a much harder time to get down everybody's throat, because they didn't have that guy in a polished three-piece suit with the short hair that spoke eloquently. So while he was robbing them blind, a guy like Jack Morrow was pushing them to the forefront.

Tom Williams: Jack Morrow was one of the most amazing managers I ever worked with. It's mostly because he could not *not* tell a lie. Ha ha ha. It's true. He was an amazing man.

I once said to him, "Jack, why don't you walk from A to B? Why do you have to do this big circle?" And he couldn't answer me. He was incapable of doing something directly. And he was a schemer. He was a great promoter, and he held together a band of people that - what'd he call them? It wasn't very flattering — oh, *pinheads*. "They're just pinheads. They don't know what they're doing for god sakes."

John Balogh: You have to remember, we were a bunch of young kids, and you were putting young people in the arena with old people to try and make money. I mean, it was really a mixed blessing, because at the end he became the thorn in the side of Teenage Head. Gordie had an accident and he's laid up in traction with a broken back, and Jack Morrow goes out and hires Dave Bendeth to play guitar for Teenage Head.

The band had always been Gordie's baby. That's like Gordie's puppy, and that must have been a little bit of a shock to his system to know that, "Hey, you know the guy that said he loved me and would look after me all my life? He's gone and hired a fuckin' replacement guitarist for me. I didn't hire him. I don't even like this guy Dave Bendeth, what's he doing playing guitar?"

Dave Rave: We got the word that they were gonna put the band together with David Bendeth and I remember going, "Why? *Why?* No, let's wait to see the results of Gordie."

Bendeth had no energy and he was a total asshole, *total* asshole. He was questioning what we listened to and what we could do. "Well, we play music here, and what do *you* do, you jive jazz man?"

Slash Booze: I was never on board with the guy they got, Bendeth. He was a good guitar player, but ... but he wasn't Gordon.

Dave Rave: That was a sad moment for rock 'n' roll, a sad moment for Hamilton, and a sad moment for Gord Lewis, the proud man that he is. The band was lost without their leader. Gord is the weight and the anchor.

Stephen Mahon: After the accident I just started not really caring. I mean, I just remember really missing him because we had to hire replacement guitar players and it just wasn't the same. It was kind of like punching the clock — "Okay, there's a gig tonight," and you did it.

Dave Rave: It was not the same, but how could it be? How could it be?

Stephen Mahon: At the time we were hot, so people came. Because this band is successful and sort of the buzzword band, people probably came that were just jumping on the bandwagon and not even know that it wasn't the right guitar player. And not even care. Just get drunk and leave; have a good time.

I was just going through the motions, really. We still had the same management. We weren't able to complete our third album when we were supposed to. We had things set up in New York to go and do a showcase. We did lose a lot that we couldn't get back.

The label couldn't wait. They needed to get the third album out. Every minute that goes by, there's another new band practicing somewhere that wants to take your place.

Gordie Lewis: I'm told that the hardest time for the band was after the car accident that I was in.

Now, what I remember about that was the band was on a roll at the time; that they were playing every night without me. They went on three months' full-time work.

I was lying in a hospital bed. I probably missed the best gigs of the whole career, ha ha ha. I missed all the fun. We were at our peak and I was out for five months, so I missed a lot.

But I've been told by the other members that that *wasn't* a fun period, and that it was like going to work for them. It just wasn't the same, and I appreciate that they would say that. And that *was* a really hard time. It definitely railroaded our momentum. I was out of commission for three months solid, and then another two. That's a whole career for some bands.

That accident really messed me up mentally, and physically, probably to this day. That stopped everything from going. That's when I lost control of the band. All the things that I wanted to have in the band I saw go away. And that was really hurtful, and I couldn't stop it.

It took a long time, it took ten years, to put it back on track again.

67.
FiFTeen-minuTe wonDer

Keith Whittaker [*Shades* no. 14, November/December 1980]: We were playing in London and a couple of guys from the college came down who were in some sort of technology course. They were just graduating and wanted to make a record as a final project or something. They asked us if we wanted some studio time and we said, "Sure."

Andy Crosbie: I was going to school at Fanshawe College, which at the time was the only school in Canada that offered a recording course. Back then it was a three-year program and at the time the Demics were playing what was called the Blue Boot. It was a really cool time because the kids would line up around the block, me being one of them, to get in there and dance. It was an amazing time because the music was really raw; it was wonderful. We would cram the dance floor and dance for hours, dripping in sweat. We were all listening to what was happening at the time coming out of England and things like that and it was really exciting. And it's funny, our teachers at school were sort of old, hippie guys and they weren't really embracing what was happening.

So one day I'm walking to school with a friend of mine named Angus MacKay and he said, "You know what we should we do?" And we were only in our second year – he said, "We should record these guys." And the more we talked about it the more I realized he was right. So we borrowed some money from our parents, each of us, and we whipped home for Christmas, did the gift thing, then whipped back to London. I mean, we had met with the band and talked to them to see if they wanted to do it and they wanted to. So we spent our Christmas holidays in a studio with the band, and another one of our fellow students, a guy named Kevin Doyle, engineered the record. And like that we made that record and then it was like, "Okay, now we've got to put it out."

Keith Whittaker [*Shades* no. 14, November/December 1980]: Initially, the record wasn't supposed to come out, and I was really surprised when it did. It happened when I was over in England again and I was furious when I came back. Suddenly the relationship changed

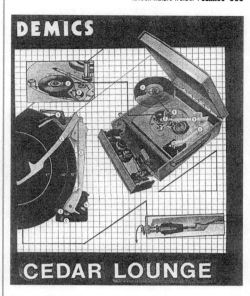

from a friendship and a learning experience to a money-making venture. I mean, these two friends were sitting across the table bargaining with us, holding these contracts ...

Andy Crosbie: One of the things that we were being taught in the recording course was to sign agreements with bands, but we stupidly went and recorded the record without doing any of that and obviously when we sat down with the band to say, "You know, we're going to start a record company, you're going to be the first record coming out on the record company and we'd like to sign you as artists." And they were flatly, "No, that's not what interests us at all."

So it was my first exposure to the School of Hard Knocks in the record business, which is, holy jeez, it is an artistic business and not everybody sees things the same way.

Keith Whittaker [*Shades* no. 14, November/December 1980]: But that's over; it did really well and won us a lot of fans. I mean, "New York City," like it or not, has done well.

Iain Atkinson: I would assume that what happened is the sentiment of the stuff transcended the fact that it didn't sound the way that we wanted.

Those guys were going to Fanshawe and – I could be making this up, but it sounds good – it was kind of like a project they had to do at the end of the year. So we did it with Kevin Doyle. I think it probably only took a couple of days to do the whole thing.

In retrospect, I would have liked to have taken a little longer to do it, but that's the amount of time that we had.

I think we hated it at the time because it wasn't like what we really sounded like. It wasn't aggressive enough. Kevin's good, I don't question that for a second, but I was hearing stuff from the UK that I thought was capturing things better. I thought it might have been stronger had it had the real sounds that I thought we were making.

We never expected that "New York City" would be received the way it was. It was written really fast; another one of those ones that kind of fell together. We wrote that on a bus. We were taking a Greyhound bus to Ottawa.

It's a weird one because there was this whole ironic element that I don't think anybody really got. There was a guy that we knew in London and he was always going on about going to New York — "Oh, it's all so much better," and then that song came out. It cuts two ways. You *did* sort of want to go there, but it was, "Would you quit with your fuckin' 'I wanna go to New York' and just fuckin' *go?!"*

Keith Whittaker [*Shades* no. 14, November/December 1980]: I think I've said everything I want to say about that song. It's a fifteen-minute wonder. I wrote it on the way to practice one day under threat from the others to write a song or else, because I was getting lazy. I had been in a pub with a guy who was always talking about New York, ramming it down your throat, and I just wrote a song from his point of view, about him and how he (was) always talking about it but never went there.

I think we're stuck with it. We play gigs and they just wait for the song. They'll sit there and be dead and we'll start that one and, *boom.*

Iain Atkinson: If you go into the arty-farty spiritual element, you're just a conduit. It's all out there in this common subconscious, and you're just pulling on that the same as many, many people are.

For musicians, even for myself, there is an element of sometimes you're playing and you have no idea what you're playing. It's coming from somewhere and you're not thinking it. I'm not sure that it's *me* doing it. I don't know what that is, but to me that's the goal: Where your hands are just going and you're not really a hundred per cent sure where the hell it's coming from.

The whole band thing was kind of like that. In London, maybe there was this pent-up demand for something to express whatever people's frustrations were or what have you, and we fit the bill at that time. I can't think it's anything else because of the enthusiastic response that we got.

Steve Koch: Keith would say what was on his mind. He would tell you the brutal, honest truth all the time and if he liked you, "You're the greatest guy in the world. You're my favourite girl in the world. You're the most beautiful girl in the world. You're the best guitar player in the world."

Real smart guy; he was university educated and everything, not that that necessarily means anything. He was pretty widely read; he was definitely into a lot of the French symbolist poetry and we were always trading tips on what book I just read. He was a real reader. Obnoxious. An obnoxious genius.

Some people say he was particularly mean to girls. Again, it's just the same thing. He would just say what was on his mind and sometimes you're supposed to give girls a little more leeway. On the other hand, lots of girls just loved him, which was also incomprehensible to me.

Keith Whittaker [*Shades* no. 14, November/December 1980]: I'd like us to be more political. When I write songs I tend to write about how I'm making out in the system and how that compares to others. Sometimes I think I write about myself too much, but when you look at it, my problems probably apply to a lot of people.

Steve Koch: He was always writing. He would be at a club and drunkenly hand you a poem he'd just wrote. "This is fucking *great,*" you know? He was in love with words.

Keith Whittaker [*Shades* no. 14, November/December 1980]: I think (the songs are) angry. I know they're angry. I mean look around, how can you not be angry? I've always felt that anger anyway, because I've never felt a part of this place since coming from England. I still don't feel completely welcome here. It's hard for an immigrant, damned hard. Can you imagine what it's like for someone who can't even speak the language? No wonder they set up their little clubs.

Steve Koch: He was a fantastic front man. So different from Leckie and Nightmare, who were all into histrionics and show biz and dressing the part and being overtly aggressive, whereas Whittaker could stand up on a stage, dressed not in any particularly noticeable manner, start singing, and he could force you to pay attention to him just through the power of his voice and his stance and his look. It was not cutting yourself or swinging a chain around or anything.

Unique. I don't know how he did it.

Andy Crosbie: My god, that guy was charismatic. He was an awesome stage performer. As was Steven Leckie, you know?

They had a really cool attitude, a really cool sound, and they had good songs. They really had a POV – point of view, you know what I mean? Rob Brent, the guitar player, had a very definitive artistic vision. They were listening to the Ramones long before anybody that I knew was listening to the Ramones. They definitely had a sound in their head.

Keith Whittaker [*Shades* no. 14, November/December 1980]: These two young producers ... saw us at the Horseshoe and we blew them away. They approached us and said, "Would you like to go in the studio?" We said yes and they said, "Wednesday?" This was Monday and it was only Steve's third gig. But we did it and when the tape came out these guys ran down to Pickwick with it. Pickwick were trying to reassemble their company in Canada at that point and they thought they could do something with us. They're really happy now because the album's doing well.

Steve Koch: It was probably more involved than we would have wanted. It was in the Nimbus 9 studio, which was the big, big Yorkville studio that Alice Cooper and the Guess Who recorded in. This guy Tom Treumuth, who was kind of our executive producer, put up the money more or less and he was involved in the mix.

Iain Atkinson: What's to tell? He's a fuckin' asshole. He's just a dick. It's unfortunate. The guy didn't have a clue about what we were doing, not at all. He was trying to push it into this middle–of–the–road, hit-on-AM-radio kind of thing and just let it get namby-pamby. He wanted to play keyboards, and I think there was a saxophone thing in one part of it and I can't remember who played it. But he was just fucking it all up.

Steve Koch: I think he wanted to do a new wave record, which means punk with the bones removed.

Basically there was only one real new song on that [album], which was "I Won't See You No More." That's the only one I got credit for. All the rest were songs that the Demics had done all along, even back in the Rob Brent days pretty much. Those were the songs that he chose that he wanted to do.

Keith Whittaker [*Shades* no. 14, November/December 1980]: I think the new record is still a little raw for me. I'm only maybe twenty-five per cent pleased with it.

Iain Atkinson: That whole thing was a massive disappointment to us, and I would say in some ways that was a catalyst in our demise. We were really unhappy with everything about that record; the artwork, everything.

Tom Treumuth was trying to force his vision of what everything was onto the thing. We didn't get the name of the record that we wanted, which was supposed to be *400 Blows*.

Keith Whittaker [*Shades* no. 14, November/December 1980]: I was really touched by that film because of my old lifestyle in England. My upbringing as a kid in Manchester was rough. Clapped around at school, clapped around at home.

Iain Atkinson: And that got vetoed because our lawyer thought Francois Truffaut would sue us. Are you fucking *kidding* me? Get a brain.

Steve Koch: We got bamboozled into doing another version of "New York City," which in no way can stand up to the original version. The original version on the EP with Rob is a million times better than the album version, and the whole album kind of got tarred by having that crappy version of "New York City" on it. They just thought they could make a whack of cash if they did it again but get rid of the swearing, so they'd play it on the radio. Well, that turned out to be the dumbest move. Ha ha ha.

I wasn't involved in their business that much, but my understanding is that re-recording it somehow got them out of their Ready Records deal.

Andy Crosbie: In the end the band would only give us the rights for that record and we did strike one consolation prize with them, which was, "Okay, if you ever record on another label any of these tracks then we are no longer obligated to pay you royalties from this record." So that was the one thing everybody could agree upon because this was going to be a one-off deal.

See, we were young. We were in college. What should have happened – what normally happens in the record business – is you sit down with an artist and you say, "We want to make a record with you and other records." But we didn't have that conversation completely with them before we recorded. We just said, "Let's make this record." Having made the record it was like, "Okay, now we'd like to represent you for other records to follow," which normally would happen in a record company. And they were like, "Well, no, you guys have no track record" – which is a valid point – "this is the first record you've ever made and blah blah blah blah." So yeah, they didn't want to enter into a recording contract. So we just struck a deal for the one record.

Iain Atkinson: We didn't do fuck all. We didn't go anywhere. We didn't go to New York City and didn't go to the UK.

In retrospect I really wish we had, because it probably would have been a much bigger entity had we gone away from here. The Canadian record business then didn't have a fucking clue what was any good or what wasn't; what could sell and what couldn't. I think American people in general are more adventurous. Maybe in the UK it's the same thing, too; people were more inclined to take a chance.

But we didn't, and it wasn't, and it's too late now. So I *could* have been famous.

Steve Koch: At first I had this crazy idea that I was gonna move to India, so I let them know that.

Basically the band seemed to be winding down; nothing was happening, there seemed to be a general reduced interest. So I thought, Maybe I'm gonna do that. But I never did do that. I think Iain basically was the first one to actually drop off.

Iain Atkinson: I don't know if I want to go into that. Keith and I had a little squabble and I just said, "Okay, that's it, we're not doing this anymore," and that was the end of it.

Steve Koch: The gigs were getting smaller and we were getting the feeling that nothing was going anywhere. So I think it just kind of disintegrated. It didn't explode; it just kind of fell apart. So my threatening to leave may have gotten people thinking about it.

Iain Atkinson: There was a lot of stuff brewing, we had an argument, and I just said, "Fuck it, I don't want to do it anymore." So that's it. Was it because we were having an argument? Probably not. I think it was on its way.

I was really fucking pissed off. I think I did it out of spite because I figured, This'll be the nastiest thing I can possibly do to you because you're pissing me off so much. And I did it. I could have recanted, but I just didn't. It had gone on for a long time.

Steve Koch: Iain and Keith kind of had a little tug of war. They're different styles. Iain's a little more conservative and more detail-oriented, whereas Keith would want to go ahead and do something without thinking it through all the way.

At first I was kind of the outsider. As the band progressed Keith and I wrote a lot of the songs together, so we kind of teamed up a little bit more than me and Jimmy or me and Ian. I probably hung out with Keith more.

Iain Atkinson: We were getting played on the radio but we weren't getting a real record deal.

We were totally unhappy with the new record and didn't think it would do anything for us other than maybe just hurt us. So I guess that's it. It was time to do something else. But it wasn't well thought out, I'll tell you that.

Steve Koch: The last show wasn't a big show; there was hardly anybody there, anyway. We just thought, Oh this is ridiculous, let's do something else. Let's start over again. Keith definitely didn't like doing "New York City" anymore. He wanted to do new stuff and I think he felt that format, this Demics thing, was like an albatross to him.

Andy Crosbie: *Chart* Magazine called ["New York City"] the Number One Canadian single of all time which I thought was hilarious, ha ha ha, because I think Neil Young and Rush might have a problem with that.

Iain Atkinson: Nobody was in this band because we wanted to remain anonymous. What "famous" meant, I'm not sure. You *were* hoping it would be a career. You *could* get famous, make money, and retire, as silly as I think that is now.

A lot of it is shit luck; being in the right place at the right time and things fall together. And in our case, it didn't really quite fall together. That being said, we did stay together for five years and all the money we made to live off of came from playing. So it made a living, as meager as it may have been. We didn't starve to death. I would have rather been more famous, but you get what you can.

68.
not be unheard of

Steven Leckie / photo by Ralph Alfonso

Tony Vincent: I started to get to know him [Steve Leckie] and I started to think, This guy's genuine. He's got a heart, he's got a soul. I started to think he was a really good person so I started to like him. We hung out together. We went to a lot of parties together; did a lot of stuff together. Sometimes we'd just hang out all day long, from like twelve o'clock right up until one, two, three o'clock in the morning when the bars would close, we'd spend that much time together.

But he was a user, too. He was using me. He uses everybody for what they're worth.

First of all, what he really used me for was to have a drummer. That's what he was using me for, musicianship. He would use other people for money, for transportation, cars, rehearsal halls. He'd try to make the person believe he was their friend, and then he would use them. That's the kind of person he is.

Sam Ferrara: I got along with Steve better in the first group because I didn't know him as well. And as I started getting to know him, I didn't get along with him that well.

One time he tried this really stupid thing where we were going to do some recording. He phones me up and goes, "If you could bring some money over to buy the tape, that would be great." I said, "Well, yeah, okay, I can do that." And I get to the recording studio and he's sitting on this tape. And I'm going, "Let me see the tape." He goes, "It's okay." "Let me see the fuckin' tape." So I pushed him away, looked at it, and said, "This is the tape I paid for about a year ago!" He'd tried to get some money off me for something I paid for a year ago. And the engineer looks at it finally and goes, "This is the wrong kind of tape anyway." I think that was the third time I quit that band.

He was an asshole. When we were in that studio, what's that chi chi place, Yorkville. We're in there with Bob Ezrin and the Garys.

Tony Vincent: That was a nightmare. We were gonna get produced by Bob Ezrin. Steve blew this one. We were gonna get a major record contract with Bob Ezrin thanks to Gary Topp and Gary Cormier from the Edge.

The first day was okay. Steve went, "I want Jack Daniels, make sure there's Kentucky Fried Chicken, a case of beer," and he started naming all these things that he wanted on the rider before he would record there. So the Garys were kind of like, "All right, we'll babysit him, we'll do it." So they gave us anything we wanted; pizza, beer. I didn't care. I wasn't even drinking then. I just wanted to play music.

Sam Ferrara: Like, okay, we have Bob here behind the glass, who did Alice Cooper, and Steve was just being such an asshole. He kept telling the Garys to fuck off. Tony and I are looking at him going, "What the fuck ...?" And he's going, "I ain't singing a note until I get some Kentucky Fried Chicken." It was like, Steve, you're not here to eat. How are you gonna sing with a mouth full of chicken? So Steve keeps telling the Garys to fuck off and finally Gary just went, "You do that one more time and I'm shutting the power off." So what does he do? Tells him to fuck off.

Dark.

He probably figured the more he pushes, the more attention he'd get. And I guess he figured, All those people I tell to fuck off, they're just gonna want more of me. But it ain't true. Ha ha ha.

Tony Vincent: We laid down the bed tracks the first night and then the next night Steve started to do the vocals. Bob Ezrin goes, "Steve, all you gotta do is sing one word, we'll punch it in. There's just one word in the song that sounds a little flat. All you gotta do is say that word in the right key. You don't have to re-do the whole song." "Whaddya mean? What are you talkin' about? I'm the greatest singer in Toronto. *Nobody* tells Steven Leckie how to sing! The song stays the way it is, and that's all there is to it."

Bob went, "Fine."

Next day we didn't have a recording. That was it.

[**Publisher's note:** When contacted for a comment, Bob Ezrin told us this incident, in fact, never happened.]

Bob Ezrin: Absolute crap. I wouldn't waste my or anyone else's time on this dog shit.

Tony Vincent: You don't screw around. Bob Ezrin is a heavyweight.

Bob Ezrin: Can you imagine me working with Nazi *anybody???*

Sam Ferrara: Man, Tony and I just wanted to kill him. There was a good chance we could do something, and he just blew it for everyone. He was always right on the edge, and then...

Tony Vincent: He's so good at doing that. I don't think Steve can handle any certain type of fame. I think it's too much for him. As soon as he gets a little bit of fame he'll get on his high horse and think that he's God.

Some people can handle being famous, some people can't. He doesn't know how to absorb it and keep it. He abuses it. He totally abuses the power that he gets, that's what he does.

Sam Ferrara: I was in the Viletones off and on. Long enough to make a mark.

I got in a fight with Steve Leckie in the early '80s. I don't know what we were fighting about. We were behind the curtains; we hadn't even started playing yet. All of a sudden both of us fall out of the curtains, onto the dance floor, and the show hasn't even started yet and people were clapping. Like, this is *not* part of the show.

I can't remember what the hell we were fighting about. It was probably something stupid. We were almost blacklisted.

When I was in the Ugly, the music was better and there wasn't any lying. Everybody was pretty up front. There was just a sinister thing about the Viletones. It was all scheming. Like, come on! We could put that energy into *music*. When I finally, really quit, it was because of Steve. I'd just had it to here. Just him ripping me off for money and credit, mostly credit. If it wasn't for Steve Koch, my name wouldn't even be on [*Saturday Night, Sunday Morning*].

He burned too many bridges. It was all the lying and trickery. I didn't trust him anymore.

Steve Leckie spray-painting his record gold — he *did*, ha ha ha. Yeah, he spray-painted it gold just to tell people he had a gold record, ha ha ha. You can tell it's spray-painted, but there were kids that would fall for it. We'd audition guitar players and he'd point at the record and kids would go, "Wow, I'm auditioning for the Viletones."

Leave now while you can.

Tony Vincent [*Shades* no. 19 + 20, October/November 1981]: After a while, people realized we couldn't play to save our lives. We went onstage and pretended we were a band. In actuality, we were only a gang of guys causing shit.

Music wasn't the first thing to Steve. Fight and image came first. When Sam and I tried to make everything sound good, he didn't give a shit.

William Cork: Nazi Dog was sort of like David Bowie's synopsis of Iggy's first book — a true rock action account of how to snatch defeat from the jaws of victory, instead of victory from the jaws of defeat. Mike Nightmare was a lot like that, too.

P.L. Noble ["Beyond Primal," *Shades* no. 19 + 20, October/November, 1981]: Parallels could be drawn between Mike Nightmare and Steven Leckie. Both singers were unforgettable personalities — but they were unable to adjust to being in a rock 'n' roll group. What it came down to was a lack of professionalism and respect for their fellow musicians. When Sam took the initiative to bring in a full time manager (Jerry Gold), Leckie cringed at the very idea. Thus came the inevitable split.

Tony Vincent: I'd had enough of Steve. It was just too much, too much.

Like, Steve, how long are you gonna be doing this for? People stopped coming to our shows; nobody liked us. The only people that ever stayed in that band was me and Sam. Every time a musician would join, he'd quit because he didn't want to play with Steve or thought Steve was an idiot. Musically it went downhill, and a lot of people didn't like Steve.

Sam Ferrara: When was the final time I quit? Ha ha ha. We have a rehearsal. Steven took out a tape recorder and was asking me, "Got any new riffs?" "Here we go again. You want to steal *these*, too?" He'd want riffs from me; bass lines and whatever.

So I just said, "Fuck you, man, you're not getting no juice from me," and that was it. Then I went and did Screamin' Sam. There wasn't that much real, raw punk around anymore.

He kept phoning me — "I wrote a song about you, Sam, I wrote a song about you. It's called 'Sam'."

Still, I think the Viletones should have been bigger than what they were. They should have given Steve Kentucky Fried Chicken that day. Bob Ezrin would have produced us, ha ha ha.

Rosy Ruin [*Shades* no. 14, November/December, 1980]: And lo also as time brought fulfillment it brought bitter fruit. The Viletones have ceased and desisted under their struggle, becoming at last a band that's expired. Yet, without fail, Steven Leckie will not be unheard of as yet.

Blair Martin: I think it was hard for people to develop musically to the next level, and I think there were some musical problems generally with everybody.

I think it was hard for the Viletones to get onto the next musical level. It was less difficult for Teenage Head. They sort of came out of the basement — already practised a couple of years.

Besides the fact that everything was poorly managed, there wasn't any real development of these people as talents, either. That's the really big rip-off. Nobody ever really invested in Steve Leckie or Mike Nightmare to see what kind of talent that would develop, which is part of the point of the exercise. It's not just, "Manage my career, sell records, hype celebrity." For me, it's the fact that these people didn't really get to develop artistically and have good people there to develop their skills. I think that's the saddest thing, truthfully.

There are a lot of terrible professional disappointments, but then again we were people who were promised a lot from being kids in the '60s. I saw the fuckin' Beatles on the *Ed Sullivan Show* when I was in kindergarten. I went to school the next day and I drew a picture of the Beatles. Just imagine the expectation I grew up with, growing up to want to be a musician. The *Beatles* — give me a fuckin' break. It's never going to happen. This is a generation of people that I don't think can avoid disappointment. It's sort built into the scenario, if you can see it from the outset. You're only going to grow up to be disappointed.

Steven Leckie: When I was, like, nine I used to play a game. My mom was young and so she had Beatles and Stones records and everything, right? And we lived next door to a young family that had a couple of daughters. And a game I would make everyone play is, chase me up the street while I've got a badminton racket, which of course was a guitar in my imagination, and you have to chase and scream to try to catch me. Because in the Beatles movie *Hard Day's Night* they're running and the girls are ...

So that was how I thought, ha ha ha, a good game should be. And the girls would completely, willingly participate. They would get a kick out of it, too, because they could be screaming girls at a rock 'n' roll show. And I confidently would tell peers, like from fourteen on, "I'm gonna be in a rock band. A really cool one."

I got the taste very young and it doesn't leave you.

And I practised for years with the headphones. I couldn't wait for my old man to leave and I would, for hours, have whole performances. Like an entire record, and I would do all the bits. And I would interview myself and I'd use an accent, and all these things all point to an absolute that *will* happen.

It wasn't a choice of vocation. It was because I had something that I felt you need to hear that no one's telling me, so I'm going to give you the penultimate anti-star in this and use metaphors of chaos and fascism to get the message across. So that's how I knew. By the time I was eighteen I'd practised being that for, like, nine or ten years.

Freddy Pompeii: Last time I talked to him, we were talking about putting together a band to open for the Sex Pistols when they were touring, because I had a connection for that.

But he didn't want to do it. I guess he wanted to do his rockabilly shit ...

Chris Haight: Even though the Dog may have thought that he was in his own little echelon or whatever — his own little thing because it was his job to deal with the press — I hope that he hasn't cut himself off from reality. Because he still has the Viletones shrine, and he still has what happened in the past about him, where the whole thing has moved. Moved on and on and on. And I just hope he doesn't get too stuck in the past to smell the roses.

Freddy Pompeii: I gotta say this. I think this is real important:

In the last few years — the last few decades, as a matter of fact — Steven has been keeping the name Viletones alive. It bothers me now, because the band has a life of its own. It has airplay. They'll play Viletones on satellite radio. But as far as maintaining the mythology, he's keeping it alive with songs that were written by *other* people.

Very early on he copyrighted everything under his name so nobody else would get anything, or if they did, he would be the one to say how much or how little. He had a handle on that from the very beginning because of his dad. What happened was when we left, Steven took all those songs that we wrote together and he changed around the writing credits. He walked away with the lion's share of the writing royalties.

To this day, we haven't seen any money from the Viletones. We haven't seen *anything*. He's seen quite a bit. It's highway robbery, really. He's stealing from the guys who helped him make a name for himself, and that's basically what I'm trying to say.

The songs were written by the original band, that being Freddy Pompeii, Steven Leckie, Mike Anderson, and Chris Haight. That was the band. He takes the same songs we wrote — "Screamin' Fist," "Possibilities," "Danger Boy," "Swastika Girl," all these songs that we did hundreds of times — he gives them to younger guys when he feels it's time to go out and do a concert every five or ten years.

He's made sure that any time there *was* a concert, he got ninety-eight percent of everything. If there was a record deal, he got ninety-five percent of everything. When people would say, "Where are the other Viletones? Why aren't they being included on this deal?" He'd say, "Well, one's a hopeless junkie and the other two are dead." People believed him because they didn't know any better.

I've talked to him about it since then, and he felt that because he was keeping the name alive and that he was doing gigs with these ringers, he deserved the money. He deserved all the proceeds, because he kept the Viletones going all these years. Maybe that's so, but he *did* get a *lot* of money.

That's always the way he did stuff. He was very sneaky all the time. You look through other rock 'n' roll bands over the years and they went through that same shit. John Lennon was always taking [Brian] Epstein aside and saying, "Hey listen, clear anything with me before saying it to these guys."

I guess it's just human nature, and what happens when someone feels like they want to be the boss.

Chris Haight: You know what? Even when he was knockin' 'em dead, he would still have that look of insecurity, looking over his shoulder like, "Am I doing okay, guys?" He was lucky to have the nice friends that he did behind him, meaning Freddy and Motor. We were pretty good to him, even though it was a debacle. We still cared for each other.

Sam Ferrara: For me, punk was just living it, not just playing like you hear this song and you learn and, "Okay, I'm a punk now." You're not.

I've got a song called "Live for Today," because to hell with tomorrow, right? I know guys from years ago and they've got jobs in offices and stuff, and man do they look old. They do. And they're younger than me. So it's a way of life; it'll keep you young.

Steven Leckie: I've still got it. Some of them look all pudgy and they've got SUVs. See, I'm a lifer; this isn't a thing I thought I'd get into for a couple years.

I'm a usurper. I'm an agent provocateur who every now and again gets lucky and gets to go to Morocco and Lisbon and Paris and has a cachet in Montreal and never has any money but will always be getting it, one day. I'm in between my millions. So I think that's how I felt.

Don Pyle: He was extremely significant to punk in Canada. He had a controversial name, he had a great band, their first single was easily the best punk single in Canada.

When that came out, it was *so* well produced, it was *so* big sounding, extremely energetic — I'm getting goose bumps thinking about the song.

That first band was extremely powerful, and I think he has been under-recognized in the whole history of punk. The Viletones' place in that is quite overlooked.

Jeremy Gluck: They would have been a really great band, but there are a *lot* of really great bands that don't get their just desserts.

They had a cultural value for Canada. They were the weirdest and wildest, and they also made one of the best records: the first EP. The Viletones had a cultural value for Canada.

Steven Leckie: A good rock band should really only last four years. The only one that didn't was the Ramones, and that's only due to Johnny forcing them to continue on. Think about this: If the Ramones had've died or stopped their career after their fourth album, they would have been a better band in history. Maybe end it with *End of the Century*, just to get a feather in your cap that you had Phil Spector do it. But to keep flogging it, the same shtick, with no intellectual anything, no. Their last albums aren't that great.

Four years seems to be the time of all good cultural revolutions. There seems to be something to that number historically, from the Pawee Indian Nation, the strong four years that they had, to the four years of the Doors. And I'm excluding three people, Elvis, the Beatles, and the Stones, but that's because that's another thing.

The career of Marilyn Monroe, it had to be short. James Dean, it had to be short.

I've overstayed my welcome.

69.
Grinding on and on

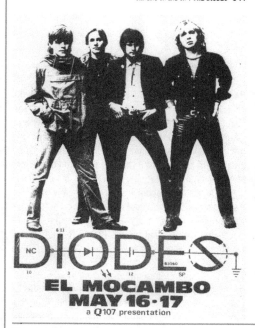

Paul Robinson: In 1980 we recorded our third album for RCA/Orient.

John Hamilton did the first two albums with us and then Mike Lengyell did the other two. It was John [Catto], Ian and I that whole way through. I think we were very, very close friends. I don't think that anybody could have that relationship that John and Ian and I had. It was camaraderie. We came from an art background. We just got what we were doing *immediately*. Everything fell into place because we just understood each other so much and so well.

Mike Lengyell: I thought we were developing some original material and still being creative, but I think some of the frustrations of things not turning out the way we'd hoped maybe put a little bit of a damper on the desire to keep pushing forward.

If I can remember, [producers] Willi [Morrison] and Ian [Guenther] had a couple of disco hits from Europe with different bands and were trying to think maybe they could get the Diodes to create a sound that was a little more radio-friendly. I mean, Blondie sort of captured that perfectly; look what happened to Blondie. Basically they were a group of rough, raw, creative people that just got molded into something really good. They kept their artistic integrity, but became really radio-friendly.

I'm not saying we wanted to be Blondie, but I think to a certain extent, sometimes you've just got to work. You've got to stay alive. You've got to have a career. And you know what? If you can't sell records and you can't get gigs, your career is over. You've *got* to make money. You've got to survive.

I'm not averse to selling records. I'm not saying I'd want to lose any creative integrity to do it, but if you don't sell records and get some kind of popular appeal, it's pretty hard to keep going as an artist.

I think Ian and Willi were trying to see if they could spark that a little bit. I don't think it was successful. On the other hand, I don't think they really felt that they wanted to alter a lot, anyway. I don't think Paul and John were willing to, anyway, even if Willi and Ian were going to push for it strongly.

You know, it was fun, I enjoyed it, but I don't think it got the result that anybody was expecting. Believe it or not, at that time they were saying, "This new wave thing, it's not gonna go big. It's gonna be Blondie and maybe one other band, and that's it. Nobody wants to put any money in the bands and it's not gonna go anywhere. It's just a short fad." That was still a pretty prevalent point of view when we were in the thick of things.

Ian Mackay: That summer of 1980, the band was at its musical peak. We were really, really good; really tight. We had an excellent sound person, Bruce Ingram. He was a good friend of John Catto's; he knew exactly what John Catto should sound like and how to contain his very big sound so everybody could be heard. He reined in Paul's voice and made it really tight and we sounded really, really good.

We played at the El Mocambo and Dave Clarkson came out with his girlfriend, came backstage and said, "That's the best I've ever heard you guys." My brothers were there, the ones who had said, "Why are you doing this?" They came backstage afterwards and said, "That was fantastic. You guys are *so* good. I can't believe how good you are, you should keep doing this" – two years later.

David Clarkson: I went to see them when they played at the El Mocambo and I felt bad for them. They had a couple of records come out and they were really good. But the shelf life of a hip band is pretty short. It happens to everybody.

You're just kind of supplanted by a bunch of other groups that come along and want to do exactly the same thing.

*   *   *   *   *

Paul Robinson: I lived at Queen Street West. It was my neighbourhood, although I really, really loved the [Toronto] islands. I used to take the ferry out to Ward's Island and just go to the beach. It kept me really sane; just getting away and going out there. Sometimes I'd be up all night and I'd go out there and sleep on the beach. I think Toronto's a great city. I *still* think it's a great city.

The one thing about Toronto that I really liked: For a very short time, I felt like I *owned* the city. To feel that you're really on top of a city, and that you can walk anywhere and feel like you belong, I think that's the best feeling that anybody can get.

Sally Cato: Toronto has the biggest inferiority complex of any major North American city. For a few minutes, a few people forgot about that completely and acted like everyone in Toronto should act all the time: They made art and stood up and did something without caring what the neighbours said. Then the media dropped the ball and left everyone hanging.

You need to understand, Toronto has one of the highest education systems and standards of living in the world. You have direct access to all American, British and world media, and a culture that is as rich as Manhattan. What happened in the Toronto scene — creatively, anyway — is expected to happen in any educated and culturally rich area.

Paul Robinson: Every once in a while, maybe in every century, a city has its moment. And I think a lot of Toronto's moment was between 1976 and 1980.

There was just an incredible amount of energy in Toronto. I think it was a pretty boring place before all of us. We kind of were the instigators in terms of changing an awful lot of the direction of the city, artistically and musically and stylistically.

People wanted Toronto to be more New York than New York, but keep its own identity. They wanted it to be important; they wanted it to matter. A lot of what I see in Toronto now is the product of what we created in a five-year period of time. Clubs, culture, fashion, art, music.

I don't want to say *we* started, because it would sound arrogant; that *we* were instigators of. I'm not saying me personally. I'm saying a group of maybe two hundred people.

Sally Cato: I left the scene in August of 1980. I rented a van and drove Bart Lewis and all of our things to New York City where he stayed with our original rhythm guitarist, Elliot. I returned to Canada to tie things up, and on December 24th, 1980 I took a train with the remainder of my personal belongings to Penn Station.

We moved because Toronto let us all down. "All" meaning Diodes, Teenage Head, B-Girls, the art scene in general, photographers, painters, conceptual artists — *everyone*. I saw amazing, honest talent and beauty deliberately ignored by an ignorant and stuffy Toronto press and media.

Here was their chance to jump on their own distinctly original and innovative cultural revolution, and wave it high and loud across the world media airwaves. And they killed it instead, like China to Tibet. At least in the UK the press are out for blood, so they at least talk about you. Toronto press are only interested in criticizing things from other countries, or saying bravo to government-subsidized art. Blondie, and Patti Smith, and the Ramones, even the Dolls, God bless 'em, and many, many more are revered here in New York. Maybe not rich, but they have always been afforded the coverage and respect they deserve for what they carved into musical and literary history. And it is reflected internationally.

Toronto media still suffers from the residue of the antiquated British class system, and are constantly shooting themselves in the foot.

Ian Mackay: That fall we released a new album and the recession hit, and it just knocked the wind out of our sails. We did try to make a go of it, and by the end of 1981 I was literally starving to death. I couldn't pay my rent.

Mike Lengyell: There was a big economic problem. So it was a tough time to try and break some new ground.

Ian Mackay: There was a vicious recession in 1981 when interest rates went up twenty per cent, and we haven't experienced anything like that since then. The gigs dried up. We *were* making good money; in 1978, '79, we'd be making fifteen hundred dollars a night, and at the end of it nobody was hiring, nobody was doing anything, nobody was going out. You'd be lucky if you got two hundred and fifty a night and all the bands were suffering.

I think that's what killed us. We couldn't sustain it. We had expenses — equipment, loans. We invested sufficiently; we could be self-sufficient, because if you're going to open for Ultravox in Montreal you've gotta have a soundman, your own monitor system, all your own equipment, if you have special lighting needs you've got to bring that. So it was turning into the rock business for us.

Mike Lengyell: It was a crazy time. A lot of record companies in the States were cutting back their rosters and cutting back their budgets for bands, so it was kind of a hard time for us to try and get to the next level.

So, we sort of stumbled a little bit.

These guys had a lot of creativity, but they hadn't played instruments a long time. I played the National Arts Centre in Ottawa when I was sixteen. I'd been playing drums for a long time. I cared about my own performance, and I cared about other people's performance. I took a lot of pride in just the craft of playing an instrument, and they didn't really come from that place. They didn't have the same kind of attitude about playing music as I did. They came from performance art, where you just kind of let it go and whatever happens is "art." So I think there was a bit of conflict in that sense; when they had a bit of an I-don't-give-a-shit attitude and got a little sloppy, and maybe they weren't as accomplished musicians as maybe I might have expected. It starts getting embarrassing.

I got mad a couple of times and I said, "We're not professional enough to be doing this. It's one thing playing a bar. It's one thing hoping you're going to get the next record deal, or the next important person is going to see you and you're going to take that next step. That's all well and good. But it's right here, right now. What are we doing *tonight*? Are you playing good, or are you just kind of not giving a shit?" That's something that I took personally, and that's where I felt that it was really starting to turn for me.

Ian Mackay: We broke up September '81. Or let me rephrase that — I left the band and they went to England to try to make a go of it.

Mike Lengyell: I think Ian was sort of hesitant about whether he wanted to stick with music. You know, these guys all had art degrees; they'd all graduated and had other interests and paths that they were maybe interested in following. I think there was maybe a little bit of a lack of interest in going all the way with it, because they could pursue other things.

Ian Mackay: I'm the organizer. I'm a little more understated. I'm back from the stage a little bit; I work with the drummer, I try to keep John Catto in line, I work with the soundman. I'm trying to unify the whole thing, whereas I would say John and Paul have more of the stage presence than I do. But we're all equally important I think. I don't think they could do it without

me, and they didn't. They needed somebody to organize them.

Ultimately, the reason I left was because I didn't believe the band had legs musically to become truly successful. We continued to develop and do well, but by that time I was in my third year of studying jazz and was doing a lot of work outside of the band. And I just didn't see the musical development of the other guys happening at the same rate. And it *needed* to happen, because if you look at the Clash's *London Calling*, that's one of the best albums ever made. Then you've got Elvis Costello, the Talking Heads evolving rapidly, and Television set the bar in the early days. This was serious music; it was no more the three-chord situation, and for people who were going to be in the scene it was no longer going to be, "Ha ha ha, let's make a song." It was all about developing musically with the scene.

Look at the finesse of a band like Blue Rodeo at their best. Parachute Club and all these bands that were coming up in the early '80s were musically more sophisticated than what we were doing in 1980, and we were starting to go in that direction, but I didn't think we were going to move fast enough. We needed to graduate.

And losing John Hamilton was one of the things that hurt me. I had more artistic solidarity with him. That coupled with what looked like the 1981 recession grinding on and on and on and on and us going hand-to-mouth. Plus at that point I was booking all the gigs, I was booking all the sound, I was doing all the work to make the gigs happen. Paul and John were just showing up; they were still the stars, but I wanted to set out on my own.

Paul Robinson: I just didn't want to do what we were doing for the rest of my life. I did not want to go up and down the Ontario bar circuit and play these shitholes. It's not what I wanted out of music.

Mike Lengyell: We all drank a little bit. I was a little bit different, believe it or not, because I could drink a lot and smoke a lot of pot, but I was also the guy that drove to and from the gig every night. I was the designated driver every night. I drove thousands of miles with that band, and I take a lot of pride in that.

I remember doing a gig in the middle of February in Guelph, and I drove non-stop after the gig to Halifax. I was the only one that could keep the vehicle on the road, and do you know how important that is? It's *really* important, because a lot of people die on the highway. And I think I was never given some of the appreciation for that effort that I should have been.

A lot of these things don't really go out with a bang.

There might be a couple of pops along the way, but not necessarily a big bang. A lot of times it kind of whimpers out — "Yeah, I can't be bothered doing this anymore and yeah, okay, no problem, see ya, goodbye."

It kind of left a sour taste in my mouth. I tried not to have hard feelings. Sometimes life just doesn't go great. Sometimes there's bad luck. Sometimes things just don't work out. Hey, you go on.

*　　*　　*　　　*　　　　*

John Catto: Paul really wanted to get out of Dodge. He came up with this idea to go over to England; his friend David from Boston had gone over a couple of years earlier as had his old girlfriend Carol, so there was a bit of infrastructure already there so it made sense. So I start selling stuff like crazy. All my guitars, clothes, everything, what the hell . . .

Paul Robinson: I think sometimes you should just stay put. Really, Toronto was our biggest market and we should have stayed and continued developing and making records.

But in a way, it's better to be somebody who burned bright and just disappeared; we didn't have to die to have this notoriety. Yet it's almost as if we died in 1980. So that in a way is good; it's like being James Dean without having to die. If you look at some of the other bands like Teenage Head, who kept going, in a way we were much wiser to be remembered for this one period where we had this enormous creativity and then disappeared.

Mike Lengyell / photo by Ralph Alfonso

Mike Lengyell: The Diodes were really groundbreaking in a number of ways, and I think one of them was in a way that maybe they didn't really foresee.

Back when I was playing in bars, very, very, very few bands, like one out of fifty or a hundred, was allowed to play their own songs. There might have been bands like Kim Mitchell and maybe Trooper, but there weren't too many bands that could go to a bar and play original material.

I think the Diodes started to really break down the barrier for the average band, if I can say that. We weren't hit-makers or high profile like the Kim Mitchells and the Troopers. We were just a — I don't want to say average, but I'll just say average for lack of a better word — Toronto band playing original material in bars. Up until that time that was unheard of, so I think we broke a lot of ground that way and paved the way for a lot of bands after that.

Not long after that it became commonplace for original bands to be able to get work in bars, which up until that point was practically impossible. So I think the Diodes broke through that wall.

John Catto: That was a very strange thing. The entire Canadian music scene changed in '83, '84 when the whole thing got re-jigged.

Paul Robinson: Thirty years later it's still probably one of the most important movements in music. It's maybe one of five seminal movements in modern music. I think it did change things. You wouldn't see the things that you see today without the influence of punk.

Ralph Alfonso: Once you got past 1978 or '79, all hell broke loose and there was the whole avalanche of the second or third wave of bands. The Diodes made it through there, but again, did it get A&R people to scout out Toronto? No. Did it get the local music industry to take notice? Not really.

But who could blame them? I was thinking about this the other day. At the time, anyway, you're dealing with bands and a genre of music which is completely based and derived from, and owes all of its existence to, music by bands who had failed. So when you're talking about the MC5, Stooges, Flamin' Groovies, Dictators, Velvet Underground even, these are all bands that, in their time, were commercial failures. None of them sold records and they all got dropped. But they were so influential that they were responsible for punk. So, ergo, the cycle will repeat itself.

If your whole music and attitude is based on bands that were commercial failures, chances are so will *your* music be a commercial failure. It's just the way it is. Your whole attitude, as valid as it is, unfortunately will not get mainstream legitimacy because they don't want it, at that particular point in time. Now, it's completely different, which is great. So that first phase is almost the martyr phase. Bands like the Stooges and Flamin' Groovies had to fail so that the Ramones, Sex Pistols, Generation X could exist. So that pattern now goes forward, so Viletones, Diodes, Teenage Head had to fail so that sadly, or not so sadly, bands like Sum 41 and the rest of them could succeed.

But there's always going to be some anger or resentment from the generation before or prior, because it's like, "Well, I was doing all this stuff and where's *my* reward," right? Well, unfortunately your reward is iconic, it's not monetary. So be happy with that.

The Diodes eventually did do well. They got out of CBS and ended up on Orient and they did get everything they wanted. I mean, it's perseverance. They kind of stuck to it and eventually got what they wanted on that level – they got the hit single and they got to tour with U2 and all that stuff. But they were never able to break out of Canada because the machinery at the time was not there to help you do that; those mechanisms weren't in place. That didn't show up until the '90s and really didn't solidify until this millennium.

To me in hindsight now, anything that will open the door into the scene and get people interested in you posthumously is a good thing. Like I said, you reap what you sow. Your success is directly related to your ambition; directly related to your hunger to make it happen. If you want it to happen, it will happen. Teenage Head perpetually kept moving forward and they made stuff happen, and the Diodes as well.

John Hamilton: One of the things that I always think about is that it was the kind of band that could have had a twenty-five year career and always done something interesting. It wasn't the kind of band that would have their four or five songs and keep playing them over and over in the same way. It was a band that really could have gone on and developed further and further, because that's what we always did. It got kind of truncated at a certain point, and I think it could have been even more influential than it has been.

Ralph Alfonso: My famous story, which is a funny one: We were playing some dive bar in Dundas, Ontario and at the time I was the Diodes' light man. And it was this club where they had strippers.

The band was supposed to go on at eight o'clock. The strippers are gone, the band isn't onstage, and I'm like, "What's going on?" So I go downstairs and there's one room where there are semi-nude women – where the strippers are changing – and in this other room there's this amazing argument coming out of the dressing room. I come in and I go, "What's going on?" And they're like, "Ralph, you've got to settle this for us." And I go, "What?" They go, "Okay, *Cabaret*, right?" I go, "Yeah?" "Is it based on *Christopher and His Kind* or *Berlin Stories?"*

And I'm like, "Is *this* what you guys are arguing about?" And they're like, "Yeah, man." It was *Christopher and His Kind,* obviously, and they're like, "That settles it. Okay." And I'm like, "Man, can't you guys argue about your farts like other bands?"

The point of that story was that as I graduated through the music industry and worked with tons of other bands, I was really spoiled. Because when your first band is *that*, you're used to this sort of interaction of higher philosophical thinking. And then when you're working with other bands; there's *none* of that. They're just guys in a band doing band stuff. It really, really spoiled me, and really made me realize what a unique moment that was in my life just to be with this crowd.

It wasn't just the Diodes, it was the circle that we had as well. You can't just close your eyes and be in a very closed scene. You've got to think sociologically of the impact of what you're doing beyond the borders of Canada; beyond the borders of the Crash 'n' Burn. How can you make an impact elsewhere? How can you transport this energy elsewhere? I remember when the Leslie Spit Treeo signed to Capitol, they came into my office and I sat them down and I go, "Okay, you've just signed to a major label. You now have the perfect, most powerful vehicle for your message if you want to do that." And they just looked at me – "*Huh?*" I'm like, "Okay, don't worry about it, we'll sell your records."

But that is the ultimate, when you can do that as a band or as a musician: You can not only create music that's accessible, but also subvert the record company machinery to your will. To have it disseminate not only your music but your philosophies, way of life, lifestyle, art.

But it's always this compromise between art and commerce. As long as you provide the commerce, then the distribution system will be there for your art. I always tell this to bands now: You can kind of do whatever you want as long as your music is good.

The Diodes on Queen St.
l-r: Mike Lengyell, John Catto,
Paul Robinson, Ian Mackay
/ photo by Ralph Alfonso

70. second wave

Blair Martin: I started the Raving Mojos in 1981. The second wave of people had shown up at that point. The first wave of people actually disappear and go home, or become the Queen Street crowd. There were people I never saw again after the first scene.

So by '81 there's this second wave of people who weren't there in the beginning, and the problem with them is that they're converts; like zealots. Henry Rollins described what the scene became like. He said how stiff punk rockers were at the time. Any hint of a guitar solo you'd get that classic comment — "Hey, man, what is this, 'Freebird'?" I remember people actually saying that in real life.

But all those people hadn't been there in the first place. They weren't the original punk rock scene. They were people who two years before had probably been listening to Led Zeppelin for the most part and living out in the suburbs. Then they would move downtown and become converts. They didn't really *get* the old scene. They could understand the prestige of something like going to a Viletones show, but I don't think they ever understood that the Viletones were a *rock 'n' roll* band, which is what they were at that point in time. They're not addressing what you want to see happening anymore.

The second wave of punk rock people had no interest in rock 'n' roll at all. They were interested in a purist form of this punk rock thing that they wanted to see that didn't really exist yet. It indicates, first of all, that punk rock was kind of getting into the mainstream. When was the Teenage Head riot, '80? Steve Goof and his buddy Greg Tynkaluk are at that thing, and apparently — and I'm remembering a really old anecdote at this point — apparently butted a cigarette out on a police horse's ass. So you can imagine who these people are and where they're coming from. It was when the hosers started getting into punk rock.

The Raving Mojos was a very ill-timed concept in that my contemporaries are people like Steve Goof. I was just being completely confrontational to what was happening. I had one vision. I particularly admired the band Teenage Head, especially Gordie's guitar playing, although when you examine them they're not always lyrically the deepest. But they're a huge influence on me and the Toronto kind of seriousness.

People from Toronto take themselves seriously, and sometimes the effect can be quite intense when the best of us do it, whether it's Marshall McLuhan or Steve Leckie or Johnny Lovesin. When a Torontonian does art, they do it very seriously. They tend not to do comedy. It's kind of in our character to do drama rather than comedy.

What I wanted to do, and under the immediate influence of the MC5, was have a rock 'n' roll band, which was about the most revolutionary fuckin' thing you could do in 1981.

Rob Sikora: I remember going to see something at the Upper Lip, I think. It was these third-string Hamilton bands, and the Raving Mojos played.

This guy wandered in and I was talking to him. We were by the window drinking beer and he's like, "This is fuckin' amazing." I'm like "Yeah, this is cool, it's four Detroit-style rock 'n' roll bands." He goes, "I'm *from* Detroit." He was in town on business and he had asked at the desk where to go to see some hard, guitar bands. Lord knows who the person was who directed him, but it made me proud of Toronto. I thought, This is unique. I'm diggin' this and I live here.

If the scene had kept being like that, I might have stayed interested. That's like a vacuum where, once again, something like Raving Mojos happens. For us, what filled the gap in Toronto was the Mojos. In Toronto, none of those bands lasted very long. They really didn't.

Hamilton kept going; Toronto didn't. Maybe in Hamilton they just had better jobs, ha ha ha. I don't know, maybe Teenage Head just really meant something in Hamilton. There weren't venues in Hamilton. Saucer used to rent the Y. People would rent halls to do shows, which meant no drinking or any of that stuff. I'm still perplexed by that.

You know, thinking back on this, Toronto had drugs. Hamilton didn't. I mean, heroin really messed up this town. Hamilton people fucked up, too, but not on the level people did in Toronto.

Dave Rave: In Toronto there were junkies, but we didn't really get that much in Hamilton. I think that's another reason why we never split up in Hamilton. When I hear stories about junk, like the Dolls, it split the group up.

The Head never got into junk. Maybe cocaine, but not junk. And Toronto had the junk. Because if you had junk, you can't trust somebody at your house. But we just had beer and pills and that stuff, and I think that's a big difference.

Tom Williams: Teenage Head came out of a steel-working town, so that's probably why they're still out there.

Frankie Venom [*Eye Weekly*, January 25, 1996]: In the early days there were bennies and Labatt's Blue and that was it. We were just wild; we didn't need the drugs that kids are doing today.

Elizabeth Aikenhead: I remember going to a reunion at the Cameron. It was in the back room, and there were lots of girls and lots of guys. This was probably 1981.

I remember seeing Anna and Nora and Nellica and a group of us were just chatting, all the girls. We were all doing things; we were going back to school, we were taking courses, we were starting jobs that we really liked, we thought we might be interested in writing a book or making a movie or becoming an architect or whatever it was. We were pulling ourselves together and we got real haircuts. Ha ha ha.

And all the guys were on the other side of the room, and they were all exactly the same. They were probably wearing the same black T-shirts they'd been wearing four years earlier. Maybe they washed them, I don't know. Then I remember seeing Crash walk in. Crash was often affiliated with heroin. I remember seeing a bunch of the guys go out and come back and then just be blobs on the table.

It was seeing all these loser guys who just hadn't moved forward. These were guys in their twenties who were totally stuck in what was their peak when they were eighteen, twenty-two, who knows what. Just stuck; totally arrested and going downhill from there.

Kerry Wade: There was a lot of heroin in Toronto. People disappearing, and then you'd go to the bathroom and there was blood on the walls and shit. It was very sad. I was right in the middle of it. I remember the biggest dealer; I was like, "I wanna try." He was like, "No, you *don't* wanna try it." He wouldn't let me do it.

Heroin never seemed to make it here in Hamilton.

Slash Booze: Don't forget, you're looking at a city of two hundred thousand versus a city of two million. When you're in Toronto, you're in the big city and you're exposed to big city habits. There's going to be that much more availability and enamour with it.

Once you're in music, too, that opens up a whole new world. Every slime bag in the world wants to give you something to ingratiate himself. They want to get in there for whatever reason; to be in with The In Crowd. So when drugs become a big part of that, that's when things get lost, right, wrong, or indifferent.

I knew lots of people sniffing and I knew lots of people speeding, but not doing needles. Maybe here a little bit, but not to the extent of Toronto.

I don't need drugs; I'm high on life. I try not to think. It disturbs my drinking.

Kerry Wade: I don't know, I think it's punk rock. That's the lifestyle. That was a huge part of it as far as Toronto goes. I know it ruined a lot of really talented people, like Handsome Ned. Who knows how far he could have gone,

he was just that fucking talented. He was amazing.

It broke a lot of hearts but as far as holding people back, like Mike Nightmare, where was he gonna go? He knew he was gonna die young. He just knew it. There was nowhere else for him to go, really.

Zero: I think Hamilton kept going strong because they were further away from us, ha ha ha. They didn't get intertwined as much; they just left and recuperated, and we just all got screwed up, ha ha ha. They had a breather in between everything so they were able to sustain a little bit easier. They didn't drown with all of us.

*   *   *   *   *

Mickey DeSadist: The drug use with us wasn't as heavy as people thought. I'm almost embarrassed to say it wasn't.

Chris Houston: I came back for summer break and we had Chuck Anarchy on drums. He played on the original demos of "Rhona Barrett" and "Surfin' on Heroin."

Mickey DeSadist: We had a gig that we had to play, Labour Day 1980. Me and Houston reformed the band again and decided to call up Cleave [Anderson] from Blue Rodeo, basically learned the songs, and went there and somebody threw a smoke grenade for a joke.

There was people gobbing. The spitters. We were covered in so much slime that we could hardly play. So when that grenade was thrown I yelled, "Fire!", the place emptied out because there was smoke everywhere, and then, because I had to get to the bus station because the buses didn't go late and I had to get to work the next day or I wouldn't get my vacation pay, I ran off after getting paid and that was the last Houston Rebels gig.

Chris Houston: Harold Kudlets wanted to manage the Rebels. He was sitting around the house and he wanted to get back into rock 'n' roll.

That was my biggest mistake. He was a real manager and I should have got him, but I thought we'd be too kooky for him, and I didn't want him telling all my friends about all the kooky antics we got up to. Then I realized how kooky the Band were, and that we were no match for them. That's kind of the weird connections in Hamilton.

Mickey had this apartment where we wrote "Surfin' On Heroin." All the *In Love With the System* was written there. We wrote a lot of those songs all in one night. Then "This Ain't Hollywood" was written because Mickey's girlfriend and her entire family were going to go into the van we were taking to a show so I blurted out, "This ain't Hollywood; only *you* get in the van."

So this is where we actually wrote everything.

It was a horrible apartment. And the other thing is that when we wrote all those hits, which was about a four-hour period, Mickey's girlfriend put on makeup the entire time. She had a little TV tray in front of her, and I remember her putting on makeup.

Mickey DeSadist: When Houston left, the songs started tilting towards more of a glitter base.

Chris Houston: I got interested in other music, and I guess the One Eyed Jacks was the band I was in right after that, with Alex and Steve [Koch]. They were really great musicians and they were nice guys. The great musicians in the Rebels were kind of hard to deal with.

I think probably at that time we thought of ourselves as a supergroup, and also we were exploring that new music that we heard — rockabilly. This is pre–Stray Cats, so it just seemed more authentic in terms of music, going back to that. Once you got into the rockabilly stuff then you got into the blues, then you got into the country, and all the southern styles of music. And that was kind of exciting. You always want to be on the ground floor of the next new movement.

That was an exciting time period. Punk rock, with all its nihilistic energy, kind of imploded, and a lot of the personalities just became stagnant. So you wanted to kind of make a break from that.

I remember talking to Mickey in the bar that was in the bus station. By the time *In Love With the System* came out, we figured it was the third gasp of punk rock; a rejuvenation in terms of it going through a cycle and getting different kids into it. Because we were definitely around at the beginning we were aware of that, so you wanted to keep moving on. The really great bands were great, but there were a lot of suspect bands that jumped on the bandwagon, and anybody that was really into music really wanted nothing to do with them. Ha ha ha.

Hamilton will never let me forget that time period. There's no other topic of discussion. I toured the Prairies numerous times. I played to lots of people. I had a career on the West Coast. They don't care about that or even know about it. It's the Rebels.

Hamilton never lets you forget.

Mickey DeSadist: Another thing that helped the Rebels out a lot, the Star Records guy Mike Shulga put out *In Love With the System*, and he also put out *This Ain't Hollywood*. Now we may have had our business disputes, but that was a very big thing for him to do and I am forever thankful to him for that. He might be very surprised when he hears me saying something nice about him, but I never say anything bad about him

anymore because I realize how important he was to the band and to our presence. I wish maybe he gave us some money, but ...

I thought that this scene was gonna get really, really, really big, and it's not that I was just in it for the money, but I thought we were gonna make a hell of a lot of money partying our way through life. And I guess it didn't quite happen that way, but it looked like it was going to. We were gonna have fun and retire young.

When did things turn pessimistic? When we realized we were too old to retire early, ha ha ha.

Stephen Burman: Mickey would go *almost* all the way, then he would stop before he got to the point where he could be commercially accessible.

I was in on the recording sessions for *This Ain't Hollywood,* which is still my favourite. There were two versions of the album, a soft mix and a harder mix. The first mix we did was really poppy. Really poppy and really musical. It was just popped to death. That could have taken them places, but they just refused to go the commercial thing. So they didn't go anywhere with it.

You can be as political as you want, but you've at least got to be approachable to the masses. They just refused to do that. They didn't want to capitulate.

It's a business. People forget that music, as culturally important as it can be and as fun as it can be, is still a business. And if you can't wrap your head around the business model and figure out what do people want, why do they like you, how do we approach more people so that we can get more money from the studios so we can make better albums, well ...

Bob Bryden: "Surfin' on Heroin" *did* make it to the Top 5 Independent Singles on the *New Musical Express* chart. It blew me away.

We found out in England, and I'll never forget it. We were in this little mall and there was a record store in a cage. We went in and told him who we were and he says, "Oh! Well, did you know you're charted here?" Then he showed us the *NME*. That was truly a divine moment. Mike and I just looked at each other and went, "Holy smoke."

Mickey DeSadist: I knew that we would get mentioned eventually, but I expected more. Because we were so much better I expected more, but I knew it would happen eventually.

It just should have happened sooner.

The media wasn't curious enough at the moment they should have been. It's like a lot of things: When you finally get it, you've waited so long that you're sick of waiting, so you don't care if you get it or not anymore.

But yeah, I expected it. See, the bands that were calling themselves punk really weren't. Teenage Head were not calling themselves a punk band, and they really were, so they deserved the mention. The Viletones were a punk band. The Ugly were a good band, they should have been mentioned. There were quite a lot of good bands in Hamilton and Toronto that also weren't really punk bands but should have been mentioned because they made the scene what it was. *Everybody* there, including the person who swept the floor at the end of the night, was important to the scene. That includes whoever owned the club, ran the club, whoever closed the club, whoever complained about the club; every single person was important. Even the people that hated the music and thought it sucked, they were important because they inspired perseverance.

Stephen Burman: If they had moved away, could they have gotten more recognition? New York, possibly. London, no, I don't think so. I think definitely in the States, particularly at the time when they came out with *This Ain't Hollywood*, because it's a very American-style album. *In Love With the System* was more British-style, but *This Ain't Hollywood* was definitely, definitely a Teenage Head, U.S.-style album.

They did a lot of international touring. They're popular still in Europe. But I guess not much happened other than that.

Mickey DeSadist: I stayed in Hamilton because I was stupid. You know, people said, "Big artists are coming out of Canada, and it's promising!" I never realized that there was not enough economic support in this nation; there's not enough of a population density to get big.

How many bands worked their butts off? If you don't play live, so what? If your record's good enough it'll get played. But no, it doesn't matter if a record's good enough. You've got to be doing favours for somebody.

I wasn't smart enough to move to New York, and in retrospect would it have even mattered? Because none of those good bands from New York actually got very big except for Blondie. She was pretty good up to what, the fifth album? Then *that* fell apart. The Clash were great and so were the Pistols in England, but what happened? What happened to all the other acts? There were great acts. And if you look at not just precedent but *quality* of other acts, I may think I've got the greatest band in the world. But so do they. You can't say the Buzzcocks were better than the Rebels, or not.

The industry is supporting its own failure. They're not smart enough to be like the sports industry.

I personally knew two guys that were drafted to the Detroit Tigers for baseball. Now, they threw their shoulders out during training, but you know what?

These were two guys that were hanging around with me at Tim Horton's. Seventeen-year-old boys when I was seventeen; guys that were in some of my classes in school. And somebody actually noticed that this guy was throwing ninety-five- to ninety-eight-mile-an-hour pitches as a little kid. So the same thing almost happened to him. He almost became a gigantic athlete, and unfortunately he injured himself.

Athletes get treated way better than musicians do, because the industry seeks out the greatness of athletes. And there is no debate when a guy makes a two-hundred-foot jump on a motorcycle. There is no debate when a guy is measured throwing a hundred-mile-an-hour baseball pitch. There's no debate when a guy hits a guy in the face solidly enough to flatten him in the first round.

But in music they say, "Well, I've got a cousin that can play like this and I've got a friend of a friend that can play like that." The industry is guided by favouritism. And if the music industry ran itself the way the sports industry did, you'd see a whole lot more artists that are very, very good, and a whole lot more changes.

Joe Csontos: I knew Mickey from my neighbourhood.

I guess this is maybe one or two incarnations of the Rebels later. They had Dave McGhee and they fired Dave or whatever and John [Welton] said, "Well, let's get Joe, he can drum." So that was it, I got the gig. I got the call and had to learn all their songs in a week because they had a gig. It was trying, but I was with them for a couple of years.

This is right after *This Ain't Hollywood*. I basically toured that record with them. We went to New York, Boston, played with the Clash — well, the later Clash, the Joe Strummer/Paul Simonon Clash. Played with the Cramps at the Masonic. Played Larry's, Kitchener, London all the time. A few years' worth of that.

Mickey DeSadist: There was lots of violence, but it wasn't between the musicians. It was between the skids, the rounders, punk rockers, and disco heads.

At one point, the people in heavy metal hated the people in disco and the people in punk hated the people in heavy metal and disco. I couldn't see the point in that ever. I just hung around with a bunch of guys. A lot of people like us for some reason, because we're silly and funny.

One time somebody slashed their wrist by accident. They fell on a glass of some type and cut their wrist and there was blood flying everywhere. I had just ordered four drinks — when they would still serve that many at a time — and it looked like somebody poured grenadine on top of them; there was blood floating in all my drinks. I was onstage at the time and I thought, Ozzy Osbourne, eat your heart out. That's what I said to the audience.

And then the person that had their wrist slashed came over to me about ten years later and thanked me for playing that night. Their wrist was cut through the veins when they fell on the dance floor and through the glass. They immediately got sewn up at the hospital. They were okay and recovered and they received some big, huge compensation package from the club. They were thanking me and I said, "Well, you might as well give me a ten per cent fee for being your agent for that one."

They made more than me that night. They made more than me and the band did in the next five nights.

Joe Csontos: When I joined, I thought their trajectory was the highest it ever was. I remember reading Greil Marcus in the *Village Voice*, and his Single of the Week was "Surfin' on Heroin." I thought, Wow, we're in the *Village Voice*. That's huge; Single of the Week. And we started getting gigs out of that.

Tom Williams: I can tell you that Sting and Stewart Copeland told me that North American bands would never make it, and the reason was because the British bands were used to sleeping on someone else's floor and having no luxuries and having no money. But the Canadian bands, when they had to go on tour, they were used to living in Don Mills. They just weren't going to put up with the hardships that the British bands would do in a heartbeat to get out of those awful council flats.

Mickey DeSadist: I toured all over Canada. It wasn't all *that* horrible. I mean, we stayed in some of the best hotels imaginable. When you phone and they say, "Okay, you're gonna stay at this great hotel; they just renovated," when they tell you they've just renovated that only means they flushed the toilets since the last customer. Air conditioning? All you had to do was put your foot through the wall. And if you paid extra they might change the sheets, but it looked like nobody ever paid the extra. They looked like they had something like dried custard on them. What I liked was sometimes you'd have to ask the squatters to leave, and when you lifted the pillow you'd have to smack the bugs off from under it. A lot of the hotels in Ontario are like that, and usually we ask for them.

But see, being from Hamilton, I'm always used to that sort of thing. I guess this is the only city where a guy like Chris Houston can come out with a quote like this; I wish this was my quote — "There are two types of people in this world. The first type sees a piece of snot hanging out of your nose and tells you, 'You've got a piece of snot hanging out of your nose' and tells you to clean it up. The second type is the one that tells everybody else that you've got a piece of snot hanging out of your nose, points at you and laughs at you." That's Houston, all right.

Always Hamilton, Toronto, London, Vancouver, Kamloops, Cranbrook were good shows. It was either Kamloops or Cranbrook, we were playing at the hockey arena, and you know the way David Lee Roth of Van Halen jumps and does the splits? Well, at the end of a song I jumped up and did the splits, and at a very inopportune moment the guitar player swung his guitar and nailed me with the head, right in my manly area. There are six hundred people in this arena. I land on the ground, face flat, spread-eagle holding my manly area. And instead of everybody cheering at the end of the song, it's six hundred people laughing at me. When I stood up, I told them they had a very uncanny sense of humour.

Actually, my favourite show of all was opening up for Ian Hunter and Mick Ronson at the Hollywood Palace, right where there's the Walk of Fame across the road from the Capitol building. That was the building that Freddy Krueger chased Andrew Dice Clay off of. And opening for the Clash in Buffalo. I was always a Clash fan.

Joe Csontos: I remember we looked at each other and went, "Holy shit, we're opening for the Clash." We're in the dressing room going, "This is *huge*."

We played for the Cramps. Things were good. Sometimes I made a lot of money for one gig. It was unbelievable. In 1985 I probably made more money in one night than I make at my job today, so that's when I knew.

We'd play one long set that was usually sixty, seventy minutes long, no break. We'd come on, we were the headliner, we'd play twenty-five songs or whatever, and that was it. It was a lot of fun. I just wish I was better in those days, but it was all about living in the moment. Now I'm a better drummer because I *care*. Then, it was just live out of the suitcase. It was the sex and drugs and rock 'n' roll thing.

Mickey DeSadist: I wish I'd played Maple Leaf Gardens, but what can you say? Maple Leaf Gardens ain't there anymore, and neither is the old guy with the beard who used to ask for money at the front. He passed away last year. Better him than me.

Our tours only ever lasted, the longest, six weeks. Who wants to be away from home for longer than six weeks? I look back at it now, I should have done it more often, but so what? I still did okay. We *all* still did okay. You can't regret anything.

Well, actually, the only thing I regret is not doing everything ten times as often as I did do. I didn't want to overwork myself, though. James Brown's the hardest working guy in show business; us guys were the biggest slackers. Still are.

That's okay. We're not even in the union. Ha ha ha.

Joe Csontos: I kind of got fed up with the business. Sometimes we'd make good money and sometimes we wouldn't. And usual squabbles: You get bitchy at each other in the van. "You missed that part," or, "Why didn't you practise more," that kind of stuff. It was like, I don't need this, you know? I'd had enough. In my mind, it wasn't going as well as it was when it started. I think it started to plateau.

I don't know if I left them in the lurch, but I think I did. But you could ask them and they'll probably say no, because then they went to Berlin.

Mickey DeSadist: When we went to Germany the places were packed, and I thank the Lord for bootleggers for that. I couldn't care less if we get bootlegged; we'll never make money off any records, so the fans might as well get it. I'd be happy if I could give away ten million albums. That way nobody gets in on the guest list and they'd charge more.

Chris Houston: I think what gives the Rebels the longevity is *In Love With the System*. A classic album in terms of production, songs, performance, that really articulates teenagers going through their difficult years. It was perfect.

Teenage Head or these other bands didn't have perfect records. They were flawed records, though they were great records. *In Love With the System* was just a perfect record. Every time that another generation of kids get into it, they always gravitate towards that record. It's a pivotal record for people in their youth, so I think that helped the Rebels out.

Mickey DeSadist: If punk never happened, I would have still become a musician and I would have still played. I consider myself a person who likes the art of making music before any scene or anything like that.

I never thought I'd be around this long. I never thought people would be interested. Yeah, I never thought people would be interested this long, but I'd still be playing whether they were or they weren't.

You know, I regret seeing that two-thirds of everybody's dead from that era, and the rest of them aren't nowhere near as good looking as me, especially when I've got my hair done. These guys, I don't know what they did to themselves. They must have burnt themselves out a little more often than I did. They never took care of themselves.

I didn't do very much drugs because I'd look at it and think, Who's gonna spend a hundred dollars for a gram of *anything?* For a hundred dollars I can get myself another guitar. And you know, I wasn't the kind of guy who'd spend two hundred dollars to share my drugs if I did buy them, you know?

Chris Houston: I'd almost say it was the early '90s that they hit their stride. That's when they started getting huge amounts of money. Plus Mickey, he always rises to the occasion in bringing that special, decadent, strange humour that he has from Hamilton wherever he goes, so it's not seeing the hits being played. It's a real show.

Mickey DeSadist: I don't know what else to say, other than there was a lot of misunderstanding at the beginning of what we were all doing. We were goofing off like kids and expecting, *expecting*, to be able to retire on it. That was always the main goal. I just wanted to get out of the working world as fast as I could. Well, I'm too old to retire young, and that's basically what happened. We carried on normal lives trying to avoid carrying on normal lives, some of us.

I guess it's better than being dead. Who knows. I think a lot of them *are* dead, even though they don't know it.

Mickey DeSadist / photo by Steve Burman

71.
THe aBsolute enD

Caroline Azar: We loved the B-Girls. When Fifth Column formed, those bands were leaving. It was sad to me because I wanted to meet them.

Actually, it was our fantasy to open for the Curse or the B-Girls. I'd see pictures of them and say, "They're from *Toronto?*!" I tell you, seeing a Toronto punk on the street was like finding a diamond. They were so beautiful. I went to New York City, and they weren't beautiful there like they were here.

Cynthia Ross: When we started playing New York again, all these bands would come out and see us, including the New York Dolls, Lenny Kaye, who played in Patti Smith's band. So we were all friends, a core group of people.

We'd go there for weekends and would stay at this guy's place. He was somehow connected to Xenia's friend's mother's friend's son. Xenia had never met him, but he said we could stay at his place. His name was Bobby Rothchild. We used to call him *Baby* Rothchild because he spoke in this really high voice. He had hair like Neil Sedaka; he had the comb-over and used tons of hairspray to keep his bald spot covered. He was probably twenty-eight or thirty; he seemed older to us. He ran a lingerie company.

So it started out by him just letting us stay there when we would come in for a weekend to do a gig. He had a bachelor apartment at this place called Waterside Towers. We would sleep on the floor, and I kept feeling like we were really imposing on this guy.

When we decided we were moving to New York, we moved into his place, all four of us. We weren't working day jobs; we were hanging out all night with all these people and we'd come in at four in the morning and there's only one room. He had two couches. He slept on one, and then there was a roll-out couch. A couple of us slept on that, we took turns; the other two slept on the floor. We totally took over this guy's life.

We were supposed to be staying there for a couple weeks until we found a place, and we just never left. It was pretty insane. Johnny Thunders was there a couple times sleeping on the couch. Bobby and Johnny actually became really good friends, which was really funny. They were such an odd pair. We would have people over for dinner, like Debbie Harry, and I realized later he was just in awe.

He thought this was amazing; that this was the coolest thing ever. We would have *Casablanca* night where we invited Stiv Bators, Johnny Thunders, Debbie Harry. We decorated the whole place like *Casablanca* and showed the movie. We all sat on pillows on the floor and wore these Moroccan bathrobes in this guy's apartment.

I ran into him about ten years ago and said, "I feel so bad about what we did," and he said, "Are you *kidding?* That was the best time of my life!"

Christmas Eve one year it was the Jim Carroll Band and the B-Girls at somebody's house uptown, and they became our brothers. We kind of had that relationship with bands. The rule was, if you opened for a band, you weren't allowed to go out with any of them. You didn't want people to think you're only getting gigs because you're sleeping with the guys in the band, so it was like professional ethics. Even though it was the punk era, we *were* pretty tame and traditional.

I was cleaning apartments for a number of stock-brokers and also for this guy who was a photographer for Andy Warhol, and I was doing window displays. I think Xenia and Marcy had waitress jobs, I'm not sure. We didn't really have a lot of expenses except food. We actually made enough playing just to get by. We made more down there than we did here.

I got all these gigs with the Clash and the B-52s and the Cramps and people were saying, "You should really get a manager; you shouldn't be doing all this yourselves." So we went around and interviewed a bunch of different managers and they all gave us these things about, "Okay, we want to manage you, you girls are great, but what we want you to do is we want to get studio musicians to play on your record.

B-Girls; Xenia, Renee / photo by Ross Taylor

And we want you to take dance lessons and get your hair cut in a certain way." It was almost like it was their fantasy to create that type of boy-band thing.

So we ended up going with this guy who was Debbie Harry's road manager, and that's when things started falling apart. We agreed that we had to give him a commission, and he got us less gigs than I was getting us. For less money. He meant well; he was a good guy. But what it showed me is that when you believe in something a hundred per cent and put your heart and soul into it, *you're* probably the better person to convince people. It's like believing in what you're selling. We had to pay him money to get out of our contract.

I had also gone out to California because we played at the Whisky a Go Go. Stiv was living in a bungalow at the Tropicana Hotel, where all the bands stayed. Two guys called the Kessel Twins came to see us at the Whisky, and they worked for Phil Spector. They're the sons of Barney Kessel, who was the guitar player on a lot of the old Ronettes and Phil Spector recordings.

The next day they came to the motel and said, "Phil would like to meet you." They said, "He's a very strange guy, he doesn't go out, but we told him all about your band and he'd like to meet you." So Stiv came with me and we went to Phil Spector's mansion, which was really, *really* weird. He had a Christmas tree up from the year before, and it was July or August. Everything was really dark and he was this very strange guy. He just came out and shook my hand, and that was it.

The Kessels said, "Okay, we've played him your stuff, he likes it, you'll hear from us." So they take us to Gold Star, the recording studio where Phil Spector did all his stuff, and we got to see that. But Debbie Harry kept warning me about not signing anything with anybody, and not recording with people because they're gonna rip you off and they're gonna take advantage of you. So I was a bit overly cautious and wasn't willing to do anything with them. At the same time Debbie was recording *Autoamerican* in L.A., so they were at the Tropicana as well. We sang backup vocals on that record, and then we just started talking about possibilities.

Xenia Splawinski: Cynthia remembers all this stuff. I came back to Toronto in '81. I was in between both worlds. I have a very sort of raw, shamanic energy to me so I could appreciate some of the rawness of punk, but I couldn't go too far into the destructive thing. And the truth is, drugs and all that sort of stuff, I had finished with that already. I had done that when I was really young. I had had my time with it, and so I was not really pulled in by all of that. And I wasn't part of their art crowd either, so I didn't really fit into either side.

There were a number of things with the band breaking up. There were some heavy addictions by the

end of the band in New York. I had gone totally the other way, practicing yoga. And it was really clear to me that *that* was what I was looking for. It was, "Okay, I've done all this stuff. I did everything I wanted to do, and I know all these people that I want to know. I've been there, I've done that."

I was looking for something else. I didn't want to act out the art anymore, I wanted to *be* the art. I didn't want to be so reflective, but transformative. I would come back up to Canada at Christmastime and I'd hook up with an old friend of mine. And she had met a man who was a teacher, a spiritual teacher. I met him while I was there, and that was it. I knew that's what I had to do.

I did go back to New York, but I was torn after that and I ended up leaving and coming back up to Canada, and then phoning and saying that I wasn't coming back. The rest of the band just fell apart from there. I was probably so scared that I don't remember what I actually said to them. It was nerve-wracking.

But people had other interests as well. People were playing with other bands and things, so it wasn't going to be like their life was over. And certainly we had enough problems within the band by that point that stuff was happening; it was getting harder and harder. I don't remember anybody yelling or screaming at me, but I'm sure they were upset.

Cynthia Ross: I think that Marcy was starting to get involved in other musical projects. So was Xenia. I was, too. I think it just ran its course. We lost that drive, and I just felt you shouldn't keep doing it if that's not there. So we never really formally broke up. We just stopped playing.

I was playing in a number of different rockabilly bands. Xenia was actually doing some of those bands with me. I was just feeling like I wanted to try some different kinds of music.

I stayed there until '86 when my daughter was a year old, but the band broke up in '83. I came back here after I'd had a child. I lived in a fifth-floor walk-up tenement in New York. I was married to Billy Rogers, who was the drummer for Johnny Thunders. Actually, he was more for moving up here than I was. I was a bit reluctant, but I guess we both felt we didn't want to raise a child being afraid to walk outside. It just wasn't a great place to raise a child. Which is funny, because now New York is very gentrified. I went back to our block on Tenth Street and it's all sushi bars and chi chi cafes. It used to be pot stores.

The B-Girls wasn't really going anywhere. We had sidestepped a couple of opportunities because we were overly cautious. We had taken Debbie's advice about how record companies would take you over and manipulate you to be something that you're not.

We really looked up to her, to the point where we had a few offers and we didn't really go with them.

In some ways I regret that, although her advice was good and made sense and I see it now. Because now, it's even *more* of a business, and I think that was exactly what she was talking about. Now record companies don't develop artists; most artists do their own thing, and it's all about distribution. So the music scene is really gone in that sense.

Xenia Splawinski: My personal feeling is that the actual energy of the band was going into a place of unnecessary investigation of self-destructive behaviour, and from that place I don't think that it could have succeeded. But if it had, I still think it wouldn't have been a good thing because then it would have been held together with all of the conflict going on at the time. It wasn't what we were about. It was appropriate. It was time for me to go.

I would say people who were drawn to that scene had that shaman energy to them. It was really about breaking form, and there were a lot of casualties and there were a lot of people who survived. It was fascinating to see who could handle what they were doing and who couldn't, and who had to go which way. I reflect back on it and I see who lived and who didn't live, and it's sad in a way. There were a lot of really cool people that were lost. They took it to the absolute end. The ones that were lost had no ability to stop themselves

Patzy and Ruby / photo by Gail Bryck

72. escape

Gail Manning: After True Confessions broke up and Ruby wasn't with them, I don't know what happened to her. It was pretty short-lived, her tenure with the band.

Karla Cranley: I was with Raymi for four years, and near the end I couldn't take it anymore. I went back to office work. I just wanted out. The Ugly had split up.

You've got to remember, the guys, they'd work to pay for a practice hall. They always had the girls more or less support or take care of the basics, you know what I'm saying? When you're in a music scene like that, you've got to work all day to pay the rent. That's primary, rent and food, and then you've got to have the extra to play the gigs. That usually interfered with your job. They'd get partying or something, they'd lose their practice hall or lose their equipment or somebody'd get busted. They couldn't get a recording contract. If they *did* manage to get it together to get into a studio, they couldn't pay for their recordings. You'd get a rehearsal space, you'd put all your money on it, and then you had to give up your job to do the gig.

Mike and Raymi just couldn't keep it together. It was really, really difficult to survive.

A few of them, like the Diodes and Teenage Head, they made it. I don't know if it was because they weren't struggling to survive; if they came from better backgrounds where they had parents to help them.

Ruby and Mike rented a warehouse down on Front Street. They were really doing good; the guys were all practicing. There was a couple of speaks in there. Everything went really good for about eight months, and then Ruby had one of her conniptions. She attempted suicide, wound up in the hospital, chewed the intravenous lines out, they lost the place.

I had had it. Raymi had gotten a rehearsal space there, too, and I refused to move down there to live in that kind of a dump. And I guess they just couldn't get the money together to keep it, so that's when they moved out west and tried to make it.

There was no future. There was *no* future. You lived for the moment. You tried to make do with what you could, and you just hoped you made it till tomorrow. I never believed there was a future. You know what I'm saying? You lived from day to day, and I really didn't believe I would live a long time. And I didn't *want* to live a long time.

I think for a lot of people it was escape and they didn't like who they were or where they came from, so they made something.

Because in the punk scene, the more different your name was — like nobody remembered Karla. Nobody remembered Eva. But as soon as she became Eva Destruction ...

Sam Ferrara: I was the one who gave her the nickname — Eva Destruction. She was nuts. I met her at Larry's Hideaway. I was just coming back from England, visiting a girlfriend; we split up there. Well, she didn't tell me that we'd *split up*. I flew all the way to friggin' England thinking we were coming back together and she didn't tell me any different.

I get there and she's living with some guy who's supposed to be gay. He's not gay – not at all. So that was over with.

The same night I got back I went to Larry's and met Eva. She picked me up. We ended up staying together for a while and she started to get more and more crazy. I used to live in this basement apartment and I used to have this huge suitcase and it was all full of fan mail from playing high schools all over northern Canada, just packed from young teenage kids writing to me. It was so cool. I came home and she'd burned them all. I don't know why. She was burning pictures of old girlfriends and stuff. A very jealous person. One night, New Year's Eve, Jimmy Paputts came by with a bottle of Jack. We did some happy New Year's stuff and Eva just went to the kitchen and grabbed this huge friggin' knife and went to stab him. Jimmy's a real skinny guy and he's against the wall, pure white, and I grabbed her hand with the knife and I'm fighting with her. She wouldn't let go and I finally slugged her and put her out. It was the first time I ever hit her – hit any woman. I don't even hit guys. Jimmy and I just looked at each other and went, "Let's get out of here," ha ha ha. We both left and took the bottle with us and I didn't come back for three days, four days or something. She wasn't home but that's when I found everything burned. Like why do you want to kill Jimmy for? He's never hurt a fly.

She started going out with Mike right in front of me. We moved to another place on Harbord and she wouldn't come home. She was with Mike. They basically just did it in front of me. I wanted her to move, but she wouldn't leave, so I phoned her dad and I said, "Can you get your daughter outta here?" So she did eventually leave, and then she got into all that stripping and stuff, which was blamed on me.

Her parents hated my guts from day one. The first night I met them I go over to their place for dinner and we're sitting in the living with a little drink and her father, and he's talking Ukrainian at me. I don't understand a word he's saying at me. Eva comes in and goes, "Let's leave." "Why?" She says, "My dad's just called you everything in the book." He was calling me anything and everything, and I'm going, "Oh man, your mom's cooking this great meal, Ukrainian meal." "No, let's go." "Okay, fine."

I got up, got my coat on, I'm almost out the door and he kicks me in the tailbone really hard and it really hurt. And my first reaction, I just turned around and I hoofed him right in the balls, ha ha ha. He fell down and we left – "Let's get outta here!" Crazy. They thought it was all my fault that Eva was this crazy girl, staying out all night. She's the one that picked *me* up.

So then I hardly saw her at all. I saw her at Lee's Palace and she scared the shit out of me. I had to leave out the backdoor because I didn't want her to know where I was going. I was supposed to meet my brother at my place who I hadn't seen in years, so my brother and some friends are there in this basement apartment on Bathurst and all of a sudden there's a big bang on the door, right? It's Eva. And my brother's going, "Who's that?" "You don't want to know."

She smashed the backdoor window and she leaves from there. In the front there's this nice oval window and she hoofs it right in. There's glass all over my bed and stuff. I run out trying to catch her and all of a sudden these cops stop her, because they actually saw her smash this window. They said, "Well, we are going to arrest her." I go, "Okay, fine, but can you just get her out of here? I'm not gonna charge her for the window, but can you just get her out of here?" And they took her away.

Then she got a motorcycle gang after me. They broke into my place and stole one of my guitars, jewelry and stuff. I know it was her because I had a dog and the dog was home and the dog knows her, so she got in through the side window and had no problem with the dog. If it was a stranger there was no way they would have walked in. And most of the jewelry that was gone was hers. I stayed at a friend's place that night and I get home and the backdoor's open and my roommate's in the hospital with a broken jaw. It was a good thing he wasn't home. Good thing *I* wasn't home. I walked in, there were empty beer bottles all over the floor. They'd drank all my beer, had a party in there. I had clothes stolen, guitars. For weeks there I was fuckin' paranoid, looking behind me coming home at night. I always had a friggin' knife in my pocket, just in case, but nothing ever happened.

Yeah, when we played at Larry's I'd put her on the guest list and she'd go, "Can you put some of my friends on the guest list?" You know, biker guys. I'd say, "Yeah, sure." They'd come walking in and they'd go, "Thanks, fag." "Okay, come on in!"

It was weird. I didn't want nothing to do with it. And then she just went way deep, deep into that shit.

Karla Cranley: Eva Destruction got me into dancing. When she moved in with me she showed me how to do it and I got into dancing, because I was too sick most of the time to go back to office work. I couldn't sit down any more because of the blood clots and everything I was getting. I wasn't allowed to sit down for any period of time because I was on anti-coagulants and if I sat down, with the deep vein thrombosis the blood clots got caught in my legs. And I mean, I still had the apartment I had to keep up, my savings were almost gone, and I had quite a bit of money. I mean, I worked seven days a week since I'd been fifteen, right?

So she got me into dancing.

For me, you had five twenty-minute shows a day, and that workout, like I put everything into the workout because that's what kept me alive. It kept my blood going and it prevented the clots. But I couldn't handle dancing in Toronto. Eva did a lot of the dancing in Toronto. Because I didn't want to do drugs. I didn't want any part of it.

Nip Kicks: I think the drugs played a real large part. I remember people going into parties and their only thing was, where are they going to get their next line? And that was a drag. It was pointless. They started acting desperately. The drugs became the cool thing instead of the music being the cool thing.

Karla Cranley: You know the best word I think I can use to describe it? It was *escape*.

Like you've got to remember, I've been a drug addict since I've been sixteen years old. But I was never a consistent addict. I would go a month, two months, six months, eight months. I wouldn't touch it. I'd be really good, then I'd fall off the wagon. I'd have a bender, I'd hate myself, and I'd stay straight again for months and months and months. It was a yo-yo thing.

To me, it was ninety per cent of who you socialized with. If it wasn't there I never went looking for it, but if it was stuck in my face I had a hard time saying no. And I think that's what happened with a lot of people in the punk scene. They weren't really into it in the beginning but I mean, it was shoved in their face. People were always offering it, giving it to you. You didn't wanna do it, but you were there, you had one or two drinks and the next thing you know you've got a needle given to you.

Nip Kicks: Heroin was a problem. But it was a more extreme problem with less people, whereas blow was almost socially acceptable and prestigious, and so that got in the way of a lot of stuff.

Alex Currie: I called the cops on Mike Nightmare. This was in the early '80s. I was living with this girl, Kelly. I was going to George Brown [College], taking carpentry. They'd been up all night shooting cocaine. Meanwhile, I'm in the other room studying geometry. Ha ha ha. All of a sudden Kelly runs out of the room. I'm going, "What the fuck's going on?"

I go in there and I see Mike Nightmare holding a bass guitar, butt naked. His guitar had just smashed this mirror. I go, "Mike, what the fuck?" And he'd go, "You're the fuckin' devil, man. You're the fuckin' devil! Get away from me."

Then he cuffs me. All of a sudden I'm bleeding. I look down at him and I'm starting to realize that he's

naked, he thinks I'm the devil, he just broke a mirror. Fuck it, I'm calling the cops.

They talk him down, he goes to the Clark Institute, and he's out by five o'clock in the afternoon. I didn't really take it personally; the guy was fucked up. I think Crash actually asked me if I wanted to get revenge on him. I think he hated Mike. I said no.

Captain Crash: We weren't on good terms because I was fucking Ruby.

Well, Ruby just wanted to get away. She was afraid of Mike and she was breaking up with him, so she said, "Will you protect me?" I had a house, I had a secure place, so I said, "You can come and crash at my place for a while." He came to the door about a week later — "Hey Crash, I need to talk to Ruby." "Well, yeah, if Ruby wants to talk to *you*," so they went out there for an hour and talked. When I seen him ten years later in Vancouver, he's got a gun in his fuckin' waistband. It was, "You're lucky, Crash. I came to the door to shoot."

But that was Mike. That's just Mike.

Chris Haight: Did I tell you about when he was shooting off his gun in the apartment?

It was like a real loft. He'd crank up the fuckin' music, pull out his .22 and shoot these great big ten-by-ten wooden pillars. Because it's only a .22, the bullet wouldn't go ten inches through the wood. One time, unfortunately I was over there, he turned the music up, he was shooting at these beams, and I remember my future wife getting all, "Fuck, you guys are out of your *mind*," and just beating it out the door. I can't blame her, because me and Mike were just having a great time.

My future wife ran and got picked up by the cops … because they thought she was a hooker. Ha ha ha. But my point is, after all that shit, we actually got married.

Alex Currie: Girls fuckin' loved [Mike], just loved him. But he was your Danger Boy.

I know he loved drugs. I heard that he shot coke in his dick once because he ran out of veins.

Rumour, though. Obviously he wasn't the brightest guy in the world; that's why he became a career criminal. His moment of brilliance was punk in '77.

Chick Parker: The Ugly had always been Mike's project and when I first joined, that was terrific. But after a while, I was basically writing all the new material. Mike would write some lyrics, but basically I wrote everything, music and lyrics, because I'm actually very good at that.

So the rest of the band started wanting to have more input, especially because we'd begun to realize that we were not getting nearly enough money at the end. We'd count the heads and he was basically rippin' us off, the same as Steve was ripping off the Viletones. Like I say, two of the same sides.

So we started to assert ourselves, and he didn't like that at all. He said, "No, it's *my* band." And I said, "Yeah, but we're doing all the work here, pal, and you're taking all the money." So he said, "Well, fuck ya." That's it. Band's dissolved.

And so he broke it up like *that*, and it's like okay, we'll go do something else. It's not as if we don't have options. And then he started phoning different members and saying, "Well, I was just talking to somebody and they say you're an asshole, but why don't you and I get together and we'll rebuild the Ugly." And then the other guy would phone me and say, "Did Mike just call you and say …?" So he was doing all this and obviously we weren't buying it. He realized it wasn't gonna work, so he figured, Fuck it, I'll find a whole bunch of new people and start something new. And he did.

William Cork: The Viletones, who I began to get closer and closer to, finally imploded and half of them went one way. The same thing happened to the Ugly. You had Sam and Tony from the Ugly going with Nazi Dog, and I came up from San Francisco, went to Mike Nightmare and started talking to him, and we decided we were going to start a band called the Wild Things. That was the other half of the Ugly. We played out here for a while, but mostly played out West a lot.

Chick Parker: I actually never even saw the Wild Things, though I heard they were pretty good. They played mostly in Kensington Market. And then I think they all went out to Vancouver, or at least Mike and Billy Cork did. Heroin capital of, well, whatever …

After the Ugly split up I went on to play with the Dorks and with Zero, so our paths didn't cross. But there was no hard feelings or anything. No, everything was rock 'n' roll: Okay, we fucked up; it's over.

And who knows, if things had gone differently, we might have picked up … Like I say, he was a great front man. It's one of those jobs where being insane sort of helps.

Sam Ferrara: The Wild Things were playing the Turning Point. I walked up and Johnny Garbagecan was at the top of the stairs. Doesn't say hi or anything, just *boom!* Breaks my nose for quitting the band. He wasn't even *in* the band.

He was another nutbar, Johnny Garbagecan.

Johnny Garbagecan: The Ugly were my anchor. I didn't even want to work with anybody else, and I didn't trust nobody else.

I'd seen the Viletones break up, and meanwhile here are all these guys who went off and did their own thing. Like the Diodes, John Hamilton walked out on them. I didn't like that kind of stuff; that they weren't loyal to each other. That really blew my mind.

The Ugly were at the point where they could have done something, and then it all fell apart.

William Cork: The rivalry between the Tones and the Ugly continued on because Steve absorbed half of the Ugly and the other half was us. We played the Polish Hall at Dufferin and Queen one night with a brand new Martin Acoustic PA with the Viletones. About four songs into our set, Steve walked to the soundboard and slammed everything in the board up full, all at once, and there was this tremendous *whomp* all over the place. It turned every speaker of this brand new Martin PA inside out.

Everything had disintegrated anyway. It all imploded at once. I had no desire to stay here at all. I grabbed Mike and the band and left immediately for Vancouver to play there a little bit more — to get seasoned before I took them down to meet the guys in San Francisco.

I was in Frisco and I heard Fred [Pompeii] got busted. It was too hot for me to come back here, for reasons that should go unexplained. I was involved with Fred and Crash.

It was real tough in those days, you know? It was sort like trying to be a hippie back in the day in Toronto. Nobody wanted to know about it, although in the 1960s it was much better. The business of being a freak in Toronto by the time punk happened was already an apocalypse from day one.

Karla Cranley: Ruby went out west, too, and tried to help the guys. They really fell on hard times. Now all of a sudden they had no girlfriends who were working. They had to do it on their own. So they resorted to going on the streets, selling their bodies, the whole kit and caboodle.

Ruby started dancing. Mike became a prostitute. And then Ruby got involved with the bikers.

William Cork: I've always had bad things happen with bikers. They can be fun people until they've done a handful of speed and they're getting real worn down and they're out of booze and they're real antsy, and then they start gritting their teeth and looking for the next person to kill. Then you've got to be with it and get the fuck out right away. If you know when to see that's coming, then you're okay. If you don't …

I think I've spent about ten per cent of my adult life escaping from some motorcycle gang through nothing I've ever had anything to do with. It's weird. All these angry women; Hell hath no fury.

Ruby and my old lady Dahlia were dancing in Vancouver when we were playing out there. Dahlia used to have two 1958 Park Lanes; big ol' party cars with whip antennas and pirate flags on them. Our bass player Richard owned them and the guys would show up at my place in Gastown in these cars and pick me up on Sunday morning. We'd go have breakfast and then go to rehearsal.

This one morning they showed up there and I was in my place in my underwear, and I saw these eyes peeking through the mailbox. It was Dahlia.

I was real angry with her. I told her not to bother coming around; I didn't want to see her anymore. She got real angry because she wanted to hang out with us and go for breakfast and go to rehearsal. She ended up kneeing me in this muscle right here in my leg and it really hurt, and I just instinctively went like *this* with the back of my hand and cut her lip. So she took off.

We went around the corner to Mike's place in Gastown to pick him up, and just as we pulled up to a stoplight you could hear *brrrrrrrrrr*. Look out the back window and it's Dahlia with the Angels coming around the corner. Ruby's on the back of one bike, Dahlia's on the back of this other bike. This guy has a big beard and he's got a Kraut helmet on with "MAD" written across the front of it. They're wearing their colours; we're wearing *our* colours in these old 1958 cars.

We hit another red light and got stopped there. First, they were riding around us like Apaches. It was like a wagon train. They pulled up to the rear passenger window of the black Park Lane. I saw in my mind's eye the back window getting kicked in right away. Everything in the car was power operated; it was like a fucking Buck Rogers car back in the 1950s. I lowered the window and the guy goes, "Is your name Will?" I said, "Yeah, man. I don't want any trouble." He goes, "You've got twenty-four hours to leave town, because the next time I see you, you're fucking dead."

And then all of a sudden his fist comes through the window, *boom, boom, boom*, and I've got blood running down my face.

This was right in front of the only police station in Vancouver. You think there's a cop anywhere? No, but just at that moment the police materialized from somewhere and the Angels decided to drive on. I could still see him shaking his finger at me: Leave town *today*.

Mike was wild, though. He walked out his door to this all happening right in front of his house, and Ruby was there going, "Yeah, you can kill *him*, too!" And Mike – a little guy, too – walked up to the curb and went, "Well, if you're gonna kill me, you better do it right here and right fucking now." And he put his fist right through the top of the metal garbage can; crushed the whole top of it.

That's when the police came, fortunately.

Karla Cranley: Everything was Ruby. She was extremely self-centred, very pretty, and as soon as she didn't get her way she became horribly destructive.

I was dancing around the country. I think I was going from Thunder Bay to, oh, I forget, Winnipeg. And I ran into Ruby on the bus one day and I thought, My God, this girl's anger. When Ruby got ticked off she became really nasty, verbally. She really hurt you. She got really, really mean in a subtle way. And she was *so* angry.

William Cork: I often wonder if people are afraid of actually succeeding. A lot of people are. I found that with Mike and his brother Raymi.

Real good friends of mine in San Francisco grew up with Iggy in Ann Arbor and they ran the Iggy Pop Fan Club in San Francisco and had the world rights to anything with Iggy's picture on it. Iggy gave it to them so they'd always have an income. Their brother Jeff was the tour manager for the Rolling Stones and Iggy and the Stooges and the Bee Gees and Etta James.

When he was tour-managing Etta James they wanted me to come down there. I had taken a tape down of the Wild Things and they super liked it. They were real dubious to begin with but then they heard it their eyes popped open and they said, "Get Mike down here right away." I got Mike and Raymi as far as Vancouver and they were just too scared to leave Canada, home boys. Plus, some people are just scared of success. They get close and then it just seems overwhelming.

I don't think drugs like heroin had anything to do with it, no, because Nazi Dog didn't even do it. With Mike and I for the first seven years we were in that band we didn't even smoke a friggin' joint. We lived in Mount Pleasant cemetery in a crypt there and we got the band together. We didn't have any money and we needed this place to rehearse. We'd get up every morning in Mount Pleasant graveyard and literally walk to Markham and back at the same pace as our heartbeats and we'd rehearse every night for four, five, six hours, five, six, seven days a week.

Fear of success happens to people everywhere. A lot of stuff kills itself on the launching pad. It happens all over the place to people, everywhere. Human nature is the same everywhere.

Karla Cranley: But that last time I saw Ruby I got really scared. I thought, My god. She's gonna wind up getting herself killed if she doesn't get rid of that vicious anger she had.

73. tHe cooL BanD

"Teenage Head Guitarist Back" [*Toronto Star*, February 13, 1981]: Guitarist Gord Lewis, severely injured in an auto crash last September, will be re-joining Teenage Head tomorrow night at Club Toronto, Queen St. West at Dufferin.

... Tomorrow night it's back to craziness as usual.

Stephen Mahon: When Gord came back, it was really hard. We'd lost it. He was able to do one set, and that was enough. It was the slow procedure of getting him up to speed.

The guy was in a body cast. He finally healed, thank God. It was a miracle, because there was a good chance he would never walk again. So just having him walk, never mind having him being able to play guitar — and turn out to be the guitar player he's turned out to be — is a miracle, I think.

But we never quite picked up where we left off.

Gordie Lewis: I kind of did a couple of shows when I was still in a body cast. I would just do half a set or something like that, so it was a gradual thing. It didn't feel very good. I was a mess, too.

I don't think I ever really fully recovered. I don't think you really do recover from one of those things, because it's so major. It's so traumatic. It's always with you somehow. It knocked the shit out of me, mentally and physically. I'm just glad it happened when I was young, and that I was strong enough to recover and everything was working okay, or as good as [it] can be or should be.

It felt great to be back but, you know, it just felt I'd lost a lot of control of the band. Up to that point I was kind of being the leader and running the show and I still had control over this manager, and when I came back it was gone. Because *I* was gone. And I couldn't get it back. And I didn't have the *strength* to get it back.

Dave Rave: When the band came back to do *Some Kinda Fun*, I thought the heart and the energy was still missing. When Gordie got back, the band did the best they could and eventually got back to where they could

play the shows and the energy was happening.

That's when that whole schism with Attic happened. They were doing *Some Kinda Fun* and they were doing great songs that were written before the accident, and the album turned out okay considering there was a fight between them and Attic and getting a deal with MCA.

Gordie Lewis [Brantford *Expositor*, June 25, 1982]: As most everyone knows by now, we have decided to leave Attic Records and we are looking for a new company. It's kind of a difficult period for us right now because we have to find a company that will be as committed to us as we are to our music, and we've also got to work on getting the records released in the States and Europe. There's not much point in our going down to play in the States if people there can't get the records and don't know our songs. We're even finding that people in western Canada have trouble getting our albums when we are touring there, and that is just ridiculous. Things have got to change real soon.

Stephen Mahon: There was a disagreement being that we felt as part of us signing to their label, they would be held responsible for trying to get the album released in the States. Which was just a no-brainer. *Everybody* knew that. It didn't matter if you were Trooper or whoever, you had to try and push your way into the States. So that's when Jack and us figured we had to do something about that.

And we didn't like the sound of *Some Kinda Fun*. We had to remix it, and that meant more money and going to another studio. And I seem to recall when we did that, our time with Attic was up and the trust level was way down. There was a hired security guard when we were remixing to make sure that X amount of tape boxes stayed in the studio, because they feared we could just walk out the door with them one night and that would be it; we could do whatever we wanted, and they owned those tapes. I do remember that.

Gord Lewis / photo by Ross Taylor

So those are the things I remember about the discrepancies with Attic. Number one: Hey, you can't seem to get us a deal in the States, so we'd like to have the option of moving on; being allowed to go to another company that may want us. That was the big one.

Tom Williams: Every Canadian band has that impatience. They don't understand.

I think there was a lot of dissension in the band. I think there was a lot of dissension between them and their management. I think maybe they hated us at times, I don't know. I mean, every band wants more than they have, and they should. If you don't have the biggest ego in the world, you really shouldn't try to make it. Talent isn't the most important thing — *ego* is; the drive. You have to live it, breathe it, eat it, sleep it, and if you don't do that you're just not going to make it. And so I don't really know what happened with them. It's kind of dim to me.

Blair Martin: You should have been able to do something with Teenage Head in the States — *something*. It seems quite incredible, but you know what? Jack Morrow and his crowd of guys, obviously they were just not extraordinarily visionary or brave or whatever it was, because as soon as they got something, all they did was do that typical Canadian thing of trying to cling on to it instead of going into the next level.

Tom Williams: We *had* offered them a new deal, I know that, and we had put up a pretty substantial budget and had a lot of stuff going, but I don't remember what happened after that. It was only when they started to get a little more power, I think, that it fell apart. And they wanted to sue Jack, they wanted to do this, they wanted to do that, and their whole career fell apart.

I'm convinced that had they stayed with Attic, at the time where we had the split, we would have broken them in the States. I'm pretty convinced we would have.

Stephen Mahon: What it's like to be financially successful, I wouldn't know. But we're well known. People that still might not know what we do, they've *heard* of us. People have definitely heard of us, so that's something.

We never lost our integrity. We always did it our way, and the fact that people liked us was a bonus. A lot of bands are sellouts. They just clone what they think is successful. That was never our way. I'm sure we did, to a certain extent, sound like Iggy and the Dolls, but we still did it our way. That was our inspiration.

But yeah, there was compromise. The name change is one example of a compromise. A small one, a silly one; one that was short-lived.

"Frank's Wild Years," by Emily Smith [*Eye Weekly*, January 25, 1996]: At the peak of their career in '83, Canada's fab four emerged worse for the wear after the aptly named *Tornado* EP. To make the release palatable to the righteous U.S. market, a sanitizing "s" was added to the band name and the sound was over-produced for commercial viability.

Stewart Pollock: They had to change their name to Teenage *Heads* for the Bible Belters. Like, who in the fuckin' Bible Belt is buying it? It doesn't matter. But the record company demanded it.

Stephen Mahon: Their whole thinking was, Good God, we can't have a band called *that*. But that's not why we called the band that in the first place. It's the whole Flamin' Groovies thing. But they never got that; people will never get that.

Gordie Lewis: It was just because of the sexual thing that they wanted us to change the name — Teenage *Head*.

It was our first American release, it was on MCA Records, and it was their suggestion. Well, not their suggestion, it was their *order* that we do it. Meanwhile, from a country that you can buy the most hardcore pornography plus a 12-gauge shotgun at every corner, they had a problem with Teenage *Head*. But that deal didn't last long.

Stephen Mahon: Within the year, we were told the people that signed the band in the Los Angeles office were no longer with MCA and, "Good luck in the future." So the "s" came right back off.

Frankie Venom [*Eye Weekly*, January 25, 1996]: It was record company manipulation and we fell for it. I said, "Put a fuckin' 'z' on it, I don't care as long as it's down in the States." And two or three weeks later we were off the label because the person who signed us got fired. That's okay. We took 'em for eighty grand ... U.S.

Gordie Lewis: If I could do it again, I would be a lot more careful who I let into my circle. I'd be very cautious of who I let handle my dream.

There's no school for this. There was nobody there to help us; there just wasn't. There was no advice and it's a really ruthless business, it really is. When you think about it, what people want to get themselves in with four snotty, twenty-year-old punk kids from Hamilton and make a living at it? We got involved with managers and things like that and were really naïve. You have to learn the hard way.

I hated our manager at the time. I hated what he had done with the band. I hated the image of the band. It was everything I didn't want it to be.

It wasn't cool. For the longest period of time we weren't doing cool things. We weren't doing cool posters. Remember I wanted to be the cool band from Canada? We started becoming the *goofy* band from Canada, in my mind, because I was dealing with a goofy manager who had goofy ideas. He was more of a carnival guy. He did real hokey, cornball promotions. Which *sold* — I'm not denying they didn't work; the people did buy it — but it was totally against everything I wanted to do.

By 1983, it was just one endless piece of crap after another, and we wound up realizing contracts that we signed had conflicts of interest. And we started to realize we had to do something about [Jack Morrow].

John Balogh: He would have been sixty, sixty-five years old, but he'd been in the School Of Hard On You all his life working with bands. So when he finally got teamed up with Teenage Head, it was an opportunity *and* an opportunity. It was an opportunity for the band, and opportunity for him. He took the ball and ran with it. He did great for Teenage Head, I think.

But when the cheques came in, mysteriously again they all went to Jack's office, and then they were distributed by Jack. The bands were the ones that were getting conned.

Had a lawyer been standing over a guy like Jack Morrow going, "Uh-uh-uh, not right Jack," that would have changed the rules. But there was nobody. So it was like giving a guy carte blanche, and he just robbed everybody. Guys like that were bandits.

Gordie Lewis: It all went downhill to the point where we had to fire him and do things on our own and try to build it up. It was a real struggle.

Larry LeBlanc: I saw Gordie just a little while ago and we were talking about those days. Where the hell were we? I saw him at a Gibson guitar thing for Neil Young, and we were talking about how I begged him not to sign with John Brower and Jack Morrow.

They were creeps. Brower's nuts. Brower was crazy. Jack Morrow meant well. And unfortunately John Brower's background was he had been involved with putting on shows at the Rock Pile, and brought John Lennon here and all that stuff. And John Lennon had denounced him in *Rolling Stone* magazine.

If you go back, you can find an old *Rolling Stone* where John Lennon — at one point he had cut off his hair and went into the middle of nowhere — denounced John Brower. I made clippings of this stuff to show Teenage

Head going, "You shouldn't sign with this guy. John Lennon thinks he's crazy."

But you know something? I was kidding Gordie and I said, "What'd you do, drive straight from my house and go over and sign?" And he said, "Larry, we were so young."

Stewart Pollock: If I remember correctly, even at the height of their career when they were making all kinds of money, the most the band got paid in salary was something like five or six hundred bucks a week. Somewhere in that area. It definitely didn't exceed a thousand. When you're taking down six grand a night, working six nights a week for it, there's a bit of a difference between thirty-six thousand dollars and sixteen hundred and fifty dollars wage. They ended up with fuck all.

Gail Manning: As the band shot forward, so did the monster machinery that kept the band running. Which was a bevy of roadies — most which were ex-bikers — massive sound systems, tour buses, riders, techs, etcetera, etcetera.

The band had all the accoutrements that any major rock band would, and all this machinery was very expensive to keep on the road. I mean, the band and the roadies and the crew all had health benefits back then, if you can believe it. As the band grew in stature, the band wanted more of the perks that go along with the job. All these things were extraordinarily expensive, so to pay for all these things the band had to go out and had to keep touring, and that's really tough, playing gig after gig after gig every night.

Stewart Pollock: Gordie took control at one point and started to monitor the managers and stayed on top of things, because he could feel he was doing all this work and wasn't really being paid for it.

Gordie Lewis: I was trying to regain control, and trying to build it up again.

Dave Rave: When finally we got rid of Jack Morrow, the energy of the band — and this is my own take on it now — instead of being stronger, it made it weaker. Before, Jack was like the whipping post. Now there was no whipping post. So I think what happened was Frank would go, "Gord, where's my paycheque?" And Gord would go, "Frank, I'm not your boss, I'm a member of your band."

So eventually tension built between him, Nick and Gord. Steve was always quiet so I don't know what he was thinking, but I could see this band — my buddies — falling apart, in a real slow, gradual way.

The energy was starting to fall, and I think finally what happened was Frank and Nick decided, "Okay, we've had it being in this band."

Gordie Lewis: First I let Nick go — "Ah, I'll just get another drummer." Nick was kind of losing it a bit, anyway. There's always one guy who isn't all there, and he would be the outsider. As great a drummer as he is, he was the one that wasn't on the same page as the rest of us. I think he didn't want to do it anymore, and he was very happy *not* doing it anymore.

But my theory and my mindset was wrong. We were just fighting a losing battle. I let *Frank* go. That was my giving up in a way, thinking I could replace him.

By that point things were just stagnant. We didn't have management at all. The band was in a mess. Nobody knew what the heck was going on.

I probably could have prevented it, but I didn't because I was so fed up with everything, too. But as I look back in hindsight, I *could* have prevented it and it would have been for the better. It was Joe Strummer from the Clash who said it: You don't mess around with the chemistry of a band. When you've got a band, you've got a good thing going. You think you can replace somebody — you think you can do this, you think you can do that — but you can't. You've built up this chemistry, and it's a magic; you can't replace the parts.

I find those words to be true. If you start screwing around with the chemistry, you're going to make a mess of things. I didn't have to let that happen, but I did.

Dave Rave: Zeke Rivers, I think they were all hanging out in a social scene, and I'm sure they were prodding Frank, like, "You're Frankie Venom, you're the star of the band," and I think he eventually fell for it.

We're in Edmonton doing a tour. Meanwhile we'd gotten a drummer; we got Mark Lockerbie, who was our

Frankie Venom / photo by Ross Taylor

lighting guy. Finally Frank quit and I remember Gord just said to me, "You're the only other guy who can sing in the band, want to be the singer?" And what am I gonna do, let the guys down? But replace *Frankie Venom?*! And they're like, "Yeah, we'll just do it."

I remember at the time saying, "Do you guys believe in me? I'm gonna do my best; I'm there."

That was a tough period, a very tough period. I got sick for about a week, and I look back now and I think I was sick because I was afraid of what was gonna happen. I remember the very first show, going on and hearing, "Where's Frankie? Where's Frankie?" *He's* the guy they wanted to see.

At first I thought, Maybe we should get a guy who's more like him. We got Blair Mojo Martin in the band for a while and I remember saying to Gord, "Why don't we just get *him* to sing?" And Gord said, "Nah, that's a second-rate Frank. We've never been second-rate." If we would have had a little Frankie guy come out, we might have been able to disguise it, but I think in the long run the integrity would have been compromised. And I love Blair — he was really important at that time because we needed somebody with that strength, who was outside of the picture saying, "Keep playing, keep playing" — but the audience would pick up [that] we just replaced Frank with a guy who's not as much as Frank.

But don't forget, I tried to give them a new energy and we had two albums with me singing and a hit single and video with "Everybody Needs Somebody". But maybe going forward wasn't where they wanted to go.

Watching their career the whole time — I joined full time in '83, I think it was — Gordie had come back from the accident and they had never lost the fans or the friends. But it was to the point where it was not routine, but *established*. Nobody from the old scene was in it anymore, and punk rock had now moved on.

They were sort of like the Ramones in a sense; it was like a parallel. Like, "Are you *still* around?" That kind of thing. Fans were loving it, press were hating it, the old fans thought you'd betrayed something.

74.
unsettled spirits

Michael Severin: I remember coming down to Maple Leaf Gardens for my birthday, Groundhog Day, to see my favourite band of all time, Emerson, Lake & Palmer.

They were playing on the second, my birthday, and the third — I couldn't get tickets for the third — so we, my old band the Roll Ons, all stumbled down the street to this place called Larry's Hideaway.

We got in. It was kind of like, "What the fuck is *this* dive?" There's this band onstage called the Battered Wives. It was just, wow — it was just smokin' energy. It was punk; it was mod. We got back in the car after and we were doing Battered Wives tunes and Iggy and all this, and people in the Sault had never heard them before so they would think they were our songs, ha ha ha. It was pretty good.

We had a chance at The Agency to get booked. It looked like a pretty good little deal, and they passed on us for a band that had a girl in it. They were called the Spoons. So that's when the Roll Ons broke up. I put my clothes and my drums on the Greyhound and came down here, and the rest is history.

That's when I met Keith. I walked down Queen Street, '80, '81. It was hot and I heard David Johansen coming out of this bar speaker; it was the Black Bull. I thought, Oh! This is kind of like home, so I walked in. There was a table of guys sitting over there and I'm looking and listening to this guy: Fuck, I know that accent, I know that voice, that tone, the timbre of the voice, "I wanna go to New York City ..." I'm hearing it. Finally, we bumped into each other and he goes, "Oi, fuck off bleeder," and I go, "That's fuckin' Keith Whittaker, isn't it?" He was a bit of a legend along the street.

Quite honestly, when I moved here, things were starting to peter out. The Mods were one of the last bands that I'd go see before I locked myself in the basement and just drummed.

David Quinton: We had one gig at the Turning Point once. Steve Leckie was there and Stiv Bators was there. It's one of the times Bators saw me in Toronto. We had them both onstage to sing "Tell Me," the old Rolling Stones song, as a duet. We were really laughing at that the other day; just how funny it was, the two of them sort of competing together onstage.

I cried at our last gig. It was awful. Guys just cry when they're really fuckin' sad. We were at the Music Hall; it was a big gig and it was very, very emotional and really tough. The funny thing, I wasn't crying at the end; I was crying in the *first* song. Because I was sad. Because I was leaving them and going to join Stiv.

Our last gig was April 11, I think, 1980, and my first gig with Stiv was in May. So I was basically on a plane to Ohio two weeks later and rehearsing with those guys. But you know, of any band that I worked with after that, I missed these guys more than anybody else, just because of the time of life we spent together.

I realized that Toronto, when I got home, really was kind of dead. When the punk thing started to die, that to me was really the end of rock 'n' roll as I knew it. Because as a drummer, the first thing that happened in the early '80s were drum machines and computers, so you can imagine how a young guy who was slightly Moon-esque in his approach felt when the drum machines invaded. It ruined my life, and it ruined the music. It absolutely fucking killed the music, and I hated what happened during the '80s. It was awful.

I knew when to get out, so in the mid-'80s when I started really hating it, I thought, I don't like the music anymore, I don't like how people are responding to it, I'm bored, so I'm going to do something completely different and freak everybody out.

I went to law school. *That* was something different.

The punk period, as short as it was, was an incredible time. The thing that bothers me more than anything when people talk about punk, is what people think punk is. Because there are very distinct eras.

When I think of it, I think 1976 to 1980. During that period it wasn't only different kinds of musical styles that were falling into the genre, there was a *musicality* to it that I found got stripped away later on. So when I was in it, you didn't see guys with mohawks that were seven feet high died blue. The music wasn't played at a breakneck speed. Listen to the Dead Boys — it's mid-tempo.

When I was back in Toronto in '81, the big thing that I noticed was there wasn't really a scene anymore. It was being replaced by different people; there seemed to be more commercialism in the air, it was less rootsy in a way.

Michael Severin: It was '80, '81, and Keith asked me to drum in his new band. He was calling it Hoi Polloi. And I was flattered; I'm a little kid from Sault Ste. Marie, Ontario, got down here, and there's this guy from the Demics. I used to *cover* his songs in Sault Ste. Marie. I was all star-struck, so I went and played with Keith.

But I couldn't keep up with the beer drinking. It was just insane. I mean, there was a case of beer at every rehearsal, and lots of drugs and whatever.

We were rehearsing at King and John Streets. Keith and his girlfriend Suzanne Timmins and Roy and myself lived there. It was a haunted house that had been vacated for at least thirty-five years and it was all boarded up.

We saw a couple of weird things, yeah. Keith was washing dishes one night. I'll never forget this. He goes, "Oi! Fucking oi!" He turned around and, "Did you see that?" I go, "What? What?" "I saw this red thing and this black thing that jumped."

I was practicing, drumming, and I heard this *ch-ch-ch-ch-ch*. I stopped, then I started playing again and I heard *ch-ch-ch-ch*. I'd stop and listen, and I kept going on, and every time it got louder and louder, and closer, and louder and louder. And I flew over to the door as fast as I could … and there's no one there. Like absolutely *no one there*, but they should have been, by the footsteps.

Suzanne Naughton: I remember we were at this speakeasy on King Street, and it wasn't a regular hangout. It had just started. It was at the corner of Peter, the southwest corner. There were some dumpy, dumpy loft spaces up there. A friend of mine lived there. He said he was sitting in his living room reading a book and the roof was right outside; his window was level with the roof. He looked out and said, "Wow, nice boots." There were these amazing knee-high boots with straps on them.

He went to the window to see who was standing out there, and there was nobody there. He realized later they were turn-of-the-century cavalry boots.

They didn't see much, but they *heard* weird things, like moans and groans and stuff; people being sick or dying.

Michael Severin: Well, we were so freaked out about this house, Suzanne [Timmins] had her parents bring in a clairvoyant. "Oh yes, well, there's a little child that's walking on the stairs there, and there's a mother doing the dishes there." We did some research and found out all the houses along King Street were barracks for Fort York back in the 1800s, so what Keith had seen was a redcoat and a piece of a leather boot, whether you want to believe it or not.

Suzanne Naughton: It used to be an army field hospital. It was what they called a fever hospital. When there were typhoid and scarlet fever outbreaks, they used to put the soldiers in there.

Michael Severin: Apparently there was a big fire and a lot of horses were lost, and a lot of guys trying to save the horses.

The other story was, we had a big party and Suzanne Timmins — she's a striking woman; Timmins of the Cowboy Junkies family — Suzanne went to bed because she had to work in the morning, and Keith and I decided just be quiet and party on in the back room.

Suzanne was just fuckin' pissed. "What are you fuckin' doing, letting these people fuckin' sleep in the fuckin' bedroom with me on the floor?" And Keith went, "Suzanne, when I left this morning there was nobody there. Nobody was in the room."

Suzanne kind of woke up just briefly, opened her eyes, and there was a guy sitting in the chair. And there was another guy lying on the floor, and there was *another* guy crouched in the corner. But there was no one in the room. Suzanne's clairvoyant said, "It's just unsettled spirits. They don't think they're dead."

I remember some of the rehearsals we had up there were really intense. Let alone the booze and the pot and whatever else was going on. I think we were pissing them off, the spirits.

Suzanne Naughton: But [that neighbourhood] is where this speakeasy was. I remember one night the people at the door didn't know who Steven Leckie was. He was freaking out; he was going to fight the guy. He was pretty hammered. I had to set them straight. I said to the guy, "Do you know who that is?" He goes, "No." I said, "Well, you fuckin' *should*."

That was when things started winding down.

Michael Severin: We did a lot of rehearsing there and I think we played one show. It was a rather rough show, and then I just decided that as much as I loved being in that circle and living with Keith, it just wasn't my avenue. I was a little more jazz oriented. Punk energy, but lots of jazz stuff. And I couldn't drink as much beer. Just forget it.

Keith always came off as a very hard, crude — especially towards women — nasty, nasty pirate. And when you saw him at home, especially with his girlfriend, who was a beautiful, beautiful woman, he'd treat her like gold. If you were to wake up with him in the morning and have your tea and your crumpets and talk English literature for, like, fucking hours — and he knew *everything* about English literature — it was just mind-boggling. And a couple of beers later, he's just fucking obnoxious.

Everybody that I know was just, "Why is he such a bastard?" He really wasn't. I'd been around with Keith a lot. Whether it was issues, or whether it was just, when he was onstage or when he went out, it was a different Keith.

Like I said, the tea in the morning …

Steven Davey: Keith Whittaker and I did music together on and off for a number of years and recorded some demo material. He actually sang with the band I had for a while after the Dishes, and that didn't work out but we remained friends. For about a year we wrote together. I've been sitting on these songs forever. We weren't very friendly when he died.

Whenever you would ask Keith, "What happened? How come you have no money? How come somebody else owns that song?" What happened was there were two versions of "New York City"; they re-recorded the song and had no recording contract. So they put papers on the old record company saying, "You have nothing on us," and the record company used that to take them to court and sue them and go, "Oh yes we do." So the court decision was that if they ever recorded any of the songs that were on the first record, the old record company didn't have to give them any more royalties. So of course what the band thought was, Well, we'll just re-record "New York City," it'll become a big hit, release it on Sony, and "Fuck you!" Right?

What happened was the version they recorded was just terrible; you wouldn't even recognize it. They changed the key, they made Keith sing higher, they took out the "fuck off" part — all the parts that made the song good. They thought, Oh, we want to get this on the radio, if it's got "fuck" on it, well, you know. The record company told them they'd be paying for everything; of course the band goes along with it. "Oh yeah, it needs a sax solo and you need some background chicks going 'whoa'." They were just spending money, that's all they were doing. And what happened? They released it as a single, CFNY played it once, and went back to playing the other one.

Then CFNY started an all-request noon hour in about 1980, 1981, and "New York City" was the Number One song for, like, three years in a row because people would call up and say, "I want to hear the song where the guy says 'fuck'." And they played it, and of course the song became bigger and bigger, and the old record started selling and eventually sold twenty thousand copies. And the band didn't get one cent. It was their own fault.

And so for the rest of Keith's life, people would come up to him non-stop and say, "You know, 'New York City's' my favourite song in the whole world. Can I buy you a drink?" And he'd go, "FUCK OFF." He wasn't a very pleasant person in public, because they'd play it on the radio everywhere he went.

Michael Severin: Bitterness? He was always bitter, other than in the morning when he'd wake up and have a cup of tea.

I think he always thought he would make it. I know he could have made it, and I think they *would* have made it if there had been someone smart enough to handle them.

Steven Davey: Unfortunately, he was sort of trapped by his image. All people wanted to hear was "New York City," and they expected him to be drunk and falling around and swearing and being that guy, and when he wasn't that guy they didn't like it. So in order to get onstage, he'd be completely loaded and would fall down and forget the words and piss the band off and people

would applaud.

He actually had a very good singing voice and had the presence. So I just used that — this was early '90s, '91, '92 — and I said, "Let's just make it bigger, more dimension to your character. Look, you've written one song, you can probably write another one." So we just started writing together with no pressure, but it just didn't work.

He was a terrible writer. Like a lot of writers, he *talked* about writing as opposed to actually writing. So I learned over the years that my job was to take notes. And every now and then he'd get a good idea. I'd just get a little snippet, like a song title. So I'd write the entire song backwards from that.

Michael Severin: And I guess I didn't see Keith a whole lot anymore because I basically got off the scene.

There are still some of us alive, which is a really nice thing. I chose to change my life when my son was born. After seven years I just went, "Fuck, no, I can't fuckin' do this anymore." And I was seeing people around me that are gone. One year we lost four or five within our circle. Three of them were in a death pact — two boys and a girl. They all hung themselves together. And Handsome Ned, he was found in his bathtub. And Brat X, he was in a band called Sturm Group.

I think the thing I remember most about Keith is his hard, hard, crusty old persona. And really, I don't know if anybody else would agree with me, but he was just such a dear, warm-hearted soul. And I guess when he found out his brother was ill, it really hit him hard. And I started to see him — I was hoping I'd see him straighten out a little bit, because he didn't look too healthy.

Iain Atkinson: Yeah, that self-destruction, I think that was there from early on. I don't know where it comes from. Maybe there's a self-destructive gene. He was abusive, drank too much, took too many drugs, would get completely out of fucking control. But then he could just turn around with the same person the next day and they'd be his best buddy.

He was an alcoholic. I think he would have been an alcoholic probably even coming out of high school.

I can't remember if he was born in Manchester or Liverpool, but I think it's hereditary. It's funny because I have a couple of other friends a little bit younger than him, and they all come from Liverpool or one of those fuckin' places and they're exactly the same. They're really smart and witty and all that stuff, but they've got this real drink-themselves-into-oblivion tendency, and their dads are the same. So it makes me wonder if it's just some kind of environmental thing or some genetic predisposition or whatever.

In a lot of ways it was really sad. He had lots of stuff to say, and it's too bad he couldn't be directed enough to actually manage to say it. He had to really be to a degree kind of coached to do stuff. The guy needed a bunch of nurturing.

Carmela Morra: Near the end, he used to go to [Kensington] Market all the time. Keith used to go to Amadeus when he started getting really ill. Friends would stop by and see him there; he'd call Amadeus and say, "Oh, if anybody comes by tell them I'm home, I'm not feeling good today." Like calling his bar sick like you would for work, ha ha ha.

But I think alcohol can do just as much damage as heroin. I mean, look at Keith.

Iain Atkinson: His brother was also a real smart guy; really well read. His brother got cancer when he was really young. I think he was dead by the time he was thirty. Keith's dad had also got cancer and died fairly young. And I've forgotten now if his younger brother also got it. So that makes me think there was some kind of environmental thing going on there; they used to live close to a river where they'd be dumping all sorts of crap, and those guys used to go swimming in there all the time when they were kids.

Maybe the cancer was kicking in a lot earlier than anybody really knew. I don't really know if his back problem was related. I can remember doing a couple of gigs with him in a wheelchair. You're a kid; you're oblivious to what the hell is going on. You'd think he hurt his back or whatever. I wouldn't even think about it. You're a kid, you're indestructible, you're going to live forever.

I was young and stupid. I didn't think about it. Now I'm old and stupid, but I am thinking about it now. It took a while. Slow learner, I guess.

Frankie Venom [CIUT-FM, Greg Dick interview, 2007]: The last time he sang was with us at the Horseshoe. I said "Keith, come on, get up." He sang "New York City." He was a good friend of mine. I miss him very much.

75. so much waste

Steven Davey: The death knell for Queen Street was when the Goodwill turned into Le Chateau in '83 or '84. That was when it started to slide.

It's kind of embarrassing living down here now. People used to walk up and down Yonge Street, and now they walk up and down Queen Street.

Karla Cranley: Near the end I wound up getting very, very sick and I had to leave Toronto. People were dying.

Chris Haight: I can't find one picture of Jimmy the Worm. After Jimmy OD'd, my mom went nutty and cut up every photograph she ever had of him. I don't know if she told me or if somebody else told me, but she just cut them all up to pieces.

Karla Cranley: I went back to Toronto one more time, when the Sidewinders were playing. I was so happy to see everybody, and then there was the back room and the heroin — the whole kit. And I just thought, *No*, I'm not going back again. I'll die coming back here.

And then Ned was dead.

Chick Parker: Handsome Ned. I hadn't thought of him in the longest time. How sad. Of course the last time I saw him, he ripped me off on a junk deal. But that's what happens. Junkies steal, they lie, and that's it. If their lips are moving, it's horseshit.

I remember at the time, there were a number of overly long articles, I think Peter Goddard did one, about heroin and how it's destroying Queen Street West.

Freddy Pompeii: When I went back ten years after with my band Thee Immaculate Hearts, the whole city was on heroin. That was in '87. I couldn't *believe* how many people were strung out.

Chick Parker: You can't deny that it killed a lot of the bright lights, like Ned and Mike, but it was there before. I think a lot of people felt compelled to live the Johnny Thunders syndrome. Everybody wants to be Keith Richards: The guitar, the hair, the junk, you know? "I'm living rock 'n' roll!"

Gambi Bowker: When I think of people like Ned I think to myself, Yeah, okay, maybe he had a bit of an identity crisis and he sort of thought he was always having to be Ned, but that was who he was.

I knew him when he was Robin — not very well, but his girlfriend was my sister's best friend, and he was always this happy-go-lucky, centre-of-the-party-talking-to-everybody, totally friendly guy. And I remember not even being able to believe it when I heard he was doing it.

Most of us, we were all pretty well in experimental stages with drugs. I tried heroin, and it wasn't for me because I was seventeen years old and I wanted to be out having a good time. No matter how good it felt, it wasn't a good time. I really think that Ned was just fooling around with it, but yeah, other people who were closer to him at that time have said there was a dark side to him.

Other people I was quite close with — one of whom is dead, two of them are not, one of whom is apparently a sixty-year-old junkie — they all had a vulnerability to them. So perhaps there is a certain attraction, to have that emotional vulnerability.

Carmen Bycok: I really thought I was gonna be dead by the time I was twenty-five. I really, sincerely thought I'd be dead. And when I turned twenty-four, that's when I had a big crisis in my life because I thought, Oh my god, I have one more year and maybe I'm *not* gonna die! What the hell am I gonna do now?

Because I wasn't thinking about the future. Because "there's no future, no future for me." I was thinking that I'd be dead and so I lived like I was gonna die. Did a lot of drugs, drank a lot, got into cars with people that I shouldn't have.

Freddy Pompeii: I got strung out, but I was in and out of it. I always refused to do drugs while I was playing. I never wanted to be stoned onstage; wouldn't even smoke a joint. In the times that we had off, the times when nothing was happening or we were waiting for gigs to come or we couldn't rehearse for one reason or another, *those* were the times I got in trouble.

It's nothing I'm proud of, and nothing I would like to talk about. Don't make it like it was a big thing; it was just something I got into and I wish it'd never happened. It was easy to get into because it was right there in your face. But I hear that it got worse and worse in the years that I was away.

Chick Parker: Definitely, it was there and we felt obliged to do it. The dark side. We personify the dark side. That's what we are. We're the bad guys.

You start out doing junk and it's great. You think it enhances your creativity, and maybe it does, but that stage disappears real quick and you know the old saying: Instead of doing the drugs, the drugs are doing you. And you spend all your time trying to get enough money and it's like clichéd shit, but it's true.

I ended up selling all my guitars. I don't even want to think about that part. So it definitely had a detrimental effect, like it always does.

Andrew McGregor: But that was part of the whole thing. Some people took the whole thing a bit too seriously, and they're long gone.

That was always in my mind, that you can't go overboard with the whole thing. If you wind up depressed and think that life really isn't worth living because your favourite songs say it isn't, you've gone too far. A lot of people fell into that and they're not with us anymore. A lot of people went into drugs because it

was fashionable. "You smoke dope? I'm cooler than you, I shoot junk." So that was a problem.

Xenia Splawinski: They're all dead. The ones that you thought were gonna die, died.

*   *   *   *   *

Mickey DeSadist: The other day I was talking with Steve Leckie and we were thinking, Who was the best band at the time?

We thought the best players were the Ugly, because they were better than the early Rebels. They were better than the early Viletones. They were way better than all of us. They couldn't keep their act together, because I guess they had a bad habit of committing criminal offences, like robberies, from what I heard. I didn't know of anything happening until years later.

I remember when Mike Nightmare passed away. I heard he died of a heart attack. Then I heard he died in a shootout with the RCMP, and this stuff flies everywhere.

Joe Keithley: Mike actually came up with one of the greatest rock 'n' roll quotes ever, and this was long after he left Toronto and was in Vancouver.

It was his thirtieth birthday and he goes, "Joe, fuck. You know what? I'm thirty years old and all I've got is a fuckin' beat-up car and a bunch of scratched Iggy Pop records." And I went, "Yeah, that sums it up." Ten, twelve years of playing rock 'n' roll and that's all he had to show for it. Everybody got paid dirt; for us to get twenty-five bucks we were amazed.

Chick Parker: After he moved out to Vancouver to, and I quote, "I'm just going to go to Vancouver and do junk the rest of my life," he ended up like a crippled criminal on the streets just doing whatever he could to maintain his junk habit.

Greg Dick: I remember Nightmare. The last time I ever saw him was at an Iggy Pop concert in Vancouver in 1988. Just by fluke, I was exiting the gig, and he was standing there. He knew me and I knew him, and I just talked to him briefly. He seemed a little bit shy for some reason, and that's the last I ever saw of him.

I really, really respected him. Just because a lot of these guys were real motherfuckers and in trouble with the law, they weren't bad guys. I know my mother wouldn't understand me saying stuff like that, but it's the truth.

Raymi Mulroney: My brother taught me some good rules. If he had five bucks, he'd give you three.

He'd punch me in the head if I had five bucks and I wouldn't give him three, ha ha ha. He'd take the shirt off his back for you.

Nora Currie: When he went out west, he reverted to doing what he did best, and that was being a second-story man.

He was on the second floor of a building, trying to do a B&E, and he fell. He hurt himself; he knocked himself out. When he woke up he was in the hospital, and every bone in his body was broken. He should have died.

I was out in Vancouver as part of a conference, so I went to visit him. He was a shadow of himself. He had lost so much weight. What he reckoned happened — although he didn't have a good memory, and this is according to the doctors and putting everything together — he had injuries from his fall, but he had also been beaten to a pulp with probably a baseball bat. So the place he was trying to break into, or some other people who were after him, took a bat to him when he was unconscious.

Anna Bourque: Can you believe the kind of bad karma you'd have to have for people to beat you up while you were *unconscious*? He must have been exuding it.

Nora Currie: He never recovered from those injuries. He walked with a cane. He did go to jail and did some pretty serious time after that; federal time. And when he came out — it was the day he was out — he had a heart attack and died at home. It was a few days before anyone found him. His system was so weakened he just couldn't survive, and that was very much about that beating that he took.

Captain Crash: I remember walking down the street — I was living in Vancouver at the time — and this skinny, skinny guy on two canes, he's talking to this guy in front of me. I didn't know it was him until I heard the story: The guy's saying to him, "You gotta get in there and fuckin' leave no trace and get the fuck out."

And I'm listening, and that voice is *really* familiar — it's fuckin' Mike Nightmare.

William Cork: I think we were still playing together up until 1996.

Mike wasn't feeling well one night. He went to an emergency ward in Vancouver and sat around there for three or four hours. He finally got pissed off and left and went to another hospital, and this went on and on. Three hospitals later at ten o'clock in the morning he was still sitting there waiting to be seen by somebody and he passed away, sitting in emergency waiting for somebody to talk to him.

Raymi, his brother who played guitar with us fairly consistently, we had a repertoire of about a hundred and sixty tunes, and about half of them were original. We had one guitar player, who lasted really for the longest time, called Bash. His family was East Indian; they came to America from South Africa. They moved to Houston, I believe, and [then] they moved here. Bash was into psychedelic garage bands; the Haunted and Question Mark and the Mysterians. I saw him at the Beverley, God rest its soul, and I went, "Oh, I'm gonna steal this guy from this band, sorry guys," and proceeded to do so. He stayed with us longer than anybody.

He overdosed on heroin, and then our lead player Grant committed suicide and Mike passed away, so there wasn't anything left to do at the time for me. It was kind of like being in the Doors and not having anything to do after Jim Morrison. There wasn't anyone I wanted to play with.

Mike was in a league of maybe about three people in North America at that time, of which Steve [Leckie], God bless him, isn't one. Mike was the real thing. I just couldn't imagine playing with anyone else.

Coincidentally, I had a child just at the same moment that he passed on, so it was a big change of lifestyle for me. I went back to work in the movie business, which was where I was from in the first place. Now my son's bugging me to buy *him* a guitar.

But Mike ... Sometimes I just stop in the street when I think of what happened to him.

Elizabeth Aikenhead: When you look at the structure of a band, the psychology of that and the dynamic, it's like a schoolyard. There's a schoolyard bully, there's a schoolyard leader, and it's not even about physical strength. Everyone falls into their role and their place, and Mike was the leader of the band and got these guys to do what he wanted them to do. Tony and Sam had backup plans. Tony always worked. He always was a painter working for his dad.

He would get up at seven o'clock in the morning and head off in his work clothes on the subway to where he had to go. He had a very strong work ethic and a lot of integrity and pride.

And yet in the end, the Sams and the Tonys are the ones who are alive and doing well and surviving, who are hard working and committed to their lives and the people in their lives, and have a certain integrity. And the Mikes and the Steves are not really at the forefront of everyday life. They're not really functioning on the same level that the Tonys and the Sams are.

*   *   *   *   *

Nora Currie: Ruby got into adult performance. She worked as a dancer and a stripper. She also got very caught up in drugs.

William Cork: Ruby and Dahlia, my girlfriend, hired the Angels to have Mike and I killed in Vancouver, and that was pretty scary.

They caught up with me three times. Each time I'd hear this huge thunder of motorcycle engines coming up behind, and every single time, whether it was in a laneway behind the Nelson Tavern or whatever the main street in Vancouver is or even the airport, the police would drive up right between me and the bikers. And the bikers would look at us and go, "Next time," and get back on their bikes.

When was the last time I saw her, 1993? Yeah. That was in Windsor, and she was about to marry this RCMP officer. I don't know what she was doing.

David Quinton: I could see how she could end up with bikers, because Mike was always a stone's throw from a biker. It's too bad, though. I always hoped that somebody like Ruby would end up sort of normalizing to a certain extent and ending up with a job, you know what I mean? It's very sad, but I don't know that she had much of a head start in life.

She was pretty young; I think she was twenty when I was in the Androids, she would have been four years older than me. It's quite amazing both of them are gone. I guess a bunch of people from those days …

Karla Cranley: Yeah, she was very, very beautiful. Which was just such a shame, you know? Waste. So much waste. That's what killed me about it, there was so much waste. But I guess that was just par for the course with life, eh?

Sam Ferrara: Mike went out with both of them, Ruby and Eva.

Eva was my girlfriend, and she went with him for a while and then she went to the bikers. That's who murdered her. Just a couple years ago I heard the guy who murdered her, he got murdered, too.

Eva and Mike got into all kinds of weird shit. When they split up she left, and one of her biker boyfriends murdered her; left her on the side of the road, dead. Ran her over with a truck a couple times, and then her dad blamed *me* for introducing her to all these weird people.

I didn't introduce her to anyone. He still blames me. There's nothing I can do.

Captain Crash: She was something else. She just didn't give a fuck. She really didn't care about anything.

If you were with her it was like this: You're gonna get in trouble, the cops are gonna come, you're gonna get searched, you're gonna get in confrontations wherever you go with people in the bar. You're gonna get thrown out of restaurants. You're gonna get thrown out of taxi cabs. You're not gonna get let into bars. And if you get let into bars you're gonna have a fight, you're gonna get cut off, you're gonna get thrown out.

You know, when they found her on the side of the road they thought she was a black girl because she was beaten so badly. It wasn't until the autopsy that they found out she was actually a white girl.

William Cork: He murdered her. Put a wrench through the back of her skull in the back of his tow truck one night. Live by the sword, die by the sword.

Sam Ferrara: It was tragic. I kind of knew that something would happen to her, but not that. No one deserves that, to be beaten and run over, beaten and run over.

Captain Crash: I guess she had her own demons. I didn't know what they were. It always seemed to me that she was kind of hurting. She just couldn't have a good time. She always had to go over the edge all the time, in excess of everything.

You know, that's the kind of life they [Eva and Ruby] led. They were really hard-nosed, tough girls. But they had this innocence in them that they really trusted everybody, and people walked all over them.

I don't know what the biker mentality is, but it's a strong, possessing, controlling one, I know that. These are who these babes went for. They went for fuckin' brutes who were mean.

I don't know; I didn't get it. Still don't.

Raymi Mulroney: Handsome Ned, that guy knew what was coming before it came and I think it was meant to be with him. But Mike, it shouldn't have been.

He was always waiting for the band to show up. I keep waiting for him to come out and go, "Hey, where *are* those guys?"

76. endless party

Dave Rave: I knew in Gord's heart that Teenage Head is Frankie Venom. In *my* heart it's Frankie Venom.

I could feel the energy ending. I remember we were playing in Mississauga and Gary Pig Gold saying to me, "I've got a feeling these guys are at the end of your line." And I remember going to Gary, "Maybe you're right."

Gary Pig Gold: I remember that night, too. It was at this club right near where I grew up that I'd played at a couple of times myself. Strangely enough, ten years earlier Simply Saucer had done their last show of the 20th Century there as well. It was that kind of place: Where bands would crawl off to when they're not well, I guess.

Dave Rave: And I remember buying a Polaroid camera and taking pictures of our last days. I had to reconcile that this might never happen again, so appreciate it and accept it, because you *have* to have acceptance.

I was ready to find a new life. I'd done my job, and the fact was that Gordie was ready to come back to Frank. I remember saying to Gord, "I really appreciate everything you've done, and I think it's time to leave. Whatever you want to do — you might want to stop Teenage Head, you might want to keep going — but I don't want to continue, because I know it's *your* band."

It was like leaving a family. This incredible journey that I had been on from 1975 to then was complete. And then new things happened.

I knew I did the best I could, and I knew that Frank should be there.

Gordie Lewis: Frankie came back and said he regretted leaving. He felt the same thing we felt: That it was wrong.

We had gone on to be Teenage Head with another singer. It didn't work; it felt awful, it didn't feel right at all. Why I let that happen, I've got no idea. Why didn't someone come and stop me? How could you let me let that happen? I remember that being a horrible time, it really was.

You don't fuck with the chemistry of your band. You don't take that for granted — "Oh, we can do this fine without so-and-so; we'll just get someone else to replace him." No, it doesn't work that way. You *can't*. You grow together, and there's a lot of emotion; a human factor to this whole thing, and you can't take people for granted. And when you *do* fuck with the chemistry, you pay a price for it. And we did.

David Liss: They just continued to tour up and down Canada, which as far as fame and industry goes — I'm sorry to report, being the proud Canadian that I am — if you want to become huge, that's not how it's done. They failed to concentrate on the all-important American audience.

In some ways you go, "Good for them," because they had a great scene *here*. There's nothing to take away from them. What, because they didn't become millionaires? Why, because they didn't become famous? Who cares. Again, that's industry stuff that in many ways goes against the original ethos of punk rock in the first place.

Mickey [DeSadist] didn't care about any of that. He had his job. He's a punk rocker and a shit disturber writing provocative songs. Whereas the Head, they wanted to be rock stars. And to become famous you have to be, even now more than then, compromising.

It's vacuous and meaningless, really. Yeah, they could have been this and they should have been that. Frank is a casualty of that, for sure.

By the time the Head had their run and imploded, or their time had passed, Steve and Gord faced the music and went out and got jobs. Frank had never had a job in his life. He didn't know what to do.

Colin Brunton: I started driving cab and very unambitiously trying to get into the business and make my own films. It was probably I would say 1986 or '87, I was driving cab and I picked up Frankie Venom from Teenage Head. I picked him up at Woodbine and Gerrard. He had to go back to jail the next day to do his weekend stint or something, and this was a guy who at that point had been playing for at least ten years ...

Paul Kobak: They had all the potential. They destroyed themselves from within as well as from without.

It's kind of ironic, because back in the '70s Goddo came out a few years before we did, and there used to be within the band as kind of a joke, "Oh, we're not gonna end up like Goddo playing the Knob Hill Hotel every second weekend." Oh! Guess what? That's what happened to you.

I was only with them for the first couple of hundred gigs, and since then they've done a couple of thousand. And I'm wondering how it's affected them, but I never get to talk to anybody except for Frank, and he's not always the most intelligible when you talk to him. Just before I went over to B.C. he was gonna stick me on the guest list. They were playing Hamilton Place opening for Helix. Talk about no management, or very bad lack of. God, *them* opening for *them?* Should have been the other way around.

I think what really happened to them, after Jack and after Gordie's accident and having guys guest in on guitar, they lost their edge. No more spark. Everybody just thinks about the old days and how great it was.

Well, too much of it is money, money, money. When guys are having a rough time coping — Nick, Gord, and Frank all went through bad breakups with their marriages while they were still relatively young, and sure, that's gonna have some effect on them — they're not gonna feel like writing songs. But then again, all's I can say is, Teenage Head was more reactionary than visionary as individuals.

It's too bad the Pistols had that title for one of their albums, otherwise I think it would have been appropriate for Teenage Head to call one of their albums *Flogging a Dead Horse.*

Stephen Mahon: Unfortunately, Paul was sort of a casualty, and to this day still harbours resentment.

He was always kind of moody like that. Too bad. Because I saw him once a few years ago show up at a show, and I remember asking him through the fence — he was looking in from the outside — and I said "Well, Paul, you want to come in? I'll get you in, come on." He just looked at me and shook his head and went, "Nah." Well, what do you mean, "Nah"? What are you here for then? You're just staring at us through the fence.

That's a good example of where he's at. So I guess for him, it's going to be a wound that will never heal. And it's not like we turned into millionaires; far from it. We didn't get much from it on a financial level. It just didn't happen for us.

Paul Kobak: I really never talked to any of the guys for over twenty years. I was so angry at the whole situation. I turned my back on everything, and every time I'd get a Teenage Head album in my store, I'd crack it over my knee. Which I figured out later on I shouldn't do, because that only escalates the value of the album when there's only so many copies left and I've destroyed a third of the ones they ever made in Canada. So I stopped doing that. But I was angry at the world for many years.

But they broke open the way for a lot of bands. There's no question they did.

John Balogh: I think punk changed a lot of things. I think it changed the way that people looked at music, ideally in general.

Stephen Mahon: It wasn't that hard in the late '70s. Just get four guys together that liked to drink beer and have a good time, and pick a funny punk name and you've got a band.

But so many of them probably never even made a 45. That was kind of the first step for any punk band: Put your seven-inch single out and now you're getting somewhere, you know? Maybe you'll sell five hundred copies. But I can't even think of that many Hamilton bands from that time, anyways. There were the Rebels, of course, and then what do you have after that? Simply Saucer. That was always a different trip than we were on, but that was still in that scene. St. Catharines; those cities probably all had some bands, and their candle was burning bright for a few minutes. The same can be said for a lot of groups like the Mods and the Viletones and

Johnny and the G-Rays. They never were successful either. In their own minds, they did what they did.

I'm proud of what we did because we rose above that, being stuck on Queen Street. We went across Canada. Those bands never did that. They never quite got beyond that. I don't think you ever heard the Viletones on Q107.

Gordie Lewis: That I wanted this to be the cool band from Canada was justified later on, because I've been told by people all over that, "You were the only Canadian band that it was okay to say you liked during high school." I've met them now, later on in life, when they come to the shows, and that's gratifying because that's what I wanted it to be. I wanted it not to be goofy to like a Canadian band. I wanted it to be okay to say that you liked this band, that they were good.

I wanted to open up doors. I wanted to open up doors right across and I think we did, because we did tour right across the country and I think we did open up a lot of doors for whatever punk or whatever new wave or whatever it was. Because we were getting played on the radio; we were touring. We were playing colleges, we were playing universities, we were playing bars, we were playing all over the place, high schools, everywhere. So *everywhere* was getting this Teenage Head fun punk band from Hamilton, and it was successful. We were pioneering the whole punk movement at the time. And that was a good feeling. I thought I was accomplishing my goals.

Stephen Mahon: Other than that, I mean, we haven't had any world tours to speak of. We cut that first record and then we kept making albums and all those highs were, for me anyways, in the first few years. And then after that, it was just going through the paces.

We realized we were probably just going to be stuck in Canada. That's one of the reasons Frank left. He was getting so bored and so jaded with the whole thing. Still, I'm really glad we're still together and still playing. So that's something; the fact that it's still intact.

People in any given city would at least say they've heard of us, and to this day people still know. Even jobs I do now on construction sites, guys'll look at me — and some guys'll figure it out and some guys won't — but someone will tell them, "Steve was in Teenage Head," and they go, "Fuck off." So they know; they've heard of it, anyways, so that's kind of cool.

Like I said, we've got our integrity intact, anyways: The band that caused the riot, ha ha ha.

Gordie Lewis: There's something I had to come to realize, too, about Frank: He's not kidding. He really *is* a punk. He's a fifty-year-old punk. Look where he's living. Look who he's hanging out with. He's not kidding. "I'll take today, you take tomorrow" — he means it. That's the way he lives, and that's the way he's *always* lived his life.

You have to understand what he does. He's the front man of a band. When you think about it, you've got to be kind of crazy when you do that. I never wanted to do that. And to be able to do that ... And he can *still* pull it off. Even at his worst he still can command a room to some degree, and that takes a rare talent. There's only a few people that have that ability to command any type of audience, and he does, and that's a true entertainer; that's what they do. That's a gift, and Frank has that gift. He has abused it, but a lot of performers and entertainers abuse that gift throughout history, and he's one of them.

When he's on, he's on. We all came from an era of music when unpredictability was the name of the game. That's what the whole punk thing was: Unpredictability.

Stewart Pollock: Frank was always really sort of the "out" guy — loud, drunk, obnoxious, could say anything to anybody. Frank could have an extremely cruel tongue on him. He had a barb on the end of his tongue that he could just lash out on people with no remorse at all.

Gordie Lewis: I've said to people, "What do you want? His name is Frankie Venom for Chrissakes," and he lives that. I think we all knew that, but it was frustrating at times, and we probably made too much of it sometimes. And sometimes our frustration was justified, to the point where we had split the band up.

Frankie Venom: You know what I did? It [*Frantic City*] went gold and platinum, right? This is when I was married. Anyways, I used to have the gold and platinum [records] on my walls and I got so fed up with looking at them; they were just bringing back memories. This was over the course of years, so when I got out of this relationship — I was with a female, obviously — I pawned them.

I didn't need the money. I just got sick of looking at them, you know what I mean? So I got into a weird altercation over something I'm not going to disclose — it was a domestic assault; I grabbed my lover, a female friend, by the arm. She charged me with assault, which is a crock of shite, okay? But I turned up in court and the cop that arrested me for this charge was there. My lawyer says, "You see the cops over there? They have your gold and platinum record." I said, "Oh, really?" He says, "Frank," he says, "do you think you could autograph something?" Talk about stickin' a dagger in and iodine to boot. Whatever, it's water under the

bridge. So now he's got my shit on his walls.

But anyways, just another war story.

Gordie Lewis: We never really split the band up. We've just *given* up.

Frank got really unhealthy for a little while. There was a short period in our career where the majority of the time he was leaving the show in an ambulance, because he would have convulsions. We would go in the van, and he would go to the hospital and stay overnight and get let go the next day.

Chick Parker: Frankie was at the bar in the Horseshoe and he had a cocaine-induced seizure. They called the emergency medical response dudes and they came in, ripped open his shirt, and he's still got the burn marks from reviving him the night before.

And they're going, "This guy, *again?*"

Gordie Lewis: One time I remember after the end of the show the ambulance came to get him, took him to the hospital, and we stopped by on our way and gave the nurse his money.

We knew the routine: He was gonna be better the next day and was gonna be at home. So we said, "Here's his cut from the show, here's his pay, can you give it to him so he has it in the morning?" and we just went home. We didn't even bother asking to see him because we knew we couldn't. We knew the program.

There was a certain point where it was just like, Okay, this is getting really out of hand. It had gotten to the point where it wasn't at the end of the show he was leaving, it was after the first couple of songs. And that was the end for about nine months. So like I said, we never split up, we've just given up. Then usually Frank would say, "Come on, man, when's the next gig? Come on, I'll be better."

And he was, for a little while. But he's been *really* good for the last two or three years. I think he's enjoying it a bit more, too. He's seeing a little bit more progress and interest in what he's doing, and it's something that he knows he does.

I think he's accepted himself — "That's what I do. I'm a singer. I sing for the band Teenage Head.

"I'm Frankie Venom."

Frankie Venom: Once the lights come on — "You ready? Gordie, you ready?" Fire up the Marshall, boom!

"Ready, Stevie?" Boom, boom!

"Ready, Jack?" Boom, boom, bass drum.

"Let's go! One-two-three!" That's it, we're off. It's rock 'n' roll. It's not a fuckin' ballet.

Rock 'n' roll, I love it.

SELECTIVE VINYL DISCOGRAPHY
OF SOUTHERN ONTARIO PUNK AND NEW WAVE BANDS, 1977-81

Compiled by Frank Manley (www.smashthestate.ca), based on bands mentioned in *Treat Me Like Dirt*.
* indicates a posthumous release.

GROUP	TITLE	FORMAT	LABEL	YEAR

63 Monroe, NFG, 12" EP, Nardem 005, **1980**

Androids, Roller Derby Queen/Over and Over, 7", Android, **1979**
Arson, (Livin' with the) White Folks/Coho? Coho!, 7", Motor 0001, **1979**

Battered Wives, Uganda Stomp/Giddy, 7", Bomb 5016, **1978**
Battered Wives, Battered Wives, LP, Bomb 7028, **1978**
Battered Wives, Cigarettes, LP, Bomb/Epic PEC 90575, **1979**
'B' Girls, Fun at the Beach/The "B" Side, 7", Bomp 123, **1979**

Cads, Do the Crabwalk, 7" EP, Bi-R 001, **1978**
Cardboard Brains, Cardboard Brains, 7" EP, Brainco Worldwide CB 7779, **1977**
Cardboard Brains, Black, 12" EP, Brainco Worldwide CB 7979, **1979**
Crash Kills Five, What Do You Do at Night?, 7" EP, N/A, **1980**
Curse, War (split 7" w/Diodes), 7", Crash and Burn (CEAC), **1977**
Curse, Shoeshine Boy/Killer Bees, 7", Hi-Fi HF 001, **1978**

Demics, Talk's Cheap, 12" EP, Ready EPRR-001, **1979**
Demics, Demics, LP, Hypnotic/Intercan IC-1010, **1980**
Diodes, War (split 7" w/Curse), 7", Crash and Burn (CEAC), **1977**
Diodes, Red Rubber Ball/We're Ripped, 7", Columbia CH-4168, **1977**
Diodes, Diodes, LP, Columbia PES-90441, **1977**
Diodes, Tired of Waking Up Tired/Child Star, 7", Epic E4-4186, **1978**
Diodes, Time/Damage, Live 1978, LP, Rave Up RUR-60, **2010***
Diodes, Released, LP, Epic/CBS PEC-80002, **1979**
Dishes, Fashion Plates, 7" EP, Regular R 001, **1977**
Dishes, Hot Property, 7" EP, Regular R-02, **1978**
Drastic Measures, Drastic Measures, LP, Columbia/Airwaves PCC 80035, **1980**
Drastic Measures, It Won't Be Long/Modern Heart, 7", Cut-Throat CUT-4, **1981**
Dream Dates, Moans on the Phone/Heart Attack Rhythm, 7", Ugly Pop UP006, **2004***
Dream Dates, The Mess You're in/Search and Destroy, 7", Ugly Pop UP0011, **2006***

Existers, Telex Love/Spadina, 7", Shy Anne CCL 45-540, **1979**

Fits, Bored of Education, 7" EP, Stage Fright, **1979**
Forgotten Rebels, Tomorrow Belongs to Us, 12" EP, S&M Smut-003, **1979**
Forgotten Rebels, In Love with the System, LP, Star SR-1846, **1980**

Government, Hemingway (Hated Disco Music)/ I Only Drive My Car at Night, 7", N/A, **1979**
Government, The Government, 7" EP, Modern World MW-1, **1979**
Government, Guest List, LP, Jackal WOW 713, **1980**

Hi-Fi's, I Don't Know Why You Love Me/Look What You've Done, 7", Showtime SHOW 001, **1980**

Johnny and the G-Rays, Every Twist Reminds, LP, Basement BASE 6003, **1980**

Jordana, Michaele, Romance at the Roxy, LP, Attic LAT 1101, **1980**
Martha and the Muffins, Insect Love/Suburban Dream, 7", Muffin Music MM-01, **1979**
Martha and the Muffins, Echo Beach/Teddy the Dink, 7" Dindisc 9, **1980**
Martha and the Muffins, Metro Music, LP, Dindisc V 2142, **1980**
Mods, Step Out Tonight/You Use Me, 7", Mod 001, **1978**

Nash the Slash, Bedside Companion, 12" EP, Cut-Throat CUT-1, **1978**
Nash the Slash, Dreams and Nightmares, LP, Cut-Throat CUT-2, **1979**
Nash the Slash, Dead Man's Curve, 7", Cut-Throat CUT-3, **1980**

Poles, CN Tower/Prime Time, 7", Nimbus 9 NN-313, **1977**

Quinton, David, David Quinton, LP, Bomb 7035, **1981**

Regulators, What's in the City/That's Right, Nothing's Left, 7", Ready BR-3, **1979**
Rough Trade, Rough Trade Live!, LP, Umbrella UMB DD1, **1977**
Rough Trade, Avoid Freud, LP, True North TN 43, **1980**
Rough Trade, High School Confidential, 7", True North TN4-159, **1980**

Scenics, Underneath the Door, LP, Bomb 113, **1979**
Scenics, Karen/See Me Smile, 7", Scenic Route 827, **1981**
Secrets, Success without College, LP, Bomb 115, **1980**
Segarini (Bob), Segarini, 7" EP, A&M AM452, **1977**
Segarini (Bob), Gotta Have Pop, LP, Bomb 7027, **1978**
Simply Saucer, She's a Dog/I Can Change My Mind, 7", Pig 1, **1978**
Simply Saucer, Cyborgs Revisited (recorded 1974-75), LP, Mole Sound, **1989***
Sofisticatos, New York Rocket (split 7" with the Sex Pistols), 7", Man's Ruin MR-056, **1997***

Teenage Head, Picture My Face/Tearin' Me Apart, 7", IGM/Epic E4-8273, **1978**
Teenage Head, Top Down/Kissin' the Carpet, 7", Epic E4-8337, **1978**
Teenage Head, Teenage Head, LP, IGM/Epic PEC 90534, **1979**
Teenage Head, Frantic City, LP, Attic LAT-1081, **1980**
Teenage Head, Somethin' on My Mind/Let's Shake, 7", Attic AT-220, **1980**
Teenage Head, King St. Teddy Boys, LP, N/A (bootleg), **2006***
Toby Swann, Lullabyes In Razorland, LP, El Mocambo ELMO 757, **1980**
Toby Swann, Somewhere over the Rainbow/Lullabyes in Razorland, 7", El Mocambo ELMO 513, **1981**
True Confessions, Give Him a Great Big Kiss/Jimmy's Fast, 7", Bomb 5019, **1979**
True Confessions, True Confessions, LP, Bomb 7033, **1980**
Tyranna, Back Off Baby, 7" EP, Boppa Do Down BDD-62048, **2008***
Tyranna, Tyranna, LP, Rave Up RUR 63, **2011***

Ugly, Stranded in the Laneway of Love/To Have Some Fun, 7", Explosion ER-101, **1978**

Viletones, Viletones, 7" EP, Vile 8277, **1977**
Viletones, Look Back in Anger, 7" EP, Razor REP-0001, **1978**

Zoom, Sweet Desperation/Massacre at Central High, 7", Riot 1001, **1980**

VA, Last Pogo (And Now Live from Toronto), LP, Bomb 7029, **1979**
VA, No Pedestrians, LP, Chameleon CR-535, **1980**

acknowledgments

This book was a labour of love that wouldn't have been made possible without the help of many generous and enthusiastic individuals.

Thanks to *Treat Me Like Dirt* editor Gary Pig Gold for all the hard work, valuable feedback, extensive archives, and great conversation. Thanks to publisher Ralph Alfonso for supporting this project so early on. And thank you to the team at ECW for keeping the momentum behind this book going. Thanks to copy editor Christine Flynn for having such an amazing eye for detail. Thanks to photographers Gail Bryck, Steve Burman, Don Pyle, Tom Robe, Edie Steiner, Ric Taylor and Ross Taylor. Thanks to Mary and Nelson for everything. Thanks to Colin Brunton, Greg Dick, and David Quinton. Thanks to Chris Houston for introducing me to the great city of Hamilton. Thanks to Margaret Barnes-DelColle and her husband Tom for letting me crash at their place. Thanks to Bob Bryden for all the encouragement and words of wisdom. Thanks to Jason Bowser for his help with the Deane Cameron interview. Thanks to Marc Coulavin for extra proofing. Thanks to Frank Manley for contributing our discography and for his pioneering work with *Smash The State*.

And of course, thanks to everyone who shared their stories for this book: Elizabeth Aikenhead, Ralph Alfonso, Cleave Anderson, Mike Anderson, Iain Atkinson, Caroline Azar, John Balogh, Christopher Barnes, Margaret Barnes-DelColle, Slash Booze Anna Bourque, Julia Bourque, Rodney Bowes, Gambi Bowker, Edgar Breau, James Bredin, Tony Brighton, AA Bronson, Wayne Brown, Colin Brunton, Bob Bryden, Stephen Burman, Carmen Bycok, David Byers, Deane Cameron, Peter Case, Sally Cato, John Catto, Fred Chagpar, Kevin Christoff, Cheetah Chrome, Richard Citroen, William Cork, Gary Cormier, Len Cramer, Karla Cranley, Captain Crash, Andy Crosbie, Joe Csontos, Alex Currie, Nora Currie, Steven Davey, Michael Dent, Mickey DeSadist, Greg Dick, Mark Dixon, Paul Eknes, Dave Elley, Bruce Eves, Barrie "Bear" Farrell, Ken Farr, Sam Ferrara, Danny Fields, Ricki Landers Friedlander, Mark Gane, Jeremy Gluck, Gary Pig Gold, Chris Haight, John Hamilton, George Higton, Chris Houston, Martha Johnson, Michaele Jordana, John Kancer, Joe Keithley, Nip Kicks, Paul Kobak, Alex Koch, Steve Koch, Imants Krumins, Bob Lanois, Larry LeBlanc, Steven Leckie, Linda Lee, Mike Lengyell, Gordie Lewis, David Liss, Pete Lotimer, Zoltan Lugosi, Lydia Lunch, Ian Mackay, Johnny MacLeod, Stephen Mahon, Fred Mamo, Gail Manning, Scott Marks, Blair Martin, Henry Martinuk, Andrew McGregor, Andy Ramesh Meyers, Carmela Morra, Bruce Farley Mowat, Raymi Mulroney, Nash the Slash, Suzanne Naughton, Jeff Ostofsky, Harri Palm, Stephen "Sparky" Park, Chick Parker, Gerard Pas, Andy Paterson, Enzo Petrungaro, Bryan Pietersma, Stewart Pollock, Freddy Pompeii, Larry Potvin, Doug Pringle, Don Pyle, David Quinton, Dave Rave, Paul Robinson, Cynthia Ross, Lucasta Ross, Glenn Schellenberg, Bob Segarini, Michael Severin, Mr. Shit, Rob Sikora, Mickey Skin, Xenia Splawinski, Sandy Stagg, Joe Sutherland, Tibor Takacs, Tank (Dave Roberts), Ross Taylor, Marty Thau, Gary Topp, Rick Trembles, Greg Trinier, Anya Varda, Tony Vincent, Kerry Wade, Tom Williams, Zero.

And finally, condolences to friends and family of Frankie Venom, who was interviewed for this book and passed away before it was published.

The Mods, Greg Trinier (seated), Mark Dixon, Scott Marks, David Quinton / press photo courtesy The Mods

Johnny & The G-Rays, John MacLeod, Harri Palm / photo by Ralph Alfonso

Lucasta Ross, Anya Varda / photo by Ralph Alfonso

Greg Shaw, Bob Segarini, Rhonda Ross (B-Girls) / photo by Ralph Alfonso

Gail Manning / photo by Ralph Alfonso